LOCOMOTIVES
of the
LNWR SOUTHERN DIVISION

LONDON & BIRMINGHAM RAILWAY
LONDON & NORTH WESTERN RAILWAY
and
WOLVERTON LOCOMOTIVE WORKS

HARRY JACK

THE RAILWAY CORRESPONDENCE AND TRAVEL SOCIETY
2001

Copyright © 2001 RCTS
ISBN 0 901115 89 4

www.rcts.org.uk

Published by The Railway Correspondence and Travel Society
121 Green End Road, Sawtry, PE28 5XA, England

Printed by The Amadeus Press, Cleckheaton
Typesetting by Highlight Type Bureau Ltd, Bradford

The right of Harry Jack to be identified as the author of this work has been
asserted by him in accordance with the Copyright, Designs and Patents Act, 1988

Cover photo: The full-size replica *Wolverton* – at Wolverton in October 1991. *(H. Jack)*

LNWR 851 *Apollo* on an Up train at Coventry c1874.

CONTENTS

PREFACE	4
Acknowledgements	5
INTRODUCTION	6
Abbreviations	8
Wheel arrangements, heating surfaces, works numbers	9
OPENING DATES	11
PERMANENT WAY	14
MAIN LINE	16
Camden incline	18
BRANCH LINES	21
WOLVERTON	25
EDWARD BURY	35
JAMES EDWARD McCONNELL	49
BALLAST ENGINES	71
LONDON & BIRMINGHAM RAILWAY, ORIGINAL ENGINES 1837-41	
1. Bury 2-2-0 12in Passenger Engines: 1-36, 49-52, A1, A2	82
2. Bury 2-2-0 13in Mail Engines: 37-48, 53-8	88
3. Bury 0-4-0 Goods Engines: 61-90	90
Rebuilding the Original Engines	93
Boiler dimensions	93
Rebuilding the 2-2-0s with bigger boilers and cylinders	94
Rebuilding as 2-2-2T	96
Rebuilding the 13in 0-4-0s	97
Original L&B engines on the LNWR and later	98
LONDON & BIRMINGHAM RAILWAY, LATER ENGINES 1845-6	
Bury, Curtis & Kennedy 14in 2-2-0 Passenger Engines: 59, 60, 91-9	110
Bury, Curtis & Kennedy 15in 2-2-2 Passenger Engines: 100-10	113
Bury, Curtis & Kennedy 15in 0-4-0 and 0-4-2 Goods Engines: 111-8	115
Tayleur, Longridge and Nasmyth long-boiler 0-6-0s: 119-44	116
SHARP STANDARD SINGLES 1845-8	
Sharp Bros 2-2-2: M&B No 8	123
Sharp Bros 2-2-2: 4/8/9, 31/5/6, 145/6, 205/7	124
CREWE ENGINES AT WOLVERTON 1845-7	129
TRENT VALLEY ENGINES 1846-7	
Bury, Curtis & Kennedy 0-6-0s: 168-71	130
Stephenson patent long-boiler passenger engines:	
Jones & Potts 4-2-0s: 147-52	131
Stephenson 4-2-0s: 153-8	132
Tayleur 4-2-0s: 159-67	135
BURY, CURTIS & KENNEDY GOODS ENGINES 1846-8	
0-4-0 4ft coal engines: 172/3	137
0-4-0 5ft goods engines: 72/4, 86/9	137
0-4-2 goods engines: 6, 16, 22, 33/4, 206	139

TWO JONES & POTTS ENGINES 1847	141
0-6-0: 174	141
4-2-0: 175	
	142
CHESTER & HOLYHEAD and LEEDS, DEWSBURY & MANCHESTER ENGINES 1847-9	143
C&H Tayleur 4-2-0s: 176-81	144
C&H Jones & Potts 4-2-0s: 182-90	146
C&H Nasmyth, Gaskell 2-2-2s: 191-6	147
LD&M Wilson 2-2-2s (outside cylinders): 201-4	148
LD&M Wilson 2-2-2s (Jenny Linds): 208/9	149
C&H Bury, Curtis & Kennedy 2-2-2s: 12/8, 65/7, 75, 218	152
C&H Haigh Foundry 4-2-0s: 202/3/4	153
C&H goods engines (note)	
LARGE EXPRESS ENGINES 1847-8	154
Crampton 4-2-0: *London* 200	158
Crampton 6-2-0: *Liverpool* 245	161
McConnell 2-2-2: 227 - 'Mac's Mangle'	162
Stephenson 4-2-2s: 233/4	
18in LONG-BOILER GOODS ENGINES 1847-55	165
4ft 6in 0-6-0 Sharp 'Atlas' type: 32	166
5ft 0-6-0s Sharp, Stephenson, Hawthorn: 85/7, 210-7/9-26/8-32/5/6/8-44/6	170
Rebuilding as 0-6-0ST	176
Wolverton: 228-30	177
Fairbairn: 257-286	
	183
The BLOOMERS, 7ft 2-2-2s - Sharp Bros 1851-3 series: 247-56/87-96	
	189
The PATENTS, 7ft 6in 2-2-2s 1852-4: 297/8, 300-9	195
Other McConnell patent 2-2-2s	
	196
CLASS A 0-4-2s 1853-5: 28, 124/48/64/92-5, 231/6	
The SMALL BLOOMERS, 6ft 6in 2-2-2s	199
Hawthorn and Vulcan Foundry 1854: 310-20	199
Wolverton Classes C, E and K 1857-61	
	204
STOTHERT 5ft 0-6-0 MINERAL ENGINES 1855: 321-31	
EXPRESS GOODS ENGINES, 5ft 6in 0-6-0s	206
Kitson, 1854: 332-42	206
Wolverton 1856-63, Kitson 1862, Fairbairn 1862	
ENGINES FROM THE SOUTH STAFFORDSHIRE RAILWAY, 1858	212
Fairbairn 2-2-2s: 297-300	216
Sharp 2-2-2s: 53, 84, 116	217
Fairbairn 0-6-0s: 307/8	217
Garforth 0-4-2: 221	218
Stephenson 0-6-0s: 309/10	218
Sharp 2-4-0Ts: 111/2	219
Wilson 0-6-0s: 301/2	220
Wilson 2-4-0s: 160/81	221
Vulcan 0-6-0s: 305/6	222
Beyer 0-4-2s: 303/4	223
Fairbairn 0-6-0s: 311-6	

ENGINES FROM THE NORTHERN DIVISION, 1860	225
1. Beyer 0-6-0s: 321/2	226
2. Crewe 7ft 2-2-2s: 320/3/4	227
3. Crewe 6ft 2-2-2s: 325-44	228
4. Crewe Goods 2-4-0s: 345-53	233
CLASS G 0-4-2T 1860: 102/10/25/74, 354	235
CLASS H Special Large Bloomers, 7ft 6in 2-2-2s 1861: 372/3/5	
The BLOOMERS, 7ft 2-2-2s - 1861-2 series:	239
Wolverton, Sharp and Kitson: 389-408	249
Modern replicas	250
CLASS M 0-4-2T 1862: 734, 974/6/82-8	
CLASS N 0-4-2 MIXED TRAFFIC ENGINES 1862: 601/6/16/88/95/6, 741/78/84/7/90, 811, 1019/20/1	253
LOCOMOTIVE CLASSIFICATION	255
Class Numbers	256
Class Letters	257
LIST OF LOCOMOTIVES BUILT AT WOLVERTON, 1845-63	261
LOCOMOTIVE NUMBERING and the DUPLICATE LISTS	
NUMERICAL LOCOMOTIVE LISTS	265
L&B and LNWR S Div List, 1837-56	271
LNWR S Div List, 1856-62	277
WOLVERTON TENDERS	282
LIVERIES and NUMBERPLATES	285
LAMPS and LAMP IRONS	286
OTHER ALTERATIONS FROM 1862	
APPENDICES:	287
1. LOCOMOTIVE PERFORMANCE, 1851	289
2. FUEL - FROM COKE TO COAL	291
3. LNWR ENGINES on the NORTH LONDON RAILWAY	294
4. LNWR ENGINES on the OXFORD, WORCESTER & WOLVERHAMPTON RAILWAY	295
5. ENGINES ON TRIAL	296
CAUTION - a note to future researchers	297
BIBLIOGRAPHY	298
ACKNOWLEDGEMENT OF PHOTOGRAPHS	

PREFACE

The first main line from London, and by far the most important railway in the land, was that between London and Birmingham. On the day it opened the four biggest towns in England - the main political, commercial and industrial centres - were for the first time linked by fast transport and brought within a few hours of each other. By joining the capital to Birmingham, whence rails already ran through the Black Country and onwards for 100 miles to Lancashire - to 'Cottonopolis' Manchester and the great port of Liverpool - the London & Birmingham Railway became the main artery of England.

When it was new it was described as "unquestionably the greatest public work ever executed, either in ancient or in modern times" and later writers have tended to concentrate on the epic drama of its construction - the excavation of its immense cuttings and awesome tunnels. Beyond that, and despite its supreme importance as a working railway, the London & Birmingham has been neglected. For whatever reason, it has not received the attention given to later and lesser lines. This applies particularly to its locomotives, which have suffered not only neglect but in some cases misrepresentation, faithfully copied from book to book. While the L&B had only a short life as an independent company, it went on to become the major constituent of Britain's biggest railway, the London & North Western, but even so the locomotives of what was thereafter known as the Southern Division of the LNWR have remained obscure. The only previous attempt to describe them all was published over a century ago.

This was a series of articles in the *Locomotive Magazine* of 1897-8 in which the engines were dealt with in the brief manner of those days: a paragraph or two and a small line drawing of almost every class. The articles were published without any author's name but later it was revealed that they were "largely based" on the notes of James Bull, who worked on the LNWR for over 56 years; after his death the magazine claimed that he had been a main line driver "and was, we believe, the last of the old Southern Division men". In fact he was not a footplateman at all, but an accounts inspector who began his long career at Peterborough in February 1847 as a 14-year old clerk. In his spare time he made notes about LNWR Southern Division engines, but it is not known for how long he kept this up. He was transferred to Crewe in 1863 and remained there until his death in 1919.

In 1896 *Moore's Monthly* (later the *Locomotive*) *Magazine* had begun a serial history detailing all the locomotives of the London, Brighton & South Coast Railway, the first time such a thing had ever been published. Seeing these articles may have prompted James Bull to pass his old notebooks to the magazine, which quickly made use of them for a serial 'The Southern Division Engines of the L&NWR' published in thirteen monthly parts from April 1897. There were 61 illustrations, drawn by Douglas Leitch using a variety of sources and it is clear that some of them were based on sketches from memory. As printed, the articles were heavily edited and contain occasional mistakes - most of them probably the fault of the editor - so it would have been useful in the light of a lot of new evidence to be able to refer back to James Bull's original work, but sadly his notebooks perished in the London Blitz. Since 1898 practically everything that has appeared in print about any of the Southern Division engines has been copied from these *Locomotive Magazine* articles. A new account is long overdue.

The present book is based mainly on the archives of the London & Birmingham and the LNWR, sources that were almost inaccessible to researchers until the 1950s. Information has been added from the records of locomotive building firms, from documents unearthed at Crewe Works since the 1960s and from LNWR drawings now held at the National Railway Museum. *The Practical Mechanic's Journal* of the 1850s contains several articles and drawings which clearly originated in the Southern Division Locomotive Dept. Useful details, otherwise unrecorded, were found in the sketches made in 1848-9 by E. T. Lane, a pupil at Swindon Works who died in 1850, aged twenty. Many observations of locomotive working were recorded in *The English Mechanic* in the 1870s, especially by an LNWR employee of Tamworth who concealed his identity by giving his name as 'Itzaex' (it's a X).

Other railway periodicals from the 1830s onwards provided occasional snippets about engines and much background material, including the letters about locomotive managers, written by the mysterious but well-informed 'Veritas Vincit', which appeared in the *Railway Times* and the *Railway Record*. Books from which additional information has been obtained are listed separately.

A lot of valuable LNWR material did not survive into modern times because of office reorganisation and wartime waste paper collections; the records of the Southern Division's Locomotive Department, the accountancy records and ledgers: all have disappeared along with countless drawings and lists. But the minute-books of the Board and various committees were preserved, together with many reports, letters and other documents, and much can be learned from them, directly or by inference. Accurate monthly lists of locomotives are available or can be reconstructed from stock totals from 1837 to 1846; this period is followed by one of near chaos in which many new engines were acquired and some were disposed of without adequate record. From September 1847 to December 1849 the minutes contain monthly locomotive lists, and there is a table giving the basic dimensions of every engine in March 1848. Unfortunately these lists contain many obvious errors and omissions and cannot always be taken at face value. The few later lists which give totals of engines by class are similarly flawed, with some baffling mysteries; from all the available evidence it has to be said that from 1847 the standard of record-keeping at the Southern Division's Wolverton Locomotive Works was poor. The worst example is the last known stock list, dated June 1855, which misleadingly puts several engines in the wrong classes. There is no complete list of Southern Division engines in the surviving archives after this; there is no list of engines built at Wolverton; many dates of delivery and withdrawal are unrecorded. Renumbering, ever the bugbear of the LNWR locomotive researcher, is especially poorly documented in the case of these engines. This shortage of vital material means that it is no longer possible to produce a locomotive history of the LNWR Southern Division with the amount of detail from official records which can be found in previous RCTS books such as Norman Groves' *Great Northern Locomotive History* or Donald Bradley's series on the Southern Railway constituents. By comparison with them this book will seem somewhat unbalanced because while much is known about certain engines, very little has been preserved about others.

The absence of authentic records allowed legends to sprout like weeds and now it can be seen that much of what has long been accepted as fact is, in reality, only guesswork and invention. There are for example at least four versions of the 'Wolverton Works list' in existence, all written by enthusiasts long after locomotive building ceased, no doubt as honest attempts to make sense of what was known.

The work of Clement Edwin Stretton (1850-1915) comes into an altogether different category, and if only to forestall readers' perplexity, some words of warning must be given. This prolific author wrote a popular book on locomotive history which, although filled with errors, ran to six editions between 1892 and 1903; he also published hundreds of quite unreliable pamphets and articles on railway and locomotive history - reference libraries throughout the land are stuffed with them. The various periodicals covering railways contain scores of his didactic letters between the 1880s and 1914. His manner towards anyone who questioned his version of events was overbearing; he was quite irrepressible. But he was often wrong, because whatever he did not know *he simply made up*.

Much of his writing about railway history, although it is always decked out with vivid and memorable details, can now be recognised as fiction. His stories about the two LNWR Southern Division locomotive superintendents, Edward Bury and James Edward McConnell, give a completely false impression but it is one which has coloured most writing about the subject for the past hundred years. His account of the Chester & Holyhead engines, which were transferred to the Southern Division and which he claimed to know all about, was accepted for a long time but can now be seen for the nonsense it always was.

He concocted many bogus works lists (such as one which claimed to enumerate the locomotives built by Bury, Curtis & Kennedy) and produced quite inaccurate drawings of engines, some of which he foisted on the Science Museum; his absurd drawing of Southern Division H class No 373 was reprinted in two books as recently as the 1980s.

In all cases he announced that his sources were official and authentic. He published so much and gave himself such an air of authority that his work will continue to be 'rediscovered' by researchers, and will continue to spread confusion. Maybe I have unwittingly included some Strettoniana in these pages; I hope not.

It is a relief to turn to those who have given valuable assistance to this project.

Acknowledgements

The curators at the British Transport Commission Archives Office gave ready access to the minute-books and other records of the L&B and LNWR, as did the staff of the Public Record Office at Kew, where the archives are now housed. Additional material was found at BTC Archives, Edinburgh, the Scottish Record Office, the General Register Office for Scotland, the National Library of Scotland, the Science Museum Library, the Patent Office Library, Somerset House, the Maritime Museum and the Picton Library in Liverpool, the Mitchell Library in Glasgow, the University of Leicester Library, the Library of the National Railway Museum, the British Museum Newspaper Library, the County of Buckingham Record Office, Wolverton Science & Art Institute, the Museum of Science & Industry in Manchester, the libraries of the Railway Club and the Stephenson Locomotive Society. The public libraries of Birmingham, Bolton, Bristol, Coventry, Crewe, Dunfermline, Edinburgh, Leamington Spa, Leicester, Manchester, Rugby, Stockport, Sutton Coldfield, Walsall and Wolverton have each provided useful facts.

Major individual contributors were: C. Williams who allowed me to copy extracts from his Crewe records; Alan G. Dunbar who gave photocopies of more recent Crewe discoveries and much else; E. Craven who sent a lot of information, especially about the Manchester & Birmingham engines and those which went from the LNWR to other railways.

Other people who helped me, in various ways and over many years, include:
Michael R. Bailey, John E. Bates, W. G. Batteson, Everard Beauchamp, John D. Blyth, W. E. Boyd, David Camis, Roger Carpenter, Reg Carter, C. R. Clinker, Arthur F. Cook, Michael Cook, J. C. Davies, Mrs F. Dewick, E. A. Eades, John Edgington, Bruce Ellis, Danny Fountain, Neil Fraser, Andrew Grant of the Powerhouse Museum, Sydney - the home of the only surviving McConnell engine, Don Hagarty, David Hanson, Les Hanson, Peter Heuzenroeder, J. R. Hollick, D. E. Jones, Frank Jones, J. Kent, Peter D. King, John E. Kite, Norman Lee, Bill Lees, Trevor Lodge, Roderick J. McConnell, Joe McLelland, Bob Meanley, M. A. Oakley, Mike Page, Anthony Parkes, David Patrick, Jim Peden, Dave Pennington, Geoff Platt, Richard Powell, Michael E. Quick, R. Michael Robbins, Richard F. Roberts, Stationmaster Tim Sheehan of Cork, in whose care rests the last Bury passenger engine, Donald H. Stuart, Thomas T. Taber, Harry Townley, John True, John Walden, Laurie Ward, Rodney Weaver, Geoffrey Webb, Gordon Webster, Bill West, G. Dudley Whitworth, and Mike Williams, Editor of the LNWR Society's excellent *Journal*.

I am very grateful to all of them, as I am to John Goodman, who carefully read through my entire original and revised drafts and gave me much valuable criticism and helpful advice.

Lastly, I know that this book would never have been finished but for the understanding, help and encouragement of my wife, Margaret.

HARRY JACK,
22 Dundas street,
Edinburgh.
October 2001

INTRODUCTION

The London & North Western Railway was formed in 1846 by the amalgamation of the London & Birmingham, the Grand Junction and the Manchester & Birmingham railways. These three constituents continued for several years just as they had before, with their own separate departments, locomotive stocks and working methods; the only obvious change was that the old railways were now known as 'Divisions' of the new LNWR. The largest of the three, the London & Birmingham, became the Southern Division. The first LNWR Southern Division locomotives were simply those of the L&B.

London & Birmingham Railway
A railway from London to Birmingham was given serious consideration as far back as 1823; surveys were made and a company was established but it failed to obtain an Act of Parliament. Other surveys were made in 1826 and 1828, prospectuses were issued and rival companies set up. The opening of the Liverpool & Manchester Railway in 1830 gave a fresh impetus to the project; the rival companies united, brought in George Stephenson and his son Robert as engineers and presented another Bill to Parliament in 1832. This too failed, but after an increase in the money paid as compensation to

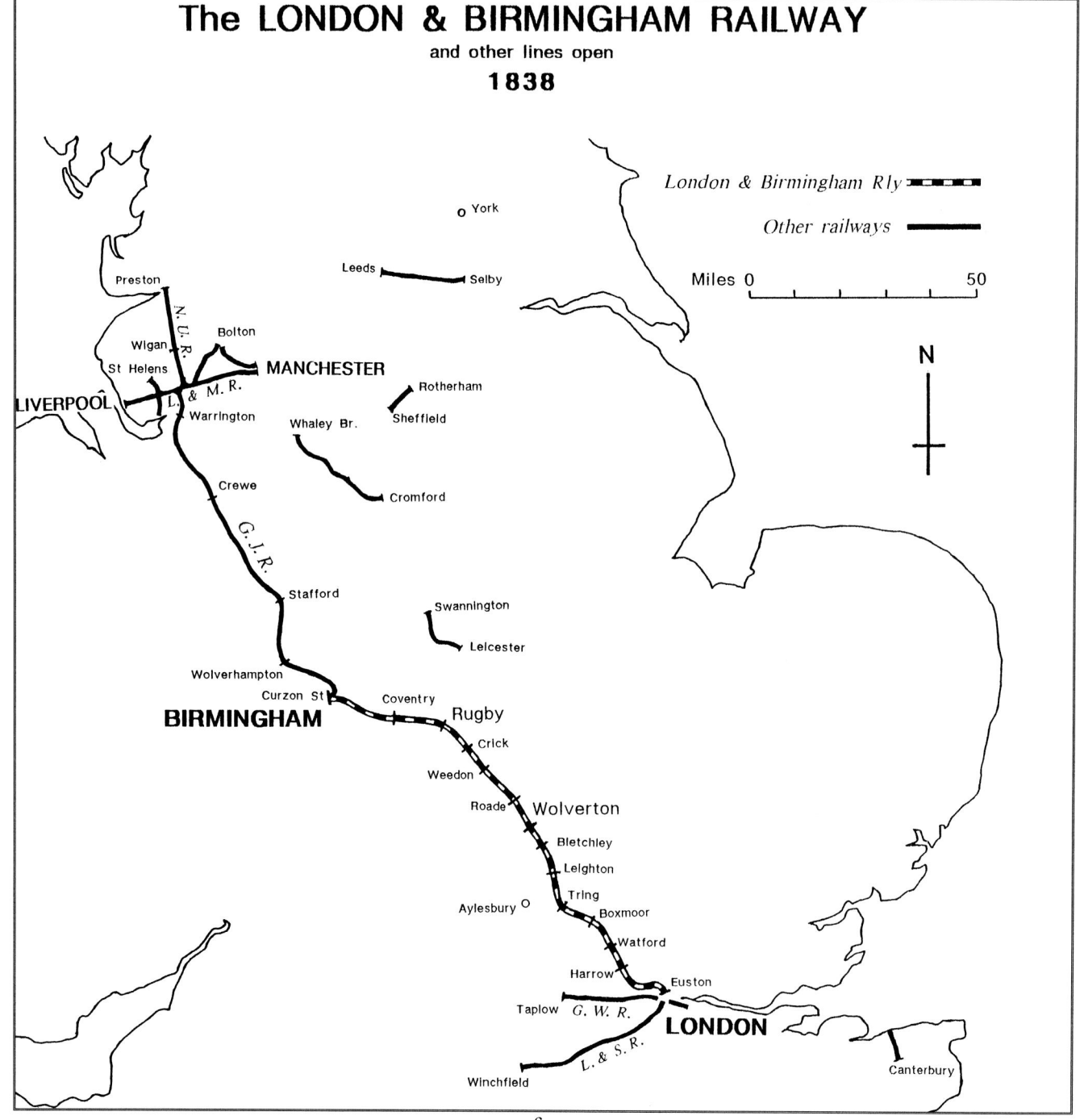

landowners, the London & Birmingham Railway Act received its Royal Assent on 6th May 1833.

This Act was for the construction of a railway of 111 miles, from Camden Town, London, to Birmingham; Robert Stephenson was appointed Engineer in Chief and the first construction contracts were awarded in April 1834. Another Act, to extend the line from Camden for about a mile nearer to the centre of London, at Euston Square, was obtained on 3rd July 1835.

The line laid out by Stephenson was very easily graded north of Camden, with no incline steeper than 1 in 326, a rise of a little over 16 feet in a mile. This was achieved by heavy earthworks: high embankments, deep cuttings, viaducts and over four miles of tunnels. On the mile-long extension line the presence of the Regent's Canal at Camden and the sudden drop to Euston necessitated a steeper incline, and stationary engines were installed at the summit to draw trains up by a rope.

The L&B was opened in four stages. The first 24½ miles from Euston to Boxmoor opened on 20th July 1837; in October the line reached Tring. In April 1838 two separate sections were opened: in the south from Tring to just beyond Bletchley and in the north, 29 miles from Birmingham to Rugby. This left an intervening gap of 35 miles containing Wolverton viaduct, Roade cutting and Kilsby tunnel; this section finally came into use in June, with the official opening of the completed railway on 17th September 1838.

In 1833, on the same day as the L&B, the Grand Junction Railway also received its Act. The GJR was in effect an 83 miles continuation from Birmingham northwards to link up with the Liverpool & Manchester Railway. It was finished first, opening on 4th July 1837, so that when the L&B line was completed from Euston to Birmingham, London was placed in direct rail communication with Manchester and Liverpool, and through-running began on 1st October 1838. In the next two years other lines made junctions with the L&B near its northern end so that by 1840 rails ran all the way to Leeds, Hull and York. For the next ten years the L&B was the only railway between London and the north of England.

The first branch from the L&B was the seven-mile line of the Aylesbury Railway, which was worked by the L&B from its opening in 1839. In 1844 another short branch was opened from Coventry to Leamington, but in the following year 47 miles were added to the L&B by the Blisworth-Northampton-Peterborough line, giving access to the rich agricultural counties of the east. In plan, the L&B was now like a giant **Y** with arms of similar length gathering all railway traffic between and beyond Birmingham and Peterborough, and funnelling it down the stem to London.

Other branches were in progress, from Bletchley to Bedford and from Leighton to Dunstable, when towards the end of 1845 the Boards of the London & Birmingham, the Grand Junction and the Manchester & Birmingham railways agreed to amalgamate. The title of the new company, the London & North Western Railway, was chosen on 13th December and a de facto working arrangement quickly followed. In the spring of 1846 the L&B purchased the Trent Valley Railway on behalf of the embryo LNWR; this line ran 50 miles from Rugby on the L&B to Stafford on the GJR, creating a shorter and more direct route to the north by avoiding the westward bend of the original lines into Birmingham.

Throughout its short but vigorous life, the L&B's locomotives were under the control of Edward Bury, initially as contractor for the working and maintenance of the company's locomotives at a set rate per mile. This system never worked in practice and in June 1839 there was a cash settlement after which Bury was employed in the normal way as Manager of the Locomotive Department. He established the L&B locomotive repair workshops at Wolverton, midway between the two ends of the main line, where the first of the planned railway towns was built - the forerunner of Crewe and Swindon. The original locomotives were to Bury's standard designs, although built by several outside firms, but from 1845 there was an influx of other types. Two engines were built at Wolverton in this period. Bury continued in charge of the Southern Division Locomotive Department after the formation of the LNWR.

LNWR Southern Division

The Act of Parliament which created the LNWR received its Royal Assent on 16th July 1846. At that time the L&B's total of 121 passenger and goods engines formed the nucleus of the LNWR Southern Division locomotive stock, retaining their L&B numbers. As further engines were added they were listed in the same numerical series, which was quite distinct from those of the other two divisions. The former Grand Junction became the Northern Division; the old Manchester & Birmingham became the M&B Division but was renamed the North Eastern Division in 1849. Like the S Div they continued to number engines in their own series, so there were many cases of three LNWR engines with the same number. On the S Div there was in addition a group of ballast engines in the hands of a contractor for the permanent way maintenance trains.

In 1847 Edward Bury resigned and was succeeded as S Div Locomotive Superintendent by James Edward McConnell who continued at his Wolverton headquarters for the ensuing fifteen years. At first the practice of obtaining engines of various types from private makers continued, with many being transferred from other sections of the LNWR, but some limited locomotive building was undertaken at Wolverton from 1848. This was quite unlike the practice on the N Div, whose Crewe Works was set up specifically for building locomotives and had turned them out in quantity since Grand Junction days. After an investigation into comparative costs conducted by experts brought in by the Board, standard S Div locomotive types were established and from 1856 these were built on a regular basis at Wolverton.

The S Div continued to grow in size by the addition of branch lines, mostly through rural areas, but in 1856 there was a major acquisition when McConnell took over the working of the independent South Staffordshire Railway, together with its locomotives. There was a further large expansion when the boundary between the divisions was moved northward and from 1860 the N Div lines south of Stafford, including the Trent Valley line, came under S Div control, with a commensurate transfer of Crewe engines to Wolverton.

With enlargement and modernisation of Wolverton Works in 1859-60, production increased dramatically and output almost matched that of Crewe. Then, following the appointment of Richard Moon as Chairman of the LNWR Board in 1861, there was a sudden change of policy.

Four years before this, in 1857 Moon had prevailed upon his fellow directors to absorb the North Eastern Division Locomotive Dept into that of the Northern Division; Moon's protégé John Ramsbottom was promoted from the NE Div to take over the enlarged N Div and Crewe Works; the existing N Div chief Francis Trevithick was dismissed. Within ten months of Moon's accession as Chairman, the N Div and S Div Locomotive Depts were amalgamated. McConnell was obliged to resign, Ramsbottom became Locomotive Superintendent of the entire LNWR, and the S Div engines were placed under the control of Crewe. Wolverton's locomotive activities were gradually brought to an end.

By the time of the amalgamation of the two divisions in March 1862, the S Div covered all LNWR lines between Euston and Stafford, from Oxford, Banbury and Wolverhampton in the west to Peterborough (and within the year, Cambridge) in the east. Including work over other companies' tracks, this was a total of more than 500 route miles.

The stock of S Div engines had grown to over 400, with numbers (still in their separate list) between 1 and 418. At that time the N Div had engines numbered from 1 to 596, so in April 1862 each S Div engine was renumbered in continuation of the N Div list by the addition of 600. Thus S Div No 1 became LNWR 601 and so on up to 1018. Engines then under construction at Wolverton filled gaps in this series and added numbers to 1021. In 1863 the final ten were built at Wolverton and were given numbers in two blocks 1056-60 and 1071-5 among groups of Crewe-built engines.

Including these last ten a total of some 632 locomotives had been built for or acquired by the London & Birmingham Railway and the LNWR Southern Division, of which 166 were built at Wolverton.

Abbreviations

a	In dates, the first half-year (e.g. a/62 = 1/12/1861 to 31/5/1862).
ADR	Alexandra (Newport) Docks Railway.
b	In dates, the second half-year (e.g. b/62 = 1/6/1862 to 30/11/1862).
B&BR	Bristol & Birmingham Railway also known as Birmingham & Bristol Rly.
B&DJ	Birmingham & Derby Junction Railway.
B&G	Birmingham & Gloucester Railway.
BC&K	Bury, Curtis & Kennedy & Co (from 1842).
BP	Beyer, Peacock & Co.
c	cab fitted to locomotive at date of rebuilding.
C&H	Chester & Holyhead Railway.
C&HPR	Cromford & High Peak Railway.
CM	Cannock Mineral Railway.
CR	Caledonian Railway.
c/u	'cut-up' number.
DP&ARJ	Dundee & Perth & Aberdeen Railway Junction.
E&GR	Edinburgh & Glasgow Railway.
E&WID&BJR	East & West India Docks & Birmingham Junction Railway (later NLR).
EB	Edward Bury & Co (to 1842, thereafter BC&K).
EBW	E. B. Wilson & Co.
ECR	Eastern Counties Railway.
FM&J	Fenton, Murray & Jackson & Co.
GER	Great Eastern Railway.
GJR	Grand Junction Railway.
GLC	General Locomotive Committee, LNWR.
GNR	Great Northern Railway.
GS&WR	Great Southern & Western Railway.
GWR	Great Western Railway.
H&C	Hesbaye & Condroz Railway.
H&M	Huddersfield & Manchester Railway.
HF	Haigh Foundry.
HJ	Hampstead Junction Railway.
IMechE	Institution of Mechanical Engineers.
J&P	Jones & Potts.
L&B	London & Birmingham Railway.
L&C	Lancaster & Carlisle Railway.
L&M	Liverpool & Manchester Railway.
L&SR	London & Southampton Railway.
LB&SC	London, Brighton & South Coast Railway.
LC	'long centres' - rebuilt with rear axle behind firebox.
LC&DR	London, Chatham & Dover Railway.
LD&M	Leeds, Dewsbury & Manchester Railway.
LFB	'large firebox' type Crewe locomotive.
LMS	London Midland & Scottish Railway.
LNER	London & North Eastern Railway.
LNWR	London & North Western Railway.
LSWR	London & South Western Railway.
M&B	Manchester & Birmingham Railway.
M&B Div	Manchester & Birmingham Division of the LNWR (NE Div from 7/1849).
M&GN	Midland & Great Northern Railway.
MCR	Midland Counties Railway.
McC	James Edward McConnell.
MR	Midland Railway.
MR&C	Monmouthshire Railway & Canal Co.
MS&F	Maudslay, Sons & Field.
N&BJ	Northampton & Banbury Junction Railway.
N&ER	Northern & Eastern Railway.
N&L	Namur & Liége Railway.
N&SWJR	North & South Western Junction Railway.
N Div	Northern Division of the LNWR.

NE Div	North Eastern Division of the LNWR (M&B Div until 7/1849).		front of firebox.
NG	Nasmyth, Gaskell & Co.	Scr	scrapped.
n/k	not known.	S Div	Southern Division of the LNWR.
NLR	North London Railway (E&WID&BJR until 1853).	SER	South Eastern Railway.
		SFB	'small firebox' type Crewe locomotive.
NSR	North Staffordshire Railway.	SSR	South Staffordshire Railway.
NUR	North Union Railway.	ST	saddle tank locomotive.
NWR	North Western Railway.	Stat	stationary engine.
OC	Outside cylinders.	SV	Stour Valley line.
OW&W	Oxford, Worcester & Wolverhampton Railway.	T	tank locomotive.
		T&L	Tulk & Ley.
PS&NWR	Potteries, Shrewsbury & North Wales Railway.	TV	Trent Valley Railway.
		VF	Vulcan Foundry (Charles Tayleur & Co until April 1847).
R&SBR	Rhondda & Swansea Bay Railway.		
RBL	R. B. Longridge & Co.	W	rebuilt at Wolverton.
RS	Robert Stephenson & Co.	W&T	Waterford & Tramore Railway.
RWH	R. & W. Hawthorn.	Wdn	withdrawn.
S	Steel boiler fitted at date of rebuilding.	WM&CQR	Wrexham, Mold & Connah's Quay Railway.
SB	Sharp Bros.		
SC	'short centres' - rebuilt with rear axle in	Wol	Wolverton Works.
		w/o	working order.

Wheel Arrangements

Fredric M. Whyte's notation (0-4-0, 2-2-2 etc) is used as a convenient way to describe wheel arrangements, although it did not come into general use in Britain until about 1906, long after the period of the locomotives described here. None of these engines had bogies so the notation as used in this book shows all leading carrying wheels grouped together. Thus Crampton's engine *Liverpool*, with three independent leading axles, is here described as 6-2-0. This is unambiguous and self-explanatory and there seems to be no advantage in the clumsier forms (2+2+2)-2-0 or 4-2-2-0 which have been used in the past. There are respectable precedents for the simpler treatment, for instance the LNER W1 class 10000 which is usually described as 4-6-4 despite its non-bogie rear carrying axles.

Heating Surface

It may be noticed that in the tables of dimensions many of the boiler heating surface figures are shown with unrealistic precision, as for example 621.323 sq ft, and that in a few cases the total heating surface is not the exact sum of firebox and tube surfaces. These are the figures given in official reports and have been left in this form because they might help to identify locomotive classes if some fragment of the missing Wolverton records is found in the future.

Works Numbers

Some firms allotted numbers to the engines they built, usually in a 'locomotives only' list but sometimes in a list which included other products or jobs undertaken. Some of these numbers are known, some are unknown and many which have appeared in print are the result of later guesswork. Many of the Sharp Bros 'works numbers' fall into the latter category, and have been omitted from this book.

Much of the Tayleur/Vulcan Foundry 'official works list' before 1853 is mere invention; it was cobbled together in the late 19th century by joining the later 'locomotives only' list to an incomplete series of earlier numbers. It is now clear that the compiler of the 'official' list simply filled the gaps by guesswork, including dozens of imaginary locomotives, while omitting several now known to have been built by the firm. Because 'works numbers' from this concocted list have been given wide currency in earlier publications, I have included an explanatory note at the appropriate places.

The published works list of Edward Bury & Co and Bury, Curtis & Kennedy, as well as that of the Haigh Foundry, are obvious fabrications by Clement Stretton, and it seems likely that the lists of Mather, Dixon and Peter Rothwell are similarly inauthentic. The alleged works numbers of these firms have been ignored, except for a few cases where the number is from a source which predates Stretton's activities.

In cases where works numbers are known for groups of engines they are given in the text, but as there are many instances where individual locomotives cannot be linked to a works number and some engines are known to have been delivered out of numerical sequence, works numbers have been omitted from some of the class summary tables.

OPENING DATES
L&B and LNWR SOUTHERN DIVISION

London & Birmingham Railway
Main Line

	Miles	Date		
London, Euston - Boxmoor	24½	20	July	1837
Boxmoor - Tring	7½	16	Oct	1837
Tring - Denbigh Hall	16	9	April	1838
Rugby - Birmingham, Curzon Street	29	9	April	1838
Denbigh Hall - Rugby	35	17	Sept	1838
Kilsby tunnel completed		21	June	1838
Limited service began on single line		24	June	1838
Limited service of 1st class through carriages and travelling post office between London, Liverpool and Manchester		1	Oct	1838
Regular goods traffic commenced		15	April	1839
Birmingham Curzon Street Jct - New Street	1	1	June	1854

LNWR Northern Division lines transferred to Southern Division, January 1860

Grand Junction Railway:				
Stafford - Birmingham, Vauxhall	28½	4	July	1837
Vauxhall - Curzon Street, junction with L&B	¾	1	Oct	1838
Curzon Street GJR station		19	Nov	1838
Trent Valley Railway - purchased by L&B in 1846 on behalf of LNWR:				
Rugby - Stafford	49½	15	Sept	1847 (limited)
		1	Dec	1847 (fully)
Stour Valley line:				
Birmingham, New Street - Bushbury Jct	14½	1	July	1852

Branches

Aylesbury Railway, leased and worked by L&B:				
Cheddington - Aylesbury	7	10	June	1839 (passrs)
(Single line)			Nov	1839 (goods)
Coventry - Leamington	8¾	9	Dec	1844
(Single line)				
West London Railway:				
West London Jct - Kensington, Canal Basin	3	27	May	1844
(Single line)				
Closed		30	Nov	1844
Reopened, worked by L&B		11	March	1845 (goods)
Leased to L&B and GWR jointly			March	1846
Doubled				1860
		2	June	1862 (passrs)
Blisworth - Northampton	4¾	13	May	1845 (passrs)
		15	Dec	1845 (goods)
Northampton - Peterborough	42¼	2	June	1845 (passrs)
(Single line)		15	Dec	1845 (goods)
2nd line, begun Oct 1845, completed			Sept	1846
Bletchley - Bedford	16¼	18	Nov	1846

	Miles	Date		
Leighton - Dunstable	6¾	29	May	1848 (goods)
		1	June	1848 (passrs)
Rugby - Market Harborough (Single line)	17¾	29	April	1850
Doubled		22	July	1878
Bletchley - Banbury	31¼	1	May	1850 (passrs)
(Single line Winslow - Banbury)		15	May	1850 (goods)
Market Harborough - Rockingham	9¾	1	June	1850
Coventry - Nuneaton	10¼	2	Sept	1850
Closed, Coventry - Counden Rd (collapse of Spon End viaduct)		26	Jan	1857
Reopened		1	Oct	1860
Winslow - Islip (Single line)	18¼	1	Oct	1850
Doubled:				
Claydon (Verney) Jct - Islip	16			1853-4
Winslow - Verney Jct	2¼	1	Dec	1875
Islip - Banbury Road	2¼	2	Dec	1850
Rugby - Leamington (Single line)	15	1	March	1851
Banbury Road - Oxford	3½	20	May	1851
Rockingham - Luffenham Jct (MR)	7¾	2	June	1851
North & South Western Junction Railway, worked by LNWR and LSWR:				
Willesden Jct - Kew Jct (LSWR)	4	15	Feb	1853 (goods)
		1	Aug	1853 (passrs, NLR)
Oxford Rd Jct - Yarnton Jct (OW&W)	1½	1	April	1854
Bletchley south-to-west curve	¼		Oct	1854
North & South Western Junction Railway:				
Hammersmith Branch (Single line)	1½	1	May	1857 (goods)
		8	April	1858 (passrs)
Watford Jct - St Albans (Single line)	6½	5	May	1858 (passrs)
		7	May	1858 (goods)
Duston Jct (West) - Market Harborough	18¼	by	Oct	1858 (goods)
		16	Feb	1859 (passrs)
(Single line Northampton - Market Harborough) Doubled in stages:				
Northampton - Kingsthorpe	1¾		Sept	1861
Kingsthorpe - Lamport	7¾		April	1862
Lamport - Market Harborough	7¾	4	Aug	1879
Hampstead Junction Railway:				
Kentish Tn Jct (NLR) - Old Oak Jct (N&SWJR)	6	2	Jan	1860
Harlesden Jct - Third Line Jct (LNWR)	¾	2	Jan	1860 (goods)
Nuneaton - Hinckley	4	1	Jan	1862
Aston - Sutton Coldfield	5	2	June	1862
Bedford - Cambridge (GER)	29½	7	July	1862 (passrs)
		1	Aug	1862 (goods)
(Single line)				

	Miles	Date		
Doubled:				
Sandy - Gamlingay	6	20	Oct	1870
Gamlingay - Cambridge	14½	10	July	1871
Watford Jct - Rickmansworth (Single line)	4¼	1	Oct	1862
West London Extension Rly (joint LNWR, GWR, LSWR, LB&SC):				
Kensington - Clapham Jct etc	5½	2	March	1863
Hinckley - Wigston Jct (MR)	11¼	1	Jan	1864

South Staffordshire Railway and Cannock Mineral line

	Miles	Date		
Walsall - Bescot (GJR)	1¾	1	Nov	1847 (passrs)
		1	March	1850 (goods)
Walsall - Wichnor Jct (MR)	17¼	9	April	1849 (passrs)
		1	March	1850 (goods)
Pleck Jct, Walsall - Dudley	5½	1	March	1850 (goods)
		1	May	1850 (passrs)
Bescot Curve	½	1	March	1850 (goods)
		1	May	1850 (passrs)
Sedgeley Jct - Dudley Port (SV)	½	2	Jan	1854
Ryecroft Jct, Walsall - Cannock	7	1	Feb	1858
Norton Branch	3	1	Feb	1858
Cannock - Rugeley (TV)	7¼	7	Nov	1859
Cannock Chase Branch	2½	7	Oct	1862
Wednesbury - James Bridge (GJR)	2½	14	Sept	1863
Wednesbury - Bloomfield Jct (SV)	2¾	14	Sept	1863

Widened Lines

	Miles	Date		
Chalk Farm - Primrose Hill (south end), 3rd and 4th lines (sidings added from 1845; there were eight tracks by 1870)				1847
3rd (Up) line:				
Primrose Hill (north end) - Watford		1	July	1858 (goods)
				1863 (passrs)
Watford - Bletchley		1	July	1859 (goods)
Watford - Tring			May	1863 (passrs)
Tring - Bletchley			May	1866 (passrs)
4th (Down) line:				
Primrose Hill (north end) - West London Jct		1	July	1858
Willesden - Watford		20	Sept	1875
Watford - Tring		8	Nov	1875

PERMANENT WAY

The design of locomotives is of course constrained by the nature of the track. It is surprising to realise that even after the introduction of large 30-ton engines in 1851 no less than 70 miles of the LNWR Southern Division main line was still laid with the original rails of 1837. Over 40 miles of it was mounted on stone blocks, each rail was shorter than an engine's wheelbase, and fishplates had only just been introduced. Little wonder that there were so many broken locomotive springs, and that there was such a wholehearted adoption of equalising levers and india-rubber springs.

The original London & Birmingham track was specified by Robert Stephenson and was the same as that which the Liverpool & Manchester Railway had been persuaded to adopt in 1833 after the failure of its original rails. It consisted of 50 lb per yard malleable-iron fishbelly rails in 15ft lengths, the half-lapped ends of which rested in a joint chair; the joint and intermediate chairs, 3ft from centre to centre, were Stephenson's patent type with iron keys. They were mounted on square stone blocks except on embankments liable to settlement, where wooden cross sleepers were used.

By February 1835 the Liverpool & Manchester found that this track was still too weak and ordered 60 lb rails of parallel form; ten months later 75 lb parallel rails were adopted as standard. On the L&B similar difficulties with Stephenson's 50 lb fishbelly rails led to a lot of discussion, argument and alteration, so that by the time the railway opened the track was a mixture of types and weights:

Rails: weight	type	distance between chair centres	
50 lb/yd	fishbelly	3ft (patent chairs)	10 miles
65 lb/yd	parallel	4ft	25 miles
75 lb/yd	parallel	5ft / 3ft 9in (cuttings & low embankments) / 2ft 6in (high embankments)	77½ miles

The rails of double-headed parallel form had been laid against Stephenson's advice. The 65 lb rail was in 16ft lengths, the 75 lb rail was 15ft; both had squared ends. The top of the rail was 2½in wide, the depth was 4½in and 5in. The rails were held by oak keys in joint and intermediate cast-iron chairs weighing 31 lb and 26½ lb respectively. Each chair sat on a sheet of tarred felt on the sleeper, to which it was fastened by two spikes. The stone sleepers were 2ft square by 1ft deep, or 1ft 3in deep if under the joint-chairs of the 75 lb rails. These expensive granite and limestone blocks, from quarries all over England, weighed 6 or 7 cwt apiece; they were set diagonally to the rails (for easier access to the sides when renewing ballast) and when bedded in position two holes were drilled in each for the 6in oak plugs which received the spikes. The wooden sleepers, mostly larch or oak and treated with Kyan's preservative, were 'half-logs' 9ft long, 9in wide and 5in deep, rounded on the bottom surface. Ballast was mainly gravel, about 2ft thick, with 10in beneath the stone blocks and 1ft 6in beneath the wooden sleepers. Some parts were ballasted with sand over a thin layer of gravel; some had mixtures of chalk and flint or chalk and gravel.

It was soon found that the wooden sleepers, which had been intended for use only until the embankments settled, gave less trouble than the stone blocks. They remained, and their use was very gradually extended.

The fishbelly rails were quickly replaced, and by 1840 only a few of them remained on the main line, at Kensal Green and Watford. Some which had been taken from the L&B and used by Stephenson in the construction of the Aylesbury Railway were found to be "worn out" by April 1844.

By February 1847 the Southern Division comprised 194½ route miles:

	Miles
Main line:	112¾
West London branch:	3 (single)
Aylesbury branch:	7 (single)
Bedford branch:	16
Peterborough branch:	47¼
Leamington branch:	8½ (single)

All but eighteen route miles of the main line was the original track of 1837-38, laid with 75 lb rails; 40½ miles of it, in cuttings, was on stone blocks. The remainder (and all the branches) was on wooden sleepers, but with a great variety of rails. About a dozen miles of the main line rails were still on chairs as much as five feet apart. From 1845 some relaying had been done, mostly with 82 lb rails, and in 1845-7 all the old 65 lb rails were removed from the main line for re-use on sidings and branches.

By the end of 1852 the main line still had 49½ miles of the original track laid in 1837-38, and there were still 40½ miles on stone blocks. The rails were now 75 lb (50½ miles), 82 lb (61¾ miles) or 90 lb (½ mile) with chairs between 2ft 9in and 3ft 9in apart. The whole line from Euston to Tring and more than three-quarters of that between Tring and Weedon had been relaid with the 82 lb rails, retaining the old stone blocks wherever possible.

As an experiment two miles had been laid in 1849 on longitudinal sleepers, but a longer-lasting improvement was the introduction of fishplates in 1851. By April 1853 some 32 miles had been 'fished'. Rail length remained at 15ft until the introduction of 21ft rails in 1853.

By 1853 the branch lines were laid with a variety of rails, all on wooden sleepers:

	Rails	Miles		Date
Aylesbury:	65 lb/yd	5½	(single)	1838
	75 lb/yd	1½	(single)	1844
Coventry-Leamington:	75 lb/yd	8½	(single)	1844
West London:	65 lb/yd	3	(single)	1844
Peterborough:	71 lb/yd	26		1845
		21¼		1846
Bedford:	70 lb/yd	16½		1846
Dunstable:	65 lb/yd	½		1847
	70 lb/yd	6½		1847

	Rails	Miles	Date
Buckinghamshire:	82 lb/yd	53 (31½ single)	1850
Rugby-Stamford:	72 lb/yd	35¼ (17¾ single)	1850
Rugby-Leamington:	82 lb/yd	15 (single)	1850
Coventry-Nuneaton:	75 lb/yd	10	1850

The distance between the centres of the chairs had been standardised at 3ft from 1846, but the light rails of the Aylesbury and the West London branches were mostly on chairs 4ft apart.

As a comparison, in 1849 the N Div main line had twenty miles of 62 lb rails and 53¼ miles of 65 lb; as much as 62¼ route miles were on stone blocks. By 1853 the line had been upgraded so that the lightest rails were now 65 lb, of which there were still 22¼ miles, and the mileage of stone blocks had been reduced to 47¼. Two N Div lines which were taken over by the S Div in 1860 were recorded in 1853:

	Rails	Miles	Date
Trent Valley:	72 lb/yd	20	1847
	75 lb/yd	29½	1847
Stour Valley:	82 lb/yd	14½	1852

During the 1850s the stone blocks were gradually removed from the S Div main line. They were replaced by wooden sleepers - creosoted from 1849 - which were now of rectangular section, 9in by 5in, instead of the old 'half-logs'. A pile of 4,000 stone blocks, lying at Berkhampstead, was sold for £170 in 1860; some of them were put to use as kerbstones in the town.

Lines opened in 1858, from Northampton to Market Harborough and from Watford to St Albans, were laid with 80 lb rails in 21ft lengths, fishplated, on creosoted timbers 9ft by 10in by 5in. There were seven sleepers to a rail, spaced closer together at the rail joints. Cast-iron chairs weighed 35 lb, held down by three spikes in trenails. The Sutton Coldfield branch, opened in 1862, was similar but with 84 lb rails.

By this time, steel rails had been introduced experimentally. In April 1861 orders were placed for five tons of steel rails from John Brown & Co and 24 cast-steel crossings from Naylor, Vickers & Co. These may have been the rails laid at Chalk Farm which are said to have remained serviceable while the adjacent iron rails were renewed seven times. Because of their expense, steel rails were at first used only at locations with the heaviest traffic. With the general substitution of steel rails for iron in the mid-1870s, the length of each rail increased from 21ft to 30ft. The Stores Committee recommended in November 1875 that in future 84 lb rails should be used on the main line and 75 lb rails on the branch lines.

The standard 60ft rails did not come into general use on the LNWR until 1894.

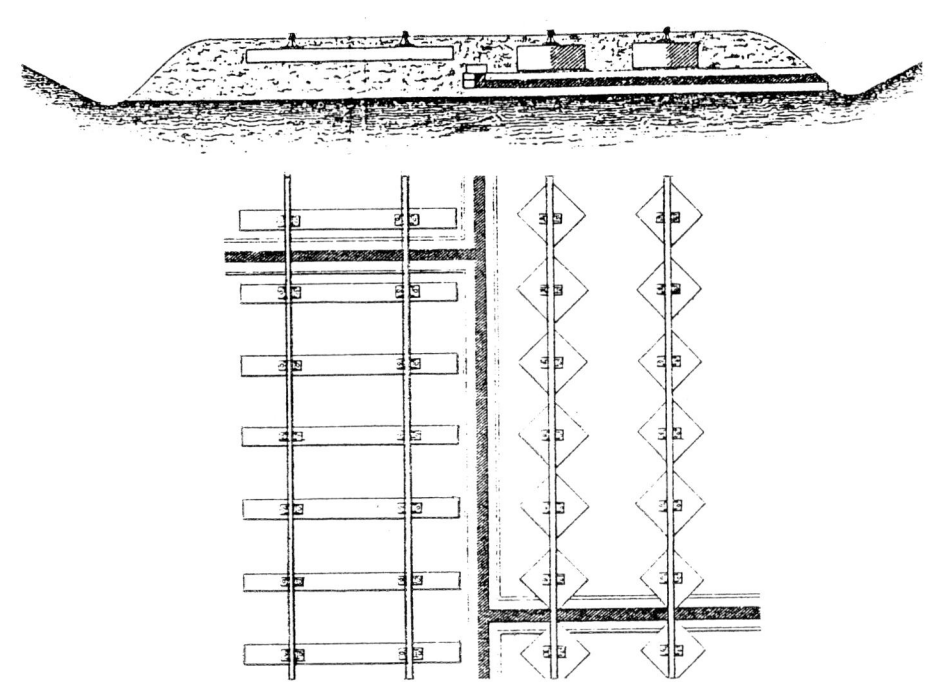

MAIN LINE

Opening to Boxmoor, 20th July 1837

Construction of the London & Birmingham Railway began in June 1834 and completion was forecast for 1837 but there were so many unforeseen difficulties and delays, as at Kilsby tunnel, that the line was opened in sections.

After the appointment of Edward Bury as contractor for motive power, 36 identical passenger locomotives were ordered from six firms of makers. The first of these engines were promised for delivery in February 1837 to be followed by the others during the next twelve months. Goods engines were also ordered but could not be expected before 1838.

Robert Stephenson had advised that no part of the line should be opened to traffic until at least three efficient passenger engines were available but the directors were naturally anxious to have a train ride and decided that 20th June 1837 would be a suitable day for a tour of inspection. Their outing had to be postponed because the first of the passenger engines was not sent off from the makers until 26th June.

On 22nd June Edward Bury felt able to tell the Board that they could announce the opening of the first section, 24½ miles from Euston to Boxmoor, for any day after 2nd July. Although no engines had arrived, Bury knew how close the first two were to delivery - they had been built at his own works in Liverpool and in the previous week one of them had a successful trial on the Liverpool & Manchester - and that another built by R. & W. Hawthorn in Newcastle was on the point of being despatched. Engines were also expected shortly from Benjamin Hick of Bolton and the Haigh Foundry at Wigan. A less confident Locomotive Committee recommended delaying the opening until after 17th July.

There were other locomotives on the line; a dozen or so were used by the building contractors, some being their own property while others had been bought by the L&B and hired to them. These formed the nucleus of the Ballast Engine stock used later in maintaining the permanent way. By contrast with the train engines these ballast engines were unnumbered but all had names. The latest addition to this stock was a big 2-4-0 built by R. Stephenson & Co for America which had been sent instead to the L&B.

Bury was asked to have an engine and train ready at 1pm on Thursday 29th June to convey the Board on their postponed trip from "the Euston Station to Box Moor" and back. At this time the stationary engines for drawing the trains up the incline to Camden were not ready and until the following October the big Stephenson 2-4-0 worked on this section.

The first trip on the L&B reported by *The Times* took place on Thursday 6th July when a train took the Engineer, the Architect and several directors, including three of the influential Liverpool group, from Euston to Boxmoor. The reporter noted that the train passed through Primrose Hill tunnel at 22mph outward and 26mph on the return journey.

Then on the 13th July there was an invitation trip consisting of two trains, each filled with directors and privileged guests. The first of these, which according to *The Times* consisted of 11 carriages hauled by one engine (presumably the 2-4-0 as far as Camden), left Euston at 1pm and reached Boxmoor in 68 minutes. The second train left at 2pm with 12 carriages and arrived at Boxmoor a few minutes after 3pm.

Nos 1, 2, and 16 were the only train engines on the line when the London & Birmingham Railway opened for public business with three trains in each direction on Thursday 20th July 1837.

Opening to Tring - 16th October 1837

On the morning the Camden incline stationary engines began regular work, Saturday 14th October 1837, about forty people, directors and friends, travelled by train to Tring (31½ miles). After being drawn up from Euston by the rope, the train of "about a dozen carriages" and an engine left Camden at 9.00am and arrived at Tring at 10.08. On the following Monday a public train service began with four trains in each direction on weekdays and three on Sundays.

Tring to Denbigh Hall and Rugby to Birmingham - 9th April 1838

The hard winter of 1837-38 delayed the opening of the next sections of line, Birmingham to Rugby and Tring to Denbigh Hall. Denbigh Hall was the new name of a small public-house (formerly the *Pig & Whistle* but renamed after a visit by Lord Denbigh) at the point where the L&B crossed the Watling Street turnpike about a mile north of Bletchley. It was adopted as a convenient end-of-track for the first through service from London to Birmingham; passengers were taken by a fleet of Chaplin & Horne's road vehicles over the intervening 36½ miles to Rugby. Five coaches, five omnibuses and a luggage van met each train. It was estimated that 250 passengers would be travelling daily in each direction, and the road journey would take four hours "including some refreshment time".

On Friday 6th April 1838 the works engines were all moved into the uncompleted Denbigh Hall - Rugby section, and on Monday the new service began, with a stock of 24 passenger locomotives, seven of them working on the Birmingham - Rugby section. On the southern section there were seven trains in each direction on weekdays and four on Sundays; between Rugby and Birmingham there were three trains on weekdays but only one on Sundays. One or two extra trains were shortly added. *The Railway Times* was impressed by the stock of locomotives, which it reckoned to be about 26 - "a supply which will obviate much of the inconvenience and prevent many of those accidents which have marked the working of the Grand Junction line."

The first train on the opening day left Euston just after 7.00am, reached Tring in under two hours and arrived at Denbigh Hall at 10.25. The first train from Birmingham left at 9.03am, took fifty minutes to Coventry (18¼ miles) where it waited for six minutes, reaching Rugby at 10.32.

For five months in 1838 Denbigh Hall was very busy and looked like a racecourse with tents everywhere, "lots of horses, coachmen, post-boys, post-horses" and as well as Chaplin & Horne's vehicles conveying passengers to and from Rugby, there were individual coaches to Newport Pagnell, Northampton, Banbury, Derby, Nottingham, Boston, Lincoln, Sheffield and Lichfield.

The normal journey time between London and Birmingham by this rail-road-rail service was 8½ hours, including 4¼ hours on the road between Denbigh Hall and Rugby; 15 minutes were allowed for refreshments when the coach stopped at Weedon, Daventry or Dunchurch.

The fastest-ever journey was recorded on Friday 20th July 1838. The Duke of Wellington had suggested laying on a special trip to impress the French Ambassador Marshal Soult - his old adversary from the Peninsular War and Waterloo. The timing was recorded by Benjamin Worthy Horne, the coach proprietor, who was in charge of the arrangements:

Euston Square	dep.:	4.20am	by rail	
Denbigh Hall	arr.:	5.55		47½ miles
" "	dep.:	6.00	by road	
Stony Stratford		6.30		
Towcester		7.10		
Foster's Booth				
Weedon (5 mins. detention)				
Daventry		8.20		72½ miles
Dunchurch				
Rugby	arr.:	9.20		84 miles
(Breakfast: 50 mins.)				
	dep.:	10.10	by rail	
Birmingham	arr.:	11.10		113 miles

This was only six hours travelling time, and no doubt the Marshal took note (as was intended) of the fearsome new possibilities of rapid troop movements from the Central Barracks at Weedon. He and the rest of the entourage were taken on from Birmingham to Liverpool by the Grand Junction Railway on which his train is said to have covered 10¾ miles in 10 minutes - 64mph!

Opened Throughout - 17th September 1838
When the long and difficult Kilsby Tunnel was at last completed on 21st June a single line was made available through the unfinished section of the railway between Denbigh Hall and Rugby; the first passenger train to make the entire journey was the 9.30am from Euston on Sunday 24th June. On the same day the first Up train left Birmingham at 10.00am for Euston. A special for the directors and their friends on Monday 20th August left Birmingham at 6.30am and after inspecting Kilsby Tunnel and Wolverton Works reached Euston at 1.00pm after only 5hr 2min travelling time, an average 22mph.

Even faster was the Directors' Special on the official opening day, Monday 17th September 1838. Leaving Euston at 7.15am it got to Birmingham just after midday. Excluding stops at Tring, at Wolverton where the engine was changed, and at Rugby, this was an average speed of over 26 mph. Public trains were to be held to a more sober speed "until the works settle".

On the same day the first public train, with at least 200 passengers distributed among sixteen first-class and mail carriages, together with four private carriages on flat trucks, was taken slowly out of Euston at 8.10am but after going up Camden Bank on the rope "did not get fairly under weigh" with the locomotive until 8.25.

Euston	dep.:	8.10am
Camden	dep.:	8.25
Watford	arr.:	9.03
	dep.:	9.06
Tring	arr.:	9.38
	dep.:	9.42½
Wolverton	arr.:	10.28
	dep.:	10.53
Roade	arr.:	11.16
	dep.:	11.26
Weedon	arr.:	11.53
	dep.:	11.56
Rugby	arr.:	12.30pm
	dep.:	12.33
Coventry	arr.:	1.06
	dep.:	1.21
Birmingham	arr.:	1.58

These were the timings recorded by those travelling on the train; at Curzon Street the clocks showed the local time to be only ten minutes to two.

The engines stationed at Denbigh Hall and Rugby had all been driven to the Central Engine Depot the night before, so from the first day of the completed London & Birmingham Railway the locomotive working was centred on Wolverton. At that station a vast crowd gathered to greet the first trains, whose elegant passengers observed the preparation of a lineside "rural feast" to celebrate the opening of the railway.

The turnplates at the temporary termini were taken up and Denbigh Hall ended its short hectic life as a station. The Denbigh Hall Inn lasted another 120 years and was demolished in 1959; the name was continued on a nearby signal box until it closed in 1965.

For running the train services there were 36 locomotives; eleven of these had been on the Rugby - Birmingham section, the remainder were from the southern section. On weekdays six trains ran in each direction from end to end of the line, with one between Euston and Wolverton and another between Wolverton and Birmingham; on Sundays there were three all the way and one between Euston and Wolverton. Very soon, with the opening of the Aylesbury branch and the connection with the Midland Counties Railway at Rugby, this pattern changed considerably, but throughout the life of the L&B and for some years beyond, all passenger trains made a stop at Wolverton.

Later Developments
For a long time the main line remained relatively unchanged. It had been well laid out and engineered, heavily built with big earthworks, tunnels and viaducts to provide a gradient nowhere steeper than 1 in 326 and with very easy curves. At Birmingham the Curzon Street terminus of the L&B was soon joined by the parallel terminus of the Grand Junction Railway whose rails also entered from the east after a circuit around the northern side of the town; a double crossover just outside the stations allowed through working of trains in each direction.

The twin stations were built on the edge of town, which did not matter much when railways were a novelty, but the distance from the centre soon became an inconvenience. Increasing traffic created congestion which was not helped by the addition of trains from the Birmingham & Derby Junction Railway (from 1839 until 1842 and again from 1851) and the Birmingham & Gloucester (from 1841). With railway developments about to take place on the west side of the town, in 1845 the L&B decided to extend its line to a new and bigger straight-through station in the middle of Birmingham, but nine years of complex inter-company manoeuvrings elapsed before the "Grand Central Station" was opened in June 1854.

The extension of the main line to New Street (as the station was more prosaically named) left the old L&B by a junction 500 yards short of the buffers at Curzon Street and ran for almost a mile into the new station; the last quarter-mile was up a sharp incline of 1 in 58, mostly in a tunnel. Curzon Street's passenger facilities were taken over as part of the goods depot.

Meanwhile other developments had taken place at the southern end of the line. Euston Station was enlarged in 1845-8, including platforms specifically for the Midland Railway traffic. In 1847-9 the whole area between the top of Camden incline and Primrose Hill tunnel was completely remodelled, with new goods sheds in a much enlarged yard and two new locomotive sheds, a roundhouse for goods engines on the Up side and a straight shed for passenger engines on the Down.

Sidings were gradually added at many places on the main line, mainly south of Rugby, and by 1852 the length of these totalled 53 miles. (By comparison, and indicating the amount of traffic handled by the S Div, the N Div main line, plus the Trent Valley, had barely 19 miles of sidings). More were added in the ensuing years, such as the extra lengths laid down in 1856 at Watford, Kings Langley, Boxmoor, Tring, Leighton, Bletchley, Blisworth, Weedon and Crick which were "rendered necessary by the increasing coal traffic". Surprisingly, it was not until that year and after a series of accidents, that short "blind sidings" or headshunts were added to each end of the main line sidings.

An enormous extension to the old main line took place early in 1860. By a revision of the interdivisional boundary the working of all lines as far north as Stafford was transferred to the S Div Locomotive Department. Three main lines were involved: from Rugby the Trent Valley line ran for 50 miles to Stafford; from Birmingham there were 29 miles of the old Grand Junction line and the 14½-mile Stour Valley line through Wolverhampton, which joined the GJR line at Bushbury. The total length of the S Div main line was now 133½ miles from Euston to Stafford by the Trent Valley, 142 miles by the GJR line and slightly less via Wolverhampton.

The introduction of the electric telegraph between Euston and Camden in 1845 and its extension along the main line in 1848 put the main stations such as Camden, Wolverton, Rugby and Birmingham in touch with each other and enabled a reduction in the number of spare engines which were kept waiting at these places. Within the next five years the wires were extended along the branches and in November 1855 the 'permissive block' signalling system, with 30 telegraph stations (or 'watchboxes', the ancestors of the signal cabin) between one and four miles apart, was introduced from Primrose Hill tunnel to Rugby. Other stations were added in 1856 between Euston and Rugby to produce the 'two-mile' telegraph system. This was also installed on the Trent Valley line.

The telegraph as an aid to more efficient train working helped to defer the laying of extra running tracks alongside the main line. These had been proposed in 1846 but it was not until 1858-9 that a third line was added for Up goods working from Bletchley southwards, with a fourth line between West London (Willesden) Junction and Primrose Hill tunnel. In the 1860s the extra goods line was made available for slow passenger trains, but bottlenecks remained at Primrose Hill and Watford tunnels until the 1870s.

Even with the universal provision of the telegraph, a modified version of the inherently dangerous 'time interval' system of working continued, with trains allowed to follow each other after a prescribed number of minutes. 'Absolute block' working, whereby only one train was allowed on the same line between one signal cabin and the next, was introduced between Willesden and Bletchley in 1869 and over the other sections of the main line between Euston, Birmingham and Stafford in 1871-4.

Camden Incline
From the Euston terminus four tracks ran for about a mile up a slope of successive gradients: 1 in 66, 1 in 110, 1 in 132 and 1 in 75 - an average of 1 in 85 - to the bridge over the Regent's Canal at Camden. The eastern pair led directly from the passenger platforms but the other two were laid on the space which had been set aside for the Great Western Railway's entrance into London. Negotiations between the L&B and the GWR had broken down in February 1836, so the extra tracks became the L&B's 'spare line' and the GWR built its own line into London with a terminus at Paddington, eventually opening from there to Maidenhead in June 1838.

The incline was to be worked by stationary engines, mainly (as it was claimed in 1839) because wealthy residents found the idea of locomotives passing their houses objectionable. Robert Stephenson's opinion was that the incline was "such that a stationary engine is better adapted ... than an assistant locomotive, which would otherwise be required" and he thought "passengers are more conveniently landed at a depot" by a stationary engine.

Immediately north of the canal bridge a vast underground complex of vaults was built to house the boilers, fuel stores, engines, workshops and rope-tensioning mechanism. It had been planned to haul trains up the two centre tracks, the intended GWR and L&B Down lines, but machinery for only the L&B half was now necessary. Winding engines for working the L&B only were ordered from the Lambeth firm of Maudslay, Sons & Field in July 1836 at a cost of £5,150. Repairs to the Regent's Canal delayed delivery and the unassembled parts did not arrive on site until just after the opening to Boxmoor in July 1837.

For twelve weeks while the winding machinery was being got ready the incline was worked by locomotive. Trains were taken up by R. Stephenson & Co's No 153, a 2-4-0 with 15in cylinders and 4ft 6in coupled wheels, the most powerful of the ballast engines. The average load was 70 tons - fourteen carriages with 148 passengers.

From the morning of 27th September 1837 some trains were taken up the incline by the stationary engines and on 14th October, two days before the opening to Tring, they began regular work. Two 60hp condensing beam engines with 43in x 48in cylinders, working side by side on a common shaft were installed in the eastern half of the engine room directly under the main line tracks. Beyond the engine room on each side were the boiler rooms each containing two boilers; all four were united by about 100ft of steam pipe. The boilers were marine-type but two of them were replaced, perhaps as late as 1844, by longer cylindrical boilers each having two flues. The boiler fuel was delivered by chute directly from the canal into two 112ft long cellars; it was smokeless anthracite at £1 10s (£1.50) a ton, expensive but necessary to protect the amenity of Camden Town, which was landmarked for a few years by the two 132ft chimneys flanking the railway. (A local publican advertised, as an attraction, that the chimneys could be seen from the windows of his bar parlour). The chimneys, coal holes and the stairway between the tracks down to the engine room were the only surface evidence of the work going on below ground.

A rope - 3,744 yards long with a circumference of 7in, weighing 11¾ tons and spliced into an endless loop - was driven by passing three times around a 20ft diameter wheel coupled directly to the engine drive-shaft. It was kept taut by means of a horizontal pulley on a sliding truck from which a chain and counterbalance weight hung down a well. The rope left its driving wheel, passed round the horizontal tensioning pulley to a vertical wheel under the centre of the southbound track, where it came up to the surface. It passed over sheaves set between the rails, passing down the line to the foot of the incline at Euston, round a pulley below rail level, and back over the sheaves of the northbound track to the driving wheel.

The bottom pulley was at bridge No 1 under Wriothesley Street (removed at the end of 1845) which stood some 250 yards from the buffers at Euston. Northbound trains were pushed by a gang of men (soon replaced by a locomotive) from the passenger platform to the bridge, where the leading carriage was attached by a short messenger rope to the endless rope. A signal was sent up to the Camden engine room by depressing a plunger at the Euston end of an air-tube; four seconds later air pressure a mile away displaced the coloured liquid in a glass indicator, also attracting the engineman's attention by a "low melancholy moan" or a "shrill whistle". The engines were started, winding the rope up to a speed of 20mph. When the carriages reached the summit, after a climb of three or four minutes, the rope was unhooked and the train rolled forward to a stop; a locomotive from the nearby engine shed then backed on for the next part of the journey. Trains coming south were detached from their locomotives at Camden and ran downhill by gravity, with the brakes in the hands of a team of 'bankriders'.

The total cost of the incline machinery was £25,000. The running cost in the second half of 1839 was £1,787, falling in succeeding half-years to £1,268, £882, £816 and £560. The cost for the whole of 1842 was £1,276 including £700 for 470 tons of fuel and £150 for wear and tear of the rope.

The original rope made by Huddart & Co of Limehouse was supplanted in October 1840 by a longer one made at Sunderland - "the longest rope on record in one unspliced piece" according to a contemporary description. This was 4,080 yards long, which would have allowed the trains to be attached at the Euston platform, but the practice continued as before, with a locomotive pushing the carriages to bridge No 1 where the rope was hooked on.

The Camden incline was an awkward and expensive mile of track and was potentially hazardous, not only from runaways (one of which occurred before the official opening) but also from the complications of rope haulage. There were many minor accidents; the messenger rope frequently slipped or broke. The signal pipe to the engine room failed occasionally. Stopping to couple and uncouple the rope, even when everything went smoothly, added many minutes to the journey. Having been planned for trains of only 12 carriages the rope was not strong enough to take the much longer trains which soon became an everyday feature. In June 1839 the morning mail train averaged 24 carriages, which meant dividing the train at Euston and taking the two sections up one after the other. On 6th July the train had 27 carriages which had to be split in three, with 29 minutes lost before the recoupled train left Camden. Assistance by banking engine was not possible because the sheaves prevented locomotives running on the roped track.

Locomotives had worked the incline before the stationary engines were installed and on later occasions, using the spare line, when they were under repair. On one such occasion in June 1839 the 11am train left Euston in drizzling rain. Reaching a spot where the rails were muddy because of recent excavations, the engine started to slip, and the following banking engine collided with the rear of the train. The only casualty was a passenger, Mr Hallam, who was bumped on the head, but the daily press sensationally reported the carriage smashed to pieces.

In October 1843 the Coaching Committee raised the whole subject: what *could* be done about the incline? Robert Stephenson, who had planned the stationary engines, suggested extending the rope to the platform to eliminate the pilot engine at Euston. The Locomotive Committee recommended a trial of locomotive working and suggested the provision of two engines with "low driving wheels" as bankers to be used behind the trains, with the train engine at the front from Euston "so as not to slacken speed at Camden. By this arrangement more time will be saved ... and the risk will be avoided that would attend the detaching of the assistant engine if in front of the train." With this foresight it is difficult to understand why front-end piloting was begun and why it was tolerated for so long.

Bury was cautious and was reluctant to abandon the stationary engine completely. Often extra carriages were added to a train at the last minute at Euston and he worried about the delay in sending down an extra engine from Camden. "I must confess the certainty of the Stationary Engines and Rope induces me to prefer it for the general business of the concern" - but he was prepared to work the Mail Trains "which the Board might consider it important to accelerate" solely by locomotive up the unroped spare line, leaving the other trains to be drawn up by rope as before. This commenced in November 1843.

The locomotive-worked mails must have been satisfactory. In June 1844 it was arranged to accelerate all the through trains by 15 minutes and on the urging of the Coaching Committee it was ordered that all trains be taken from Euston by locomotive from Monday, 15th July 1844.

This also proved satisfactory and in December the Camden engineman Mr Dakers was moved to a clerical job. In July 1845 and again a year later the stationary engines were ordered to be sold but it was not until 15th June 1847 that they were put up for auction. Job Wright & Co got them for £2,000. They were then sent to Russia, for work at a flax mill and a silver mine. The rope was bought by Huddart & Co of Limehouse for £14 per ton. The two large chimneys were demolished in 1849, but the empty underground vaults were simply sealed up. Filled with mud and water they remained as a hazard to those tunnelling under them over a century later.

Some northbound trains were assisted by a locomotive in front which could slip its coupling at the top of the bank and run forward into a long siding; the points were then quickly changed to the main line for the following engine and train. To indicate if the leading engine of a double-headed train was to enter the siding, the driver signalled to the pointsman by a leftward wave of his hand by day, or his handlamp by night. No signal meant both engines would go ahead.

An inadequate handlamp signal on 24th January 1853 sent the entire 5.20pm train into the siding and in the following month a whistle code was introduced - one crow when the leading engine was going on with the train, two when it was to be turned into the siding. There was another near-disaster on 24th April 1855, when an engine ran alone onto the main line, while its tender and the carriages of the 4pm Rugby train went into the siding. Despite the potential danger and - probably - many unreported near-misses, the practice of slipping the front pilot engine endured without major mishap for 25 years.

In January 1862 it was suggested by General Manager William Cawkwell and District Superintendent Henry Bruyeres that the assisting engine should be at the rear of the train to avoid the risk at the facing points, but for whatever reason this practice did not begin until 1st January 1869.

Locomotives were taken off southbound trains at Camden and the carriages went down by gravity in charge of bankriders until 1857. In that year many delays occurred because trains were held at the top when the arrival platform could not be cleared quickly enough; in July it was arranged that trains would in future go down to Euston with the engine attached, to be used to take away the empty train as soon as it was unloaded. In practice, engines of main line trains continued to be detached at the Camden ticket platform, being replaced by one of the pilot engines for the descent. Local trains however continued down to Euston with their own engines.

SUMMIT of CAMDEN INCLINE

with Stationary Engine Chimneys and Engine Shed.

BRANCH LINES

Aylesbury Branch   **1839**

The first branch from the main line was the locally-promoted Aylesbury Railway which joined the L&B by a trailing junction about 36 miles from Euston. The branch was seven miles of single track, practically level all the way. It was worked by the L&B from its opening in June 1839, and was leased to that company until July 1844; the lease was then renewed for a further seven years but on the formation of the LNWR in 1846 the line was purchased outright. From its earliest days there were schemes to extend the branch westward but no connections were ever made and Aylesbury remained a terminus to the end.

At first the branch passenger trains ran to connect with main line trains but soon one of them became a daily through train between Aylesbury and London.

	Passenger trains in each direction	
Year	Weekdays	Sundays
1839	3	2
1841	3	2
1845	4	2
1850	4	2
1863	7	1
1868	7½ (7 Down, 8 Up)	2

In 1852 two goods trains ran on weekdays, three on Sundays.

Several L&B engines worked on the branch in 1839:

No.	Type	Mileage 1/7/39 to 15/12/39	
		Aylesbury	Main line
17	2-2-0	5,776	2,109
23	”	3,152	3,937
1	”	1,904	7,059
21	”	336	7,294
18	”	256	7,606
2	”	192	5,532
15	”	112	8,036
25	”	112	5,590
79	0-4-0	112	6,010

In January 1840 two 2-2-0s were delivered to the L&B from Benjamin Hick & Co and were allocated to the branch as Aylesbury Railway Nos 1 and 2. These two were housed in the small shed at Aylesbury but their working was not confined to the branch. The through London train left Aylesbury with the engine running tender first as far as the junction at Cheddington where the same engine was coupled to the other end of the train and ran forward to Camden. Other L&B engines continued to work on the branch.

As built, the branch had an engine shed at each end, but that at Cheddington was taken down in 1840. By 1855 there were four engines (one spare) at the Aylesbury shed, which had room for only two.

Originally two drivers and two firemen were based at Aylesbury, the man in charge being the senior driver, Charles Callan. He had been a driver on the Liverpool & Manchester, where he was sentenced to a month on the treadmill for going on strike, and had been taken on by Bury before the opening of the L&B. He was unable to read, but his wife was "a good scholar" and helped with written instructions, and was described by the Chief Foreman as "about the best engineman we have". He was the driver of Aylesbury No 2 in the accident near Berkhampstead in December 1842.

Poor track near Aylesbury caused the derailment of 2-2-0 No 49 in June 1842 and in April 1844 it was reported that two miles of the branch rails - old fishbelly rails from the main line - were worn out. They were replaced but complaints continued and in January 1852 it was ordered that only small engines (with 14in cylinders or less) be used until "the road is in a fit state to run heavier engines, if required"; in the following month 14in 0-4-0 No 76 was recorded at Aylesbury. "Weak rails" were mentioned when one of the 14in 2-2-0s was derailed in June and in August McConnell was again told not to run heavy engines on the branch. More pointedly he was told to withdraw his heavy engines in May 1855.

With its closeness to London, light traffic and straight and level track, the branch was convenient for trying out new systems, as in 1855 when it was the scene of experiments with Professor Glückmann's apparatus for communication by electric bell between train guard and driver, and a mysterious "train indicator" system for checking guards' reports.

Leamington Branch   **1844**

The Warwick & Leamington Union Railway was promoted locally to link these towns with the L&B at Coventry. In 1843 before construction commenced it was purchased by the L&B and was built by that company as cheaply as possible, an undulating 8¾-mile single line with 1 in 80 gradients. It was opened in December 1844 from a junction just east of Coventry station to a terminus at Milverton, between Leamington and Warwick. Before opening it was thought that one engine would be sufficient for the work of the branch but this was quickly shown to be an underestimate.

	Passenger trains in each direction	
Year	Weekdays	Sundays
1844	6	2
1845	7	2
1850	9	2
1852	9	3
1863	9	4

In 1852 there was a total of four goods trains on weekdays, and two on Sundays. Three drivers and three firemen were based at Milverton in 1848-9.

For over six years Milverton remained the terminus of a simple branch but in 1851 an extension of 15 miles was added forming a loop to rejoin the main line at Rugby. On this single line section there were five passenger trains on weekdays in each direction. At first there were no trains on Sunday but a solitary train was put on by 1863. An 1853 return shows no goods-only trains at all. In 1855 there were six engines at Milverton, two of them spare.

The GWR opened its mixed-gauge line through Leamington in 1852, running close by the LNWR line, but no physical connection was made until 1864.

West London Railway   1844
This was an independent venture originally known as the Birmingham, Bristol & Thames Junction Railway. A wide canal ran from the Thames at Chelsea for 1½ miles to a basin at Kensington; the railway was projected as a continuation northwards to connect with the GWR, the Grand Junction Canal and finally the L&B Railway near Willesden. Construction was very slow and it was eight years before the three miles of single line across open country was opened as the West London Railway in 1844. Apart from a sharp dip of 1 in 36 shortly after leaving the L&B to tunnel under the Grand Junction Canal, the line was almost level. Four passenger trains daily from Kensington were scheduled to connect with L&B Down trains at West London Junction, and all the L&B "short trains" stopped there when signalled to do so. For lack of custom the WLR was closed after six months.

The L&B, which had twice loaned an engine for short periods, took over the working (and the outstanding debts) by agreement in March 1845, and thereafter ran some goods trains. A year later the line was leased jointly to the L&B and the GWR. As on the Aylesbury branch the original 65 lb rails precluded the use of heavy engines until the middle 1850s. The line was doubled in 1860 and a passenger service to Kensington began in 1862, with trains from Harrow and Camden (reversing at West London Junction). Those from Camden ran in connection with NLR trains to Chalk Farm, the two stations being joined by a long footbridge.

The line was extended to the Clapham Junction complex in 1863 as a joint venture by the LNWR, GWR, LSWR and LB&SC called the West London Extension Railway. Within a few years LNWR trains were running to London Bridge, Cannon Street, Victoria and other points south of the Thames.

Northampton & Peterborough Branch   1845
The L&B had a monopoly of the traffic between London and the North but this was threatened by proposals to build a line directly north from London through the eastern counties. In 1842 the L&B attempted to forestall competition in this area by proposing a branch from the main line at Blisworth to run 47 miles north-east down the valley of the River Nene to Peterborough. An Act was obtained in the following year; the line was built quickly, as cheaply as possible, and was opened for passengers in the summer of 1845 and for goods at the end of the year. Beyond the first five miles to Northampton the branch was single all the way. For the first two miles it fell away from the main line at 1 in 100, beside the locks of the Grand Junction Canal; thereafter, running close to the river, it was lightly graded. It was equipped with the electric telegraph from its opening.

At first there was a daily pick-up goods train in each direction between Peterborough and Camden. During 1846 the whole line east of Northampton was doubled and as soon as this was completed the long-awaited cattle traffic commenced in September, with two extra locomotives set aside for the work. In December an end-on connection was formed with the Eastern Counties Railway at Peterborough, giving access to East Anglia. By 1852 there were six weekday goods trains on the branch plus an extra goods train and one of empties on the section between Wellingborough and Blisworth. Sunday goods traffic was limited to two trains between Blisworth and Northampton.

| | *Passenger trains in each direction* | |
Year	Weekdays	Sundays
	Blisworth-Northampton:	
1845	5	1
1850	10	3
1863	17	4
	Northampton-Peterborough:	
1845	3	1
1850	5	1
1863	5	1

The number of footplatemen employed on the branch in 1848 was 44 (compared with 227 on the main line) but this was reduced to 29 in 1849. There were two engine sheds, at Northampton and Peterborough; in 1855 Northampton had space for fourteen engines, but only seven were allocated; Peterborough had six. Engines recorded on the branch were the Bury 0-4-0s Nos 62, 73 and 85 in 1846 and No 72 in 1850, and Wolverton-built 0-6-0 228 in 1852. Later that year such heavy engines were banned from the branch but a big Fairbairn 2-2-2, 297 from the South Staffordshire Railway, was on the line from 1859 to 1864.

Bedford Branch   1846
Locally promoted but leased to the L&B "in perpetuity" from June 1845, this sixteen-mile branch was opened from the main line at Bletchley to Bedford in November 1846, and was the first new line opened by the LNWR. After seven miles of easy grades the line fell towards the valley of the Ouse with 2¾ miles of 1 in 129 as the steepest section.

| | *Passenger trains in each direction* | |
Year	Weekdays	Sundays
1846	5	2
1850	4	1
1861	4	1
1863	6	1

By 1852 there were three goods and one coal train on weekdays only.

Eight footplatemen were based at Bedford in 1848-9, with a shed which had room for four engines. By 1855 there were only two engines (one of them spare) following the construction of Bletchley shed. Early in 1847 2-2-0 No 34 was stationed at Bedford and in the summer of 1858 a similar engine No 51 was working on the branch.

The Midland Railway's Leicester to Hitchin line opened in 1857, crossing the branch on the level with a spur giving access to Bedford LNWR station, which was used by the MR until its own station was completed two years later.

Bedford remained a terminus until 1862 when the branch was extended by 30 miles of single line to join the Great Eastern Railway at Cambridge, with a goods connection to the Great Northern at Sandy. The section between Sandy and Cambridge, which included the minute Sandy & Potton Railway, was doubled in 1870-1. At first there were five passenger trains daily in each direction, weekdays only, but one Sunday train was added in 1864. By that year there was a total of six goods trains and one coal train daily between Bletchley and Cambridge.

Dunstable Branch 1848

A railway seven miles long from the main line at Leighton eastwards to Dunstable was promoted locally but leased to the L&B "in perpetuity" from June 1845. Its main feature was a steep incline climbing towards Dunstable, the original plan for which was a rope-worked self-acting plane. As built and opened in 1848 the incline was 1¼ miles at 1 in 40, worked by adhesion. The small-wheeled 0-4-0s 172 and 173 worked goods and passenger trains on the branch and 2-2-0 Nos 43 and 57 (or 58) were fitted with small driving wheels for this task. At first the two branch engines were stabled at a tiny shed at Dunstable with room for only one. In 1852 there was a total of one mineral, one empties and two goods trains on weekdays only. The passenger service of two trains each way on weekdays only was increased to six (and for a time as many as nine) after 1858, when the branch was joined at Dunstable by the Luton, Dunstable & Welwyn Junction Railway's 5½-mile line to Luton, which was extended to Welwyn and taken over by the GNR in 1861. Until then, LNWR trains were hired to the Luton line, which had a service of five trains daily in each direction. In 1859 a shed for four engines was built at Leighton.

Rugby to Stamford 1850-1

This line, the last for which the L&B obtained an Act before the creation of the LNWR, was a long, cheaply-built and partly single cross-country line running north-eastwards from Rugby, mostly along the valleys of the Avon and the Welland. In its 35 miles it passed through only one sizeable town, Market Harborough, and ended in a junction at Luffenham with the Midland Railway, over whose rails LNWR trains ran for the last six miles to Stamford. The MR continued for another thirteen miles to Peterborough; the L&B's promotion of this second route to that city appears to have been another attempt to block competing lines.

Construction began in 1847 but the branch did not open until 1850-1. It was easily-graded with nothing steeper than a half-mile of 1 in 121 near Market Harborough. There was a weekdays-only service of one goods and three passenger trains in each direction. Three LNWR engines (one of them spare) were stabled in the Midland shed at Stamford in 1855.

The MR line from Leicester to Hitchin opened in 1857, using a mile of the LNWR branch through Market Harborough station; in 1859 the LNWR branch from Northampton was added, joining on the Rugby side of Market Harborough. The service of three daily passenger trains was augmented by an extra train in each direction between Stamford and Northampton.

A photograph taken in 1857-60 shows Sharp 2-2-2 No 35 on a Rugby or Northampton train at Market Harborough (Fig 33).

Banbury and Oxford Branches 1850-1

The Buckinghamshire Railway was an amalgamation of two lines promoted locally but backed by the L&B as part of a scheme to reach much further west, and was leased to the LNWR. Opening in 1850-1 it ran west from the main line at Bletchley for ten miles, then split at Claydon Junction into two 21-mile branches: south-west to Oxford, and north-west through the town of Buckingham to Banbury. The Banbury branch was a single line, and remained so; most of the Oxford line was single at first but it was doubled throughout by 1854. Although connections through exchange sidings were made later to the GWR at both Oxford and Banbury, each LNWR station remained a terminus. Gradients were relatively easy, the steepest being 1½ miles of 1 in 120 falling towards Banbury and a three mile climb out of Bletchley at 1 in 142 and 150.

In the early 1850s the Oxford branch had five weekday passenger trains in each direction and one on Sundays; the Banbury branch had four passenger trains on weekdays and one on Sundays. The total number of goods trains daily was: Oxford branch, two coal, two empties and two goods; Banbury branch, one coal and two goods, with a train of empties four times a week. In 1853 extra trains came to the Oxford branch from the Oxford, Worcester & Wolverhampton Railway, which for eight years routed all its London traffic via the LNWR. This was simplified in 1854 by the construction of a link joining the southern end of the OW&W at Yarnton with the Oxford branch near its western end, cutting out the GWR altogether, and at the eastern end by a short curve southwards from the branch to the LNWR main line to avoid reversing at Bletchley. For a short period in 1857 OW&W trains to Oxford used the LNWR station via a west-to-south chord from the Yarnton loop, but London trains continued using the branch until 1861. In that year the GWR agreed to amalgamate with the OW&W, or the West Midland Railway as it had become, and working over the LNWR came to a sudden end. Thereafter during the 1860s branch train services were only slightly better than in 1850, with six weekday passenger trains each way on the Oxford branch, four or five on the Banbury branch, and one on each on Sundays.

In August 1851 it was stated that the Buckinghamshire lines required eighteen engines, in use and in reserve; some of them were based at Bletchley where a shed had just been built. From the beginning there was ample accommodation for locomotives at the ends of the branches, probably born of schemes for possible LNWR westward expansion. The shed at Oxford had room for nine engines and in 1855 seven engines (including two spare) were based there; OW&W engines had the use of the shed from 1853. Banbury shed was also bigger than required; four engines (one spare) were in a building with space for six.

At first the Banbury branch was worked by Bury four-wheelers with 14in cylinders, but by 1853 two 15in engines were being used for goods traffic. Some engines which worked the Oxford line are known from accident reports: 4-2-0s 148 and 149 and 0-6-0s 124 and 220 in 1851-3. Four which worked with OW&W trains were 0-6-0s 220, 260, 267 and 276.

The Oxford branch was the scene of McConnell's

patent steam sledge brake trials on 19th January 1858 when a Bloomer with a 20-carriage train made a series of emergency stops between Bletchley and Islip from speeds of up to 43mph. The train probably reversed on the Oxford Rd Jct - Woodstock Rd Jct triangle at the end of the Yarnton Loop before returning to Bletchley, making more stops on the way back.

Coventry to Nuneaton 1850

Connecting the old L&B main line with the Trent Valley line, this ten-mile link had a complex history, having been proposed as part of an Oxford, Coventry & Burton-on-Trent Railway, but was built by the LNWR as a convenient means of tapping the coal mines of the district. It opened in 1850 with three short branches to collieries at Griff, Bedworth and Hawkesbury, but unfortunately the coal did not produce coke of a quality suitable for locomotives.

Starting with five, there were seven passenger trains in each direction, weekdays only, by 1852. Surprisingly, there was only one coal train and one of empties each day. In 1855 a small engine shed at Nuneaton accommodated three engines (one spare) for working the branch.

In 1857 a 28-arch viaduct on the line suddenly collapsed. This was at Spon End, within a mile of the junction at Coventry, so the branch was severed at its southern end for almost four years until an embankment and a shorter viaduct were completed.

In 1863 there were five weekday passenger trains in each direction, with two on Sundays.

North & South Western Junction Railway 1853

This four-mile link between the LNWR at West London Jct (later Willesden) and the London & South Western Railway at Kew was worked jointly by these two companies, but they seem to have made little use of it and the North London Railway provided the passenger trains. The NLR lay four miles to the east over LNWR metals so, to avoid congestion on its main line and the bottleneck of Primrose Hill Tunnel, the LNWR promoted the Hampstead Junction line. This opened in 1860 and joined the NLR to the N&SWJ, crossing over the main line by a bridge at Willesden; there was also a connection for goods, from the LNWR main line at Third Line Jct to the HJ line at Harlesden Jct.

St Albans Branch 1858

This 6½-mile single-line branch ran north-east from the main line at Watford to a terminus at St Albans. It was opened in 1858 but despite an 1866 branch of the GNR into the same station and a connection to the new MR main line in 1867, St Albans station remained a terminus.

A turntable was installed at Watford (on Board of Trade insistence) in addition to that at St Albans, but all passenger trains ran between St Albans and Euston with the same engine all the way. At first there were six weekday passenger trains in each direction, increased to eight by 1863, and two on Sundays. The ex-South Staffordshire 2-2-2 *Wednesbury* was on this service within a few weeks of the opening of the branch, as were Sharp 2-2-2 Nos 31, 35, 36, 145 and 205 in the 1860s.

Northampton to Market Harborough 1859

This was an 18-mile link between two LNWR branches, Blisworth-Peterborough and Rugby-Stamford. Built under an Act obtained in 1853 as a counter to the Midland Railway's proposed line from Leicester to the Great Northern at Hitchin, construction was delayed as long as possible. It was also done as cheaply as possible, the line closely following the level of the ground with few earthworks and about four miles of 1 in 100 and a mile of 1 in 130. It was mostly single line but by three years after opening ten miles at the southern end had been doubled.

At first there were two passenger trains daily in each direction on weekdays only, but this was soon increased to four, one of them continuing along the Stamford branch beyond Market Harborough.

Nuneaton to Leicester 1862-4

The South Leicestershire Railway ran east from the Trent Valley line at Nuneaton to join the Midland Railway at Wigston, three miles from Leicester. Its first section, four miles from Nuneaton to Hinckley, opened in 1862 when it was leased by the LNWR. The remaining eleven miles opened two years later.

There were four passenger trains in each direction between Nuneaton and Hinckley, but after the line was completed there were nine trains (four of them MR) on weekdays and two on Sundays between Nuneaton and Leicester. Working was by locomotives from the Coventry and Nuneaton line.

Engines known to have worked on the line in the 1860s include a G class 0-4-2T and the ex-Birkenhead Railway Sharp 2-2-2ST 316. For much of the 1870s the entire passenger service was worked by similar Sharp saddle tanks, among them ex-South Staffordshire 684, and at the end of the decade Small Bloomers 615, 717 and 978 were on this duty.

Sutton Coldfield Branch 1862

This was a locally-promoted line which the LNWR took over and built to prevent a similar scheme with MR connections; it opened in 1862. The branch left the old GJR line (from 1860 under S Div control) at Aston; in its five miles it rose over 100 feet, including a mile of 1 in 95, before descending by easier grades to reach the terminus at Sutton Coldfield. The branch was not extended to Lichfield until 1884.

All passenger trains ran between Sutton Coldfield and Birmingham New Street and at first there were seven in each direction on weekdays and three on Sundays; by 1863 this had only increased by one weekday train but by 1870 the service had more than doubled.

M class 0-4-2T 734 was photographed on a branch train of seven four-wheeled carriages at Sutton Coldfield in 1863 (Fig 129).

Rickmansworth Branch 1862

The Watford & Rickmansworth Railway was "a private enterprise of Lord Ebury's" (Neele) with LNWR support and was worked by that company from its opening in 1862. A single line, it ran four miles from Watford Junction and although alongside a riverbank for most of the way it had many short up and down gradients. It provided a station in the centre of Watford and a weekdays-only service of seven trains each way.

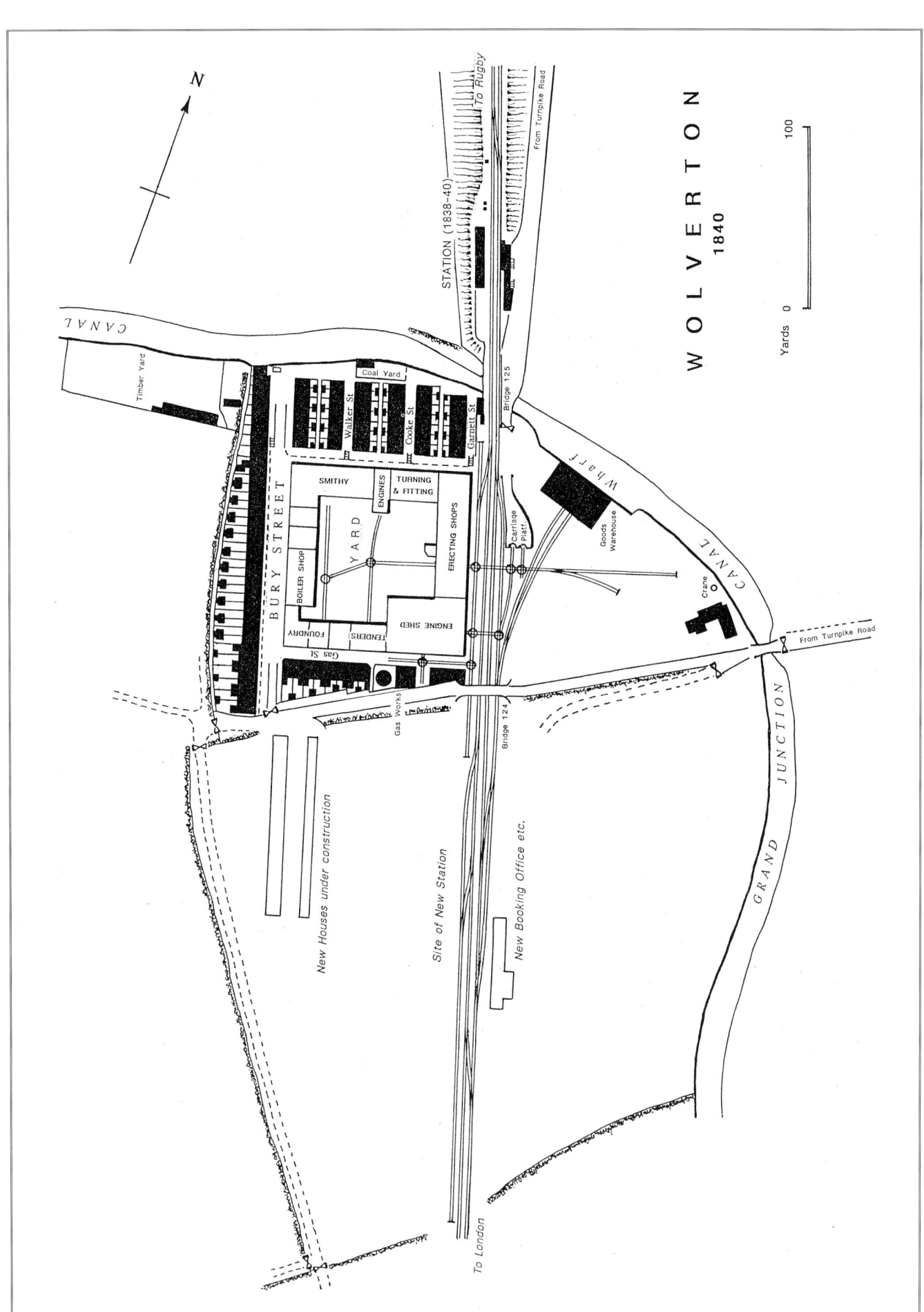

WOLVERTON

The Central Locomotive Repair Works

Robert Stephenson, the Engineer-in-Chief, reckoned that while the railway was being built he had walked the entire length from London to Birmingham about fifteen times. He was out on the line with Edward Bury in the second week of October, 1836, looking at possible sites for stations. Among the quiet meadows of north Buckinghamshire they came to the south bank of the Grand Junction Canal, which made a sharp bend at this point in its meandering course from the Thames to the Midlands, crossing the intended line of the railway and heading westward towards the village of Wolverton, about a mile away. Bury pointed out to Stephenson the field known as Roger's Holm which was enclosed by the canal bend and was now cut in two by the strip of land taken for the L&B. At 52½ miles from Euston and 60 from Birmingham this was about as near as could be to the half-way point, with the advantage of the canal for bringing in building materials, machinery, coal and coke. Also, the London to Birmingham mail-coach road was only two miles away at Stony Stratford. This field, they decided, was the ideal site for the locomotive repair shops.

Repair shops were necessary somewhere, and on an unprecedentedly long line such as the L&B a central position had advantages. Engines would be changed there; it would, as Bury said "decrease the chances of delay by running the engines a short distance." A more important consideration was that 5½ hours on an open footplate, especially in bad weather, would be too much for the engine crews; driving to Wolverton and back was much the same distance as going all the way, but with "a little rest in between, the men would be more active and more able to carry on the work." Similarly, passengers would welcome a brief escape from their cramped compartments. Out in the country land was cheaper and there was room for possible expansion.

The owners of the field (reduced to about eight acres by the land already taken by the railway) were the Trustees of Dr John Radcliffe. A quick sale was arranged and the L&B took possession in May 1837. The construction of Wolverton Works began at once.

The workshops were built on the west side of the line. The outside walls formed a square, each side 314ft long. The general design was prepared by George Aitchison, the Company's Architect, but Bury wrote to the Secretary Capt Moorsom: "I much fear damage may be done if the architects get hold of the drawings - they want appearance, I want convenience and light" and he urged against any decrease in the windows of the workshops.

Soon, like some great barracks or workhouse, the imposing brick structure rose above the surrounding fields. The uniform 28ft high walls were strengthened by stone pilasters and were crowned by a heavy stone cornice which almost hid the low roofs within. Between the pilasters the 15ft 6in tall round-topped windows with dozens of small square panes in their iron frames had a functional appearance which did not detract from the classical regularity of the block. It might have been taken for a hospital or a very large bank.

The eastern wall, alongside the railway, had in its centre a fortress-like gateway leading into the enclosed courtyard. On each side brick buildings for the various repair shops pressed up to the outer wall, leaving a central open space which was mostly 216ft across, slightly less in places. A line of rails left the siding beside the Down main line from a turnplate, entered by the central gateway and crossed to a turnplate in the middle of the yard, whence lines radiated to shops on each side.

On the right (north) side of the central gateway was the large erecting shop, 146ft long by 50ft wide; rails ran along its centre from a 12ft diameter turnplate within the gateway. On the left of the gateway was the small erecting shop, 56ft long by 50ft wide, also having rails along its centre from the same turnplate. Both shops had short engine bays connected by 12ft turnplates to the central track. Next to the small erecting shop and taking up the south-east corner of the block was the engine shed, 90ft wide and 130ft in length along the south outer wall. A central track, at right angles to that through the erecting shops, ran along the centre of the shed across nine turnplates, each giving access to an engine pit on each side, left and right, with a total capacity of 18 engines and tenders. The engine shed had its direct egress to the running lines by another doorway in the east wall through which the central track ran onto a turnplate.

Beyond the engine shed, next along the south wall was the tender shop, 60ft long by 50ft wide, with four bays from the rails which continued along one side from the engine shed next door. One of the turnplates gave access to a line across the courtyard to the central turnplate and back to the main gateway. Next to the tender shop were stores and a brass foundry. Another 60ft by 50ft shop for the iron foundry took up the south-west corner of the block.

Along the back (west) wall the boiler shop, 95ft by 40ft, contained two hearths, two drills and a punch. Next was the hooping furnace, then the joiners' shop with pattern stores above. The north-west corner contained the smithy, L-shaped in plan, 40ft wide and taking up 76ft of the west wall and 136ft of the north wall. This contained 18 single and three double hearths. In the centre of the north wall was the engine-house with its two 14in x 48in beam engines. These pumped water from a well into two tanks, one above the engine-house holding 16,000 gallons and another of 24,000 gallons over the main gateway; they also drove machinery in the shops and worked blowing cylinders for the smithy hearths. The boilers were in a sunk area to the south of the engine-house, projecting into the courtyard; fuel was brought to them by rail across the yard.

Next to the engine-house, the turnery (99ft by 40ft) occupied the remainder of the north wall; this was on two floors, with eight lathes upstairs and fourteen downstairs. Lastly, the lodge, superintendent's office and drawing office were in a block of tiny rooms in the courtyard just inside the gateway on the right side.

Francis Whishaw, from whose 1840 description some

Fig. 1 Wolverton – the south-east corner of the Old Works of 1838 looking across the former main line; the gable-ended roof was added later replacing the original hipped roof which was lower and had a louvred smoke ventilator along the ridge. Looking west, August 1970. (H. Jack)

of these details have been taken, was for once understating the case when he said Wolverton was "perhaps one of the most complete establishments of the kind in the world."

Opposite the Works, on the east side between the railway and the canal there were other developments. Relations with the canal's owners had never been good; the Grand Junction Canal Co's opposition to the L&B Bill was followed by physical confrontation, as at Wolverton in 1834 when canal navvies destroyed railway construction works and had to be restrained by a legal injunction. Then the railway, cutting through the Chiltern chalk ridge at Tring, severed a supply of water to the canal's summit level and during the dry summer of 1838 it became apparent that this section would have to be closed. Pickford & Co, a major user of the canal, appealed to the L&B for help. They asked for a wharf on the canal "at a place called Wolverton" whence goods could be taken by rail to London.

The new wharf was built on the canal's south bank a short distance east of the railway and was used by Pickford & Co as a canal-rail interchange during the stoppage of boat traffic at Tring from September 1838 to January 1839. About 70 or 80 tons were transhipped each day. By the time the L&B's regular goods service began in April 1839 a warehouse had been built on the wharf with rails into its upper floor and cranes to exchange goods between canal boat and railway wagon. Its roof extended as a wide awning over the canal.

In the angle between the rails from the warehouse and the main line was a two-bay loading dock for wheeling road carriages onto flat railway trucks. Road access was over the canal, on a widening of the railway bridge, from the Newport Pagnell - Stony Stratford turnpike road 300 yards to the north. This access also served as the public approach to the passenger station, which was built on the embankment north of the canal. The traffic anticipated there is suggested by a map published in March 1838 showing coach roads from as far away as Peterborough and Stamford leading directly to the "Grand Railway Station at Wolverton".

The First Railway Town

Wolverton Works was completed about September 1839

and by the end of the year the workforce consisted of 203 men and boys, most of whom had come from a distance.

Accommodation was a problem; in August Edward Bury reported "a very strong prejudice against the Company's servants in most of the places adjacent to the railway; parties having rooms or houses give the preference to anyone not connected with the line." In December he wrote: "It is not necessary to remark the entire uselessness of that large establishment if there be not hands to set it in motion, nor to point out that as it is an isolated place, to keep the men in a state of quiet and content their wives and families ought to be provided with suitable residences." From May 1841 Bury himself lived at the Parsonage House in Great Linford, two miles away to the east or as he put it: "within a reasonable walk" from the Works. Most of the men lodged in the villages up to a four-mile walk away.

The area taken up by the Works was 2¼ acres. Except on the east, where the Works wall was next to the railway (at this point widened to four tracks by a siding on each side) the remainder of the original field formed an unoccupied belt of grass. The canal was fifty yards away down a slope to the north, the field boundary hedge thirty or more to the west. On the south side an access road was laid in from the Newport Pagnell turnpike (and was extended westwards in 1841 toward Stony Stratford, the present Stratford Road) with a three-arch bridge over the line, but this still left open ground between the road and the Works. All this space might have been reserved for future extensions (as, eventually, it was used) but at that time, with no precedent for guidance, no clear idea about how the traffic might develop, and with a central open yard into which the shops could be extended - should this ever prove necessary - the decision was taken to fill the surrounding space with cottages.

With hindsight, obviously it would have been more sensible to put the cottages on the vacant land east of the line, but this area had been used for the canal warehouse and was earmarked for future goods yard extension. Building anywhere else would have meant buying more land, but the Radcliffe Trustees were reluctant and very unco-operative. They laid down conditions, one of which was that the L&B should bind itself to stop every train at Wolverton. During 1839 there were meetings and discussions with the Trustees and the L&B's Chairman Glyn and Superintendent Baxendale both made fruitless efforts to persuade them to part with as little as two acres beside the line. But with no agreement in sight, and no other land forthcoming, the tidy solution was adopted; streets were laid out beside the Works wall in 1839 and the first cottages were begun; by the end of the year 62 had been built. In 1840 the entire space was covered and the Works was completely hemmed in by eight rows of houses.

Along the back (west) wall Bury Street ran from the access road to the canal bank. Filling the space to the north were the parallel rows of Walker, Cooke and Garnett Streets, named after members of the Board: Joseph Walker, Thomas Cooke and Robert Garnett; Gas Street ran along the south wall and contained a small gasworks. At the canal end of Bury Street eight of the houses had ground-floor shops; at the other end six with three storeys were for clerks and foremen, as were the eight in Gas Street. The remainder were 'two up, two down' cottages. In February 1840 the Board announced proudly that, on what had recently been "little more than open fields - we have now established what may almost be called a town".

Before these 85 houses were finished it was obvious that many more would be needed. And at last in June 1840 the Radcliffe Trustees were persuaded to sell the 14-acre Shrub Field south of the access road. On this land twenty houses were begun at once, continuing the line of Bury Street to the south but named Creed Street (after the Secretary, Richard Creed) with twenty backing onto them on the east in a street named after the Deputy Chairman, Joseph Frederick Ledsam. The Ledsam Street cottages were minute, with two rooms only, one on each floor. Fifteen years later they were doubled in size by breaching the alternate party-walls. They were still tiny, but were occupied until their demolition in 1965.

The first passenger station, north of the canal, had a very short life. Building work began about November 1838 but was suspended in May 1839 for a report by Bury and Superintendent Joseph Baxendale. The incomplete station at that time consisted of two small brick buildings facing each other across the two tracks; that on the Up side was the booking office, with adjoining waiting and refreshment sheds along the unfinished platform. The Down building held three tiny waiting rooms and a porters' room, with long rows of urinals and closets in extensions on each side. Public access was inconvenient; its position on the embankment required massive retaining walls and flights of steps; any enlargement would be costly. With the development of New Wolverton now under way on the other side of the canal, the station was obviously in the wrong place and as soon as the extra land was purchased in June 1840 work began on a new site south of the three-arch bridge. Here a much bigger station was planned on level ground with room for expansion. There were two 400ft platforms facing each

Fig. 2 Wolverton – railway cottages in Ledsam Street, built 1840, demolished 1965. Looking south-east, August 1962. (H. Jack)

other across four tracks, with a large two-storey block containing a booking office and refreshment rooms on the Up side. This was quickly followed by a similar structure on the Down platform. Each platform was covered by an awning which extended over the adjacent track to a line of columns beyond, leaving the two central through lines open to the sky. On the Up side, kitchens, stables, piggeries and an underground ice-house were added. The new station was opened in November 1840. For many years every Up and Down train made a long stop there, while engines were changed and passengers surged into the refreshment rooms. This station lasted until 1881, when the main line was re-aligned on a long deviation passing east of the Works.

Through the 1840s additional cottages were built; Young Street (Thomas Young, another director) and Glyn Square (George Carr Glyn, Chairman and later Baron Wolverton) continued the grid-pattern. With the addition of a school in Creed Street, allotment gardens behind Bury Street, two public houses just outside the Company boundary, six semi-detached villas for officers and clerks near the canal, and a Market House built in 1843, Wolverton was almost complete. "A little red-brick town composed of 242 little red-brick houses" as a much-quoted description put it in 1848. Most of this brickwork had been laid by the firm of Richard Dunkley of Blisworth.

Bury reported in July 1841 that the school had started; fees were 2d per week for boys, and 1d for infants. Evening classes were begun at the same time for the workmen.

The Radcliffe Trustees gave a piece of land for a church (suitably, to early Victorian wags, in line with streets whose names suggested creeds and burial) and offered to pay half the cost of building a church and a parsonage if the L&B would put up a like amount. The total cost was to be £4,000. The first impulse of the Company, on 7th August 1840 ("at the suggestion of a Dissenter") was to give £1,000, but this led to wrangling about the *proper* function of a commercial enterprise, for many of the shareholders were dissenting Dissenters. Twenty-eight Quaker shareholders sent in a memorial objecting to the money being given, and the Board was obliged to offer to hand back their share of the £1,000 to any who asked for it. Ninety-seven did so and got £55 12s 9d between them. The remaining sum required to make up the half-cost of the church was contributed by individuals. The Chairman, George Carr Glyn, led off with £50 to pay for the communion plate. Edward Bury gave £50, as did the Quaker, Edward Cropper. Several other directors and the two secretaries, Creed and Moorsom, gave £20 each, Robert Stephenson gave £1 and £5 3s 3d was collected from the workmen - a respectable sum as only about a dozen of them were churchgoers.

The foundation stone of the Church was laid on 4th July 1843. The building was in the Early English style, of local stone and with an octagonal spire at the north-east corner. It was consecrated on 28th May 1844 and given the name of St George the Martyr, from the church in Southwark where the new Wolverton parson, the Rev George Weight, had served as curate.

Wolverton was the first of the planned Railway Towns. The land for Crewe was only bought in July 1840, and the decision to build Swindon was not taken until October. Both began to function in 1843. There is no doubt that the example of Wolverton was carefully studied by the Grand Junction and Great Western engineers - who profited from the London & Birmingham's pioneering mistakes. Indeed, Bury was consulted by the GWR about Swindon. Doncaster lay far in the future, but there too Bury played a large part in its inception.

By February 1844 the Chairman could tell the shareholders: "We are beginning to find more fully the economic result of the establishment of Wolverton." He went on, to cries of "Hear! hear!" and applause: "When I look, gentlemen, at Wolverton, I always think with the greatest satisfaction of the expenditure which has been incurred there. I do not say this for the purpose of boasting of what we have done, for it is not much after all, and was perhaps somewhat tardy, but the results have been so gratifying that we allude to it for the purpose of encouraging other companies to follow our example. We were obliged to collect at Wolverton a population from nearly every part of the kingdom, who settled there without any local attachments and without any of the domestic ties of home to bind them together, but who are now, I believe, taking them all-in-all, as quiet, orderly and industrious a set of inhabitants as can be pointed out in any part of the country."

Workmen had come from all over Britain, and beyond, to Wolverton. One of them, Hugh Stowell Brown, later wrote about his experiences from his arrival in August 1840 until his departure at the beginning of 1844. He had two lodgings, both in Old Wolverton village; at the first his fellow-lodger was an engine fitter from London, the second he shared with three young journeymen mechanics from Manchester, Derbyshire and Scotland. Other workmates came from Yorkshire, Birmingham, Wales, Ireland and in one case, Poland. Brown himself was from the Isle of Man. His foreman was the Scotsman William Paton who left Wolverton in 1842 to become Locomotive Superintendent of the Edinburgh & Glasgow Railway which was in many ways similar to the L&B and even had a mile-long rope-worked incline out of its main terminus. The similarity would become even more striking when Paton ordered Bury engines for his new line.

In January 1837 Bury engaged William Andrews, previously with Jesse Hartley of Liverpool Docks, as his "superintendent of engine power" or Chief Foreman at £400 a year, to reside at the Central Repairing Shop at Wolverton when this was ready; until then he was based at Camden engine shed. Andrews duly moved to Wolverton but was there for only two years. The next Chief Foreman was Frederick Parker who had worked at Bury's Clarence Foundry since 1832; Bury had a high opinion of him and brought him south to take over from Andrews at Camden in 1838 and then at Wolverton in 1840. Parker remained there through the L&B period and beyond Bury's departure but did not last long after McConnell was brought in as Locomotive Superintendent in 1847. In August 1848 he gave evidence to the Board of Trade inspector about the incompetence of blackleg drivers during the footplatemen's strike and was promptly sacked. On Bury's recommendation he was then appointed second-in-command of the Great Northern

Fig. 3　Wolverton Works – looking north from Stratford Road bridge (No 124, later 171B) along the former main line in August 1962. Old Works of 1838 on left, new repair shop of 1846 on right, with extension for traverser. The trees mark the position of the canal underbridge; the carriage storage buildings beyond were built in the 1880s on the site of the engine shed of 1846. (H. Jack)

Railway Locomotive Department, and was Works Manager at Doncaster until 1865.

Parker was replaced as McConnell's Chief Foreman at Wolverton by Thomas Forsyth. Forsyth gave support to McConnell's proposal to pay engine drivers on a contract basis instead of by day wages, and said this would almost eliminate engine failures. Shortly afterwards, at the end of 1854, he left for a job with Sharp, Stewart & Co at Manchester, where four years later he was killed by a boiler explosion. He was succeeded at Wolverton by William Rowland - at a wage of £250 a year, rising to £300 in 1856 - who held the post to the end of the separate Southern Division.

Expansion of the Works and Town

Until 1845 the total number of locomotives in stock remained at 90 but by the middle of that year, with new engines arriving and orders placed for another 40, some enlargement of the Works had become urgent. Bit by bit the open central yard was roofed over, providing additional turning and fitting shops. Extension northwards was considered, but it would have involved the demolition of 41 cottages in Garnett, Cooke, Walker and Bury Streets, tucked down below the north wall of the Works, confined by the canal at the end of the streets and the railway embankment on the east. "From their situation they are not considered so eligible by the inhabitants as any others in Wolverton" the Locomotive Committee reported, contemplating the destruction of dwellings only six years old. Instead it was decided to build on the site of the goods yard east of the line, opposite the Works entrance. The old goods shed, its canal transhipment facilities having served their purpose, was demolished at the end of the year and a new goods shed and yard were established south of the passenger station, on the west side of the line and without direct canal access.

On the site of the old goods yard a new repair shop was built 150ft wide by 200ft long, with a central traverser which conveyed locomotives sideways directly from a siding beside the main line and down the length of the shop. There were 16 bays on each side, each with an inspection pit and facilities for light repairs; in design it was similar to the engine house/repair shop which had

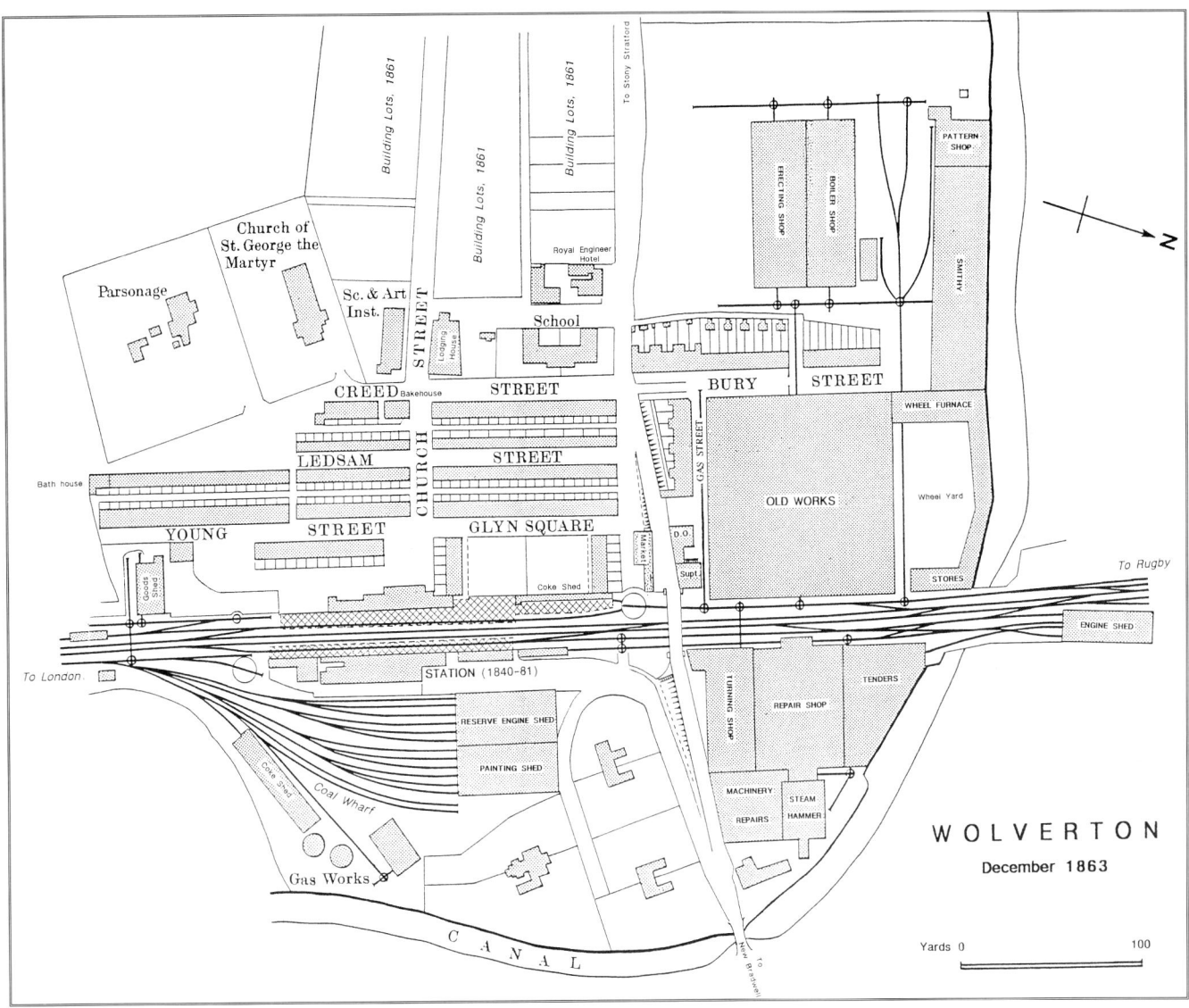

recently been built by the GWR at Swindon. The repair shop was soon flanked by a new turning shop and a tender shop and by 1850 practically the whole area between the railway and the canal was built up. The main line now ran between the two blocks of works buildings, which were connected by rails crossing it at right angles from the Old Works to the new turning shop.

About the same time as the new repair shop was built a new wooden engine shed, 155ft long with four straight through-roads, was built north of the canal bridge on the Up side. These additional stabling facilities allowed the original engine shed in the south-east corner of the Old Works to be altered for use as another erecting or heavy repair shop. Lighting for the new shops required more gas than the gasworks could provide; twice as many retorts were now needed but the Gas Street location was too cramped for expansion. A bigger gasworks was built in 1847/8 on the canal bank east of the station; the old retort house was converted into a drawing office, while the Superintendent's new office was built over the adjoining former coke store.

A 30-cwt steam hammer was ordered in January 1847 and at first worked in the open yard but late in 1848 it was roofed in, using materials from the original L&B engine shed at Camden which was then being taken down. In 1849 a separate foundry was set up to make axleboxes and gas pipes. In 1855 the cottages north of the Old Works were at last demolished and their foundations built over by extensions of the workshops, right down to and along the canal. These shops contained a wheel furnace and store rooms and enclosed an open wheel yard.

To the south, behind the station Up side buildings, another engine shed was built in 1856. This was a six-road brick structure 164ft long with a double roof, the twin end-gables of which had the three standard louvred ventilators typical of so many LNWR engine and goods sheds of the period; shortly afterwards an identical building was added, as an extension on its east side. This became the paint shop, outside which the four well-known photographs of Wolverton's latest locomotives were taken in 1861.

By the late 1850s the original 22-acre site astride the railway was crammed with workshops, passenger station, gas works, coal wharf, goods yard, six officers' villas with large gardens, 225 cottages, a lodging house, market hall, school, bath house, bakehouse and a Wesleyan chapel. On an adjoining three acres stood the C of E church and parsonage.

Unable to persuade the owners to sell any more of the surrounding land for expansion, in 1852 the LNWR purchased "fifteen acres of corn fields" half a mile to the east and began building an overspill village known as Stantonbury or New Bradwell. By 1859 there were about 120 houses - increasing to almost 200 in the following year - in parallel rows along the unimaginatively-named High, Middle and Top streets; there was a post office, butcher's and grocer's shops, the Railway Tavern and a Baptist chapel. A large steam-driven flour mill, a school for 300 children and a C of E church were being built.

Then at last the Radcliffe Trustees agreed to sell, and In 1859 the Works broke out into the newly-acquired land to the west. Two cottages in the middle of Bury Street were demolished and a line of rails was extended from the Old Works through the gap into open ground where two adjoining glass-roofed workshops were quickly built, each 260ft long by 86ft wide; these were the new boiler and erecting shops.

The boiler shop contained 21 forges and a steam hammer, two plate-bending rolls with reversing gear, ten drilling machines, several punching and shearing machines and a 1,000rpm circular saw for cutting hot angle iron. There was a steam rivet-making machine which could turn out 17 rivets a minute and a steam riveter which was capable of completing an 820-rivet boiler barrel in ten hours. Overhead were two travelling cranes. The erecting shop, adjoining to the south, also had two travelling cranes of 40 tons capacity.

To the north of the boiler shop was an open yard of east-west sidings which had a new connection to the main line, by rails which ran alongside the north wall of the Old Works. Beyond this open yard a huge smithy was built in 1860/1, adjoining the wheel furnace of 1855, over the site of more demolished houses at the foot of Bury Street and stretching for 326ft along the edge of the canal. The smithy contained 100 forges ranged along each side, with six 15-cwt Nasmyth steam hammers down the middle. At its western end and continuing the same 90ft wide block was a pattern shop. The ten most northerly remaining cottages in Bury Street were now within the Works, cut off behind a new entrance gate. The northern limit of the workshops was now an unbroken 730ft wall of buildings, west from the main line and forming the side of the canal.

This was the start of the great westward expansion of the Works, with the parallel expansion of the town on the other side of the road to Stony Stratford. The south side of this road and Church Street behind it were quickly set out for housing. One of the first buildings was a 'model' lodging house for single men, a big three-storey block on the corner of Creed Street and Church Street and extending into the newly-acquired field. It was built in 1860 but had a very short life; by 1877 it had been demolished and its site was proposed for a skating rink. Much longer lasting was the Science & Art Institute on the opposite corner. McConnell proposed this new mechanics' institute at a meeting of the men in the Works on 25th April 1861; it was to contain a lecture room, concert hall, classrooms and a library. Within a month £500 had been subscribed by the workmen and the foundation stone was laid. In June an enlarged plan was adopted but thereafter it was a long struggle to raise the necessary funds and opening did not take place until May 1864. This was after McConnell's departure, but he remained on the Committee of Trustees - perhaps his last active connection with Wolverton.

The workforce had risen steadily. At the start in 1838 there were about 100 men; by 1851 there were 775; by 1859 there were 1,300 and a maximum of 2,400 was reached in 1861. The town's population had likewise grown, and continued to grow:

Population

Year	Wolverton	New Bradwell
1831	417	—
1841	1,261	—
1851	2,070	—
1861	2,370	1,658
1871	2,804	2,409

About half of the Wolverton workforce lived in New Bradwell in 1862.

By 1862 the Old Works had been equipped with modern slotting machines, hydraulic presses, a 50-cwt steam hammer and a large cupola furnace in the foundry, where castings of up to 9 tons had been made. In all there were now ten steam hammers, with 145 lathes and almost 200 other machines driven by 11 stationary steam engines.

This rapid expansion of the Works made it the biggest on the LNWR. In August 1859 the floor area of Crewe Works was 3¼ acres, Longsight had less than an acre, but Wolverton Works was bigger than both of them combined, with 4.54 acres of ground floor space and 0.43 acres in the upper storeys. "Money" as the future Chairman Richard Moon said disapprovingly "was spent like water at Wolverton."

Locomotive Construction
Wolverton Works was originally built solely for the repair and maintenance of the locomotive stock. Expert opinion in the 1830s was that construction of locomotives by a railway company would be wasteful, so Wolverton had not been equipped with the necessary facilities and all new engines were obtained from outside firms. Later, with increasing experience, several railways went over to building their own engines and evidently found this to be worthwhile: the Liverpool & Manchester from 1841 at Edge Hill; the Grand Junction from 1842 also at Edge Hill and from 1843 at Crewe. On the London & Birmingham in 1845 there was a sudden and acute shortage of motive power which outside makers were unable to satisfy. This led Bury to construct two of his 14in 2-2-0s at Wolverton, the first to be built there, but probably they were simply put together from spare parts held in the stores, plus finished components supplied by his firm at Liverpool. These two engines were numbered 92 and 95.

Before coming to Wolverton in 1847, McConnell had already built a locomotive in the very cramped workshops at Bromsgrove. Within a fortnight of his arrival he suggested that Wolverton be used for construction, and a month later he was authorised to build one large passenger engine of his own design. This was completed in 1848 as No 227, but became known among the men as 'Mac's Mangle'. As soon as it was out of the shops three more engines were begun, in order to provide work for the many extra hands taken on to defeat the footplatemen's strike in August of that year. These three were copies of Sharp Bros powerful 0-6-0 goods engines, but work on them was halted during a period of cost cutting when the Wolverton mechanics were put on 'short time' - a 4½-day week - and the engines 228-230 were not completed until 1851.

Early in that year, with the prospect of increasing traffic, ten more goods engines were authorised, to be built mostly from spare parts. These were copies of the 0-4-2 class built by Bury, Curtis & Kennedy in 1847-8. Construction began in February 1851 and continued slowly through the next four years, until the last of the ten was completed in 1855. In March of that year another period of financial retrenchment put a stop to locomotive building at Wolverton.

Meanwhile a searching investigation into the relative cost of the LNWR's Southern and Northern locomotive departments resulted in a change of policy. S Div locomotives were no longer to be purchased from outside firms; instead, like Crewe, Wolverton would build its own.

Locomotive construction began in earnest in 1856. At first, two standard types were undertaken, Express Goods 0-6-0s and Small Bloomer 2-2-2s, reproducing the classes built by private firms in 1854. Eventually 86 Express Goods and twenty Small Bloomers would be built at Wolverton but other types were added to the repertoire from 1860: two classes of 0-4-2 tank engines; two classes of Bloomers; 0-4-2 'Mixed Traffic' tender engines. In 1859 eleven new engines were completed and 300 were repaired, but these totals were quite eclipsed after the opening of the new erecting and boiler shops.

Eighteen new engines were built in 1860 and as many as 41 in 1861. By the end of that year nine repairs were completed and one new locomotive was turned out every week. This compared well with the N Div where Ramsbottom had built 43 engines in 1860 and it began to look as if Crewe's output would be matched, and perhaps overtaken, by that of Wolverton. From a slow start, locomotive building had suddenly taken off. Then, with the amalgamation of the two LNWR locomotive departments and McConnell's departure, it nose-dived.

After McConnell
John Ramsbottom, with his headquarters at Crewe, took over as all-LNWR Locomotive Superintendent on 29th March 1862. At once the old S Div received an influx of new managers from the north, while many Wolverton men were transferred to Crewe. Ramsbottom's 'Indoor Assistant' (or 'Resident Chief Officer') at Wolverton was Henry Peet, the former Locomotive Superintendent of the Lancaster & Carlisle Railway and more recently the LNWR Foreman at Carlisle shed, who came south on 1st April. Thomas Wheatley, a Yorkshireman from the Manchester, Sheffield & Lincolnshire was appointed 'Outdoor Assistant' at Wolverton from 1st May and at the same time A. L. Mumford was transferred from Crewe as Chief Draughtsman. Peet died in February 1865 and was succeeded by Mumford as Works Manager. While he was at Wolverton, Mumford completed a magnificent model (now in Rugby Library) of Ramsbottom's *Lady of the Lake*, finished with LNWR green paint but with the old-style elliptical Wolverton numberplates.

On his first tour of inspection Ramsbottom was amazed to discover that there was no spring-making machinery in Wolverton; all springs were made and repaired by hand. He installed the necessary eccentric rolls and punching and shearing machine for £220 in June 1862. He was also critical of the way steam was produced for the steam hammers and for the engine which drove the circular saws and woodworking machinery; it came from two old locomotives standing in the yard - "a very costly method of raising steam" he said. In February 1863 a new boiler was made and put down at the west end of the Joiners' Shop, with a proper chimney stack. Several old locomotives stood about the Works doing similar duty; in 1860 there had been at least seven. They were all taken away in the mid-1860s and Crewe records indicate that twelve Bury 13in passenger engines were cut up in the 1863-6 period; presumably these included most of the Wolverton stationaries, although one survived to be photographed at Crewe in 1879 (Fig 14).

It was quickly decided that all future LNWR locomotive construction was to be at Crewe and in July 1862 Ramsbottom said that when the engines in hand at Wolverton were completed, the staff would be considerably reduced. There were then about 2,000 men employed.

Despite the curtailment of new construction, another 37 engines were completed during 1862 and in the following year a final ten were built, to use up spare parts. The last locomotive of all, Wolverton Express Goods No 1075, was turned out in September 1863. In its entire history some 166 new engines had been built at Wolverton; this total includes two which were nominally rebuilt from Crampton passenger singles but which were completely transformed into new goods engines, Nos 200 and 245.

Rebuilding and repair of locomotives continued, but In May 1864 it was decided to move construction and repair of LNWR carriages from Saltley, Birmingham, to Wolverton. At the same time an improved rail access into the western extension of the Works was authorised; a new bridge was to be built over the canal with a double track line curving in from the north, avoiding the Old Works and passing through the wheel yard and forge into the sidings between the new boiler shop and the smithy. To make way for this new curve and the erection of a new carriage stores warehouse the demolition of the ten Bury Street cottages within the Works was ordered in February 1865. More land was bought to the west of the 1859 extension for a new sawmill and carriage body shop.

One by one the locomotive shops were handed over to Richard Bore, Superintendent of the Carriage Department. The first to go were on the east side of the main line, the tender shop and turning shop, initially to be used for light repairs to carriages which commenced in January 1865 when the first group of workmen arrived from Saltley. The last of the men were transferred on completion of the new sawmill and carriage body shop in June, when the building of new carriages began at Wolverton. The LNWR's lease of Saltley Works was transferred for £10,000 to the Metropolitan Railway Carriage & Wagon Co, who took possession on 1st July 1865.

The last portion of the locomotive shops east of the main line was given up in February 1866; the entire block became a carriage painting shop. Towards the end of 1867 part of the foundry and all the westward extensions of 1859 were transferred, the boiler and erecting shops becoming carriage lifting and repair shops.

Following the success of the system at Crewe Works, 1,180 yards of 18in tramway were ordered to be laid at Wolverton Works in October 1865 at a cost of £590 - with £250 for the engine. Whether one of the Crewe tramway engines *Pet*, *Nipper* or *Topsy* ever went to Wolverton has not been recorded and perhaps the provision of a narrow-gauge engine was found to be unnecessary after the new rail access into the works from the north was completed in the same year. A small standard-gauge 0-4-0T with 3ft 9in wheels was sent from Crewe to Wolverton "to shunt for the Works there" in September 1865. This was a Sharp Bros product of 1850 which had been built for the Coed Talon colliery near Mold, had briefly shunted for the Chester & Holyhead with the name *Diamond* before passing to the Birkenhead Railway as their No 27. The LNWR acquired it in November 1860, naming it *Memnon*. It went swiftly into the duplicate list, first as 356A, then as 1118 in April 1862. From 1865 it was exclusively employed at Wolverton Works and in September 1869 it was transferred to the Carriage Dept, losing its number but acquiring yet another name, *Acton*.

In March 1871 *Acton* was sold to the Shropshire Union Railway & Canal Co for £581 and was replaced in the Works by one of Ramsbottom's standard 0-4-0ST shunters. This engine retained its running number, but from 1877 a series of engines was transferred to Wolverton, renumbered as Carriage Dept No 1, 2 etc, a system which continued for the ensuing 82 years.

Meanwhile main line engine shed accommodation was reduced until only the shed behind the station was left. Under the 1863 shedcode system, Wolverton shed became No 5; it held 22 engines in 1866, down to half of its allocation eleven years before. In a corner of the Old Works nineteen former S Div engines were undergoing repair as late as October 1871, but by then even little Longsight Works had better facilities and most Wolverton engines were being serviced at Crewe. The engine shed, at the end reduced to only three roads, was given up entirely in August 1874 when its engines were transferred to Northampton. There were no more locomotive repairs at Wolverton after 1877 when in February the few remaining shops were ordered to be handed over to the Carriage Dept. The old erecting shop roof was dismantled and taken away for re-use in an extension of Willesden shed to house the Metropolitan "and other heavy engines" shedded there.

Thomas Wheatley had resigned on 28th February 1867 to join the North British Railway as Locomotive Superintendent at Cowlairs Works, Glasgow. This led to a further decline in the status of the S Div. Ramsbottom's N Div Outdoor Assistant, John Rigg, was given oversight of the S Div, retaining his office at Crewe, and Wheatley's reduced post was taken by George Lord. In November 1871 A. L. Mumford took over as S Div Outdoor Assistant with headquarters at Rugby.

The last Locomotive Department Manager at Wolverton was H. W. Kampf, who had started there under Bury in 1841. He became a draughtsman and was transferred to Crewe in 1862, being promoted to Chief Draughtsman before returning to Wolverton in November 1871 to take over A. L. Mumford's post. With the ending of locomotive activity at Wolverton he was transferred to Carlisle Shed in November 1877.

To the end of the century the Carriage Works continued its westward expansion until it stretched for more than a half mile beyond the original boundary of 1837, and there were other additions at the eastern end following a radical realignment of the main line. Since the construction of the locomotive erecting shop on the east side in 1845, the main line had passed through the Works. This awkward arrangement persisted for 36 years, and although the right-angled rail crossing between the shops was eliminated after the Locomotive Dept relinquished the Up side shops, there was still a lot of shunting across the running lines. In 1878 it was decided to divert the main line to pass clear of the Works on its east side. The deviated line of four tracks was about 1½ miles long and opened, with a new Wolverton passenger station, on 1st August 1881.

Despite the many changes and enlargements of the Carriage Works, and of Wolverton itself, much of the fabric of the original Locomotive Works and most of the streets of railway cottages survived into recent times, but virtually nothing remains today. Gas Street and the last of Bury Street were removed to make room for additional workshops as long ago as 1890, but the cottages built from 1840 - Creed Street, Ledsam Street, Young Street and the south side of Glyn Square - lasted until they were razed in the mid-1960s. The Science & Art Institute was gutted by fire in 1970, and was subsequently demolished. The outer walls of the original Works of 1838 remained, much modified but still recognisable, until 1991. The old buildings were then demolished and the site is now covered by Tesco's carpark.

At the time of writing (August 2000) the only surviving fragment of the London & Birmingham Railway's Wolverton Locomotive Works is the extension east of the old main line, the oldest part of which dates from 1845.

EDWARD BURY

The Locomotive Power Contract

As with many railways in the 1830s there was a strong contingent of the 'Liverpool Party' among the London & Birmingham Railway proprietors; this was a group of merchants with an influential Quaker element, several of whom had been involved with the Liverpool & Manchester Railway.

Certain members of this Liverpool group had come to distrust the Stephensons. The cause of this has never been adequately explained, and in the past it has been put down simply to the alleged narrow-minded spitefulness of their "ringleader" James Cropper. There is no shred of evidence for this accusation. It is difficult to believe that these serious Quakers and Unitarians, businessmen of long experience and undisputed integrity, straightforward, honest and philanthropic, could have adopted their determined anti-Stephenson stance because of pique or petty spite. It is more likely that they suspected malpractice, and that these suspicions were aroused by the virtual monopoly in locomotive manufacture which was being assumed by the Stephensons, with their extended family of associated companies supplying other railway equipment, and their pushing of their own patents when alternative products were available. It is easier to believe that *if* Cropper and his colleagues discovered evidence of some unethical business practice - a wangled contract perhaps - they would not make a great public scene of it, but would make certain it could not happen again on any railway in which they had an interest.

On the London & Birmingham, where Robert Stephenson was Chief Engineer, they were determined to prevent the purchase of any locomotives from Stephenson's Newcastle works. Their first move came in October 1834, only four months after the construction of the railway had begun, with the suggestion by the director Theodore Woolman Rathbone, a leading figure in Liverpool, that it might be more profitable for the Company to pay a contractor to work the line and maintain the engines and rolling stock. Joseph Pease of the Stockton & Darlington wrote: "You are right, I believe, in not taking this troublesome department into your own hands" - and he sent a sheaf of figures to prove it. Robert Stephenson was also consulted and estimated a 20 to 25% saving by contracting, adding: "Edge Hill manufacture is a source of great waste and expense to the Liverpool & Manchester."

Charles Tayleur of the Vulcan Foundry (in which Robert Stephenson was a partner) proposed a contract in September 1835 whereby Tayleur would supply, work and maintain all London & Birmingham locomotives. This would not have been to the liking of the Liverpool directors, who would see it as another attempt to create a Stephenson monopoly.

Instead of taking up Tayleur's offer, in November 1835 the Board placed this advertisement in London and provincial newspapers:

LONDON & BIRMINGHAM RAILWAY

Contracts for Locomotive Power:- The Directors are ready to receive TENDERS for the SUPPLYING, UPHOLDING and WORKING LOCOMOTIVE ENGINES requisite for working the whole or any part of this railway between the Company's depots at Camden-town, London, and at Nova Scotia, Birmingham, being a distance of 112 miles to commence on the 1st day of January 1837, on that portion of the line then open between Camden-town and King's Langley.

Tenders will be received and considered either simply for the supply of engines delivered at stated periods on the line of railway, or for the supply and maintenance of such engines at a specific sum per trip, or for a given number of miles, or at a specific rate per passenger and per ton for different descriptions of traffic; or such other mode of payment as the parties tendering suggest.

Though the Directors think it desirable to leave parties tendering at liberty to state the conditions under which they are prepared to supply, uphold and work the requisite number of locomotive engines it must be understood that a preference will be given to tenders for supplying the power at a specific price per trip or for a given number of miles or per passenger and per ton, and engaging at the same time to find and supply, independently of the Railway Company everything that may be required to keep and maintain, in complete working order, the number of engines necessary to perform the work contracted for.

For working the portion of the line from Camden-town to King's Langley already mentioned, ten engines will be required, five of which must be delivered on or before the 10th day of December 1836.

Parties tendering for the supply and maintenance of power, on conditions in uniformity to those above described will be required to give security for the due performance of their respective contracts. Tenders will be received up to Wednesday the 2nd of December next, on which day the Directors will meet.

Further information, with every particular respecting the inclination of the line and a specification of the engine, may be obtained on application to the Secretary by letter, to Richard Creed Esq., Railway Office, Cornhill; Capt. Moorsom R.N., Railway Office, Birmingham; S. Woods jun. Esq., India-buildings, Liverpool. By Order

Nov. 6   RICHARD CREED
*   Secretaries to the Board.*
*   C. R. MOORSOM*

Long before this, some of the Party had their fellow-townsman Edward Bury in mind for the position. He was the proprietor of an iron foundry and machine shop in Liverpool and had several years' experience of locomotive construction.

A locomotive of his had been delivered to the Leicester & Swannington Railway in July 1834 (ordered at the suggestion of the Liverpool directors of that line) and Bury's foreman was later to say that the satisfaction given by this engine resulted in Bury's connection with the L&B. Perhaps the engine was a practical test of his fitness for the post.

Fig. 4   Edward Bury, 1794-1858. Contractor for working the London & Birmingham Railway, 1836-9; Manager of the L&B Locomotive Department, 1839-46; Locomotive Superintendent, LNWR Southern Division 1846-7.

On 13th February 1835 the Liverpool directors persuaded the L&B Board to pass a resolution to the effect that no director, engineer or any servant of the company should have any connection, directly or indirectly, with any contract for the supply of rails or locomotives. Robert Stephenson wrote home bitterly: "The *revenge* of these people is quite insatiable ... The Liverpool people do not disguise that this is aimed especially at me. This has all sprung from the Quakers, and Bury, our Liverpool rival." *Revenge* - but for what? Had there been some fiddled Stephenson contract on the Liverpool & Manchester? Whatever it was it had thoroughly spoiled the Stephensons' chances of lucrative orders and a splendid shop window for their locomotives on the foremost railway in the world.

In response to the advertisement, a Mr Morton Jones offered to work the L&B but his terms seemed rather high. It was a month before Edward Bury made an offer - "through the urgent request of Mr Theodore Rathbone and Mr Boothby and not by my own seeking" as he later put it. James Brownell Boothby was another Liverpool director of the L&B who acted as a guarantor of Bury's tender; the second guarantor was Sir Thomas Brancker, a prominent Liverpool citizen and head of a large sugar-refining business.

Meanwhile, as Chief Engineer, Robert Stephenson had prepared his specification for the locomotives that would be required; it was, naturally, his patent 2-2-2 with outside wooden frames. As soon as he learned of Bury's proposal and realised that this would not be in the Newcastle firm's interests, he rushed to get one of his new six-wheeled engines to the London & Birmingham, to show off to the directors. Somehow he persuaded one of the contractors building the line to take (of all things) a 2-2-2. A series of these was just then being built at Newcastle for Belgium; one of them was sent instead to London and arrived on the Berkhampstead excavations on 28th December.

He was too late. The next day a committee of three, Rathbone, John L. Prevost and Joseph F. Ledsam, recommended Bury as the most suitable candidate for the contract. The committee was then enlarged to five to work out the details. The two new members were Robert Garnett and Edward Cropper, son of James Cropper, Liverpool Quaker and foremost critic of the Stephensons. Then followed months of wrangling about terms.

In this interval Stephenson tried again. On 13th January 1836 he told the London Committee of the L&B that the opening of the line would have to be delayed unless twelve locomotives were ordered immediately. They straightaway placed orders for ten 2-2-2 engines of Stephenson's patent design: six from Tayleur, two from Stephenson and two from R. & W. Hawthorn.

They had been too hasty. Two days later the Birmingham Committee, which included the Liverpool directors, declared that the proposed contract which was being discussed with Bury was in the best interests of the L&B and that no arrangement should be entered into which might interfere with it. "That consequently the locomotive engines now ordered should be of Mr Bury's specification, particularly as he states that it is essential to the success of his plan that all the engines should be exact facsimiles of each other."

So the three orders for Stephenson 2-2-2 'Patentees' were cancelled. On 11th February the London Committee ordered four contractors' ballast engines, two each from Stephenson and Tayleur, no doubt as compensation for the lost train-engine orders. If there was an arrangement with R. & W. Hawthorn over their lost order, it has not been identified but it may be relevant that six months later a tender for passenger engines was accepted from this firm.

During the long arguments about the terms of the contract Bury managed to get rid of Robert Stephenson's specification. "I must respectfully decline entering into any contract for working the locomotive power on your road if you insist upon the engines having six wheels" he wrote to the L&B's Secretary at one point. In April he seemed quite weary of the arguments and was ready to abandon the whole idea, but at last the contract was signed and sealed on 11th May 1836.

Bury and the Clarence Foundry

Edward Bury was 41 years old, having been born on 22nd October 1794 the younger son of a wealthy timber merchant in Salford, Lancashire. The family name would have been pronounced 'Burry' originally but, in the south at least, he was known as 'Berry'. He was given a good education at Chester School and is said to have been something of an amateur mechanic at a very early age. By 1823 he was a partner in Gregson & Bury's steam sawmill at Toxteth Park, Liverpool, but in 1826 he set himself up as an iron-founder and engineer. He had a 'boiler-yard' at Gregson's sawmill but his new office and works were half a mile away in Tabley Street. This was an astute move: the proposed Wapping goods terminus of the Liverpool & Manchester Railway was nearby and the first L&M workshops were established in Tabley Street in the same year.

As his foreman, Bury took on James Kennedy, an Edinburgh-born millwright who had packed a lifetime of experience into his 30 years, including eighteen months at Stephenson's Newcastle works, where he claimed to have had a hand in the design and building of the first three Stockton & Darlington engines *Locomotion*, *Hope* and *Black Diamond*. After this he moved to Mather, Dixon & Co at Liverpool at the end of 1825. It has been said that he was the brother of John Kennedy, the Rainhill Trials judge, but this is untrue.

Shortly afterwards Bury moved his works to new premises in Love Lane, backing onto the Leeds-Liverpool Canal and not far from the Clarence Dock on the Mersey, hence the name Clarence Foundry & Steam Engine Works. This was on the northern edge of the rapidly expanding town, where old windmills still stood among the new rows of houses, and across the canal were the six new gas holders of the Vauxhall Gasworks. In the same vicinity were other engineering firms, Mather, Dixon & Co, George Forrester & Co, and Thomas Vernon & Co, whose slip Bury later hired for shipbuilding orders.

The Clarence Foundry eventually covered 3 acres and at its height employed 1600 men. About 415 locomotives were manufactured there as well as all manner of other metal goods from marine engines to church bells. The works had a frontage to Love Lane of about 400 feet, south from the corner of Burlington Street; today the site is covered by Eldonian Avenue, Jack McBane Court and neighbouring streets.

Bury lived in Crabtree Lane, nearly two miles away on the east side of town, but convenient for the Liverpool & Manchester station at Crown Street and very close to the new railway workshops. Crabtree Lane was later renamed Falkner Street; Edward Deane Falkner was a rich merchant who lived nearby and in 1830 his daughter Priscilla Susan Falkner and Edward Bury were married.

Bury's first locomotive, *Dreadnought*, an 0-6-0 with horizontal outside 10in x 24in cylinders, an intermediate shaft and chain drive to the wheels, was intended for the Rainhill Trials but could not be finished in time. It is said to have had a cut-off valve for working expansively, a very early if not the first example of this. It did some ballasting work on the Liverpool & Manchester from March 1830 where Lecount says it "was much objected to" because it was on six wheels. It was sold to John Hargreaves and thereafter worked on the Bolton & Leigh Railway.

Bury's second engine was a four-wheeler but the objection this time was to the size of the wheels: at 6ft diameter they were described as "dangerous" by the L&M's Engineer, George Stephenson. As originally built - it appeared in July 1830 - it had a boiler, according to Edward Woods, "with a number of convoluted flues" whatever that means. Bury's widow said it was a modification of Marc Seguin's multitubular boiler patent of February 1828. After rebuilding in May 1831 its boiler contained 131 small, straight tubes. This engine, *Liverpool*, established Bury's standard design practice: simple wrought-iron bar frame inside the wheels with only two bearings on each axle, near-horizontal inside 12in x 18in cylinders and a round firebox in the shape of a vertical cylinder with a hemispherical top and a grate which was **D**-shaped in plan. The 6ft coupled wheels were the largest seen up to that time, but after a high-speed derailment at Atherton on the Bolton & Leigh in July 1831 they were probably reduced to 4ft 6in. In this form *Liverpool* can be seen passing Parkside in one of the famous Ackermann 'long prints' of trains on the Liverpool & Manchester, published in November 1831.

This was a remarkable design then, when Stephenson and allied firms were using outside wooden frames plus four internal sub-frames; it was obviously the product of much serious thinking, and it lasted. In gradually increasing sizes, the same frame design - rectangular-section bars for the top members and round-section bars for the bottom trusses - was continued successfully for twenty years.

The round firebox, said Bury, was superior to a square one "inasmuch as the corners, in which the combustion is always languid, are avoided." The curves of its hemispherical top "are such as to enable the plates to resist the pressure of the steam without the assistance of ribs or stays, which so materially prevent the circulation of the water over square fireboxes." The domed outer firebox enclosed a large steam space, ensuring an adequate supply of dry steam and reducing the risk of priming.

Bury said in 1840: "I have always been in opposition to the plan of engine adopted on the other roads. I adopted a certain class of engine and the engine of the present day is a copy of my original engine *Liverpool* .... it was commenced in October 1829 and set to work on the Liverpool & Manchester Railway in July 1830; since that period many improvements in the details have been introduced, but the general plan of construction has been steadily adhered to." He built the same general type for many British and overseas customers.

Although Bury built engines for local buyers, the Liverpool & Manchester would take only one, *Liver* (L&M No 26) and insisted, at George Stephenson's urging, on outside frames. In a trial between Bury's *Liver* and Stephenson's *Planet* for six days in June 1832 the Bury engine was found to do the same work while burning less coke - 0.49 lb per ton per mile against *Planet*'s 0.54 lb - and this despite an attempt by a Stephenson supporter to feed *Planet* with better coke while also screwing down its safety valves. A widely-published magazine article about the L&M complained in October 1832 that "all the engineers employed, all the firemen ... are the nominees of Mr Stephenson and are his zealous and unflinching partisans" and that they had "secretly inflicted injuries" on non-Stephenson engines "for the purpose of disabling them or impairing their performance". The L&M director Hardman Earle had to admit this behaviour from "some of the servants of the Company, under the mistaken notion that they were promoting thereby the interests of their kind patron" George Stephenson. For a time Bury did repairs to L&M

engines but gave this up in December 1834 "on account of the difficulty of giving satisfaction to the foremen and enginemen…"

Thwarted by Stephenson and so failing to obtain more than a toehold on the L&M, Bury quickly established an export trade with the USA. In the 1830s he sold at least 28 engines there, more than any other British maker except R. Stephenson & Co with 35. Bury was the Stephensons' biggest competitor at this period and they had good reason to worry about him. His engines quickly gained a reputation for good workmanship, cheapness and reliability. From his exports to the USA the bar frame became standard there. Like the bar frame, the domed-top firebox increased in size over the years; it too was taken up by American builders such as Norris, Rogers and Baldwin and was used by them into the mid-1850s.

The Clarence Foundry prospered; Bury took his foreman James Kennedy into partnership and in 1842, with additional partners Timothy Abraham Curtis and John Vernon, the firm became Bury, Curtis & Kennedy.

Bury and the L&B
The earliest official contact between the London & Birmingham Railway and Bury came on 18th December 1834 when Secretary Richard Creed wrote to ask if he could supply one engine by the end of March. His price was £1,050, plus £120 for a tender, but he could not deliver before June. Earlier delivery was promised by both Stephenson and Charles Tayleur, and an engine was ordered from each of these firms for the use of the contractors building the railway. These orders with the two Stephenson companies roused Rathbone and Cropper to push through the resolution barring Stephenson-built locomotives. Rathbone was perhaps already cajoling Bury, who was eventually persuaded to respond on 5th December 1835 to the advertisement for a contractor to work the railway.

His original estimate of the likely cost of working was based on a train speed of 22½ mph which the Board stipulated, and trains of not more than twelve carriages. The journey time between London and Birmingham would take 5½ hours, including half an hour for taking on water and fuel. "I thought it might be done at ¼d per passenger per mile and leave something very handsome for the contractor. I took 250 passengers as the number a train could take, but made a calculation on half of that" he later explained.

The contract which was finally agreed in May 1836 laid down that the Company would provide engines to Bury's specification, while he would maintain them in good repair and convey each passenger at ¼d (0.104p) per mile and each ton of goods at ½d (0.208p) per mile, the speed not to exceed 22½ miles per hour. This was to be in force for three years, coming into effect from the opening of the line, which was forecast for October 1837. He began by recommending that 36 passenger engines be ordered as soon as possible.

At the end of January 1836 nineteen firms had been asked to say, tentatively, how many locomotives they could promise by June 1837. The list is an interesting mixture of firms well-known, obscure and unknown which built - or were thought to build - locomotives in 1836:

Newcastle:	Robert Stephenson; R. & W. Hawthorn.
Liverpool:	Edward Bury; Mather, Dixon; George Forrester.
Manchester:	Sharp, Roberts; William Fairbairn; Galloway & Bowman; Thomas Sherratt; Thomas Banks.
Bolton:	Benjamin Hick; Peter Rothwell.
Leeds:	Fenton, Murray & Jackson.
Wigan:	Haigh Foundry.
Warrington:	Charles Tayleur.
St Helens:	Lee Watson.
Wednesbury:	Marshall & Sons.
London:	Maudslay, Sons & Field; Braithwaite & Milner.

As tenders were to be sought from a number of firms Bury's specification went into minute detail, for he insisted that all the engines were to be built in absolute fidelity to the same plan; thus engines by different makers would have standard parts to make maintenance and repair easier. Daniel Gooch and Joseph Locke have both been credited with the first such scheme, but Edward Bury was earlier. As things turned out he was, alas, too early. Some makers were unable, or unwilling, to build in strict accordance with his plans; some of them could not see why it was so important.

In the early summer of 1836 full-size drawings and templates were circulated among the manufacturers with whom orders were quickly placed: Hick; Rothwell; Mather, Dixon; Haigh Foundry; Bury's own firm; and Hawthorn - who offered to build "any number". All these were at the same price: £1,120, engine only. Hawthorn's inclusion in what otherwise looks like a Lancashire pricing-ring may have been to compensate for their lost London Committee order for two engines in January. In July another Northumbrian firm offered to build four engines for £1,120 each; this was the Bedlington Iron Co, whose Michael Longridge was about to resign as Stephenson's manager and begin building locomotives on his own account. Bury said he was unable to recommend them and as 33 passenger engines had already been ordered - and the Locomotive Committee wanted to have some engines built in London - it was resolved to turn down Longridge's tender. Robert Stephenson & Co wrote asking if their tender would be entertained, in view of their chief's connection with the L&B. The reply could not have been an outright refusal, but their offer to build two engines was declined; £1,175 each was considered too much.

Despite the directors' anxiety to give contracts to London firms, none of these had troubled to send in tenders. Maudslay, Sons & Field did not seem to want the job, but were persuaded to quote. They did, but their price of £1,350 per engine was too high.

While the passenger engine drawings were being circulated, the goods design was prepared. This was very similar, but had four coupled 5ft wheels, a bigger boiler and 13in cylinders, slightly inclined (just like the old *Liverpool*) and working below the leading axle. Drawings were finished by November 1836 and once again detailed tenders came in from the northern firms, though only Bury's was eventually accepted. The London Committee set about trying to persuade a London firm to make an offer. After coaxing, Maudslay at last consented to build six engines. Their offer was accepted before a formal tender was received and this prior acceptance was confirmed on 13th February 1837 at £1,300 each.

In October 1836 Bury visited Nottingham to inspect Samuel Hall's patent coal-burning boiler which might be applicable to locomotives but found it "far from matured" so coke ovens were ordered for the L&B. In the same month he was out on the line with the Engineer, Robert Stephenson, arranging the positions for the fuel and water stations and selecting the site near the village of Wolverton for the Central Repairing Station. In November he was in Yorkshire at the Bowling and Low Moor ironworks trying to speed up the production of boiler plates for the locomotive builders.

Meanwhile the directors meddled and criticised. In November Bury had to explain why he wanted *spare parts* for the engines. He had to explain precisely what he meant by the terms *firebox*, *wheel* and *crank*, and to explain that, as the drawings already showed the dimensions of the axle in four different places it was hardly necessary also to include them on the attached specification. In February 1837 they worked out a system of numbering for their as-yet-unbuilt engines on a geographical basis - those built furthest north coming first and gradually progressing southwards. Within a week they produced another number list running from south to north, apparently to give a London-made engine the honour of being Number One. Bury ignored both lists, as well as a later minute drawing attention to the *necessity* of carrying out the 'London first' scheme.

At this period it was customary to give names to railway engines, just like horses or ships. The L&B created a precedent with the decision in August 1836 that "the engines be simply numbered instead of named." After all, this was the nation's new rapid transport system, to be conducted in a sober, businesslike manner without needless frills.

Even before the railway had begun operating, the contract with Bury caused other companies to think this system might benefit them. In April 1837 the Grand Junction advertised for a contractor to work their line, and in May the Liverpool & Manchester prepared a contract after asking if they could look over the L&B document. Perhaps there were no takers; nothing more is known of either scheme. As late as March 1839 the Midland Counties Railway were considering working by a contractor.

Bury gave his views on the contract system of working to the Parliamentary Select Committee in 1839. He agreed that it was "the natural interest of the contractor to keep the establishment as low as the traffic will require" and said "I think the contractor would do it more economically than the railway company could, because he would look into things more closely." He certainly looked into details very closely, as his records of work done and the breakdown of costs of each engine amply demonstrate. In a note to the Chairman and again before the Parliamentary Select Committee he claimed that the total cost of working the entire stock of L&B locomotives - coke, oil, repairs and wages - in the first half of 1839 was only £16,000, contrasting this with the slightly smaller Grand Junction which was spending £36,000.

Nevertheless, on the L&B the contract system never worked as it was intended. The railway took almost a year longer to complete than had been forecast in 1836, but was still opened "much too soon" for Bury's liking, as he was without adequate repair facilities until late in 1839 and without means of obtaining suitable coke at the northern end. The unforeseen working of two separate sections, London - Denbigh Hall and Birmingham - Rugby, led to differences in interpreting the contract and differences of opinion about how much Bury should be paid for his work in this period. As early as January 1838 he was writing to complain about the illiberal and "most rigorous construction" which was becoming apparent in the Board's reading of his contract and that he was not being given due credit for working the line successfully despite the imperfect state of the track and the lack of watering and repair facilities. He said he did not have the time or money to spend on litigation or arbitration and he would prefer to abandon the contract on the best terms he could.

A revised contract was drawn up and agreed in June 1838 but the problems continued. With only one coupled engine delivered, the Board acceded to Pickford & Co's request to carry goods between Wolverton and London while the Grand Junction Canal was stopped for lack of water on the Tring summit level. This lasted from mid-September 1838 to January 1839. Another two firms of carriers were given the same facilities, although warehouses were not ready and there were insufficient wagons. The traffic did not amount to much, 70 or 80 tons a day, but other carriers were turned away because the L&B could not cope with more. A regular goods service began on 15th April 1839 by which time only sixteen of the thirty goods engines had been delivered and there were still too few wagons.

For Bury the crunch came in June 1839 when, still without proper repair shops, he was asked to increase the mail train speeds from the 20th. "I protested against the acceleration as much as I could" he said; there would be more accidents and wear and tear, and until Wolverton was ready he foresaw difficulties. He agreed to comply "out of civility" but he gave notice that this would be an infringement of his contract, and on the 31st July the contract was annulled. Bury was paid £4,000 in lieu of salary for his past "zealous services" and awarded £10,000 as compensation. His engagement as Manager of the Locomotive Department was backdated to 1st July, from which time he was to be paid £1,000 a year, with a bonus of £200 for every 1% rise in the share dividend above 7%.

He had been in charge of the troublesome Coke Department since October 1838 and now his duties were further increased to include control of the Camden Incline winding engines and all other stationary engines, as well as the ballast locomotives and their sheds previously under the Engineer's Department "together with the general superintendence of the machinery of the Company".

There were other small irritations. One very obvious difference between Bury's engines and the ballast engines built by Stephenson and Tayleur was that the chimneys of the latter were capped with prominent bonnets of wire mesh. Seeing these spark arresters prompted one of the secretaries, Capt Moorsom, to write to Bury in December 1838. Bury's reply was brief. "I am in receipt of your letter of the 29th inst: 'The engines shall have wires on their chimnies.' They will not prevent the sparks but impede the draft." But Moorsom was co-opted to the Board in 1839 and quickly raised the matter again. In June the Board told Bury to give his attention to the subject. He waited until November before replying that he had considered the "wire fire guards" but that the only remedy for the spark problem was coke of good quality "the means for the preparation of which are not yet provided by the Company at Birmingham." No more is heard about spark arresters in Bury's time, but his complaints about the lack of adequate coking facilities continued.

Bury's 'Dual Role'
Much was written, then and ever since, about Bury's dual role as railway manager and manufacturer and supplier of locomotives; it was also discussed by the Board. In August 1840 he took three weeks off, saying that his partner James Kennedy would act for him if any problems came up. No doubt this was only meant to be helpful, but it drew attention to his position as chief of Bury & Co. Some wagon wheels had recently been purchased from the firm and director Edward Cropper was unhappy about it. He moved: "that in order to relieve Mr Bury from the improper position of being at once the manufacturer and judge of articles supplied to the Company it is expedient that he be no longer employed by them for the supply of any articles whatever, excepting only locomotive engines."

Cropper's motion was voted down on 27th November 1840 but at the next meeting Capt Moorsom returned to the same subject. His motion was more explicit:

"1. Mr Bury, having to judge the quality of various articles, cannot be expected to be impartial. It is certain that no manufacturers will continue to enter into competition ... this will give Bury the monopoly.
2. That it is inexpedient to continue this system.
3. That as the Act of Incorporation prohibits any Director being interested in any contract, it is expedient similarly to apply this principle to all servants of the Company.
4. It is expedient to depart from this as to admit Mr Bury to supply *Locomotive Engines* on this consideration, that he first brought forward and has gradually improved a plan of engine which so far appears to have answered the contemplated purpose and that he is confessedly a superior manufacturer of such engines..." Moorsom thought Bury was making a sufficient profit already, without extra profits from other articles supplied.

The *Railway Times* somehow got hold of the story and printed a comic paragraph about "the great talents of Mr Bury's family ... 'Edward Bury' being engineer of the line ... 'Edward Bury' contractor for building their locomotives ... 'Mr Edward Bury' is at the same time the consulting engineer as to the merits of all new plans, springs, wheels ..."

Moorsom's motion also failed, and the Board gave an effective vote of confidence in their locomotive superintendent. It was agreed that Bury's duties had been carried out with fidelity; in his admittedly delicate position he had conducted himself with great care; there was no sign of backwardness by manufacturers in tendering. Although of course servants should not have an interest in any contract, this was a special case. In any event, orders were placed with Bury & Co *only* when it was in the L&B's interest to do so, so the question of his extra profit did not arise.

This was a repetition of the Liverpool & Manchester Railway controversy of 1832-3, when the influential *Edinburgh Review* had criticised George Stephenson's dual role as a manufacturer and as an arbiter of other suppliers' materials. The L&M director Hardman Earle, well known as a Stephenson supporter, wrote a rebuttal of the charges, but some of the other directors, including James Cropper, remained unconvinced.

Locomotive Stock Increased and Improved
In February 1837 Bury gave his estimate of the number of engines required as 36 passenger and 30 goods, but Hardman Earle disagreed. Earle, who was an L&B director for a short period in 1836-7, was firmly in the pro-Stephenson camp and could therefore be expected to try to destabilise Bury. At his first meeting as a member of the Locomotive Committee he contended that only twenty goods engines were necessary, with nine more passenger engines than Bury had recommended. In having to justify his ideas about the engines he needed to fulfil his contract, Bury said that coupled engines would probably be necessary for some passenger trains. The other directors took Bury's side.

The initial orders for 36 passenger and 30 goods engines were divided among seven manufacturers and all the passenger engines and seven of the goods were at work by the end of 1838. Earlier in that year, with the benefit of working experience on the partly-opened line, fifteen more passengers engines had been ordered to the same design as before, so that the intended complement for the completed railway stood at 51 passenger engines and 30 goods. Two extra passenger engines were ordered in January 1839 for working the Aylesbury Railway, the seven-mile branch from the L&B main line.

Other factors - the demand for faster trains and the ending of Bury's contract - soon brought changes. The L&B had begun carrying mail for the General Post Office on 21st May 1838, some four months before the line was opened throughout, and a travelling post office commenced running between London and Liverpool on 1st October. Almost at once the GPO began pressing for higher speed.

As contractor for the working of the line, Edward Bury's payment was per passenger and per ton carried. Out of this he had to maintain the engine fleet and, to keep his repair bills to a minimum, it was advantageous to have engines to the same pattern. With twelve-carriage trains and a 22½ mph speed as the basis of his contract he had adopted 12in cylinders for the passenger engines. After the contract was ended in July 1839 he was on a salary and no longer had to pay the maintenance and repair bills and in these new circumstances and amid calls for greater speed he quickly opted for bigger cylinders. The 13in goods engines had been used on passenger trains with good results and in August 1839 Bury proposed that the passenger engines then on order should have 13in cylinders.

The first of these new 13in passenger engines arrived in October and were a success from the start. They were put on the mail trains and became known as the Mail Engines.

A new source of traffic was in prospect with the completion of the Midland Counties Railway, which was to join the L&B at Rugby and would extend the rail network through the East Midlands. On 18th February 1840 the L&B agreed to provide separate engines for working the MCR's through mail trains south of Rugby *at the expense of the MCR*. The junction was made at Rugby in August but whether the Midland Counties actually paid for the L&B engines is not known; presumably this scheme was superseded in December 1840 by the MCR/L&B through-booking arrangement and the creation of the Railway Clearing House (on the initiative of the L&B) in 1841. Six more Mail Engines were ordered for the MCR trains, which with a slight rearrangement of the earlier order brought the total stock of locomotives to 90, all of which were on the line by June 1841.

London & Birmingham Railway locomotive stock, June 1841:
60 passenger engines:
2-2-0 12in cylinders: Nos 1-36, 49-52, Aylesbury 1 and 2.
2-2-0 13in cylinders: Nos 37-48, 53-58.

30 goods engines:
0-4-0 13in cylinders: Nos 61-90.

As soon as the last of the 90 engines had been delivered, Bury recommended upgrading the 12in passenger engines; whenever one of them needed a thorough repair it was to be rebuilt with 13in cylinders and a larger boiler. A first trial conversion was undertaken at Bury's Clarence Foundry and cost £400; on its completion nine further rebuilds were authorised, to be done at Wolverton. Similar rebuilding, latterly with 14in cylinders, continued steadily throughout the L&B period and beyond.

Four v Six Wheels
Bury had plenty of experience of six-wheeled locomotives; his first, *Dreadnought*, had been an 0-6-0 but thereafter he stuck with great persistence to his belief that four wheels were better than six. In any case, for a long time the available six-wheeled engines were certainly inferior to his four-wheelers.

Bury has been accused of 'crippling' the L&B by his four-wheeled engines but this is to think of that line as though it had the functions of a modern railway; it was in fact something very different. The L&B was conceived primarily as a fast long-distance passenger and mail line. Although cheap-fare excursionists were catered for in roofless carriages during the early months of operation, only first and second-class passengers were carried after the opening to Tring in October 1837. Third-class passengers were not carried until 5th October 1840, and local suburban trains were not introduced until 1842; before then such traffic was thought unprofitable and not worth the trouble. Goods traffic did not properly commence until 15th April 1839 and was entirely in the hands of firms of carriers such as Pickford & Co, who to a great extent continued their use of the parallel Grand Junction Canal. As a contemporary commentator put it: "Under this system, while carriers grew rich, the goods traffic remained stationary." It was stated officially in 1840 that the L&B did not desire a large goods traffic and that a service of two goods trains a day was the optimum. In 1839 and again in 1841 the Company declared "they were not and did not intend to become carriers." There was little cattle traffic and coal was not carried at all until 1845, apart from six wagons a day from the MCR between Rugby and the canal at Crick.

From the start the line was equipped with a fleet of the most up-to-date motive power and facilities, planned to the last detail for the purpose intended. By 1841 the 90 engines, consisting of just three classes, were in marked contrast to the wild variety of engines on other lines and presented a unique model of standardisation for those days. They were well-designed and sturdy machines which long outlasted their contemporaries.

Bury's dislike of six-wheeled engines was confirmed after the opening of the Birmingham & Derby Junction Railway in August 1839. This line joined the L&B at Hampton and it had been arranged that the B&DJ's 2-2-2 locomotives would work its trains between there and Birmingham along nine miles of the L&B. But on 21st September the Board decided to withdraw permission and the practice ended in the following month. This was perhaps just as well, for in June 1840 the B&DJ Sharp single *Dove* tore up the junction points at Hampton. It was found to be out of gauge and was forthwith banned from all L&B metals.

The Copyhold accident on the London & Brighton Railway in October 1841 aroused some anxiety about Bury's policy. The engine driver involved claimed that his engine, a Bury four-wheeler, had left the track because of its faulty design. This led the inquest jury to recommend that four-wheeled engines should be taken out of service, and although the Board of Trade inspector found that the accident was not caused by the design of the engine but by excessive speed on wet rails, the jury's opinion created great public excitement. Bury had already given his reasons for preferring four-wheeled engines to the Parliamentary Select Committee in the previous year and about the same time he presented an authoritative paper to the Institution of Civil Engineers which also went into the subject.

Bury said that four-wheeled engines were cheaper, simpler to construct, more compact and although lighter, had better adhesion with the same weight on the driving wheels however uneven the track. Having fewer parts they were less liable to derangement, with less friction. They were easier to repair and were more economical in working. They held the track better on curves. The turntables and sheds could be smaller and cheaper, and with fewer parts to maintain, the outlay on tools was less.

He also set out the advantages of inside frames: as there were only two bearings on each axle (instead of six with outside frames - two in the main frame and four between the wheels) there was less friction and strain on the crank axle and less strain on the boiler. In the event of an axle breaking, the wheels of an inside-framed engine would be less likely to derail. The unencumbered layout of the inside bar frames enabled the driver to oversee the valve gear from the footplate.

Bury's engines aroused no serious criticism (except from manufacturers of six-wheeled engines and their advocates) until 1842. On 8th May of that year on the Paris-Versailles line an outside-framed 'Planet' type 2-2-0 broke a leading axle, went down, and caused a catastrophic accident. To demonstrate that his engines were immune from such calamities he took the 2-2-0 No 18 which was in Wolverton for repair, and had the fore axle partially sawn through close to one of the journals, leaving only a one-inch thickness. On 23rd the engine left Wolverton and travelled north until the axle broke in two, as intended; it continued as far as Roade and returned without mishap. The following day the engine with its broken axle set off from Wolverton hauling six wagons weighing 32 tons and ran at 25mph as far as Watford, where one of the leading wheels left the rails. It was replaced and the train continued. Two miles beyond Harrow, going at 15-20mph, the wheel slipped off again, the train travelling 200 yards before stopping. The engine was still upright on arrival at Camden 3½ hours after leaving Wolverton.

Up to that time there had been no case of an accidentally broken fore axle, and in every case of a crank axle breaking the engine had travelled to Wolverton for repair on its own wheels, usually after taking its train on to the next station.

This stainless record was broken on Thursday 8th December 1842 when a flawed leading axle fractured in its journal. A Hick-built 2-2-0, Aylesbury No 2, was travelling about a mile north of Northchurch Tunnel on the 11am Aylesbury-London train when the break occurred; the nearside front wheel fell off and the engine was derailed. A woman in the leading carriage was killed.

Bury was shaken. He confessed: "I should have said on Thursday morning that such an accident could not have taken place." But it was the only case of its kind, and led to a series of comparative tests of solid and hollow axles at Camden in January 1843. Hollow axles, being found stronger, were used to some extent after this, but details are not known. In the same year Bury designed a dynamometer carriage and carried out a series of tests with Bryan Donkin on L&B engines; this was four years before the more widely publicised dynamometer experiments of Daniel Gooch.

Increasing Passenger Traffic
Despite the Board's rather restricted ideas about the proper function of the L&B, changes were forced upon it by its connections with other railways. As the only railway between the capital and the north, traffic came to it in increasing quantity from an ever-expanding catchment area. In 1838 London was linked by rail to Birmingham and the West Midlands and to Liverpool, Manchester and manufacturing towns in Lancashire as far north as Preston, and by connecting steamer services to Ireland and Scotland. Within two years rails reached out from the northern end of the L&B into the other side of the country through the East Midlands, Leicester, Nottingham and Derby to Yorkshire: Sheffield, Leeds and Hull. In 1844 through trains ran from Euston as far as the Tyne. From there rails had crossed England to Carlisle since 1838.

This increasing volume of traffic meant heavier and more frequent trains. In 1839 seven passenger trains left Euston daily; by 1841 there were thirteen and by 1845 nineteen. Train speeds also increased. In 1839 the fastest train was scheduled to reach Birmingham in 5½ hours; the others took 6 hours. By 1841 Birmingham could be reached by mail train in 4¾ hours; the others took 5 to 5¾ hours. In 1844 the fastest took 4 hours, reduced to only 3 hours in 1845. There was also a daily third-class slow train, with long intermediate stops to allow other trains to pass, but even this was speeded up between 1841 and 1845 from 8½ hours to 7 hours 40 minutes.

There were the beginnings of a suburban service at both ends of the line; in 1842 stations for new "short trains" were opened at Willesden (Acton Lane), Sudbury, Pinner and Bushey and in 1844 at the (Willesden) junction with the West London Railway to connect with that company's trains. Docker's Lane (Berkswell), Marston Green and Stechford were opened in 1844 for a service of "short trains" between Birmingham and Leamington using the new 8¾-mile branch from Coventry. A mile was added to locomotive working on the main line in July 1844 with the abandonment of rope haulage on the Camden Incline.

During this period no additions were made to the original stock of 90 engines; the only authorised increase in locomotive power was Bury's rebuilding programme, which was gradually equipping engines with bigger boilers and cylinders. Not until the middle of 1844, with the opening of the 47-mile Peterborough branch less than a year away, was consideration given to any increase in the locomotive stock, and then all the Board wanted were two express engines for the prestige mail trains. These two were not delivered until the following year.

Nevertheless, at the end of 1844, the trains were being worked in an efficient and orderly manner - without, as far as can be seen, complaint from any quarter. Even the fiercely critical 'Veritas Vincit' was moved to write in November: "I have not the smallest intention to find fault with the locomotive management of [the L&B ... and I can] bear ample testimony to the excellence of all the internal arrangements Mr Bury has adopted; they are nearly perfect and complete, as far as present principles in locomotive management can suggest."

Early in 1845 Bury told the Locomotive Committee that increasing traffic would require twenty new passenger engines, or eighteen in addition to the two which were then on order. These two were being built by Bury, Curtis & Kennedy as the best the firm could provide for the fast mail trains and were 14in 2-2-0s with 5ft 9in driving wheels. An order for a further eighteen of the type from BC&K was conditional upon the satisfactory performance of the first two, but delays caused by some fault in construction held back the trial of the engines and the order was not confirmed until May 1845. Delivery could not be promised before November.

By this time the sudden and rapid increase in passenger traffic was causing real anxiety. The Board received complaints from Bury that insufficient notice had been given of demands on his department so that the existing locomotive stock might not be able to cope. The Locomotive Committee complained about the "dead weight" of carriages and suggested the adoption of a rigid rule that passengers must fill up carriages from the front end of the train, with extra vehicles added only where necessary.

When it was learned that no new engines could be expected quickly from anywhere because all manufacturers were swamped with orders (this was the period of the 'Railway Mania'), the Locomotive Committee looked around for some stop-gap solution. An attempt was made in April to purchase "five or six" old Bury 12in engines from the Midland Railway, with the intention of converting them to 13in engines "and thus be made equal to the best on the line" but the engines had already been sold. The Manchester & Birmingham Railway was next approached with a request to borrow or purchase four engines "which it is believed they can spare from their stock".

The M&B responded with the loan of their No 8, a brand new Sharp Bros 2-2-2. Its outside frames and six wheels were the antithesis of Bury's ideas about locomotive design but its 14¾in cylinders made it the most powerful engine on the line. Bury's new 14in engines were speedy with light loads but the sudden onset of much heavier trains required something with more power; No 8 was well able to cope and its performance greatly impressed the directors. Within a month of its arrival Bury, Curtis & Kennedy were authorised to increase the size of the engines they were building and six months later a further increase was ordered.

Because of these changes the twenty BC&K express passenger engines came in three distinct lots - the first three were to the original design of October 1844, the next six as revised in June 1845 had bigger boilers than M&B No 8. These were all 2-2-0s with 14in cylinders and 5ft 9in driving wheels. Only the first three and one of the revised design were delivered from BC&K in 1845, but two more were begun at Wolverton Works, the first locomotives ever built there; one of them was at work by the end of the year. The last eleven of the BC&K order were to be 2-2-2s with much bigger boilers, 15in cylinders and 6ft driving wheels.

On 17th October 1845 it was announced that the L&B, the Grand Junction and the Manchester & Birmingham planned to amalgamate. Although the necessary Act of Parliament was not obtained until the following July, the new joint Board met for the first time on 13th December and adopted the title 'The London & North Western Railway Company'. Shortly after this two engines of the 2-2-2 Crewe type were loaned by the GJR to the hard-pressed L&B, bringing the total of passenger engines to 68 at the end of the year. These consisted of the 60 original 2-2-0s, five of the new 14in 2-2-0s, one 2-2-2 borrowed from the M&B and two 2-2-2s borrowed from the GJR.

During 1846 the second Wolverton engine was completed, the other BC&K 14in 2-2-0s arrived, followed by the same firm's 15in 2-2-2s and Sharp Bros supplied another of their singles like M&B No 8. Six engines of a quite different character also appeared, the first outside-cylinder engines owned by the L&B. These were 4-2-0s "of the greatest power" which had been ordered for the not-yet-open Trent Valley Railway; they were by Jones & Potts but any relief they offered was offset by their poor construction and the repairs which were immediately necessary. Before the end of the year two of them were laid up with burst fireboxes.

A Tidal Wave of Goods Traffic
For several years the L&B did not carry coal. "What! Coal by railway? They will be asking us to carry dung next!" as Superintendent Bruyeres famously exclaimed when the Midland Counties Railway proposed sending coal to London over the L&B. In September 1841 the Board allowed one train a day, limited to six tarpaulin-covered wagons, on the eight miles between Rugby and Crick, where the coal was discreetly transferred to canal boats. The train was worked by the permanent way maintenance contractor Thomas Jackson, using one of his ballast engines.

The Board does not appear to have considered doing any more about coal until prompted by a proposal from Richard Madigan. Madigan had been an employee of Jackson's and was shortly to be engaged by the L&B for the haulage of permanent way maintenance materials. In January 1845 he suggested a contract whereby he would be responsible for the transport of not less than 200 tons of coal per day between Rugby and London. The Locomotive Committee seemed surprised by the quantity but knowing that there were insufficient engines to cope with this extra traffic, turned down his offer on 8th January. Two days later the Board decided that the L&B Company would itself become a carrier of coal. Coal sidings were put in hand at Kilburn, beside the main line and within two miles of Camden. Bury's opinion was that sixteen more engines would be needed for the expected slow and heavy coal trains; the Board then resolved that they "should be of much greater power and weight than any hitherto employed on this line" and recommended that they should be on six wheels. The Locomotive Committee placed orders for the sixteen engines on 16th February, eight of them to be built by Bury, Curtis & Kennedy. Two of these were to be 0-4-2s but on Bury's comment that four-wheeled engines would be better, the other six were to be 0-4-0s. All would have 15in cylinders.

When these orders for engines were placed the Committee had already been negotiating with Robert Stephenson for eight of his patent 15in "large 6-wheeled engines suitable for heavy goods traffic, which will be built on his plan and specification and under his inspection and responsibility by Messrs Nasmyth, Gaskell & Co of Patricroft, it being out of his power to take the order himself at present."

This is a strange and unexpected move by the directors, who had resolved ten years before to purchase no Stephenson engines. There had certainly been denigration of Bury from various quarters and no doubt there had been lobbying on behalf of the Stephenson firm and its allies. The coal which the L&B now intended to convey was from the Clay Cross pits owned by George Stephenson & Co, preliminary discussions with whom may have influenced the Board in favour of six-wheeled engines, in particular those of Stephenson design.

As early as 25th January there was a leak to the press. Herapath's *Railway Magazine* announced that the L&B had "ordered several new engines on the plan and of equal weight with the new ones of the Midland Co, for the purpose of taking the large mineral traffic they have arranged to carry."

At this time the L&B Board was deep into negotiations for amalgamation with the M&B and other intervening lines which would give a new route to Manchester, free of the GJR, and other schemes were being furthered to outflank the GJR via Shrewsbury to the Mersey and Holyhead. The old concept of the L&B was being completely transformed and these big ideas suggested bigger engines. The amalgamation scheme and the ordering of the big engines for mineral traffic, to be carried at low rates, were announced on 12th February.

On 9th May another six of the patent engines were ordered, to be built by Tayleur & Co of Vulcan Foundry "under Mr Stephenson's direction" and on 6th August the Board authorised the order of ten more "on Robert Stephenson's patent". With 24 of the patent goods engines on order the L&B Secretary wrote in October to Robert Stephenson & Co offering to place further large orders with the firm. His letter contained an extraordinary proposal: the L&B was "prepared to deal with you for a supply of engines to an extent that would probably make it worth your while to *devote your establishment to the execution of our orders exclusively.*" This was before a single Stephenson patent engine had been delivered.

About the same time the L&B Locomotive Committee placed orders for 29 six-wheeled engines for the Trent Valley Railway; Bury, Curtis & Kennedy offered to build fifteen but were fobbed off with an order for only four, all the others were to be "upon Mr Stephenson's plan" with ten by Stephenson & Co, nine by Tayleur and six by Jones & Potts.

Early in 1845 came the first murmurs of the approaching surge of traffic. Camden goods yard was becoming congested and the directors had the idea of looking for land at Wolverton for a goods yard there. Bury saw no point in this and urged the enlargement of Camden; sidings were laid between Chalk Farm and Primrose Hill tunnel later in the year. The first coal train, from Clay Cross, arrived at Kilburn in July.

The Board had involved the line in heavy goods traffic without first obtaining locomotives to deal with it. In the second half of 1845 the tonnage of goods carried by the L&B shot up by no less than 80%. The line was suddenly overwhelmed with more traffic than the engines could handle. A long series of complaints about delays and late arrivals began in July 1845.

In 1845 there was one goods train daily in each direction between Rugby and Camden and two between Birmingham and Camden, each of which conveyed all manner of goods and empty wagons, stopping anywhere as required to take up and deliver at the various stations en route. Engines were normally changed at Wolverton. This arrangement had been adequate hitherto but by August some of these trains were over 100 wagons long, hauled by up to four engines. Broken wagon couplings and delays became endemic. There was a crisis on Saturday 9th August when all six goods trains arrived at their destinations very late. On the previous day the 3rd Down goods - 96 wagons headed by three 0-4-0s Nos 72, 88 and 90 and 2-2-0 No 56 - left Camden 40 minutes late and stopped twelve times to leave and pick up wagons, so that the total number varied between 68 and 105. On the journey one of the couplings parted, there was a derailment, time was lost in having to separate and shunt wagons into sidings and in shunting out of the way of passenger trains and eventually 78 wagons behind 0-4-0s Nos 62, 63 and 84 arrived at Birmingham 6hr 30min late. On the first Up train on the 9th two 0-4-0s Nos 70 and 74 heading 47 wagons (30 goods, 8 cattle, 8 coke, 1 empty) began to slip inside Kilsby tunnel and were stuck there for an hour and fifty minutes. Camden was reached 3hr 35min late, by which time the train consisted of 59 wagons (31 goods, 21 cattle, 4 coke, 3 empties) hauled by 0-4-0s Nos 73 and 64. The other five trains that day, each consisting of up to 80 wagons, arrived between 1hr 40min and 4hr 50min late, in part because of another derailment and three broken couplings. Delayed arrivals had a cumulative effect; engineless trains were stuck at Rugby and Birmingham until northbound trains came in and at Wolverton both Up and Down trains were delayed "waiting for engines".

An attempt was made to overcome these difficulties by running the engines straight through between Birmingham and Camden, and trying to limit each train to one engine and 24 wagons as had been normal up to the previous year. By the following month the longer trains were being divided into sections, but wagon couplings were still failing. On 25th September 2-2-0 No 15 and 0-4-0 No 67 were on the second part of an Up goods train of 37 wagons and started away from a signal at Pinner with such vigour that the coupling between the seventh and eighth wagons parted; in the dark the enginemen were unaware of what had happened until they stopped south of Harrow, when the 30 wagons rolling downhill caught up with them; in the collision three wagons were derailed, one each from the L&B, GJR and M&B. In the early hours of the following day the first part of a Down goods train consisted of 24 wagons pulled by 0-4-0 No 89; the last five wagons broke away in dense fog in Kensal Green tunnel and were rammed by the second part of the train, 2-2-0 No 51, 0-4-0s Nos 69 and 87 and fifty wagons.

Between September 1845 and the end of the year Bury, Curtis & Kennedy supplied six 15in four-wheelers; these were the first additions to the original goods stock. The Board had insisted on Stephenson long-boiler 0-6-0 engines for the coal trains but the first one only arrived in December and was almost immediately sent away for repair.

In October 1845 the Goods Committee's complaint about delays was repeated - there was a lack of engines to take the trains. On 12th December "although several new engines have lately been delivered" - actually only five from BC&K and the one from Tayleur which had been sent away - "no improvement has taken place with the working of the goods trains which still keep very bad time, creating great irregularity and confusion in the Goods Dept and causing numerous heavy claims from carriers and others in consequence." In December

'Veritas Vincit' told *Railway Times* readers of his sorrow that the L&B had fallen from being a first-rate railway to "below third-rate". The engines were "overburdened and overworked".

There was some revision of the goods train timetable early in 1846, with more but shorter trains, and at last some commonsense attempt to allocate specific duties to each train. Now ten goods trains left Camden every day and ten arrived, plus a cattle train on Thursdays and Saturdays; there were also nightly coal trains from Rugby to Kilburn. The Peterborough branch had one daily goods train each way. The suggestion was made to add separate tracks to the main line for goods traffic but this was still a dozen years away.

The complaints of goods train delays went on through 1846, blamed on the greatly increased tonnage to be dealt with. Bury's stock was stretched to the limit but his requests for the provision of more engines were ignored; the Locomotive Committee seemed to be oblivious, or worse. Its members were still dazzled by the prospect of the wonderful Stephenson engines, which - when they had all arrived - would provide an instant cure. The Committee knew all about Bury's difficulties in trying to find engines for the goods trains but when Richard Madigan (by now operating permanent way maintenance trains) mentioned a deficiency in his ballast engines, Bury was told to lend him two of his engines "forthwith". He must have complained loudly about this inconsiderate poaching of his inadequate stock because later the same day, 6th August 1846, the Board ruled that Madigan should purchase two engines from outside.

Then Bury was asked to provide two engines for working the new cattle trains from Peterborough, which had been arranged to start in September as soon as the doubling of the branch was completed. He wrote to Thomas Smith of the Locomotive Committee that he had arranged to "squeeze power from our own stock" for this, but that the engines were being worked very hard, "too much for continuance". He asked Smith to urge the Committee to recommend obtaining more engines. The Committee's puny response was to ask to borrow two Crewe Goods from the Northern Division.

In the same month Edward Tootal of the Trent Valley Railway asked for an engine to work on that line, which was on the point of completing its junction at Rugby; Bury replied that he was quite unable to help, adding that he had the greatest difficulty finding two engines for the Peterborough cattle trains. Four of the engines ordered for the Trent Valley, Stephenson patent long-boiler 4-2-0s, had already arrived from Jones & Potts but brought extra worries with them: leaky tubes, a cracked tubeplate, a replacement firebox required.

The relief promised by the new patent six-wheeled engines had proved illusory. Four of the Tayleur 0-6-0s arrived by March 1846 but the first impression was that they were no better than the new four-wheeled goods engines from BC&K: "about 35 loaded wagons is as much as any of them can take at the required speed." And like the Jones & Potts, they were poorly constructed. Bury wrote to Tayleur early in September to complain about "defective workmanship" on two of them, which had kept them in the shops nearly as much as they were at work. By the end of October twelve had been delivered, another two from Tayleur and six from Longridge, whose wheels gave trouble from the start and in many cases had to be replaced within weeks. They were indifferent performers, had been badly made and were constantly breaking down. It was hardly an encouraging prospect that fourteen more of this type were still to come from Longridge and Nasmyth.

Hitherto, as shown by monthly returns, it was normal for 90% or more of the stock to be in good working order, with between four and ten engines in for repair at any one time. Now, with the old engines overworked and the new patent long-boilers failing as soon as they arrived, the proportion of engines undergoing repair was rising month by month. In early September 1846 Bury was struggling to make do with 82 passenger and 47 goods engines. These were:

Type			*Total*
12in	2-2-0	1837-40 Bury type:	20
13in	2-2-0	1839-41, & rebuilds of 12in engines, Bury type:	35
14in	2-2-0	1845-6, & rebuilds of 12in & 13in engines, Bury type:	16
14¾in	2-2-2	1845 Sharp Bros, on loan from M&B Div:	1
15in	2-2-2	1846 Sharp Bros:	1
15in	2-2-2 OC	1845 Crewe, on loan from N Div:	2
15in	2-2-2	1846 Bury, Curtis & Kennedy:	3
15in	4-2-0 OC	1846 Jones & Potts:	4*
13in	0-4-0	1838-9 Bury type:	29
14in	0-4-0	rebuild of 13in engine, Bury type:	1
15in	0-4-0	1845 Bury, Curtis & Kennedy:	6
15in	0-4-2	1846 Bury, Curtis & Kennedy:	2
15in	0-6-0	1845-6 Tayleur:	5*
15in	0-6-0	1846 Longridge:	4*

OC - outside cylinders
*Stephenson patent long-boiler engines

Of these 129 engines on 8th September, 112 (86.8%) were in working order. During the following month eight more new engines arrived but the number of engines in working order only increased to 114 and in November was down to 111 (81%). On 12th December the total stock was 137 but the number of engines fit for work had fallen to 108 (78.8%).

Despite this depressing overall trend, the locomotive shortage only affected the goods traffic; there was now an adequate stock of efficient passenger engines. Although the new 4-2-0s from Jones & Potts gave a lot of trouble - two of the six were returned to the makers before the end of the year - the big BC&K 2-2-2s began to arrive in August and produced such an improvement that a month later Bury was able to return the borrowed Sharp single to the M&B Division. The two borrowed N Div singles went back to Crewe in November. Early in December the S Div passenger train working was pronounced satisfactory.

The problem of inadequacy and failure of the goods engines remained. On 13th October 1846 a special meeting of the Locomotive Committee was attended by Bury and Stephenson to discuss the defective state of the patent engines. It should have been a showdown, but the Committee seemed paralysed. The only outcome was a squad of men sent down from Newcastle under William Ferguson (who was paid £300 a year by the LNWR) to try to keep the Stephenson engines in repair.

Ferguson and his men arrived on 3rd November and established themselves in the new engine house on the east side at Wolverton. Ten days later the Locomotive Committee reported that "owing to the imperfect performance and continual want of repair of the goods engines on Mr Stephenson's specification, as well as the increasing traffic, a further supply of goods engines will be required." Before considering placing orders with private firms, the Committee suggested asking Crewe for help.

Bury's position was intolerable; his carefully considered and systematic plan of management had been undermined, Stephenson's men were within the gates, and relief, in the shape of adequate goods engines, seemed unlikely.

He had written to the new Manager, Capt Mark Huish, on several occasions complaining that he did not have sufficient goods engines. Machines and men were much overworked and the old engines, he said, were "done" - had any others been available he "would have taken them off a long time ago". He wrote again on the 20th November - he was "fearfully short of power." As usual, there was no response.

Bury's Resignation
"Soon after the amalgamation under the name of the 'London and North-western' Mr Bury began to find his position on the line was changed, and the constant pressure of the heavy responsibilites that rested upon him, without the possession of adequate power and authority to meet them, preyed so much upon his health..." This was how Mrs Bury later described her husband's situation.

On 27th November Bury wrote to Huish again saying he was unable to attend the Joint Locomotive Committee meeting the next day because he had a cold, then ended: "I have already intimated to Mr Creed my intention to retire from the service of the Company..."

Huish replied on 30th: "... I was very sorry to read the concluding para of your note, and hope you will proceed cautiously. I have no clue to your reasons for desiring to retire from the important post you have so long and so ably filled but I conclude it proceeds from the state of your health, and I am anxious that *this* should not be *misunderstood*. Looking to the difficulties that beset the Southern Division in consequence of the state of its power, I feel that your sudden retirement might be misinterpreted, and remarks be made which would be painful to all parties. I have no right in any way to constitute myself the judge of your proceedings, and I hope you will pardon the freedom I have taken. I do it in good feeling, and I confess I am anxious you should withdraw leaving the 'Birmingham' free from those pressing claims which *cannot* be met, but which I presume will shortly be removed by the arrangements you have made... Yours truly, Mark Huish."

To this piece of ambiguous bluster from 'the wily Captain', Bury's reply was dignified:

"Wolverton Dec 1st 1846
You need be under no apprehension that my departure from the service of the Company will be in any other way than will best suit the interest and convenience of the Directors. Most probably I shall remain at my present residence and I shall only be too happy to render the best assistance possible to my successor to enable him to carry on the department so as to produce the best effect and with as little annoyance from the change as possible... I am yours truly, Edward Bury."

At the very next meeting of the S Div Locomotive Committee, Bury finally got his point across: at least twenty new goods engines were needed. He presented a report on the insufficiency of the present engines for the increased goods traffic, comparing the performance of the Stephenson 0-6-0 long-boiler engines with the N Div Crewe Goods and with his own 0-4-2 and 0-4-0 classes. Most of the long-boiler class were out of action, but when they were at work they were no more powerful than the others.

He preferred the 0-4-0 15in class, Nos 111-6, and recommended more of them "with some small alterations by which their power would be much increased".

On 18th December there was a lively meeting of the General Locomotive Committee; the subject for discussion was twenty goods engines required immediately for the S Div. With the poor performance of the Stephenson patent 0-6-0s and the inadequate power of the Crewe Goods 2-4-0s having been demonstrated, the Committee heard the opinions of several authorities on the relative merits of four- and six-wheeled goods engines. Bury, as always, was firm in his advocacy of four wheels and produced supporting letters from John Hawkshaw, Chief Engineer of the heavily-graded Manchester & Leeds which had both four- and six-wheeled goods engines and from Henry Houldsworth, Chairman of that line. Also in favour of four wheels were William Fairbairn of Manchester and Benjamin Cubitt, formerly manager of Rothwell's of Bolton, later Locomotive Engineer of the Brighton, Croydon & Dover Railways Joint Committee and recently appointed Locomotive Superintendent of the Great Northern.

Hardman Earle (in his usual role as a Stephenson apologist) had gathered letters of support for six-wheeled engines from Joseph Locke, J. E. McConnell of the Bristol & Birmingham, Matthew Kirtley, Locomotive Superintendent of the Midland Railway, Thomas Cabry, Engineer of the York & North Midland, and Edward Woods, Engineer of the Liverpool & Manchester section of the LNWR.

The LNWR engineers present at the meeting were asked for their opinions. Francis Trevithick was in favour of six wheels, but was not practically acquainted with the work of four-wheeled engines; John Ramsbottom was in favour of six wheels if the engine was over 18 tons. R. B. Dockray, with the effect on the track in mind, preferred six wheels in engines over 16 tons. R. S. Norris, the N Div Superintendent, thought that six wheels were less liable to slip than four. Henry Bruyeres, S Div Superintendent, said that BC&K 0-4-2s Nos 117 and 118 were the best goods engines on the line. The minutes simply record that "a long and interesting discussion ensued."

Certainly, the patent 0-6-0 goods engines which had been delivered to the LNWR were a dismal failure; the L&B sheds and workshops had been equipped for short, four-wheeled engines, and having to alter so many buildings and enlarge all the turnplates and turntables must have seemed an expensive and pointless task, merely to accommodate engines of no greater power but with the needless complication of an extra pair of wheels. Bury still argued in favour of four-wheeled engines for the S Div when he had already resigned from the railway; as a manufacturer (and if he had been the acute businessman of legend) perhaps he should have been urging the LNWR to buy bigger and more complex engines, to bring his firm a bigger profit. BC&K were, after all, perfectly capable and willing to build big engines, very good six-wheelers of their own design. In the autumn of 1846 their large 2-2-2s cured the S Div passenger train problem.

Meanwhile, with a hugely increasing tonnage and decreasing locomotive availability, the goods traffic working was steadily deteriorating. And again BC&K came to the rescue. In 1845 they had offered to build fifteen 16in 0-6-0s for the Trent Valley line but, as the directors were then beguiled by the promise of Stephenson's patent long-boilers, only four had been ordered from the Liverpool firm. The first of the four, by far the most powerful engine yet seen on the S Div, arrived early in December 1846 and was quickly followed by the other three. If Bury's employers insisted - misguidedly, as he thought - on an extra pair of wheels, then this was how six-wheeled engines ought to be. Soon afterwards came two 15in 0-4-0 'coal engines' with 4ft wheels, which had been ordered by the Manchester & Birmingham but were instead sent to Wolverton. With these six BC&K engines added to stock - and these only, with a little help from a borrowed Crewe Goods - the Goods Committee was able to report on 4th March 1847 that goods traffic on the S Div was now being worked satisfactorily. On the following day Bury attended his last meeting of the General Locomotive Committee and so had the gratification of knowing that he had seen the crisis through and was leaving the S Div adequately provided with locomotives. He might have regretted that they were not all four-wheelers but he could be content with this demonstration that his firm's engines had, in the end, succeeded where those of his great rival had failed.

As promised, he had remained in attendance until his successor McConnell settled in. Having seen the Locomotive Department restored to normality after almost two years of frustration, worry and panic, and with McConnell in his first three weeks already pushing on with ideas of his own, Edward Bury left the LNWR.

The Board recorded "their sense of his systematic arrangements and his able and zealous services" and presented him with a service of plate "of the value of £500 in token of esteem from the Directors". Mrs Bury wrote that a more highly prized testimonial was a "massive, handsome silver candelabrum" and the signatures of 300 voluntary subscribers.

Bury was 54 years old but he had worn himself out; his doctor recommended rest and he spent the spring and summer of 1847 recuperating, on holiday in Europe.

Bury after the LNWR
In 1848 Sir William Cubitt persuaded him to accept the job of Locomotive Engineer on the new Great Northern Railway. The GNR Board recorded the appointment on 22nd February at a salary of £2,000. He created such a good impression that in June 1849 he was also appointed General Manager, while retaining the Locomotive Department under his control. He prepared the first plans for Doncaster 'Plant'.

Frederick Parker, Chief Foreman (works manager) at Wolverton, had become dissatisfied with the new regime there and after giving evidence at an accident enquiry about the incompetence of McConnell's blackleg drivers, he followed Bury to the Great Northern in November 1848. He was appointed Bury's deputy and remained on the GNR until 1865. Many others were unhappy that Bury was no longer in charge on the S Div; during the drivers' strike in August 1848 the men proposed that he be brought in as an arbitrator - as (unlike his successor McConnell) "a gentleman of long experience of locomotive management."

One of Bury's long-lasting innovations on the GNR was the varnished teak carriage livery, which was not only cheaper but made it harder to disguise inferior wood or workmanship.

He left the GNR in March 1850 after complaints that he had placed orders for ironwork with firms with which he was associated. R. B. Dockray the LNWR Engineer wrote in his diary that Charles Fox of Fox, Henderson & Co was "the presiding fiend in this ... his imagination and malevolence will supply abundance of suspicious facts. I shall be curious to know how so experienced and I believe really upright a man as Bury will clear himself." The ironwork in question was 30 sets of spare carriage wheels, a minor item when Bury was then involved in seeking tenders from nine firms (none of them Bury, Curtis & Kennedy) for 20 passenger and goods engines. Perhaps it was a slip; perhaps he was too preoccupied trying to get the GNR started.

Meanwhile Bury's firm had suffered a heavy loss on a large swing bridge across the Neva at St Petersburg for which they designed and produced most of the ironwork, filling the yard of the Clarence Foundry with the erected sections. The Russian Government defaulted on the bill, which was never paid although the bridge was opened by Tsar Nicholas in November 1850. The Liverpool shipbuilding trade was in serious decline at the same period, and although BC&K had taken over Vernon's shipyard, the largest in Liverpool, the workforce had been reduced to 170 by mid-1851. The Clarence Foundry closed down shortly afterwards and there was a huge auction of equipment lasting 34 days in July and August.

In 1852 Bury went into partnership in a steelworks with Charles Cammell and lived for a time at Hillsborough Hall just outside Sheffield; in 1855 he started another successful steelworks with his son William Tarleton Bury and John Bedford, as Bedford, Burys & Co, Regent Works, Sheffield. Once this was established Bury himself withdrew, buying Croft Lodge, near Ambleside in the Lake District, with a fine view down Windermere. Sadly he was able to enjoy his retirement there for only a few years.

In August 1858 he became ill and was taken to Harrogate, then to Scarborough, where he died at East Villa on 25th November 1858. He was 64; his death certificate reads: "cerebral disease, 4 months; dropsy 3 weeks." He was buried at Scarborough on 2nd December, but his gravestone has been tidied away, and cannot now be traced.

Writers of railway history have not been kind to Edward Bury. He has been derided as a builder of tiny old-fashioned engines, obstructively stuck in the past while greater men were pushing locomotive development forward. He has been denigrated by authors from Stretton onwards. He was described by Ahrons as "endowed richly with the commercial instinct" and by a more recent writer as "above all a business man" but in reality it seems that the money-making instinct was the very thing Bury lacked. His first concern was always in running the railway efficiently; if he placed orders with his own firm it was because he knew he could rely on his own products. Kennedy was later to complain that if he had only had a good commercial man as partner he would have carried on with the Clarence Foundry.

All the evidence shows that Bury was liked and respected by his men. "By a union of strictness and kindness" he gained their confidence in his judgment and integrity. 'Veritas Vincit' said he was "the most particular Superintendent in England in the selection of enginemen" and Bury himself described his L&B footplatemen as regular and well-behaved who gave him no trouble. In 1839 he said that although without powers to do so, he had fined one or two of them a sovereign each, but gave out rewards for good work. Some men took to the work at once, he said, but others would never make engine drivers; he had already promoted five or six firemen to drivers. Mostly labourers originally, the L&B engine drivers were "men of great activity and of great ability to get out of a difficulty."

At first the L&B did not carry third-class passengers because the directors could see no profit in it, but Bury argued that they had a duty to do so, because "the railways have, or will destroy all other means of communication" including the stage wagons and carriers' carts used by the poor. He spoke to the Board repeatedly about this, until eventually one daily slow train was put on to carry third-class passengers - albeit at the fairly expensive fare of 1½d a mile - in October 1840.

Bury's legacy, from the railway workshops at Wolverton and Doncaster down to such details as the net parcel rack and the varnished teak livery, undoubtedly includes many improvements in locomotive design which have been credited to others. A rather reserved, cultured and speculative product of the eighteenth century, he was very unlike the generation of locomotive superintendents which succeeded him. His was no rags-to-riches story and was therefore of no interest to Samuel (*Self-help*) Smiles who wrote so many popular biographies of engineers; it was left to Bury's widow to publish a short memoir, which few could have seen.

Now Edward Bury can be recognised as a great railway organiser, as well as one of the greatest locomotive pioneers. It was not for nothing that he was elected a Fellow of the Royal Society in 1844, the only locomotive engineer so honoured until Sir William Stanier a century later.

His widow believed Bury had "devoted the best energies of his life to the success of the London & Birmingham Railway".

JAMES EDWARD McCONNELL

Edward Bury mentioned his intention to retire from the LNWR to the Manager, Mark Huish on 27th November 1846, and to the Secretary, Richard Creed shortly before. On the following day the first meeting of the new Joint Locomotive Committee took place at Birmingham, attended by representative directors of all three constituent companies and by Trevithick and Ramsbottom. One of the matters discussed - after the surprising news about Bury - was a valuation of locomotive stock which it was decided would take place annually on 30th November. Trevithick was to list the Northern engines, with assistance from Ramsbottom for the M&B section, while Bury covered the S Div - assisted by Mr McConnell of the Bristol & Birmingham Railway. This is the first mention of McConnell in the LNWR records. His involvement *may* have been suggested by Bury, to give him an introduction to the LNWR and sound him out as a possible successor, but Bury was not present at the meeting because he had a cold and there is no mention of McConnell in any of the letters about the meeting between Bury, Creed and Huish. It is far more likely that McConnell's name was brought up by Capt Moorsom. Moorsom had known and been impressed by McConnell since 1841; Bury's views about who should take over after his departure - if indeed he had any by this stage - are not known.

On 12th December the entire Board learned of Bury's impending resignation and a committee of three (Chairman Glyn, Capt Moorsom and Thomas Smith) was appointed to consider the subject and, in conjunction with the Joint Locomotive Committee, make arrangements for Bury's successor. Within days a rumour was circulating (and reported by 'Veritas Vincit') that "Mr Stephenson will endeavour to put on a gentleman from the North". But on 9th January 1847 Moorsom reported that they recommended the appointment of McConnell to succeed Bury at Wolverton, at £700 a year, a lot less than Bury's basic salary but the same as Trevithick's and more than twice that of John Ramsbottom.

Creed wrote to McConnell on 14th January, offering him the job; four days later McConnell wrote back from Bromsgrove, accepting. Together with Bury he attended a meeting of the renamed General Locomotive Committee on 4th February and started work at Wolverton on Monday 15th February. He was 32 years old and had been in charge of the locomotives on the Birmingham & Gloucester line for almost five years.

The new Superintendent was very different from his predecessor in background, education, wealth and status as well as in age. For many generations McConnell's family had been handloom weavers and small tenant farmers at Watshouse near the village of Dailly in south Ayrshire. Towards the end of the eighteenth century, with the opening of coal pits and the growth of small industries in the neighbourhood, some of the younger members began to take up other trades, such as that of blacksmith. Some of them moved out of the district; Quentin McConnell, born at Dailly in 1785, became a

Fig. 5   James Edward McConnell, 1815-83. Locomotive Superintendent, LNWR Southern Division 1847-62.
(Science & Art Institute, Wolverton)

millwright and left Scotland for Ireland. At Cork in 1813 he married Elizabeth Bradbury from Manchester and their son was born at the garrison town of Fermoy, Co Cork, on New Year's Day, 1815. Quentin was then still working as a millwright (the story that he was the proprietor of a "large ironworks" at Fermoy is a much later piece of fantasy) but in 1821 he died and young James Edward McConnell was sent back to Watshouse in the care of his uncle. He lived there until aged about 13, when "owing to a difference with his uncle he was launched on the world with a capital of ten shillings" - according to the account of his early struggles in one of his obituaries.

One of his father's cousins had progressed from the smithy into the ironmongery business and went on to marry the sister of a partner in an ironworks. This was the firm of Claud Girdwood & Co of Gorbals, Glasgow, machine makers and iron-founders, which had begun in the 1790s by making looms and spinning mules for cotton mills; by 1824 they were building an iron lighthouse for the Broomielaw Quay and making all the machinery for the first steam bucket-dredger used in deepening the Clyde. Young McConnell went to Glasgow and was taken on as an apprentice at Girdwood's in 1828, about which time they were building an enormous beam engine for Newcraighall Colliery, Edinburgh; with its 80in diameter cylinder it was the largest in Scotland. At

Girdwood's he is said to have been "regarded as a steady and reliable workman, assisting the foremen and managers against the frequent difficulties arising through trades-unions and strikes."

Claud Girdwood went bankrupt in 1837, but by then McConnell was working as a fitter at Edward Bury's Clarence Foundry in Liverpool. He was there for three years and quickly rose, via the drawing office, to the position of underforeman. Then he "gave some offence to Bury" and moved to Bury's associates, Thomas Vernon & Co of the nearby Regent Street Foundry, with whom he acted as foreman at the erection of the Earl of Clare's great glasshouses at Mountshannon near Limerick, designed - forerunners of the Crystal Palace - by Joseph Paxton. After ten months at Vernon's he was for a short time a foreman in a machine shop in Manchester.

While in Liverpool he spent a lot of his spare time at the Mechanics' Institute, to which he later attributed much of his success in life. According to 'Veritas Vincit' he gave lectures there on the steam engine.

In 1841 at the age of 26 he applied for a job with the Birmingham & Gloucester Railway.

The Birmingham & Gloucester Railway
The B&G was a 50-mile line which had only opened in the previous year and was notorious for its Lickey incline, over two miles at 1 in 37.7. All but six of its 27 engines were 4-2-0 outside-cylinder Norris-type and three more of these were on order. The management, finances and working practices were in the middle of reorganisation after a period of near chaos, when one last catastrophe showed up the appalling state of the B&G's Locomotive Department. After a heavy drinking session in the Vigo Bank alehouse the superintendent, his foreman, the foreman's wife and one of Nasmyth's men were being brought home down the Lickey on the footplate of *Boston*, a Norris 4-2-0 driven by the fireman, when an insecure plug blew out of the tubeplate and a sudden rush of steam and boiling water came through the firehole. Superintendent William Creuze was scalded to death, the four others escaped with minor injuries. This was on 6th April 1841. Changes were immediately made among the staff and at the end of the month the B&G placed an advertisement in the railway papers:

"Wanted, a competent FOREMAN for the workshops of the Locomotive Department of this Railway. He must be sufficiently educated to be able to understand accounts and express his ideas clearly by letter..."

Applications, with satisfactory testimonials and references were required by 8th May.

The chairman of the B&G was Capt C. R. Moorsom, who had been one of the secretaries of the L&B, and was now a director of that company. McConnell applied for the job, with a reference from Edward Bury; it was offered to him on 2nd July. Having accepted, he said he also wanted the job of locomotive superintendent, held by the newly-appointed G. D. Bishopp, but the B&G would not agree to this, so he began his duties as foreman at Bromsgrove on 14th July.

He was very energetic and his ability clearly impressed Moorsom, who backed him from the beginning. Within three weeks of his appointment he suggested, as an experiment, fitting 5ft wheels in place of 4ft on one of the Norris engines, which were rough runners at more than 20mph. Three were altered by February 1842 and were a success. Another aid to steadier running was the addition of balance weights to the driving wheels, put on in 1842 at the suggestion of George Heaton of Birmingham, who had been balancing stationary engines in this manner for thirty years. McConnell continued Bishopp's scheme of adding a saddle tank to some of the Norris engines for use as banking engines. This also was a success, resulting in a 23% reduction in coke consumption.

The B&G was under a certain amount of London & Birmingham influence at this time. As well as the chairman, other directors had family connections with the L&B Board and Edward Bury had been brought in at the beginning to advise on the laying out of Bromsgrove Works and on the procurement of locomotives, but his advice had only been followed in part, hence the stock of small American engines. These had been obtained on the strength of the exaggerated claims of their maker, William Norris of Philadelphia.

Bury had been present when the first of the American engines began its trials and was unimpressed. When in 1839 the House of Commons Select Committee asked his opinion of the result he said "there was no occasion to send to America for engines." He considered the engine a failure. On the Grand Junction it had been carefully timed with 30 trains, but a GJR engine took one of the same trains in 28 minutes less time. "I think there has been a mistake made about that engine from the United States. The engineer who ordered it left the pressure of the steam an open question. I have no doubt that the engine has been working at at least 100 lbs on the inch." This reply would hardly endear Bury to the engineer in question, William Scarth Moorsom, brother of the L&B director.

Two years later, on the same day in August 1841 that the line was connected to the L&B and trains were at last able to run into Curzon Street, the B&G Birmingham Committee wrote to Bury saying that they would be glad to have one of his engines tried on the Lickey incline. On 23rd August he took an L&B goods engine to Bromsgrove with a train of weighted wagons for test purposes. The engine was No 65, an 0-4-0 with 13in cylinders and 5ft wheels which, after stalling on the incline with five vehicles behind the tender (31.3 tons), completed the ascent four times with successively reduced loads. Also present was the B&G 4-2-0 *Philadelphia*, a Norris A-Extra type delivered in May 1840 and fitted with a newly devised sanding gear; having 12½in cylinders, 4ft driving wheels and an undisclosed but higher boiler pressure it was more powerful than the L&B engine. It was tried with the same loads as those of No 65's successful ascents; with four (24.6 tons) and three vehicles (17.9 tons) it ran up the bank at greater speeds than the L&B engine. The whole affair looks like a publicity stunt arranged by W. S. Moorsom, on behalf of the Philadelphia firm and to justify himself to the B&G Board for having purchased expensive American engines. McConnell himself later said "the pressure on the American engines was very fallacious, for the spring balance only indicated about one-third of the actual pressure, which was really about 100 lb."

By June 1842 the only engines on the line with cylinders of so large a diameter as 13in were four by Forrester, bought on Bury's advice in 1838/9 and two by Bury, Curtis & Kennedy. The rest were between 10½in and 12½in, presumably kept going by their undisclosed high boiler pressure.

McConnell meanwhile had extended his scope by a redefinition of his duties and those of Locomotive Superintendent Bishopp in October 1841; six months later Bishopp resigned and McConnell got his job. The first meeting of the Board he was summoned to attend was on 23rd August 1842.

At the end of the following year he recommended ordering two 0-6-0 goods engines of Stephenson's patent long-boiler type, with 15in x 24in cylinders and 4ft 3in wheels. Told to consult the *best* engine makers he consulted eight firms, five of whom tendered for engines to his specification at these prices:

Bury, Curtis & Kennedy:	£1,490
R Stephenson:	£1,575
Kitson, Thompson & Hewitson:	£1,500
Stothert, Slaughter:	£1,700
Jones & Potts:	£1,357

Shepherd & Todd, of the Railway Foundry, Leeds, offered to build engines at £1,550 each, but they would have 16in cylinders, 5ft wheels and iron tubes instead of brass as specified. BC&K proposed as an alternative an 0-4-0 with 14in cylinders for £1,360, and Stephenson suggested iron instead of brass tubes for a price reduced by £75 each. Two firms declined to tender: Neath Abbey Ironworks because they could not finish the engines by the date required, and Sharp Bros, who were too busy and could not start until autumn.

McConnell visited Jones & Potts and found them "fully competent so far as tools and machinery." He reported on 9th January 1844 that he was preparing drawings which might cause some alteration to the firm's offer. The changes probably included an increase in wheel size to 4ft 6in; Jones & Potts said their price would remain the same but asked if the B&G would pay Stephenson's patent royalty of £50. This was declined. The engines were delivered in June and July 1844, and were named *Bristol*, in celebration of the opening of the adjoining Bristol & Gloucester Railway, and *Hercules*.

On a recent visit to Glasgow McConnell had seen another *Hercules* which began banking on the Edinburgh & Glasgow Railway's 1 in 41 Cowlairs incline in January. In March 1844 he was given permission to build an engine at Bromsgrove, specifically for banking on the Lickey incline. This was to be an 0-6-0 tank engine similar to William Paton and John Miller's very successful *Hercules* which was thought to be the most powerful locomotive in the world; it had 15½in outside cylinders and 4ft 3½in wheels. In McConnell's engine, which was named *Great Britain* to emphasise its un-American origin, the cylinders were increased to 18in and the wheels were reduced to 3ft 10in; the tank was placed over the boiler. The width of the firebox - 4ft 4¼in - suggests that it probably had outside frames. The weight was 30 tons, 3½ tons greater than the E&GR *Hercules* and "the largest engine known" according to Sir Charles Pasley, Inspector General of Railways. It created a sensation when it was completed in June 1845 and began banking on the Lickey.

In 1845 the B&G and its broad gauge continuation southwards, the Bristol & Gloucester, had come together in a de facto amalgamation as the 'Bristol & Birmingham'. Motive power for the Bristol & Gloucester had been supplied, maintained and worked under a contract with Stothert, Slaughter & Co, which did not expire until the end of the year. Meanwhile the Midland Railway leased both companies from May.

For the B&G section of the Bristol & Birmingham, McConnell was authorised to prepare specifications for two new engines on 30th July; estimates were obtained and on 3rd September an order was placed with Charles Tayleur & Co of the Vulcan Foundry for two passenger engines and tenders at £2,050 each and two goods engines and tenders at £2,150 each. In November McConnell asked for four extra engines, one passenger and three goods, but this was refused because the price had gone up by £250 each.

These engines were certainly needed; in 1845 the B&BR experienced a shortage of locomotives so severe that three old engines were bought from John Hargreaves of the Bolton & Leigh Railway, which had just been taken over by the Grand Junction. Two of these were Tayleur 0-4-2s of 1836 and 1838, *Wellington* and *Pandora*. The third, named *Camilla*, was probably a 14in 2-2-2 built by Nasmyth in 1839 and known only as *No 1* on the Bolton & Leigh.

The four new engines from the Vulcan Foundry were the patent long-boiler type with inside cylinders, inside frames and all wheels in front of the firebox, but were not Tayleur's normal type. They had some curious features, presumably specified by McConnell; they are the earliest designs of his of which authentic drawings survive. The boiler was the same design on both types, with a large dome on the raised firebox and a slim safety valve trumpet on the middle of the barrel. The T-iron wheels had central balance weights; the leading axle was sprung normally, but a single large inverted spring transmitted the load to the second and third axles on each side. The 2-4-0 passenger engine had its driving wheels coupled closely together, like the middle and trailing wheels of the 0-6-0; in both types the centre pair were flanged, unlike the standard Stephenson long-boiler engines.

The cylinders on both were horizontal and in the goods engine were centred immediately in front of the leading axle. The axle was avoided by each cylinder having *two* piston rods 12in apart, one above and one below the axle. Behind the axle they were united in a common crosshead. The valves lay between the cylinders, each valve rod having a stirrup-shaped eye encircling the leading axle.

All four engines were delivered in mid-1846. The two goods engines were Tayleur's working numbers 740/1, the two passengers were 744/5; tenders were 742/3/6/7 (Tayleur's alleged 'rotation numbers' 237-40 are later conjectures). They were taken into Midland stock in 1847 as 165/6 (2-4-0) and 169/70 (0-6-0) and were scrapped in 1858-63.

Dimensions

	2-4-0	0-6-0
Cylinders (2 inside)	16" x 22"	16" x 24"
Boiler		
Diameter	3' 8"	
Length of barrel	13' 9"	
Pitch	6' 1"	5' 7"
Length of firebox casing	4' 0"	
Heating surface		
Tubes (131, 1¾ dia, 14' long)	840 sq ft	
Firebox	277 sq ft	
Total	1117 sq ft	
Grate area	11.6 sq ft	
Diameter of wheels		
Leading	3' 6"	—
Coupled	5' 6¾"	4' 7½"
Length over bufferbeam	23' 6"	23' 6"
Wheelbase	5' 6" + 5' 10" =11' 4"	6' 4" + 4' 10" =11' 2"

In February 1846 Stephenson offered three engines "now building" by Tayleur for £2,400 each. These had been ordered by the Chester & Holyhead for delivery in July and August but the C&H was nowhere near ready for them. They were patent long-boiler 4-2-0s with 6ft driving wheels, 15in x 24in outside cylinders and Gothic firebox. These were purchased, as were two Sharp singles. With the locomotive shortage overcome, McConnell resumed trying to get rid of the light American engines.

On 19th January 1847 the B&BR Board was shown the letter from Richard Creed to McConnell "announcing his appointment to the Locomotive Department of the L&NWR" and it was arranged that Matthew Kirtley, Locomotive Superintendent of the Midland would take over his duties. On 27th February, after McConnell had departed it was ordered that he be told that Kirtley was now in charge "and that the Secretary do assure Mr McConnell that the Directors are much gratified that his efficiency on the Bristol & Birmingham Railway has ended in promotion to his present important position."

McConnell on the LNWR

On his first day at Wolverton, 15th February, McConnell wrote to Moorsom, asking when it would be convenient to see him. "Several very important matters require my immediate attention" but he was happy to say that "there appears a general good feeling towards me on the part of the officers and workmen... all are anxious to work *with* me."

Some of his new colleagues recorded their impressions of McConnell. David Stevenson, the Camden Goods Manager, described him as "a strong and determined man of the rough sort." Robert Benson Dockray, the LNWR Engineer wrote in his diary: "There is no doubt of his being intellectually a very clever man, full of energy, but he has some sad moral blemishes which will always prevent his occupying the position he otherwise could do. He is cunning and wants straightforwardness." Superintendent Bruyeres also said McConnell was not straightforward and "works for his own department as though it were not part of the general concern." The anonymous writer in the railway papers of the 1840s who signed himself 'Veritas Vincit' had some very caustic things to say about McConnell: "this youthful superintendent has an immeasurable conceit of his own talents" (April 1843); his "usual flurried manner in giving directions" (April 1845); there "is not a locomotive superintendent in the kingdom who has wasted more money or failed in his attempts at improvement ... pushing himself forward in the company of men of talent, hearing their opinions on scientific subjects, and advancing them in other quarters as his own. This is no secret, it is often alluded to." He "knows nothing but what he copies, and what he does copy is usually fallacious" (February 1847). The last outburst was prompted by hearing about McConnell's appointment to the LNWR, which had completely astonished 'Veritas Vincit'. He thought the appointment had to be because of some private motive - "it cannot have been based on the qualifications of McConnell."

During his last months in office Bury appealed repeatedly for new locomotives because the old ones were worn out but he received scant and tardy response from the directors. McConnell's way was different. After observing the members of the two locomotive committees at meetings on 4th and 13th February, and after taking up his duties at Wolverton on 15th, he fired a broadside. He read a damning report to the S Div Locomotive Committee on 3rd March, full of figures which don't add up (or which came so thick and fast that the minute-clerk became confused) saying that all engines with cylinders smaller than 14in diameter should be sold or scrapped. No fewer than 47 engines with 12in and 13in cylinders were quite inadequate and their state of repair was mostly such that selling or scrapping was "the only alternative". The imminent failure of many of the old engines was "a matter of certainty"; they were not worth the expense of rebuilding and he recommended that *forty* of Sharp Bros 18in goods 0-6-0s be ordered, as well as twenty passenger engines, these to be 6ft singles with outside cylinders at least 16in by 21in. He also criticised Wolverton Works, suggesting it should become a manufactory, with repairs being done at Rugby - presumably in new shops to be erected there.

These sweeping and radical recommendations must have overwhelmed the directors, who gave him a lot of what he wanted. Sales of old engines began at once, the S Div Committee agreed that forty big goods engines of the Sharp type should be ordered (although this was cut back to twelve by the General Committee) and he was given the go-ahead to build a passenger engine at Wolverton "of as large dimensions as he may consider suitable". He had certainly got off to a flying start.

Whatever McConnell thought about his new colleagues being anxious to work with him, his reputation as a reducer of footplatemen's wages on the Birmingham & Gloucester had gone before him. One of his first acts was to introduce piece-work at Wolverton. His behaviour soon upset the drivers, and by July the Board was receiving anonymous letters from "old servants" filled with serious grievances and complaints of mismanagement in the Locomotive Department. A notice was posted at Wolverton inviting the writers to send their names to the Secretary and promising to investigate the complaints.

A year later, in August 1848, practically all the footplatemen, 115 drivers and a similar number of firemen, went on strike; only 13 men remained at work. Their wages had been reduced and this, according to the *Railway Chronicle* was coupled with a general dislike among the men for McConnell's system of management. "So obnoxious has this officer rendered himself that the men have expressed a disinclination to work under him." Just before the strike began some drivers mounted brooms on their engines, to show they were 'to let'. One driver trailed a long rope over the side: "To catch that **** McConnell."

McConnell recruited blacklegs from Woolwich Arsenal, Thames riverboats and redundant railwaymen from other lines; 50 Wolverton fitters became drivers. The use of these inexperienced men soon led to accidents; questions were asked in Parliament. A Quaker shareholder likened the position on the S Div to that of McConnell's old line, the B&G, "where life was lost for the saving of a few shillings."

The strikers held a meeting on 17th and proposed to submit their case to the arbitration of Edward Bury, Daniel Gooch and Richard Madigan who were all gentlemen "of long experience of locomotive management." The Chairman consulted Madigan and it was arranged that McConnell's system of classification of drivers should be withdrawn.

The strike lasted from 7th to 23rd August; after it was over McConnell kept on many of the new recruits, but had to write to the Secretary on 26th: "I have endeavoured to comply with your request only to employ competent drivers. On receipt of your letter I issued immediate orders that all the trains on the Main Line should be driven by old drivers, and this I believe has been attended to with the exception of the case to which you allude..."

McConnell was successful in his aim of reducing the number of footplatemen. In November 1848 there were 289 on the S Div; a year later the total was down to 220.

The strike-breaking fitters of Wolverton wrote to the Chairman, incensed by their treatment in the press. They considered themselves as good as - or better than - drivers. Having taken on all the extra hands, whose pay increased the wage bill by 28% for the half-year, work had to be found for them. Some of them were set to work on two of the old engines which had been condemned as not worth repairing, 2-2-0s Nos 47 and 56.

Wolverton was put on 'short time' - a 4½-day week. In 1848-9 another five condemned engines (Nos 14, 20, 43, 62/3) were thoroughly repaired and two (90 and 2, renumbered 237) were completely rebuilt. The construction of three new engines was begun, but shortly afterwards suspended; these were copies of Sharp long-boiler 0-6-0 goods engines, and were eventually turned out in 1851 as 228-30.

McConnell had other strikes to contend with, but he was skilled in subduing them. Perhaps he was unlucky in that his arrival coincided with an economy drive and a Board decision to reduce wages; perhaps his success in carrying through a similar exercise on the B&G was among the reasons for his surprising appointment to the LNWR. Perhaps Bury, who seems to have been liked and respected by his workmen, was lucky in not having to implement a similar policy.

Another difference from Bury is revealed in a gushing letter from the Wolverton parson to the Chairman: "Mr McConnell attends the church very regularly - he requires the apprentices also to attend and his wise example, of course, cannot be without effect. I see a great change since *he* came -"

A Surplus of Engines

It was McConnell's good fortune that his arrival on the LNWR in February 1847 coincided exactly with the end of the locomotive shortage on the S Div. Five months before, Bury had been trying desperately to make do with 129 engines, 112 of them in working order. Since then several reliable engines had been added, and both passenger and goods traffic were being worked satisfactorily. McConnell found 158 engines under his control when he arrived at Wolverton, 123 of which were in working order. Later in the year he claimed that the locomotive stock when he took over was "in a ruinous state" but this was something of an exaggeration and was simply the customary claim of a new man on the job; in due course similar disparaging remarks would be made by his successor after McConnell's departure.

Apart from two which had been scrapped following a collision in January, all the original L&B engines were still at work, many of them rebuilt with bigger boilers and cylinders. Their longevity was a complete contrast to those on McConnell's old line, or for that matter on the Grand Junction, but within six months he had sold a dozen of the smaller ones to contractors. After this first flush, and despite the influx of new engines, fewer were sold. Some became stationary pumping engines or were used to drive machinery in Wolverton Works. Ten of the 13in engines were in regular use on trains from Euston late in 1847 and five of the original L&B engines of 1837-40 were still working on the line at the end of McConnell's term on the LNWR.

More Stephenson patent long-boiler 4-2-0s arrived on the S Div in 1847 as the orders for the Trent Valley line were completed and several of the same type, which the Chester & Holyhead Railway had ordered, were sent instead to McConnell. Other new passenger engines included Sharp singles and the Crampton *London* with 8ft diameter driving wheels. Another Crampton, *Namur*, was on loan to the LNWR and Stephenson & Co had sent a big 3-cylinder engine for trials.

New goods engines included more of the Stephenson patent long-boiler 0-6-0s, ordered in 1845, four BC&K 15in 0-4-0s, one 0-6-0 from Jones & Potts and one of Sharp Bros powerful 'Atlas' type 18in 0-6-0s, transferred from the M&B Division.

In twelve months the S Div stock increased by more than a third. Whatever McConnell's problems were, shortage of engines was not one of them.

On 7th September 1847 there were 111 passenger and 63 goods engines:

Type		Total
12in 2-2-0	1837-8 Bury type:	8
13in 2-2-0	1839-41 & rebuilds of 12in engines, Bury type:	30
14in 2-2-0	1845-6 & rebuilds of 12in & 13in engines, Bury type:	22
15in 2-2-2	1846 Sharp Bros:	3
15in 2-2-2 OC	1845-7 Crewe, on loan from N Div:	4
15in 2-2-2	1846 Bury, Curtis & Kennedy:	11
15in 4-2-0 OC	1846-7 Jones & Potts:	11
15in 4-2-0 OC	1847 Stephenson:	6
15in 4-2-0 OC	1847 Tayleur:	15
18in 4-2-0 OC	1847 Crampton *London*:	1
13in 0-4-0	1838-9 Bury type:	15
14in 0-4-0	rebuilds of 13in engines, Bury type:	8
15in 0-4-0	1845-7 Bury, Curtis & Kennedy:	9
15in 0-4-2	1846 Bury, Curtis & Kennedy:	2
15in 0-6-0	1845-6 Tayleur:	6
15in 0-6-0	1846-7 Longridge:	8
15in 0-6-0	1847 Nasmyth:	7
15in 2-4-0 OC	1846 Crewe, on loan from N Div:	2
16in 0-6-0	1846 Bury, Curtis & Kennedy:	4
16in 0-6-0	1847 Jones & Potts:	1
18in 0-6-0	1847 Sharp Bros:	1

Of these 174 engines, 146 were in working order; four of the smaller 2-2-0s were listed as "for sale" but only one was sold in 1848; the other three later became tank engines.

As many as 68 new engines arrived on the S Div during the year 1847 and by the end of 1848 there were 230 engines in stock, including eight 'for sale' and no fewer than 25 of the big Sharp-type 18in 0-6-0s. There was now a large surplus of engines and in a new period of financial stringency McConnell was told to put as many in store as possible "to reduce the number in ordinary work to the amount that may be absolutely necessary". The stored engines were to be kept for use on new branches when these were brought into use but the changed financial climate led to a cutback of capital expenditure and the slowing down of railway construction; only 6¾ miles were added to the S Div between 1846 and 1850. By the end of January 1849 there were 25 engines in storage, mostly quite new and including ten of the big Sharp-type goods.

During 1848-9 more small classes of various types of engines arrived at Wolverton which had been built for lines taken over by the LNWR: the Chester & Holyhead, the Leeds, Dewsbury & Manchester and the Huddersfield & Manchester. Trevithick did not want them on the N Div, and as Crewe, unlike Wolverton, was organised as a locomotive-building works from the outset, he was able to continue on his division with his own standard types. Whatever McConnell's views about them, the miscellaneous engines continued to arrive on the S Div. Some of them were undoubtedly poor machines which McConnell was probably content to put into store; later he was able to transfer a few of them away from the S Div when he was told to send engines from store to the Yorkshire lines; unfortunately nine of the Sharp-type 0-6-0s went too.

Thomas Russell Crampton persuaded the Board to order another of his patent singles which materialised as the monster 6-2-0 *Liverpool* in 1848 and which despite its fame did little work. McConnell's own Wolverton-built prodigy, known as 'Mac's Mangle', was completed in the same year but remained the only one of its type.

On 4th December 1849 there were 135 passenger and 94 goods engines:

Type		Total
12in 2-2-0	1837-8 Bury type:	5
13in 2-2-0	1839-41 & rebuilds of 12in engines, Bury type:	33
14in 2-2-0	1845-6 & rebuilds of 12in & 13in engines, Bury type:	22
15in 2-2-2	1846-8 Sharp Bros:	9
15in 2-2-2	1846 Bury, Curtis & Kennedy:	11
15in 4-2-0 OC	1846-8 Jones & Potts:	16
15in 4-2-0 OC	1847 Stephenson:	6
15in 4-2-0 OC	1847 Tayleur:	15
15in 2-2-2 OC	1847 Wilson:	1
15in 4-2-0 OC	1849 Haigh Foundry:	3
15in 2-2-2	1848 Wilson, Jenny Lind type:	2
16in 2-2-2	1848 Sharp Bros:	1
16in 2-2-2	1848 Bury, Curtis & Kennedy:	6
18in 4-2-0 OC	1847 Crampton *London*:	1
18in 4-2-2 OC	1848 Stephenson:	2
18in 2-2-2 OC	1848 Wolverton, McConnell:	1
18in 6-2-0 OC	1848 Crampton *Liverpool*:	1
13in 0-4-0	1838-9 Bury type:	10
14in 0-4-0	rebuilds of 13in engines, Bury type:	8
15in 0-4-0	1845-7 Bury, Curtis & Kennedy:	12
15in 0-4-2	1846 Bury, Curtis & Kennedy:	2
15in 0-6-0	1845-6 Tayleur:	6
15in 0-6-0	1846-8 Longridge:	12
15in 0-6-0	1847 Nasmyth:	8
16in 0-4-2	1848 Bury, Curtis & Kennedy:	6
16in 0-6-0	1846 Bury, Curtis & Kennedy:	4
16in 0-6-0	1847 Jones & Potts:	1
18in 0-6-0	1847-9 Sharp Bros:	8
18in 0-6-0	1848-9 Hawthorn:	9
18in 0-6-0	1848-9 Stephenson:	8

Of these, 170 were in working order. The five 12in were 'for sale' and 21 were in store: a Sharp single, the three Haigh 4-2-0s, the two Stephenson 4-2-2s, McConnell's 2-2-2, the 6-2-0 *Liverpool*, five Longridge 0-6-0s, a BC&K 0-6-0 and seven of the 25 big Sharp-type 0-6-0s.

By March 1850 the total in store had grown to 31, but with the opening of more than 100 miles of new branch lines in the following twelve months, all the stored engines were gradually put to work. The total stock remained at around 230 engines throughout this period; no more were added in the two years from September 1849.

The best of the goods engines were the 18in 0-6-0s and McConnell adopted this as his standard type. He built three more of them at Wolverton and in 1851, when rising traffic required additional goods engines, further batches were ordered from Fairbairn & Sons. Of the passenger engines the 42 long-boiler 4-2-0s and 4-2-2s were the most numerous type, (although divided into ten distinct groups) but no more of these were obtained.

When new passenger engines were needed the Cramptons and McConnell's own express engine were disregarded; the best and most reliable engines were the six Bury, Curtis & Kennedy singles of 1848 and they became the prototype for the express engines ordered from 1851 - the Bloomers, the most celebrated of S Div locomotives. All subsequent fast passenger engines built for the line in the McConnell period were to be based on this design.

North v South Comparisons
The S Div Locomotive Committee with Capt Moorsom in the chair gave McConnell constant backing, but in the early years of the LNWR the General Locomotive Committee was the overall controlling body, to which the three divisional committees reported. The GLC may have been intended to co-ordinate the working of the distinct parts of the new company, but old Grand Junction and London & Birmingham prejudices were still alive and its meetings were often the scene of inter-divisional bickering. Capt Moorsom - Rear Admiral Moorsom from 1851 - was a member of the GLC, as was his N Div counterpart Hardman Earle. At the very start of the company's existence, Earle had led the attack on Bury's four-wheeled engines. Now he opposed McConnell's large-engine policy.

With separate locomotive departments it was only sensible to compare the performance of each, and the GLC did so, studying the various costs and statistics of the three divisions. One item recorded was the monthly total of engines on each division which had failed when on trains, and for whatever reason the S Div almost always had the worst record of the three. More importantly, expenditure was always highest on the S Div, and the General Manager Mark Huish was not slow to point out "the great apparent disproportion of the Establishments of the three divisions" - the much lower mileage per day of each S Div engine and the higher cost of train working, of repairs and of footplatemen's wages. Huish had of course come from the Grand Junction, and the S Div Committee tried to explain that conditions in the south were different, with faster and heavier trains, and that a lot of the extra expense was because of the higher cost of locomotive coke. In 1852 the average cost of coke in the north was 14s 6.75d (72.81p) per ton; in the south it was £1 0s 2.55d (101.06p).

Nevertheless, McConnell was under pressure to improve the S Div record, and his efforts led him to explore and recommend some unusual remedies.

Broken Springs
It was inevitable, given the age and condition of the L&B trackwork, that engine and tender springs would often fail, but they were breaking at the enormous rate of between 100 and 180 a month. Other breakages followed: "links, pins and joints - solid good material is wrenched asunder almost every trip" as McConnell wrote to the Chairman. Rubber springs seemed to offer a cure.

Shortly after Charles de Bergue had taken out his patent, in December 1847 McConnell made a trial of india-rubber springs in the buffers of one engine and tender, and early in 1849 six wagons were also fitted experimentally. In May 1852 he equipped one engine with rubber carrying-springs, and these proved so successful that in July it was arranged that his new Patent class express engines would be built with them.

The patent springs were hollow cylinders of thick rubber, confined within the socket when used for buffers, and in a brass casing, or held within iron rings, when used above or below the axlebox. The rubber cylinders were compressed endwise by pressure and were intended to return to their original form when the pressure was released.

In July 1852 400 rubber springs were purchased from Moulton & Co for £96, with more in October but supplies from this firm were stopped in March 1853 following a dispute between the various patentees. In November McConnell described J. E. Coleman's rubber springs as superior to any description in use; he had used them for twelve months, during which time there had not been a single failure. This he contrasted with the record of steel springs which were failing at an average rate of 147 each month. A year later he was still enthusiastically recommending their extended use.

In the six months to the end of November 1854 there had been 297 failures of springs at a total cost of £466 2s 7d (£466.13):

199 engines with steel springs:
    292 failures   £425 19s 3d   (£425.96)

34 engines with rubber springs:
    1 failure   £3 2s 4d   (£3.12)
4 cases or rings originally
too tight: £37 1s 0d   (£37.05)
                    £40 3s 4d   (£40.17)

The 34 engines with rubber springs included eleven of the Patent class and the eleven Small Bloomers, and perhaps also 'Mac's Mangle' 227. The other eleven are not known.

Rubber springs were fitted to Wolverton-built engines in 1857, but in that year McConnell complained to the manufacturers, Spencer & Co, that one of their springs had "no more elasticity than a block of wood" and sent back 45 of them because they had acquired a permanent 'set'. Nothing is recorded on the subject after this and later new engines were built with steel springs. No doubt the introduction of longer rails and fishplates helped to reduce the number of failures.

Ramsbottom got rid of the rubber buffer springs soon after taking over; rubber bearing springs were gradually replaced by steel, although many tenders still had them into the late 1870s.

McConnell's Contract System
In a report to the GLC in 1852 the wage bills of the three divisions were compared and the S Div, as usual, was conspicuous:

	Drivers	Miles per day	Wage per man per mile	Average wage per day
S Div	154	76	1.346d	7s 2.33d (35.97p)
N Div	157	96	0.852d	6s 9.76d (34.07p)
NE Div	38	88	0.826d	6s 0.68d (30.28p)
Firemen				
S Div	170	69 ¼	0.64d	3s 8.35d (18.48p)
N Div	174	86 ½	0.50d	3s 7.4d (18.08p)
NE Div	37	84 ¾	0.58d	4s 1.29d (20.54p)

The S Div Committee said it was not possible to reduce the wages, but McConnell thought he saw a way to do it.

Working the trains by paying a fixed sum to a contractor had been tried in early L&B days and had been abandoned as unworkable. Maintenance of the permanent way on a flat-rate contract system had been in operation for many years but was also being abandoned. Experience had shown that contracting in this way produced its own complications and disputes, and sometimes inefficiency by negligent work. In November 1853 McConnell suggested engine driving by contract.

Under this system each driver would be paid a fixed sum per train-mile worked, out of which he would pay the wages of his fireman and cleaner, and purchase fuel, oil, brake blocks etc. He would also pay for repairs to slide valves, piston packing, glands, connecting rod brasses, pumps and general maintenance to keep the engine "in perfect working order".

In February 1854 the contract system was started on Watford, Tring and Aylesbury trains, and in the same month the first contract was let for working a train to Rugby and back. As many as 31 drivers had applied for contracts by the end of May and in June McConnell reported to Moorsom, comparing the low cost of drivers under contract with those on the old day-wage system. There were then 328 footplatemen on the S Div and he estimated that the wholesale adoption of contracting would allow 54 of them to be dispensed with. Paying the reduced staff by contract instead of day wages would bring in a profit of £14,698, which he suggested could be increased later, by lowering the contract rates.

Thomas Forsyth, the Head Foreman at Wolverton, predicted that "engine failures would all but, if not entirely disappear", punctuality would improve, and there would be an annual saving on repairs of £20,000.

Initially the rates paid to drivers per train-mile were:

Main line passenger:	4d	(1.67p)
Branch line passenger:	3 ¾d	(1.56p)
Main line goods:	6 ½d	(2.71p)
Branch line goods:	6d	(2.5p)

In July there were further requests from drivers to be placed on contract, but some of those already on the system had begun to complain and on 9th August a deputation of drivers presented their grievances to the Board. They were "against the system of contract which Mr McConnell wishes to introduce which would ... compel men to do more than they are capable of." Under the system men were to be seen "fast asleep on their engines on the road" in charge of trains of 50-60 wagons. One Rugby driver came on duty at 7pm on Friday 28th July, was on piloting until 2.30am on Saturday, drove from Rugby to Rockingham and back (54 miles) then to London and back (163 miles) and finished work at 1am on Sunday, "without time for any refreshment except on the engine". They said this was a regular occurrence. Some drivers were accused of illicitly burning coal instead of the more expensive coke.

McConnell claimed that contracting had dramatically reduced the number of engines failing when on trains. Although the system led to at least one strike, was blamed for causing accidents by making men work extra hours to keep up their incomes, and was mostly to their disadvantage, some drivers were still contracting as late as 1858. The prices drivers then had to pay for stores were:

Coke	£1 2s 0d (£1.10)	per ton
Coal	12s 6d (62.5p)	per ton
Oil	5d (2.08p)	per pint
Tallow	6½d (2.71p)	per lb
Yellow grease	2d (0.83p)	per lb
Cotton waste	2d (0.83p)	per lb
Firewood	6d (2.5p)	per cwt
Tender hosepipes	3s 6d (17.5p)	per foot
Gauge glasses	1s 2d (5.83p)	each
Tender brake blocks	7d (2.92p)	each
Flax for dressings	6d (2.5p)	per lb
Spun yarn	4d (1.67p)	per lb
Cotton wick	1s 0d (5p)	per lb

By this time, as McConnell had planned, the contract rates had been reduced substantially; a main line goods train driver was paid 5d (2.08p) per train mile.

McConnell's Boiler Experiments
In August 1851 McConnell obtained a patent which covered various "improvements in locomotive engines" including wrought iron cylinders and steel or wrought iron pistons, tubular frames and motion rods, tubular stays to supply air to the firebox, a system of heating the feedwater by passing it through the smokebox, and "indenting" the boiler over the crank axle "thereby allowing the centre of gravity to be lowered". The accompanying drawings show a boiler with a large firebox and combustion chamber and comparatively short tubes.

In November he proposed trying a new boiler with a big firebox and short tubes on 125, one of the Longridge long-boiler goods engines. He expected his new boiler would save between 7% and 10% of coke. Six months later he reported that in its new form 125 was over 13% more economical, although the total heating surface had been considerably reduced.

Other patents followed, including one at the end of 1852 in which air was heated in the smokebox and fed, with jets of steam, into the firebox, whose heating surface was enlarged further by means of three midfeathers. "By these arrangements anthracite and other fuels more difficult of combustion than coke may be employed" he claimed, almost as an aside.

The S Div Locomotive Committee was enthusiastic

about McConnell's firebox and the savings it would bring, and favoured its widespread adoption. It was recommended for fitting to the other 15in long-boiler goods and all the 4-2-0 long-boiler passenger engines, a total of 56, as well as for new engines on order. But some members of the General Locomotive Committee remained unconvinced.

Locomotive Exchanges - Wolverton v Crewe
The old enmity between the L&B and the GJ continued. Even after three years of the LNWR, Hardman Earle seemed to be unable to forget that he had been a Grand Junction director. In June 1849 as Chairman of the General Locomotive Committee, he asked for a trial of "a GJ engine on some average train in and out of London" to compare the "value and utility" of N Div and S Div locomotives.

Four new 6ft singles were sent from Crewe and were put on the 9am Down express. On 8th August McConnell said he had had to take them off after complaints from the Traffic Committee. Hardman Earle made excuses, blaming McConnell for exaggerating the "alleged loss of time". The visitors were tried on more leisurely trains, the 6.15, 10.00 and 10.30am - with McConnell offering to help by double-heading with S Div engines.

The N Div 2-2-2s were:

234	*Mazeppa*	built Crewe, March 1849
237	*Blenheim*	built Crewe, May 1849
238	*President*	built Edge Hill, May 1849 (in store, entered stock as 34 *Phoebus*, ½ yr ending May 1850)
239	*Powis*	built Edge Hill, April 1849 (in store, entered stock as 125 *Soho*, ½ yr ending May 1850)

Four S Div engines were ordered to the N Div in exchange. According to the stock list of 8th August *five* engines were sent: Nos 8 and 9 (Sharp singles), 67 (BC&K 2-2-2) and 85 and 87 (18in 0-6-0s). The Sharps and the goods engines were similar to engines already on the NE Div and in fact 85 and 87 had come from there just twelve months before; the Bury had originally been built for the Chester & Holyhead, so in a sense they were all northern engines to start with. On 14th August they were sent south again "having done considerable damage to the permanent way ... Mr Earle having already ordered their removal as a matter of safety." McConnell replied by offering ten engines "suitable for the Crewe line" - all tiny 13in four-wheelers - but got no answer.

After their uninspiring performances the four N Div engines were sent back to Crewe by early September.

This exchange seems to have been singularly futile and to have convinced nobody of anything.

In defence of the big-engine policy McConnell claimed a 20% loss of power when "yoking two or more engines to a train as compared to the capacity of the same engines if separately attached." "A loose and extravagant assertion" said Hardman Earle, and put it to the test. On Tuesday 29th April 1851 a train of Ince Hall coal from Wigan to London, 56 wagons and two 5-ton brake vans, a total of 493 tons 17 cwt, was drawn out of Crewe by two 'Old Crewe' Goods engines, N Div 239 *Powis* and 257 *Stanley* (both built May 1850). At Madeley the train was divided, each engine continuing with half. The result proved to Earle the "superiority of multiple small engines" but McConnell, who was present at the trial, replied with a mass of figures demonstrating the opposite and suggested a *series* of trials on the 1 in 30 Chequerbent Incline on the N Div Bolton Branch.

He described to the directors the policy on other lines - the Midland, the Great Northern (where orders had been placed for forty goods engines even larger than his) and most striking of all, the Great Western, where double-heading was unknown on passenger trains and rare on goods. He quoted Daniel Gooch, who was in no doubt "that it is a very bad and extravagant way of working any kind of traffic by multiplying the engines on the train, both in money and power." As for charges that the S Div engines were too heavy for the road, the weight on each axle, at most 9 tons, was the same as on the driving wheels of a Crewe Goods. McConnell ended: "I am quite willing for the most rigid trial, and if necessary to draw the number of wagons with one of our engines and at the same speed that is taken by two of those on the N Div." So a trial was arranged between single and double engines in May 1851 at Crewe. Naturally, this settled nothing.

Trevithick produced some timings of the 11.15am train from Liverpool on the 10 mile climb from Crewe to Whitmore:

22nd April 1851:	N Div 177 *Chimera*:	with 24 coaches took 28 minutes.
23rd April 1851:	N Div 45 *Sybil*:	with 23 coaches took 21 minutes.
24th April 1851:	N Div 211 *Onyx*:	with 19 coaches took 25 minutes.

But McConnell had travelled back from the trials at Crewe on 29th April by the 5.15pm Manchester-Birmingham express, a train of 20 carriages which required two engines: 188 *Colonel* and 69 *Python*. He had timed the train, and even with two engines it took 20 minutes and 40 seconds to get from Crewe to Whitmore; could Trevithick explain this? The inter-divisional sniping went on.

The N Div engines at this period had prominent wire bonnets on their chimneys and in June 1851 McConnell was told to direct his attention to fires caused by hot cinders from his engines. He replied that the fires were mostly caused by cinders falling from ashpans and began fitting vertical plates between the tender guard irons, which were introduced at this time for backwards running. How efficacious these plates were, or how long they lasted, is not known, but by October 1851 he was putting wire spark arresters on his chimney tops. These were flat discs of half-inch mesh which sat out of sight just inside the chimney rim; they quickly wore out, and seem to have been quietly abandoned, for they are never heard of again.

It remained an undeniable fact that the cost of running trains on the S Div was higher than in the north. Manager Mark Huish, assisted by Edward Watkin, brought this before the General Locomotive Committee on 2nd April 1852.

Costs per mile were:

COMPARATIVE EXPERIMENTS ON THE LONDON AND NORTH-WESTERN RAILWAY,
AND BIRMINGHAM, FEBRUARY

	\multicolumn{14}{c}{PASSENGER ENGINES.}													
Number of Experiment, Date of Experiment,	1 Feb. 24.		2 Feb. 25.		3 Feb. 26.		4 Feb. 28.		5 March 1.		6 March 4.		7 March 5.	
Name or Number of Engine,	N. 291	Rocket	N. 291	Rocket	N. 291	Heron	N. 291	Heron	N. 291	Heron	N. 300	Heron	N. 300	Heron
Division, South or North,	S.	N.	S.	N.	S.	N.	S.	N.	S.	N.	S.	N.	S.	N.
Experimenter, Mr. Marshall or Mr. Woods,	W.	M.	W.	M.	W.	M.	W.	M.	W.	M.	W.	M.	W.	M.
Distance run, miles,	111	111	111	111	111	111	111	111	111	111	111	111	111	111
Direction,	Up	Up	Down	Down	Up	Up	Down	Down	Up	Up	Down	Down	Up	Up
Number of Carriages,	9	9	13	13	17	17	21	21	25	25	17	17	17	17
Weight of Train, tons,	46	46	66	66	86	86	106	106	126	126	86	86	86	86
Do., including tender, ,,	62	56	82	76	102	96	122	116	142	136	103	96	103	96
Do., including Engine and Tender, ,,	92	76	112	96	132	114	152	134	172	154	134	114	134	114
Coke consumed, lbs.	2,465	2,190	3,310	3,480	3,041	2,871	3,420	3,374	3,346	3,144	3,220	3,179	2,938	2,815
Do., per mile,	22·20	19·73	29·82	31·35	27·41	25·86	30·81	30·40	30·15	28·32	29·01	28·64	26·47	25·37
Do., per ton per mile, ,,	·483	·429	·452	·475	·319	·301	·291	·287	·239	·225	·337	·333	·308	·295
Do., do., including difference in weight of Tenders, ,,	·427	·429	·414	·475	·298	·301	·275	·287	·228	·225	·312	·333	·281	·295
Water consumed,	15,853	16,132	23,364	25,214	19,304	22,526	23,481	26,010	23,704	23,774	25,106	24,357	24,431	21,619
Water evaporated per lb. of Coke,	6·43	7·37	7·05	7·25	6·35	7·85	6·86	7·71	7·08	7·53	7·80	7·66	8·32	7·68
Number of Stoppages,	3	3	5	5	7	7	9	9	11	12	5	5	5	5
Time of ditto, minutes,	5	11	12	14	14	15	48	16	18	27	12	12	11	13
Time of Running, ,,	162	156	182	193	195	208	215	222	232	228	188	202	174	186
Ditto allowed, ,,	158	158	175	175	196	196	215	215	237	237	175	175	175	175
Time lost, ,,	4	..	7	..	..	12	..	7	..	..	13	27	..	11
Ditto gained, ,,	..	2	..	..	1	..	..	..	5	9	..	..	1	..
Time from lighting fire to starting,	170	169	206	182	209	161	210	218	202	200	140	205	153	201
Speed, running greatest, miles per hour,	56	51	49	45	53	45	44	41	48	45	45	42	53	48
Ditto, average, ,,	41·11	42·69	36·50	34·51	34·15	32·02	30·88	30·00	28·71	29·14	35·46	32·97	38·27	35·81
Ditto, allowed, ,,	42	42	38	38	34	34	31	31	28	28	38	38	38	38
Ditto, lost per cent.,	2	..	·4	9	..	6	..	3	..	..	7	13	..	6
Ditto, gained per cent.,	..	1	..	..	..	..	..	..	2	4	..	..	..	..
Pressure, average, lbs. p. inch,	111	114	110	102	101	114	111	115	111	110	106	98	116	113
Ditto, greatest, ,,	130	122	127	125	128	130	122	127	126	125	123	128	134	127
Ditto, least, ,,	65	105	79	79	51	95	77	103	82	95	79	71	84	100
Do., on safety valves, ,,	120	120	120	120	120	120	120	120	120	120	130	130	130	130
Wind,	Calm.	Side-wind.	Brisk head-wind.	Strong head-wind.	Strong side-wind.	Strong side-wind.	Strong head-wind.	Strong head-wind.	Moderate side-wind.	Calm.	Strong head-wind.	Strong head-wind.	Calm.	Moderate wind behind.
Weather,	Fair. Frosty.	Fair. Frosty.	Fair.	Fair.	Fair.	Fair.	Fair.	Fair.	Snow showers.	Snow and sleet.	Fair.	Fair.	Mist.	Rain and fog.
Remarks,	Steam not fully up at starting.		Carriage axles oiled. Bad coke at starting.		Rails greasy.	Rails greasy.	Stopped to repair steam-chest joint.		Rails in bad state.	Rails in bad state.	Bad coke at starting.	Bad coke at starting.		

* Powis dropped some fire-bars on the trip, causing a little loss of coke, and an obstruction

WITH ENGINES OF THE SOUTHERN AND NORTHERN DIVISIONS, BETWEEN LONDON 24 TO MARCH 19, 1853, INCLUSIVE.

			Goods Engines.					
8 March 7.	9 March 8.			10 March 18.			11 March 19.	
N. 300	N. 291	N. 300	{ Heron and P. of Wales. }	..	N. 277	{ Hector and Powis }	..	N. 277	{ Hector and Powis }
S.	S.	S.	N.	..	S.	N.	..	S.	N.
W.	W.	M.	W.	..	Holt	M.	..	Holt	M.
111 Down 17 86 103 134	111 Down 17 86 102 132	111 Up 34 171 188 219	111 Up 34 171 191 227	..	Rugby to London 81¼ Up 53 451 468 501	81¼ Up 53 450 472 511	..	Rugby to London 81¼ Up 45 402 419 452	81¼ Up 45 401 423 462
3,157 28·44 ·331 ·306	3,210 28·91 ·336 ·314	4,529 40·80 ·239 ·239	4,851 43·70 ·255 ·251	{ 2,481 Heron 2,370 P. of W 22·35 Heron 21·35 P. of W. }	5,319 65·26 ·145 ·145	6,328 77·64 ·173 ·171	{ 3,149 Hector 3,179 Powis 38·64 Hector 39·00 Powis }	4,435 54·42 ·135 ·135	4,409 54·09 ·134 ·133	{ 2,196 Hector. 2,213 Powis. 26·94 Hector. 27·15 Powis. }
26,100 8·27	22,719 7·07	36,189 7·99	40,453 8·34	{ 20,563 Heron 19,890 P. of W. 8·29 Heron 8·39 P. of W. }	46,031 8·65	47,257 7·47	{ 23,728 Hector 23,529 Powis 7·54 Hector 7·40 Powis }	39,514 8·91	36,963 8·38	{ 18,689 Hector. 18,274 Powis. 8·51 Hector. 8·26 Powis. }
5 12 175 175	5 14 172 175 .. 3	5 12 183 175 8 ..	5 14 193 175 18 ..	..	11 97 327 288 39 ..	9 117 277 288 .. 11	..	9 64 286 288 .. 2	11 61 279 288 .. 9
208	216	208	204	..	188	182	..	175	166
52 38·00 38	52 38·52 38 .. 1	54 36·39 38 4 ..	48 34·51 38 9 ..	..	26 14·95 17 12 ..	31 17·65 17 .. 4	..	31 17·10 17 .. 1	35 17·53 17 .. 3
				Heron. P. of W.			Hector. Powis.			Hector. Powis.
113 130 92 130	114 130 88 130	118 130 90 130	92 116 65 130	95 90 120 113 72 58 130 130	109 130 70 130	106 119 84 130	109 103 123 116 82 87 130 130	117 132 82 130	100 123 75 130	108 92 127 120 90 60 130 130
Calm.	Calm.	Calm.	Calm.		Side-wind.	Side-wind.		Little side-wind.	Little side-wind.
Rain.	Rain.	Fair.	Fair.		Snow showers.	Snow showers.		Fair. Frosty.	Fair. Frosty.
			Bad coke for lighting fires.						Powis dropped some fire-bars.*

to the draught, from bricks put into the ash-pan to support the bars temporarily.

N Div: passenger   6.48d   goods   8.9d.
S Div: passenger 10.39d   goods 13.7d.

According to Huish the fault lay with the type of engine in the south. This forced the S Div Locomotive Committee to ask for a thorough investigation of the whole subject which "must be undertaken by parties *having no bias* to mislead their judgment and *who are competent* to appreciate the differences affecting the cost of each Division."

The Woods and Marshall Reports

During 1852 McConnell had presented three reports demonstrating the great advantages of replacing the small engines by larger ones. In December he said that if the Board would sanction 30 large engines this would complete the replacement of the small ones. Just as the orders were being placed it was discovered that McConnell's statement was incorrect: a further 27 would be needed to complete the substitution.

This, coming on top of Huish's allegations of possibly wasteful expenditure, monthly returns of engine failures which showed Wolverton consistently worse than Crewe and the complaint that McConnell's engines were too big and dangerously heavy, prompted the GLC to ask for an independent inquiry into the locomotive accounts of the three divisions for the year 1852.

On 14th January 1853 "two professional men of high standing", Edward Woods and William Prime Marshall, were commissioned to make this investigation. Both were in private practice as consulting engineers; Woods had been Chief Engineer of the Liverpool & Manchester and until the previous year was the LNWR's Engineer on that section; Marshall was the Secretary of the Institution of Mechanical Engineers, and had been Locomotive Superintendent of the North Midland Rly and the Norfolk Rly.

If Woods had N Div leanings they were balanced by Marshall's friendship with McConnell who was a founder member and Vice President of the IMechE; Marshall and McConnell later became partners in private practice and Marshall was named as a trustee in McConnell's will.

The contracts for the thirty new engines were suspended on 11th February and Woods and Marshall were asked to look into their design. McConnell had just been authorised to alter the fireboxes of 56 long-boiler engines to his patent system, but this too was suspended pending the outcome of the investigation.

From February to April 1853 Woods and Marshall, with the assistance of a Mr Holt, conducted a series of locomotive trials on the S Div main line. Crewe and Wolverton engines were pitted against each other with a variety of trains, from 9 to 34 carriages and from 45 to 53 goods wagons. The engines tested were Trevithick's first 7ft single *Rocket*, six months old and the prototype of a proposed new class, two of his 6ft singles and two Crewe Goods *versus* S Div Bloomer 291, Patent 300 and a brand-new Fairbairn Goods 277. The passenger engines were run Up and Down on alternate days between Birmingham and Camden; the two goods trials were with Up trains from Rugby. For seven days the Bloomer and the Patent were matched against Crewe singles; on one day the Patent took on two Crewe singles double-headed, and on another there was a real battle of the giants when the Patent ran against the Bloomer. In the goods tests the Fairbairn ran against the double-headed Crewe Goods.

The results of these trials are set out in the table which is taken from the official report.

One point that should be mentioned is the boiler pressure. Ahrons and Nock believed that the Wolverton engines were handicapped by having their pressure reduced to 120 lb/sq in to correspond with that of the Crewe engines. The normal pressure of the Bloomers and Patents at that period *was* 120 lb/sq in; the 150 lb traditionally associated with McConnell was not used at Wolverton until 1860. In fact the pressure was *raised* to 130 lb/sq in for all the tests involving the Patent and Fairbairn Goods.

Woods and Marshall's Report came out in three parts, the first on 5th April 1853. This merely described the work done so far. They reported that the Patent and all the N Div engines had a "great and equal steadiness at all speeds" and that the Bloomer had a rougher motion, especially at higher speeds. The test results were undramatic, but showed clearly the higher speed and greater power of the Wolverton engines and that a Fairbairn 0-6-0 could do the work of two Crewe Goods. The value of McConnell's patent boiler was "not proven": they were not yet convinced of its superiority and could not recommend it for any large class of engine.

Meanwhile the tests went on. During March and April six Crewe 6ft singles worked six regular trains daily from Euston to Rugby - the 6.30am, 9.15, 12 noon, 4.00pm, 5.00 and 8.45 Down - returning to Camden with the corresponding Up trains. The engines involved were:

N Div	Name	Built	Period on S Div
28	*Prometheus*	11/1849	28/3/53 to 23/4/53
139	*Cygnet*	9/1852	31/3/53 to 19/4/53
7	*Scorpion*	4/1852	31/3/53 to 23/4/53
130	*Heron*	5/1852	1/4/53 to 22/4/53
291	*Prince of Wales*	11/1852	1/4/53 to 21/4/53
125	*Soho* (ex-*Powis*)	4/1849	2/4/53 to 23/4/53

Similar trials were made with two Tayleur long-boiler 4-2-0 engines: 178 - with its original boiler - from 16th to 20th May, and 179 - with a McConnell firebox - from 25th May until 11th June 1853.

The thirty suspended engines had been planned as ten 16in singles and twenty 18in long-boiler goods, all equipped with the patent boiler. The passenger engine was to be like a Bloomer but with a low-pitched indented boiler and with three longitudinal midfeathers in the firebox. McConnell's original scheme was for goods engines with 19in cylinders and 5ft 6in wheels "for through express goods trains" but this was quietly dropped in January when the GLC began its investigation. Orders had been placed on 25th January 1853 with Kitson and Stothert for ten goods engines each and with Vulcan for four passenger engines and Hawthorn for six. The orders were suspended "for a month" on 11th February for Woods and Marshall's opinion; their inconclusive first report led the GLC to ask them to reconsider the design of these engines (together with the S Div Committee) with the aim of reducing their weight. McConnell toed the line: his patent boiler was shelved. "While the engines are in every respect the most eligible and best suited to the work" he wrote "still I am willing to concede to some extent a diminution of power." He produced new specifications with the passenger engine reduced to 24 tons and the goods to 27 tons - limits prescribed by Huish, Watkin and Henry Woodhouse, the Permanent Way Superintendent, in a report on the state of the track. McConnell's revised designs came before the GLC on 3rd May.

Engines as ordered on 25th January 1853:

	10 Passenger	*20 Goods*
Cylinders:	16 x 22"	18 x 24"
Driving wheel:	7' 0"	5' 0"
Weight:	29 tons	30 tons
on leading axle:		8 tons
on driving axle:	10½ - 12 tons	10 tons
on trailing axle:		12 tons
Firebox heating surface:	296 sq ft	339 sq ft
Tube heating surface:	805 sq ft	913 sq ft
Total heating surface:	1101 sq ft	1252 sq ft

As revised by McConnell, 3rd May:

	10 Passenger	*10 Goods*	*10 Mineral*
Cylinders:	16 x 21"	16 x 24"	18 x 24"
Driving wheel:	6' 6"	5' 6"	5' 0"
Weight:	24 tons	27 tons	
on leading axle:	10 tons	10 tons	
on driving axle:	9 tons	10 tons	
on trailing axle:	5 tons	7 tons	
Firebox heating surface:	104.0 sq ft	101.75 sq ft	
Tube heating surface:	993.4 sq ft	1107.28 sq ft	
Total heating surface:	1097.4 sq ft	1209.03 sq ft	
Tube length:	10' 7"	10' 4"	

Six days later Woods and Marshall's second report appeared. They recommended:

	Passenger	*Goods*
Cylinders:	16 x 20" (outside)	16 x 24"
Driving wheel:	6' 6"	5' 0"
Weight:	23 tons	25 tons
on driving axle:	10 tons	10 tons
Firebox heating surface:		80 sq ft
Tube heating surface:		900 sq ft
Total heating surface:		980 sq ft

On 13th May Woods and Marshall were quizzed by the GLC; Woods explained his preference for outside cylinders from his Liverpool & Manchester experience of broken crank-axles. Both admitted that if trains of 400 tons became necessary then 19in or even 20in cylinders would be required. Pressed for more data and their reasons for restricting the weight to well below even Huish's limit, they began to hedge: "We do not wish to commit ourselves to these precise weights, or to assume reponsibility for the design... and consequent interference with the duties of your Locomotive Superintendent."

The two investigators then left the room and the Committee got down to debating what should be done about the thirty suspended engines. G. H. Lawrence (N Div) moved, Hardman Earle seconding, that Woods and Marshall's specification be adopted instead of McConnell's. This was defeated by six votes to four. Theodore Rathbone (N Div) then moved that the new engines be built to Trevithick's Crewe design. This too was defeated, six to four. The Committee's chairman, Admiral Moorsom, then moved that McConnell's revised designs be adopted. Fortunately for McConnell, the North Eastern directors voted with the Southern, united perhaps in a common distrust of Crewe. The motion was carried by five votes to four. McConnell had come very close to being Trevithick's Wolverton foreman, perhaps building Crewe Goods to work in permanent pairs.

The manufacturers were given the revised designs and after some desperate bargaining, they all offered lower prices. The orders, except for that to Vulcan Foundry, were increased accordingly:

		Original orders, 25.1.53	New orders, 10.6.53
Passenger engines:	Hawthorn	6 @ £3,200	7 @ £2,743
	Vulcan	4 @ £2,850	4 @ £2,700
Goods engines:	Kitson	10 @ £3,200	11 @ £2,909
Mineral engines:	Stothert	10 @ £3,200	11 @ £2,909

These became, respectively, the original Small Bloomers, the original Wolverton Express Goods and the Stothert Goods.

Meanwhile, rumours of extravagance on the S Div had begun to circulate among the shareholders. At the half-yearly meeting on 18th February, Joseph Locke rose from the body of the hall to ask if figures of comparative costs of the Crewe and Wolverton engines could be produced. "I ask this question because I have reason to believe that there is a difference, not to be counted by tens, fifties or hundreds of pounds, but by thousands." Locke had been practically the creator of Crewe, and he was famous for his interest in railway costing. On this occasion he failed to get a satisfactory answer from the Chairman, Major-General Anson, and at the next meeting in August he said bluntly: "It has been stated out-of-doors that a difference exists between Wolverton and Crewe of from £200,000 to £300,000 dating from the time of the amalgamation. This demands explanation." He had heard that Woods and Marshall had estimated a difference of about 30%. If this was so he wished for an official statement from the Board. He had no personal interest, neither as a locomotive builder *nor as a patentee*. All he wanted was that the Company got the greatest amount of work done for the lowest price. "A prima facie case has been made out and I think the proprietors would be fools if they did not look into it." He asked that the auditors advise on the expediency of introducing the Crewe system on the S Div.

This put the whole affair on a very serious footing. No longer could the Report be merely an instrument of inter-divisional bickering. It now involved "more serious responsibilities, requiring a more comprehensive enquiry embracing the longest period which the accounts will admit of." More data were ordered to be passed to Woods and Marshall. The third instalment of their Report came out at the end of the year. They analysed the accounts thoroughly and concluded that the high cost of the S Div Locomotive Department was caused by:

1. Too many different types of engine. There were 253 engines in more than thirty distinct classes.
2. The large amount of renewal by rebuilding which

had been done at Wolverton; at Crewe the policy was to build some new engines each year out of revenue.
3. The purchase of engines from outside firms - there were "scarcely any built by the Company."
4. The size and type of the engines. They were larger therefore more expensive in first cost, in heating and in dismantling, and heavier on the track. Their inside cylinders made them less accessible for repair.
5. The inadequacy of Wolverton Works for repairs.

Further, there were the high wages which had to be paid at Wolverton because of the shortage of housing there, the extra wear-and-tear on the engines caused by the heavy Exhibition traffic of 1851, and the higher cost of coke. The remoteness of the coalfields put up the price per ton to £1 0s 1d (£1.004) which was 37% more than on the N Div.

Finally, they recommended a reorganisation of the goods traffic by creating a class of through trains avoiding unnecessary stops, additional sidings and a more extended use of the electric telegraph, and greater uniformity in classes of engines, referring again to their previous specifications. And, though the new engines on the S Div were undoubtedly faster and more powerful than their N Div counterparts "advantage cannot be taken of this superiority, simply because the circumstances of the traffic do not require it; consequently the surplus size and weight of such engines entail a loss in interest on excess of capital invested in purchase, heavier working expenses, and a greater damage to the permanent way."

At the next half-yearly meeting of shareholders on 22nd February 1854 the new Chairman, the Marquis of Chandos, claimed that Woods and Marshall had shown "there really is no difference, or only a very trifling one." Joseph Locke rose. Experiments at Crewe, he said, had proved that the heavy Southern engines were *unnecessary* and were destroying the Company's track. Hardman Earle joined in, and he had a copy of the actual Report. Even allowing for the high price of coke, he said, there was still an excess of 25% spent at Wolverton.

The reason for this, it was explained, was the inadequacy of Wolverton Works, and that because of the pressure of traffic many repair jobs had to be done at night. The remedy, obviously, was enlargement of the shops and a bigger stock of engines.

In the same month, the S Div Committee counter-attacked with figures to show that the engines on the N Div burned 37% more coke per ton moved. They explained in detail the peculiar disadvantages of their Division: many undersized Bury engines, the tidal wave of traffic in 1845-46, the desperate measures to cope which meant acquiring engines of any type that could be had, the transfer to the S Div of the Chester & Holyhead and Yorkshire lines stock: all this accounted for the variety of locomotive types. The LNWR, they said, might yet be compelled by competition to increase the speed of their trains, and they recommended that the experience of other railways should be studied. It was decided that Woods and Marshall should confer with *all three superintendents,* to set up new engine standards, and that they should prepare drawings of their ideal locomotive types.

Answering a shareholder at the next meeting in August, Chandos said that no more of the heavy engines were being ordered, so it "would not be necessary to revive the topic mentioned by Mr Locke." In March 1855, McConnell, Trevithick and Ramsbottom reported on the Woods and Marshall designs. They each disapproved, and saw no reason to advise their adoption.

Another phase of the north v south struggle blew itself out. The cost of all the Woods and Marshall experiments was about £3,500, apart from inconvenience to ordinary traffic. Nothing was proved, but there were results: McConnell's heavy engines and his patent boiler were checked - for a time - and the Wolverton Express Goods and Small Bloomers were begun, both successful and eventually large classes. The eleven Stothert Goods were not perpetuated; they were not very successful, probably crippled by shortage of steam to fill their 18-inch cylinders by Woods and Marshall's insistence on small boilers.

The most striking result of the investigation was the great development of Wolverton Works. Five years later the S Div workshops covered a bigger area than Crewe and Longsight combined.

Meanwhile Capt Huish kept up his intermittent gadfly attacks on McConnell, who reacted angrily - and was reprimanded for it. Moorsom's description of Huish as an "intriguing, web-weaving protocoller" is famous, as is his letter to Thomas Smith, another member of the S Div Locomotive Committee:

> "November 2nd 1854
> ... If we had a manager who instead of sitting all day on a Tripod - like a Delphick oracle of old - fulminating prophecies, were to occupy himself out of doors on the line (as Seymour Clarke [GNR] and Saunders [GWR] do) and learn by his own knowledge the real facts instead of taking for granted every scrap of paper that every body writes against the Locomotives, the Directors would be spared much trouble that it is not their place to take and our affairs would be more satisfactorily managed ..."

The End of the North Eastern Division
The creation of a single Locomotive Department had been an obvious possibility from the start of the LNWR; the appointment of one overall chief would mean subservience, or dismissal for two or all of the three locomotive engineers.

Easy-going Trevithick, at Crewe from its foundation, probably just hoped things would go on as they were. In any case he seemed to be ahead of his southern rival; years of boardroom criticism of McConnell's big engines had culminated in outside experts damning them as wasteful; despite their smallness his own N Div engines had performed respectably at the trials and powerful voices had been heard in Crewe's favour.

McConnell, brought to Wolverton after the formation of the LNWR, was ambitious and determined. If amalgamation came it would be an opportunity for another step up, and he was untiringly active in showing off his ability and the rightness of his policy. He too had strong support.

John Ramsbottom probably saw little chance for himself. His works at Longsight was tiny by comparison with the other two and even the name 'North Eastern Division' sounded like a minor backwater. The north v south struggle was played out with scant reference to him.

But Woods and Marshall had made the Board think and the dust from the Report had barely settled when the first positive move was made towards uniting the three departments. On 10th March 1855, having just heard the various opinions of their three locomotive superintendents about Woods and Marshall's recommendations, the Board set up a special committee to consider the wisdom of maintaining the three separate bodies. This committee consisted of the Chairman Lord Chandos, Hardman Earle (N Div), Matthew Lyon (NE Div) and two from the S Div, Admiral Moorsom and Henry Wollaston Blake. They reported, Lyon dissenting, that "a consolidation of the various Locomotive Departments is very desirable" with one overall superintendent, and an assistant at each of the three works. No immediate or violent change was advised, but advantage should be taken of any opportunity as it presented itself. A strong possibility was that McConnell would take over the whole line if Trevithick could be got rid of. This was certainly Moorsom's idea, and probably the way it would have worked out, but for Richard Moon.

Moon joined the Board only in 1851, so his keen eye was unclouded by any Grand Junction or Euston prejudice. He was impressed by Ramsbottom's matter-of-fact efficiency and was scathingly critical of the diffident, gentlemanly Trevithick. He put forward an amendment to the Special Committee's report on 29th March 1856, that the Board "as a first step resolve that the Locomotive Departments of the present Northern and North Eastern Divisions be placed under one management, and that Mr Ramsbottom be appointed superintendent of the amalgamated Division."

To Ramsbottom this was an eye-opener. The director from his division on the Special Committee, Matthew Lyon (who was quite lamb-like in discussion, according to Neele) had gone so far as to object to the amalgamation of the locomotive departments, among which the NE Div's Longsight was the smallest and most vulnerable, but active support from this new patron gave Ramsbottom real hope. Though Moon's amendment was rejected by eleven votes to eight, it raised his sights.

He quickly wrote to the Chairman asking for an interview to "discuss the propriety of applying" for the post of locomotive superintendent on the Eastern Counties Railway. At such an interview he would be able to put his cards on the table. Almost at once he was given an extra salaried job as manager of the 'California' rail-rolling mill at Crewe. This must have shaken Trevithick, but worse was to come.

In July 1857 the LNWR was due to relinquish working the Lancaster & Carlisle Railway. The ninety miles thus lost to the N Div were almost equal to the mileage of the NE Div. In April the Board decided to consolidate the two divisions. Ramsbottom told Moon that he would take on the job as chief of the new N Div, but he wanted a salary of £1,200 - otherwise he would look elsewhere.

On 9th May the salaries of the locomotive superintendents of the S Div and the new amalgamated division were fixed at £1,000. The new post was to be offered to Ramsbottom, with an extra £200 for the rail works. Hardman Earle tried to thwart this by proposing, Lawrence seconding, that there was no need for amalgamation, and no need for the retirement or removal of either superintendent. This was lost by seventeen votes to eight. Rathbone said amalgamation was necessary but Trevithick should stay. Earle then moved that Trevithick be offered the superintendence of the united divisions. This also fell, nineteen to five. Voting for Ramsbottom was eighteen to seven. Any feelings of uneasiness were salved by a unanimous resolution to present a huge gratuity of £3,000 to Trevithick for his "long and valued services" and "in testimony of the high sense which the Board entertains of his honourable personal character."

Trevithick was dismayed - he was only 45 - but he had to go. He went home to Cornwall and, bitterly angry, wrote a long letter of self-justification. But soon he found that "having lost the honour of being in the company of railway directors" (as he sarcastically put it) he had also lost his nervous facial twitch.

His successor John Ramsbottom entered his new office at Crewe on 1st August 1857. From this date McConnell had a really formidable rival in the north.

Territorial Ambitions

At first the Southern Division met the Northern Division only at Birmingham, but new lines spreading across the Midlands produced more points of contact, and more areas of contention.

The Trent Valley Railway, linking the London & Birmingham at Rugby to the Grand Junction at Stafford, bypassing Birmingham with a more direct route to the North, had been purchased by the L&B in the spring of 1846 on behalf of the embryonic LNWR, but was not opened until after the amalgamation. Which division of the LNWR should work it? It would naturally have fallen to Wolverton, but the tidal wave of extra traffic then pouring down the L&B from the ever-growing catchment area of the Midlands and North East took all the engines they had. So in May 1847 Crewe was asked to take it on, as a temporary measure, until Wolverton could get back on its feet. A temporary engine shed "as limited as possible" was built on the Down side at Rugby for six or eight Crewe engines. The Trent Valley line was worked by N Div engines from its opening in September 1847.

The branch from Coventry on the L&B main line to Nuneaton on the Trent Valley was worked by McConnell from the opening in 1850, with a small engine shed at Nuneaton.

The Stour Valley line from Birmingham New Street via Dudley Port to Wolverhampton and joining the GJR just north of there at Bushbury was opened in 1852 (after a lot of procrastination) and was worked by the N Div, whose main line ran parallel.

The South Staffordshire Railway lay west and north of Birmingham, crossing the Stour Valley, the GJ main line and the Trent Valley at right angles and when the LNWR took over its working in 1852, this duty naturally fell to the N Div. But it was a very troublesome line and after four years of near chaos the working was transferred to the S Div in April 1856. When the Cannock Mineral line - the extension from Cannock on the SSR north to

Rugeley on the Trent Valley - was opened in 1859, the S Div worked that too.

On the Trent Valley line the N Div working began as planned in September 1847 with a limited service of two local passenger trains each way and through goods trains. On Wednesday 1st December a full train service began but at the end of the following week the General Locomotive Committee complained loudly about the "lamentable manner of working the Trent Valley line". Soon McConnell was reporting the savings he could make if only the N Div and the Midland were more punctual at Rugby. But despite constant complaints the N Div working went on, although control of the line was transferred to the Southern Outdoor Superintendent Henry P. Bruyeres in January 1856.

Trevithick sent his new 7ft singles to the Trent Valley, fresh from Crewe Works: No 12 *Centaur*, 31 *Pegasus*, 134 *Owl*, 144 *Raven*, 325 *Chandos*, 342 *Amphion* and 343 *Etna* are known to have been there for long periods in 1854-56. Two new 6ft singles, 364 *Latona* and 367 *Nightingale*, are also recorded from June 1855 to August 1856. Some if not all of these were still there in 1860.

By 1858 McConnell badly needed the Trent Valley. The LNWR was growing like a tree, branches into Yorkshire, Wales and the Marches and the probable grafting-on of the Lancaster & Carlisle. Further yet - Scotland perhaps? It would have seemed possible then, with the LNWR financial interest in lines as far as Aberdeen. Meanwhile, the old trunk, from its root at Euston, was hemmed in on both flanks by rival growths - the Great Western and the Great Northern. All expansion was in - or radiating out from - the Northern Division and, apart from the troublesome South Staffordshire enclave, the S Div was stuck at Birmingham.

John Ramsbottom had leapt from the nowhere of Longsight to the top job at Crewe. It was obvious that when the day came for the entire Locomotive Department to be placed under one chief, Ramsbottom's growing responsibilities and expanding territory would give him the advantage. McConnell had to recover parity somehow, or Crewe would simply annex Wolverton, and he would be sacked like Trevithick. The only direction he could advance was north. He began to campaign for the Trent Valley.

He wrote to the Chairman, Lord Chandos, to explain why Wolverton cost more than Doncaster. The Great Northern main line, he said, allowed a more favourable engine mileage. A similar benefit could be got by lengthening the S Div main line - by adding the Trent Valley and running on to Stafford.

McConnell promoted his cause with other influential directors. In September 1858, travelling down from London with Richard Moon, he mentioned three N Div engines he had seen standing idly blowing off steam at Coventry "having by some chance got out of their beat". N Div train working around the Birmingham area was in "a shocking state. A night or two ago there was nothing to take on the Liverpool express but a goods engine and consequently she did not arrive until after midnight. On Wednesday night the Scotch express was an hour late." McConnell told Moon: "I'll be hanged if I couldn't make better arrangements!"

The next year, 1859, it was arranged that the Lancaster & Carlisle was to return to the LNWR, after a short interlude of independence. The N Div was to take over the working from the end of December. This gave McConnell an opportunity to press his case. On 6th September he wrote to Chandos, with a copy to his old patron Admiral Moorsom:

"We could take the working of the Trent Valley line at once without the slightest difficulty, by which I could engage the trains would arrive more correctly to time both up and down at Stafford and London, and avoid the risk and expense of running so many Specials from Rugby as we do at present owing to irregular arrivals. The run to Crewe including the Shrewsbury loop could also be accomplished with advantage, but the greatest saving could be effected by working the Stour in conjunction with the Trent Valley by this Division entirely.

"Our South Staffordshire engines, for want of a further run which the Stour would give, run only about half the mileage proper for engines - the eight passenger engines getting only seventy miles per day on the average and the ten goods engines only forty-eight miles per day. With these eighteen engines in steam on the South Staffordshire I believe nearly the whole of the Stour Valley could be worked, and the whole of the stock of engines and men on that railway be set at liberty. This is most important for your Lordship's consideration as no outlay for buildings or shops would be required there. With regard to the Trent, a very few engines, in addition to our main line engines getting more mileage, will work that line.

"We run on the Trent now at Nuneaton, Lichfield and next month Rugeley to Colwich, and the S D manage the traffic. No outlay for sheds at Stafford would be required if we were allowed to put our four or five engines to be stabled there along with the N D, as their engines do now in our shed at Rugby."

[The "temporary" Rugby shed had become dilapidated by 1853 and thereafter the N Div engines shared the S Div shed]. McConnell went on:

"I repectfully submit that as it is well known we do our work better, we do it considerably cheaper taking loads into account, and even as cheap per mile run (although not fair as a comparison as our trains will average nearly double the weight) and as we have good and powerful engines in steam and reserve daily and fully competent for the duty, there seems no good reason, if your Lordship approves, that we should not do the work and save the Company a large expenditure.

"A large expenditure would be saved not only chargeable to revenue but also a threatened demand for extension which I contend is not at all required."

[This referred to proposed capital expenditure on new engines at Crewe].

"I am quite satisfied that the present engine stock of the Company is amply sufficient to meet the increasing wants of the traffic for a long time to come provided that it is fully and properly maintained and its efficiency gradually increased by adopting the improvements of the period.

"This Division working the Stour and Trent Valley Railways which I now officially offer to do, working both to Stafford, with my present stock, would liberate a large number of engines of the Northern Division, *save any outlay* for engines from *capital* and largely *reduce* the current expenditure."

Chandos at once wrote to the Traffic Committee suggesting a "revision of the locomotive arrangements, looking to the disproportionate mileage and resources of the two Divisions and the large additional duty about to devolve on the Northern Division." A Special Committee on Locomotive Arrangements was formed to look into this, and it was suggested that either Stafford *or Crewe* might be the new divisional boundary. The Special Committee included Richard Moon, who was chairman of the Locomotive and Stores Committee.

Ramsbottom of course was very reluctant to part with the Trent Valley. He was scornful of McConnell's promised savings. "I have read Mr McConnell's report several times but am yet unable to discover how he arrives at some of his conclusions ... how the 1500 miles daily between Rugby and Stafford is to be worked by the S Div engines already in steam. N Div passenger engines running in that district are averaging nearly 150 miles per day, goods engines about 132, hence the low cost of working ... it would be difficult to improve on this, an average much greater than the average of either Division." Any advantage to Wolverton would be at Crewe's expense; consequently McConnell's claimed saving of £5,000 "falls to the ground. This cannot be saved by the removal of 11 engines whose mileage has to be worked by others ..."

At the same time he had to admit being very hard-pressed for goods engines, and claimed that the addition of the Lancaster & Carlisle mileage, despite the accompanying locomotive stock, would bring him no overall relief. The L&C engines were practically all of the Trevithick type, and most of them had been built at Crewe. He wanted to build thirty more of his DX 0-6-0 goods engines, and had the backing of Moon.

The Special Committee on Locomotive Arrangements met on 27th November 1859; Chandos, Moorsom, Bancroft, Earle, Lyon, Tootal and Moon were present. After discussion and a proposal to ask Ramsbottom and McConnell on the likely effects of a Stafford or Crewe boundary between them, Moon moved an amendment:

"That the Stores Committee having unanimously recommended that no change be made in the present division of the line and that the working of the Lancaster & Carlisle may fall into the present Northern Division, the Board be recommended to leave the Locomotive Departments as at present defined." After voting (and we can guess who voted for what) this amendment was carried.

But the proposed outlay for building 30 new N Div engines alarmed the Board; it would probably mean paying overtime wages at Crewe. Ramsbottom was told to see if he could buy engines from private firms - he got four from Beyer, Peacock & Co - and an enlarged Committee recommended (Moon still dissenting) a reduction in the size of the N Div. The Board confirmed this on 22nd December.

Moon felt badly snubbed by this decision. A few months before he had been thwarted in an attempt to enlarge Crewe. He may have been "the ablest railway administrator who ever lived" as one of his latter-day fans has written, but he was certainly ruthless and opinionated. As the Camden District Goods Manager, David Stevenson wrote: "Many of the Directors, and more of the officers, from the Manager downwards, decried his recommendations and opposed him. He was condemned as mean, self-seeking, and petty, partial in his appointment of officers and ungrateful for earnest services, unjust to old servants, and capricious and conceited in his own views."

Furious at his "humiliation", Moon bombarded Chandos with letters full of boiling resentment, petulance and self-pity. On the day of the Special Committee's decision, 22nd December 1859, he resigned from the chairmanship of his committee (although he later allowed himself to be coaxed to stay on) and on 31st December wrote:

"My real objection is the want of support and confidence in my management, that I was defeated not by force of arguments but by the necessities of the N Division, *that having no confidence in McConnell's upright truthfulness and disbelieving his statements and report*, which I am certain are misleading, it should have come almost to a personal issue, in which one of our colleagues, Admiral M[oorsom], could use *in McConnell's presence*, as an argument, that he would take his opinion against mine, and that McConnell had been in communication even with yourself ... If my views as to Crewe had been carried out ... and if we could believe our friend McConnell to be undoubtedly truthful and honest as well as clever, I should not have been found so determinedly opposing the wishes from colleagues as I do now when *I put no confidence in McConnell*... As it is, whoever takes charge will have to begin again with both divisions, *McConnell's ambition to go to Crewe still keeping up the old irritation* - having before him the absurd idea of Admiral M. that if North were worked as South, or rather, by McConnell, a great saving would ensue. I would ask you how, after my plans have been spoiled, I can feel otherwise than humiliated and unwilling to have anything more to do with a concern where there is no consideration for my labour or care or time to work out a plan, but the whole is overthrown and *the triumphant party allowed to trample on the other* ... I am certain 12 or 18 months will show I was right ..."

Chandos met him in the Euston Hotel on the night of 5th January and tried to placate him. The next day Moon sent him another letter:

"... After the severe rebuff I have sustained I can only adhere to the resignation ... The decision of the Special Committee has satisfied me on one point - which will serve as a warning to others who may serve the L&NW Co faithfully in the vain imagination that it will be thought for the interest of the Company to reward such service with success and honour viz: the result to myself of nine years uninterrupted labour that I was a fool for my pains. Having awoke to the consciousness of this disagreeable fact I ask myself *cui bono?*"

As for McConnell, at the moment of achieving his long-desired extension along the Trent Valley to Stafford, and whether he was fully aware of it or not, he had acquired an implacable enemy. Within a few days of sending this letter Moon changed his mind; he remained in the chair of the Locomotive and Stores Committee.

Meanwhile Ramsbottom and McConnell had been ordered to co-operate on the redrawing of the interdivisional boundary and reported to Chandos:

"Euston Station
19 Decr 1859

My Lord

... After discussing the whole subject fully we have agreed that the following is, upon the whole, the best plan to be adopted.
1st   That Stafford be the limit of both Divisions.
2nd   That an independent Engine Shed be erected at Stafford for the Southern Division.
3rd   That the length from Stafford to Bushbury be worked jointly as it may be best found to suit Time Bills.
4th   That the Southern Division receive a proportionate number of engines for this work.

The proposed arrangement giving different conditions of loads and shorter lengths of run will prejudicially affect the Northern Division in future comparisons.

We are,
My Lord,
Yours respectfully,
J. E. McConnell.
J. Ramsbottom.

PS Without the Lancaster & Carlisle Mr McConnell agrees to the latter clause, but with that line added he considers there are no grounds for such a statement as that embodied in the last paragraph."

They were in agreement that the N Div lines south of Stafford were the work of 73 or 75 engines. McConnell estimated that he could do the work with 44 engines in addition to his spare power. Of the 73 Crewe engines then working south of Stafford, 39 were to be sent north for duties elsewhere, the remaining 34 to be transferred to McConnell for his extended territory. To make up his estimated total he was authorised to build ten goods engines at Wolverton. On the question of the *types* of engine to be transferred they were deadlocked. Ramsbottom wrote to Chandos:

"We agree that 22 passenger and 12 goods of average quality should be taken from Rugby, Birmingham and Wolverhampton. Owing to great pressure upon this Division as re Goods Traffic however, it is much to be desired that we should retain the whole of our new [DX] goods engines, of which we have yet only 25. There are now 5 of these at Rugby, two having been added this month and one in October. To compensate for the retention of these I have proposed to transfer the whole of our new 7-feet passenger engines, of which type we have 16, towards the 22 required. This will certainly take away 16 of our best passenger engines but as they are exceptional in type it is of less consequence. It will also prevent the introduction of one additional type to the Southern Division."

Far better that McConnell take away the Trevithick 'Rockets' in their entirety than that he get his hands on any DX goods engines! But McConnell was not taken in. On the same day, 27th December, he wrote:

"I object, as I understood I was to have a *fair sample* of those working on the lines I aim to work transferred. I am sure *we* will *not* settle this question and I beg to suggest that your Lordship decide - *nothing prevents the transfer but this* and having made great saving of engines I cannot afford also being put off with the inferior class for goods altogether."

And on the next day:

"I can begin on the first of January, but I must have a fair sample of the engines, and not as Mr Ramsbottom may choose to select as *least useful* to him. I see no chance or hope of the question being disposed of by Ramsbottom and myself."

In the end, 23 passenger engines were handed over, only three of them 7ft singles, and the eleven goods did include two 0-6-0s. They were not of the DX class, but were two of the four which Ramsbottom had just selected for purchase from the stock of spare engines in Beyer, Peacock & Co's Manchester works.

Ramsbottom was in no hurry. He had to take over the Lancaster & Carlisle on New Year's Day, so he suggested delaying the transfer until the middle of the month. "By that time the steam shed at Bushbury may be nearly completed and the difficulty of providing shed accommodation at Stafford will be partly overcome."

A fortnight later the first two Beyer, Peacock 0-6-0s were handed over to the LNWR and on the following day, Friday the thirteenth of January 1860, Chandos wrote to each superintendent:

"You may proceed to arrange the details of the transfer of working and to carry it out on Monday and following days as you may both think fit."

Then, the Special Committee on Locomotive Arrangements having reported to the Board, Ramsbottom and McConnell were told to refer for all further instruction to the committee whose chairman was Richard Moon.

After the 34 N Div engines had been transferred, Ramsbottom asked if he could have his nameplates back. On 2nd February the Locomotive & Stores Committee instructed McConnell to return the nameplates. McConnell, it is said, loaded them into a wagon boldly labelled: TRASH - FOR CREWE.

It can be imagined that from this time Moon's relations with McConnell were cool. If there were any letters between them they have not survived and minutes of the Locomotive & Stores Committee meetings give little away. But McConnell's campaign had succeeded, so far. He had pushed the S Div to within 25 miles of Crewe and had won through to what he probably saw as the first of his objectives, Stafford.

Later in 1860 there were festivities at Wolverton; the Bishop of Oxford preached before a gathering of workmen in the new erecting shop with a platform party including McConnell, LNWR Secretary C. E. Stewart, William Fairbairn of Manchester, the wealthy philanthropist Angela Burdett-Coutts, Lord Leigh and other notables. The Bishop inaugurated the font in the new church at Stantonbury, Wolverton's overspill village, by christening McConnell's four-months-old son with the names Ronald Stafford. Lord Chandos proposed the health of Mr and Mrs McConnell, with three cheers, and an extra cheer for the baby. Richard Moon was also there (his habitual frown would deepen when he heard the baby's middle name) but played such a low-key role that a reporter asked him who he was. His short reply "R.Moon" got him into the local paper among the also-present as "Mr Harmoon".

The End of the Southern Division

Towards the end of 1860 a scheme was drafted by which the LNWR and the GNR would jointly take over the Manchester Sheffield & Lincolnshire Railway. The LNWR Board voted 25 to 1 in favour, the dissentient vote being cast by the Chairman, Lord Chandos, who believed the takeover was not in his shareholders' interests. (The GNR Board agreed with Chandos and rejected the proposal). Feeling he had no other course he promptly resigned on 5th January 1861; his place was taken by the Deputy Chairman, Admiral Moorsom. This must have been good news for McConnell, but a month later the position of Deputy Chairman was filled by Richard Moon.

Moon lost little time. On 13th April he brought up the question of the great expenditure at Wolverton consequent on the change in the boundary of the locomotive departments and on his motion a Special Committee was set up to enquire "how far McConnell's explanation is borne out by the facts."

In the next few weeks McConnell and Moorsom met often, and a number of orders for new locomotives, to be built at Wolverton and by outside firms, were passed by the Board. On 18th May Moorsom attended a meeting of the Board; eight days later he was dead.

For McConnell and the S Div Locomotive Department this was only one of several blows in a terrible year. Early on 11th June one of the heavy Fairbairn Goods engines fell through a bridge near Kenilworth, killing both enginemen. Although the cause of the accident was eventually found to be a badly repaired cast-iron beam in the bridge, the weight of McConnell's engines again came under scrutiny. Moon was now Chairman and a change of tone is evident at a meeting of the Locomotive Committee on 20th June where it was

> "Ordered that Mr McConnell's attention be specially called to the following minute of this Committee: No 40 of the 26th October 1859, viz.: Ordered that the Superintendents report the weight of each engine and tender separately, turned out of the shops during the last ½ year, and that this be done at the end of each future ½ year ..."

The first of McConnell's H class Special Large Bloomers had just been completed at Wolverton; it was heavier than had been specified and weighed more than 34½ tons. These engines were bound to be looked at critically.

Then on 4th July the boiler of a Bloomer on the Down Irish Mail exploded, focussing attention on the subject of boiler pressure. McConnell had been building engines with a pressure of 150 lb/sq inch since early in the previous year; Ramsbottom's highest was 120.

Back in January, McConnell had estimated that he would need eight extra engines for working the South Leicestershire branch, the first section of which was to open early in 1862, but G. P. Neele, newly appointed as Superintendent of the Rugby-Stafford district, suggested instead "extending the trips of the Coventry and Nuneaton service and avoid any extra engine; the idea exactly fitted the Chairman's notions." No doubt Moon would probe very closely into McConnell's other estimates of engines required: five for the Sutton Coldfield branch, eight for the Cambridge and three for the tiny Watford and Rickmansworth line.

The Special Committee looking into the large expense at Wolverton consisted of Moon, Bancroft, Wollaston Blake, Birley, Bramley-Moore, Clements, Edward Cropper, Dean, Hardman Earle, Matthew Lyon and Westhead. They sat on several occasions during the year at what must have been stormy meetings. Their first report was submitted to the Board who sent it back to them to reconsider. At last, a resolution was composed and voted on in committee: 8 for and 2 against. It was laid before the Board on 21st December, but a decision was put off until 15th January and a further report from McConnell.

Moon's report detailed the financial outcome of the transfer of the Trent Valley. In November 1859 McConnell had stated that if his Division were extended to Stafford he could do the extra work, provided the following outlay were made:

An engine shed at Stafford:	£1,200
Sundry works at Wolverton (already under consideration):	£6,478
Small further addition there:	£ 950
Total:	£8,628

Since 1st January 1860 there had been a gross expenditure of £78,010 against McConnell's estimate of £8,628 "and the ultimate vote of the Board, to include everything, of £21,000." Moon concluded:

> "On a review of all the evidence, documentary and otherwise which has been presented to us in this case, we are of opinion that the results of the change in the boundary of the locomotive departments recommended by Mr McConnell do not bear out the statements of his reports of November 1859 nor of the subsequent representations which led to the resolution of 22nd December of that year. We find that the expenditure actually incurred exceeds Mr McConnell's largest estimate to the extent of £44,275 and we regret to state that no part of the anticipated saving of £12,080 3s 9d yearly as set forth in his reports of 30th November 1859 has been realised. Whilst as regards the question 'How far Mr McConnell's statements have been affected by other circumstances?' we do not see that any change has taken place in the policy of the Board nor has extension of traffic ensued which can with propriety be assigned as the cause of the failure of those statements. We are therefore reluctantly led

to the resolution already submitted to the Board on the 21st ultimo:

> That this Committee is unwilling to impute to Mr McConnell an intention to mislead the Board, but find that his statements of the probable outlay on Capital Account have been so much at variance with the real facts of the case as seriously to shake the confidence which the Board ought to have in the reports and statements of an officer holding so reponsible a situation."

One member of the Committee, Henry Wollaston Blake, wrote to Moon accusing him of preparing a one-sided report and railroading it through when in fact members of the Committee were not unanimous in their views. He said the report was inaccurate; he disputed Moon's figures and his conclusions. He listed ten points in Moon's report, with a comment on each point beginning: "It is not true ..."

Another director, Ross Donnelly Mangles (1801-1877; former Chairman of the East India Company and MP for Guildford) wrote to Moon because he was unable to be present at the Board on 15th January. He said he thought the resolution of censure on McConnell was far too severe, unjust, unfair and unreasonable. He ended:

> "The fact seems to me to be clear that Mr McConnell has been acting throughout as an honest man in his position would act and ought to act - in the persuasion that he enjoys the confidence of his employers and that he was working in unison with the Committee and the Board in carrying out plans which he sincerely believed to be for the best for the Company without a suspicion that there were eyes upon him to watch whether he did not exceed estimates given upon limited plans months before and persons ready to trip up his heels if he failed to make things tally which admitted in their nature and extent of no common measure.
>
> "In my humble judgement whatever fault Mr McConnell has been guilty of would be adequately punished by a mild censure and admonition instead of such a sweeping condemnation as it has been proposed to inflict upon him."

But it was all too late. Moon was as unswayed by Mangles' "sense of justice due to an old and highly deserving servant of the Company" as by Wollaston Blake's accusations of inaccuracy. He would have his revenge for being shown up in front of McConnell, and after a lot of argument across the table, he was able to get his resolution accepted. The voting was: for, 14; against, 11.

McConnell received the news the following day in a letter from Charles E. Stewart, the Company Secretary. He must have spent a thoughtful month before scribbling out his resignation:

> "Euston Feb. 20 1862
>
> Dear Sir,
> Referring to the Resolution of the Board communicated in your letter of the 16th January last - I am not able to admit the justice of the conclusion therein stated - on the contrary I feel it due to myself to *protest against* it but as it is apparent that I cannot either with satisfaction to myself or advantage to the Company continue to act I resign the office which I have now held for fifteen years reserving to myself the right to adopt such course hereafter as I may think necessary for the justification of my character.
> Yrs truly
> J. E. McConnell"

The same day the Board resolved: "That the resignation of Mr McConnell be accepted. That considering the additional expenses to which Mr McConnell will be subjected by reason of the sudden removal from his present residence, the sum of £1,000 be voted to him on account of a half year salary and such expenses."

On 5th March he attended his last Locomotive & Stores Committee meeting, where he learned that someone called Peter Salmon from Glasgow, the inventor of a steam heating system for carriages, had already applied for his job.

McConnell's last official act as Locomotive Superintendent was a two-sentence letter to Stewart: "Mr Ramsbottom has now taken charge of this Dept. Will you please note this as an official intimation." This was dated from the LNWR Locomotive Department, Wolverton Station, 29th March 1862.

Ramsbottom had been appointed Chief Locomotive Superintendent on 22nd March at £2,000 a year. He wrote a more effusive note to Moon, acknowledging his minute of that date which "has done me the honour to appoint me Superintendent of the whole of the Locomotive Department of this Company. For this substantial mark of your confidence I beg to tender my warmest thanks and to assure you that it shall be my constant study to shew that it has not been misplaced."

McConnell beyond the LNWR

The news of McConnell's resignation surprised Wolverton. On Saturday 1st March 1862 he was the guest of honour at a Freemasons' banquet at the Victoria Hotel. A week later he was on the platform before a large meeting of the LNWR staff in the Works Carpenters' Shop, with the Rural Dean, Rev R. M. Russell, in the chair. The Chief Foreman, William Rowland, who was himself to leave Wolverton within the month, made the presentation. McConnell was given "an elegant and massive silver epergne or candelabrum, with a cut-glass centre dish for flowers, and six branches supporting cut-glass dishes which may be removed for holding candles..." The triangular base had an inscription in one panel from the officers and workmen of the S Div "as a testimonial of regard and esteem ... and of their grateful appreciation of the great interest he has invariably taken in their welfare." The second panel had the McConnell crest and motto, an arm holding a cross-crosslet fitchée and "Prêt, toujours prêt" - "Ready, aye ready". The third panel contained an engraving of a locomotive and tender - perhaps his latest H class, 373? There was also an address signed by 1,966 subscribers.

Since 1847 McConnell had lived at Park House, usually known as Wolverton Park, a substantial villa on the edge of Old Wolverton, a mile west of the Works. In February 1848 he married Charlotte Bowton Addison, the daughter of a surgeon in Burnham, Essex and they had eight children, born from 1848 to 1864. On resigning from the LNWR he moved 25 miles south into the Chiltern Hills where he bought The Woodlands, a large country mansion with a surrounding estate lying in the broad valley known as the Wendover Gap, not far from the village of Great Missenden. Later he added the adjoining Road Farm and Dutchlands Farm. Perhaps it was about this time that he acquired a long and quite fantastic family tree which purported to trace his ancestry, via kilted Highland clansmen who fought at Culloden for Bonnie Prince Charlie, right back to the Lords of the Isles.

McConnell took an office at 2 Dean's Yard, Westminster, and for several years practised as a consultant engineer. At the International Exhibition of 1862 he was on the jury for railways, which awarded a bronze medal to Ramsbottom's *Lady of the Lake*; he was also a juror representing the interests of English railways at the Paris Exhibition of 1867. He appeared as an expert witness at many railway enquiries. During his time on the LNWR he had taken out over a dozen patents which, according to David Stevenson "brought him wealth", although how any of those for "improvements to locomotives" could have produced much of an income is unclear. He took out his last three patents in 1863 in association with a partner, George H. Bovill of Millwall, for chains, the treatment of worn railway tyres and the manufacture of thick wrought-iron plates.

He had long concerned himself in railways beyond the LNWR and in 1853 was appointed consultant to the Sydney Railway, for which he produced a design of 0-4-2 (Fig 144); four of these were built by R. Stephenson & Co, completed in September 1854 and delivered to Australia in January 1855. They were a slightly smaller version of the Kitson 0-6-0 of the same period, with the rear drivers replaced by trailing wheels, and had many typical McConnell features. India-rubber springs were mounted over each wheel, the straight axles were hollow, the reversing rod, on the left, was carried below the driving axle to valve gear arranged as in most S Div engines after the Bury singles of 1848; the tender was the normal six-wheeled S Div type with rubber springs. In superficial details - the shape of the splashers and the square sandbox between them, the cornered dome and safety valve cover, the footstep, even the positioning of the engine number on the chimney front and the very form of the brass numerals - the engines were LNWR S Div in all but name. Happily, one of them survived and, thoroughly restored to near-original condition, may be seen today in the Powerhouse Museum, Sydney.

When the engines arrived in Australia they were supervised by William Scott, who had been sent out by McConnell. Scott had worked at Wolverton for three years, latterly as a foreman erector; he remained in Australia and eventually became the New South Wales Locomotive Engineer. McConnell was apparently able to make "offers of appointments on foreign railways" to other members of the LNWR staff, including David Stevenson the Camden Goods Manager, which suggests an involvement in other far-flung ventures, well outside his duties on the S Div. On the evidence of the appearance of their locomotives, many overseas railways seem to have consulted McConnell.

Nearer home, he was consulted by the Portpatrick Railway, a line being built over 61 hilly miles through Galloway to create a new route to Ireland with a short sea-crossing. In March 1860 he presented the Portpatrick with drawings and specifications for an 0-4-2 tender engine, very like those for the Sydney Railway. The design seems to have been prepared in Wolverton Works, and shared many features with the S Div G class tanks whose drawings were being made at the same time, but the Portpatrick engines were smaller, with 5ft driving wheels and 15in x 22in cylinders, and were without McConnell's patent boiler and corniced dome as fitted to the G class. Six were ordered from Sharp, Stewart & Co, but in May the order was changed to four of the 0-4-2s and two 2-2-2s, which were also to McConnell's drawings. The singles too had 15in x 22in cylinders and with 6ft driving wheels on a 14ft 9in wheelbase were like very small Bloomers with plain domes. The six Portpatrick engines became Caledonian Railway 262-5 and 267/8 and apart from one destroyed in an accident, survived until 1888/90.

After his departure from the LNWR he produced further locomotive specifications for small railways, one of which was the Northampton & Banbury Junction, an impoverished little company with big ideas. The N&BJ, also known as the Midland Counties & South Wales Railway, was building fifteen miles of single track between the LNWR main line at Blisworth and Cockley Brake on the Banbury branch. Once again the engines McConnell specified were 0-4-2s and the N&BJ ordered ten engines to his design from Neilson & Co of Glasgow on 5th June 1865: five 0-4-2 tender engines and five 0-4-2 tanks, to be delivered between February and December 1866. The driving wheels were to be 5ft 6in diameter with inside cylinders of 16in x 20in. Typically, McConnell then sent a series of letters to Neilson's asking for modifications to the design: on 28th June, length of outside crank to be 13in, not 10in as formerly requested; on 17th August, Krupp's patent steel tyres on all wheels; on 24th November, right-hand crank to lead.

These engines were similar to the LNWR M and N classes, but had a plain dome on the boiler and the splashers had Beyer-type brass rims. For the N&BJ they were to be painted green and numbered in brass figures from 1 to 10 on the boiler side. After five were completed it was learned that the N&BJ could not pay, so no more were built. The first one (works No 1216), a tank engine, was sold by Neilson & Co to the Athens & Piraeus Railway in April 1869; the other four (works Nos 1217-20), two tender engines and two tanks, lay in Neilson's yard until sold to the Caledonian Railway on 15th September 1870. Before leaving the works all were fitted with cabs "to the satisfaction of Mr Conner" the CR Locomotive Superintendent, and were given CR numbers 452/3 (tender engines) and 540/1 (tanks). None ever carried Solway Junction Railway numbers and the legend that they did so seems to be based on Neilson's works photograph of a tank engine with a boilerside N&BJ numberplate "No 1". They lasted until 1899-1906.

McConnell was a director of various concerns, notably of Fairbairn's, the Manchester firm which built many S Div locomotives. At the other end of the scale he was briefly a director of the Colne Valley & Halstead Railway for which in May 1864 he tried to obtain old engines from the LNWR on deferred terms. The Stores Committee minute recording this is marked: "Referred to Mr Moon" - and there was no sale. He was also a director of the Thames Subway Co, formed to construct a tunnel from Deptford to the Isle of Dogs, and of the London & Aylesbury Railway, which materialised nine years after his death as the Metropolitan line running along the valley, in sight of The Woodlands and between his two farms.

In 1871 he went into partnership for ten years with William P. Marshall, making valuations and assessments of railway property. Marshall had been associated with Edward Woods in the LNWR locomotive trials of 1853/4 and was Secretary of the Institution of Mechanical Engineers from 1849 to 1877. McConnell was one of the founder members of the IMechE in 1846 and was for many years on its Council, serving as a Vice President from 1847 to 1853 and from 1855 to 1857. He read several papers and made lively contributions to most discussions. He stood for election as Vice President again in November 1860, but Ramsbottom was elected instead. Thereafter McConnell left the IMechE.

At this distance it is difficult to know what to make of McConnell. He had been an ambitious young man in a hurry - "a strong and determined man of the rough sort" - everyone agreed he was very energetic and clever, some said cunning; Richard Moon thought him untruthful and the caustic 'Veritas Vincit' accused him of passing off other men's ideas as his own, and worse. He seems to have provoked strong reactions in everyone; his patron Admiral Moorsom believed in him absolutely and gave him consistent backing for twenty years; the LNWR Board almost tore itself in half over the motion of censure which forced his resignation. Certainly his written reports are unlike those of his predecessor, Bury, or of his successor Ramsbottom: they are vague and misleading where they should be concise, and much of his paperwork is full of inaccuracies. Perhaps these were overlooked because most directors were simply baffled by the details, or else they were charmed by his bluff, outspoken ways. He is said to have been well-liked in Wolverton, latterly at least, organising all manner of social activities in the town, annual excursions, sports days, a savings bank. As a great enthusiast for technical education, night schools and self-improvement he reinvigorated the Wolverton Mechanics' Institute in 1856 and went on to be the prime mover in the creation of the more ambitious and comprehensive Wolverton Science & Art Institute.

He played an active part in local politics; he was a Liberal and a long-standing member of the Reform Club. He became a magistrate in 1870, and sometimes sat on the bench at Aylesbury with Disraeli. In 1873 he was appointed High Sheriff of Buckinghamshire.

He had come a long way, from fatherless apprentice to country gentleman. His initial "capital of ten shillings" had increased mightily. Although his salary on the LNWR had risen from £700 in 1847 by modest increments to £1,200 in 1860, he now owned a mansion and estate, farms, various houses and plots of land. He had amassed over £28,000, and at today's prices he would be a millionaire.

Then, at the end of 1882, McConnell's bailiff at Road Farm was summoned for neglecting to report an outbreak of swine fever among his 58 pigs. The case was dismissed, with a pointed "no comment as to the conduct of his master". On 13th January 1883 McConnell himself appeared before his fellow magistrates, was convicted under the Contagious Diseases Act and fined £2, with costs. The case excited great local attention and when he appealed against his conviction at the Quarter Sessions in April he was told bluntly that he ought to have suspected that his pigs were diseased. His appeal was dismissed "with the usual costs".

In the following month he suddenly fell ill. He died on 11th June 1883 from heart failure and pneumonia. He was 68.

His grave, on the hill above the parish church of SS Peter & Paul in Great Missenden, records that his widow survived him by only three years; it is surmounted by a white marble angel, winged and pointing upwards.

PRÊT, TOUJOURS PRÊT

McCONNELL.

BALLAST ENGINES 1834-56

The first locomotives on the London & Birmingham Railway were quite separate from those which worked the traffic. On the advice of Robert Stephenson several engines were purchased by the L&B for use by the contractors who built the line; they were mostly small 0-4-0s of Stephenson type, with outside wooden frames and four inside iron sub-frames between firebox and smokebox, 4ft 6in wheels and inside cylinders 12 x 18in. They were hired to the contractors at 5% a year interest on the value of each engine, plus the difference in valuation when returned at the end of the contract.

After the opening of the line most of these engines formed the nucleus of the Ballast Engine stock, used in the maintenance of the permanent way. They were all named, and in 1847 the survivors were given numbers in their own series, distinct from the traffic engines.

Permanent way maintenance
At first, the track was the responsibility of the Chief Engineer, Robert Stephenson, who had charge of the ballast engines. They were first based at Camden, then were moved to Watford when a separate repair shop was opened there. From April 1839 Stephenson's role was that of Consulting Engineer and in August the ballast engines became part of Edward Bury's responsibilities.

In September, exactly one year after the L&B opened throughout, permanent way maintenance was placed in the hands of two contractors: Thomas Jackson took over the London to Rugby section, for which he was paid £345 per mile per annum; John Cummings took Rugby to Birmingham at £300 per mile and also had responsibility for the Aylesbury branch. Under this arrangement the contractors had to provide labour, tools and all materials except iron rails, but all wagons and locomotives were hired to them by the L&B. The engines were supplied from the stock of ballast engines at Wolverton but Bury also loaned some of his standard goods engines, probably because the ballast engines were by this time in poor repair.

This system of hiring engines as required created problems. After two years the contracts were renewed but under the new arrangements Jackson and Cummings had to provide their own locomotives - which had to be approved by Bury. It seems likely that they took over some of the L&B ballast engines at that time and in January 1842 a separate ballast engine depot for their use was built on the Down side at Camden.

Jackson's contract was terminated in April 1845 (he was blamed for letting the line get into a rough state) and in May the contract for maintaining the London - Rugby line and the Aylesbury branch was awarded to Messrs Cardus & Fawcett, but the ballast engines and wagons on these sections were taken over on 1st March 1845 by one of Jackson's old employees, Richard Madigan, who under a separate contract became responsible for the haulage of permanent way materials.

In June 1846 the ballast engine depot at Camden was removed to make way for the new passenger engine shed and the ballast engines then went back to Watford.

On the expiry of the contract with Cummings in September 1846, Cardus & Fawcett took over his section and so had the maintenance of the whole line from London to Birmingham, with haulage by Madigan, who acquired Cummings' ballast engine. Contracts were renewed in May 1848: with Cardus until May 1853, and with Madigan until June 1851.

By 1849 Mr Cardus was the contractor for the maintenance of the entire main line from London to Birmingham and the Aylesbury, Bedford and Leamington branches, while Mr Brown maintained the Peterborough branch. Rates were much lower than before:

Section	Rate per mile per year
London - Wolverton	£165
Wolverton - Birmingham	£123.95
Bletchley - Bedford	£135.99
Aylesbury branch (single)	£ 69.97
Leamington branch (single)	£ 62.18
Blisworth - Peterborough	£ 82.03

Under his separate contract Richard Madigan took care of all haulage and loading and unloading of materials. The LNWR provided him with workshops and sheds at Watford, sheds at Leighton and shops at Hillmorton ballast pits for a rent of £210 a year, and engines and wagons on an annual payment of 5% of the value. The total stock was valued at £33,000 for the use of which he paid £1,656.50 a year. The LNWR paid him 3¼d (1.35p) per wagon per mile for haulage and for loading and unloading, 2s 6d (12.5p) per wagon of ballast or excavated material, and 5s 0d (25p) per wagon of screened gravel. For the use of one locomotive and twelve wagons he received £4 10s (£4.50) per day.

This cumbersome system of contracts lasted until 15th August 1849, when the LNWR took haulage of permanent way materials into its own hands. The Watford ballast engine shops were closed forthwith, and from then all repairs to the engines were done at Wolverton.

Summary of Main Line Permanent Way Maintenance Contracts

London - Rugby
Period	Maintenance	Provision of ballast engines
9/39 - 9/41	Jackson	L&B
9/41 - 4/45	Jackson	Jackson
5/45 - 5/53	Cardus & Fawcett	Madigan (to 8/49) LNWR (from 8/49)

Rugby - Birmingham
Period	Maintenance	Provision of ballast engines
9/39 - 9/41	Cummings	L&B
9/41 - 9/46	Cummings	Cummings
9/46 - 5/53	Cardus & Fawcett	Madigan (to 8/49) LNWR (from 8/49)

Locomotives used in making the L&B
The construction of the line was divided into thirty separate contracts distributed among large and small firms, almost a third of which got into financial

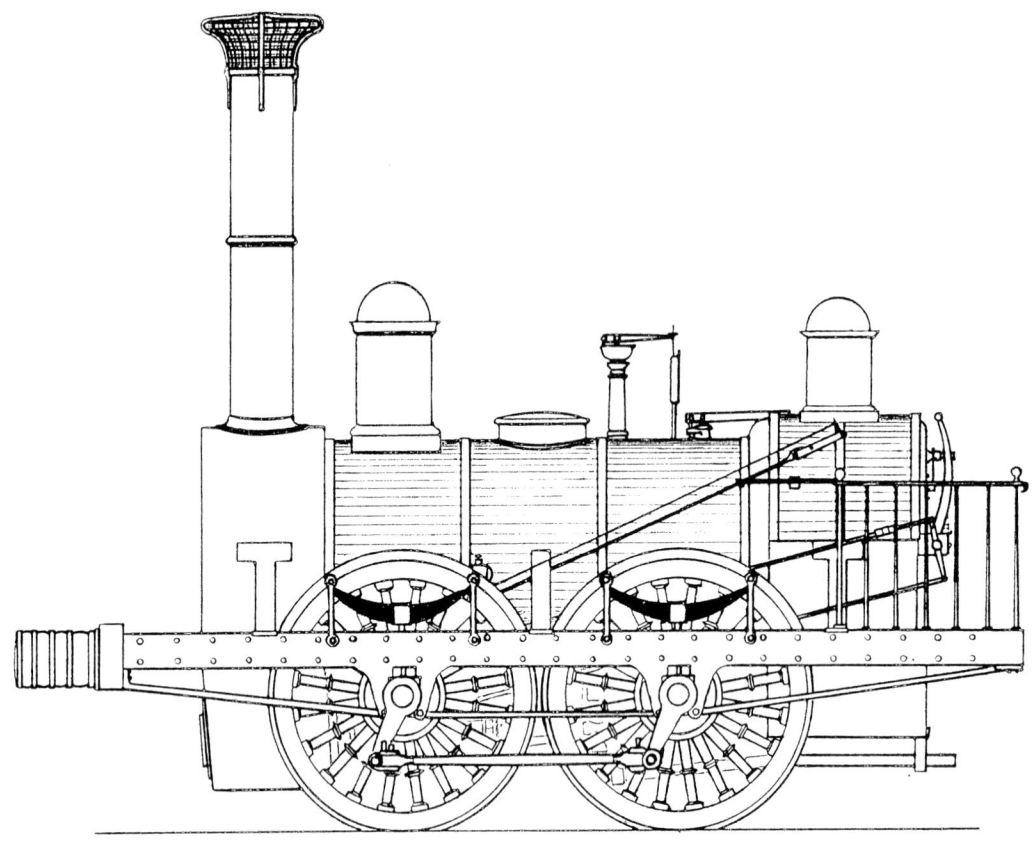

Fig. 6 Standard 0-4-0 ballast engine by Chas Tayleur & Co of the Vulcan Foundry. During 1835-7 seven of these were built by Tayleur; Stephenson built four similar, while Mather, Dixon and Fenton, Murray & Jackson built one each.

Fig. 7 Leicester & Swannington Railway *Phœnix* built in 1832 by Robert Stephenson & Co; purchased by the L&B in 1835 for use in constructing the line and employed as a ballast engine until 1844.

difficulties. Administration was in the hands of two committees of directors, known as the London Committee and the Birmingham Committee. Each committee purchased engines for use in the building of its own section, with Wolverton as the boundary.

On Robert Stephenson's recommendation the London Committee ordered two engines on 24th December 1834, one from Charles Tayleur & Co and one from R. Stephenson & Co, and began negotiations with the Leicester & Swannington Railway who had replied to an L&B advertisement and wished to dispose of an engine.

The Stephenson engine (works No 111) was reported by letter of 11th April 1835 to have been shipped from Newcastle to the Thames. It was at work at Willesden by June.

The Tayleur engine was paid for on 22nd July 1835 and was maker's number 18. At first it worked on the Primrose Hill cuttings but was probably the engine ordered to be transferred to the Birmingham Committee on 27th January 1836 for the Berkswell contract. Later Tayleur's No 18 acquired the name *Brockhall* from the contract north of Weedon on which engines were first used in September 1837.

The Leicester & Swannington engine, No 2 *Phœnix*, was another similar Stephenson engine, maker's number 6 of August 1832, which the L&S were glad to sell because it was too small for their needs. After repairs it arrived on the L&B in May-July 1835. It probably kept its name.

The Birmingham Committee ordered six ballast engines in January 1836. Three of these were from Charles Tayleur & Co, whose first one was to be sent to the London end as a replacement for the engine (*Brockhall*) transferred to Birmingham in that month; the other three were from Stephenson & Co, Mather, Dixon & Co and Fenton, Murray & Jackson. The Liverpool & Manchester Railway offered their famous old *Northumbrian* for £450, and Rothwell & Co of Bolton offered an engine called *Hercules* for £600, or £760 including a tender, but neither was taken because they were not to the Company's specification.

The first of the Birmingham Committee's Tayleurs was tested on the Warrington & Newton Railway (which ran past Tayleur's Vulcan Foundry) at the end of May; it was sent off on 6th June and arrived by canal in London on Monday 13th June 1836. The second Tayleur was ready in the same month, Stephenson's arrived at Kensal Green about the same time and by the end of the year all had been delivered except that from Fenton, Murray & Jackson, which was sent by sea from Hull to the Thames in January 1837. Mather, Dixon's engine was working on the Coventry contract by May 1837 when it was seized for the £900 debt of a bankrupt contractor, and had to be bought back from the Sheriff.

The London Committee ordered four more in February 1836, two from Stephenson and two from Tayleur. These were evidently to compensate for cancelled train engine orders of the previous month; Stephenson's two were built under works numbers 141/2 which had been allocated to the L&B's cancelled 2-2-2 order. The Tayleurs were received at Wolverton on 10th February 1837.

In October 1836 Robert Stephenson wrote to the Birmingham Committee recommending the purchase of an engine from his firm. The engine would cost £1,575, the tender £220. From the price this was clearly a six-wheeled engine; his offer was not taken up.

Another standard ballast engine "like those already supplied" offered by Tayleur at the end of December 1836 was accepted and in September 1837 it was delivered at Coventry canal wharf. This was presumably Tayleur's No 61. The name *Franklin* is assigned to 61 in the Tayleur works list but an old Vulcan Foundry drawing shows *Franklin* to have been a very small 2-2-0 on a Bury-type bar frame which (together with the name) suggests that this engine was destined for the American market. Linking this drawing with No 61 is just another bad guess on the part of the compiler of the 'official' works list, which is crammed with errors in the period 1833-45. The name *Franklin* appears nowhere in the L&B records and there can be little doubt that 61 was a standard 0-4-0.

A Vulcan Foundry drawing dated June 1836 shows an 0-4-0 outside-framed engine for the London & Birmingham with 4ft 6in wheels and 12 x 18in inside cylinders. Works numbers 36, 37 and 42 are quoted and the figure '7' is added, which may represent the total built of this type for the L&B.

Dimensions of standard 0-4-0 ballast engine
(from a specification of 1836)

Cylinders (2 inside)	12" x 18"
Boiler	
Diameter	3' 4"
Length of barrel	7' 6"
Tubes (86, 2" dia.)	
Firebox (copper)	
Length	2' 4¾"
Width	3' 5"
Depth	3' 0"
Frames	
Outside: ash planks (plated both sides with ¼" iron)	4"x7"
Inside: four wrought-iron frames between smokebox and firebox	
Diameter of wheels	4' 6"
Wheelbase (from VF drawing)	4' 10½"

Whishaw (1840) describes Tayleur's seven engines (including No 61) as coupled engines with 4' 6" wheels and gives boiler dimensions as follows:

Tayleur's No 18 *Brockhall:*
Boiler	
Diameter	3' 0"
Length of barrel	8' 0"
Heating surface	
Tubes (89, 2" dia, 8' 6" long)	394.09 sq ft
Firebox (2' long, 3'5¾" wide, 4'3" high)	36.26 sq ft
Total	430.35 sq ft

Tayleur's Nos 36, 37, 42, 43, 44, 61:
Boiler	
Diameter	3' 4"
Length of barrel	7' 6"
Heating surface	
Tubes (88, 2" dia, 8' long)	366.78 sq ft
Firebox (2' 4" long, 3' 5" wide, 3' 8" high)	33.81 sq ft
Total	400.59 sq ft

Miscellaneous engines

The Birmingham Committee reported on 30th September 1836:

"The following locomotive engines, with their tenders, have been supplied by the Company:

    Berkswell contract: two
    Blisworth contract: two
    Coventry contract: one

besides the one procured by Mr Thornton for which the Company advanced the money, and another engine now due from Messrs Fenton, Murray & Jackson which will be supplied to the Rugby contract."

The engine ordered by the contractor Joseph Thornton was delivered on 27th July 1836 by John Jones (later of Jones & Potts) and cost £970 including tender. Thornton had another engine at work on his Yardley contract by October 1835 when it hauled an inspection train. After he finished work there in autumn 1837 he probably transferred the two engines to his other contracts at Long Buckby and Brockhall where locomotives started working in September. After finishing on the L&B Thornton might have moved his two engines to other construction work on the North Midland Railway.

Daniel Pritchard, a contractor at Berkswell, bought himself an engine for £200 on 18th September 1835. This was the 2-2-0 'Planet' type *Sun*, No 17 of the Liverpool & Manchester Railway. Robert Stephenson commented: "On the Berkswell contract two good engines will be needed instead of which Pritchard has got himself one bad one and it is certain the contractors will get bad second hand engines or imperfect new ones." It was "out of order" in May 1836 and was not taken over by the L&B.

Samuel Hemming had his own engine at work at Brandon by October 1836, supplemented by L&B-owned engines later. He possibly took his engine away in October 1837 for work on the Bristol & Exeter Railway.

John Chapman purchased a locomotive for use at Bugbrook shortly before 31st October 1837; this may have gone to further contracts on the North Midland.

On the Blisworth contract William Hughes & Son obtained their own engine in February 1836, which was joined by the L&B's *Tayleur* (37) in June. Following the death of Hughes senior in November the firm went bankrupt and the L&B took over its plant. It is possible that Hughes' engine was *Hercules* offered by Rothwell & Co on 11th January; an engine with that name was included in the later ballast stock.

A curious purchase was *Caledonian*, No 28 of the Liverpool & Manchester. Built by Galloway, Bowman & Glasgow of the Caledonian Foundry, Manchester in 1832, it was an 0-4-0 with vertical cylinders amidships working a dummy crankshaft. The L&B bought it in May 1837 for £400 when there was a need for more engines on the Blisworth contract, but ordered its sale in December, when it was valued at £200. Probably it went in 1838 to a contractor building the Midland Counties Railway where, renamed *Mersey*, it featured in the opening celebrations of the Nottingham - Derby section on 30th May 1839.

On 3rd October 1837 G. & J. Rennie of Blackfriars, London, asked for a trial of two engines on the L&B. One engine, "Rennie's experimental engine, the *Victoria*" certainly arrived and was probably put to work by the contractors. On 21st October it collided with three wagons loaded with rails at Tring, whereupon Messrs Rennie were asked to remove it.

Harvey Combe

Best known of all the ballast engines was another non-standard machine, the 2-2-2 *Harvey Combe*. The use of a passenger single as a ballast engine has always seemed puzzling, but it can now be seen as part of Stephenson & Co's campaign to promote their patent locomotive.

Just at the time the L&B directors were considering candidates for the position of Locomotive Power Contractor, Robert Stephenson persuaded W. & L. Cubitt & Co to take one of his firm's Patentee type as a works engine for their contract on the L&B. An engine (RS 123) which had just been completed for Belgium was quickly diverted south, arriving on Cubitt & Co's Berkhampstead contract on 28th December 1835. It was named *Harvey Combe* after the Master of the Old Berkeley Hunt, whose territory was disturbed by the building of the L&B in Hertfordshire. Stephenson was clearly trying to use this indirect means to show off his patent six-wheeled passenger engine to the directors in the hope of procuring orders for the Newcastle firm or, failing that, obtaining royalties if orders were placed elsewhere.

The artist John Bourne included *Harvey Combe* in his lithograph of a construction train at Berkhampstead dated 10th June 1837.

In October 1837 Robert Stephenson recommended that the L&B should buy it from Cubitt for use as a ballast engine; the Board agreed, but by the next meeting had second thoughts: *Harvey Combe* was too expensive, had been too long at work, and in any case was a passenger engine. But then it was revealed that it had already been taken away "by order of Mr Stephenson" and because of this Cubitt & Co had missed another chance to sell it. The Board, under a moral obligation, agreed to buy it on 25th October 1837 but only at a price reduced from the £900 originally asked. It had only done a year's work and "would be suitable for drawing ballast trains down the incline from Watford". It was working at Watford Heath by 31st October, when it was derailed on a temporary crossover.

The design was a development of the Planet type, with a trailing axle added behind the firebox for steadiness. It had outside wood and iron sandwich frames, flangeless driving wheels, horizontal cylinders and the four-handle loose eccentric gear. In 1838 a very full 64-page description of what appeared to be this engine was published, elaborately illustrated with large sheets of engravings. The text was written by William P. Marshall "under the direction of Mr Stephenson" and the engine was described as having been "made for Messrs Cubitt, the contractors for a part of the London & Birmingham Railway near Berkhampstead ... purchased by the railway company ... in which work it is now employed." Clearly this could only be *Harvey Combe* but the details given were, misleadingly, of a later and improved version of the same type with more boiler tubes and with the new four-eccentric large gab valve gear operated by a single reversing lever.

Fig. 8 *Harvey Combe* built by Robert Stephenson & Co in 1835. Used in line construction and as a ballast engine until 1840.

Dimensions of 2-2-2 *Harvey Combe*

Cylinders (2 inside)	12" x 18"
Boiler	
Diameter	3' 6"
Length of barrel	7' 6"
Heating surface	
Tubes (102, 1⅝" dia, 8' long)	345.98 sq ft
Firebox	
(3' 0½" long, 3' 4½" wide, 3' 2" high)	43.38 sq ft
Total	389.36 sq ft
Grate area	10.25 sq ft
Diameter of wheels	
Leading and trailing	3' 6"
Driving	5' 0"
Wheelbase	5' 0" + 5' 4" = 10' 4"
Weight	11 tons 17½ cwt

Locomotive for Camden incline

By May 1837 the first section of the railway was within a few weeks of opening but the Camden stationary engines were far from ready; in fact, the components had not yet been brought to the site and were to be further delayed by repairs to the Regent's Canal. Bury told the Locomotive Committee that until rope working commenced it would be necessary to use coupled engines as bankers. But none of the goods engines could be expected before the end of the year and the only coupled engines available were the puny ballast engines.

At the same time there was another crisis, a shortage of engines on the Blisworth contract, and on 19th May the L&B Secretary Richard Creed asked Robert Stephenson if he could "procure a locomotive and tender from his connection at Newcastle, within a month." Just then Robert Stephenson & Co were in the middle of an order for six 2-4-0 engines (works numbers 151-6) for America via the agents G. & A. Ralston. The first two had been sent to London en route for the Baltimore & Susquehanna Railroad in January and March and the third left Newcastle on 31st May. Meanwhile G. & A. Ralston had got themselves into financial difficulties and the latter part of their order was cancelled. Construction of the last two engines was abandoned while the fourth was sold to the Paris & Versailles left bank line as *La Victorieuse*. The third engine (153) arrived in London early in June and Stephenson appears to have transferred it to the L&B for delivery by canal to the Blisworth contract. "By chance" it was unloaded at Camden and remained there. The invoice was sent to Creed on 5th June and the London Committee recorded the payment of £1,750 to Stephenson on 12th July. One of Tayleur's ballast engines was sent to Blisworth in its place.

The 2-4-0 arrangement was a novelty and the engine was large and powerful for its time. The inside cylinders were horizontal, with the slide bars over the low leading axle; the valves were operated by the new four-eccentric gear with large gabs, controlled by a single reversing lever. Framing was the normal Stephenson outside sandwich type.

Fig. 9   Robert Stephenson & Co's 153; worked the trains on Camden incline during 1837. Later used as a ballast engine until 1843, and was probably named *Leviathan*.

Dimensions of Stephenson No 153 2-4-0

Cylinders (2 inside)	15" x 18"
Boiler	
Diameter	3' 9"
Length of barrel	8' 6"
Firebox (iron)	
Length	3' 2⅞"
Width	3' 5½"
Depth	3' 8¼"
Grate area	11.29 sq ft
Heating surface	
Tubes (145, 1⅝" dia, 8' 11½" long)	545.5 sq ft
Firebox	50.4 sq ft
Total	595.9 sq ft
Outside frame members	4" x 7½"
Diameter of wheels	
Leading	3' 2"
Coupled	4' 6"
Wheelbase	4' 10" + 6' 11" = 11' 9"
Weight	about 13 tons

This was the "large engine" referred to by Stephenson on 27th July 1837 when he was asked by the Locomotive Committee about "the future disposal of the *Wharncliffe* and *Skipwith* engines now at Camden." He said he intended "to retain the *Wharncliffe* and the large engine in London", to send the *Skipwith* to Wolverton and "Messrs Tayleur's engine to Blisworth."

Skipwith and another named *Firefly* are mentioned by Peter Lecount (1839) as engines used in the construction of the L&B. *Wharncliffe* (or *Lord Wharncliffe*) and *Firefly* appear in later records, but *Skipwith* does not and may have been renamed.

The first part of the line was opened on 20th July 1837. Lecount describes an average of fourteen trips from Euston "with the great engine made by Robert Stephenson & Company to work the trains up the inclination till the fixed engine was ready [which] amounted to 15 miles an hour with 70 tons, viz. 14 carriages and 148 passengers, at a steam pressure of 50 lbs per square inch."

After the Camden stationary engine began regular work in October, the 2-4-0 appears to have gone into the ballast stock and was probably named *Leviathan*.

Summary: Ballast Engines to 1837

1. London Committee:

Ordered	Maker	Cost	Delivered	Name
24/12/1834	Stephenson (111)	£1,124	4/35	
24/12/1834	Tayleur (18)	£1,170	7/35	Brockhall
12/1834	Stephenson (6)	£ 615	5-7/35	Phœnix
11/ 2/1836	Stephenson (141)	£1,230	c6/36	
11/ 2/1836	Stephenson (142)	£1,230	c8/36	
11/ 2/1836	Tayleur (43)	£1,250	10/2/37	
11/ 2/1836	Tayleur (44)	£1,250	10/2/37	
19/ 5/1837	Stephenson (153)	£1,750	6/37	Leviathan (?)
25/10/1837	Stephenson (123)	under £900	10/37	Harvey Combe

2. Birmingham Committee:

Ordered	Maker	Cost	Delivered	Name
1/1836	Tayleur (36)	£1,204	13/6/36 (London)	
1/1836	Tayleur (37)	£1,204	6/36	
1/1836	Tayleur (42)	£1,204	c12/36	
1/1836	Stephenson (140)	£1,177	c6/36	
1/1836	Mather, Dixon	£1,368	c9/36	
15/ 1/1836	Fenton, Murray & Jackson	£1,125	1/37	Leeds (?)
—	Rothwell?		c12/36	Hercules (?)
23/12/1836	Tayleur (61)	£1,430	9/37	
15/ 5/1837	Galloway	£ 400	5/37	Caledonian

Of the eighteen engines listed above, all but four (*Harvey Combe*, *Caledonian*, *Hercules* and Stephenson's 153) were standard 0-4-0s.

Fig. 10 Dr William Church's engine, built by John Inshaw in 1837. Used on L&B ballast trains during 1838. Exploded at Bromsgrove in 1840.

Ballast engines from 1837 to 1845

From January 1838 Dr William Church's engine worked on ballast trains on the L&B where it is said to have pulled 100 tons "with ease" and run light at 60mph, according to D. K. Clark. It was a quaint 2-2-0 well tank with a patent boiler, built by John Inshaw at Birmingham in 1837 for Samuel Aspinall Goddard to the design of Dr Church and had driving wheels of 6ft 2½in diameter and 11½in x 24in outside cylinders. It worked for a few months but was not taken by the L&B; it then went to the Grand Junction Railway where it was named *Victoria*. After standing out of use at Vauxhall for some months it was sent for trial on the Birmingham & Gloucester Railway in 1840 with the name *Surprise* but on 10th November its boiler exploded at Bromsgrove. Rebuilt with a normal boiler and renamed *Eclipse* it may have been given another trial on the B&G in 1844, and was at Camp Hill station on that line in 1850. About 1857/8 it was rebuilt as an 0-6-0 tank by the Swansea Vale Railway and was still working at Swansea in 1861.

Leviathan was involved in an accident at Harrow in May 1838 when "carrying Mr Bramah's men".

Lord Wharncliffe made trial trips on the Aylesbury branch in May 1839 before the line opened.

The Engineer's Department relinquished control of the ballast engines in August 1839, when they were placed under Edward Bury. Seven were needed daily on the line but such was their state that he had to use his own goods engines for the work; Nos 80, 81 and 88 put in a total of over 20,000 miles "ballasting" during the next four months.

In November 1840 there were nominally fourteen ballast engines in stock but only four of them were in working order. In December *Harvey Combe* was put to work on passenger trains and by March 1841 another (unidentified) ballast engine was got rid of, reducing the total to twelve.

In April 1841, with five of them under repair "from wear" and three "laid up", Bury recommended selling the twelve and replacing them with four new standard goods engines. The Board agreed to sell the old ballast stock but declined to buy new engines, saying that three or four of the goods engines could be appropriated as necessary. After this unhelpful response Bury kept the ballast engines at work and made no attempt to sell them, so there were still twelve in stock (seven of them in working order) in January 1842.

From March 1841 a series of reports lists the ballast engines by their names:

Date of report:	3/41	4/41	5/41	6/41	7/41	9/41	10/41	11/41	12/41	1/42
Osiris	in working order									
Leeds	in working order									
Vulcan	w/o	under repair*				in working order				
Blisworth	w/o	under repair				in working order				
Firefly	w/o	repair**		in working order						
Lord Wharncliffe	in working order									
Phœnix	w/o	repair				w/o		laid up		
Leviathan	under repair									
Brockhall	rep	in working order								
Avon	laid up									
Ashton	laid up									
Hercules	laid up									

* broken cylinder.
** new firebox.

In 1838 *Harvey Combe* had been used in tests by Nicholas Wood for his report to the Great Western directors; it performed well against the GWR's *North Star* and the published results showed the L&B engine was "very superior and more economical" according to letters in the railway papers in 1840. In December of that year it was taken out of the ballast stock and was tried on passenger trains for a few months. This might have been arranged as a response to the publicity, to appease the vocal Stephenson supporters on the Board, or maybe it was just Bury's way of demonstrating that a six-wheeled engine had no advantage over his four-wheelers. From the very detailed results which were published it is clear that *Harvey Combe* was a poor performer by comparison with the Bury engines. It was slower, consumed far more coke and oil and was heavier on repairs. It broke an eccentric rod in April 1841, but was back working as a traffic engine in June. Its last appearance in the monthly lists was on 8th September 1841; thereafter it disappears from L&B records and is listed neither as a ballast nor as a traffic engine.

Evidently it remained L&B property. Late in 1843, at the request of the contractor Thomas Jackson, it was altered at Wolverton to the 5ft gauge of the Northern & Eastern Railway; Jackson had a contract with that line and needed engines there. *Harvey Combe* was transferred to him on 15th December on payment of 5% interest on the valuation, on condition that he bought it outright at the end of his contract.

One other surplus ballast engine went to him at the same time. This was probably *Leviathan* whose last mention in the records is its derailment on 23rd August 1843; when running from Roade to the Watford ballast pits it collided with a "lurry" near Leighton. If this was in fact Stephenson's 153, Bury would be quite content to see the last of it and *Harvey Combe* simply to rid himself of six-wheeled engines, for as long as they remained on the L&B they would always have been a potential source of irritation to him.

On 10th November 1843 the Board ordered that the old engines "which were employed in the construction of a portion of the line and are now lying in the yard at Wolverton and the remainder of the useless materials accumulated there" were to be removed to Birmingham Goods Station and sold by auction. The auction was held on 20th February 1844, and according to the prospectus ten engines were involved:

Leeds - 12 x 18in cylinders, 4ft 6in wheels, copper firebox, brass tubes.

Ashton, Avon, Lord Wharncliffe, Osiris, Phœnix, Victoria, Watford - engines and tenders of similar construction and dimensions.

Hercules - 12 x 18in cylinders; two wheels 5ft 3in, two wheels 2ft 6in.

One engine boiler with wheels and axles.

Victoria and *Watford* appear here for the first time. Perhaps, like *Harvey Combe*, they had been lying out of use and for some reason were not included in the 1841 lists; perhaps they were old engines renamed.

Four ballast engines which are known to have been in use later were omitted from the auction, presumably because they were then in the possession of one of the contractors: *Blisworth, Brockhall, Firefly* and *Vulcan*.

The auction realised £2,253 14s 11d (£2,253.75) from "the sale of old engine stock and materials". *Victoria* was bought by the contractor Jackson but when his contract was terminated in April 1845 he still owed £150 for it, plus other larger sums, and it came back into the L&B ballast stock.

From later lists of ballast engines it looks as if *Ashton, Avon, Osiris, Phœnix* and *Watford* may have been sold at the auction or at about this time. One L&B engine with 12¼ x 18in cylinders, almost certainly one of these five, was sold on 3rd May 1845 and sent to Sheerness Dockyard where Maudslay, Sons & Field were preparing the two ships of Sir John Franklin's expedition to find the North-west Passage and circumnavigate America. The L&B engine was installed athwartships in the afterhold of HMS *Terror*, its driving axle extended aft to the screw propeller. *Terror* and *Erebus* (which was similarly equipped with locomotive No 4 from the London & Greenwich Railway) set sail on 19th May, but were abandoned in the ice of the Canadian Arctic in April 1848 and are believed to have sunk off King William Island somewhere about Lat 69°50'N and Long 98°47'W.

Names
Trying to link the names of the ballast engines to those known to have been ordered is difficult, but some clues can be given:

Lord Wharncliffe was named after Baron Wharncliffe of Wortley, Lord Privy Seal; a Stephenson engine?

Leeds was probably the Fenton, Murray & Jackson engine.

Vulcan was probably a Tayleur engine.

Ashton, Avon, Blisworth, Brockhall are all names of places in the Birmingham Committee's area. *Brockhall* was repaired and fitted with George Heaton's system of balance weights by William Middleton of the Vulcan Iron Foundry, Birmingham, paid for by the Birmingham Committee in April 1839.

Skipwith - a Stephenson engine? - was evidently named after Sir Grey Skipwith of Newbold near Rugby; he had been an MP for South Warwickshire and was a candidate for the North Warwickshire seat in the August 1837 election.

Firefly was repaired in September 1838 by Middleton and paid for by the Birmingham Committee.

Hercules was a 2-2-0 and was perhaps Rothwell's *Hercules* of 1836.

Victoria is an unlikely name before Queen Victoria's accession (21st June 1837); possibly it was the last Tayleur engine (61) of September 1837. An L&B engine with this name was repaired by the Horseley Co about August 1838 for the Birmingham Committee.

Ballast engines under Richard Madigan, 1845-9
A former employee of Jackson's, Richard Madigan, took over the working of the ballast engines and wagons on 1st March 1845. His stock consisted of seven engines: *Blisworth, Brockhall, Firefly, Leeds, Wharncliffe, Victoria* and *Vulcan* with a total valuation of £3,630.

On 21st January 1846 another engine *Contractor* was bought for him from Tayleur for £1,100. A possible candidate is that advertised by Tayleur in the *Railway Times* in November 1845: "Locomotive engine and tender to be disposed of with copper firebox and brass tubes, cylinders 13 inch by 18 inch, driving wheels coupled 4ft 6in diameter and tender 750 gallons."

In August 1846 Madigan was authorised to purchase two more ballast engines, but instead one engine, *Albert*, was bought for him for £700 from John Cummings, whose contract came to an end in September. This was probably one of the original ballast engines with a new name, bestowed at some time after February 1840 - the date of Queen Victoria's marriage to Prince Albert.

In April 1847 one of the L&B goods engines, Bury 0-4-0 No 71, was transferred to Madigan, at a valuation of £1,050.

The ballast engines were numbered in a list dated 1st June 1847:

No.	Name	In Madigan's possession	Acquired	Days of 10 hours at work
1	*Victoria*	27 months	3/45	484
2	*Wharncliffe*	27 "	3/45	341
3	*Blisworth*	27 "	3/45	506
4	*Brockhall*	27 "	3/45	609
5	*Contractor*	17 "	1/46	367
6	*Leeds*	27 "	3/45	453
7	*Camden* (late *Vulcan*)	27 "	3/45	53
8	*Albert*	9 "	9/46	208
9	*L&B No 71*	2 "	4/47	45
10	*Firefly*	27 "	3/45	none

E. T. Lane made a sketch of *Camden* in 1848-9, which confirms the general appearance of the former *Vulcan* as an 0-4-0 with heavily-bolted outside wooden frames. There is a typical Tayleur small dome just behind the chimney and a larger one over the firebox, with a Salter safety valve and a wide steam escape. The other boiler mountings shown on the original Tayleur drawing of 1836 - the manhole and the safety valve columns - do not appear, and there is a simple reversing lever on the right side of the footplate. The nameplate is on the middle boiler-ring.

Ballast engine No 1 *Victoria* was involved in a collision while shunting wagons at Linslade ballast pit sidings at 3am on 5th September 1848.

By 9th March 1848 Madigan's stock had increased to eleven engines and tenders by the addition of *Hercules* (without a number). The ex-L&B goods engine 71, now ballast engine No 9, had been named *Bury* in memory of the lately departed locomotive superintendent.

Madigan's contract was renewed on 31st May 1848, to run until the end of June 1851. His stock of locomotives was revalued at £9,450:

No.	Name		Value
1	*Victoria*		£700
2	*Wharncliffe*		£1,200
3	*Blisworth*		£700
4	*Brockhall*		£800
5	*Contractor*	& tenders	£1,200
6	*Leeds*		£1,150
7	*Camden*		£1,250
8	*Albert*		£750
9	*Bury*		£950
10	*Firefly*		£400
—	*Hercules*		£350

Early in June 1848 another goods engine was transferred to Madigan's stock, Bury 0-4-0 No 65; it was probably named *Kennedy*.

Also about this time he bought two engines, 96 and 97, from the London Brighton & South Coast Railway for £800 each (LB&SC minutes: sold on 17th May, paid for on 14th June 1848).

These were Bury, Curtis & Kennedy 0-4-0s delivered to the Joint Committee of the Croydon and South Eastern Railways on 13th December 1843 and 28th November 1844 as 38 *Gog* and 83 *Forester*. In 1845 they were allotted to the London & Brighton Railway, becoming their Nos 9 and 10, and LB&SC No 96 and 97 in 1848. Both had 5ft wheels but the cylinders of 96 were 14x20in (or perhaps 22in) while those of 97 were 14x24in.

Ballast engines from 1849

Madigan gave up his contract in July 1849 - he was in some financial difficulty - and on 15th August it was decided that the Works Committee would take over the ballasting and haulage of materials. Five of the ballast engines were to be considered as special ballast stock and "the remainder be devoted to traffic or sent to other Divisions of the Company's lines." In September it was resolved that the nine surplus engines should be handed over to the S Div Locomotive Dept.

Whatever happened to them it is certain that McConnell did not at once number them in the S Div stock.

On 7th November 1849 *Brockhall* and *Victoria* were sold to Thomas Brassey for £1,650 for the two. They had been valued in August at £1,900, but they were "of a class unsuitable for this line." In February-March 1850 *Brockhall* was back at Wolverton, being repaired at Brassey's expense.

On 5th December 1849 McConnell reported having hired *Kennedy* to Brassey for £50 per month and had offered to sell it to him for the surprisingly large sum of £1,250, but had received no reply. Some exchange of nameplates may have taken place and perhaps this engine was one of the two newer and bigger engines from the Brighton line.

On 7th October 1850 it was arranged for T. Smith to hire three ballast engines for twelve months for £1,200, with the option of outright purchase for £2,000 after that.

Two ballast engines were being repaired at Wolverton in July 1850 and two are recorded as additions to S Div working stock in the half-year ending May 1851 - probably between 8th January and 11th February. They may have been the former LB&SC engines; a June 1852 list of engines giving totals in each class and basic dimensions includes a solitary goods engine with 14x24in cylinders and 5ft wheels, probably 0-4-0 because of its boiler whose total heating surface was 761.46 sq ft. This engine is not mentioned anywhere else and is untraceable, but might be ex-LB&SC 97 taken over by the LNWR from Madigan in the settlement of his debt.

Madigan's other ex-LB&SC engine 96 was (according to a note in the LB&SC records) sold on 10th July 1852 to the Rhymney Iron Co, who scrapped it in 1859 following a boiler explosion; there is no mention of the sale in the LNWR minutes.

It seems likely that *Kennedy*, *Bury* and at least one of the LB&SC engines were taken into S Div stock in 1851-3 but the available evidence is sparse and confusing.

By the end of 1853 only two Bury-type 13in 0-4-0s remained in S Div working stock, Nos 61 and 82. According to James Bull, *Kennedy* and *Bury* were given these numbers; 61 went from stock in 1855/6 but 82 remained to the end of 1858 when it was sold to the contractor Tredwell for £375.

On 8th November 1853 *Leeds* and *Contractor* were sold to the Rhymney Railway for £600 each "to be put in order and delivered at Gloster". On 21st February 1854 it was reported that the Rhymney Railway Co were refusing to accept the engines "in their present condition" and on 7th March the English Copper Co's offer of £1,100 was accepted for the two engines at Gloucester.

A list of S Div engine accommodation dated 12th April 1855 includes five ballast engines "in steam". These were presumably the five set aside for ballast duties in August 1849.

By elimination, they were probably No 2 *Lord Wharncliffe*, No 3 *Blisworth*, No 7 *Camden*, No 8 *Albert* and No 10 *Firefly*.

The last record of the surviving ballast engines is a minute of 13th June 1856: "Mr McConnell reported that three old ballast engines, two boilers and one firebox, part of Madigan's stock, were useless except for scrap."

They were ordered to be scrapped.

Summary: Ballast Engines 1837-56

Name	Date acqd.	Type	D.W.	Cyls.	Maker	No. (1847)
Leviathan (? =)	6/1837	2-4-0	4' 6"	15x18"	RS 153 (6/37)	
Harvey Combe	10/1837	2-2-2	5' 0"	12x18"	RS 123 (10/37)	
Osiris		0-4-0	4' 6"	12x18"		
Phœnix	5-7/1835	0-4-0	4' 6"	12x18"	RS 6 (8/32)	
Avon		0-4-0	4' 6"	12x18"		
Ashton		0-4-0	4' 6"	12x18"		
Watford		0-4-0	4' 6"	12x18"		
Hercules	?12/1836	2-2-0	5' 3"	12x18"	?Rothwell	—
Victoria	by 1838	0-4-0	4' 6"	12x18"		1
Lord Wharncliffe	by 7/1837	0-4-0	4' 6"	12x18"	?RS	2
Blisworth						3
Brockhall	7/1835	0-4-0	4' 6"	12x18"	VF 18 (7/35)	4
Contractor	1/1846				VF	5
Leeds (? =)	1/1837	0-4-0	4' 6"	12x18"	FM&J (1/37)	6
Vulcan/Camden		0-4-0	4' 6"	12x18"	?VF	7
Albert	9/1846					8
L&B 71 *Bury*	4/1847	0-4-0	5' 0"	13x18"	EB (5/39)	9
Firefly	by 1837					10
L&B 65 *Kennedy*	6/1848	0-4-0	5' 0"	13x18"	EB (1/39)	?
LB&SC 96	6/1848	0-4-0	5' 0"	14x20"	BC&K (12/43)	?
LB&SC 97	6/1848	0-4-0	5' 0"	14x24"	BC&K (11/44)	?

Disposal

No.	Name	Remarks
	Leviathan	? Sold to Thos Jackson for his N&ER contract 12/43
	Harvey Combe	Sold to Thos Jackson for his N&ER contract 12/43
	Osiris	? Sold 2/44 }
	Phœnix	? Sold 2/44 }
	Avon	? Sold 2/44 } ? One of these to Sir John Franklin's
	Ashton	? Sold 2/44 } Expedition, in HMS *Terror*, 5/45
	Watford	? Sold 2/44 }
—	*Hercules*	? Scr c/50
1	*Victoria*	Sold to Thos Brassey 11/49
2	*Lord Wharncliffe*	? Scr /56
3	*Blisworth*	? Scr /56
4	*Brockhall*	Sold to Thos Brassey 11/49
5	*Contractor*	Sold to English Copper Co 3/54
6	*Leeds*	Sold to English Copper Co 3/54
7	*Camden*	? Scr /56
8	*Albert*	? Scr /56
9	*Bury*	Returned to S Div goods stock in /51 and reno'd 82 in /52-3
10	*Firefly*	? Scr /56
?	*Kennedy*	Returned to S Div goods stock in /51 and reno'd 61 in /52-3
?	ex-LB&SC 96	? To S Div goods stock 1/51. Sold to Rhymney Iron Co 7/52; boiler exploded 18/8/59, scrapped.
?	ex-LB&SC 97	? To S Div goods stock 1/51. Withdrawn /52 or /53

LONDON & BIRMINGHAM RAILWAY
ORIGINAL ENGINES 1837-41

1. Bury 2-2-0 Passenger Engines with 12-inch cylinders Nos 1-36, 49-52, Aylesbury Railway 1 & 2

Bury's drawings for the first passenger engines were approved by the Locomotive Committee on 20th June 1836 when he recommended that a maximum of 36 engines to this design should be contracted for without delay. Orders for passenger engines were placed as follows

Maker	Ordered	No.	Price each	For delivery
Mather, Dixon	24/6/1836	6	£1,120	6/37-12/37
Benjamin Hick	30/6/1836	6	£1,120	2/37-10/37
Peter Rothwell	22/7/1836	6	£1,120	4/37-9/37
Haigh Foundry	23/7/1836	3	£1,120	3/37-12/37
R. & W. Hawthorn	1/8/1836	6	£1,120	3/37-2/38
Edward Bury	19/8/1836	6	£1,120	by 1/38

Carriage to London was an extra £20 each in the case of the Hawthorn engines.

With these 33 engines ordered, the Committee was "anxious to leave a few of the passenger engines open for a contract in London" but Maudslay, Sons & Field of Lambeth did not tender until almost three months after receiving the drawings, when they offered to build three engines for £1,350 each. This was declined on 12th December, and Bury's offer was accepted:

Maker	Ordered	No.	Price each
Edward Bury	13/2/1837	3	£1,120

These contracts were for engines only, the tenders were obtained separately; Bury provided the drawings for these at the end of July 1836, and offered to build them for £150 each. Twenty were ordered from "respectable manufacturers." Others were ordered from Bury at £180 each on 12th February 1838.

Makers' works numbers have been published for most of these engines in the past, but only those of Hawthorn's six - 220-5 - can be substantiated.

Engines were given running numbers at the various makers' works; each fitted brass numerals to the chimney fronts and oval brass numberplates (supplied by Whinfield & Co) to the boiler sides. The number scheme

Fig. 11   Bury's original L&B passenger engine, 1837. 12in x 18in cylinders, 5ft 6in dia driving wheels.

adopted was:

Engines	Maker	Engines	Maker
1 to 9:	Edward Bury	22 to 24:	Haigh Foundry
10 to 15:	Benjamin Hick	25 to 30:	Peter Rothwell
16 to 21:	R. & W. Hawthorn	31 to 36:	Mather, Dixon

With this scheme of numbering Bury blithely ignored the directors' order of 13th February 1837 and a reminder of 13th November about the "necessity" of giving a London-built engine the magic number 1.

The first engines to arrive were from Bury & Co. James Kennedy tried out No 1 on 15th June 1837, taking eight wagons the thirty miles from Liverpool to Manchester in 1½ hours and returning with a fast train of nine carriages in 70 minutes, "not having had assistance" on the 1 in 96 Sutton incline. Nos 1 and 2 were sent off by canal on 26th June. Next came an engine from R. & W. Hawthorn. A strike had delayed construction but their first, No 16, left the Tyne for the Thames on 5th July aboard the *Esk*. These three were the only train engines in stock when the first part of the London & Birmingham Railway was opened on Thursday, 20th July. Benjamin Hick's first, No 10, was sent from Manchester "by Pickford's canal conveyance" on 22nd July and arrived in London on 28th.

Haigh Foundry's first engine, No 22, was working on the line by 27th August; their second arrived at Lower Place, Willesden, on 19th September and their third about the end of the month. No 31, the first from Mather, Dixon & Co, arrived in October.

By 23rd November ten engines had been received (Nos 1, 2, 10/6/7/8, 22/3/4, 31) and four more (11/9, 25, 32) were expected shortly. Bury said that these, plus the other two from Hawthorn (20/1), would be sufficient for the London end and that he proposed to send all the others to Birmingham.

Hick's No 11 was sent off by canal in December and on 14th January 1838 Hawthorn wrote that No 20 was "ship'd on board the *Halcyon* and will sail from here whenever the Wind is favourable which we trust will be in a few days." It was on the line by 10th February. The last engine of their order, No 21, was given a successful works trial on 24th February when it was expected to be shipped to London on 28th.

The engines for the Birmingham end of the line were sent by the Grand Junction Railway which had been opened in the previous July. Some, or all, of Hick's No 13, Rothwell's 26/7/9 and Mather, Dixon's 33/4/5 were held up by the partial collapse on 10th March of the short tunnel at Dutton on the GJR, when the line was blocked until 21st March.

There was no service on the isolated northern end of the L&B until 9th April 1838, when the line was opened between Birmingham and Rugby; on 24th August 1838 engines working on this section were Nos 5, 6, 12/3, 26/7/9 and 33-36.

The last of the 36 engines ordered in 1836-7 was on the line by October 1838.

Bury's plan in February 1837 had been to work the line with 36 passenger and 30 coupled engines but he considered that some of the coupled engines would be necessary for passenger trains. By February 1838, with practical experience of operating the railway and with a much heavier traffic than predicted, he revised his estimate of the number of passenger engines that would be required. Tenders were accepted for another fifteen to the same design as before on 30th March and orders were placed:

Maker	Ordered	No.	Price each	Delivery
Edward Bury	30/3/1838	9	not known	not known
Benjamin Hick	14/5/1838	6	£1,235	by 3/39

In response to Bury's request to the Board on 14th December 1838 for "one or two" engines for the Aylesbury line, a further order was placed:

Maker	Ordered	No.	Price each
Benjamin Hick	7/1/1839	2	£1,250, tender £180

The contracts for these seventeen engines became the subject of some revision in August and September. By then, the Board having agreed with the Post Office to speed up the mail trains and with his working contract ended, Bury proposed that the engines on order should have 13in cylinders. He visited Bolton but finding Hick's were too near completion to be altered he suggested that his firm build all seventeen with 13in cylinders and that Hick's engines be sent to another railway "in fulfilment of engagements which he expects to effect". This was the Midland Counties, which had ordered engines from Bury and Hick, but unfortunately the MCR Board now also wanted 13in engines. In the end Hick supplied six 12in engines to the L&B while Bury & Co turned out twelve as 13in Mail Engines, to be described later.

The six engines from Hick (No 49-52 and Aylesbury Railway Nos 1 and 2) did not arrive until January-March 1840.

Dimensions

Cylinders (2 inside)	12"x18"
Boiler	
Diameter	3' 2"
Length of barrel	8' 0"
Pitch	5' 5"
Heating surface	
Tubes (86, 2¼" dia, 8' 5" long)	426.33 sq ft
Firebox	37.64 sq ft
Total	463.97 sq ft
Boiler pressure	50lb/sq in
Diameter of wheels	
Leading	*4' 0"
Driving	5' 6"
Wheelbase	5' 6"
Length over buffers (engine)	17' 9"
Weight	
On leading axle	3 tons 19.25 cwt
On driving axle	5 tons 17.5 cwt
Total	9 tons 16.75 cwt
Tender (4 wheel) capacity	coke 21cwt
	water 700 gal

*Leading wheels of Nos 31-36 (Mather, Dixon): 4' 6" dia.

These engines naturally followed Bury's well-known precepts - inside iron bar frame, round dome-top firebox, four wheels - but the design itself was a new one, intended specifically for a long main line railway.

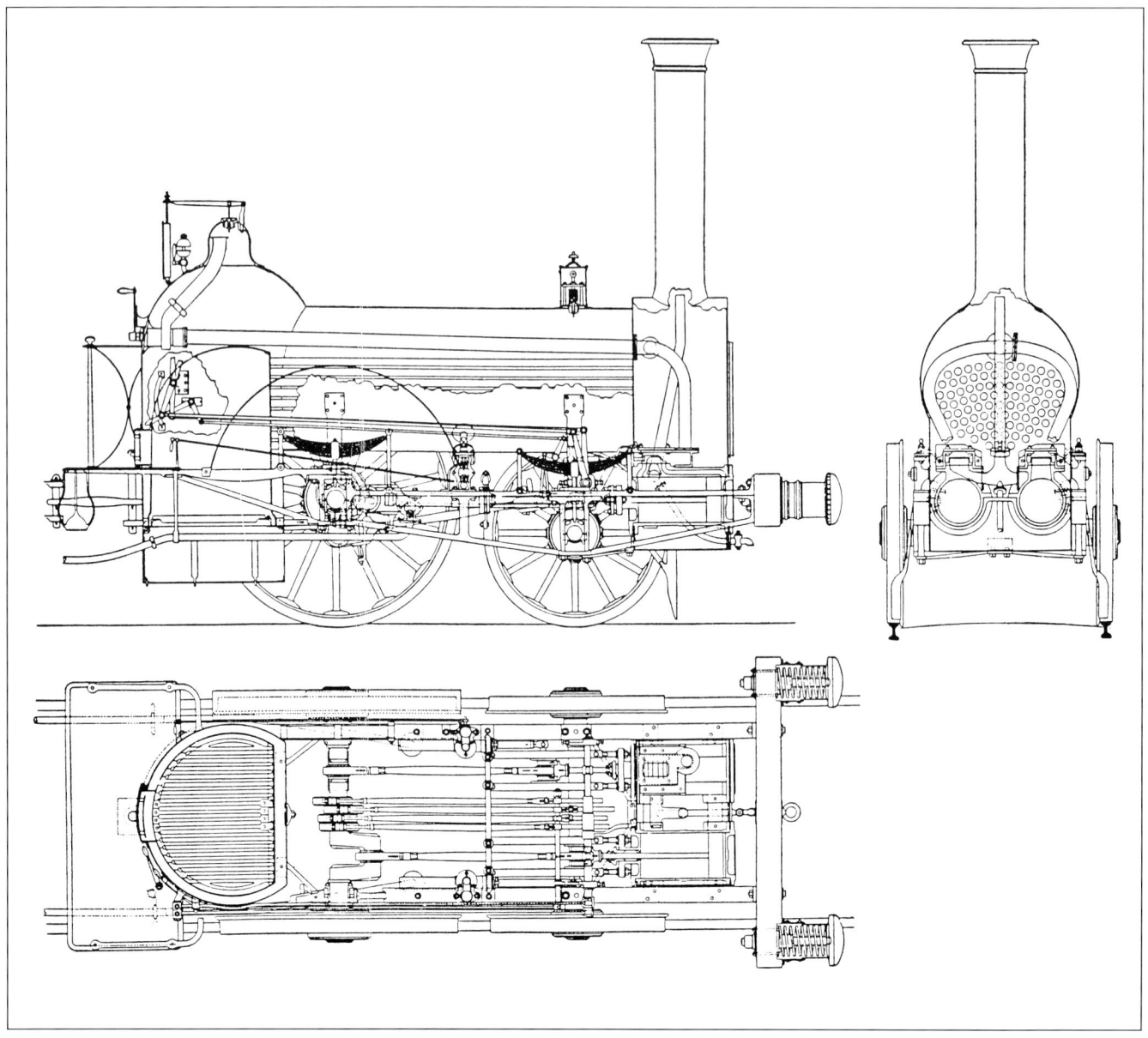

Fig. 12   Sectional views of Bury 2-2-0.

Bury's Specification

The specification stipulated that the framing was to be of best hammered wrought iron with all pins of joints to be hardened steel; the crank axle to be of Backbarrow iron, cut from one solid piece, and the straight axle of best scrap iron. Each cast-iron wheel-nave was to be secured to the axle by two 1in square steel keys at right angles; spokes were to be wrought iron, fitted into the nave and riveted to the inner tyre, which was to be $\frac{5}{8}$in thick best Staffordshire iron; the outer tyre rolled in one piece of the very best Low Moor or Bowling iron, finished $1\frac{5}{8}$in thick, shrunk on and turned. The boiler and firebox were to be made entirely with the best Yorkshire plates, Bowling or Low Moor, the firebox being welded so as not to have rivets or lap joints exposed to the fire. Plate thicknesses were to be: firebox: $\frac{3}{8}$in; tubeplates $\frac{1}{2}$in; barrel $\frac{5}{16}$in. A $\frac{5}{8}$in fusible plug was to be riveted in the centre of the firebox crown. Tubes were to be 2in inside diameter of best rolled sheet brass, secured with steel hoops at the firebox end and iron hoops at the smokebox. The smokebox and chimney to be of Staffordshire iron sheets, with a brass frame around the smokebox door and a brass handle on the small door in the middle of the large one.

Boiler lagging was to consist of at least three thicknesses of felt, with a thin sheet of lead 3ft 6in wide over this on top of the barrel, and wooden strips $\frac{1}{2}$in thick fastened by four boiler bands, with a $2\frac{1}{2}$in brass strip under the front hoop to cover the rivet heads at the junction with the smokebox.

The outer firebox was to be surrounded by wooden lagging, fastened by two hoops on its lower part and covered with copper sheet above; an iron sheet, 6ft by 2ft 3in surrounding the firehole door, with another iron sheet under the wooden lagging, 6in wide at the sides and 10in above. There were to be three brass water gauge cocks, one glass water gauge with a lampstand; a brass-covered lock-up safety valve; a powerful whistle.

The single slide valves were to be brass and the sprung pistons of gunmetal with cast-iron packing and there was to be an oil cup at the end of each cylinder. Two pumps, one attached to each crosshead, were to be made of good brass, with Mackintosh's hose pipes with brass couplings between engine and tender.

All iron working parts were to be case-hardened and furnished with oil cups. The buffers were to be spirally sprung, and mounted on the "front wood guard" which was to have a 2in x $\frac{3}{4}$in steel drawbar, chain and shackle at its centre. At the tender end the coupling was a drawpin and loop.

Each engine was to be finished with two coats of paint and two of best varnish, and have a complete set of screw keys.

Spare parts were to include, for every three engines supplied, a spare firebox and one set of axles and wheels.

Each engine was to be guaranteed to run 1,000 miles within its first 14 days with no work allowed except the tightening of cotters; an engineman was to be sent with every engine to start it in working order.

Drawings were to be "accurately followed in every part, no deviation whatever can be allowed and in case any further description is wanted ... Mr Edward Bury ... will give any information required."

Despite the unambiguous specification and the provision of templates and complete sets of full-size drawings, on his monthly visits to the manufacturers Bury soon found that things were not going according to plan: engines were being built with variations. In March 1837 he ordered inaccurate parts to be removed from Mather, Dixon's engines and in the same month halted work on the eccentrics of one of Haigh Foundry's engines. In April he found deviations from the specification in engines at Hawthorn's, but had to overlook this because of the urgency.

Later he was to complain that - with the exception of Hick's No 15, which was extremely well made, and Hawthorn's, which were less inaccurate than the others - the engines differed not only from the drawings and specification but from each other, even from others by the same maker. The cranks in Mather, Dixon engines were $\frac{3}{8}$in too large; the leading wheels were 6in oversize; the fireboxes were too small.

The worst offenders were the three engines from Haigh Foundry. Their No 22 had framing so inaccurate it had to be cut in three places, necessitating a new set of pumps; the same engine needed a new firebox and tubes after only 14,000 miles. Haigh Foundry said their No 23 had worked satisfactorily for a week on the North Union Railway in August 1837 before delivery to the L&B and they objected to the reports about their engines which were "injurious to our professional reputation". They said the "supposed defects" in their engines included lead instead of double brass joints in the pumps and a different form of joint between the cylinders and the frame, different positioning of the spokes in the wheel tyre and the general construction of the wheels. "A bracket or flange was omitted in our pumps - we have remedied this defect by attaching a substantial iron one." Within a month of delivery both pumps on No 23 failed while it was working the 5.00pm Down train on 15th October, causing a delay at Watford Heath; the following day the 7.00pm Up train was stopped at Kensal Green because No 23 lost its steam - "a screw in the boiler at the smokebox end" had worked loose. The disagreement between Haigh and Bury eventually went to the arbitration of Joshua Field of Maudslay's; the outcome has not survived, but Bury later found that Maudslay's goods engines were themselves badly made.

The boiler had a small lock-up safety valve towards the front end, and a spring balance valve on a small brass dome on top of the domed firebox. Steam was collected in the small dome, passed to a plug regulator just behind the footplate control handle and thence through a $3\frac{1}{2}$in diameter pipe running the length of the boiler to the smokebox where it divided into two, one pipe to each valve chest.

Each row of boiler tubes was arranged in an arc, with the middle tubes higher than those at the sides; this was intended to promote a more rapid circulation, and would also prevent any of the tubes being uncovered when the water was thrown to the side by centrifugal force on sharp bends.

The pumps delivered through clack valves low down and half way along the boiler sides.

The firebox was in the form of a vertical cylinder, with a flat tube plate so that the grate was in the shape of a **D**. The middle four grate-bars were loosely hooked at the front end and could be dropped. The inner firebox was made of iron, for lightness, and had a domed top. The only stays were between the flat plates at the front of the firebox, everywhere else the strength of the firebox came from the curvature of the plates. The domed top of the outer firebox, notwithstanding its apparent prominence in most illustrations, rose less than nine inches above the lagged boiler barrel in these first engines.

The top member of the iron frame was a rectangular bar, 4in wide by $1\frac{3}{4}$in deep; the bottom truss was a rod of circular section, $1\frac{3}{4}$in diameter. The separate components were held together by cotters and bolts; the axle horns were bolted between the upper and lower frame bars. The two sides of the frame were joined in five places: at the back by a large C-shaped member which encompassed the firebox; amidships by a transverse $1\frac{3}{4}$in rod which supported the ends of the slide bars; by two $3\frac{3}{4}$in x 1in straps which passed under and supported the cylinders; and at the front by the 14in x 7in oak bufferbeam. The boiler was supported by two brackets on each side, one over each axle bearing; another four brackets supported the firebox. It has often been said (following D. K. Clark) that Bury's engines were at fault in that the cylinders had no direct connection with the frame and that the strain was passed via the smokebox to the boiler. This is quite untrue; the cylinders *were* bolted to the cross-members of the frame, and as Bury said in 1840: "the force of the engine is exerted directly through the line of the framing, and thus any strain is diverted from the boiler." The drawbar was attached to the rear frame member. By contrast, the drawbar in Stephenson and other contemporary engines was riveted directly to the back of the firebox.

The valve gear had four fixed eccentrics, a recently introduced feature. All four lay between the cranks and were fixed to give a cut-off $2\frac{3}{4}$in before the end of the piston stroke. Control was by three levers on the right side of the footplate. The lowest of these was the disengaging lever by which the fore ends of one pair of

Fig. 13 A contemporary impression of No 34. Built by Mather, Dixon & Co in 1838.

eccentric rods could be raised clear, while the other pair was lowered so that their hooks engaged with cranks on a transverse rocking shaft which worked the valve rods. The other two levers or 'gearing handles' were connected via the rocking shaft to the valve rods, which could be moved into position to receive the eccentric rod hooks. The 'rocking shaft' was actually a solid shaft within a sleeve; the internal shaft worked the left valve, while the hollow shaft worked the right valve. The two gearing handles, each linked to one of these shafts, rocked constantly back and forth while the engine was in motion.

The wheels had solid round wrought-iron spokes, with turned conical ends keyed into holes bored in the cast-iron nave, and forged T heads which were riveted to the ⅝in thick wrought-iron wheel rim. On this was shrunk a 1⅝in tyre, 4½in wide. The spokes were staggered so that from the rim they inclined inwards and outwards alternately to the back and front of the nave.

At first there were no splashers, but plain brass mudguards were fitted over the driving wheels within a very short time. Similar splashers were fitted over the leading wheels from about 1840. Originally the footplate was protected only by a small wrought-iron fence, but this was boxed-in in the 1840s.

The tender was mounted on a frame of oak or ash, bolted together and with iron corners. The four wheels were cast-iron, 3ft diameter on 3¼in axles. Outside the tender on the right side a long diagonal handle worked brakes on all four wheels.

They were sturdy and compact engines and were not particularly small for the period. Their driving wheels were larger than those of contemporary Grand Junction or Liverpool & Manchester engines, but because of the absence of the heavy outside frame, to some contemporary onlookers they had a 'wiry' or 'spidery' appearance and were regarded as top-heavy.

Practice and Performance

At the beginning there was an unexpectedly heavy traffic of sightseers and a few engines were permanently coupled together: Nos 1 & 24 and 8 & 32 were recorded in March and April 1838. At the end of May it was decided to divide the trains when they were too heavy for one engine. This seems to mark the ending of the permanently coupled engines, but it was by no means the end of double-heading.

In November 1837 Bury had to issue an order to enginemen to use the brakes instead of throwing the engine into reverse when stopping.

A series of train timings in 1837-9 shows trains of between seven and fifteen vehicles with one engine, but longer trains were double-headed. Average speeds were from 17mph, on 26th July 1837 (within a week of the opening day) with a heavily-laden fourteen-carriage train of sightseers (62 tons), to 29mph on 12th December 1839 when No 18 took thirteen carriages (48 tons) from Tring to Wolverton with one stop; the highest speed on this journey was 41mph running down the 1 in 440 approaching Wolverton. The average speed of 22 trains, six of them double-headed, was 24mph. The highest speed recorded was on 6th August 1839, when a 62-ton double-headed train from Birmingham composed of three 1st class carriages, five 2nd class, five horseboxes and eight trucks went up the 1 in 849 through Stowe Hill Tunnel at over 46mph.

Lecount writing in 1839 describes a run on 3rd October 1838, when No 7 *with only one cylinder working* covered ten miles in ten minutes start to stop. This was presumably a trial with a light engine; high train speeds were discouraged as wasteful while Bury's contract was in force, the terms being based on an average of 22½mph.

Secretary Richard Creed timed his train between Watford and Camden on 22nd October 1838 at a speed of 41¼mph. He complained to Bury: "Is not this *rather* fast for night work?" Bury agreed that it was far too fast.

In September 1842, with higher speeds required, trains hauled by 12in 2-2-0 engines were double-headed when the number of carriages exceeded twelve.

The Aylesbury Railway was opened in June 1839, but the two engines allocated to it had not yet been delivered; No 17 spent most of the next six months on the branch assisted by Nos 1 and 23. Other engines which did occasional work there in that period were Nos 2, 15, 18, 21 and 25.

In the year 1839 engines 1-36 averaged a mileage of 12,965 each. The Hick and Hawthorn engines were about average, Rothwell and Mather, Dixon slightly below average, but the Haigh Foundry engines were well below, 18% down. By contrast the engines built by Bury had a mileage 26% above average. The amount spent on repairs per mile told a similar story, with engines by Bury, Hick and Hawthorn costing significantly less than the others, with the three by Haigh Foundry as the worst.

Average coke consumption in 1840 was 36.575 lb per mile and 0.913 lb per ton per mile.

In 1851, probably because of better quality coke by then, average consumption was 31.18 and 0.779 lb respectively.

Fig. 14   The remains of one of the original 12in engines in Crewe Works in 1879. Presumably this was one of the engines used as stationary boilers at Wolverton; the connecting rods, valve gear and the lower components of the frame have been removed. The locomotive retains its original 5ft 6in wheelbase and had been withdrawn from working stock in the 1840s. The elusive No 27, perhaps?   *(LNWR photo)*

Fig. 15   The engine in Fig. 14 as sketched by a Crewe draughtsman.

Accidents

Because of inexperience and the unsettled state of the road, many mishaps befell the first engines in their early months.

On 31st July 1837 No 16 (Hawthorn) was in collision at Boxmoor with No 10 (Hick) which was on its first day's duty with a test train of stone wagons. Next it was derailed at the points at Chalk Farm bridge when on the last Up train on 7th August 1837. In the evening of Saturday 4th November 1837 it ran off the line in Kenton cutting with an Up train. Driver George Robson and Hawthorn's mechanic Chicken, who was on the engine, were both drunk, the train had been going at 40mph over unsettled track. Robson was horribly injured; No 16 was badly damaged. The same Mr Chicken was on the tender of No 18 (Hawthorn) on the 2.00pm Down train which ran for several miles at 34mph on 20th November; he was promptly barred from riding on any of the engines.

Driver Forsyth was sacked for derailing No 22 (Haigh) at Harrow on 27th August 1837, causing delays to the evening Up and Down trains.

On 5th November 1838 Driver William Hogg was on No 14 (Hick) with the 5.00pm Down train; he had just left Tring Cutting when he collided with a ballast engine whose driver was so drunk (according to Hogg) that he did not know which line he was on. Driver Hogg and his fireman escaped by jumping off, but No 14 had to go into the shops for two months to be fitted with a new firebox and a new tender tank.

No 15 (Hick), a Camden engine with Driver William Mills, was on the 11.30pm Up mail train on 8th November 1838 when about three miles south of Leighton the embankment subsided under it. The engine capsized; repairs were completed at Camden by 8th December, but three days later it was again derailed on the points at Chalk Farm bridge.

This was not the end of its troubles. Less than two years later, on 12th November 1840, it was rammed by an Up goods train at Harrow. It had been standing light in the station, waiting to take supplies to men clearing the line after a wagon derailment near Kenton, when the train - 27 wagons double-headed by No 1 (Bury) and 0-4-0 No 82 - passed a red signal and ran into No 15 before it could draw clear. Fireman Finch jumped off and escaped; Driver Bradburn had left the engine shortly before the accident. Fireman Dawson on No 1, which had been returning to Camden after repair at Wolverton, and Driver Simpson on No 82 were both killled.

No 15 was in another accident at Harrow, on 25th September 1845, involving runaway wagons as described on p44; on that occasion the engine escaped serious damage.

2. Bury 2-2-0 Passenger Engines with 13-inch cylinders
Mail Engines Nos 37-48, 53-58

Seventeen more 12in passenger engines were on order when Bury's contract was terminated in July 1839. In August he suggested that they should have cylinders of 13in diameter; this was agreed but the engines being built by Hick & Co were too near completion to be altered. Bury & Co built twelve instead of the nine ordered; the first two arrived in October, with 13in cylinders and the same boiler as the 0-4-0 goods engines. They were an immediate success and were put on the mail trains, the prestige expresses which carried only mail and first-class passengers for a half-crown (12.5p) supplement, and as a result became known as the Mail Engines.

Ten were delivered by April 1840 and the last two in October. Numbers were 37-48.

Dimensions

Cylinders (2 inside)	13" x 18"
Boiler	
Diameter	3' 4"
Length of barrel	8' 8"
Heating surface	
Tubes (96, 2¼" dia, 9' long)	508.89 sq ft
Firebox	43.00 sq ft
Total	551.89 sq ft
Diameter of wheels	
Leading	4' 3"
Driving	5' 6"
Wheelbase	6' 0"
Weight	
On leading axle	4 tons 19 cwt
On driving axle	6 tons 11 cwt
Total	11 tons 10 cwt

The boiler was larger and pitched higher (perhaps to 5ft 8in) than on the 12in engines. The editor of *Herapath's Railway Magazine* inspected No 41 at Camden Town in 1841 and was impressed that it was much higher than the 12in engines.

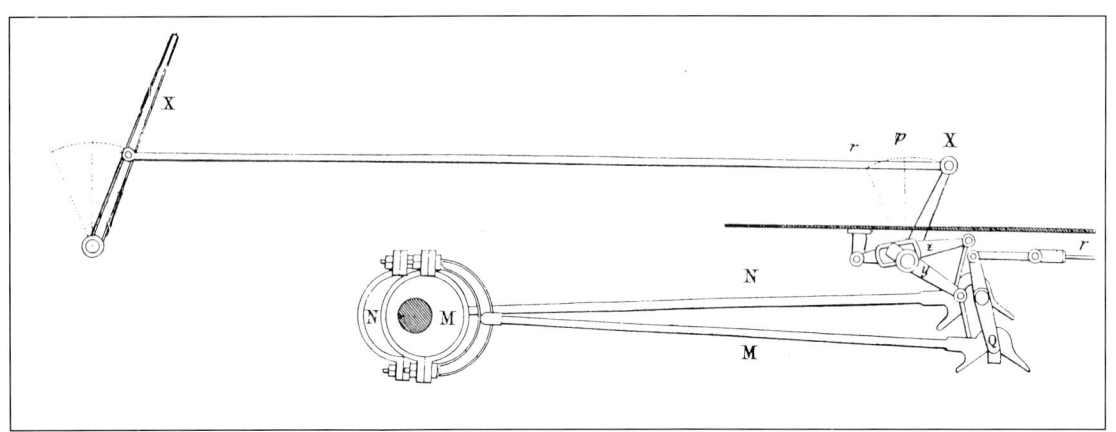

Fig. 16 Bury's large gab valve gear operated by a single reversing lever; introduced in January 1840.

The valve gear of the first three, 37/8/9, was the same as that on the 12in passenger engines, with a disengaging lever and two gearing handles on the footplate, but a simplified control system was adopted on 40 and the subsequent Mail Engines. In this, one two-position lever did all the work required for reversing the engine. It was mounted on the right of the footplate; by one movement through its quadrant it operated a system of levers which simultaneously raised one pair of eccentric rods while lowering the other pair. The fore-end of each eccentric rod had a downward facing gab, a ∧-shaped notch whose jaws were sufficiently wide to engage a pin on the rocking shaft lever at any valve position. As the gab was lowered, the moving diagonal of its inside edge acted on the pin to move the valve to the correct position.

On 6th May 1840, with ten of them in stock, the Locomotive Committee reported. "It is hardly necessary to remark that the Mail Engines which have been furnished by Mr Bury are the most perfect which have yet been used upon the line, the manner in which they have performed the work for which they were intended is a sufficient proof of their excellence." Bury himself said: "great care and pains have been taken to arrive as much at perfection as possible, and I do not assert too much when I state that the Mail Engines are without exception the best yet set to work on any line of Railway." He said that apart from the first three, in which there was a difference in the valve gear, all parts of the engines were interchangeable.

A further batch of 13in Mail Engines was ordered for working the Midland Counties Railway's through mail trains south of Rugby. On 27th March 1840 the Board invited tenders from the firms of Hawthorn, Bury, Nasmyth and Hick for six more "like Bury's No 45" which was the latest of the class, just delivered. Nasmyth, Gaskell & Co, of the Bridgewater Foundry, Patricroft replied at once. They were ignorant of the specific nature of No 45, they wrote, but had already turned out engines of the Bury type for the London & South Western and the Midland Counties railways; if the proposed engine was uncoupled their price was £1,160, if coupled, £1,210. Tenders were £150 each (including a brake and tool box). Delivery would be in six months.

When he received the L&B reply that Bury's 45 was *not* like the LSWR or MCR engines, James Nasmyth himself travelled to Birmingham station, inspected No 45 and repeated his offer of £1,160. Bury & Co's tender was £1,300, but Nasmyth's seemed such a bargain that on 24th April the Board accepted it.

This decision upset Bury. Having designed and produced such a fine machine, he was dismayed at the prospect of another firm turning out an inferior copy; Nasmyth, Gaskell & Co had built only about sixteen engines up to that time, and the inaccurate versions of his earlier engines, badly made by other hands, were fresh in his mind. "Though other makers might copy No 45 with great exactness" he told the Board "yet there are numerous points which all require to be correctly adjusted to produce the greatest effect, and which experience alone can furnish the necessary guide for." There was evidence that his engines were better made; his Nos 1 and 7 had been retubed after running 36,490 and 34,000 miles, while the average for engines by other makers was 29,000, and only Hawthorn's No 17 had exceeded 31,000 before retubing.

On 6th May he offered to lower his price to £1,250 "feeling quite assured that the system of uniformity cannot possibly be carried out by having Engines made by different individuals however anxious they may be to adhere strictly to drawings and specifications." Two days later the Board gave the order for the six engines to Bury. Nasmyth's contract was annulled, with the polite lie that "Mr Bury had the option" and with compensation in the form of an order for a 6hp engine, a pump and 100 yards of 5in pipe for Wolverton Works.

Orders for 13in Mail Engines:

Maker	Ordered	Number	Price each
Edward Bury	30/3/1838 as 12"	9	
	8/1839 revised as 13"	12	£1,545 including tender
Edward Bury	8/5/1840 for MCR trains	6	£1,250

The six engines for the Midland Counties mail trains were delivered between February and June 1841, and were numbered 53-8.

The Mail Engines kept time with sixteen carriages in all weathers and could take eighteen when it was fine.

Whishaw timed No 39 on two trains on 12th December 1839 and 22nd February 1840. On the former occasion, when the engine was only days old, the train left London with eight coaches, a travelling post office and an empty truck (total weight 43.2 tons) and reached Tring in 1 hour 19 minutes, including three stops. The average speed was 25½mph, with a top speed of almost 47mph at Boxmoor.

John Herapath described his journey on the footplate of No 41 on the morning mail train on 15th November 1841. He said this engine ran the Up night mail and the Down morning mail between Camden and Wolverton every day, and had no material repairs for eight months; an average 12 cwt of coke was burned on each trip. A 'ballast gauge' had been fitted to the engine in the form of a bar hanging low down between the leading wheels; when struck by too-high ballast it sounded a whistle. Herapath concluded: "As far as I have seen, Bury's engines do not deserve the character given them of being 'top heavy'."

The average coke consumption in 1840 was 34.687 lb per mile and 0.726 lb per ton per mile. In 1851 the average was 32.04 and 0.74 lb.

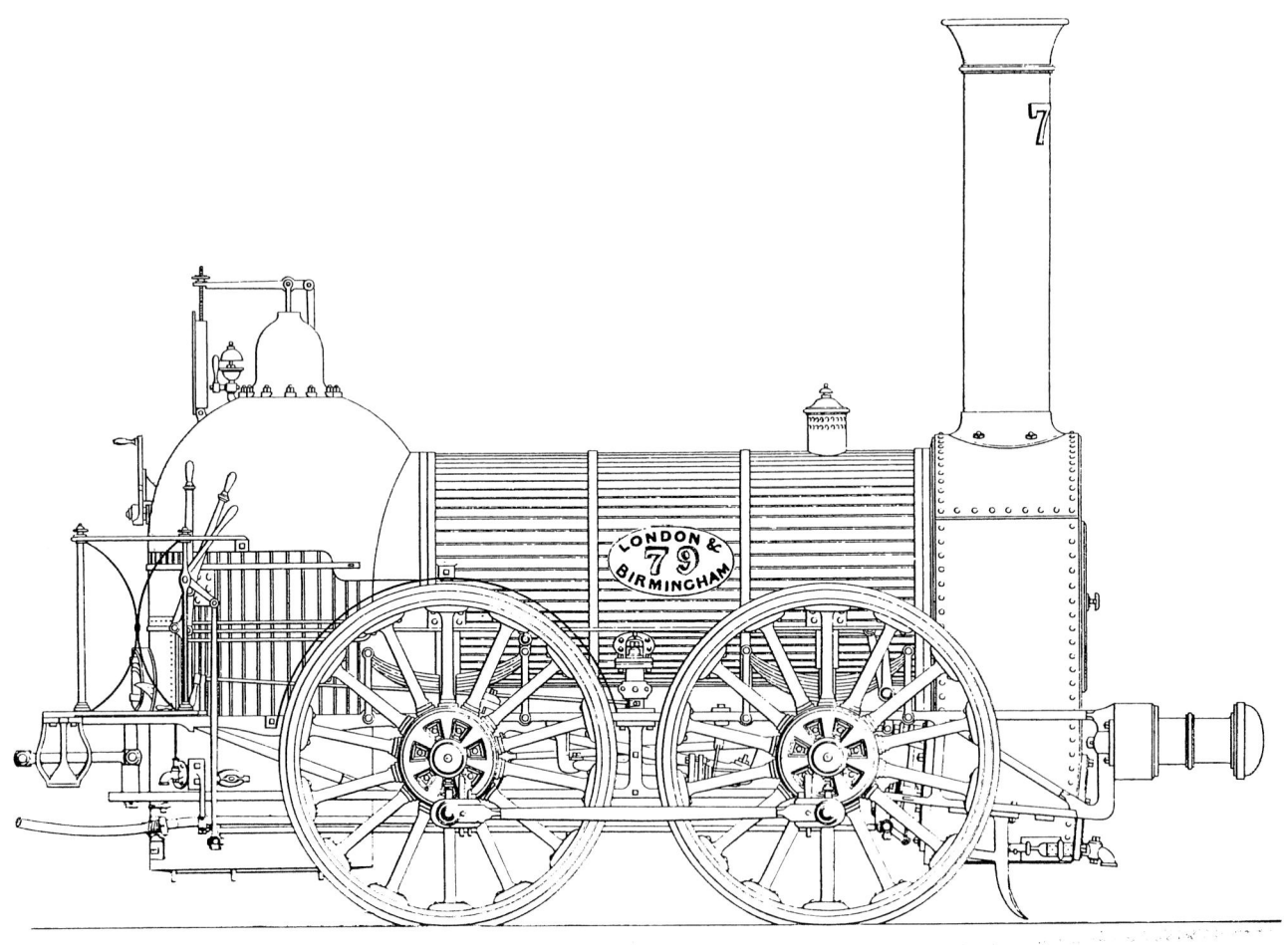

Fig. 17   Bury's original L&B goods engine, 1838.
13in x 18in cylinders, 5ft dia wheels.

3. Bury 0-4-0 Goods Engines
Nos 61-90

Bury estimated that thirty coupled goods engines would be needed and said in July 1836 that it would take him about three months to prepare drawings and specifications. They were laid before the Locomotive Committee on 12th November. Advertisements were published for thirty engines, all to be delivered in the month of December 1837 at "the Company's stations at Camden Town, London - or Nova Scotia, Birmingham at the Company's option." Tenders were to be sent in by 10th January 1837. Six manufacturers sent in offers and these were discussed on the 18th:

Maker	No.	Price	incl spares	Tenders
Bedlington Iron Co, Morpeth	6	£1,250	£1,333.66	£180
R. & W. Hawthorn, Newcastle	3	£1,225	£1,300	£165
Peter Rothwell, Bolton	12	-	£1,400	£165
Thos Vernon, Liverpool	3	£1,250	£1,300	-
Benjamin Hick, Bolton	6	£1,310	£1,361.66	£160
Edward Bury, Liverpool	6	-	£1,350	£170

After a long discussion it was agreed to offer contracts to Hick, Rothwell and Hawthorn if early delivery could be promised, and Bury was persuaded to revise his offer and build twelve engines by the end of 1837, with a 5% penalty on deliveries after 21st June 1838. The London Committee members would try "to induce, if practicable" Maudslay, Sons & Field of Lambeth to submit a tender for six engines.

On 8th February it was learned that Rothwell and Hick wanted higher prices for quick delivery and also that Maudslay had at last consented to make an offer for six goods engines. Maudslay's offer was accepted at once, without any formal advice of cost or delivery date, and the following week the order was confirmed. At this point the directors produced their revised engine numbering scheme; the goods engines were to be 1-30, beginning with those built in London.

Bury, when asked In May 1837 if he could build more goods engines, replied that he could only offer six more but that they would not be ready until 1839, and in April 1838 he suggested that an order for the last six engines be given to Maudslay, Sons & Field.

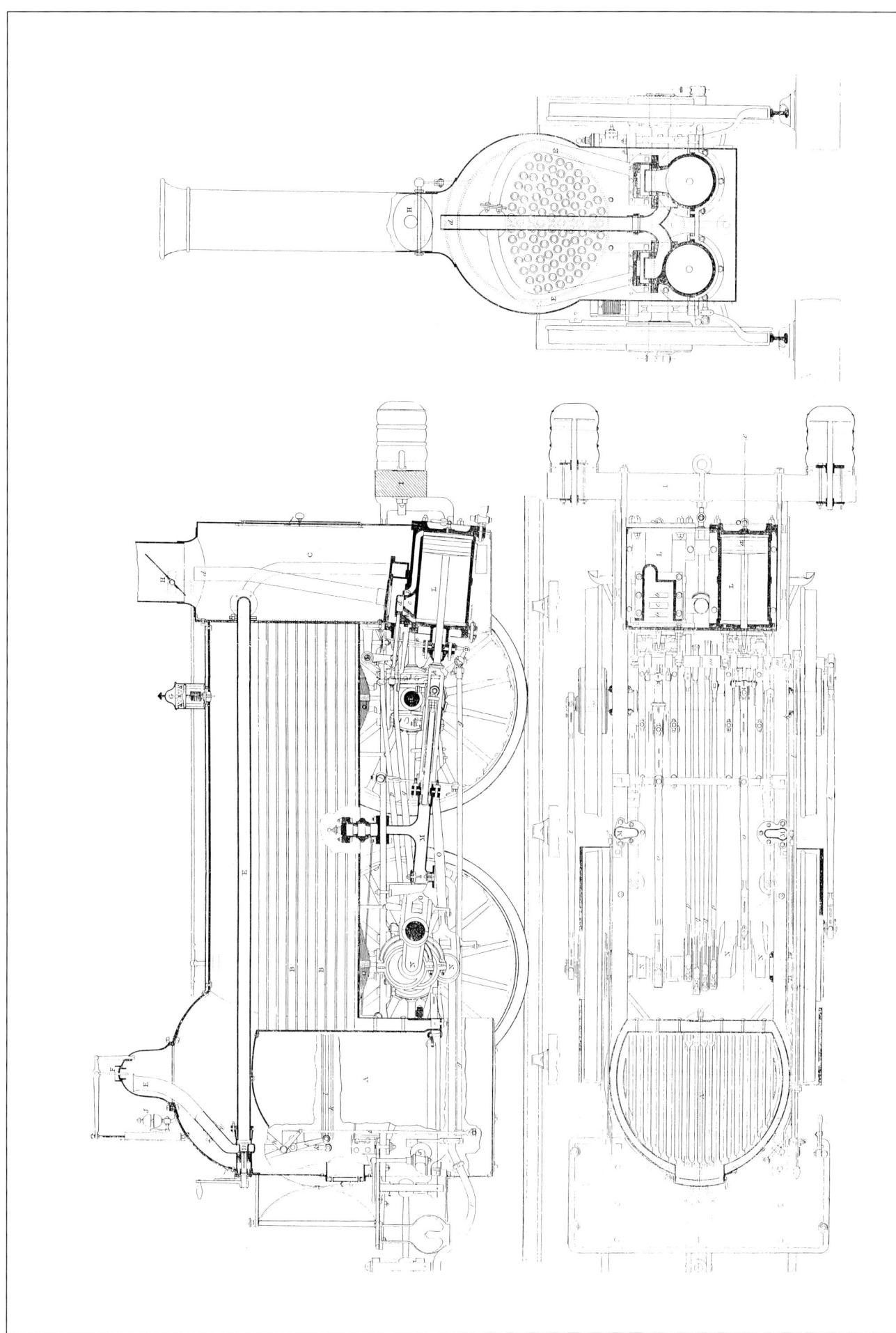

Fig. 18 Sectional views of Bury 0-4-0.

Orders were placed as follows:

Maker	Ordered	No.	Price each	For delivery
Edward Bury	18/1/1837	12	£1,300*	by 1/38
Maudslay, Sons & Field	8/2/1837	6	£1,300	by 7/38
Edward Bury	22/6/1837	6	£1,300*	by 7/39
Maudslay, Sons & Field	11/4/1838	6	£1,400	by 12/39

*increased to £1,350, 20/2/38

The numbers actually given were Bury: 61-78; Maudslay: 79-90.

The first engine to arrive was 79 from Maudslay in September 1838, with the remainder of their first six at the rate of one a month. After building the first three, Maudslay asked for an increase in the price of their engines; the Board declared this inadmissable but had allowed Bury an increase of £50 on each of his in February, probably as compensation for a reduction in his working contract rate. Bury's first did not appear until November 1838 but thereafter deliveries continued steadily until the last of each firm's engines came in November 1839.

Dimensions

Cylinders (2 inside)	13" x 18"
Boiler	
Diameter	3' 4"
Length of barrel	8' 8"
Pitch	5' 4"
Heating surface	
Tubes (96, 2¼" dia, 9' long)	508.89 sq ft
Firebox	43.00 sq ft
Total	551.89 sq ft
Diameter of wheels	5' 0"
Wheelbase	5' 10"
Length over buffers (engine)	18' 6"

Weight

	Herapath, Dec 1841	Bury, Nov 1846
On leading axle	5 tons 2 cwt	5 tons 4 cwt
On driving axle	6 tons 11 cwt	7 tons 14 cwt
Total	11 tons 13 cwt	12 tons 18 cwt

The design was a coupled version of the passenger engine with smaller driving wheels and a bigger boiler and cylinders. Because of the height of the leading axle the cylinders were positioned lower than in the 2-2-0, hanging down at the front at an angle of 5°, with the piston rods working under the axle and the valve rods working above it. Similarly, the valve gear layout was slightly modified. To reverse the engine the eccentric rod ends were simultaneously raised and lowered by pendulum links from cranks on a cross shaft which was located underneath the frame, instead of above as in the passenger engines. This cross shaft passed below the right-hand piston rod, and could be rotated, through bevel gears, by a 10ft horizontal shaft which came forward just behind the wheels from beneath the footplate, where it was turned by a crank and a long vertical link from the disengaging handle on the right side footplate handrail. When disengaged, the valves were moved into position for the changeover to the other pair of eccentrics by two gearing handles, as in the passenger engine. The coupling rod was round in section, 1⅝in diameter thickening to 2in in the centre and held by a ball pin on one crank and a parallel pin on the other.

The specification was similar to and as detailed as that for the passenger engines, with the same clause: "Drawings to be accurately followed in every part, no deviation whatever will be allowed."

Disappointingly, even the firm founded by Henry Maudslay, the pioneer of precision, seemed unable to work to the drawings. No 82 was described in the month of its arrival as "a bad and defective job." The cylinder cover broke and was found to be ⅜in out, and the wheels would "not fit under any other on the line." A man from Maudslay's was summoned to examine it and when their account was finally settled, there was a deduction of £100 for "a bad firebox".

Performance

On goods trains they achieved an average speed of 20mph. However, as Bury predicted, many were used on passenger trains, often running without their coupling rods. During 1840 about half the class was so employed, running at an average speed of about 25mph.

Francis Whishaw timed five of them on passenger trains between August 1839 and February 1840. On 27th August No 72 took a train from Coventry to Birmingham comprising four 1st class carriages, two road carriages on trucks and a wagon (26.86 tons) at an average 28mph with one intermediate stop; the highest speed was almost 43mph, approaching Hampton down the 1 in 330. On 12th October No 75 ran north from Wolverton with three 1sts, two 2nds, four carriages on trucks and a horse box (37.47 tons); its greatest speed was 50mph on the same stretch of track, two miles east of Hampton. Whishaw's other timings are incomplete, but seem to indicate an average speed of something over 26mph.

In the second half of 1839, No 79 was used occasionally on the Aylesbury branch, while 80 and 81 spent most of the six months ballasting. No 88 also spent much of its first three months at this work.

After hearing about Samuel Hall's patent coal-burning system in two locomotives on the Midland Counties Railway, the Locomotive Committee asked Bury in June 1842 to try it out on a goods engine. One of the engines in Wolverton for repair, 79, was to be sent to Camden for this. The system consisted of boiler tubes extended through the smokebox with bell mouths to force air into the firebox, but probably nothing was done to 79 because in August Josiah Kearsley, Locomotive Superintendent of the MCR, published a detailed report concluding that any savings were not worth the expense of maintenance.

Average coke consumption in 1839 was 41.66 lb per mile, 0.591 lb per ton per mile. In 1851 figures for the remaining unrebuilt engines were 38.56 lb and 0.477 lb respectively.

Accidents

On 12th November 1840 Driver Simpson and Fireman Quinlan were on No 82, the second engine on a goods train which ran through a red signal at Harrow and collided with a light engine (No 15). Simpson was said to be a reckless driver in the habit of "running hard", seldom looking ahead and "very fond of sitting down on the seat by the handrailing of the footplate"; he was killed, but Quinlan jumped off before the crash. The engine was found to be in full forward gear although it was certain that Simpson had seen the danger signal.

No 67 was involved in a collision with runaway wagons at Harrow on 25th September 1845, as described on p44. Fifteen months later it was scrapped after an accident at Kings Langley.

During the doubling of the Northampton to Peterborough line in 1846, three engines of this class came to grief. According to James Bull a Down goods train was allowed to leave Northampton with 62 and 85, while a ballast train with 73 left Wellingborough in the opposite direction. "They met at Cogenhoe crossing, about half way between Wellingborough and Northampton, all the engines being very badly damaged, but the men jumped off and were not much hurt."

Rebuilding the Original Engines
From 1841 to 1849 many of the original engines were upgraded to meet increasing demands by rebuilding with bigger boilers and bigger cylinders, and in the case of some of the passenger engines, with driving wheels of larger diameter. Later, some passenger engines were converted to 2-2-2 tank engines.

Bury boiler dimensions
The gradual enlargement of Bury's four-wheeled engines produced a variety of sizes of boiler and firebox. For each class of engine, the number and length of tubes and the heating surfaces of tubes and firebox are given in McConnell's report of 3rd May 1853. From the class totals and other details it is possible to deduce which engines received which size of boiler. For easier reference, the various boiler and firebox sizes have been coded as 1a, 3c etc in the following table, but it must be stressed that this coding has been invented for this book and was *not* used on the railway.

Boilers:

Code	Number of tubes	Tube length	Tube heating surface	Tube dia
1	86	8' 5"	426.33 sq ft	2¼"
2	86	10' 0"	506.41 sq ft	2¼"
3	96	9' 0"	508.89 sq ft	2¼"
4	96	10' 0"	565.46 sq ft	2¼"
5	96	10' 10"	612.56 sq ft	2¼"
6	96	11' 0"	621.98 sq ft	2¼"
7	110	10' 6"	680.29 sq ft	2¼"
8	108	10' 10"	689.70 sq ft	2¼"
9	110	11' 1"	712.69 sq ft	2¼"/2⅛"?

Fireboxes:

Code	Firebox heating surface
a	37.64 sq ft
b	41.27 sq ft
c	43.00 sq ft
d	43.30 sq ft
e	46.48 sq ft
f	46.50 sq ft
g	48.77 sq ft
h	72.46 sq ft

Thus, total heating surfaces indicate boiler and firebox combinations:

sq ft:	463.97	544.05	551.89	606.71	637.92	659.06
code:	1a	2a	3c	4b	4h	5f

sq.ft:	665.284	726.77	735.12	761.46
code:	6d	7e	8f	9g

(It may be noticed that 4b and 8f show inexact totals; these are taken from McConnell's reports of June 1852 and May 1853. The tube and firebox surfaces are from the May 1853 report).

These boilers were utilised as follows:
1a - the original 12in 2-2-0s of 1837-40.
2a - 2-2-0s rebuilt with 13in cylinders 1842-4.
3c - the original 0-4-0s of 1838/9 and the 13in Mail 2-2-0s of 1839-41.
4b - 2-2-0s rebuilt with 13in cylinders 1844-6.
4h - 2-2-0s rebuilt with 13in cylinders 1849- .
5f - 14in 2-2-0s 59, 60, 91 of 1845.
6d - 2-2-0s rebuilt with 13in and 14in cylinders 1846-9.
7e - 2-2-0 rebuilt with 14in cylinders 1846.
8f - 14in 2-2-0s 93/4/6-9 of 1845/6.
9g - 14in 2-2-0s 92/5 of 1845/6 and 0-4-0s rebuilt with 14in cylinders 1846-8.

Although all the 12in passenger engine boilers (1a) were *nominally* the same when built, with 86 tubes 8ft 5in long giving a heating surface of 426.33 sq ft, boilers by different makers are known to have varied in detail as shown in the table below.

Hick's details are from the firm's records; the other dimensions are as given by Whishaw. The tube diameters seem to be a mixture of internal and external measurements. Tubes of two inches internal diameter were specified.

Wheel diameters
In Bury passenger engines the size of the leading wheels bore a fixed relationship to the size of the driving wheels. When an engine was rebuilt with a different size of driving wheel, the leading wheels were also changed to those of the appropriate size.

Maker	Barrel Dia	Barrel Length	Tubes No	Firebox Dia	Length	Width	Height
Hick:	3' 2"	8' 0"	84	2⅛"			
			2	1⅞"			
Hawthorn:	3' 2"	8' 0"	86	2⅛"	2' 11"	3' 7"	3' 7½"
Haigh:	3' 2"	8' 0"	86	2"	2' 9"	4' 2"	3' 9"
Rothwell:	3' 1½"	8' 0"	86	2"	3' 7½"	--	3' 8"
Mather:	3' 6"	8' 0"	90	2¼"	2' 6"	3' 4"	3' 3"

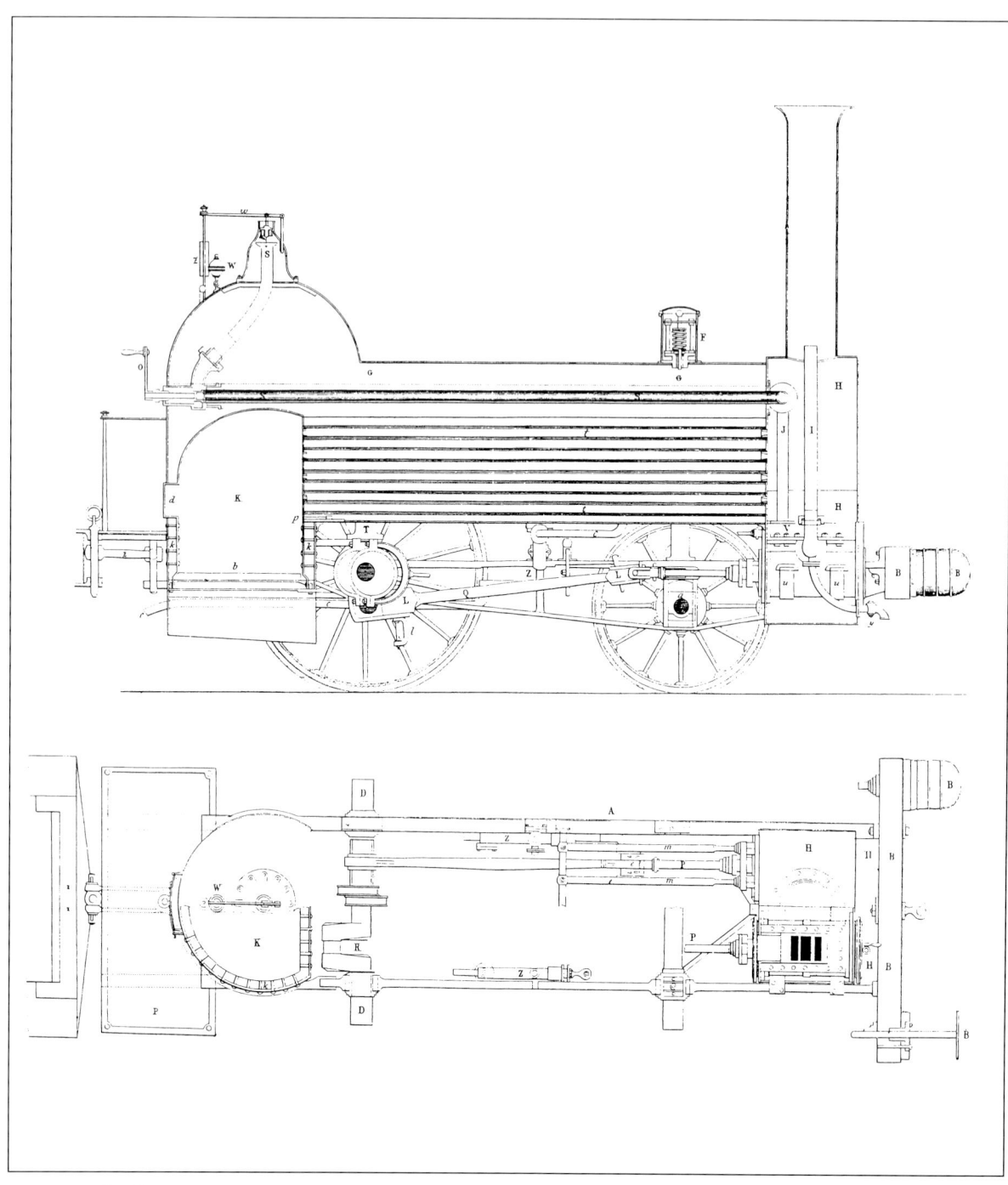

Fig. 19 A Bury, Curtis & Kennedy design of 1842 which although similar to the rebuilt L&B engines cannot be identified with any individual group of these. Although the boiler has 11ft tubes and the wheelbase is 7ft 6in, the driving wheels are of the earlier diameter, 5ft 6in.

Driving wheel diameter	*Leading wheel diameter*
5ft 0in	3ft 6in
5ft 6in	4ft 0in
5ft 9in	4ft 3in
6ft 0in	4ft 6in

Rebuilding the Passenger Engines

From their arrival the eighteen Mail Engines were such a success that in June 1841 it was decided to upgrade the original 12in cylinder passenger engines. Whenever one of them needed a thorough repair, it was to be fitted with 13in cylinders.

One of the Rothwell engines, No 25, required a general overhaul in September 1841 and was sent off to Bury's Clarence Foundry at Liverpool. On 7th October Bury reported satisfactory progress with the fitting of new 13in cylinders "and other necessary alterations consequent on this change." The engine was returned in March 1842. The boiler barrel had been lengthened; the number of tubes remained the same as originally but were now 10ft - some nineteen inches longer than originally and a foot longer than those in the Mail Engines. The wheelbase was increased to 6ft 6in. The cost of the rebuilding - new boiler plates, new tubes, new cylinders and new frame members - was £400, on top of £400 for the original repairs. After tests 25 was declared on 7th April to be "quite equal to the best Mail Engines". Nine other similar conversions were authorised by the Board, to be undertaken at Wolverton. In these the wheelbase was lengthened to 7ft.

Five sets of cylinder castings were ordered in August and the first two engines were taken in hand in October. For the next six years there were usually three or four engines in Wolverton undergoing enlargement. Rebuilds were turned out at the rate of one about every two months, each engine having been out of service for four or five months.

With the first rebuilding programme almost completed, another ten were authorised on 8th November 1843. After two of these had been done the design was improved, and from the end of 1844 rebuilding involved a boiler of the same length as in the previous rebuilds but with ten more tubes and a larger firebox. The driving wheels were increased to 5ft 9in and in one case (No 24) to 6ft. Aylesbury Railway No 2 was one of this batch, but there is doubt about Aylesbury No 1, which was sold in August 1847 and was afterwards recorded in retrospective lists among both rebuilt and unrebuilt engines. In 1845 the weight in working order of the 13in rebuilds was given as 12 tons.

A year later, after the introduction of a new class of engines with 14in cylinders, and against a background discussion by the Locomotive Committee of the need for bigger heating surfaces and 6ft wheels, further enlargements were incorporated in the rebuilt engines.

No 40, a 13in Mail Engine, was rebuilt with 14in cylinders and 6ft driving wheels. A firebox similar to that of the new 14in engines was fitted and the new boiler had 110 tubes longer by eighteen inches. This gave the biggest heating surface so far, 727 sq ft, an increase of 31% on its original boiler, and 10% greater than that of the first three of the new 14in engines. A spring balance safety valve replaced the old lock-up on the boiler barrel.

For whatever reason, the other ten engines rebuilt with 14in cylinders were given 5ft 9in wheels and a different boiler, with 96 tubes as in the last 13in rebuilds, but increased in length by a foot. The tubes were two inches longer than those in the 14in engines so that although the firebox was smaller, the total heating surface was slightly bigger. In these rebuilds the two safety valves were mounted in a small dome on the firebox top, with fore-and-aft levers. In March 1848 the weight of the 14in rebuilds was given as 15 tons 2 cwt, with 9 tons 9 cwt on the driving wheels.

In November 1845 five engines (23, 26, 50, 51 and 52) were undergoing rebuilding at Wolverton; for No 50 this was its second conversion, having already been rebuilt with 13in cylinders three years before. Another 12in engine (No 13) was also rebuilt with 14in cylinders by July 1847.

By this time McConnell had taken over and the 12in and 13in engines were being sold off. Even so, rebuilding did not entirely cease but continued in a leisurely manner; another 12in engine, No 14, went into Wolverton in August 1847 joining three engines already there - two 12in, Nos 28 and 30 and one 13in, No 43. No 28 was finished at the end of the year, 30 in October 1848 and the last two not until May 1849.

According to James Bull, 43 and 57 had their driving wheels reduced to 5ft diameter (leading wheels reduced to 3ft 6in) for working the Dunstable Branch which contained a 1$\frac{1}{4}$-mile 1 in 40 incline. This branch opened in May 1848, but 43 was in Wolverton at the time and did not emerge (with 14in cylinders) until a year later. Presumably this is when it was given 5ft wheels, but there is no confirmation of this in the LNWR records and it had 5ft 9in driving wheels by 1859.

No 57 was recorded with 5ft 6in driving wheels in March 1848 and June 1852, and again there is no official confirmation of a change to 5ft. Not mentioned by Bull is 58, which definitely had 5ft wheels by March 1848 and still had them in 1852. This engine may have been so altered for banking duties on Camden Incline.

Another 2-2-0 rebuilt with a bigger boiler in 1849 was No 2. It had received 13in cylinders in 1843 and was sold to a contractor in May 1847. He returned it in January 1849 when it was renumbered 237, its original number having been given meanwhile to the former Aylesbury No 2. It went into Wolverton in February and emerged in June 1849, rebuilt with a large boiler of the type used on the 14in 5ft 9in rebuilds, with link motion, but retaining its 13in cylinders and 5ft 6in wheels. In this state it was the most powerful of the 13in engines and was nicknamed 'The Little Wonder'.

It appears that two more 13in engines were rebuilt in 1849-51 with boilers like those fitted to the 13in rebuilds of 1845, with 96 10ft tubes. They retained their old cylinders but the driving wheels were increased to 5ft 9in, and new fireboxes of a much larger size were fitted. From the heating surface, 72.46 sq ft (in a report of 1852) they cannot have been Bury fireboxes and may have been McConnell's first step in the direction of the very large fireboxes which were shortly to become his trademark.

By elimination, these two engines seem likely to have been 48 and 56. In 1847, 56 was a 13in engine with 5ft 6in wheels. In January 1848 it was withdrawn and put on the "for sale" list, where it lay until November, when it went into Wolverton "for general repairs". It came out in March 1849. Thereafter it is recorded as in working order, being among ten 13in four-wheelers offered to Crewe as suitable for the Northern Division in September 1849. It was withdrawn in 1852/3.

The other engine, 48, was also a 5ft 6in 13in engine in 1848 and must have been rebuilt after December 1849. It was withdrawn in 1856.

These two rebuilds were not a success; according to a report of June 1852 the remaining engine (presumably 48) took the smallest average load of any on the line and was very costly on repairs, which might suggest that it was being used for experimental work.

Some were reboilered by McConnell but no details are known. No 3 (formerly 26) is said to have had a domed boiler with a small square firebox and long cylindrical combustion chamber, with very short (only 1ft 6in!) tubes when it was sold to the LC&DR in 1860.

Summary: 2-2-0s rebuilt with 13in and 14in cylinders and bigger boilers

(i) 12in engines rebuilt with 13in x 18in cylinders, 2a boiler, 6ft 6in (No 25) or 7ft 0in wheelbase, retaining the 5ft 6in driving wheels:

No.	Date completed
25	3/42
2	3/43
50	4/43
1, 16	6/43
20	b /43
15, 49	a /44
3, 4, 10	/44
21	11/44

(ii) 12in engines rebuilt with 13in x 18in cylinders, 4b boiler, 7ft 0in wheelbase, 5ft 9in driving wheels:

11	11/44
19	1/45
17	2/45
24 (6ft driving wheels)	/45
29, 7	/45
Aylesbury 2 (and perhaps Aylesbury 1)	/46

(iii) 13in engine rebuilt with 14in x 18in cylinders, 7e boiler, 7ft 0in wheelbase, 6ft 0in driving wheels:

40	/46

(iv) 12in and 13in engines rebuilt with 14in x 18in cylinders, 6d boiler, 7ft 6in wheelbase, 5ft 9in driving wheels:

23, 26, 50*, 51, 52	/46
13	a /47
28	12/47
30	10/48
14	5/49
43* (? with 5ft 0in driving wheels)	5/49

* 43 and 50 rebuilt from 13in engines; others from 12in.

(v) 13in engine rebuilt with 6d boiler, link motion, 7ft 6in wheelbase; retaining 13in x 18in cylinders and 5ft 6in driving wheels:

237 (ex-2)	6/49

(vi) 13in engines rebuilt with 4h boiler, 5ft 9in driving wheels; retaining 13in x 18in cylinders:

56	3/49
48	/50 (?)

Rebuilding as 2-2-2 Tank Engines

By 1849 most of the original passenger engines had been rebuilt with bigger cylinders, sold or scrapped; only five 12in engines remained in stock, Nos 12, 18, 31/2/5, all on the 'for sale' list. In December one of them, number unknown, was sent to the Construction Dept at Camden, probably to drive machinery.

In May 1850 it was decided to convert the other four to 2-2-2 tank engines for branch line work at a cost of £100 each; three months later they were joined by a fifth, 22, which had been driving a pump at Leighton since 1847. A June 1852 list shows these five 12in tank engines as Nos 5, 27, 191, 198 and 199. All had been renumbered on their return to working stock from the sales list, because their original numbers had been taken by new engines. James Bull records that No 12 was renumbered 5, but does not mention the others. Four 13in engines were also converted to tanks in 1850/1: Nos 25, 45/7 and 54.

By the end of 1850 "several" of the 'condemned for sale' engines were being "altered and adapted for the East & West India Docks line" (later the North London Railway) and five were recorded as being under reconstruction to tank engines on 11th February 1851; a month later there were only two in the shops.

The conversion involved the addition of a plate frame behind the original bar frame to take a trailing axle with 4ft or 4ft 3in diameter wheels, extending the wheelbase by 8ft 4in. A bunker was mounted at the back, similar to the Jones & Potts engines of the London & Blackwall Railway, but with a bigger tank beneath the footplate. This tank was deep at the front and back, with an arch in the middle over the trailing axle.

Some of the 12in tanks were sent to work on the Docks line from its opening, but were quickly replaced by the 13in tanks. Nos 47 and 54 were working there, presumably as tank engines, by 28th January 1851.

The five 12in tank engines were sold in 1852 and delivered in the following year to Wm Fairbairn & Sons who altered two of them to the 5ft 3in gauge and shipped them to Ireland to work on the Waterford & Tramore Railway. Another 2-2-2T sent to the W&T at the same time had been rebuilt by Fairbairn from one of the Bury 13in 2-2-0 tender engines.

On 16th April 1856 McConnell reported that he had arranged to sell three old engines to the Wiesbaden Railway for £1,650. These were 47, 37 and 39 "altered to tank engines at an expense of £100 each" - the LNWR keeping the tenders.

All the Bury tank engines went from the S Div between 1853 and 1856 but McConnell reported on 13th May 1858 that he was adding tanks to three 14in engines. He was told to convert only two.

One of these may have been 43, by then renumbered 10, of which a drawing exists dated 23rd May 1859, showing the alterations required to convert it to a 2-2-2 tank. The plate frame extension had a 3ft 6in trailing wheel, centred 9ft 4in behind the 5ft 9in driving wheel. The cylinder stroke had been increased to 20in. The other was probably No 14, renumbered 1, which is said to have been converted to a tank in 1859.

These two of the original passenger engines survived to be renumbered in the capital list in April 1862 and are believed to have been tanks. Rosling Bennett recalled seeing two Bury well tanks which had been rebuilt with McConnell boilers; this was at Addison Road, Kensington, and he gives the date as 1865. Nos 1 and 10 were renumbered 1167 and 1127 in 1862, but one of them (1167) was replaced in the following year, so is unlikely to have been at Kensington in 1865. Perhaps Bennett misremembered the year when he saw the two tank engines - he would have been 14 or 15 in 1865 - or there was at least one other tank conversion of which there is no record.

Fig. 20   No 25 built by Rothwell in 1837, rebuilt as 2-2-2T in 1850/1 and sold to the North London Railway in 1855. Photographed as NLR 15A at Hammersmith N&SWJ station in the 1870s.
(Stephenson Locomotive Society)

Summary: 2-2-0s rebuilt as 2-2-2 tanks

No.	Date
12, reno'd 5 (/50)	1850/1
22, and three of 18, 31, 32, 35 reno'd as 27, 191, 198, 199 (/50)	1850/1
25, 45, 47, 54	1850/1
37, 39	before sale to Wiesbaden Rly, 4/1856

Other tank conversions include two in 1859, probably No 10 (ex-43) and No 1 (ex-14), but details have not survived.

Rebuilding the 13in 0-4-0 Goods Engines

About 1844-6 Nos 65/6/8, 72, 85/8 were fitted with copper fireboxes and spring balance safety valves on the boiler barrel.

The first of the 15in 0-4-0 class arrived in September 1845 and shortly afterwards four of the old goods engines were taken into Wolverton for rebuilding with 14in cylinders; these were 70, 79, 81 and 64. Of these only one was completed by September 1846, another two following in October. In all, eight engines were so rebuilt, the last being completed in May 1848.

New 14in x 20in cylinders were fitted and the wheelbase was lengthened to 8ft to accommodate a larger boiler of the same type as used for two 2-2-0 14in passenger engines built at Wolverton in 1845/6, Nos 92 and 95. The domed top of the enlarged firebox was made higher than before, rising to 16in above the boiler barrel and fitted with two fore-and-aft safety valves on the small brass dome, like those on 95.

Heating surface
Tubes (110, 2¼" dia, 11' 1" long)	712.69 sq ft
Firebox	48.77 sq ft
Total	761.46 sq ft

The last three rebuilds, 69, 78 and 80 were given link motion.

The weight was given variously in official reports:

	Nov 1846	March 1848	Oct 1860
On leading axle	6.7 tons	5.875 tons	6.775 tons
On driving axle	9.3 tons	8.5 tons	8.85 tons
Total	16.0 tons	14.375 tons	15.625 tons

During 1848/9 three 13in engines Nos 62, 63 and 90 were rebuilt in their original form to give employment to extra hands taken on during the footplatemen's strike.

Two 0-4-0s 65 and 71 were transferred in 1847/8 to Richard Madigan's ballast stock; they were returned in 1849 and were later renumbered 61 and 82. According to the somewhat confused account in the 1897 *Locomotive Magazine* they had 13in cylinders and 5ft wheels, but a 7ft wheelbase, and very low grates without ashpans. The accompanying sketch shows 61 with safety valves inset in the domed firebox top and with fore-and-aft levers, as in the passenger engines of 1845, Nos 59, 60 and 91. If these details are correct, the two engines must have been rebuilt at some time, either while in Madigan's hands or later, perhaps using second-hand fireboxes.

Summary: 13in 0-4-0s rebuilt
13in engines rebuilt with 14in x 20in cylinders, 9g boiler, 8ft wheelbase:

No.	Date completed
79	by 11/46 ⎫
70	by 11/46 ⎬ one of these by 8/9/46
81	by 11/46 ⎭
64	between 11/46 and 9/47
76	between 11/46 and 9/47
69 (with link motion)	between 11/46 and 9/47
78 " " "	10/47
80 " " "	5/48

Rebuilt but retaining the original 3c boiler and 13in cylinders:

62	2/49
63	3/49
90	6/49

Perhaps rebuilt with longer boilers and bigger fireboxes (5f?), 7ft wheelbase:

61 ex-65	after /48?
82 ex-71	after /47?

The original London & Birmingham engines on the LNWR and later

The ninety original 2-2-0 and 0-4-0 engines were all still at work until the beginning of 1847. Within a week two were destroyed in accidents; in the following month McConnell arrived and by the end of the year another seventeen had gone, sold or put to work as stationary engines, with another four "condemned for sale". Even so, single 13in passenger engines were still regularly working trains of up to eleven carriages out of Euston, and were often used to assist bigger engines on trains of fifteen or more carriages.

The last of the unrebuilt 12in 2-2-0 engines were sold in 1853 but two years later, of the original 90 there were still 23 in capital stock, with another eighteen on the duplicate list. At the end of the 1850s several of them were at work on the Peterborough and Bedford branches; others were shunting at Camden and Watford. Five of them survived in capital stock until 1862: three singles of 1837/8/40 and two goods of 1839. In 1862 several more were on the duplicate list, with a dozen others still in service as stationary engines at Wolverton Works and elsewhere. The last one in the duplicate list was retubed (with a second-hand set of Everett's tubes) as late as August 1868, and was taken out of stock - perhaps to see further service hauling materials inside Crewe Works - in the second half of 1869. This engine had been built by Hick in March 1840.

Their longevity reflects great credit on Edward Bury and demonstrates that their original design was well thought out and that they were built to last; they long outlived their contemporaries on other lines, such as the Grand Junction. On the LNWR some worked as locomotives into the 1880s; one (at least) continued as a stationary engine into the twentieth century. Several of the engines which were sold had lengthy second careers - notably the tank engine which worked on the Waterford & Tramore Railway until 1906 and was not scrapped until 1912; this must be a record for a locomotive built in the 1830s.

16 and 67
These were the first engines withdrawn. On 5th January 1847 No 16 was on an Up goods train, double headed with 115 (a 15in 0-4-0 of 1845), when it ran into the back of a coal train standing at Kings Langley and had to be scrapped. During the single line working following this accident, 67 collided with No 1 and also had to be scrapped.

Under McConnell, from March 1847
On 1st March 1847 McConnell recommended that all engines with cylinders smaller than 14in diameter should be sold or scrapped. Disposals began at once. Many engines were sold in the normal cash-down manner to purchasers such as collieries, but for contractors there was another system whereby payment was deferred to the end of the contract. Cash prices were normally around £600, but the deferred-payment price was £1,000 or £1,050. Probably this was simply an inflated valuation on which the contractor paid interest, and some engines described in the records as 'sold' were later returned to the LNWR. Sometimes an engine 'sold' in this way had its running number kept open in its absence and got it back on its return; evidently in these cases the engine was hired with an option to purchase outright at the end of the contract. In other cases an engine was returned after its original number had already been taken by a new engine; it was then renumbered, but some of the details are unknown.

McConnell found another use for the small locomotives; from 1847 some were set up as stationary engines for driving machinery in Wolverton Works and at other places on the line. One of the Aylesbury engines - probably No 1 - is said to have driven the traverser in the

Totals in capital stock:

Originally built as:	12/1846	12/1847	12/1848	12/1849	-/1853	6/1855	4/1856	4/1862
12in 2-2-0	42	30	25	26	19	10	7	2
13in 2-2-0	18	15	15	18	13	5	4	1
13in 0-4-0	30	22	17	18	10	8	8	2
Total:	90	67	57	62	42	23	19	5
Plus duplicate engines for sale:		4	8	5	n/k	18	n/k	n/k

east shops at Wolverton from early in 1847 (*The Engineer*, 12/1884). After Aylesbury No 1 was sold the traverser was worked by No 36.

Others were used as stationary boilers, one of which was photographed at Crewe in 1879 (Fig 14). This was one of the unrebuilt 2-2-0s, but its precise identity is unknown. The connecting rods, valve gear, and lower frame trusses had been removed, and a blower, steam valve and delivery pipe from the top of the firebox had been fitted.

In stock, 7th December 1847:

		Nos	
2-2-0	12in	5/9, 12/8, 31/2/5/6	(8)
2-2-0	13in	A2, 1/3/4/7, 10/1/5/7/9, 20/1/4/5/9, 37-9, 41/2/4/6-9, 53/5-8	(30)
2-2-0	14in	13, 23/6, 40, 50-2; plus 14, 28, 30, 43 being rebuilt	(11)
0-4-0	13in	61/2/5/6/8, 73/5/7, 83/4/5/7/8, 90	(14)
0-4-0	14in	64/9, 70/6/8/9, 81; plus 80 being rebuilt	(8)
		Total:	71

Nos 9, 12, 35 and 47 were "condemned for sale." Apart from these, the five being rebuilt and two under repair, all were in working order.

In stock, 4th December 1849:

		Nos	
2-2-0	12in	12/8, 31/2/5	(5)
2-2-0	13in	1-4, 7, 10/1/5/7/9, 20/1/4/5/9, 37-9, 41/2/4-9, 53-8, 237	(33)
2-2-0	14in	13/4, 23/6/8, 30, 40/3, 50-2	(11)
0-4-0	13in	61/2/3/6/8, 73/7, 84/8, 90	(10)
0-4-0	14in	64/9, 70/6/8/9, 80/1	(8)
		Total:	67

The five 12in engines were on the "condemned for sale" list; all the others were in working order (53) or under repair (9).

In stock, 7th June 1852:

	Boiler	Driving wheels	Nos	
2-2-2T	12in	1a	5ft 6in	5, 27, 191/8/9	(5)
2-2-0	13in	2a	5ft 6in	1, 3, 4, 10/5, 20/1, 49	(8)
2-2-2T	13in	2a	5ft 6in	25	(1)
2-2-0	13in	3c	5ft 6in	37/8/9, 41/2/4/6, 53/5/7, 71*	(11)
2-2-0	13in	3c	5ft 0in	58	(1)
2-2-2T	13in	3c	5ft 6in	47, 54	(2)
2-2-0	13in	4b	5ft 9in	2, 7, 11/7/9, 29	(6)
2-2-0	13in	4b	6ft 0in	24	(1)
2-2-0	13in	6d	5ft 6in	237	(1)
2-2-0	13in	4h	5ft 9in	48, 56	(2)
2-2-0	14in	6d	5ft 9in	13/4, 23/6/8, 30, 43, 50/1/2	(10)
2-2-0	14in	7e	6ft 0in	40	(1)
0-4-0	13in	3c	5ft 0in	61/2/3/6/8, 77, 83/4/8, 90	(10)
0-4-0	14in	9g	5ft 0in	64/9, 70/6/8/9, 80/1	(8)
				Total:	67

* 71 was a renumbered engine so far unidentified.

In stock, 5th June 1855:

		Nos	
2-2-0	13in	20, 48, 237	(3)
2-2-2T	13in	47, 54	(2)
2-2-0	14in	13/4, 23/6, 30, 40/3, 50/1/2	(10)
0-4-0	13in	82	(1)
0-4-0	14in	69, 70/6/8-81	(7)
		Total:	23

For sale (all 13in) were:

2-2-0 Nos 2/7, 11/7/9, 21/9, 37/8/9, 42/4/6/9, 57/8	(16)
2-2-2T No 25	(1)
0-4-0 No 61	(1)
Total:	18

8 and Aylesbury 1

were sold in August 1847 for £1,050 the pair (valuation £800) to Benjamin Greene, described as "a director of the Rhymney Railway". This was the 'Old Rumney' tramroad connecting Rhymney ironworks with the Monmouthshire Canal system.

Aylesbury 2

was renumbered 2 in September 1848, old L&B No 2 having been sold. It was taken out of capital stock in 1852/3. After the cost of special water heating apparatus had been looked at in November 1855, No 2 was installed in Birmingham New Street Station to provide hot water for filling carriage footwarmers. A very tall chimney was fitted to carry away the coke fumes and it was looked after by two young cleaners from Vauxhall shed. It was renumbered 2S about January 1859 but McConnell's request to list it as a stationary engine, charged to the Traffic Dept at £200, was refused by the Auditor who ordered that it be considered as a locomotive in store. It was still in New Street in September 1867 when it was seen by Isaac Watt Boulton who recorded 13½in cylinders and "old motion". It was taken away shortly afterwards.

1, 3, 4, 10, 15

These five were among ten old engines sold to Wm Fairbairn & Sons in June 1852 for £450 each in part payment for new engines built by the firm. The original agreement was for the firm to take six 13in engines in good working order at £500 each but they were persuaded to accept ten, these five 13in tender engines plus five 12in tank engines (see below, No 12 etc) which were not guaranteed to be in good working order. Fairbairn said that they would have great difficulty in getting rid of them "in fact we might even have to break some of them up." Repairs were done at Wolverton to two of the ten old engines for £318 16s 11d (£318.85) and two of the 13in were taken away by January 1853. The others followed soon after, two being recorded as sent to Manchester by goods train for £16 17s 6d (£16.87) about March 1853. One of the 13in engines seems to have been converted to a tank engine by Fairbairn who sold three 2-2-2T - one 13in and two 12in - altered to the 5ft 3in gauge to William Dargan the Irish railway contractor; they were delivered to him in May, August and September. No other sales by Fairbairn of the ex-L&B engines have been traced. Dargan numbered them 1 to 3 and used them in the construction and working of the Waterford & Tramore Railway, which opened in September 1853. In December 1854 the W&T decided to keep the 13in engine and Dargan took away the two 12in. The railway obtained two new engines from Fairbairn in 1855 which were numbered W&T 1 and 2; the old 13in engine then became No 3, renumbered 4 in 1861. In 1867 it was reboiled with a large dome just behind the chimney and in 1880 was fitted with new cylinders and driving wheels, but retaining its Bury domed firebox. The *Locomotive Magazine* in 1900 said "it is undoubtedly the oldest locomotive running passenger trains in Great Britain, probably in the world." It remained at work until September 1906 when it was laid aside as "incapacitated through age and not worth repairing". It lay out of use in the Waterford workshops until it was sold for scrap about September 1912.

It was said in 1900 that it bore the number 191 somewhere (perhaps stamped on the motion or regulator) which has led to its identification as ex-LNWR 191, a 12in engine, but its 13in cylinders and its 7ft leading to driving wheelbase make it seem more likely that it was one of 1/3/4/10/5. As the bunker extension was unlike that of other Wolverton tank engines it was probably converted to a 2-2-2T by Fairbairn. Perhaps some parts of a cannibalised 12in engine were used in this rebuilding, hence the '191' story.

2

was sold in May/June 1847 to Elisha Wright Oldham, contractor on the "West Yorkshire Railway" for £1,000. He returned it in January 1849 and because its old number was now occupied it was renumbered 237. It was at once rebuilt with link motion and the large boiler as used in the 14in conversions. In this form (the only 13in engine so rebuilt) it was evidently a great success; known as 'The Little Wonder' it lasted to the end of the separate S Div, being renumbered 837 in April 1862, then into the duplicate list in November 1862. It was probably scrapped in the first half of 1863.

5 and 9

No 9 was on the "condemned for sale" list by September 1847 and was joined there in January 1848 by No 5. In March 1848 they were sold to Blaina Iron Works for £1,050 (the pair). No 5 was valued at £300, No 9 at £500. They were used by F. Levick & Co of Cwm Celyn & Blaina Ironworks on the Western Valley section of the Monmouthshire Rly between Newport and Blaina as Nos 1 and 2 until the regular Monmouthshire engines came into use in August 1849.

6

went from stock between January and September 1847 and was recorded in June 1848 as "turning lathes etc" at Wolverton and was still there at the end of 1849.

7, 11, 17, 19, 21, 29 and 49

were taken from capital stock in 1853-5 and were last heard of in the sales list of 5th June 1855. All were replaced in 1856.

12, 18, 22, 31, 32, 35

Nos 12 and 35 were on the "condemned for sale" list from September 1847, No 18 from December 1848 and 31/2 from January 1848. All five were still on the sales list at the end of 1849 when one of them (unidentified) was sent to work machinery in the Construction Dept's wagon shops; No 18 had been adapted for stationary work and had been pumping at Northampton from December 1847 to October 1848 and may have been the one selected. An old engine (perhaps this one) was sent from the wagon shops to the auction held at Birmingham on 20th August 1858, where four S Div engines identified only as E, H, G and Q raised £171-£174 each.

On 6th May 1850 the other four 12in "now lying unemployed" were ordered to be repaired and converted to 2-2-2 tank engines at a cost of £100 each for branch line work. Three months later another 12in 2-2-0, No 22, which had been working a pump at Leighton since 1847, was replaced there by a small stationary engine brought from the recently-closed ballast engine depot at Watford. The locomotive was taken to Wolverton and converted to a tank engine.

These five 12in tanks, when returned to stock, had to be renumbered because their numbers had been taken by new engines. No 12 became 5; the other four took 27, 191, 198 and 199. Exactly how these four new numbers were allocated is unknown.

No. in 1849	No. in 1850
12	5 tank engine
18	— stationary engine, to Construction Dept, 12/49
22	27 tank engine
31	191 tank engine
32	198 tank engine
35	199 tank engine

5, 27 and 191 were numbers left vacant by engines removed from stock; 198 and 199 had not been used before.

The tank engines were sent to the East & West India Docks line in September 1850, but they proved inadequate, and on 22nd June 1852 it was arranged to sell them to Wm Fairbairn & Sons (with Nos 1, 3, 4, 10 and 15 above) for £450 each as part payment of an order for new engines. They were still in LNWR hands in January 1853 but went shortly afterwards. In that year two of them appear to have been altered by Fairbairn to the Irish 5ft 3in gauge and sold to William Dargan for the construction and working of the Waterford & Tramore Railway. They were removed from that line in December 1854 and one of them went to the Waterford & Limerick Railway, where it "was kept for odd jobs for some time." (*Locomotive Magazine*, 1908 p66).

13 and 50

The seven-mile Balaklava Railway was built in February-August 1855 for military operations in the Crimea. The LNWR was asked if it could supply locomotives and McConnell wrote on 4th September that as they were "willing to oblige the Government" he thought he could dispose of two "of the small class" Nos 13 and 50.

Although they were not on the "condemned for sale list" then, he thought they would form part of his next list. (50 had been working on the North London line, whence it had been returned in May "minus all wheels"). Both had 14in x 18in cylinders, weighed 14 tons 9 cwt and worked satisfactorily at a pressure of 85 to 90 lb per square inch. With fittings to connect them with a rope for working an incline, and all duplicate parts supplied they would cost £800 per engine. The sale was minuted on 14th September as two engines without tenders at £800 each, but the War Office records show that £1,800 was paid for the LNWR engines to Peto, Brassey & Betts who were acting as agents. Presumably Nos 13 and 50 were used as stationary engines on the inclines. After the war ended the Balaklava Railway was dismantled in May-June 1856 and sold to Turkey so perhaps Nos 13 and 50 went there too.

14
was renumbered 1 in April 1856, was converted to a tank engine in 1859 and is believed to have been renumbered 1167 in May 1862, although it was not replaced until the following September; it probably became a stationary engine about 1863 and was said in 1878 to be working a pump at Coalville. In 1908 it was noted in the *Railway Club Journal* that No 1 had been pumping water at the joint shed at Coalville (Charnwood Forest Jct) as recently as 1896 but had since been removed.

20
was fitted with iron tubes in April 1852 and ran 63,458 miles between then and the report in February 1856. It was in working order in June 1855, but was taken from capital stock by April 1856.

23
was renumbered 2 in April 1856 and was taken from capital stock by July 1858.

24
worked as a stationary engine from early 1855, possibly on a pump at Northampton. The locomotive there, on being replaced by a vertical stationary table engine in August 1858, was put in order and placed in store at Wolverton. It was probably scrapped in 1866.

25
Rebuilt as a 2-2-2T in 1850/1, 25 was hired with several others to the North London Railway in 1854/5. They came back in bad condition; 25 was put on the sales list and was sold to the NLR in October 1855 for £500. It became NLR No 15, then 15A from 1869. It was reboilered in 1864 and worked, latterly on the N&SWJR Hammersmith Branch (where it was photographed, Fig 20) until c1877.

26
Renumbered 3 in April 1856 it was replaced in October 1859, when it presumably became 1003 in the duplicate list. By then it had been rebuilt with a McConnell boiler, having a small square firebox and a long cylindrical combustion chamber which reduced the tube length to about 1ft 6in.

It was purchased for £500 in September 1860 by the London Chatham & Dover Railway and delivered by road from Camden to Battersea on 9th November. It was named *Wasp* in January 1861, was laid aside as unserviceable in June of that year but was later employed pumping water at Battersea. It was dumped on a siding at Canterbury at the end of 1863 and was sold for scrap in April 1864.

27
was taken out of stock sometime between January and September 1847. It does not appear in the monthly lists of engines, available from 7th September 1847 to 4th December 1849, except once, on 5th May 1848, as a 12in engine for sale. In a table dated 2nd March 1848 it makes another appearance, as a 5ft 6in passenger engine with 12in x 18in cylinders. Apart from these two entries there is no mention of 27 in any of the lists: neither as working stock, stock for sale, already sold, scrapped, nor stationary. (Because of its mysterious disappearance the suggestion has been made that 27 was the L&B engine installed in HMS *Terror* in May 1845 for the Franklin Expedition, but there is no evidence for this, and much to be said against it. In April 1845, so far from selling traffic engines, the L&B was trying to *buy* 12in Bury engines from the Midland Railway; at about the same time the L&B was selling ballast engines; HMS *Terror* was the smaller of Sir John Franklin's two vessels, but 27 was larger than the London & Greenwich Railway engine known to have been installed in the other, HMS *Erebus*. The L&B monthly stock totals confirm that no engine was taken away in 1845). That the engine is unaccounted for can only be put down to McConnell's careless way with records. Its number was not taken by another engine until 1850.

28
was taken out of capital stock in 1853 and was sold or scrapped before June 1855.

30
was renumbered 5 in April 1856 and was replaced in September 1860. It was renumbered 1005 in 1860, and 1180 in May 1862. It worked on the Cromford & High Peak line from July 1862 for two years, before being sent to Longsight in July 1864. It was sold in June 1865 to Whitwick Colliery, Coalville for £700. The Crewe notebook entry which records "Loco Machinery No 30 from Wolverton, old Bury's" scrapped in No 1 Erecting Shop on 26th June 1877 presumably refers to some other engine, employed as a stationary in the workshops.

33
was sold in March 1847 for £560 to a contractor on the Rugby & Stamford line, Mr Burton. On Burton's bankruptcy, in September 1847 Thomas Dyson took over his contract together with this engine. In April 1848, following complaints by Dyson about its defective state, 33 was fitted with 5ft driving wheels at Wolverton.

34
was sold in June 1847 to McKenzie & Brassey for £700. In February 1848 they wrote complaining about it and were

allowed £50 off the price. McKenzie & Brassey sold it in December 1849 to another contractor, Edmund Sharpe, who put it to work on the (Little) North Western Railway and gave it the name *Helvellyn*. The Midland Railway worked the NWR from June 1852 and took over the locomotives; *Helvellyn* became MR 151. In January 1853 it was rebuilt as a 2-2-2 tank engine by Wm Fairbairn & Sons, and was scrapped in December 1858.

36
was installed in December 1847 on the traverser in the new shop on the east side at Wolverton. It was still there in February 1866 when I. W. Boulton visited the works and wanted to buy it. It is said to have been used for shunting in Crewe Works in 1884.

37, 39 and 47
For some reason 47 spent a long time (unusual for a 13in engine) in the sales list, from September 1847 until March 1849. It then worked for four months before going back on sale in July, but was again at work from October and was altered to a 2-2-2T in 1850/1 for the North London line. 37 was taken from capital stock in 1852/3; 39 in 1853-5; 47 was working in June 1855 and was allocated the number 11 in the April 1856 renumbering scheme. All three were sold to the Wiesbaden Railway in April 1856 for a total £1,650. Before being sent to Germany, 37 and 39 were altered to tanks for £100 each. The sale had been arranged between McConnell and the engineer of the Wiesbaden line, C. B. Vignoles, and (unusually) the engines had been sent off before payment was received. In September 1859 the LNWR threatened proceedings against Vignoles for the unpaid bill plus interest from the date of the sale; in December 1860 the money for two of the engines had still not been paid, and further solicitor's letters were sent off. What became of the engines is not known. There seems to be no record of three Bury tanks on the Wiesbadener, the first part of which opened from Rüdesheim to Mosbach on 24th July 1856, or on its successor the Nassauische Eisenbahn.

38, 44 and 46
were put to stationary work in Wolverton in 1856. 38 went from capital stock in 1852/3, the other two in 1853-5.

40
was renumbered 7 in April 1856 and was replaced in August 1857. As No 7(A) it was one of seven engines offered to the Portsmouth Railway Co for £800 each (but not taken) in August 1858. At that time McConnell said it would be broken up in the current half-year.

41
was taken from capital stock in 1853-5 and in 1855 was put to working a pump on the canal bank on the east side of the line at Wolverton. It was probably scrapped in 1864.

42
was taken from capital stock in 1853-5 and was sold In August 1856 to "Mr Hayton" for £500, the purchaser also paying for the engine's overhaul. This may be the contractor Thomas Hayton who had by then almost completed the Stamford & Essendine Railway (opened 1st November) and who was involved in the construction of the Hampstead Junction Railway just before his death later in 1856.

43
was renumbered 10 in April 1856, rebuilt as a 2-2-2 tank in 1859, renumbered 610 in April 1862, replaced and put on the duplicate list as 1127 in December 1862 and probably withdrawn for sale or scrapping in 1866.

45 and 54
were sold in April 1847 for £1,000 each to Thomas Brown of Leeds. Both engines were returned in February 1849. 45 was converted to a 2-2-2 tank in 1850/1, and following Ramsbottom's request for the loan of a tank engine for the Macclesfield branch in April 1851, was transferred to Longsight and arrived there on 27th January 1852, becoming NE Div 70. On the amalgamation of the Northern and North Eastern Divisions it was renumbered 470 and was withdrawn in 1858 (possibly auctioned for £165 in August).

54 was also converted to a tank and worked on the North London Railway from 1851 to 1854. In December 1854 Mr Palmer, of Marley Hill Colliery, Durham, offered to buy it and another tank, 47; the price was £900 for the two, but there was no sale at that time. It was working on 5th June 1855, but was 'for sale' at Camden on 27th, when George Richardson of 10 Craig's Court, Charing Cross made enquiries on behalf of a purchaser at the West India Docks. This was probably John Bowes & Partners, owners of Marley Hill Colliery and also of the Northumberland & Durham Coal Co which operated coal trains with its own locomotives from the docks over the NLR. In its $14\tfrac{1}{4}$ years 54 had run 199,986 miles and McConnell suggested a price of £550, but would accept £500 "as it stands" without any guarantee as to condition. Nothing further is recorded in the LNWR archives, but a Bury-type ex-LNWR 54 is said to have been delivered to Marley Hill in December 1855, perhaps becoming their No 7 or 8 in 1860 and working on into the 1870s (*Industrial Locomotives of Durham* p43).

48
was renumbered 19 in April 1856, but was replaced in July.

51
was working on the Bedford Branch in July/August 1858 when a spark set fire to five or six acres of wheat near Ampthill. It was replaced in September 1860, presumably becoming 1051 in the S Div duplicate list, then 1182 in May 1862 and was withdrawn the same year.

52
worked on the NLR in 1855, fitted with rubber springs. It was replaced in August 1861 and put in the S Div duplicate list as 1052 and was renumbered 1181 in the combined list in May 1862. It was retubed at Crewe in August 1868 and withdrawn towards the end of the following year.

Fig. 21 Bury 0-4-0 66, 68 and 73 as rebuilt at Perth in 1854 for the Dundee & Newtyle Railway. *(L. Ward)*

53
was taken out of capital stock in 1852/3 and was working as a stationary engine in Wolverton before June 1855.

55
was taken out of capital stock in 1853-5 and set up in Wolverton Works to provide steam for the steam hammer, replacing 75 on this duty.

56
was in the sales list from January to October 1848, after which it spent five months undergoing a general repair. It was taken out of capital stock in 1852/3 and put to stationary work in Wolverton by June 1855.

57
was taken out of capital stock in 1853-5, was on sale in June 1855 and is said by Bull to have been sold in 1856. Possibly this was the unspecified "old engine" sold to the Peebles Railway in October 1855 for £800. The Peebles accounts show that payment was made on 19th for a second-hand locomotive from Camden. The line had opened in the previous July with two Neilson 2-4-0 tanks having 5ft driving wheels and 15in cylinders. In view of the gradients on the Peebles line a 13in 5ft 6in Bury 2-2-0 seems an unlikely choice for a third engine. Perhaps 57 *had* been altered, as Bull says, to 5ft wheels for the Dunstable Branch, but if so this would have been after June 1852. In August 1856 the Peebles Rly advertised an engine and tender for sale for £850 which was described as having 5ft driving wheels and 14in x 20in cylinders; this may have been the ex-LNWR engine, which was eventually sold for £250 in January 1858. The purchaser was Hawthorn of Leith, who supplied two 0-4-2s to the Peebles company, with 4ft 6in driving wheels and 16in cylinders.

58
was taken from capital stock in 1853-5 and was on sale in June 1855. After the cost of water-heating apparatus had been looked into in November 1855, 58 was installed at Euston to provide hot water for carriage footwarmers. It was renumbered 58Z about January 1859 and was still at Euston in January 1860 when McConnell was told (at the request of the Auditor) not to consider it as a stationary engine but as a locomotive in store.

61
was sold in March 1848 to Messrs Duckett & Co for £1,050 (valued at £800). It was returned in May, possibly on the completion of this firm's contract on the Leeds & Thirsk Railway, but was taken out of stock again in February 1849, presumably on a further hire, and was returned in September. It was still in stock in June 1852, but was probably sold or scrapped shortly afterwards as Madigan's ballast engine *Kennedy* seems to have taken the number 61 in 1852/3.

62
was sold in May 1853 to the Swansea Vale Railway for £600. It retained its LNWR number on that line and was sold in February 1858 to C. H. Smith, a coalowner of Swansea, for £250.

63

was sold in June 1847 to "Mr Bewick, East Anglian Railways" for £1,000. Messrs Bewick & Burrows were contractors on the Swaffham-Dereham section, which opened in September 1848. The engine was returned in December, resumed its old number, and was finally sold to an unnamed purchaser in April 1853 for £600.

64

was sold in January 1855 for £500 to the Llanelly Railway & Dock Co who named it *Princess Helena*. It was rebuilt in 1857 and renamed *Helena*. It was put to stationary work, driving a sawmill, in January 1871.

65

On 6th May 1848 Richard Madigan asked for the loan of two engines to augment his ballast engine stock. Early in June, 65 was transferred to him and was probably named *Kennedy* as a partner for his engine *Bury* (formerly 71). After the ending of Madigan's contract *Kennedy* was handed back to the Locomotive Dept and in November 1849 was hired to Brassey for £50 per month for ballasting. Because its old number was then occupied it was renumbered 61, probably in 1852/3, and was for sale in June 1855. It may be the "old engine" sold in October 1855 to the Peebles Railway for £800 (but see 57 above).

66, 68 and **73**

73 was sold (with 82) in March 1847 to Mr Waring, a contractor on the East Lincolnshire Railway, for £1,050. He gave up part of this contract to Peto & Betts and returned 73 in September 1847. It was still in working stock at the end of 1849 but in 1851-3 it was away again, possibly on hire.

On 27th September 1853 McConnell reported that he was "in treaty" with the Scottish Central Railway for the sale of three small engines, but he did not expect to get £600 each for them. The Locomotive Committee sanctioned a drop of £100 on the total price "if necessary" and on 11th October he reported the sale of 66, 68 and 73 for £1,700 to the Dundee, Perth & Aberdeen Railway Junction. Delivery was at Preston, at that time the northern end of the LNWR. All three were taken to the Scottish Central Railway workshops at Perth and rebuilt with 14in x 20in cylinders and a 7ft wheelbase. Then they were sent to the DP&ARJ's Dundee & Newtyle branch where they were numbered 10, 11 and 12 and are said to have been named *Balbeuchly*, *Hatton* and *Law*, which were places on the eleven-mile Newtyle line with rope-worked inclines. They were known locally as 'Toads' - perhaps because they were green and rather squat. Around 1855 one of them worked on the pier line at Broughty Ferry and one was later sent to the steep (1 in 36) Carmyllie Branch. The Scottish Central Railway took them over in 1863, allocating numbers 63, 64 and 65, but they were quickly scrapped.

69

was renumbered 191 in April 1856, and was given duplicate number 1191 in 1862, being replaced in October. On 19th February 1863 it was sold for £500 to Edward Preston of Rhyl.

70

was renumbered 53 in April 1856 and was offered to the Portsmouth Railway Co in August 1858 for £800. It was not taken and was probably scrapped later in that year.

71

was transferred in April 1847 (at a valuation of £1,050) to Richard Madigan, the contractor for the permanent way maintenance trains. It was No 9 in his ballast stock and received the name *Bury* by March 1848. In September 1849 after the ending of Madigan's contract it was handed back to the Locomotive Dept and because its old number was occupied by another engine (shown in a list of June 1852) it was renumbered 82, probably in 1852/3. It was sold in November 1858 to Mr Tredwell for £375.

72

was sold in August 1847 for £1,150 (having just been valued at £700) to Thomas Oldham, of Bridge of Earn, Perth. He had been the contractor for the Errol section of the Dundee & Perth Railway, which had recently opened, so 72 probably went to work on one of his other contracts. It was not returned to the LNWR before the end of 1849; its number had been taken by another engine soon after it was sold to Oldham so if it did return it would have been renumbered.

74

was sold In September 1847 for £1,000 (valuation £800) to "Mr Collier, Llanelly Rly", on which line it was named *Princess Alice*. It was rebuilt at Llanelly as an 0-4-2 in 1858/9, was renamed *Alice* and became GWR 896 in 1873. It was withdrawn at the end of 1877.

75

Wolverton obtained its first steam hammer in 1847 and 75 was installed in the Works yard in May 1848 to provide steam. The hammer was roofed over in September but the engine remained outside. It was replaced on this duty by 55 in the first half of 1855.

76

On 10th February 1852 76 was at Aylesbury, where it was turned into a siding by mistake and crashed into some coal wagons; the engine was "disabled". It was renumbered 66 in April 1856 and replaced in August 1859, when it became 1066 in the S Div duplicate list. As 1066 it was sold in November 1859 to the Rhymney Iron Co for £400. A previous engine of theirs was another 0-4-0 Bury, ex-LB&SC 97, which Richard Madigan had once owned, and which exploded on 18th August 1859.

77

was sold in October 1853 to the Llanelly Railway & Dock Co for £600, and delivered at Gloucester. It was named *Prince Alfred*, then renamed *Alfred* and rebuilt as an 0-4-2 in 1862/3. It became GWR 897 in 1873 and was withdrawn at the end of 1877.

78

McConnell reported on 11th April 1848 that (at the request of Capt Moorsom) he had sent 78 to construction contract No 9 of the Chester & Holyhead

Railway. A section of this contract of Thomas Jackson's between Bangor and the Menai Strait was seriously behind schedule, and Moorsom told the C&HR Board that an engine had gone from Wolverton to work there and as it was a 14in coupled engine "may usefully be employed in Anglesey when the line is open". This did not happen; the line was opened as far as Bangor on 1st May but the engine was sent back to the S Div by 5th May and remained there.

On 2nd June 1853 the boiler of 78 exploded. When the engine was rebuilt in October 1847 the inner firebox had been enlarged, "the previous spherical crown, with the pressure on it balanced, was departed from by extending the firebox forward, and to support the unbalanced portion of the crown, four small roof-girders were fixed upon it. These girders had not sufficient support and when the plate became overheated one of the girders tore through the crown, causing an explosion." (W. P. Marshall, 1898)

It was renumbered 83 in April 1856 and was replaced in 1859, becoming 1083 in the S Div duplicate list. 1083 was sold in November 1859 to S. Clarkson for £400 "including £50 for putting her in repair".

79

was renumbered 84 in April 1856 and was hired to Brassey at £5 per day in May 1859 for ballasting on the Cannock Mineral line, which opened in November. It was replaced in July 1859, and if still working, would then have become 1084, but nothing further is known.

80

was renumbered 88 in April 1856 and went into the duplicate list as 1179 in May 1862, although it was not replaced until the following October. It was sold to Thomas Nelson of York for £600 on 31st March 1863.

81

was renumbered 90 in April 1856 and was replaced in September 1856.

82

was sold (with 73) in March 1847 to Mr Waring, a contractor on the East Lincolnshire Railway, for £1,050. Although its number was kept vacant, it did not return and was possibly the engine sold by Waring & Sons to the Monmouthshire Railway & Canal Co in September 1849 for £950; this engine became MR&C No 11 and was scrapped in 1870.

83

was sold in December 1847 to Marley Hill Coking Co for £825 (valued at £600); twelve months later a Mr Crawford was given £25 commission for arranging the sale.

84

was sold in November 1853 to Messrs Prothero for £600, delivered at Birmingham.

85 and 87

On 31st May 1848 the Huddersfield & Manchester Railway offered to exchange two heavy 18in 0-6-0 goods engines for two 13in 0-4-0s "at a valuation for each description." The new H&M engines were £2,500 each; the two 0-4-0s 85 and 87, valued at £800 and £900, were sent north in January 1849 and became NE Div 68 and 69 in July. By July 1853 neither had done much work (69's total mileage was only 688) and in 1855 Ramsbottom reported that they were "old contractor's engines, much worn when received" from the S Div and were then in store. Described as "nearly useless" 68 was sold for £380 to Mr Tredwell, contractor on the Oldham branch, in July 1856. 69 was described in January 1857 as a ballast engine "too light for the general purposes" of the NE Div and was hired to Davidson & Co, contractors on the Stockport, Disley & Whaley Bridge line for £4 per day. It was renumbered 469 in August 1857 after the amalgamation of the North Eastern and Northern Divisions, then became 469A on the N Div duplicate list in 1858; it worked on the Birstall branch about this time. It was renumbered 1131 in the combined duplicate list in April 1862 and was scrapped in the first half of 1864.

86

was sold in March 1847 to Mr Tredwell, contractor on the Oxford, Worcester & Wolverhampton Railway, for £1,050. It was still with him at the end of 1849; if it was returned it would have been renumbered.

88

was sold in May 1853 to the Swansea Vale Railway for £600. It retained its LNWR number but was named *Bee* by 1861. It was withdrawn in 1862.

89

was sold in September 1847 to Thomas Dyson for £1,000 (valuation £600). He complained about its defective state in April 1848 but was told that Wolverton was unable to provide new tubes. It was repaired at Wolverton at his expense in May, but he returned it early in 1850 and paid £150 compensation for not taking it, which was "to be placed against the amount expended on No 89 at Dyson's instructions." On its return to stock it would have been renumbered. A possibility is that the work done at Wolverton involved conversion to 2-2-0 (his other engine, 33, was a single with 5ft driving wheels fitted at his request) and that it took the vacant number 71. An otherwise inexplicable 71 is listed, with a 3c boiler, 5ft 6in driving wheels and 13in cylinders, among small engines for disposal on 7th June 1852.

Another possibility is that the returned 89 took the vacant number 83. The original 83 had been sold to the Marley Hill Coking Co in 1847, but an 83 reappears in the June 1852 list. This 83 was sold in November 1853 to A. & G. Holmes for £600, delivered at Wigan.

90

was sold in March 1853 to Mr Locke, acting on behalf of "the representatives of the late Sir John Guest" for £600.

Summary: Bury 2-2-0 Passenger Engines of 1837-41

1. Engines built with 12in cylinders:

No.	Maker	Delivered	Rebuilt	Remarks	No.	Maker	Delivered	Rebuilt	Remarks
1	Bury	7/1837	2a 13" 6/43	Sold 6/52 Wm Fairbairn & Sons, £450	14	Hick	6/1838	6d 14" 5'9" 5/49 2-2-2T /59	Reno'd 1 (4/56) Reno'd 1167 (5/62) replaced 9/63 Stat, Coalville (pump) from 1870s to c1900
2	Bury	7/1837	2a 13" 3/43 6d 6/49	Sold 5/47 Elisha W. Oldham, West Yorks Rly, £1,000 Returned 1/49 Reno'd 237 (1/49) Reno'd 837 (4/62) Reno'd 1201 (11/62) Scr a /63	15	Hick	7/1838	2a 13" a/44	Sold 6/52 Wm Fairbairn & Sons, £450
					16	Hawthorn	7/1837	2a 13" 6/43	Scr after collision at Kings Langley, 5/1/47
3	Bury	8/1838	2a 13" /44	Sold 6/52 Wm Fairbairn & Sons, £450	17	Hawthorn	10/1837	4b 13" 5'9" 3/45	Wdn /53-/55 For sale 6/55
4	Bury	8/1838	2a 13" /44	Sold 6/52 Wm Fairbairn & Sons, £450	18	Hawthorn	11/1837		Stat, Northampton (pump), 12/47-10/48 (? to Constrn Dept 12/49)
5	Bury	7/1838		Sold 3/48 Blaina Iron Wks (with No 9) total £1,050	19	Hawthorn	12/1837	4b 13" 5'9" 1/45	Wdn /53-/55 For sale 6/55
6	Bury	8/1838		Stat, Wol. (lathes) /47	20	Hawthorn	2/1838	2a 13" b/43	Wdn /55-/56
7	Bury	9/1838	4b 13" 5'9" /45	Wdn /53-/55 For sale 6/55	21	Hawthorn	3/1838	2a 13" 11/44	Wdn /53-/55 For sale 6/55
8	Bury	9/1838		Sold 8/47 Benjamin Greene, Rhymney Rly (with Aylesbury No 1) total £1,050	22	Haigh	8/1837	 2-2-2T /50-/51	Stat, Leighton (pump), 9/47-8/50 (? Reno'd 27 (/50) and sold 6/5 Wm Fairbairn & Sons, £450)
9	Bury	10/1838		Sold 3/48 Blaina Iron Wks, (with No 5)	23	Haigh	9/1837	6d 14" 5'9" /46	Reno'd 2 (4/56) Replaced 7/58
10	Hick	7/1837	2a 13" /44	Sold 6/52 Wm Fairbairn & Sons, £450	24	Haigh	10/1837	4b 13" 6'0" /45	Stat (?Northampton, pump, a /55-8/58 To store, Wol. 8/58)
11	Hick	1/1838	4b 13" 5'9" 11/44	Wdn /53-/55 For sale 6/55					
12	Hick	2/1838	2-2-2T /50-/51	Reno'd 5 (/50) Sold 6/52 Wm Fairbairn & Sons, £450	25	Rothwell	12/1837	2a 13" 3/42 2-2-2T /50-/51	Sold 10/55 NLR, £500
13	Hick	4/1838	6d 14" 5'9" a/47	Sold 9/55 HM Govt, £800 for Balaklava Rly, Crimea	26	Rothwell	3/1838	6d 14" 5'9" /46	Reno'd 3 (4/56) Reno'd 1003 (10/59) Sold 9/60 LC&DR, £500
					27	Rothwell	3/1838		Wdn between 1/47 & 9/47

No.	Maker	Delivered	Rebuilt	Remarks
28	Rothwell	8/1838	6d 14" 5'9" 12/47	Wdn /53; gone by 6/55
29	Rothwell	4/1838	4b 13" 5'9" /45	Wdn /53-/55 For sale 6/55
30	Rothwell	8/1838	6d 14" 5'9" 10/48	Reno'd 5 (4/56) Reno'd 1005 (9/60) Reno'd 1180 (5/62) Sold 19/6/65 Whitwick Colly, Coalville, £700
31	Mather	10/1837	(? 2-2-2T /50-/51)	(? Reno'd 191 (/50) and sold 6/52 Wm Fairbairn & Sons, £450)
32	Mather	12/1837	(? 2-2-2T /50-/51)	(? Reno'd 198 (/50) and sold 6/52 Wm Fairbairn & Sons, £450)
33	Mather	3/1838		Sold 3/47 Mr Burton, contractor, Rugby & Stamford Rly, £560 Transferred Thos Dyson 9/47
34	Mather	3/1838		Sold 6/47 McKenzie & Brassey, £650
35	Mather	4/1838	(? 2-2-2T /50-/51)	(? Reno'd 199 (/50) and sold 6/52 Wm Fairbairn & Sons, £450)
36	Mather	7/1838		Stat, Wol. (traverser) 12/47 Still there 2/66 ? Shunting at Crewe /84
49	Hick	1/1840	2a 13" a/44	Wdn /53-/55 For sale 6/55
50	Hick	1/1840	2a 13" 4/43 6d 14" 5'9" /46	Sold 9/55 HM Govt, £800 for Balaklava Rly, Crimea
51	Hick	2/1840	6d 14" 5'9" /46	Reno'd 1051 (9/60) Reno'd 1182 (5/62) Wdn /62

No.	Maker	Delivered	Rebuilt	Remarks
52	Hick	3/1840	6d 14" 5'9" /46	Reno'd 1052 (7/61) Reno'd 1181 (5/62) Wdn b /69

Two engines built for the Aylesbury Railway:

No.	Maker	Delivered	Rebuilt	Remarks
Aylesbury 1	Hick	1/1840	(? 13" 5'9" /46)	Sold 8/47 Benjamin Greene, Rhymney Rly (with No 8)
Aylesbury 2	Hick	1/1840	4b 13" 5'9" /46	Reno'd 2 (9/48) Wdn /52-/53 Stat, Birmingham New St (foot-warmers), 11/55 Reno'd 2S (c1/59) Still at B'ham 9/67 Taken away c/68

2. Engines built with 13in cylinders:

No.	Maker	Delivered	Rebuilt	Remarks
37	Bury	10/1839		Wdn /52-/53 Sold 4/56 Wiesbaden Rly, £550, as tank
38	Bury	10/1839		Wdn /52-/53 Stat, Wol. /56
39	Bury	11/1839		Wdn /53-/55 Sold 4/56 Wiesbaden Rly, £550, as tank
40	Bury	1/1840	7e 14" 6'0" /46	Reno'd 7(4/56) Reno'd 7A (8/57) Scr /58-/59
41	Bury	1/1840		Wdn /53-/55 Stat, Wol. (pump) a /55
42	Bury	2/1840		Wdn /53-/55 Sold 8/56 Mr Hayton, £500
43	Bury	2/1840	6d 14" 5'9" 5/49 2-2-2T /59	Reno'd 10(4/56) Reno'd 610 (4/62) Reno'd 1127 (12/62) Wdn /66?
44	Bury	3/1840		Wdn /53-/55 Stat, Wol. /56

No.	Maker	Delivered	Rebuilt	Remarks
45	Bury	3/1840	2-2-2T /50-/51	Sold 4/47 Thos Brown, Leeds, £1,000 Returned 2/49 Sent to NE Div 1/52 Reno'd NE Div 70 Reno'd 470 (8/57) Replaced 11/58
46	Bury	4/1840		Wdn /53-/55 Stat, Wol. /56
47	Bury	10/1840	2-2-2T /50-/51	Reno'd 11 (4/56) Sold 4/56 Wiesbaden Rly, £550
48	Bury	10/1840	4h 5'9" c/50	Reno'd 19 (4/56) Replaced 7/56
53	Bury	2/1841		Wdn /52-/53 Stat, Wol. by 6/55
54	Bury	3/1841	2-2-2T /50-/51	Sold 4/47 Thos Brown, Leeds, £1,000 Returned 2/49 Wdn 6/55 ? Sold Marley Hill Colly, 12/55
55	Bury	3/1841		Wdn /53-/55 Stat, Wol. (steam hammer) a /55 (replacing No 75)
56	Bury	3/1841	4h 5'9" 3/49	Wdn /52-/53 Stat, Wol. a /55
57	Bury	5/1841		Wdn /53-/55 For sale 6/55 ? Sold /55-/56
58	Bury	6/1841	5' DW before 9/47	Wdn /53-/55 Stat, Euston (footwarmers) 11/55 Reno'd 58Z (c1/59) Still at Euston 1/60

Summary: Bury 0-4-0 Goods Engines of 1838/9

No.	Maker	Delivered	Rebuilt	Remarks
61	Bury	11/1838		Sold 3/48 Duckett & Co, £1,050 Returned 5/48 Gone 2/49 Returned 9/49 Wdn /52-/53
62	Bury	11/1838	2/49	Sold 5/53 Swansea Vale Rly, £600
63	Bury	11/1838	3/49	Sold 6/47 Mr Bewick, East Anglian Rlys, £1,000 Returned 12/48 Sold 4/53, £600
64	Bury	1/1839	9g 14" x 20" /47	Sold 1/55 Llanelly Rly & Dock Co, £500
65	Bury	1/1839		Transf'd 6/48 to Rd Madigan, ballast engine *Kennedy* Reno'd 61 (/52-/53?) For sale 6/55
66	Bury	2/1839		Sold 10/53 Dundee, Perth & Aberdeen Rly Jct (with 68 & 73) total £1,700
67	Bury	2/1839		Scr after collision at Kings Langley 5/1/47
68	Bury	3/1839		Sold 10/53 DP&ARJ (with 66 & 73)
69	Bury	4/1839	9g 14" x 20" /47	Reno'd 191 (4/56) Reno'd 1191 (5/62) Sold 19/2/63 Edward Preston, Rhyl, £500
70	Bury	4/1839	9g 14" x 20" b/46	Reno'd 53 (4/56) ? Scr b /58.
71	Bury	5/1839		Transf'd 4/47 to Rd Madigan, ballast engine No 9, *Bury* Reno'd 82 (/52-/53) Sold 11/58 Mr Tredwell, £375
72	Bury	5/1839		Sold 8/47 Thos Oldham, Bridge of Earn, Perth, £1,150

No.	Maker	Delivered	Rebuilt	Remarks
73	Bury	6/1839		Sold 3/47 Mr Waring, contractor, East Lincs Rly, £1,050 Returned 9/47 Gone /51-/53 Sold 10/53 DP&ARJ (with 66 & 68)
74	Bury	7/1839		Sold 9/47 Mr Collier, Llanelly Rly, £1,000
75	Bury	7/1839		Stat Wol. (steam hammer), 5/48 - a /55
76	Bury	8/1839	9g 14" x 20" /47	Reno'd 66 (4/56) Reno'd 1066 (8/59) Sold 11/59, Rhymney Iron Co, £400
77	Bury	9/1839		Sold 10/53 Llanelly Rly & Dock Co, £600
78	Bury	11/1839	9g 14" x 20" 10/47	Reno'd 83 (4/56) Reno'd 1083 (/59) Sold 11/59 S. Clarkson, £400
79	Maudslay	9/1838	9g 14" x 20" b/46	Reno'd 84 (4/56) Replaced 7/59
80	Maudslay	10/1838	9g 14" x 20" 5/48	Reno'd 88 (4/56) Reno'd 1179 (5/62) Sold 31/3/63 Thos Nelson, York, £600
81	Maudslay	11/1838	9g 14"20" b/46	Reno'd 90 (4/56) Replaced 9/56
82	Maudslay	12/1838		Sold 3/47 Mr Waring, contractor, East Lincs Rly, £1,050
83	Maudslay	2/1839		Sold 12/47 Marley Hill Coking Co, £825
84	Maudslay	2/1839		Sold 11/53 Messrs Prothero, £600
85	Maudslay	7/1839		Transferred 1/49 Huddersfield & Manchester Rly Reno'd NE Div 68 (7/49) Sold 7/56 Mr Tredwell, contractor, Oldham branch, £380
86	Maudslay	8/1839		Sold 3/47 Mr Tredwell, contractor, OW&W Rly, £1,050
87	Maudslay	9/1839		Transferred 1/49 Huddersfield & Manchester Rly Reno'd NE Div 69 (7/49) Reno'd 469 (8/57) Reno'd 469A (/58) Reno'd 1131 (4/62) Scr a /64
88	Maudslay	10/1839		Sold 5/53 Swansea Vale Rly, £600
89	Maudslay	11/1839		Sold 9/47 Thos Dyson, £1,000 Returned 4/50 *Then:* Reno'd 71 (/50) as 2-2-0 Replaced 4/56 *Or:* Reno'd 83 (/50). Sold 11/53 A & G Holmes, £600
90	Maudslay	11/1839	6/49	Sold 3/53 Mr Locke, for the reps of late Sir John Guest, £600

LONDON & BIRMINGHAM RAILWAY
LATER ENGINES 1845-6

Bury, Curtis & Kennedy 14-inch 2-2-0 Passenger Engines Nos 59, 60, 91-99

In November 1843 the mail trains began climbing Camden incline without assistance from the rope, and from July 1844 every train went up unaided. All the through trains had already been speeded up by fifteen minutes and the 10am Down Mail had been retimed to take four hours to Birmingham.

Because of these accelerations the Locomotive Committee recommended on 13th June that Bury be given carte blanche "without reference to cost" to build two engines, the best that his firm was able to make for the service required. The following day the Board resolved that Bury, Curtis & Kennedy be authorised to prepare drawings (at L&B expense, up to £100) for the two new engines which would be delivered within three months. The drawings were finished in October, and Bury expected that the first engine would be delivered about the end of the year. The engine was designed to run eight carriages (38 tons including the six-ton tender) from London to Birmingham in three hours; allowing for the slower speed on Camden incline and 15 minutes for stoppages this meant a capability of at least 45 mph. Cylinders would be 14in diameter, pressure 60 lb/sq inch and driving wheels 5ft 9in.

Cylinders of 14in diameter were not a new thing for Bury; as far back as July 1841 he had tried out two engines on the London & Birmingham which Clarence Foundry had built for the London & Brighton Railway. They were 2-2-0 Nos 17/8, later LB&SC Nos 3/7.

From June 1844 through trains worked between Euston and the Tyne, passenger traffic was increasing and the 47-mile Peterborough branch was nearing completion but the total locomotive stock was still 90. The two new engines had not arrived when Bury told the Committee on 8th January 1845 that increasing traffic would require twenty passenger engines; the Board agreed and an order was to be placed with BC&K for another eighteen, delivered at one per week from 20th May, provided that the two being built were satisfactory. They arrived at the end of February and Bury said that the morning mail would now be able to get to Birmingham in 3½ hours, provided the carriages were limited to eight. The cost of each engine was £1,330, plus £200 for the tender and a delivery charge of £10. There was also some form of guard welded to the framing and "preparation in the wheels for preventing accidents from the breakage of axles" which added another £30, making a total of £1,570. BC&K wrote on 11th March that they would reduce the price by £5 per engine if the order for 18 more was confirmed; if ordered soon delivery would be in 4½ months at the rate of one every fortnight, alternately with engines they were building for the Irish Great Southern & Western Railway. The two new engines were numbered 59 and 60.

The Committee was present at trials in March 1845, when a four-carriage train was taken to Birmingham in 2 hours 51 minutes exclusive of eleven minutes for stoppages; it was clear that there would be no difficulty in maintaining a three hour schedule with a limited train. But there was something wrong with the engines and overall the results were disappointing. Bury identified the cause as a departure from the drawings, a mistake by his works foreman. The engines were sent back to Liverpool for correction, which took a fortnight. The first of them returned and started work on 1st May. Some fast running followed. On the first day the new regular mail train took only 2 hours and 58 minutes to Birmingham and on the 7th only 2½ hours, excluding five minutes for stoppages. The train was praised for its easy uniform speed and freedom from oscillation.

In the same month the other engine was returned, followed by a third, which was numbered 91; on 6th May the Committee asked Bury to proceed as fast as possible with the rest of the order, which had been suspended pending the outcome of the trials. But this was at the beginning of the chaotic period known as the Railway Mania, and all locomotive manufacturers were being swamped with orders. Bury, Curtis & Kennedy could not now promise their first delivery until November. The price per engine and tender was reduced to £1,565.

Shortly after the 14in four-wheelers began work, a 14¾in engine was borrowed from the Manchester & Birmingham Railway. This was M&B No 8, a Sharp Bros 2-2-2, which from its arrival created a big impression among the directors. Bury's new engine had been very fast with short trains but the Down Day Mail now consisted of at least nine carriages and averaged nearly eleven and it was timed to get to Birmingham in 3½ hours. With this in mind on 12th June the Committee authorised Bury to alter two or more of the engines on order to a larger size.

BC&K had stopped other work to push on with L&B orders; with Clarence Foundry fully occupied, Bury used the facilities at Wolverton Works to build two similar but slightly bigger engines. They had a heating surface greater than that of M&B No 8.

They were not part of the BC&K order, and there is no mention of their building or any purchase of components in the surviving L&B records. Their construction seems to have been initiated by Bury during the locomotive shortage in response to the Committee's request for two enlarged engines and as his answer to the widely proclaimed superiority of M&B No 8. Probably the engines were built from spare parts in the Wolverton stores. They were given bigger boilers than the other 14in passenger engines; the same size of boiler was used in the rebuilding of the goods engines with 14in cylinders from mid-1846. The first Wolverton-built engine, No 92, came out about November 1845; the second, No 95, appeared two months later.

Apart from the first three, none of the passenger engines ordered from BC&K had been completed when on 7th October 1845 the Committee asked if they could

Fig. 22
No 92, the first locomotive built at Wolverton Works, 1845. *(LNWR)*

be given the largest possible heating surface, and whether 6ft driving wheels might be more suitable. The construction of many of the engines was too far ahead to permit these alterations but on 12th December it was arranged that the last eleven would have boilers increased to 1,000 sq ft heating surface, and that they would be 2-2-2s.

Deliveries of the BC&K engines began on 29th December 1845 when No 93, the first of the six 14in engines, was sent off from Liverpool via the GJR. The others, up to No 99, had arrived by July 1846. Because of the increases in size of the boiler and firebox to meet the wishes of the Committee, the price had gone up to £1,658 10s (£1,658.50) each.

Dimensions

Nos 59/60/91

Cylinders (2 inside)	14" x 18"
Heating surface	
Tubes (96, 2¼" dia, 10' 10" long)	612.56 sq ft
Firebox	46.50 sq ft
Total	659.06 sq ft
Diameter of wheels	
Leading	4' 3"
Driving	5' 9"
Wheelbase	8' 0"
Weight	
On leading wheels	5 tons 17.5 cwt
On driving wheels	8 tons 10.0 cwt
Total	14 tons 7.5 cwt

Nos 92/5 (built at Wolverton)

Cylinders, wheels and weights as above.

Heating surface	
Tubes (110, 2¼" dia, 11' 1" long)	712.69 sq ft
Firebox	48.77 sq ft
Total	761.46 sq ft

Nos 93/4/6-9

Cylinders, wheels and weights as above.

Heating surface	
Tubes (108, 2¼" dia, 10' 10" long)	689.70 sq ft
Firebox	46.50 sq ft
Total	*735.12 sq ft

See note on heating surfaces in Introduction.

Apart from the boiler size there were several differences in this group of engines, notably in the valve gear. According to Bull, No 59 and 60 had motion similar to that of the early engines, with gearing handles, the difference being that the rocking shaft was mounted well behind the leading axle instead of above and just in front of it. This reversion to the old form of gear is difficult to understand unless it had proved more reliable in use than the large gab gear with its single control lever. Perhaps it had some advantage in high speed running; perhaps drivers preferred its complexity (as some present-day car drivers scorn the automatic gear change) or perhaps it was a makeshift alteration, made when the two engines were sent back to Liverpool, as the easiest way to remodel a failed original gear.

Nos 92/5, built at Wolverton, also had the old form of gear, which is understandable if they were put together from spare parts. No 91 had the large gab gear but 93/4/6-99 had link motion as built, and were the first L&B engines to be so fitted from new.

According to James Bull the valves on No 96 were between the cylinders; on all the others they were above, as in the previous Bury engines.

Nos 59/60 and 91 were without the small brass dome; instead the safety valves, with levers fore-and-aft, were set directly in the firebox top. The others had the small dome with fore-and-aft levers but later some were given a spring balance safety valve near the front end of the boiler, replacing one of the valves on the dome. Bull says the Wolverton engine 92 was like this and the photograph of 96 toward the end of its life shows the same arrangement. All except 92/5 had copper capped chimneys. Early in their careers balance weights were added to the driving wheel centres and later some were given leading wheels with plain spokes.

There are scanty records of them in service. Two were involved in accidents at Camden, 91 on 29th July 1845 and 95 on 30th May 1847. On 17th August 1848 during the footplatemen's strike the Up York mail, despite having three red tail lights, was rammed in the rear by No 98 with the following Peterborough mail. No 98 was being driven by Thomas Richardson, a fitter promoted to the footplate by McConnell only nine days before.

All except 94 and 96 are recorded with trains leaving Euston during the months of July and November 1847, taking up to fifteen carriages alone.

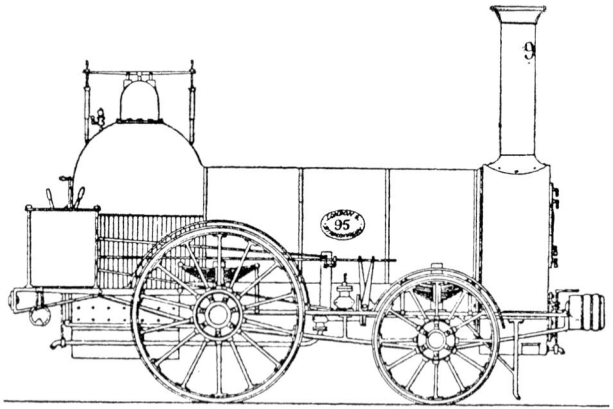

Fig. 23 No 95, the second locomotive built at Wolverton, 1846.
(D.Leitch)

In August 1860 the London Chatham & Dover Railway, being very short of motive power pending the arrival of engines ordered, asked if the LNWR had any to spare. Three long-boiler Jones & Potts 4-2-0s were suggested and an offer of £500 each was accepted on 13th September. But the cost of repairs, estimated at £418 extra, was considered too much and instead the LC&DR bought three Bury singles at the same price but with repairs at Wolverton thrown in free. The £1,500 was paid in two lots, £1,000 on 16th November 1860 and £500 on 17th January 1861. The engines were No 3 (formerly 26) and two of the 1845 14in engines, 50 (formerly 60) and 91. They were taken through the London streets from Camden to Battersea by Pickfords, 50 on 3rd November and 91 on the 4th. In January 1861 they were named *Gadfly* (50) and *Hornet* (91) with brass nameplates on the boiler side. By May *Hornet* had run a mere 1,624 miles on the LC&DR. *Gadfly* was tried on the Sheerness branch in April 1861. Both are said to have been tender engines, with hollow leading axles and link motion, and a dome close behind the chimney, on which were two spring balance safety valves; there was another spring balance valve on the raised firebox top. In July 1863 they were dumped on a siding at Canterbury, where they were later joined by ex-26 *Wasp*. All three were sold for scrap in April 1864.

Of the other 14in 2-2-0s, 59 was renumbered 21 in 1856 and thereafter disappears from view, being replaced in 1857; six more were replaced in 1861 leaving two, 95/6, in capital stock at the end of that year; these two joined the other six in Ramsbottom's duplicate list in May 1862. Contractors bought at least three of them, including the two built at Wolverton, early in 1863. In January 92 went for £600 to Joseph Firbank described as "contractor on the Bedford and Cambridge line" while 95 was sold to Robert Morris of Liverpool for £500. In February 94 was sold to Tredwell of Handsworth, also for £500. 99 was probably sold or scrapped in 1863, and 97/8 seem to have been the two sold for £400 each in April 1864 to the Mersey Docks & Harbour Board, which employed a variety of old locomotives, some as stationary pumping engines.

The remaining two are recorded in the earliest-known complete duplicate list which is dated 30th November 1867; these were 1157 and 1160, ex-93 and 96. Both were withdrawn in the first half of 1869, but 1160 having been retubed as recently as July 1867 saw several years of further service in Crewe Works where it was used for hauling materials between the shops. Its number was painted out and was replaced by the words LOCO MACHINERY in 1½-inch letters.

It survived to be recorded by the official photographer about 1880. For ten years from 1904 the LNWR issued reproductions of this photograph in its popular series of postcards, captioned "Old Passenger Locomotive" but with the absurd description: "Built in 1835 for the Liverpool and Manchester Railway. The first engine with inside cylinders."

Summary: 2-2-0s built by Bury, Curtis & Kennedy and at Wolverton Works, 1845-6

No.	Maker	Date	Renumbered	Remarks
59	BC&K	2/1845	21(4/56)	Replaced 7/57
60	BC&K	2/1845	50(4/56), 1050(11/59)	Sold 11/60 LC&DR, £500
91	BC&K	5/1845	1091(8/59)	Sold 11/60 LC&DR, £500
92	Wolverton	11/1845	1092(6/61), 1156(5/62)	Sold 5/1/63 Mr Firbank, contractor, Bedford & Cambridge line, £600
93	BC&K	12/1845	1093(1/61), 1157(5/62)	Wdn a /69
94	BC&K	1/1846	1094(6/61), 1158(5/62)	Sold 16/2/63 Mr Tredwell, Handsworth, £500
95	Wolverton	1/1846	1159(5/62)	Sold 29/1/63 Robt Morris, Liverpool, £500
96	BC&K	3/1846	1160(5/62)	Wdn a /69 Transferred to Crewe Works as *Loco Machinery*, /69 Still there c1880
97	BC&K	4/1846	1097(8/61), 1161(5/62)	Sold 1/4/64 Mersey Docks & Harbour Board, £400
98	BC&K	7/1846	1098(6/61), 1162(5/62)	Sold 1/4/64 Mersey Docks & Harbour Board, £400
99	BC&K	7/1846	1099(7/61), 1163(5/62)	Wdn /63

Fig. 24   14in passenger engine built by Bury, Curtis & Kennedy in 1846, originally 96; renumbered 1160 in 1862, withdrawn from stock in 1869 and used to transport materials within Crewe Works. Photographed at Crewe about 1880. Changes since building include the addition of a safety valve on the front of the boiler and the removal of one of those on the firebox; the reversing gear has been altered and moved to the left side. The valves appear to be above the cylinders, operated through rocking shafts; as built 96 is said to have had the valves between the cylinders. The chimney is not the original and is the type used by Benjamin Hick & Co in the 1840s; it may have been attached for the photograph, because only one nutted bolt is visible among eight holes in the chimney base and smokebox.

(LNWR photo)

Bury, Curtis & Kennedy 15-inch 2-2-2 Passenger Engines Nos 100-110

As arranged on 12th December 1845, the last eleven of the engines ordered in the preceding May were to be on six wheels with bigger boilers. The first of these 2-2-2s arrived in August 1846 and was given the number 100; the remaining engines of the order, 101-10, were on the line by the end of the year. They were a simple enlargement of the 14in engines, with a trailing axle added under the footplate and cylinders increased by one inch in diameter and two inches in stroke. The boiler was longer and fatter with many more tubes and its centre line was about 6ft 6in above the rails; the round firebox was increased to its maximum possible size, with a very high domed top which gave the engines the nickname 'Haystacks'. Like the 14in 2-2-0s they had copper chimney caps. It has been said that they had the large gab valve gear, and were the last new engines on the S Div so equipped. The use of this gear sounds unlikely, and they certainly had link motion by 1850. A good idea of their appearance can be obtained from GS&WR No 36, now preserved at Cork, which is from a series built about the same time and (apart from being 6½ inches wider in gauge) is generally similar in design. In this engine the valves are above the cylinders, worked by indirect link motion through rocking shafts.

The price of 100-10 was £2,150 each.

Dimensions

Cylinders (2 inside)	15" x 20"
Heating surface	
Tubes (152, 12' 0" long)	1,032.12 sq ft
Firebox	62.22 sq ft
Total	1,094.34 sq ft
Grate area	11.0 sq ft
Boiler pressure	75 lb/sq in
Diameter of wheels	
Leading	4' 6"
Driving	6' 0"
Trailing	4' 0"
Wheelbase	8' 0" + 7' 0" = 15' 0"
Weight	
On leading wheels	7 tons 6 cwt
On driving wheels	11 tons 10 cwt
On trailing wheels	2 tons 10 cwt
Total	21 tons 6 cwt

The heating surface and tube details are from McConnell's report of May 1853 and may suggest that some increase had taken place since building. The near-contemporary GS&WR engine is said to have 151 tubes of $2\frac{1}{8}$in diameter, 11ft 11in long, with approximate heating surfaces of 1000 sq ft (tubes) and 1060 sq ft (total).

From their arrival these engines made a dramatic improvement to passenger train working and allowed

Fig. 25   Bury, Curtis & Kennedy 2-2-2 36 of the Great Southern & Western Railway, very similar to the contemporary L&BR Nos 100-110, the 'Haystacks'.

Fig. 26   Bury, Curtis & Kennedy 2-2-2 36 of the Great Southern & Western Railway, as preserved at Glanmire Road (Kent) station, Cork. September 1993.

(H. Jack)

the borrowed Sharp single to be returned to the M&B Division at the end of September. Every engine of the class was recorded on trains leaving Euston in 1847, taking up to 29 carriages alone, but usually double-headed on trains of over twenty.

On 20th July 1847 the twelve-carriage 2.45pm Down train was headed by 108 when it was involved in a collision at Tring. The driver was Clayton, an ex-fitter and according to 'Veritas Vincit' one of McConnell's favourites. On becoming a driver "he said he would show the ****s what driving was, and he has kept his word." He was sacked the next day.

On the evening of 28th January 1850 the Up Newcastle express, consisting of seven carriages and a brake van, was headed by 102; the engine was derailed by a broken 75 lb rail on a stone-sleepered section in Roade cutting. Both lines were blocked until the following morning.

Crampton's *Namur* was tested against 102 but the report of 23rd March 1847 has not survived. In connection with McConnell's search for a better boiler, 104 was the subject of an experiment in May 1852 to ascertain the amount of coke consumed while stationary. The only details known from the report are the grate area, given as 11 sq ft, and the boiler pressure, 75 lb/sq in.

None of the 2-2-2s are known to have been rebuilt. One (103) was replaced in 1857, another nine were replaced by McConnell but survived into the 1862 duplicate list, to be scrapped quickly thereafter. Only 106 remained in the capital list in 1861 but it went into the 11xx duplicate list with the others and in August 1862 became the first S Div engine to be replaced by a Crewe product. Its duplicate list number is not known (it is unlikely to have been 1160 or 1180, both of which have been suggested) and it seems to be the 15in engine recorded as scrapped in the half-year ending November 1864.

Summary: 2-2-2s built by Bury, Curtis & Kennedy, 1846

No.	Date	Renumbered	Remarks
100	8/1846	1100(11/60), 1147(5/62)	Wdn by 2/63
101	5/9/1846	1101(10/60), 1148(5/62)	Wdn by 2/63
102	9/1846	1102(8/60), 1149(5/62)	Wdn by 2/63
103	9/1846		Replaced 5/57
104	9/1846	1104(9/60), 1150(5/62)	Wdn by 2/63
105	10/1846	1105(11/60), 1151(5/62)	Wdn by 2/63
106	10/1846	11xx (5/62)	Scr b /64
107	10/1846	1107(11/60), 1152(5/62)	Wdn by 2/63
108	11/1846	1108(1/61), 1153(5/62)	Wdn by 5/63
109	11/1846	1109(1/61), 1154(5/62)	Wdn by 5/63
110	12/1846	1110(8/60), 1155(5/62)	Wdn by 5/63

Bury, Curtis & Kennedy Goods Engines 1845-6
Nos 111-118

The Board decided in January 1845 that the L&B should begin carrying coal; Bury's opinion was that sixteen engines were needed and the Locomotive Committee placed orders for sixteen on 11th February, eight of which were to be built by Bury, Curtis & Kennedy. Two of these were to be 0-4-2 type "similar to the one furnished to the Northern & Eastern Railway" but Bury was convinced that four-wheeled engines would "answer better than engines on six wheels" so the other six were to be 0-4-0s, costing £1,890 each including tender. All were to have 15in cylinders and 5ft driving wheels with delivery commencing in July.

The first one, an 0-4-0, began work on 24th September 1845; the second followed three weeks later. BC&K wrote to the LNWR Secretary on 17th October saying they had stopped all other work "to push your engines through" and asked for payment on credit to "Roberts, Curtis & Co."

After the first three had been tried out it was reported that they were capable of drawing 35 wagons without losing time, but with 40 they lost about an hour on the journey. All six four-wheelers were on the line by December numbered 111-6 and the two 0-4-2s 117/8 followed in February 1846. They were standard Bury designs with inside iron bar-frames and round, domed fireboxes similar in size to those of the 15in 2-2-2s. The chimneys had copper caps.

Dimensions

0-4-0 Nos 111-6

Cylinders (2 inside)	15" x 20"
Heating surface	
Tubes (121, 2¼" dia, 11' 6" long)	819.59 sq ft
Firebox	57.28 sq ft
Total	876.87 sq ft
Boiler pressure	70 lb/sq in
Diameter of wheels	5' 0"
Wheelbase	8' 0"
Weight	
On leading wheels	7 tons 2 cwt
On driving wheels	10 tons 12 cwt
Total	17 tons 14 cwt

0-4-2 Nos 117/8

Cylinders (2 inside)	15" x 20"
Heating surface	
Tubes (129, 2¼" dia, 10' 10" long)	823.12 sq ft
Firebox	63.60 sq ft
Total	886.72 sq ft
Boiler pressure	70 lb/sq in
Diameter of wheels	
Coupled	5' 0"
Trailing	3' 6"
Wheelbase	8' 0" + 6' 0" = 14' 0"
Weight	
On leading wheels	7 tons 11 cwt
On driving wheels	7 tons 15 cwt
On trailing wheels	3 tons 3 cwt
Total	18 tons 9 cwt

Bury reported on all the goods engines in November 1846. He said 117 and 118 were the most powerful on the line but were to some extent crippled by the addition of the third pair of wheels which detracted from the adhesive weight, increased the friction on curves and added to the weight to be moved. The four-wheeled engines, which he had recommended, had much the same power but with better adhesion, were more compact and required less repair. The daily average of 111-6 was 75.09 miles, with 132 tons; 117/8 averaged 88.33 miles with 136 tons. Coke consumption of 117/8 was 55.5 lb per mile; that of 111-6 was greater (58.4) because they did more shunting than other classes. The 0-4-0s were handy engines and "do all the drudgery of the line." Should the directors ask what engines were best for the future service on the line "I can urge with perfect confidence and certainty in the results the adoption of this class of engine with some small alterations by which their power would be much increased."

The L&B Superintendent Henry Pringle Bruyeres gave his opinion that 117/8 were the best engines on the line and on 18th December the newly formed General Locomotive Committee, consisting of directors from the three constituent companies, decided that the six-wheeled 117 should be adopted as the pattern for engines about to be ordered for the London & Birmingham Division.

A report of June 1852 gave the average loads taken as:
    0-4-0s 111-6:   113 tons
    0-4-2s 117/8:   125 tons.

By then the total mileage of the 0-4-0s far exceeded that of other goods engines except the originals of 1838.

In June 1854 112 was fitted experimentally with a set of iron tubes, and ran 32,106 miles between then and the date of the report, 28th February 1856. In 1853/4 115 was fitted with rubber springs and in 1854/5 112/3/5 were loaned to the North London Railway.

Accidents

On 5th January 1847 115 was with 2-2-0 No 16 on a double-headed Up goods train which collided with the rear of a coal train standing in Kings Langley station. The drivers and firemen of both engines were killed. On 24th May 1850 the engine of the 8.00pm Peterborough-London goods train, 118, was derailed at Hanslope by a bale of wool which had fallen from an earlier train. The engine fell into the field on its left side and the dome was cut in two by wagons piling over it. The driver, John Hague, was "frightfully scalded" but survived. In an uncharacteristic spasm of compassion the Board awarded him 40 guineas (£42), presumably in lieu of wages, and a year later paid his surgeon's account for £29 7s (£29.35). In December 1852, not long after his return to work, he was involved in a collision at Kilburn, for which he lost his annual gratuity and was fined £1, and in 1854 he was fined again for crashing through level crossing gates on the Bedford branch.

Disposal

All were replaced before the divisions were amalgamated, but some entered the 11xx duplicate list in May 1862. 117 was replaced in May 1859 and was given the suffix D; as 117D it was hired for ballasting to Mr Maxwell of the Redditch Railway in July 1859 for £3 10s (£3.50) per day paid in advance "exclusive of working expenses". The Redditch Railway (MR) opened on 19th September the same year, and the engine was sold in November to the Clay Cross Co for £500 plus £50 for repairs.

113 is believed to be the engine sold as 1175 on 25th October 1865 for £850 to the contractors Kirk & Parry of London. After completing their work on the Barking-Upminster-Pitsea line of the London, Tilbury & Southend Railway in 1888, they offered this engine (still numbered 1175) for sale.

Summary:

1. 0-4-0s built by Bury, Curtis & Kennedy, 1845

No.	Date	Renumbered	Remarks
111	24/9/1845		Replaced 7/59
112	14/10/1845		Replaced 7/59
113	26/10/1845	1113(6/61), 1175(5/62)	Sold 25/10/65 Kirk & Parry, London, £850
114	18/11/1845	1114(3/61), 1176(5/62)	Wdn by 2/65
115	2/12/1845	1115(3/61), 1177(5/62)	Wdn by 1/66
116	18/12/1845		Replaced 7/59

2. 0-4-2s built by Bury, Curtis & Kennedy, 1846

No.	Date	Renumbered	Remarks
117	6/2/1846	117D(5/59)	Sold 11/59 Clay Cross Co, £550
118	16/2/1846	1118(4/61), 1170(5/62)	Wdn by 8/63

Tayleur, Longridge and Nasmyth 0-6-0 Goods Engines, 1845-48   Nos 119-144

In January 1845 the Locomotive Committee began negotiations with Robert Stephenson for eight of his patent 0-6-0s but as his firm was then unable to take the order it was sub-contracted to Nasmyth, Gaskell & Co of Patricroft. On 9th May another six were ordered, to be built by Charles Tayleur & Co of Vulcan Foundry, Newton-le-Willows, one to be delivered in November, three in December and two in January 1846. On 6th August the Board authorised the order of ten more and in October the goods engines ordered so far were listed as:

Tayleur: 8 engines, delivery from November 1845.
Jones & Potts: 8 engines, delivery from March 1846.
Nasmyth: 8 engines, delivery from end of 1846.

Just after this the order was further increased to 26 engines, and some reallocation of the Stephenson sub-contracts took place; Jones & Potts dropped out and R. B. Longridge & Co of Bedlington Ironworks, Morpeth, were brought in to build twelve of the engines. There is

Fig. 27
Stephenson patent long-boiler 0-6-0 'Mammoth' type, 1845.

no record of this firm's first order but it was evidently in November; they offered six more engines "on the same terms" which was accepted on 12th December. The orders finally arranged were:

Maker	Date		L&B/LNWR Nos
Nasmyth, Gaskell:	11/2/1845	8 engines	137-44
Tayleur:	9/5/1845	6 engines	119-24
Longridge:	11/1845	6 engines	125-30
Longridge:	12/12/1845	6 engines	131-6

Prices appear to have been: Tayleur: £2,105; Nasmyth: £2,388; Longridge: £2,455.

The first to arrive was 120 from Tayleur on 4th December 1845. There was something wrong with it so it was almost immediately sent to the Midland Railway, where others of the type were in use. The Midland discovered a defect in the blast pipe, repaired it and returned 120 early in February 1846. By the middle of March five of them were on the line, but the first impression was that they were no better than the other new goods engines from Bury, Curtis & Kennedy.

Works or so-called 'rotation' numbers 225-30 have often been quoted for Tayleur's six engines but these are doubtful, having been estimated in the 1890s. Tayleur also had a series of 'working numbers' which were given to all jobs - not merely new locomotive construction. Working numbers for these six were 608-13 (engines) and 614-9 (tenders).

The first of Longridge's engines, L&B 125/6, arrived in May and 127 in June. By 9th July the Locomotive Committee was complaining that they were "imperfect." They had iron tubes; future engines were requested to have brass. An engine from Longridge arrived on 15th September, without a tender, and Bury's letter enquiring about this quotes the Longridge works number 201. This was either LNWR 129 or 130, which started work on 2nd October and 21st September respectively.

Nasmyth's first three engines arrived in April 1847, the last in November; their works numbers were 64-71. The last engine of all, LNWR 136 of Longridge's second order, was not delivered until the first week of March 1848.

They were all Stephenson's patent long-boiler 0-6-0 'Mammoth' type with 15in x 24in inside cylinders inclined 8° upwards to the front and T-iron wheels, the centre pair of which were flangeless. It is quite apparent, and was admitted by Stephenson, that the design was influenced by the success of Bury's engines; the framing, of iron only, was inside and had only two bearings on each axle. It consisted of two straight iron plates, each 1 inch thick and 8 inches deep, to which the horn plates were riveted. The horns were stayed at the bottom by horizontal iron bars and by diagonal bars to the frame plate at its ends. The outer firebox had a tall vaulted top, a square version of Bury's domed type but with flat and heavily stayed sides. There was a single steam chest between the cylinders; the feed pumps, located between the frames in front of the rear axle, were worked from the backward-gear eccentrics. The long boiler was designed to increase the tube heating surface without enlarging the diameter of the barrel.

In certain details the engines supplied by the three manufacturers differed, and in addition there were other variations within the Tayleur and Longridge batches. For example the wheels of the Nasmyth engines had been ordered as 4ft 9in diameter, but were 4ft 6in as delivered. The Tayleurs were 4ft 6in also, but Longridge's had 5ft wheels. The second group from Longridge had a cast-iron balance weight on each wheel boss, opposite the crank, added at McConnell's suggestion. The boilers also differed in details and dimensions; the last two from Tayleur were the smallest of all. James Bull says the first group from Longridge had the regulator handles "rather awkwardly placed" between the safety valve spring-tubes, but in the second group the regulator handles were "of the ordinary type" and both spring balance levers were angled to the left side of the footplate.

Dimensions

Tayleur Nos 119/24

Cylinders (2 inside)	15" x 24"
Boiler (oval)	
Vertical diameter	3' 6"
Horizontal diameter	about 3' 1"
Length of barrel	12' 5¾"
Heating surface	
Tubes (115, 2" dia, 12' 9" long)	767.70 sq ft
Firebox	54.65 sq ft
Total	822.35 sq ft
Grate area	10.4 sq ft
Boiler pressure	70 lb/sq in
Diameter of wheels	4' 6"
Wheelbase	5' 11" + 5' 0" = 10' 11"
Weight	
On leading wheels	5 tons 18 cwt
On driving wheels	9 tons
On trailing wheels	8 tons 0.5 cwt
Total	22 tons 18.5 cwt
Tender (6 wheel) capacity	coke 105 cu ft
	water 1000 gal

Tayleur Nos 120-3

Cylinders, pressure, wheels and weights as above

Heating surface	
Tubes (147, 1⅝" dia, 12' 9" long)	797.33 sq ft
Firebox	52.40 sq ft
Total	*849.82 sq ft
Wheelbase	6' 0" + 5' 4" = 11' 4" (?)

Longridge Nos 125-36

Cylinders as above

Heating surface	
Tubes (156, 1¾" dia, 13' 4½" long)	952.95 sq ft
Firebox	61.50 sq ft
Total	*1,014.49 sq ft
Grate area	10.20 sq ft
Diameter of wheels	5' 0"
Wheelbase	6' 0½" + 5' 4" = 11' 4½"

Weight

	Nos 125-32	*Nos 133-6*
On leading wheels	6 tons 3.0 cwt	6 tons 13.25 cwt
On driving wheels	8 tons 3.5 cwt	8 tons 1.0 cwt
On trailing wheels	8 tons 7.0 cwt	8 tons 6.0 cwt
Total	22 tons 13.5 cwt	23 tons 0.25 cwt

Nasmyth Nos 137-44

Cylinders as above

Heating surface	
Tubes (151, 1¾" dia, 12' 9" long)	881.92 sq ft
Firebox	52.40 sq ft
Total	*934.40 sq ft
Diameter of wheels	4' 6"
Wheelbase	6' 0" + 5' 4" = 11' 4" (?)
Weight	
On leading wheels	6 tons 14.5 cwt
On driving wheels	6 tons 4.0 cwt
On trailing wheels	9 tons 5.5 cwt
Total	22 tons 4.0 cwt

See note on heating surfaces in Introduction.

Unsatisfactory performance

On 2nd September 1846 Bury had written to Tayleur about defective workmanship on 120 and 123; the engines were nearly as much in the shops as at work. This was not entirely due to bad workmanship, he said, but it had much to do with it. On 23rd he wrote again, asking for "much wanted" new wheels for their engines, and on 26th to Longridge urging them to send wheels. As a stopgap on 2nd October he asked Nasmyth, Gaskell to let him have a set of wheels from the engines they were making, and a fortnight later extended the order to two sets, engine and tender wheels, axles and axle boxes; on 15th he ordered other sets of wheels and axles from Longridge and Tayleur for their engines.

On 13th October 1846 there was a special meeting of the Locomotive Committee attended by Bury and Stephenson to discuss the "defective state of the engines supplied by Tayleur and Longridge"; a month later the Committee complained of the "imperfect performance and continual want of repair of the goods engines on Mr Stephenson's specification."

On 2nd November Bury wrote to Stephenson reporting that 125 (Longridge) which had been delivered six months before was in the shops for a change of wheels after only 13,959 miles, less than Tayleur's 120. He did not think 5ft wheels had much advantage over 4ft 6in. The following day William Ferguson was sent by Stephenson to Wolverton "with two or three hands accustomed to erection" to try to keep the patent engines in repair.

On 24th November, in response to a request from the Board, Bury reported on the long-boiler goods engines:

"A defect exists in the ratio of the wheel to the stroke, which renders these engines useless for the purposes of the Company, as the speed at which the piston has to travel to obtain the requisite progressive motion on the road is far too rapid either for durability or economy. This violent action of the piston, assisted by the angle at which the cylinder is placed and the shortness of the connecting rod, is very soon visible on the tyres of the middle or crank wheels, for in the course of working over a few thousand miles, a certain portion of the tread of the wheels is worn into a groove. This being only on one pair of wheels, and on those, not at the same place or to the same depth, a large amount of slipping takes place and the engine soon becomes useless. This is no longer an opinion. Nos 120, 121, 122, 125 and 126 have all been sent into the shops for the same defect after about 15,000 miles each. The daily performances of these engines exhibit a capability of only about 36 waggons, a weight far below their apparent power, which at 9 lbs friction per ton on the level with 7 lbs gravity should be about 400 tons, whereas it is only about 250. This discrepancy can only be accounted for by the excessive speed and friction of the engine, and it entirely corroborates my frequent assertion that six-wheeled coupled engines are badly adapted to any traffic, but on a line similarly situated to the Southern Division of the L&NW, most improper."

He added that these engines were never

employed in shunting, because of a weak front end and that their average daily mileage was only 67.08 with an average load of 131 tons.

On 4th December Bury wrote to Capt Mark Huish, the new Manager, complaining about lack of power. The large engines, of which 26 had been ordered, did not perform well. Of the twelve so far delivered, six were in the shops and were likely to remain there for two months; six were at work, but one of them had broken down and would be out of use for at least a week and the other five were not likely to continue for any length of time. The other engines being built by Longridge and Nasmyth would not be delivered for several months. In late December four engines were sent back to their makers for repairs, two to Tayleur, two to Newcastle.

Longridge & Co offered to build eight or ten more of these engines, but the offer was declined in March 1847.

McConnell said in August 1847 that repairs to the Stephenson long-boiler engines were so heavy because the engines had been built in a hurry. Expensive alterations had been necessary to connecting rod ends, iron tubes, tender springs and valve motion.

R Stephenson & Co were paid £600 in July 1847 for repairs to Tayleur's 120 and 122. When the balance of Nasmyth's account was paid in January 1848 there was a deduction of £304 for repairs necessary to their eight engines.

Simply put, the vaunted Stephenson patent six-wheeled goods engines were a disaster. Their failure cannot be blamed on Bury's antipathy or prejudice; after he had been succeeded by McConnell the monthly returns of engines show a continuing heavy rate of repairs. In this respect they were by far the worst engines on the line. In the last four months of 1847 an average of 19% of the class was out of service for repairs; in 1848 the average was 30% under repair, with half the class out of action in July. In December 1848 125 and 137 were put into store as surplus to requirements, and were joined in January 1849 by 132/9/40. Of the 21 remaining, between two and eight, averaging 20% of the total, were under repair at the date of each return in that year.

Figures for average loads taken in 1851 were:

Tayleur 119/24:	132 tons
Tayleur 120-3:	130 tons
Longridge 125-36:	132 tons
Nasmyth 137-44:	117 tons

New wheels were obtained in August 1849 - 26 sets at a cost of £1,738 - but this did not fully solve the problem for in May 1851 McConnell said that he had put an additional tyre "on top of the ordinary one, with the twofold object of increasing the wheel's diameter and also of strengthening the rim of the wheels which from experience we have found necessary." This probably refers to the 5ft Longridge engines, whose wheels are usually described as 5ft 2in diameter in later records. Some of the Tayleurs and Nasmyths were also given 5ft 2in wheels.

In November 1851 McConnell proposed trying an improved boiler on 125. This boiler had a large firebox and combustion chamber and short tubes which reduced the total heating surface by 60% and, according to the trial results in April 1852, was 6% more economical than the old boiler. McConnell estimated a fuel saving of 7 to 10%. Another of the class, 132, was given the new boiler in 1852 and on 25th January 1853 the S Div Locomotive Committee authorised the conversion of the remaining 24 engines. Unfortunately for McConnell this coincided with the investigation into the relative costs of the divisional locomotive departments and the substitution of the boilers was suspended by the General Locomotive Committee on 11th February.

A new boiler for engines 128-31 is shown in a drawing dated 4th June 1853. This had an 11ft barrel, 4ft 1in diameter, with a 5ft 5in long flush-topped firebox. There were 209 tubes with a distance between tubeplates of 10ft 7in. The grate area was 17.75 sq ft.

In 1854 coal was being tried out experimentally as locomotive fuel and on 25th July McConnell was authorised to use it in the large firebox engines 125 and 132 "and to report the effect, with a view to determine whether the engines of the same description now wanting material repairs of boiler shall be altered in a similar manner." McConnell boilers were also authorised for two 4-2-0 passenger engines 175/9; these four were the only coal-burning engines on the S Div in 1854.

In May 1855 McConnell recommended the gradual replacement of the old long boilers with boilers of a better form and with shorter tubes and more firebox heating surface at a cost of about £238 per engine. He proposed to alter twenty engines at the rate of two a month. Completion of three already started was authorised, but Hardman Earle insisted that Stephenson ought to be consulted before any general alteration of the long boilers took place.

132 had been fitted with iron tubes in August 1853, had survived being rammed by another engine in January 1855, and had run 45,020 miles by the date of the report on the tubes in February 1856.

The boiler of 140 exploded in December 1856 and McConnell said the rest of the long-boiler engines "might be expected to fail almost simultaneously, they having all been put to work at the same time." This probably led to more of the class being reboilered, but details are not known.

The new McConnell boilers appear to have had a barrel of about 10ft long and 3ft 6in diameter with a raised outer firebox about 7ft long. A combustion chamber of 2ft 10½in reduced the length of the tubes to 11ft. Photographs of two of these engines purchased by I. W. Boulton, as well as a GWR diagram of one purchased by the West Cornwall Railway show boilers like this with McConnell's dome and lock-up safety valve.

By the end of 1862 most of the engines surviving in capital stock had been given 5ft 2in diameter wheels; these were: Tayleur 121/2; Longridge 126/8-32/6; Nasmyth 137/9/42. Wheels of 4ft 6in diameter were retained by Tayleur 119/23 and Nasmyth 138. Longridge 133/5 retained 5ft 0in wheels.

Two were rebuilt by Ramsbottom in 1867, 1182 (ex-122) and 1186 (ex-126); they were given new boilers which (according to a Wolverton drawing dated 30th January 1867) were 13ft long and 3ft 6in diameter containing 92 tubes, 2⅛in diameter, 13ft 3in between tubeplates. The grate area was 11.23 sq ft.

Fig. 28
Stephenson patent long-boiler 0-6-0 built R.B. Longridge & Co, 1846, as rebuilt with a McConnell boiler in the 1850s.

Disposal
The first to be withdrawn was 124, which was destroyed in a collision on 3rd January 1853. During heavy rain and flooding in late 1852, a part of Wolvercote tunnel just north of Oxford had collapsed; during the repairs the contractors had sole possession of the Down line, traffic working in both directions being confined to the Up line. The 5.30pm passenger train, Jones & Potts 4-2-0 148 with three carriages and a guard's van, left the terminus by a mistake of the driver and less than a mile out collided with an incoming coal train consisting of 44 wagons and a brake van, double-headed by 124 and 220. The passenger engine was turned right round and thrown off to the left where it came to rest upside down in the ditch between the LNWR and GWR tracks. 124 was thrown to its right and fell on top of 148 so that their wheels were locked together. The drivers of 124 (R. Law) and 148 (J. Tarry) were killed, as were all three firemen.

In December 1856 when working on the Leamington branch 140 was destroyed by the explosion of its boiler. Two others, 120/5, were replaced by McConnell in 1859/60 and seem to have been scrapped or sold by 1862.

In 1861 another five were removed from capital stock, 127/34/41/3/4, which went into the duplicate list some months before being replaced by new engines. The replacements were built at Wolverton: 734/41 (May and August 1862) and at Crewe: 743/4 and 727 (August and October 1862).

The seventeen remaining comprised four built by Tayleur, 119/21/2/3, nine by Longridge, 126/8-33/5/6 and four by Nasmyth, 137/8/9/42; they were renumbered by the addition of 600 in April 1862.

Five of these were replaced in 1863 and the remaining twelve in 1864. These engines were all renumbered in the 11xx duplicate list at a particularly obscure period and some of the numbers are doubtful. Several which have been published are the result of attempts to fill the blanks by deduction and conjecture. The earliest available complete duplicate list is dated November 1867 and contains five described as Longridge engines: 1131, 1158, 1171, 1186 and 1193; another, 1182, is included in a miscellaneous group of Wolverton goods engines, presumably because it was not by Longridge. 1182/6 survived to be renumbered in the 18xx duplicate list in December 1871, where they are identified as the former 722/6, both with 5ft 2in wheels and 15in x 24in cylinders, built in 1846 by Tayleur and Longridge respectively.

Despite the difficulty in identifying individual engines because of renumbering it seems likely that at least one of these engines went to the Grand Trunk Railway of Canada; a minute of 16th August 1864 records the sale of 1150 and 1166 to that line for £700 each; from Crewe records the actual date of sale was 1st July. 1150 is believed to have been the former 119 and 1166 may also have been of this class but seems more likely to have been an E. B. Wilson 0-6-0 from the South Staffordshire Railway. They were bought by the Grand Trunk because delivery of locomotives from American builders had been interrupted by the Civil War; on arrival in Montreal they were completely rebuilt as 4-4-0s with 5ft 6in driving wheels and 16in x 26in cylinders. They worked on the Grand Trunk's standard gauge Port Huron - Detroit section in the USA and were scrapped in 1886 and 1889.

Two were sold to Messrs Hunt & Sacré; 1135 was minuted on 18th January 1866 as sold for £800 ("cash before delivery") and 1107 on 9th February 1866 for £750 ("cash had been paid before delivery"). C. Williams recorded the actual dates of sale (probably from the now lost account books) as 1135 on 22nd November 1865 and 1107 on 9th January 1866. Hunt & Sacré sold them on to the West Cornwall Railway, whose Joint Committee had authorised the purchases in September and November 1865. On that line they were named *Nestor* and *Apollo* and are recorded as having McConnell boilers with 156 tubes of 1¾in diameter, 9ft 6in long. Tube heating surface was 683.7 sq ft, firebox 68.02 and the grate area of 11.24 sq ft. The wheel diameters are quoted variously as 4ft 10in, 5ft 1in and 5ft 2in. These two became GWR 1387/8 in 1876 and were withdrawn in 1881.

The two engines rebuilt by Ramsbottom also went to the West Cornwall Railway, whose locomotives were by then being provided by the South Devon Railway. No 1864 was sold on 2nd April 1874 to the South Devon Railway for £550; 1826 was sold on 1st September 1875 to the "South Devon & West Cornwall Rly Co" for £500. On the West Cornwall they were named *Cyclops* and *Ceres*, became GWR 1389/90 in 1876, and were withdrawn in 1881.

Isaac Watt Boulton of Ashton-under-Lyne, Lancashire,

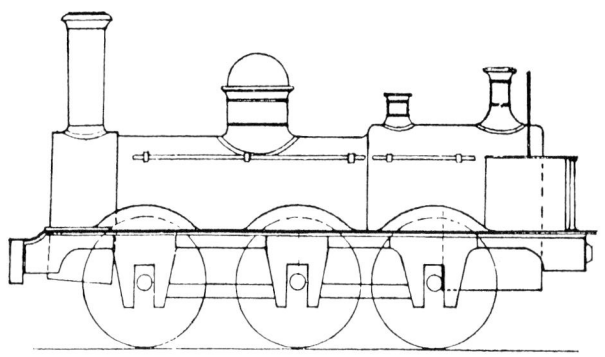

Fig. 29   Longridge 0-6-0 LNWR 1135 (ex-S Div 131) which became West Cornwall Railway *Nestor* – as shown in a GWR diagram.

bought some of them, all (according to Rosling Bennett) fitted with McConnell combustion chambers about 3ft long. Two of them he converted to saddle tanks with 3ft 6in wheels; one which he named *Achilles* was sold to the Welch Freehold & Iron Co, Briton Ferry, the other named *Queen* went to Ilkeston Colliery for £800 in 1881/2. A third, bought at Wolverton and given the name *Cotton*, was not rebuilt and was hired out as a stationary engine to drive cotton mill machinery; it was scrapped about 1875. Bennett says Boulton acquired five of this class, but among them he includes LNWR 1140 which was something else - the former 368 from the Birkenhead Railway, a 2-4-0 which Boulton named *Cavendish*. Not all the engines sold to Boulton are mentioned in the LNWR minutes, so he may well have taken four of this class, but only three are recorded. On 12th January 1872 two are minuted as sold to Isaac Boulton: 1171 for £450, and 1131 (without wheels) for £200. On 9th February 1872 another sale is minuted to I. W. Boulton: 1193 for £550. The engine named *Achilles* is said by Bennett to have been bought at Crewe as LNWR 1173, but this is almost certainly a misreading of either 1171 or 1193. *Achilles* and *Cotton* had 5ft wheels when purchased, whereas those of *Queen* were 4ft 6in diameter with a wheelbase of 11ft, so it must have been one of the Tayleur or Nasmyth engines.

There is a photograph in *The Chronicles of Boulton's Siding* showing *Cotton* working as a stationary engine in a mill; the engine has McConnell's extended firebox, dome and safety valves and a Ramsbottom chimney.

Past attempts to sort out the 11xx numbers have been complicated by some LNWR records which describe all the engines with 5ft 2in wheels as by Longridge. Several cut-up numbers and scrap dates have appeared in print but these seem to conflict with an official table which shows eight of the engines scrapped at Crewe, four each by Longridge and Nasmyth, but none by Tayleur.

Fig. 30   Stephenson patent long-boiler 0-6-0 built by Longridge in 1846, as rebuilt with a McConnell boiler in the 1850s. Photographed after sale to Isaac Watt Boulton, on his siding at Ashton-under-Lyne, 1872-3.

121

Summary: 0-6-0s built by C. Tayleur, R. B. Longridge and Nasmyth, Gaskell, 1845-8

No.	Maker	Date	Reno'd 4/62	Rebt	Reno'd	Withdrawn
119	Tayleur	20/10/1846	719		1150(2/63)	Sold 1/7/64 Grand Trunk Rly, Canada, £700
120	Tayleur	4/12/1845	-			Replaced 10/59
121	Tayleur	11/2/1846	721		1221(3/64)	Wdn by 1/66
122	Tayleur	18/2/1846	722	b /67	1182(3/64), 1826(12/71)	Sold 1/9/75 South Devon & West Cornwall Rly, £500
123	Tayleur	25/2/1846	723		1151(2/63)	Sold? Wdn by 2/67
124	Tayleur	3/1846	-		In Oxford collision 3/1/53	Scr 1/53
125	Longridge	14/5/1846	-	/52		Replaced 7/60
126	Longridge	7/5/1846	726	/67	1186(3/64), 1864(12/71)	Sold 2/4/74 South Devon Rly, £550
127	Longridge	23/6/1846			1127(/61), 1193(5/62)	Sold 1/72 I. W. Boulton, £550
128	Longridge	30/7/1846	728		1158(3/64)	Scr /68
129	Longridge	2/10/1846	729		1171(3/64)	Sold 12/71 I. W. Boulton, £450
130	Longridge	21/9/1846	730		1222(3/64)	Scr 5/64?
131	Longridge	/1847	731		1135(7/64)	Sold 22/11/65 Hunt & Sacré, £800 To West Cornwall Rly
132	Longridge	/1847	732	/52	1131(7/64)	Sold 12/71 (no wheels) I. W. Boulton, £200
133	Longridge	10/1847	733		1155(5/63)	Wdn by 7/65
134	Longridge	12/1847			1134(/61), 1164(5/62)	Wdn by 8/63
135	Longridge	12/1847	735		1156(5/63)	Wdn by 8/64
136	Longridge	3/1848	736		1107(7/64)	Sold 9/1/66 Hunt & Sacré, £750 To West Cornwall Rly
137	Nasmyth	4/1847	737		1150?(7/64)	Sold 26/1/66 Kirk & Parry Sleaford, £800
138	Nasmyth	4/1847	738		1158(5/63)	Scr 11/63?
139	Nasmyth	4/1847	739		1165?(7/64)	Wdn by 5/66
140	Nasmyth	5/1847	-		Boiler explosion 12/56	Scr 12/56
141	Nasmyth	6/1847			1141(/61), 1165(5/62)	Wdn by 8/63
142	Nasmyth	7/1847	742		1166(7/64)	Wdn by 7/65
143	Nasmyth	7/1847			1143(/61), 1182(5/62)	Wdn by 3/64
144	Nasmyth	11/1847			1144(/61), 1183(5/62)	Wdn by 6/67

Tayleur working numbers were 608-13 (engines) and 614-9 (tenders). Nasmyth works numbers were 64-71.
Longridge works number 201 was either LNWR 129 or 130.

SHARP STANDARD SINGLES

Manchester & Birmingham Railway Sharp Bros 2-2-2, 1845-6

M&B No 8

Because the sudden growth of traffic created such a shortage of motive power, in April 1845 the L&B asked the Manchester & Birmingham Railway if they would lend or sell four of their spare engines. On 3rd May the M&B took delivery of a new passenger engine from Sharp Bros; this was No 8, the second to hold that number, the first one having been sold to the South Eastern Railway three years before. On Thursday 8th May the M&B wrote that No 8 would be sent "for a trial" on the L&B in a few days, and it arrived at Wolverton the following weekend.

It was a typical Sharp 2-2-2 with outside frames, inside cylinders and 5ft 6in driving wheels, and from the first it was a great success on the L&B. It was the first six-wheeled engine on that line since the departure of *Harvey Combe* and it made a big impression on the directors.

On 23rd May 1845 No 8 took the 8.30pm train from Euston. This was the thirteen-carriage night mail to Birmingham and the north and despite a delay on the part of the Post Office resulting in a fifteen minutes late start, it reached Wolverton at 10.17pm, eight minutes ahead of time.

It was also tried on heavier trains. On 5th June 1845 it took the 2.30pm Up 3rd class from Birmingham and "held its time" with 27 heavily loaded carriages, comprising eleven horse boxes each containing three horses from Rugeley Fair, ten third class carriages, three luggage vans and three carriage trucks with private carriages of luggage. There was a late start from Birmingham and five more minutes were lost at Hampton by loading parcels making the train fifteen minutes behind time at Coventry. Three carriages were detached at Rugby and the train had lost a further two minutes on arrival at Weedon, where the engine took on coke, making it 22 minutes late arriving at Blisworth. Henry P. Bruyeres, Superintendent of the Line, was on the train and marvelled that No 8 started away smartly up the 1 in 330 gradient "without reversing to slack the couplings".

Bury reported on 12th June that No 8 was working very satisfactorily, and when Sharp Bros wrote (perhaps fishing for compliments) that they had heard of complaints about their engine the Board replied that "the performance of this engine has been highly creditable to it and in all respects satisfactory to the Company" and sent a report on its working. This led Sharp Bros to offer engines in ones and twos from stock directly to the Board - at a time when all manufacturers were extremely busy with orders. The Board's acceptance of one of these was conditional on its being "in all respects similar to Engine No 8".

M&B No 8 was on the L&B/S Div for over sixteen months until, with the arrival of the first of his own big 2-2-2s, Bury was able to return it. On 29th September 1846 he wrote to the M&B Div Secretary, J. Latham, saying No 8 would be sent north the following day and that it had performed very well.

Over its entire period on the L&B its average had been 109 miles per day. In a letter to McConnell on 22nd December 1846, Bury gave these mileages:

To 31 May 1845	2,060
1 June to 30 Nov 1845	19,290
1 Dec 1845 to 31 May 1846	18,705
1 June to 29 Sept 1846	15,065
Total	55,120

M&B No 8 became 408 when the NE Div engines were renumbered into N Div stock in August 1857 and was converted to a saddle tank at Longsight in 1859. It survived until September 1878.

Dimensions

Cylinders (2 inside)	14¾" x 20"
Boiler	
Diameter	3' 6"
Length of barrel	9' 6"
Heating surface	
Tubes (147, 1¾" dia, 9' 9" long)	656.6 sq ft
Firebox	60.6 sq ft
Total	717.2 sq ft
Diameter of wheels	
Leading	3' 6"
Driving	5' 6"
Trailing	3' 6"
Tender (6 wheel) capacity	water 1,000 gal

Summary: 2-2-2 on loan from Manchester & Birmingham Rly, 1845-6

M&BR No.	Maker	Delivered	On L&B/S Div	Reno'd	Scrapped
8	Sharp Bros(291)	3/5/1845	11/5/45 to 30/9/46	408(8/57) 1858(9/74)	10/9/78

Fig. 31 No 31 built by Sharp Bros, 1846, photographed about 1860; four-wheeled Wolverton tender with rubber springs.

Sharp Bros 2-2-2 Passenger Engines 1846-8
Nos 4, 8, 9, 31/5/6, 145/6, 205/7

No 31 (M&B 31)
Taking advantage of the good impression created by M&B No 8, Sharp Bros offered a similar engine on 11th February 1846 at a price of £1,760. The offer was accepted at once and the engine was on the line before 13th March.

Although delivered to and paid for by the L&B this engine was clearly intended for the Manchester & Birmingham, and arrived bearing the M&B number 31 and probably 'M&BR' on its tender sides. Perhaps there was an arrangement for the L&B to send the new engine to the M&B instead of returning their No 8. The M&B had done this before, hiring out four old engines to the South Eastern Railway, then persuading the SER to buy four new ones for the M&B. If this was the plan, it fell through with the amalgamation; the S Div having paid for M&B 31, kept it and returned No 8. While there is no documentary evidence for this, it is difficult to think of any other reason why an engine on the S Div should be known as M&B 31. It retained this identity until October 1848, when it became simply 31, the former No 31 having been on the "condemned for sale" list since the end of 1847.

It has been tentatively identified as Sharp's order 168, progressive No 335, which the firm's order book records was built "for stock" with a 9ft 6in boiler barrel like M&B No 8; the sparse LNWR evidence suggests it had a 10ft boiler.

The photograph of 31, unfortunately heavily retouched, was taken in late S Div days at an unknown location; it is seen coupled to a four-wheeled McConnell tender fitted with india-rubber springs.

Nos 145, 146
On 9th October 1846 Sharp Bros offered another engine which the Board accepted ("provided it is in all respects similar to No 8") for delivery in February 1847. In fact two engines were delivered "out of stock" under order No 196, one in October 1846 at £1,800 and one in December 1846 at £1,860, plus tenders at £450 and £460. Sharp's progressive numbers were 384 and 387. Their S Div numbers filled two blanks which had been in the list from May 1846, possibly for the two Aylesbury engines, or held open for M&B Nos 8 and 31 whose future disposal was then uncertain because of the impending formation of the LNWR.

Nos 8, 9
Sharp Bros made another offer of two passenger engines, which was accepted on 3rd March 1847. They were promised for May but the first (order No 189) was not delivered until 15th October; the second arrived a year later in November 1848. These delays, in contrast to the prompt arrival of the others, suggest that alterations had been requested; it is known that McConnell asked for a 1,500-gallon tender for one of them (instead of the normal 1,000-gallon type) on 26th June 1847. Sharp's progressive numbers are thought to have been 448 and 547. They were given S Div numbers of engines which had been sold, 8 and 9.

They were not alike. Their boilers differed from each other and both were bigger than those of the standard Sharp singles; 8 had 5ft 6in driving wheels as before, but had 16in cylinders; 9 had 15in cylinders as before, but had 6ft driving wheels. The cost of No 8 is not recorded, but £2,730 was paid for No 9 after delivery.

There is no foundation for the 1897 *Locomotive Magazine* story that this No 8 was transferred from the NE Div; presumably the explanation is that James Bull had heard about M&B No 8 having come south and believed the similar S Div No 8 was the same engine. The claim that it had been NE Div 59 is a later elaboration by someone trying to apportion the doubtful Sharp works numbers.

E. T. Lane made a sketch of No 9 in 1849, showing the reversing lever on the right side and an oval number plate on the middle of the boiler.

Fig. 32
No 9 built by
Sharp Bros, 1848.

Nos 35, 36, 205, 207

Four more singles were offered by Sharp Bros on 13th August 1847 "similar to M&B No 8 which was at work on this portion of the line for a considerable period and was found most effective." They were ordered (No 213) on 12th October, just three days before the arrival of the S Div's own No 8; Sharp's progressive numbers seem to lie between 462 and 470. These four were the same type as LNWR 145/6 and cost £1,860 each, tenders £460. They were all delivered within eleven weeks.

The first to arrive, on 3rd December 1847, was given the number 36; the old engine with that number was put to work on the traverser at Wolverton in the same month. The next one took the number of one of the old "condemned for sale" engines, 35, and the other two took new numbers at the end of the list, 205 and 207.

No 4 *Saddleworth*

The Huddersfield & Manchester Railway ordered their fourth engine, a Sharp 2-2-2 with 5ft driving wheels, on 21st January 1847 at a price of £1,860 plus £380 for the four-wheeled 850-gallon tender; it was Sharp's order 201, progressive number 473, and was named *Saddleworth* as requested by the H&M, after a village on that line. By the time it was ready, painted green, with nameplates on the boiler side, lettered 'H&MR' on the tender and numbered 4 on the bufferplank, the LNWR had agreed to take over the H&M. On 8th October 1847 the LNWR General Locomotive Committee decided that surplus engines for the Yorkshire lines should be transferred to the main line for working the Chester & Holyhead Railway, so when *Saddleworth* was delivered on 24th December it was sent to Crewe. It was still there on 13th July 1848, when it was ordered to be transferred to the S Div.

It was not at the time renumbered into S Div stock, perhaps because of the possibility that it would not stay long. It appears to have kept its H&M number 4, but at first was referred to only by its name because S Div No 4 was still in the working stock. About 1850-2 the old engine was condemned and *Saddleworth* became S Div No 4.

All these engines were standard Sharp Bros outside-frame singles with the dome close behind the chimney. Apart from No 9 which had the smoother, more modern boiler mountings typical of its later date, all had square pedestals at the base of the chimney and dome.

Dimensions

Nos 31/5/6, 145/6, 205/7

Cylinders (2 inside)	15" x 20"
Boiler	
Diameter	3' 6"
Length of barrel	10' 0"
Heating surface	
Tubes (147, 1¾" dia, 10' 3" long)	690.21 sq ft
Firebox (3' 0" long, 3' 6½" wide)	60.60 sq ft
Total	750.81 sq ft
Grate area	10.62 sq ft
Diameter of wheels	
Leading	3' 6"
Driving	5' 6"
Trailing	3' 6"
Wheelbase	5' 10" + 6' 11" = 12' 9"

Weight

	Nos 145/6	*Nos 31/5/6/205/7*
On leading wheels	5 tons 10 cwt	6 tons 7.25 cwt
On driving wheels	9 tons 12.5 cwt	8 tons 9 cwt
On trailing wheels	2 tons 18.5 cwt	2 tons 17.5 cwt
Total	18 tons 1 cwt	17 tons 13.75 cwt

Tender (6 wheel) capacity   coke 2 tons
    water 1,000 gal

Fig. 33   No 35 built by Sharp Bros, 1847. Photographed on a Rugby or Northampton train at Market Harborough, 1857-60.
(J.C. Davies collection)

No 8

Cylinders (2 inside)	16" x 20"
Heating surface	
Tubes (161, 2" dia, 10' 4" long)	871.09 sq ft
Firebox	93.90 sq ft
Total	964.99 sq ft
Diameter of driving wheels	5' 6"

Weight	As built	Sept 1858
On leading wheels	5 tons 9.75 cwt	7 tons 5 cwt
On driving wheels	12 tons 19 cwt	10 tons 5 cwt
On trailing wheels	3 tons 4.25 cwt	4 tons 0 cwt
Total	21 tons 13 cwt	21 tons 10 cwt

Tender (6 wheel) capacity water 1,500 gal

No 9

Cylinders (2 inside)	15" x 20"
Heating surface	
Tubes (177, 2" dia, 10' 5½" long)	969.24 sq ft
Firebox	84.70 sq ft
Total	*1,053.97 sq ft
Diameter of wheels	
Leading	4' 0"
Driving	6' 0"
Trailing	4' 0"

See note on heating surfaces in Introduction.

No 4 *Saddleworth*

As built:

Cylinders (2 inside)	15" x 20"
Boiler	
Diameter	3' 6"
Length of barrel	10' 0"
Heating surface	
Tubes (147, 1¾" dia, 10' 3" long)	690.21 sq ft
Firebox (3' 0" long, 3' 6½" wide)	60.60 sq ft
Total	750.81 sq ft
Grate area	10.62 sq ft
Diameter of wheels	
Leading	3' 6"
Driving	5' 0"
Trailing	3' 6"
Wheelbase	5' 9" + 6' 11" = 12' 8"
Tender (4 wheel) capacity	water 850 gal

In 1853 boiler details were:

Heating surface	
Tubes (178, 1¾" dia, 10' 4¼" long)	844.72 sq ft
Firebox	60.00 sq ft
Total	904.72 sq ft

Average loads taken in 1851 were:

No 4:	35 tons.
Nos 31/5/6/145/6/205/7:	57 tons.
No 8:	64 tons.
No 9:	68 tons.

Fig. 34 Sharp Bros *Saddleworth* built in 1847 for the Huddersfield & Manchester Railway; became LNWR S Div No. 4.

Rebuilding

Engines known to have been rebuilt at Wolverton are: No 8 in June 1858; 4/35/6 in 1860; 145 in 1861 and 146 in June 1862. Of these, 35/6 and 145 were reboilered with domes on the centre of the barrel, the old dome covers being re-used. No 4 was given a McConnell boiler with a combustion chamber, which it retained until it was scrapped in 1875. It is believed that 146 was rebuilt without a dome but with McConnell's lock-up safety valve on the boiler centre. In 1862, the firebox of 146 was lengthened to 3ft 10½in, with a grate area of 13.88 sq ft. Probably the other rebuilds were similar.

Engines in the 1860s whose dome remained in the original position close behind the chimney were Nos 31 and 205. The firebox of No 31 was still its original size in 1862.

Two engines, ex-31 and ex-207, were rebuilt as saddle tanks (probably at Longsight) in the Ramsbottom period. A Crewe diagram dated April 1877 of "Sharp's Common Passenger Saddle Tank" shows a 5ft 6in engine with a wheelbase of 5ft 8in + 7ft and a length over the buffers of 24ft 5in. The weight is given as:

On leading wheels	7 tons	2 cwt
On driving wheels	11 tons	
On trailing wheels	5 tons	10 cwt
Total	23 tons	12 cwt

Work

From an analysis of trains leaving Euston in July and November 1847, it is known that Nos 8, M&B 31, 145 and 146 were used singly on trains of up to 19 carriages, although usually the load was much lighter.

As a new engine surplus to immediate requirements, No 9 was put into store in December 1848 but was brought out in June 1849 and in the following month was sent with No 8 and three other engines (Nos 65, 85, 87) to work on the N Div, in exchange for four Crewe singles. All were quickly returned; No 8 resumed work on the S Div and No 9 went back to store where it remained until 1850. It was used for some time on the Royal Train.

145 was hired to the North London Railway in 1855.

The suburban service from Euston to Watford and St Albans was worked almost exclusively by these engines in the 1860s and early 1870s.

Accidents

No 36 was involved in a collision at Weedon on 3rd March 1848, and was damaged at Birmingham on 5th September 1849. No 35 collided with 2-2-0 No 29 at Birmingham on 7th April 1849. When hauling the 6.30am London-Leamington train on 26th February 1859, No 8 ran off the line on the curve just a mile short of its destination. Fireman John Pilkington and two passengers were killed and No 8's tender was destroyed. The engine had a mileage of 238,000 at that time.

On 4th December 1872 No 745 was in an accident at Blisworth, running past a red signal through the trap points and down the canal bank. Driver John James was killed. The engine was taken to Wolverton and scrapped, the boiler being put to stationary work.

Disposal

Apart from 745, all reached the 18xx duplicate list in the 1870s and were scrapped at Crewe, the tender engines in 1874/5 and the two saddle tanks in 1878/80.

Summary: 2-2-2s built by Sharp Bros, 1846-8

No.	Date	Sharp No.	Reno'd 4/62	Rebt.	Reno'd.	Scrapped
31	2/1846 (listed as M&B 31 until 10/48)	335	631	11/70 ST	1937 (10/74)	7/1/80
145	10/1846	384	745	/61	Accident 4/12/72	1/73 at Wol.
146	12/1846	387	746	6/62	1141 (1/66), 1931 (12/71)	4/74
8	15/10/1847	448	608	6/58	1247 (12/66), 1934 (12/71)	4/74
36	3/12/1847		636	/60	1933 (9/73)	4/74
35	8/12/1847		635	/60	1916 (9/73)	4/74
205	14/12/1847		805		1937 (9/73)	6/74
207	28/12/1847		807	12/68 ST	1936 (1/75)	17/12/78
4	24/12/1847 to S Div 7/48 Named *Saddleworth* (not listed as S Div No 4 until 1850-2)	473	604	12/60	1900 (9/73)	8/75
9	11/1848	547	609		1180 (12/65), 1930 (12/71)	6/74

CREWE ENGINES AT WOLVERTON 1845-7

The L&B goods train crisis was at its worst in the autumn of 1845 when the agreement to amalgamate with the Grand Junction Railway was suddenly announced. The news broke on 17th October and at once the L&B Goods Committee asked if Crewe could help by lending such goods engines as they might have spare. The GJR made an offer of two engines, which was accepted on 6th November.

Perhaps Crewe had no goods engines to spare after all, for two passenger engines arrived towards the end of the year. They were GJR No 74 *Deva* and 77 *Mersey*, 2-2-2s of what was known later as the 'Old Crewe' type, with 6ft driving wheels and 14¼in (or 15in - both are recorded) outside cylinders. They were quite new having been built at Crewe only a few weeks earlier in the same batch as *Columbine*, now preserved in the National Railway Museum.

Nine months later, with the doubling of the Northampton and Peterborough line, extra trains were planned for conveying cattle from the eastern counties, for which two extra engines were needed; Bury said he had "the greatest difficulty" providing them. This prompted another request to Crewe, and this time two new goods engines were sent, No 88 *Lune* and No 90 *Lowther*, 2-4-0s with 5ft driving wheels and 15in outside cylinders. They arrived at Wolverton on 12th and 14th September 1846, allowing the Peterborough cattle traffic to begin on Tuesday 15th.

In November Bury gave the weight of the two Crewe Goods engines as 18 tons 6 cwt; the weight on the coupled wheels was 8 tons 7cwt and 4 tons, a total of 12 tons 7 cwt. This was the lowest adhesive weight of any goods engine on the line, 5½ tons less than the latest 0-4-0s - and actually 11 cwt less than the current weight of the original 0-4-0s of 1838. They took an average load of 126.4 tons, somewhat less than the S Div's own new engines. He thought the inclined cylinders and the short connecting rods were a disadvantage but "these objections are rendered less apparent in consequence of the very excellent workmanship and care with which the engines are put together, which is visible in every part of them." Their boiler pressure was 70 lb/sq in when on the S Div. *Lune* was reckoned able to work 30 wagons and was put on the Rugby goods trains in December.

In September *Mersey* was found to be getting flats on its tyres. It and *Deva* were reported to be in good order (except for the pistons) on 7th November, but within a fortnight they were both sent to Crewe for repairs. *Mersey* remained at Crewe for several weeks and did not return to the S Div until early 1847. *Deva* never returned, but another goods engine (built in July in the same batch as *Lune* and *Lowther*) came south on 19th December. This was No 87 *Eden*; when it was inspected on arrival it was found to have leaky tubes and worn pistons so it did no work on the S Div until the following month.

Meanwhile the new General Locomotive Committee of the LNWR at its second meeting, on 18th December 1846, decreed that the next three goods engines built at Crewe "on the model of *Lowther*" should be sent to Wolverton. In fact three new passenger engines went to the S Div, No 95 *Hydra* at the very end of December and Nos 9 and 98, *Alecto* and *Dædalus* in January or February 1847. When Trevithick reported on 4th February that the first of the three goods engines would be ready for the S Div in three weeks, he was told to send it to the Manchester & Birmingham section, because a large engine for the M&B by Sharp Bros was nearly ready and could be sent to Wolverton instead. Thus in March 1847 N Div 102 *Marquis* went new to Longsight, where it became M&B Div No 31, and the Sharp 0-6-0 went to Wolverton, eventually to become S Div No 32.

On 25th January 1847 *Lune* was involved in an accident; it was sent to Crewe for repairs and did not come back to the S Div.

Before McConnell took over he was asked to report on the N Div goods engines because Crewe had offered to build a further fifteen of them for the S Div in 1847; he responded on 1st March by saying that the least effective of the modern goods engines on the line was *Eden*. Crewe's offer was not taken up.

It is known that during the month of July 1847 three Crewe 2-2-2s *Dædalus*, *Hydra* and *Mersey* worked trains from Euston. *Mersey* is recorded as taking unassisted a train of 21 carriages, but normal practice was to double-head trains of more than seventeen. *Alecto* was probably at work on the Wolverton-Birmingham section at this time and in the first available monthly return in September these four passenger engines were listed in S Div stock together with two goods engines, *Eden* and *Lowther*. All six remained in the south for the next three months and *Dædalus*, *Hydra* and *Mersey* were still working trains of six to seventeen carriages from Euston throughout November.

In that month the General Manager Mark Huish proposed that the Crewe engines should be returned north in exchange for four that had been built for the Leeds, Dewsbury & Manchester Railway and so the Wilson singles (S Div 201-4) promptly arrived at Wolverton and McConnell said on 9th December that the six N Div engines would be returned. They were back on the N Div before 11th January 1848; all necessary repairs were carried out at Crewe but charged to Wolverton.

Summary: Crewe engines working on the S Div, 1845-7

No.	Name	Type	Built	Sent to Wolverton	Returned to Crewe
74	Deva	2-2-2	10/1845	12/45	20/11/46
77	Mersey	2-2-2	11/1845	12/45	12/47
88	Lune	2-4-0	8/1846	12/9/46	25/1/47
90	Lowther	2-4-0	9/1846	14/9/46	12/47
87	Eden	2-4-0	7/1846*	19/12/46	12/47
95	Hydra	2-2-2	12/1846	1/47	12/47
9	Alecto	2-2-2	1/1847	1 or 2/47	12/47
98	Dædalus	2-2-2	1/1847	1 or 2/47	12/47

Eden completed 15/7/46, to stock 8/46

TRENT VALLEY ENGINES 1846-7

Nos 147-171

The promotion of the Trent Valley Railway, a 50-mile link between the London & Birmingham at Rugby and the Grand Junction at Stafford had been a cause of strife between these two companies. Under pressure from their shareholders, and with the construction of the line a certainty, in the autumn of 1845 both Boards of Directors suddenly saw the virtue of co-operation.

On 17th October 1845 it was announced that agreement had been reached between the L&B, the GJR and the M&B that these three companies would amalgamate. On 13th December the new body was given a name: The London & North Western Railway Company. The necessary Act of Parliament was not obtained until the following July, but long before then the constituent companies were acting in close collaboration.

The L&B already had a £70,000 stake in the Trent Valley line with the option of outright purchase, and on 15th April 1846 - "as representatives of the new company" - the L&B exercised this option and paid the sum required, £584,000.

Months before this negotiations had been taking place behind the scenes. Early in September 1845 the L&B Board had raised the subject of "new engines required for the Trent Valley Railway". On 7th October the Locomotive Committee recommended that 30 engines should be obtained at the earliest possible date, twenty of them to be passenger engines with 6ft driving wheels, 16in x 20in cylinders and 1,000 sq ft heating surface, and ten goods engines with 5ft driving wheels, 16in x 24in cylinders and 800-900 sq ft heating surface. The Board endorsed the order three days later but said that the engines should be "of the greatest power that may be advantageously employed" and that all should have a heating surface of not less than 1,000 sq ft. Advertisements were to be published immediately.

Only 25 engines appear to have been built as a result of this. The creation of the LNWR, a period of slow deliveries from very busy manufacturers and the purchase of miscellaneous engines in ones and twos has obscured the rest of the story. The Trent Valley line was opened in September 1847, but was worked by the N Div; the engines bought for it remained in S Div stock.

Bury, Curtis & Kennedy 0-6-0 Goods Engines, 1846
Nos 168-171

The advertisement for engines required for the TV line having 1,000 sq ft heating surface which appeared in the *Liverpool Courier* on 15th October 1845 brought a swift response from Bury, Curtis & Kennedy who offered to provide fifteen engines of the type required. Their letter has survived, and it bears an endorsement on the back: "Accept four of these engines on condition that Messrs BC&K deliver them before the 1st July 1846. Loco Ctee, 7 Nov 1845, J.L.P." This curt note from the director John L. Prevost is in complete contrast to the Board's assiduous courtship of Stephenson & Co, and is the sole reference in the L&B records to this BC&K order.

The first of the four engines came early in December 1846 - probably on the 4th - and the others followed later in that month. They were by far the biggest and most powerful engines seen on the line. The design was a much enlarged version of 117 with the usual Bury bar frames adapted for a coupled axle behind the firebox. It looks as if Bury had been stung by the Board's infatuation with the Stephenson patent engines and decided to show what a really big engine could be like.

The firebox was of maximum size, even bigger than that of the 2-2-2 passenger engines. While the high domed top was retained, the sides had to be made flat to avoid undesirable outward bending of the frame bars; the cylinders were arranged as on the earlier Bury goods engines, down at the front end and working under the leading axle. They became known as the 'Goods Haystacks'.

They were numbered 168-71 following the block of numbers allocated to the TV passenger engines.

Dimensions

Cylinders (2 inside)	16" x 24"
Heating surface	
Tubes (160, 2¼" dia, 12' 0" long)	1,130.88 sq ft
Firebox	78.00 sq ft
Total	1,208.88 sq ft
Diameter of wheels	5' 0"
Wheelbase	8' 0" + 8' 0" = 16' 0"
Weight	
On leading wheels	9 tons 0 cwt
On driving wheels	9 tons 4.5 cwt
On trailing wheels	5 tons 5 cwt
Total	23 tons 9.5 cwt

Their arrival on the S Div, although late, was timely. Before they came complaints of goods train delays were frequent and were becoming worse. There was an acute shortage of goods engines, all of which were being overworked. Of the twelve long-boiler 0-6-0s so far delivered, six were undergoing heavy repairs and another five were thought likely to break down soon. This state of near chaos was ended with the delivery of the four Goods Haystacks, which worked a transformation in goods haulage. These, and two small-wheeled 0-4-0s (172/3, also from BC&K) in the following month, were the only goods engines added to stock before the Goods Committee's report on 4th March 1847 that the traffic was being worked satisfactorily.

As usual, not much was recorded of them in service. On 5th September 1848 170 was on the 12.30am Down goods train; emerging from Linslade Tunnel Driver Beston did not have time to pull up before crashing into some wagons which were being shunted by the ballast engine No 1 *Victoria* at the ballast pit siding. The 0-6-0 was thrown off the line and was then rammed by the Up York Mail, headed by Jones & Potts single 183, which also capsized. The 4-2-0 was in Wolverton for repairs for the next seven months, but the Bury engine was out again after "slight repairs" within the month.

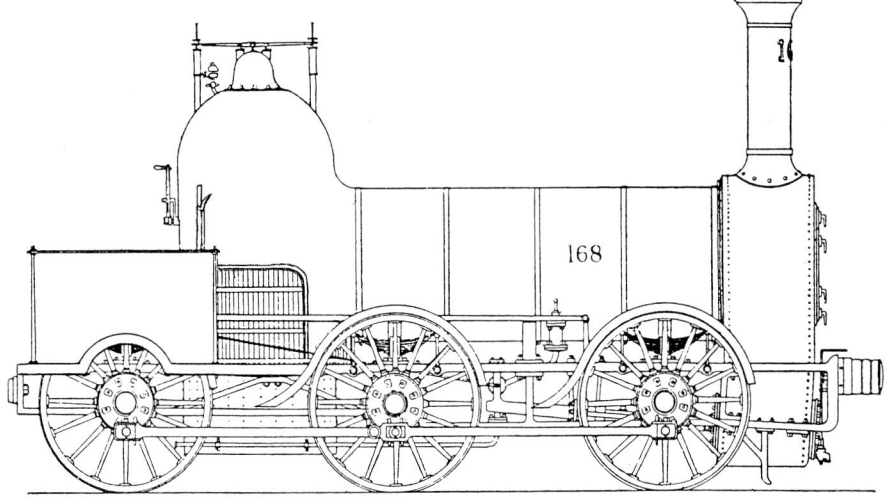

Fig. 35 Bury, Curtis & Kennedy 0-6-0 of 1846; 168-171 ordered for the Trent Valley Railway.

With fourteen other goods engines 169 was placed in store in January 1849 and remained there until 1850.

In the 1853 report this class took the heaviest average load - 160 tons - of any except the Sharp 'Atlas' and 'Sphynx' type of 1847-9.

Disposal

All four were replaced in 1858-60. The first one to go, in February 1858, may (on circumstantial evidence) have been sold to the St Helens Railway in that year, becoming StHR No 16 *Mersey*. In 1864 this engine came into LNWR stock as 1382 and was reboilered at Wolverton in the September; described in a Crewe notebook as "one of Bury's six wheel coupled" it was renumbered 1132 on 28th December 1865, and sold for £450 to contractor Wm Moss of Stafford on 4th January 1870.

Summary: TV 0-6-0s built by Bury, Curtis & Kennedy, 1846-7

No.	Date	Replaced	
168	12/1846	2/58	Possibly sold to St Helens Rly in /58: No 16, *Mersey*.
169	12/1846	10/60	
170	12/1846	10/60	
171	12/1846 or 1/1847	10/60	

Stephenson Patent Long-boiler 4-2-0 Passenger Engines

Although a total of twenty passenger engines had been authorised for the TV, in fact orders were placed for 25. All were to be of Stephenson's patent long-boiler outside-cylinder 4-2-0 type, with all wheels in front of the firebox and the centre pair flangeless. They were ordered from Jones & Potts of the Viaduct Foundry, Newton-le-Willows, from Charles Tayleur & Co of the Vulcan Foundry, Newton-le-Willows, and from Robert Stephenson & Co. Each maker's engines were different from the others in the boilers, cylinders and wheels as well as in superficial details. The design was a development of the earlier outside-cylinder long-boiler 2-2-2 which had proved to be unsteady at speeds over 35mph; by putting the driving wheels behind the carrying wheels the cylinders were brought back towards the middle of the engine for improved stability.

The frame was similar to that of the long-boiler 0-6-0, a straight plate on each side about 22ft long by 8in deep and 1in thick, with separate horns riveted on for the driving axle, and a massive forging for the two carrying axles and to support the cylinder which was outside with the valve chest inside. Stay bars linked the horn plates underneath and ran up to the front and back of the main frame plate; stay rods held the two sides together.

Each connecting rod was split for most of its length in the shape of a tuning fork, to clear a stout bracket supporting the slide bar ends. The pumps lay forward of the driving axle and were worked from two additional eccentrics.

The boilers were oval in section, narrowed to sink as low as possible between the frames and achieve the lowest possible centre of gravity. The reversing gear weighshaft was curved downwards to clear the underside of the boiler. On most of the engines the regulator shaft was a mere 2ft 4in above the footplate, making the handle about waist-high for an average-size driver.

Tayleur's offer was dated 24th October 1845 promising nine engines and tenders at £2,230 each, with delivery dates between October 1846 and the end of that year. This was accepted "by order of Mr Smith" of the Locomotive Committee on 24th October, with an instruction to the L&B Secretary: "Mr Creed in accepting should specify that the engines and tenders are to be upon Mr Stephenson's plan and according to his specifications."

Stephenson & Co's order dated 19th November 1845 was for six engines, to be delivered between July and December 1846; more were then requested on condition that they would be delivered in 1846 and the order was quickly increased to a total of ten.

No trace remains of the Jones & Potts order, but their six engines were the first to arrive, from May 1846. They were numbered from 147, which left two blanks after the last engine then on order.

The first of the Stephenson and Tayleur engines did not arrive until December 1846 and were given numbers in blocks following the Jones & Potts.

Jones & Potts 4-2-0 Passenger Engines, 1846
Nos 147-152

Apart from the borrowed Crewe engines these were the first with outside cylinders on the line. They had square Gothic fireboxes similar to those of the long-boiler goods engines, all springs were mounted above the frames, and the wheels had T-iron spokes.

Fig. 36 Jones & Potts long-boiler 4-2-0 of 1846; 147-152.

Dimensions

Cylinders (2 outside)	15" x 24"
Boiler: length of barrel	13' 6"
Heating surface	
Tubes (140, 2" dia, 13' 10½" long)	1,017.06 sq ft
Firebox	60.61 sq ft
Total	1,077.67 sq ft
Diameter of wheels	
Leading and middle	4' 0"
Driving	6' 6"
Wheelbase	7' 0" + 5' 6" = 12' 6"

Weight

	March 1848	April 1853
On leading wheels	6 tons 19 cwt	6 tons 2 cwt
On middle wheels	4 tons 12 cwt	4 tons 1 cwt
On driving wheels	11 tons 6.5 cwt	13 tons 2 cwt
Total	22 tons 17.5 cwt	23 tons 5 cwt

The first of them had not long arrived when the Locomotive Committee recorded their dissatisfaction, contending that they were "imperfect." They had been built with iron tubes; all future engines were ordered to have brass tubes, the LNWR paying the difference in price.

On 21st September 1846 Bury wrote to tell Jones & Potts that 148 was giving constant trouble. It had leaky tubes and a cracked tubeplate; the boiler was useless and it required a new firebox after running only 8,226 miles. On 16th December he wrote again complaining that two of their engines were laid up with burst fireboxes. On the 22nd these two were sent back to Newton-le-Willows to be put right, along with two of Tayleur's goods engines. Two were able to be sent on their own wheels, but the other two had to go in iron wagons which Bury had built for transporting crippled locomotives.

Work and Disposal

Every engine in the class worked trains from Euston in July or November 1847, taking a maximum of nineteen carriages alone, but usually double-headed with more than seventeen. They were heavy on repairs; in 1847-9 it was a rare monthly report which did not include at least one of them in Wolverton. The worst report was that of 7th June 1848 when all except 147 were in for repair.

They were most expensive machines; Jones & Potts were paid £464 in February 1848 for their repair of 148, and it is clear that McConnell did not consider them worth fitting with his new boiler in his scheme of January 1853.

Two of them are known to have worked on the Oxford line in the early 1850s. On 6th September 1851 a fourteen-carriage Great Exhibition excursion train returning from London was being taken from Bletchley to Oxford by Driver Carrier with 149. The engine was derailed on the crossover points at Bicester level crossing; the engine swung sharply right and almost hit the stationmaster's house; six passengers were killed. In the Oxford collision of 3rd January 1853, 148 was destroyed when Driver Tarry took his train out of the station believing the line to be clear and collided with an incoming coal train.

Another four were replaced in 1856/7 leaving only one (152) in capital stock at the end of the separate S Div. It went into the duplicate list and was probably scrapped in 1863.

Summary: TV 4-2-0s built by Jones & Potts, 1846

No.	Date	Replaced	Reno'd 4/62	Reno'd	Withdrawn
147	5/1846	12/56	-		
148	7/1846	In Oxford collision 3/1/53			Scr 1/53
149	7/1846	8/56	-		
150	8/1846	5/56	-		
151	9/1846	6/57	-		
152	12/1846		752	1159 (5/63)	?Scr/63

Stephenson 4-2-0 Passenger Engines, 1847
Nos 153-158

These engines had a raised, straight-topped firebox and a large brass dome on the middle of the boiler barrel; the dome had a directly-loaded safety valve with a steam escape like the bell of a trumpet; a manhole on the firebox held two spring balance safety valves contained within a tall brass column and with levers to the firebox back. The wheels were of malleable iron and did not have the usual T-iron spokes; the frame likewise differed from the original design in that instead of having the usual driving axle hornplates a large rectangular plate was attached to the main frame, covering the whole of the lower side of the firebox and extending forward with a vertical slot for the driving axle bearing. The springs on each axle were located differently; the middle axle springs were above the main frame-plate, whereas the leading springs were below it and those for the driving

Fig. 37
Stephenson long-boiler 4-2-0 of 1847; 6ft 6in driving wheels, 153 and 157.

Fig. 38
Stephenson long-boiler 4-2-0 of 1847; 7ft driving wheels, 154/5/6/8.

axle were underhung. The running board dipped down at the footplate end.

Ten were ordered, four of them being conditional on delivery during 1846, so only six were taken by the LNWR. Stephenson & Co had allocated works numbers 561-70 to the ten, but the firm received an order from a new customer who also insisted on quick delivery, so 561-4 were sent to the Eastern Counties Railway between October 1846 and January 1847. The other six, comprising two (565/6) of the original order and the four extras (567-70) were sent to the LNWR as follows:

567	8/1/47	
565	13/2/47	
569	15/2/47	
568	22/2/47	
566	1/3/47	(its tender No 662 sent 22/3/47)
570	22/3/47	(its tender No 552 sent 22/3/47)

Tenders were evidently numbered in a separate series. Stephenson works numbers 567-70 cannot be linked with certainty to LNWR numbers, but LNWR 153 and 157 were the two from the first batch 565/6, and as 157 is said (in an accident report) to have entered service in April 1847 it was probably 566. The two batches differed from each other: those of the original order, the ECR engines and LNWR 153/7, had 6ft 6in diameter driving wheels; the driving wheels of the other four were 7ft. There were also differences in the spacing of the wheels and the pitch of the boiler. It was reported that one of the 7ft engines was at work by mid-February; this would be Stephenson's 567, but the LNWR number is not given.

According to a surviving invoice each engine came with a set of screw keys, a monkey-wrench, a set of fire irons, a set of oilcans, hammers and chisels; the cost was £1,950 per engine, and £430 per tender.

Dimensions

Cylinders (2 outside)			15" x 24"
Boiler			
Length of barrel			12' 9"
Diameter (vertical)			3' 8"
		Nos 153/7	*Nos 154/5/6/8*
Pitch		5' 8"	6' 2"
Heating surface			
Tubes (125, 2" dia, 13' 4½" long)			875.36 sq ft
Firebox			65.40 sq ft
Total			*940.84 sq ft
Grate area			11.45 sq ft
Diameter of wheels		*Nos 153/7*	*Nos 154/5/6/8*
Leading and middle		3' 9"	4' 0"
Driving		6' 6"	7' 0"
Tender		3' 6"	
Wheelbase		*Nos 153/7*	*Nos 154/5/6/8*
		7' 9" + 5' 3"	7' 6" + 5' 6"
		= 13' 0"	= 13' 0"
Weight		*March 1848*	*April 1853*
On leading wheels		6 tons 0.25 cwt	6 tons 3 cwt
On middle wheels		5 tons 0 cwt	4 tons 15.5 cwt
On driving wheels		12 tons 13.5 cwt	13 tons 4 cwt
Total		23 tons 13.75 cwt	24 tons 2.5 cwt
Tender (6 wheels) capacity			water 1,200 gal

See note on heating surfaces in Introduction.

Rebuilding

Perhaps because of the unusual construction of the rear end of the frame of this class, McConnell fitted "improved stronger framings" to 153-6 and 158 in 1848 at a cost of £100 each. At the end of 1848 the two Stephenson 4-2-2s (233/4) arrived and early in 1849 McConnell added trailing wheels to 153 and 157 "with a view to lightening the effect on the road". He reported favourably on the alteration on 29th May, when six more were authorised to "engines of similar character" but no others are known.

The new trailing wheels had a diameter of 3ft 9in and the wheelbase was:

7ft 9in + 5ft 3in + 5ft 7in, total 18ft 7in.

As 4-2-2s they retained the same boiler dimensions as originally.

The class was proposed for McConnell's patent firebox and combustion chamber in January 1853 but this was suspended in the following month pending the Woods & Marshall trials. By 1858 some of the engines (including 153/7) had McConnell boilers with a long raised firebox plus combustion chamber, 6ft 9in outside, and a 10ft boiler barrel. The grate area was 15 sq ft.

Work and Accidents

On 28th April 1847 a five-carriage racegoers' special left Euston for Chester behind 157. According to contemporary newspapers the top speed, for over a mile, was 75mph and the last 21 miles to Wolverton were covered in 21 minutes.

While still a 4-2-0, 153 was in an accident on 5th June 1847. With Driver William Manners and Fireman Edward Bradbury it was heading the nineteen-carriage 8.45pm Down Liverpool Mail when it was turned by mistake into a siding at the south end of Wolverton where it collided with a train of wagons; seven people were killed.

At Wolverton on 26th March 1850 the boiler of 157 exploded. The safety valves were normally set at 60 lb/sq in but had been screwed down to 95 lb/sq in by a labourer working on a neighbouring engine to prevent the annoying sound of steam escaping. When the driver opened the regulator to start his day's work the boiler barrel ripped along the bottom, and was bent flat, with parts of it being thrown over the Works roof and landing in gardens 400 yards away. The frame was buckled and one of the driving wheels was blown off, but the only casualty was the labourer who had screwed down the valve: he was scalded and one of his ears was cut off. According to McConnell 157 was different from the others of the class in that the crank axle had a central bearing whose guides were bolted to the boiler; the boiler was weakened at the bottom because of the number of bolts and repeated blows from the axle bearing. A claim was lodged against R. Stephenson & Co for the damage to 157 caused by "defective workmanship". The engine was rebuilt at a cost of £506.

On 2nd August 1852 153 was on an Up train just south of Hampton when its ashpan, which had been fitted at Wolverton in September 1851, fell off and fouled the leading brake van, thus derailing the train whose carriages were then hit by a Down train. Two people were killed.

Disposal

Four were in capital stock at the end of the separate S Div, but were replaced and put on the duplicate list in 1862/3. Two were still on the duplicate list in November 1867, 1202/3. They were scrapped in 1871 and 1869.

Summary: TV 4-2-0s built by R. Stephenson & Co, 1847

No.	Date	Rebuilt	Reno'd 4/62	Reno'd	Withdrawn
153	2/1847	as 4-2-2, 2/49	753	1202(9/63)	Scr b /71
154	1/1847			1200(5/62)	Scr /65
155	2/1847			1184(5/62)	Scr /66
156	2/1847		756	1203(9/63)	Scr /69
157	3/1847	as 4-2-2, 4/49	757	11xx(5/63)	? Scr 5/63
158	3/1847		758	11xx(5/63)	? Scr /63

Stephenson works numbers were 565-70.

Fig. 39
Tayleur long-boiler 4-2-0 of 1846/7; 159-167.

Tayleur 4-2-0 Passenger Engines, 1846-7
Nos 159-167

These nine engines had Gothic fireboxes, all springs above the axles and were generally similar to the Jones & Potts batch 147-52. Their delivery dates are not precisely known, but McConnell stated in 1853 that these and the later Tayleurs (176-81) started work in January-May 1847.

Tayleur works 'rotation' numbers 254-62 are doubtful, having been estimated at a later period. Working numbers were 834-42 (engines) and 843-51 (tenders).

Dimensions

Cylinders (2 outside)	15" x 22"
Boiler (oval)	
Vertical diameter	3' 6"
Horizontal diameter	3' 3"
Length of barrel	13' 6"
Pitch	5' 6½"
Heating surface	
Tubes (125, 2" dia, 13' 10½" long)	908.89 sq ft
Firebox	56.17 sq ft
Total	*965.072 sq ft
Diameter of wheels	
Leading and middle	3' 6"
Driving	6' 0"
Length over buffers (engine)	24' 10½"
Wheelbase	
Engine	6' 9" + 5' 3" = 12' 0"
Tender (6 wheels)	12' 0"
Total	33' 7½"

Weight	March 1848	April 1853
On leading wheels	6 tons 19 cwt	6 tons 3 cwt
On middle wheels	4 tons 12 cwt	4 tons 0 cwt
On driving wheels	11 tons 6.5 cwt	13 tons 1 cwt
Total	22 tons 17.5 cwt	23 tons 4 cwt

See note on heating surfaces in Introduction.

Accidents

Three drivers were sacked in 1848 for burning fireboxes: Driver Brandwood with 167 in May and Drivers Shepherd and Ince with 160 and 166 in July. All three engines were in Wolverton for general repairs until September.

167 was soon back in the shops. On 31st October 1848 it was on the seven-carriage 9.00am Down Caledonian express when it was derailed on the curve at Weedon, the sharpest on the line. The curve had recently been relaid and realigned, with new wooden sleepers in place of stone blocks and the rails were found to be ¼in too close together. The engine and tender had solid buffers between them and the coupling was screwed up tight thus forming "an unyielding mass 40ft long on twelve wheels". McConnell said he was already putting on spring buffers, but all engines and tenders with solid buffers were ordered to be taken out of service "at once".

The boiler of 164 exploded on 5th April 1855 while the engine was shunting wagons at the coking stage at Rugby. Up to December 1853 it had run 141,986 miles and put in 260 hours of ballasting work. It was then retubed and had run a further 11,750 miles with trains and had been used as a shunter for 1,140 hours. The safety valves were set at 50 lb/sq in but had been screwed down to "at least" 200 lb/sq in. The explosion decapitated a young cleaner, threw half a ton of boiler 150 yards and other pieces much further; the engine was blown over on its side, a complete wreck. It was scrapped.

This prompted McConnell to recommend (again) his large firebox and short tube boiler which he proposed to fit to twenty Stephenson long-boiler engines. He had previously wanted to reboiler 56 engines, including Tayleur's 159-67, but this had been blocked by the General Locomotive Committee in February 1853.

Disposal

159 and 167 were replaced in 1856 and 166 in 1857. 166 was on the sales list, but still running with its old number until November 1858, when it became 'B' in the S Div 'letter series' and probably 166B shortly afterwards. In August 1858 McConnell said 160 and 165 would be broken up "this half year" if not sold; they were offered to the Portsmouth Railway for £800 each but were not

taken. 165 was replaced by a Small Bloomer in October 1858 and the number 160 was given to a South Staffordshire Railway engine in July 1859. 161/2/3 were still in capital stock in 1861 and 163 was renumbered by the addition of 600 in April 1862, but joined the others in the 11xx duplicate list in the next twelve months. The last of them was scrapped in 1866.

Summary: TV 4-2-0s built by Chas Tayleur & Co, 1846-7

No.	Date	Replaced		Reno'd	Withdrawn
159	12/1846	8/56			
160	12/1846	7/59	On sale 8/58		? Scr /58
161	12/1846	11/62		1196(5/62)	Scr /66
162	1/1847	11/62		1197(5/62)	Scr /65
163	1/1847	5/63		763(4/62), 1178(5/63)	Scr /64
164	2/1847	5/55	Boiler explosion 5/4/55		Scr 4/55
165	2/1847	10/58	On sale 8/58		? Scr /58
166	2/1847	7/57	Reno'd 166B(11/58)		
167	3/1847	12/56			

Tayleur working numbers were 834-42 (engines) and 843-51 (tenders).

BURY GOODS ENGINES 1846-8

Bury, Curtis & Kennedy 0-4-0 Coal Engines, 1846
Nos 172, 173

In December 1846 Bury told the Locomotive Committee that at least twenty new goods engines were needed to cope with the rising traffic. The new LNWR Joint Locomotive Committee was consulted to see if Crewe could supply any and in the discussions which followed various transfers of engines between the divisions were arranged. Two which had been ordered by the Manchester & Birmingham Railway from Bury, Curtis & Kennedy were diverted to the S Div; these were 0-4-0 "coal engines" having 4ft diameter cast-iron wheels with H-section spokes, very like those used many years later at Crewe. The domed firebox had flat sides in order to fit between the frames. These two engines arrived on the S Div at the end of 1846 and were numbered 172/3 following the BC&K large 0-6-0 class.

Dimensions

Cylinders (2 inside)	15" x 20"
Heating surface	
Tubes (133, 2¼" dia, 11' 6" long)	900.87 sq ft
Firebox	72.81 sq ft
Total	973.68 sq ft
Diameter of wheels	4' 0"
Wheelbase	8' 0"

Their small driving wheels made them suitable for hill climbing and according to James Bull they worked goods and passenger trains on the Dunstable Branch (opened May 1848) which contained a 1¼ mile incline of 1 in 40. In December 1849 173 was sent for trial on the Mold Branch of the Chester & Holyhead Railway which had a long 1 in 43 gradient. In March 1850 172 was hired to a contractor for £50 a month working on the East & West India Docks line. Because of a shortage of engines on the Stockton & Darlington Railway two were sent from the S Div in February 1854; 173 was one of them and was returned in May having worked 35 days on that line for £3 15s (£3.75) per day.

172 was replaced at the end of 1858, being renumbered in the 1000 S Div duplicate list during 1859, and minuted on 12th April 1860 as sold to a Mr Knight. 173 is believed to have been the engine 1178 sold on 22nd April 1863 to J. Roscoe Allen of Westminster.

One of the two, or an engine of the same type, came to be owned by J. B. Wilson of Wingfield Manor Colliery and survived long enough to be photographed at Wingfield MR station. It was sold to Frodingham Ironworks in 1890 and was scrapped six years later.

Summary: 0-4-0s built by Bury, Curtis & Kennedy, 1846

No.	Date	Replaced	Renumbered	Withdrawn
172	12/1846	12/58	1172(/59)	Sold 4/60 Mr Knight, £550
173	12/1846	3/61	1173(3/61), 1178(5/62)	Sold 22/4/63 J. Roscoe Allen, Westminster, £550

Bury, Curtis & Kennedy 0-4-0 Goods Engines, 1847
Nos 72, 74, 86, 89

The sudden rise in goods traffic, coupled with the Board's commitment to the unreliable long-boiler 0-6-0 type, resulted in an acute shortage of power. Bury, Curtis & Kennedy took the initiative on 3rd September 1846 by writing with a promise to make every exertion to help the S Div out of their difficulty. On the recommendation of S Div Superintendent Henry P. Bruyeres, the General Locomotive Committee agreed that BC&K's 0-4-2 117 should be the pattern for the new engines so urgently needed, and sought tenders from several manufacturers.

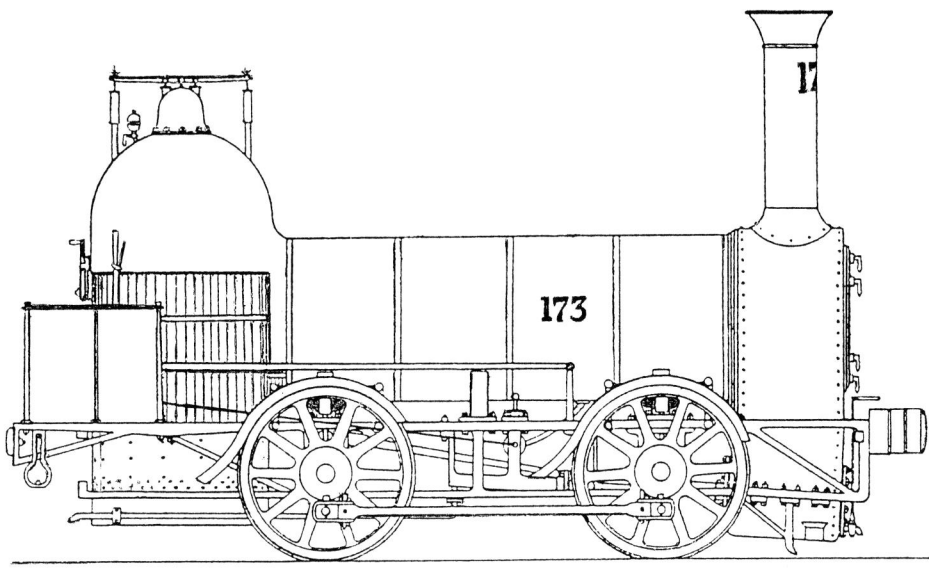

Fig. 40
Bury, Curtis & Kennedy 0-4-0 Coal Engine, 1846; 172/3.

Fig. 41   Bury, Curtis & Kennedy Engine believed to be ex-173, at Wingfield station, Midland Railway, 1890.

The replies were discouraging, for such was the the state of their order books that only BC&K and Nasmyth Gaskell could promise delivery of *any* engines in 1847; BC&K could provide six, and Nasmyth four but these only towards the end of the year. Crewe Works could make fifteen, but stipulated that they would have to be of their standard type. The outlook was bleak. Bury's partner Timothy Curtis attended the GLC meeting on 5th March 1847 and suggested that if the Chester & Holyhead Railway could be persuaded to postpone delivery of engines to them until March 1848, BC&K would be in a position to supply the LNWR with eight goods engines in 1847. This was agreed by all parties and BC&K's offer was accepted. Six of the engines were to be 0-4-2s like 117, and on Bury's contention that he could supply an even better engine on four wheels, two were to be 0-4-0s.

In fact four 0-4-0s were delivered in 1847, two of which had been diverted from some other line's order. They arrived from June to October and were given the numbers of old engines which had recently been sold, 72/4, 86/9. This was a departure from previous practice in that until then new engines had always been numbered consecutively in classes.

Nos 86/9 had high-domed haystack fireboxes like those on 168-71, whereas 72/4 had the lower, straight-top firebox with a rounded back of the type adopted by BC&K at this period. According to James Bull they had gab gear and his sketch shows mudguard splashers. Apart from the firebox shape of 72/4, all four were similar in size and type to the standard goods engines running at the time on the Lancashire & Yorkshire Railway and were slightly bigger than Furness Railway No 3 'Old Coppernob' now preserved at the National Railway Museum.

Dimensions

Cylinders (2 inside)	15" x 24"
Heating surface	
Tubes (135, 2¼" dia, 12' 0" long)	954.18 sq ft
Firebox	64.60 sq ft
Total	1,018.78 sq ft
Diameter of wheels	4' 9"
Wheelbase	8' 0"

Weight

	Nos 72/4	*Nos 86/9*
On leading wheels	8 tons 4.5 cwt	8 tons 7.5 cwt
On driving wheels	11 tons 2.0 cwt	10 tons 6.0 cwt
Total	19 tons 6.5 cwt	18 tons 13.5 cwt

Practically the only references in the LNWR records are that in February 1850 No 72 suffered a burnt firebox at Northampton, and that in August 1858 No 86 was among engines offered for sale to the Portsmouth Railway Co, but not taken.

All four were replaced in 1861 and all are believed to have survived into the 1862 duplicate list as 1171-4. One of them, 1173 ex-86, was sent to the High Peak line on 30th June 1864 and worked between High Peak junction and Cromford. In April 1865 it was installed at the top of the 1 in 8½ Sheep Pasture incline while the regular stationary engine was being repaired; this duty ended on 19th August 1865 and 1173 was returned to Crewe, whence it was sold two months later to the Whitwick Colliery Co.

Two other disposals are recorded: 1172 sold on 30th July 1862 to William Tredwell, Birmingham, and 1174 sold on 27th February 1865 to the Dowlais Iron Co, Merthyr.

Summary: 0-4-0s built by Bury, Curtis & Kennedy, 1847

No.	Date	Renumbered	Remarks
86	6/1847	1086(7/61), 1173(5/62)	Sold 17/10/65 Whitwick Colly, Coalville, £600
72	9/1847	1072(11/61), 1171(5/62)	Wdn /63
74	9/1847	1074(1/61), 1172(5/62)	Sold 30/7/62 Wm Tredwell, Birmingham, £500
89	10/1847	1089(11/61), 1174(5/62)	Sold 27/2/65 Dowlais Iron Co, Merthyr, £750

Bury, Curtis & Kennedy 0-4-2 Goods Engines, 1847-8
Nos 6, 16, 22, 33, 34, 206

The six engines "like 117" ordered on 5th March 1847 were much bigger than the original 0-4-2 class. As in all BC&K goods engines the cylinders were inclined down to the front and worked under the leading axle; the frames were the usual Bury bar-type and the driving wheels had brass mudguard splashers. They cost £2,468 10s (£2,468.50) each and were delivered from October 1847 to January 1848. At the time of their arrival they were the second most powerful class on the line, surpassed only by the BC&K 0-6-0 'Haystack Goods'. Five were given the numbers of old engines that had been scrapped or sold, 6, 16, 22, 33/4, but although there were other vacant numbers, the last engine but one received a new number at the end of the list, 206.

Dimensions

Cylinders (2 inside)	16" x 24"
Heating surface	
Tubes (157, 2¼" dia, 12' 1½" long)	1,121.33 sq ft
Firebox	77.20 sq ft
Total	1,198.53 sq ft
Diameter of wheels	
Coupled	5' 0"
Trailing	3' 4"
Wheelbase	8' 0" + 6' 9" = 14' 9"
Weight	
On leading wheels	10 tons 2 cwt
On driving wheels	10 tons 10 cwt
On trailing wheels	2 tons 15 cwt
Total	23 tons 7 cwt

In the 1850s McConnell equipped at least three (22, 33/4) with outside footplating and splashers, which made them look like his A-class 0-4-2s, but without domes. A photograph of 1859 (ex-34) taken in the early 1870s shows that this engine had also been given other McConnell features. No 34 was fitted with iron tubes in June 1854 and at the time of the report made in February 1856, had run 33,845 miles in this condition.

Only one is known to have been rebuilt, 206 in 1861.

Accidents

On 3rd March 1848 No 6 was on a goods train and because the swing bridge at Weedon had been left open, fell into the canal; Driver Beston was suspended for not stopping in time.

On the night of 8th September 1853 Driver Worrall took No 16 to look for an object said to be lying on the track ¾ mile south of Wolverton. Despite carrying red lights front

Fig. 42
Bury, Curtis & Kennedy 0-4-2 34 built 1847. At Shrewsbury Abbey station in 1872-4 after sale to the Potteries, Shrewsbury & North Wales Railway; still carrying its last LNWR number 1859. Changes by McConnell include running plate, splashers, sandboxes, smokebox door, extra lock-up safety valve, blower pipe, water delivery at front of boiler. Subsequent Ramsbottom fittings include chimney, buffers, lubricators, front handrail and weatherboard.
(A.G. Dunbar collection)

Fig. 43
Bury, Curtis & Kennedy 0-4-2 as built, 1847.

and rear, the engine was run into by a Down train.

Disposal

Four were renumbered into the capital list by the addition of 600 in April 1862; the other two (6 and 16) appear to have gone directly into the 11xx duplicate list although they were not replaced until the following July and September. The four capital engines were replaced in 1863, two of them surviving to be renumbered in the 18xx duplicate list at the end of 1871.

1153 (ex-33) was sold to an unrecorded purchaser on 17th March 1864.

1143 (ex-22) was sold on 9th October 1865 to Messrs Knight & Gorton of Manchester for £700.

1859 (ex-34) was sold on 31st May 1872 to the Potteries, Shrewsbury & North Wales Railway for £500. It became their No 10 and was known as 'Black Tom' but was disposed of in 1874.

1858 (ex-206) was sold on 18th April 1873 to Wm Moss, railway contractor of Stafford, for £600 plus his old engine, which was cut up at Crewe on 4th May "in lieu of 1858" and is described as an old Stephenson engine from the North Staffordshire Railway. Its successor 1858 was on a Peterborough branch ballast train just east of Northampton on 18th October 1877 when it was in collision with Midland Railway 2-4-0 191. It was badly damaged and was sent to Crewe where it was scrapped under cut-up number 1808 on 5th December 1877. On payment of £150 Moss was given Class A 1171 in part exchange.

Summary: 0-4-2s built by Bury, Curtis & Kennedy, 1847-8

No.	Date	Reno'd 4/62	Rebt	Reno'd	Withdrawn
22	10/1847	622		1143(1/63)	Sold 9/10/65, Knight & Gorton, £700
33	10/1847	633		1153(5/63)	Sold 17/3/64
34	11/1847	634		1154(5/63), 1859(12/71)	Sold 31/5/72 PS&NWR, £500
6	11/1847			1168(5/62)	Scr /63
206	12/1847	806	/61	1148(2/63), 1858(12/71)	Sold 18/4/73 Wm Moss, £600 c/u 1808 Scr 5/12/77
16	1/1848			1169(5/62)	Scr /63

TWO JONES & POTTS ENGINES 1847

Jones & Potts 0-6-0 Goods Engine
No 174

Following the General Locomotive Committee's quest among the manufacturers in January 1847, Jones & Potts of the Viaduct Foundry, Newton-le-Willows responded on 27th February with an offer of one passenger and one goods engine. McConnell was sent to inspect them, and their purchase was agreed on 4th March. The goods engine was an outside-framed 0-6-0 with the rear axle behind the firebox, a boiler which contained the surprisingly large number of 224 tubes, a square-based dome with a spring balance safety valve just behind the chimney, another spring balance safety valve on a column on the boiler top, and a second square-based dome on the raised firebox. It arrived on the S Div late in March 1847 and was given the number 174, after the Bury coal engines.

It may have been similar to the two engines offered by Jones & Potts to the N Div in November 1846 which Trevithick had refused and which went to the Lancaster & Carlisle Railway instead, later becoming N Div 214 *Shap* and 215 *Spitfire*.

Dimensions

Cylinders (2 inside)	16" x 22"
Heating surface	
Tubes (224, 2" dia, 10' 1½" long)	1,187.52 sq ft
Firebox	74.60 sq ft
Total	*1,262.14 sq ft
Diameter of wheels	5' 0"
Wheelbase	6' 6" + 6' 6" = 13' 0"
Weight	
On leading wheels	7 tons 14.5 cwt
On driving wheels	8 tons 4.0 cwt
On trailing wheels	2 tons 16.5 cwt
Total	18 tons 15.0 cwt

See note on heating surfaces in Introduction.

By the end of 1851 it had run 32,470 miles; its average load was 146 tons.

Presumably it went into the S Div duplicate list in 1860; its precise fate is unknown.

Summary: 0-6-0 built by Jones & Potts

No.	Maker	Date	Replaced
174	J&P	3/1847	9/60

Jones & Potts 4-2-0 Passenger Engine
No 175

The passenger engine offered by Jones & Potts on 27th February 1847 and accepted on 4th March was an outside cylinder long-boiler of similar type to those already obtained and in process of delivery. It is said by the usually reliable Sekon to have been named *Snake*. This name may have been that selected by Jones & Potts' original customer; it is not mentioned in LNWR records and may have been a nickname provoked by McConnell's balancing experiments.

The firebox was like that of Stephenson's engines 153-8, with a straight top. There was a large brass dome on the boiler, with a spring balance safety valve on a column behind it. Another spring balance safety valve was mounted on a manhole on the firebox top. The wheels had plain spokes.

It probably arrived in April 1847 following the Jones & Potts goods engine 174 and was numbered 175.

Dimensions

Cylinders (2 outside)	15" x 22"
Heating surface	
Tubes (117, 2¼" dia, 13' 10½" long)	946.90 sq ft
Firebox	65.80 sq ft
Total	*1,012.76 sq ft
Diameter of wheels	
Leading and middle	3' 10"
Driving	6' 5"
Wheelbase	7' 0" + 5' 5" = 12' 5"
Weight	
On leading wheels	5 tons 19.0 cwt
On middle wheels	5 tons 19.25 cwt
On driving wheels	10 tons 18.0 cwt
Total	22 tons 16.25 cwt

See note on heating surfaces in Introduction.

It was tried against Crampton's *London* in September 1847 with the result that another Crampton was ordered, the 6-2-0 *Liverpool*.

In July 1848 McConnell was authorised to try out a system of compensating balances to the outside cylinder engines "to avoid the lateral motion to which they are subject" and 175 was the engine selected for the trial. The scheme involved adding a connecting rod to the driving crank, which worked a sliding block of the same weight as the piston, but behind the driving wheel. The experiment was not a success. According to Sekon "the result was a rude disilluson of the idea ... the engine breaking down on its first trip after being fitted with the reciprocating counterbalance."

The provision of a McConnell patent boiler was sanctioned in November 1852, the second passenger engine (after 179) to be so fitted. Because of its large firebox 175 was one of the four engines permitted to use coal from 25th July 1854.

It was replaced in November 1859, offered for sale to the London, Chatham & Dover Railway in September 1860 and was probably scrapped shortly afterwards.

Summary: 4-2-0 built by Jones & Potts

No.	Maker	Date	Replaced	Withdrawn
175	J&P	4/1847	11/59	Probably scrapped b/60 or /61

CHESTER & HOLYHEAD
AND
LEEDS, DEWSBURY & MANCHESTER ENGINES

1. Chester & Holyhead Railway

The C&H was an independent line, with close ties to the L&B despite the distance which separated them; the L&B had a £300,000 investment in it and several directors sat on both boards. The C&H had ordered fifty engines in 1845/6 on the advice of Robert Stephenson which were all of his patent long-boiler type; thirty were to be 6ft 4-2-0 passenger engines with 15in x 24in outside cylinders, the other twenty were 4ft 6in 0-6-0 goods.

The orders are listed in a C&H document dated April 1846:

"Contractor	No of Engines	Price per Engine & Tender	Total amount of contract	Remarks
Bury & Co	6	£2,000	£12,000	2 in Jan, 2 in Feb, 2 in Mar, 1847.
Jones & Potts	6	£2,000	£12,000	March 1847.
	3	£2,260	£6,780	1 March 1848.
Nasmyth & Co	6	£2,000	£12,000	In the course of 1846.
Tayleur & Co	6	£2,000	£12,000	2 in July, 2 in Aug, 2 in Sept, 1846.
Haigh Foundry	3	£2,250	£6,750	1 March 1848, not later.
PASSENGER ENGINES	30		£61,530	
Stephenson & Co	6	£2,100	£12,600	Jan 1848
	8	£2,380	£19,040	2 in Jan, 2 in March, 2 in May, 2 in July, 1848.
Hawthorn	6	£2,305*	£13,830	2 in Feb, 2 in March, 2 in April, 1848.
GOODS ENGINES	20		£45,470	

*Contract with Hawthorn at £2,275 per Engine and Tender, the Company paying the patent right, amounting to £30, making a total of £2,305 per Engine and Tender."

By this time the first of the disastrous patent long-boiler 0-6-0 goods engines had arrived on the L&B, to be joined in the following month by the equally dismal 4-2-0 version. Capt C. R. Moorsom, who was a director of both companies, wrote to the C&H secretary in September 1846, saying that the Stephenson patent engines supplied to the LNWR by Tayleur, Longridge and Jones & Potts were not working "altogether satisfactorily" and he asked about the state of the fifty engines being built, so that "if necessary the manufacturers may be communicated with". This led to some revision of the original designs.

Financial difficulties before the line was ready for opening led in 1847 to an agreement with the LNWR under which the latter would work the line, provide engines and rolling stock and would take over the engines being built for the C&H.

Several C&H engines were completed long before the line was ready. This caused Moorsom (probably prompted by McConnell) to suggest in March 1847 that some of the superfluous locomotives might be transferred to Wolverton.

Eventually all the C&H engines went from the makers to the S Div. When the LNWR General Manager Mark Huish proposed in March 1848 that some of the still-undelivered engines be sent instead to the N Div, the S Div Locomotive Committee decreed that they should be sent south like the others, although "Mr Trevithick is to have as many as he may require". He didn't ask for any.

The story that the C&H engines were delivered by sea and erected at Holyhead shed, and then worked on that line, and that they were renumbered into the LNWR series "on the night of 18th March 1859" (*Locomotive Magazine*, pp52 & 67, 1909, and other publications) is complete nonsense. A series of letters between McConnell and the C&H preserved in the LNWR archives puts this beyond any doubt.

2. Leeds, Dewsbury & Manchester Railway

This line was taken over by the LNWR before opening. Six of its engines were sent to Wolverton in 1847-8 and were given S Div numbers. Three of them were returned

Fig. 44 Tayleur long-boiler 4-2-0 of 1847, ordered for the Chester & Holyhead Railway; LNWR S Div 176-181.

to the north in 1848, and in the following year their numbers were taken by the last three of the Chester & Holyhead engines.

Tayleur 4-2-0 Passenger Engines, 1847 Nos 176-181

The original order for these six engines was dated 10th September 1845. Charles Tayleur & Co began immediately, and in February 1846 Robert Stephenson wrote to the Bristol & Birmingham Railway offering three engines then being built by Tayleur for the Chester & Holyhead, but not yet required by that line. The price asked was £2,400 each (20% more than the C&H price) which the B&BR paid. The other three engines of this order were taken by the Norfolk Railway in July 1846. Tayleur then went on to build six replacements to a revised design for the C&H.

On 6th March 1847 Edward Tayleur wrote from the Vulcan Foundry to tell the C&H that their first engine was complete and "if it remains here it will be a serious inconvenience to us". His postscript: "There will be a new one ready every week" must have embarrassed the C&H, until Moorsom and the S Div came to the rescue.

On 18th March McConnell wrote to the C&H asking to arrange the transfer: "I assure you we shall be very happy to see them on this line, being very short of power at present."

The first three of the C&H engines were sent straight from the Vulcan Foundry to Wolverton on Saturday 27th March 1847. The fourth was sent off on 1st April, and arrived at Wolverton on 2nd with a broken wheel which was replaced by Tayleur in the next fortnight. The fifth arrived by 13th April and the sixth and last on 1st May.

They are said to have been named *Britannia, Menai, Bangor, Carnarvon, Flint* and *Chester* but this seems very unlikely and there is no mention of any of these names in the LNWR records. Tayleur's works 'rotation numbers' have been quoted as 263-8 but these too are doubtful, having been estimated in the 1890s. The recorded 'working numbers' were 960-5 (engines) and 966-71 (tenders). The final price of each was £2,045 which probably covered some improvement specified after Moorsom's complaint of September 1846. On the S Div they were numbered 176-81 in order of arrival.

They were Stephenson patent long-boiler 4-2-0s similar to Tayleur's 159-67 obtained for the Trent Valley line; they had the same T-iron wheels but differences included a straight-topped firebox and a large dome immediately behind the chimney. Two spring balance safety valves sat side by side on a manhole on the firebox top, with splayed levers to springs mounted on each side of the firebox; an elegantly curved column enclosed the valves. The driving axle springs were underhung, the boiler centre line was slightly higher, there was a cast balance weight on the driving wheel boss opposite the crank and the bracket holding the slide bars was modified to support the running board. Otherwise the engines were almost identical with the earlier batch.

A Vulcan Foundry outline drawing was published in the 1909 *Locomotive Magazine* showing the dome situated towards the back of the boiler barrel, but a Vulcan general arrangement drawing dated 5th June 1847 shows the engines as built, with the dome close behind the chimney. A sketch by E. T. Lane dated June 1848 confirms the forward position as does James Bull, whose drawing also shows the engine number 176 on the side of the dome.

Dimensions

Cylinders (2 outside)	15" x 22"
Boiler (oval)	
Diameter, vertical	3' 6"
horizontal	3' 2"
Length of barrel	13' 6"
Pitch	5' 8"
Length of firebox casing	4' 2"
Heating surface	
Tubes (125, 2" dia, 13' 10½" long)	908.89 sq ft
Firebox	62.46 sq ft
Total	971.35 sq ft
Grate area	10.25 sq ft
Diameter of wheels	
Leading and middle	3' 6"
Driving	6' 0"
Wheelbase	
Engine	6' 9" + 5' 3" = 12' 0"
Tender	5' 4" + 4' 10" = 10' 2"

Weight	March 1848	April 1853
On leading wheels	6 tons 2 cwt	6 tons 3 cwt
On middle wheels	5 tons 3.75 cwt	4 tons 0 cwt
On driving wheels	11 tons 1 cwt	13 tons 1 cwt
Total	22 tons 6.75 cwt	23 tons 4 cwt

Tender (6 wheel) capacity	coke 112 cu ft
	water 1,000 gal

McConnell's patent boiler was fitted to 179, the first passenger engine to be so treated, in April-June 1852. He reported its working from July 1852 to April 1853, and compared it favourably with four of the same class which had not been rebuilt, claiming that 179 consumed 29% less coke per ton/mile than the others, and providing other details of the work of these engines:

July 1852 - April 1853:
Engine number:	176	177	178	179	180
Miles run with load:	7,531	5,739	11,912	11,287	17,223
Total miles excl. of shunting:	8,655	6,538	12,127	11,716	17,816
Hours shunting:	661	201	187	30	83
Hours stationary:	124.5	468	461	903	1511.7

McConnell wanted to apply the new boiler to the others of the class, but this was suspended by the General Locomotive Committee in February 1853. On 25th July 1854, authority was given to him to use coal in 179 (as also with 0-6-0s 125/32, and Jones & Potts 4-2-0 175) "and to report the effect, with a view to determine whether the engines of the same description now wanting material repairs of the boiler shall be altered in a similar manner."

Disposal
179 was the first to be replaced, in May 1857. In August 1858 180 was offered to the Portsmouth Railway for £800, but was probably scrapped in the same year; it was replaced in November 1858. One of the South Staffordshire Railway engines replaced 181 in July 1859. The other three survived to the end of the separate S Div, but then went into the 11xx duplicate list and were scrapped shortly afterwards.

Summary: C&H 4-2-0s built by Chas Tayleur & Co, 1847

No.	Date	Replaced	Reno'd	Withdrawn
176	29/3/1847	8/62	1185(5/62)	? Scr /67
177	29/3/1847	8/62	1186(5/62)	? Scr 1/64
178	29/3/1847	8/62	1143(5/62)	? Scr /62
179	2/4/1847	6/57		
180	13/4/1847	12/58		? Scr /58
181	1/5/1847	7/59		

Tayleur working numbers were 960-5 (engines) and 966-71 (tenders).

Jones & Potts 4-2-0 Passenger Engines, 1847-8
Nos 182-190
The Chester & Holyhead had ordered six engines from Jones & Potts on 18th August 1845, and another three in January 1846. McConnell reported the arrival of the first of them on 25th May 1847. The invoice from "Jones & Potts, Viaduct Foundry, Newton, manufacturers of Land, Marine & Locomotive Engines" survives:

"1 six-wheeled locomotive engine
 'Stephenson's Patent': £1,650
 1 six-wheeled locomotive tender: £350
 £2,000

This engine & tender is received & is numbered on the Company's list as Nº 182

J. E. McConnell, 25 May 47"

As he was not fully aware at that time of the number of C&H engines he could expect, he wrote to the C&H secretary for a list.

Another two arrived in June, and one more in August, by which time McConnell had asked if the engines being built could have brass tubes instead of iron, and other modifications. Jones & Potts wrote on 25th August that the additional cost of McConnell's requirements on the five outstanding engines would be £162 10s 11d (£162.55) each, making a total price of £2,350 each engine and tender. Some further alterations were probably asked for and when 186-90 at last arrived in May-October 1848 the price had gone up again to £2,450 each. The driving wheels were six inches larger than in the first engines, the firebox was increased in size and there were fewer but larger tubes.

According to S. S. Scott (source unknown) S Div 185 was J&P works number 155.

The nine were outwardly similar to 175 purchased from the same maker in April 1847, with a large brass dome on the boiler and two spring balance safety valves on columns behind.

Dimensions, Nos 182-5

Cylinders (2 outside)	15" x 22"
Heating surface	
Tubes (140, 2" dia, 13' 10½" long)	1,017.06 sq ft
Firebox	58.44 sq ft
Total	*1,075.56 sq ft
Diameter of wheels	
Leading and middle	3' 10"
Driving	6' 0"
Wheelbase	7' 0" + 5' 5" = 12' 5"

Weight

	March 1848	April 1853
On leading wheels	6 tons 5 cwt	5 tons 17 cwt
On middle wheels	5 tons 7 cwt	4 tons 0 cwt
On driving wheels	10 tons 12 cwt	13 tons 6 cwt
Total	22 tons 4 cwt	23 tons 3 cwt

Dimensions, Nos 186-90

Cylinders (2 outside)	15" x 22"
Heating surface	
Tubes (117, 2¼" dia, 13' 10½" long)	946.90 sq ft
Firebox	62.80 sq ft
Total	*1,016.25 sq ft
Grate area	12.5 sq ft
Diameter of wheels	
Leading and middle	3' 10"
Driving	6' 6"
Wheelbase	7' 0" + 5' 5" = 12' 5"
Weight	
On leading wheels	6 tons 5 cwt
On middle wheels	4 tons 6 cwt
On driving wheels	13 tons 6 cwt
Total	23 tons 17 cwt

See note on heating surfaces in Introduction.

A photograph of 189 (Fig 45) was taken c1858/9 at Birmingham with Driver Bowker on the footplate. By then a weatherboard and sandboxes had been added, the middle wheels had flanged tyres, the leading wheels had solid disc centres and both carrying axles were

Fig. 45 189 built for the Chester & Holyhead Rly by Jones & Potts, 1848. Disc wheels (McConnell's patent of July 1854) have been fitted to the hollow leading axle. Other changes include spring buffers, sand boxes and a very low weatherboard. Photographed at Curzon Street station, Birmingham, with Driver Bowker of Vauxhall shed on the footplate, probably in 1858/9.
(W.H.Whitworth collection)

Fig. 46 Jones & Potts long-boiler 4-2-0 of 1847/8. The ten engines of this general type, 175 and 182-190, were not all alike; the driving wheel diameter and internal boiler details varied.

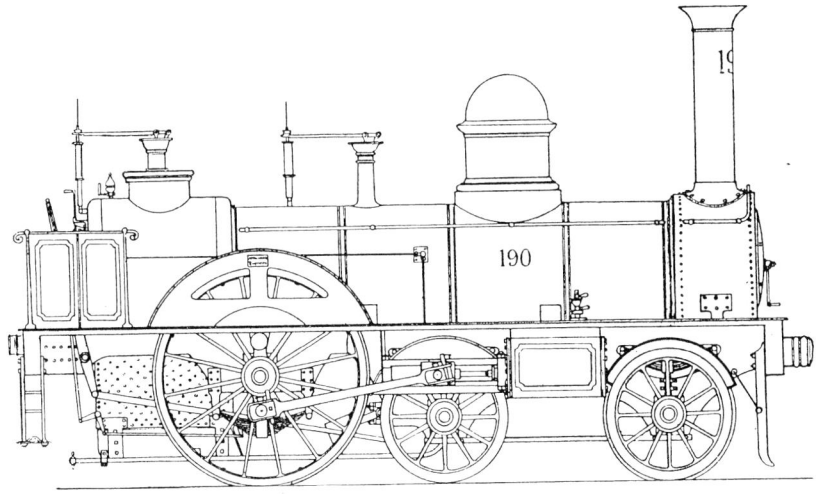

hollow. Weights given by Bowker were:

On leading wheels	5 tons	16 cwt
On middle wheels	5 tons	18 cwt
On driving wheels	13 tons	12 cwt
Total	25 tons	6 cwt

Accidents

A few days after its delivery 188 was bringing the Up York Mail from Rugby on 17th August 1848 when it collided at Roade with the Peterborough Mail, headed by 98. This happened during the footplatemen's strike when both engines were being driven by strike-breaking fitters; William Cumberlidge was in charge of the York Mail as his fourth experience of driving. The accident report concluded that "from his replies to a number of questions he obviously does not know how to handle an engine." Another fitter Thomas Richardson was driving 98 after nine days on the job; the inspector unhesitatingly pronounced both men incompetent to drive. When Jones & Potts' bill for 188 was paid on 7th September, the engine was already in Wolverton for repair.

On 5th September 1848, 183 was on the Up York Mail with Driver Ross on the footplate when at about 3.00am it ran into the large Bury 0-6-0 170 derailed at the north end of Linslade Tunnel. As a result it was out of action until the following April; repairs to the two engines cost £800, most of it for the 4-2-0.

One of the 182-5 series was derailed at Watford on 6th August 1856 while working the then fastest train on the LNWR, the 6.15am Up Wolverhampton-Euston; the inspecting officer commented that the centre of gravity of the engine was only 4ft 1½in in front of the rear wheels and that the type was not the best or safest for running very fast trains. His was not the first such criticism; five years earlier long-boiler engines had been banned from working fast trains in Prussia after the Gütersloh derailment of 21st January 1851.

Disposal

The first one, 182, was replaced in July 1857 and was offered to the Portsmouth Railway in August 1858 for

£800. McConnell said it would be broken up in the current half year, but in November 1858 at the start of the S Div duplicate listing it was ordered to be lettered 'C' so became No 182C. It was offered for sale to the LC&DR in September 1860, and was probably broken up soon afterwards.

183 and 189 were replaced in 1859, 183 being offered in September 1860 to the LC&DR (it should have been S Div duplicate 1183 by then) but it was probably broken up.

Five were in capital stock in 1861 but these and one from the S Div duplicate stock went into the 11xx duplicate list in 1862. One, ex-185, is believed to be the engine sold as 1190 to Benjamin Piercy of Westminster for £850 on 13th June 1865. Piercy was the engineer of railways as various as the Hoylake and the Royal Sardinian but what he did with a Jones & Potts 4-2-0 is not known. The last survivors of the class, ex-186/8, were scrapped in 1867.

Summary: C&H 4-2-0s built by Jones & Potts, 1847-8

No.	Date	Replaced	Reno'd	Withdrawn
182	25/5/1847	7/57	182C(11/58)	? Scr /61
183	6/1847	10/59		? Scr /61
184	6/1847	9/62	1144(5/62)	? Scr 9/62
185	8/1847	10/62	1190(5/62)	Sold 13/6/65 B.Piercy, £850
186	5/1848	10/62	1188(5/62)	? Scr 2/67
187	6/1848	11/62	1145(5/62)	? Scr 11/62
188	8/1848	10/62	1194(5/62)	? Scr 2/67
189	9/1848	7/59		
190	10/1848	8/62	1146(5/62)	? Scr 10/62

Nasmyth, Gaskell 2-2-2 Passenger Engines, 1847-8
Nos 191-196

Six passenger engines were ordered by the Chester & Holyhead Railway from Nasmyth, Gaskell & Co of Bridgewater Foundry, Patricroft on 18th August 1845. Delivery was to be during 1846; the price of each engine was £1,650 plus £350 for the tender. According to the specification they were to be Stephenson's patent long-boiler 4-2-0 type, like the others ordered by the C&H, but this was revised after Moorsom's complaint about the LNWR engines of this pattern. The Nasmyth engines as built had the patent long boiler and outside cylinders but were 2-2-2s with the trailing axle behind a Gothic firebox; for the time they must have had a very long wheelbase. The order having been diverted to the LNWR S Div, they arrived at Wolverton between November 1847 and March 1848; the maker's numbers were 80-5. They were given S Div numbers 191-6.

The price was £2,350 each, the £350 increase no doubt because of the change of design. Only £2,333 5s (£2,333.25) per engine was paid; £16 15s (£16.75) was deducted as the "cost of putting the engine in working order."

Dimensions

Cylinders (2 outside)	15" x 22"
Diameter of driving wheels	6' 0"
Weight	
On leading wheels	8 tons 3 cwt
On driving wheels	10 tons 10 cwt
On trailing wheels	4 tons 9.3 cwt
Total	23 tons 2.3 cwt

Nothing is known of their work on the S Div, where they remained for only a short time. All are recorded in S Div working stock each month from their delivery until mid-December 1848.

By October 1848 the LNWR had a surfeit of engines and there were more on order. The General Locomotive Committee decided that all engines surplus to requirements should be placed in store, for use on new branch lines when they were opened. In the second half of December 1848 three of the Nasmyth singles 191/2/5 were given an overhaul and put into store, being joined there in January 1849 by the other three.

They did not remain long in store for on 13th April 1849 the GLC ordered that 191-6 be transferred north for the forthcoming opening of the Huddersfield & Manchester line. They were not what Ramsbottom would have preferred - he wanted engines with smaller driving wheels and inside cylinders for steadier running on the tight curves of the Huddersfield line. It looks very much as if McConnell was glad to be rid of them. At the end of April he said they were "out of store and being thoroughly repaired for the Yorkshire lines"; on 23rd May the M&B Div Committee learned from him that they were ready for delivery and ordered that they be sent to Longsight immediately. They arrived there at the end of the month, recorded as "much worn when received". In August Ramsbottom complained that the "long-boiler engines from Wolverton were in very bad condition" and that for the efficient working of the Stockport-Stalybridge branch it was absolutely necessary to take two Sharp singles (M&B Div Nos 8 and 9) out of store. The wheels of the Nasmyth engines were described as "dangerous" in September when new wheels were to be put under them. Extra wheels and axles had already been ordered to be sent from Wolverton to Longsight. In a report by Ramsbottom in July 1853, all six engines had low mileages on the NE Div and had a boiler pressure of 80 lb/sq in.

They became NE Div 47-52 and were renumbered by the addition of 400 in August 1857 when the N and NE Divisions were combined.

Fig. 47   Old sketch of 2-2-2 built by Nasmyth, Gaskell 1847-8 for the Chester & Holyhead Railway; became LNWR S Div 191-6 briefly before transfer to the Manchester & Birmingham Division. Not to scale.

Summary: C&H 2-2-2s built by Nasmyth, Gaskell & Co, 1847-8

No.	Date		NE Div No.	Renumbered	Scrapped
191	11/1847	to M&B Div 5/49	47	447(8/57), 447A(5/59)	b /61
192	12/1847	to M&B Div 5/49	48	448(8/57), 448A(7/59)	b /61
193	12/1847	to M&B Div 5/49	49	449(8/57), 449A(7/59)	b /61
194	1/1848	to M&B Div 5/49	50	450(8/57), 450A(9/59)	b /61
195	1/1848	to M&B Div 5/49	51	451(8/57), 451A(9/59)	b /61
196	3/1848	to M&B Div 5/49	52	452(8/57), 452A(9/59)	b /61

Nasmyth works numbers were 80-5.

E. B. Wilson 2-2-2 Passenger Engines, 1847
Nos 201-204

The Leeds, Dewsbury & Manchester Railway ordered six outside-cylinder singles from Fenton, Craven & Co of Leeds about February 1846. Some were ready by December but the railway was not, so it was agreed that the firm - now renamed E. B. Wilson & Co - would store them until required. Wilson asked for an advance of £3,000 on account of the engines already built but when the LD&M demurred he decided to sell the first two to the Eastern Counties Railway and proposed replacing them later with two of his firm's new standard 'Jenny Lind' type. These were now being built continuously for stock, so that two for the LD&M could be delivered at a week's notice. On 25th May 1847 the ECR received the two engines for £2,501.25 each; they became their Nos 115/6 later renumbered 215/6.

The other four remained with Wilson. Meanwhile the LD&M was taken over by the LNWR and in November the LNWR Manager Mark Huish proposed that the four engines at Leeds be sent to the S Div, in exchange for the N Div engines then at work there which were required back at Crewe. The Wilson engines arrived at Wolverton by 7th December and were numbered 201-4.

They had Gothic fireboxes, which like the boilers, were covered with painted wooden lagging. According to the *Locomotive Magazine* of 1897 the wheels were painted red which led to the nickname 'Jenny Red Legs' - a story which the magazine repeated later about the Eastern Counties engines of the same type. There are two sketches of 202 dated July 1848 by E. T. Lane.

The maker's number of 201 was 43 according to Douglas Leitch's drawing in the 1897 *Locomotive Magazine* but his source for this is unknown.

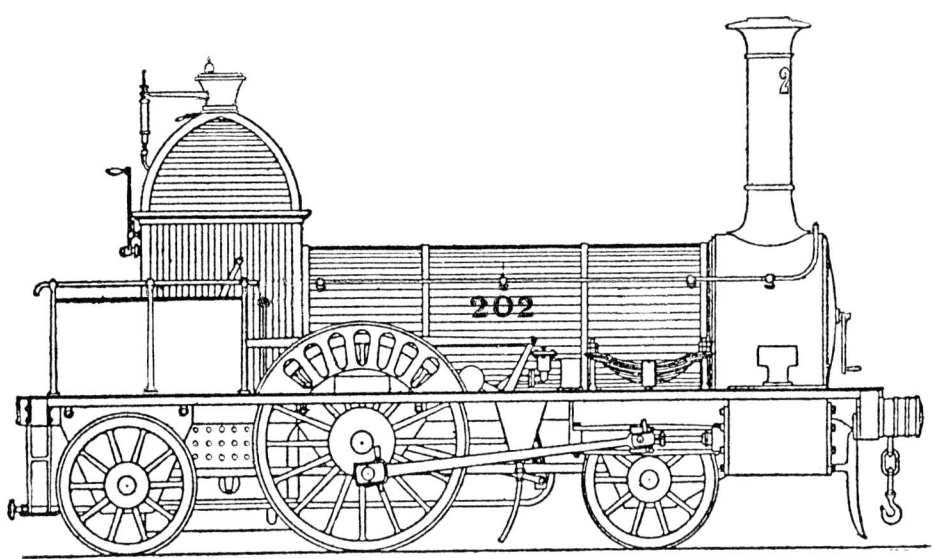

Fig. 48   E. B. Wilson 2-2-2 for the Leeds, Dewsbury & Manchester Railway, 1847. Became LNWR S Div 201-204.

Dimensions

Cylinders (2 outside)	15" x 20"
Boiler (oval)	
Diameter, vertical	3' 7"
horizontal	3' 4"
Length of barrel	11' 0"
Pitch	5' 10½"
Heating surface	
Tubes (107, 1¾" dia, 11' 5½" long)	561.80 sq ft
Firebox	59.50 sq ft
Total	*621.323 sq ft
Grate area	9.84 sq ft
Boiler pressure	80 lb/sq in
Diameter of wheels	
Leading	3' 6"
Driving	5' 6"
Trailing	3' 6"
Wheelbase	7' 8" + 6' 1" = 13' 9"
Weight	
On leading wheels	9 tons 3 cwt
On driving wheels	9 tons 10.5 cwt
On trailing wheels	3 tons 2 cwt
Total	21 tons 15.5 cwt

See note on heating surfaces in Introduction.

Summary: LD&M 2-2-2s (OC) built by E. B. Wilson

No.	Built	Date to S Div	Date to LD&M	Renumbered	Withdrawn
201	1846/7	11/1847	—	1192(5/62)	Scr /67
202	1846/7	11/1847	9/48	NE Div 40(7/49), N Div 440(8/57), 440A(8/60)	? Scr a /62
203	1846/7	11/1847	9/48	NE Div 41(7/49), N Div 441(8/57), 441A(10/59)	Sold 10/4/60, Henry Clements, Cardiff, £500
204	1846/7	11/1847	9/48	NE Div 42(7/49), N Div 442(8/57), 442A(11/60), 1129(4/62)	? Scr 2/71

By all accounts they were not a very good type, and when McConnell was given the chance to discard them he took it. On 7th September 1848 he was told to send two of them back for the imminent opening of the Leeds & Dewsbury line with "another suitable for their traffic - the three to be on the L&D line within a week". He sent all four Wilsons, according to the monthly returns for 10th October and 8th November, but this may have been wishful thinking, for 201 was again listed in S Div stock by mid December. The other three, 202/3/4, were recorded as "part-worn when received" in Yorkshire.

The Leeds line was isolated from the rest of the LNWR until Standedge tunnel opened in 1849, when the three engines were taken into NE Div stock with the numbers 40/1/2. Later they were given 6ft driving wheels at Longsight.

S Div 201 remained in the south and for several years was used as a banking engine between Euston and Camden.

This engine and one of the NE Div trio lasted long enough to go into the 11xx duplicate list in 1862. Isaac Watt Boulton bought one of them, 1129 ex-204, on 13th March 1866 for £350, but must have returned it to Crewe very quickly because it remained in duplicate stock and is believed to have been scrapped in February 1871. The other, 1192 ex-201, was scrapped in 1867.

E. B. Wilson 2-2-2 Passenger Engines - 'Jenny Lind' type, 1848
Nos 208, 209

The S Div had agreed to take four engines from the Leeds, Dewsbury & Manchester which became Nos 201-4 in November 1847, and McConnell was surprised by the arrival of two more in January 1848. These were the two engines which E. B. Wilson & Co built for the LD&M to replace two of their order sold to the Eastern Counties Railway. They were of a much better design and McConnell wanted to keep them "being the more suitable for the work of this Division" and send back two of the outside-cylinder engines in their place, but for the time being all the LD&M engines remained in the south.

In April the LNWR paid the LD&M £13,200 for all six, the new arrivals having been taken into S Div stock as 208/9 about the middle of March 1848.

E. B. Wilson built engines of this type for several railways; the first one for the London Brighton & South Coast was named *Jenny Lind* after the sensational Swedish soprano whose London debut was in May 1847, just as the first engine was completed. At least two others of the type were given the same name (on the York & North Midland and the Manchester Sheffield & Lincolnshire) and it quickly caught on as the name for the class.

They had outside frames with outside bearings for the leading and trailing wheels; inside frames with the driving axle bearings were attached to the front of the wide firebox. They had Wilson's typical finish - cast-iron dome and safety valve covers with fluted sides, and boiler lagged with strips of varnished mahogany. Ahrons attributed their great success largely to the high boiler pressure, which is said to have been 120 lb per square inch. This is unlikely to have been the case on the S Div,

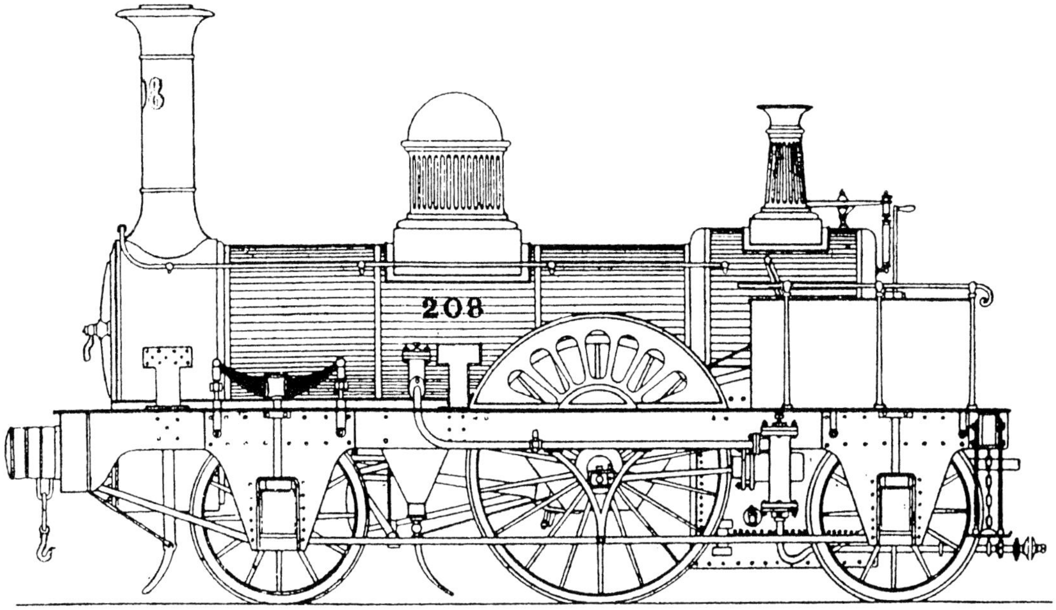

Fig. 49
E.B. Wilson 'Jenny Lind' type built for the Leeds, Dewsbury & Manchester Rly, 1847. Became LNWR S Div Nos 208/9.

where boiler pressures did not officially exceed 85 lb until 1851. It is possible they were among the 45 S Div engines with the highest boiler pressure (120 lb) in 1856.

Dimensions

Cylinders (2 inside)	15" x 20"
Boiler	
Diameter	3' 7"
Length of barrel	10' 6½"
Pitch	5' 9"
Heating surface	
Tubes (124, 2" dia, 10' 11" long)	708.77 sq ft
Firebox (3' 6" long, 3'6½" wide, 5' 1" high)	75.20 sq ft
Total	*784.01 sq ft
Grate area	12.7 sq ft
Diameter of wheels	
Leading	4' 0"
Driving	6' 0"
Trailing	4' 0"
Wheelbase	7' 0" + 6' 6" = 13' 6"
Weight	
On leading wheels	7 tons 17.5 cwt
On driving wheels	10 tons 19 cwt
On trailing wheels	4 tons 14.5 cwt
Total	23 tons 11 cwt
Tender (6 wheel) capacity	coke 2½ tons
	water 800 gal

*See note on heating surfaces in Introduction.

When engines were ordered to be sent back for the opening of the Leeds line, McConnell was able to unload most of the inferior outside-cylinder type, keeping the Jenny Linds.

E. T. Lane made sketches of 208 in October 1848. Although both engines lasted well beyond the end of the separate S Div there is no record of their work.

Summary: LD&M 'Jenny Lind' type 2-2-2s built by E. B. Wilson, 1848

No.	Date to S Div	Reno'd 4/62	Reno'd	Scrapped
208	3/1848	808	1204(9/63)	5/68
209	3/1848	809	1206(9/63), 1937(12/71)	25/4/73

Bury Curtis & Kennedy 2-2-2 Passenger Engines, 1848 Nos 12, 18, 65, 67, 75, 218

These six engines were ordered in August 1845 by the Chester & Holyhead Railway. The cost was to be £2,000 each with delivery between January and March 1847, but on the 5th of the latter month it was arranged between Timothy Curtis of BC&K, the C&H and the LNWR, that completion would be postponed until eight goods engines had been delivered to the S Div.

In fact ten goods engines arrived at Wolverton from BC&K between June 1847 and January 1848, followed in May 1848 by the first of the singles which the S Div had agreed to take. The price of each of these was now £2,613 10s (£2,613.50).

They had Bury's bar frames "of best hammered iron" proportionately bigger but similar in form to the frames of his earliest L&B engines. The top frame member was of rectangular cross section, mainly 4¼in wide by 2¼in deep, but thickened near the axles and flattened along the firebox sides to 1¾in wide by 4¾in deep; forward of the driving wheel the bottom truss consisted of 2¾in diameter rods. The driving and trailing axlebox horns were welded to the framing but the leading horns were bolted on. The two sides were united by the oak buffer plank, the inside cylinder assembly, transverse stay rods and behind the firebox by a forging which carried the drawbar pin.

Fig. 50 Bury, Curtis & Kennedy 2-2-2 ordered for the Chester & Holyhead Rly and delivered to the LNWR S Div in 1848, becoming Nos 12, 18, 65, 67, 75 and 218. They were later fitted with a dome on the boiler barrel, outside footplating and splashers. The Bloomers were closely based on this design.

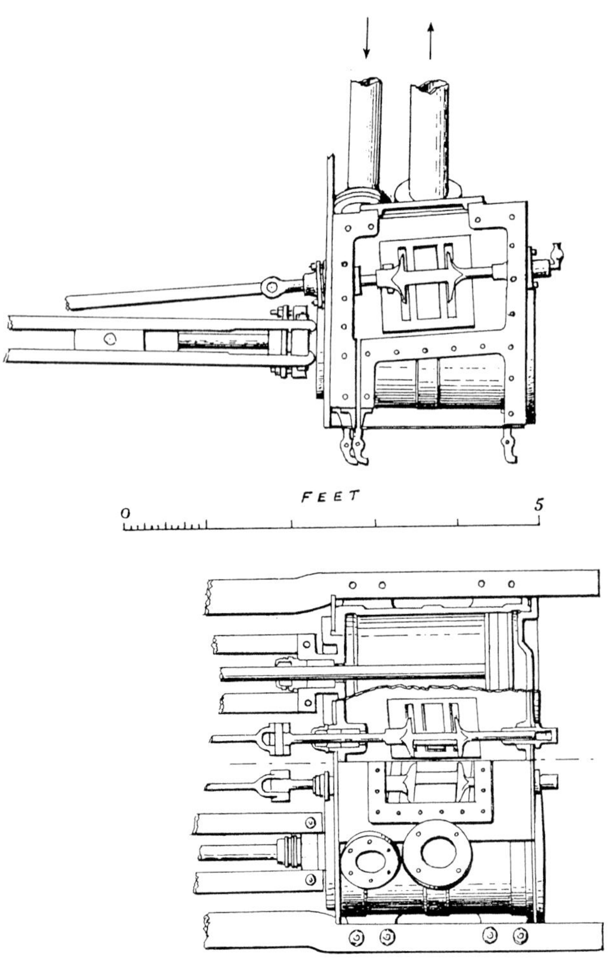

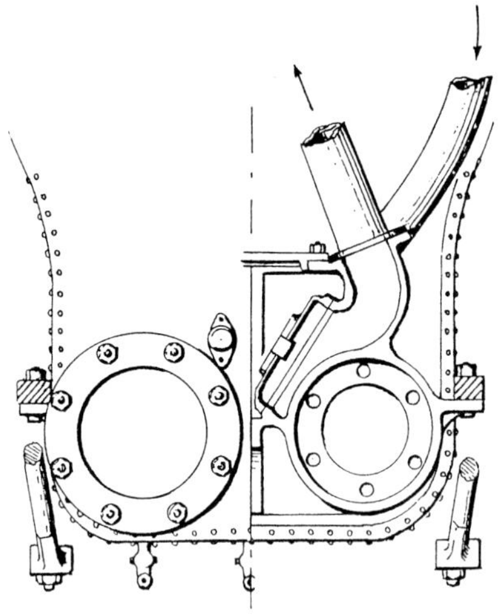

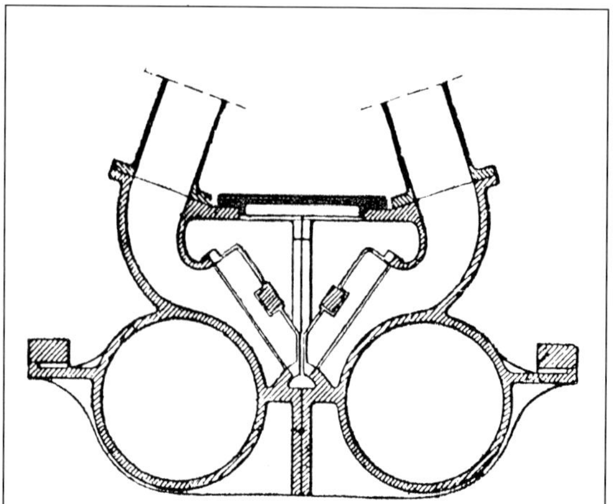

Fig. 52 Cylinders of Bury, Curtis & Kennedy 2-2-2.

Fig. 51 Bury's cylinders, from D.K. Clark's *Railway Machinery*.

Wheel rims and spokes were of welded wrought iron; the naves were cast iron. The driving wheels had narrow balance weights embracing three spokes on the rim.

The boiler was domeless with three rings, of which the middle ring had the greater diameter, and a firebox with straight sides and top. Bury's pattern of double-beat regulator was in the smokebox, with a long collecting pipe through the boiler from a position over the flat firebox crown; the shaft from the regulator handle passed through this pipe, which collected steam through a narrow slit along the top. A warming cock on the firebox just behind the whistle turned steam into both feedwater pipes between the tender and the pumps. The rectangular grate was so made that the fire could be dropped quickly; the middle five grate bars were loosely hooked at the front and could be lowered at the back end by means of a lever under the footplate.

Above and between the inside cylinders was a large single steam chest containing both valves; in cross section it was V-shaped with the valve faces set at an angle, and the valves themselves almost touching at their lower edges. On the flat top of the steam chest a big removable plate gave convenient access to the valves. The cylinders were inclined very slightly downwards towards the front, while the valve spindles inclined upwards. Four eccentrics between the cranks worked the valve gear, whose links were raised and lowered by a reversing lever on the right side of the footplate. The pumps were just inside the top frame member and were driven directly by the crossheads. Laminated springs were above the leading and driving axles, but the trailing axle was close behind the ashpan and had helical springs. The whole layout was simple and straightforward, with good accessibility everywhere.

All subsequent S Div express passenger engines - the three Bloomer classes and the Patents - were closely based on this design, which was Bury, Curtis & Kennedy's own. It was nothing like the outside cylinder long-boiler singles which Robert Stephenson had recommended for the C&H, but was a bigger version of BC&K's *Wrekin* built in 1849 for the Shrewsbury & Birmingham Railway and of which detailed drawings were published in Tredgold's *Locomotive Engines, 8th Paper* (1850). Another similar BC&K product was the 2-4-0 No 100 for the Great Northern Railway in April 1849.

A BC&K general arrangement drawing dated 28th November 1847 shows the straight-topped firebox and this is confirmed by E. T. Lane's measured sketches of No 65 of August 1848 and No 12 dated 23rd November 1849. These are sufficient to dismiss as spurious the drawing by Stretton showing one of this class as a much smaller engine with a round-backed firebox. Like other misleading material from him it was published by the Science Museum and seems to be the source of the drawing and incorrect data in the *Locomotive Magazine* vol 2, p144.

These engines were big and had a distinctive appearance; there was a lot of brightwork on them. The firebox was almost entirely covered by a sheet of copper, the chimney cap was copper, the safety valve cover was brass and the smokebox had a brass-framed door, rounded at top and bottom, straight at the sides, hinged on the right and with a central locking handle. There was a brass moulding between the smokebox and the boiler barrel, brass wheel centres and brass mudguard splashers over the leading and driving wheels.

They were numbered 12/8, 65/7, 75 and 218; all but the last were numbers left vacant by withdrawals. One of the last delivered, No 12 of August 1848, was BC&K works number 280 according to E. T. Lane's sketch. Works numbers 301/3/4/5 have been quoted for 12, 65/7 and 75 but these are probably Stretton inventions.

Although they were domeless, the raised firebox sheathed in copper suggested a cut-down 'haystack' and for this reason they became known as 'Bury's low-domed engines' being so described in a McConnell report of 1853, and by enthusiasts writing to the *English Mechanic* in the 1870s.

Dimensions

Cylinders (2 inside)	16" x 20"
Boiler	
Diameter	4' 1"
Length of barrel	12' 8"
Pitch	6' 6"
Heating surface	
Tubes (178, 2¼" dia, 13' 0" long)	1,363.55 sq ft
Firebox	86.70 sq ft
Total	*1,449.66 sq ft
Grate area	**16 sq ft
Diameter of wheels	
Leading	4' 6"
Driving	6' 0"
Trailing	3' 7"
Wheelbase	8' 2" + 7' 10" = 16' 0"
Weight	
On leading wheels	9 tons
On driving wheels	10 tons
On trailing wheels	5 tons
Total	24 tons

*See note on heating surfaces in the Introduction.
** The grate area of No 12 was recorded as 16.75 sq ft in 1853; a drawing of this engine's firebox dated July 1862 shows a length of 4ft 9¾in and a width of 3ft 6¾in, a grate area of 17 sq ft.

The average load taken was 66 tons according to a report of 1853 and their maximum speed was rated by McConnell as 48.3mph, compared with his estimate of 52.98mph for the Small Bloomers then proposed.

Outside footplating and splashers were fitted in the 1850s, a dome was added to the middle ring of the boiler and the water delivery clack valve was moved to the front ring. Not surprisingly, in this guise they looked like a smaller version of the Bloomers.

In 1849 the permanent way contractors complained that these engines (and some others) were too heavy; but even so they were kept at work and not put into store as many others were. They were evidently fine machines and ran the main line expresses until the advent of the Bloomers in the 1850s.

During July and August 1849 No 67 worked for a short time on the Northern Division in the locomotive exchange.

Two of them are mentioned in minor accidents: No 67

was started by its fireman and damaged at Birmingham in January 1849, and No 18 was derailed at Tring in February 1851.

All were put on the duplicate list in 1863, but shortly thereafter they were rebuilt at Wolverton with new three-ring boilers and the usual Ramsbottom mountings. A drawing of the new boiler dated 14th January 1865 shows a wheelbase of 8ft $2^{1}/_{2}$in + 7ft $11^{1}/_{4}$in. The total length of the bar frame was 23ft $5^{3}/_{4}$in. The boiler barrel was 12ft $7^{1}/_{2}$in long and the grate area was 14.9 sq ft.

At the end of 1871 they were restored to the capital list as 1182-7, and in the following year they were given names previously borne by Crewe Goods engines. The standard LNWR nameplates bore the misleading words:

CREWE WORKS 1848

In July 1869 all six were shedded at Northampton, but in the 1870s they were at Bletchley. All were scrapped in 1877-80 at Crewe, whose No 1 Erecting Shop notebook records the actual dates and the cut-up numbers of the first four, the remaining two having received second 18xx series duplicate numbers in September 1878.

Strangely, these successful and very influential locomotives were quickly forgotten; no photographs are known and they were hardly mentioned by any of the railway authors. Even their names were lost sight of for many years.

Livery

E. T. Lane's November 1849 drawing is coloured thus:
Frame, smokebox, chimney, boiler bands: black.
Boiler, wheels, footplate side sheet,
bufferplank end, wooden lagging on
firebox side: dark green.
Splashers, axle ends, safety valve cover,
ring between smokebox and boiler barrel: brass.
Firebox covering, chimney cap: copper.

Summary: C&H 2-2-2s built by Bury, Curtis & Kennedy, 1848

No.	Date	Reno'd	Rebt.	Name /72	Dup List	Scrapped
65	5/1848	665(4/62)				
		1144(1/63)	a /66			
		1184(12/71)		General	c/u 1983	26/6/77
67	6/1848	667(4/62)				
		1145(1/63)	a /67			
		1185(12/71)		Cuckoo	c/u 1984	26/6/77
75	6/1848	675(4/62)				
		1146(2/63)	a /65			
		1186(12/71)		Allerton	c/u 1898	8/5/78
12*	8/1848	612(4/62)				
		1128(1/63)	/66			
		1182(12/71)		Eglinton	c/u 1999	5/12/77
18	8/1848	618(4/62)				
		1139(1/63)	a /67			
		1183(12/71)		Conway	1810(9/78)	30/9/79
218	8/1848	818(4/62)				
		1149(2/63)	b /66			
		1187(12/71)		Derby	1811(9/78)	14/5/80

* No 12 was probably BC&K No 280

Haigh 4-2-0 Passenger Engines, 1849
Nos 202, 203, 204

These outside-cylinder long-boiler engines were the last of the Chester & Holyhead passenger engines. Three were ordered by the C&H from the Haigh Foundry Co, Wigan, at some date between January and April 1846. They were to cost £2,250 each and be ready by 1st March 1848.

While they were under construction, in January 1848 McConnell asked for some alterations to the engines, which Haigh agreed to do for £150 extra. In March he asked that wrought-iron flat-spoked wheels be fitted - instead, presumably, of the intended wheels with T-iron spokes. Haigh agreed to this without extra charge, the final cost being £2,406 per engine.

They did not arrive at Wolverton until 1849, when they were given numbers 202/3/4, previously held by engines sent back to the Leeds & Dewsbury, and were immediately placed in store. The only known illustration is a rough sketch of one of them (no running number visible) made by E. T. Lane in 1849. He made a note of the builder's plate:

Haigh Foundry Co, Wigan
No. Stephenson's Patent 43

43 appears to be the works number; the Haigh Foundry works list published by Stretton in which he gives these three engines as "89-91" is simply guesswork.

According to this sketch the driving axle springs were underhung, while the middle axle springs were mounted above the running plate; those of the leading axle were enclosed within an aperture in the frame. In these details they were like Stephenson & Co's own 153-8 and the later Jones & Potts series. The driving wheels had eighteen spokes, the leading wheels twelve. The driving wheel splasher had five radial apertures; the dome, which was on the second boiler ring and centred (as in the later Jones & Potts version) above the rear of the cylinders, was bell-shaped on a square plinth and was surmounted by a spring balance safety valve. Another safety valve was on a column which rose from a manhole on the slightly-raised firebox top.

They were first put to work early in 1851.

Dimensions

Cylinders (2 outside)	15" x 22"
Heating surface	
Tubes (117, 2¼" diam, 14' 2" long)	976.3 sq ft
Firebox	65.8 sq ft
Total	1,042.1 sq ft
Diameter of wheels	
Leading and middle	3' 10"
Driving	6' 5"
Wheelbase	7' 0" + 5' 6" = 12' 6"

They appear to have been the poorest performers of all the long-boiler 4-2-0 classes.

They were among the 56 patent long-boiler engines ordered to be fitted with McConnell fireboxes in January 1853 but the order was countermanded the following month.

All three survived in capital stock to the end of the S Div, but went into the duplicate list in 1862/3; surprisingly, two of them lasted until 1867.

Summary: C&H 4-2-0s built by Haigh Foundry, 1849

No.	Date	Reno'd 4/62	Reno'd	Scrapped
202	1/1849	802	1147(2/63)	4/67
203	7/1849		1198(5/62)	2/67
204	9/1849		1199(5/62)	by 9/63

Chester & Holyhead Railway Stephenson and Hawthorn Goods Engines

Twenty goods engines of Stephenson's 15in x 24in 0-6-0 type had been ordered by the Chester & Holyhead Railway, fourteen from Stephenson and six from Hawthorn, but in August 1847 the design was altered on McConnell's recommendation to that of the Sharp 'Sphynx' type 18in goods. The six Hawthorns and twelve of the Stephensons were delivered in 1848-9 and were numbered, together with those of the same type from Sharp Bros, within the block 210-44; details of all three makers' engines will be found on pp166-175.

Two of the Stephenson engines were not delivered to the S Div and appear to have been sold to the South Staffordshire Railway in 1851. In their place, Stephenson sent two 4-2-2 passenger engines to the S Div in 1848, Nos 233/4, for which see pp162-4.

The South Staffordshire engines (SSR Nos 12/3) eventually became S Div 309/10, for which see p218.

LARGE EXPRESS ENGINES 1847-8

Crampton 4-2-0 Express Passenger Engine, 1847
No 200 *London*
To show what the GWR broad gauge could accomplish, Daniel Gooch's big new engine *Great Western* took a train from Paddington to Exeter and back at an average speed of over 55mph on 1st June 1846. This came as a bombshell to the narrow-gauge companies.

Eleven days later the L&B Locomotive Committee accepted an offer from Thomas Russell Crampton to build an engine capable of taking a train of 100 tons at 50mph "according to his own plan and dimensions - the engine not to exceed 26 tons in weight and to be delivered on 15th January next."

Bury was sceptical, but the directors were impressed by Crampton's presentation of his revolutionary patent design which promised high speeds on the 4ft 8½in gauge with perfect safety. Large diameter driving wheels were achieved by mounting the axle behind the firebox instead of in front, allowing the boiler to be set just above the carrying wheel axles and giving the low centre of gravity considered necessary for safety. In this position the boiler could be bigger than would have been possible with normal standard-gauge engines, and able to produce an adequate steam supply to the outside cylinders at high speeds.

Crampton's *Namur*
The Namur & Liége Railway, a Belgian line financed in Britain, had already ordered the first Crampton engines which were being built by the firm of Tulk & Ley of the Lowca Foundry at Whitehaven. The first of them, appropriately named *Namur*, left the works on 2nd February 1847. It was a typical Crampton, 4-2-0 with 7ft driving wheels and 16in x 20in outside cylinders.

With their own similar and very unusual engine on order, the LNWR took the opportunity to try out the Belgian. Just ten days after starting in his new job at Wolverton, McConnell reported on 25th February: "Crampton's engine brought 15 wagons, gross weight 80 tons, from Camden to Wolverton today in two hours, 20 minutes of which were lost by stoppages." The engine had been steady at 40-50mph and had burned 35 lb of coke per mile and Crampton himself claimed that this train of coke trucks had reached 51mph. The *Railway Chronicle* commented on 27th February: "the *soi-disant* impossibility of using a 7ft wheel on the 4ft 9in gauge has at last ceased to be an impossibility."

The day before this the Namur & Liége Railway's secretary had written from his office at 52 Moorgate Street, London, asking if the new engine could be used on the LNWR for a short excursion for his directors. By 4th March *Namur* had been at work on the line "for the last few days" and on 11th March it took a regular Down train of nine carriages to Wolverton in 1¼ hours, including four stops. According to the *Railway Chronicle* the speed was often over 60mph. But in answer to a note from the S Div Secretary Richard Creed, McConnell said "I have been cautious in entrusting so important and difficult a train as the 10am Down Mail with Mr Crampton's engine." One of the pumps had been faulty, but he had given instructions to put *Namur* on that train the following day, 20th March.

Crampton read a paper to the Society of Arts on 31st March, claiming that *Namur* had reached 62 mph on a passenger train between Tring and Wolverton, and reached 75mph "with satisfactory steadiness" when running light between Willesden and Harrow on a demonstration for the Board of Trade inspector, Major-General Pasley. On 8th April McConnell reported on its comparative performance against the Bury 2-2-2 102 but the minutes merely record that the statement was "laid on the table".

In all, *Namur* ran over 2,300 miles on the LNWR. Nevertheless, when on 13th April the engine was offered to the LNWR for £3,150, because the opening of the Belgian railway had been deferred for eight months, it was refused and the engine was stored, probably in the roundhouse, at Camden. Another offer in June 1848 was also refused, as was the Belgian company's request in December to steam the engine once a month.

While it lay at Camden, E. T. Lane made a drawing of *Namur* on 22nd October 1849 which records what was presumably the livery of the N&L, red boiler, firebox, frame, splasher, wheels; black smokebox, chimney and boiler bands; dark red lining; the wooden-lagged dome barrel was red, between a brass plinth and the brass top and safety valve.

At the end of 1849 and while still at Camden, *Namur* was purchased by the South Eastern Railway, together with the other two N&L engines which had remained at Tulk & Ley's works, for a total price of £4,000. None of them ever reached Belgium, and in January 1850 they became SER 81, 83 and 85. The Namur & Liége Railway did not open until November of that year.

London
The LNWR's own engine was also built by Tulk & Ley, and is said to have been their No 12 and the third by them on Crampton's system. While still in the maker's hands it is believed that it was tried on the York, Newcastle & Berwick Railway and that during the trials the motion had been shorn off by fouling a wooden platform, a mishap which may account in part for the delayed delivery, which only took place in June 1847. It left the Lowca Foundry early on the 15th, travelled by rail via Carlisle, and reached Wolverton on the 17th.

It was an enlarged and more powerful version of *Namur*. Boiler and cylinders were bigger and the driving wheels were 8ft in diameter, unprecedented on the standard gauge and the same as those of Gooch's broad-gauge express engine. Unlike *Namur*, whose driving axle spring crossed the footplate above the firehole, the new engine had separate springs over each axlebox. The boiler was oval in cross-section, with flat sides; it was stayed throughout its length by 22 wrought-iron transverse stays. Steam was taken by separate outside pipes to a slide-valve regulator above each cylinder; the regulators were controlled by separate rods from a horizontal shaft across the back of the firebox, worked by

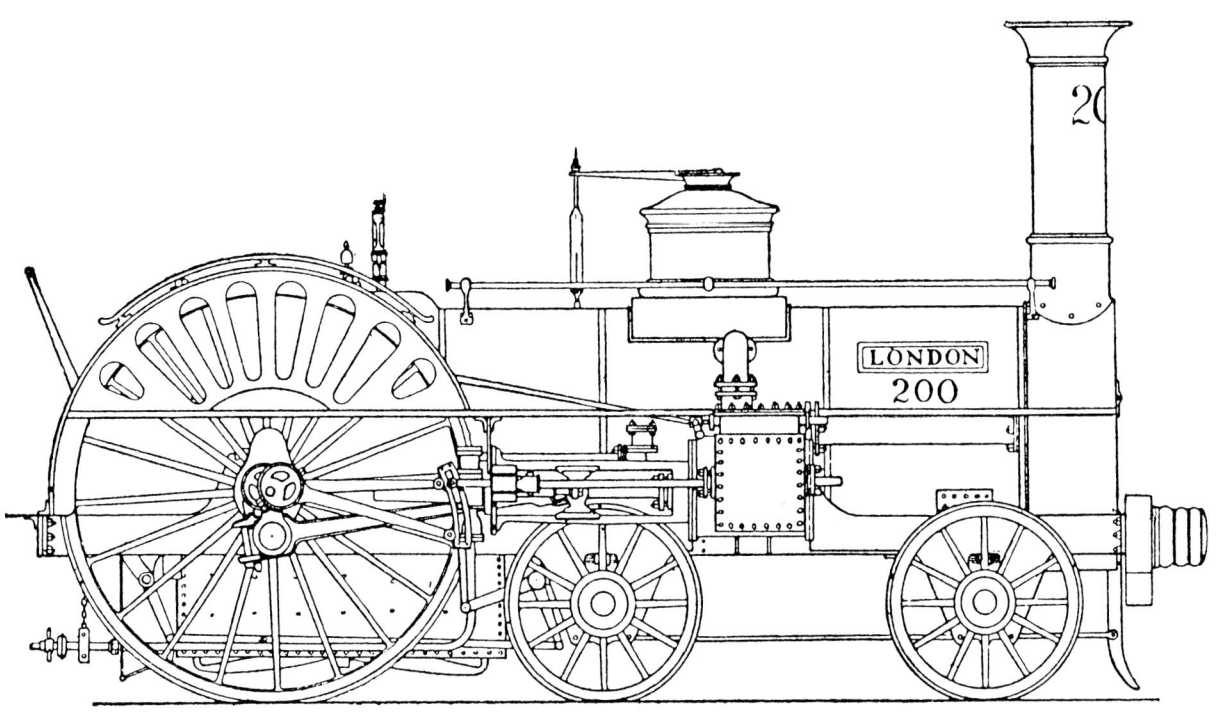

Fig. 53   Crampton's 200 *London* built by Tulk & Ley of Lowca Foundry, Whitehaven, 1847.

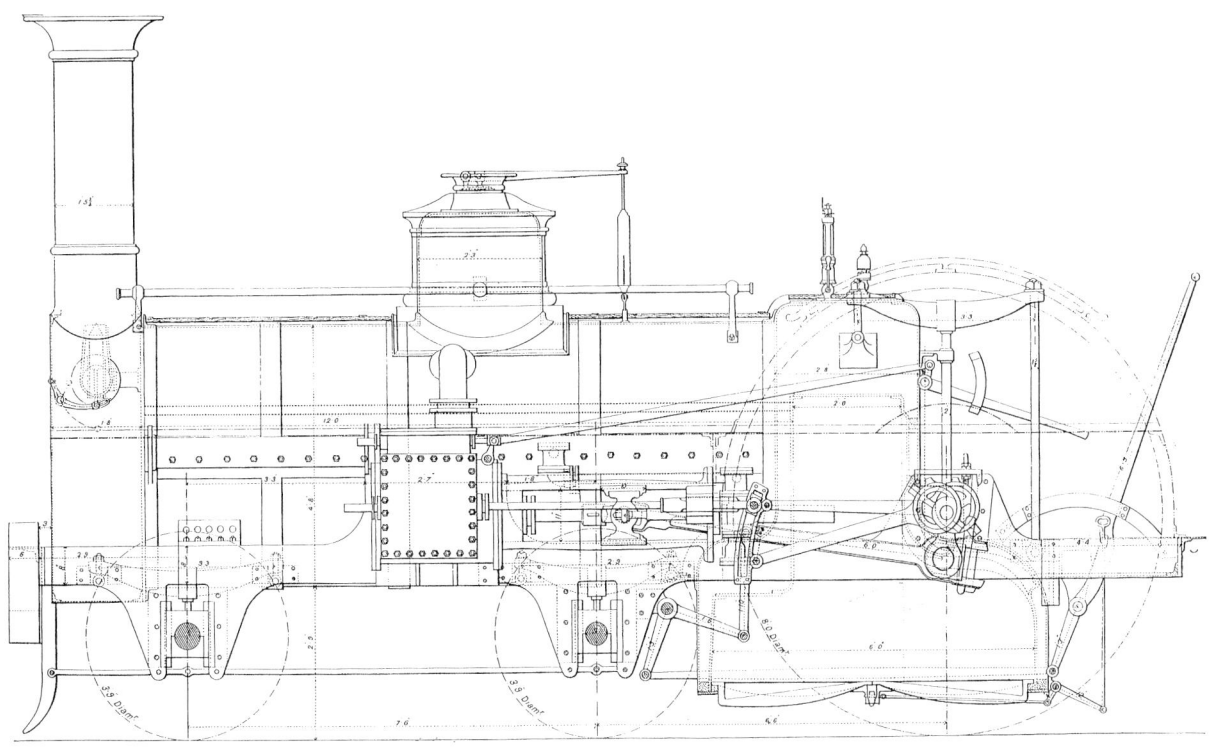

Fig. 54   200 *London* as built.

a handle moving vertically in a quadrant on the inside of the right-hand splasher. The reversing lever was also on the right side, moving the links by a rod running alongside the bottom of the firebox. There was a linkage from the footplate floor for rocking the grate bars - or perhaps for lifting them in the middle, to spread the fuel into the front and back of the grate. A variable exhaust was achieved by a movable cone in the blast pipe.

Dimensions

Cylinders (2 outside)		18" x 20"
Boiler (oval)		
Diameter, vertical		4' 8"
horizontal		3' 10"
Length of barrel		12' 0"
Pitch		5' 0"
Heating surface		
Tubes (229, 2" dia, 1⅞" at firebox, 12' long)		1,438 sq ft
Firebox		91 sq ft
Total		1,529 sq ft
Grate area		21.5 sq ft
Boiler pressure		100 lb/sq in
Diameter of wheels		
Carrying		3' 9"
Driving		8' 0"
Wheelbase		7' 6" + 6' 6" = 14' 0"
Weight		
On leading wheels	8 tons	3 cwt
On middle wheels	5 tons	15 cwt
On driving wheels	11 tons	14 cwt
Total	25 tons	12 cwt
Tender (loaded)	18 tons	10 cwt

The above heating surface details are from *The Engineer* of 28th November 1890, apparently quoting from the makers' records.

It cost £3,848 4s (£3,848.20) and great things were expected of it. Previous L&B and Southern Division engines had been known only by a number but this new reply to the GWR challenge was given a big nameplate bearing the name of the capital. Its number was likewise selected to impress; no railway at that time owned an engine with so high a running number; the S Div had a stock of 172, but by jumping ahead beyond the highest-numbered engine, and leaving a few blanks for engines on order, the number 200 was awarded to the new Crampton.

Within 24 hours of its arrival it was out on the road, running with a 60-ton train of twelve carriages from Wolverton to London and recording a speed of between 57 and 65mph south of Watford. With eleven carriages (55 tons) it covered 30 miles at 53.4mph. But McConnell was unimpressed and said so, which Crampton quickly got to hear about. He wrote to the S Div Secretary:

"18 Adam St, Adelphi
June 30th 1847

Richd. Creed esq.
Sir,
It is very painfull to me to be compelled to throw myself upon your kindness by writing so soon on a subject that in no way interests you but am induced to do so, trusting that you will make use of the information in such a manner that I may be put into a proper position and not prejudiced.

I think it was admitted by Mr McConnel that the *London* had settled the question of speed on the narrow gauge from the first trip taken by it, at which time it was driven by Callan, who knows more about the engine than anybody else. Since then we have had two other drivers neither of whom have had sufficient experience to do justice to the engine, in fact I am confident that one man must be kept to the engine to do it justice. You are doubtless aware that the *London* ran over 4 or 5 cross sleepers near Whitehaven in consequence of the rails being up. This I am satisfied jarred the frame behind to a certain extent, also a pilot engine ran into her and broke the buffer board. Every trip since this last accident the leading bearings heated but not previously. I have ascertained that the front part of the frame was sprung which caused the heating of the axles. The valves have never been looked at, in fact nothing has been attempted to put the engine in good working condition yet under these circumstances Mr McConnel told Mr Tulk yesterday that the *London* had failed to do what I had undertaken, that it was useless to the Company, that it was wrong in principle and the Driving Wheel not in the best position. Sir, I cannot tell what Mr McConnel's motive can be but I do think he is a little hasty in forming such an opinion before any thing like a trial has taken place and I do not see that I can be heartily assisted when such opinions are held by the party having the power to do as he likes. If you sir can do anything that will enable me to have proper trials I shall feel gratefull. Of course, I do not wish Mr McConnel to know of this letter because if he did there would be an end of my engine on the L&NW Railway. In fact I consider that no engine can do its best unless it is very carefully looked after. More particularly with my firebox, which I admit requires more than ordinary attention but which I will take care to remedy in future by making them of the ordinary form. Previously to seeing Mr Tulk this morning, I wrote to Mr McConnel telling him what I thought should be done before trials were made. Trusting you will excuse my thus intruding upon your time,
I remain Sir, Your obedient servant
T. R. Crampton."

Creed passed this letter to Thomas Smith of the Locomotive Committee with a covering note: "McConnell may be right but ... I should be very sorry that his engine proved a failure though Bury certainly anticipated this result." Smith discussed the matter with Moorsom and on 8th July McConnell was told "to make all the alterations sanctioned by Mr Crampton."

On Wednesday 21st July *London* worked the noon train (11 carriages) from Euston. This was its first and only appearance on a regular train from Euston that month. Two days later McConnell told Creed that the engine was undergoing a "heavy reconstruction" at Wolverton; "the alteration, required to remedy a great error in the original construction, will require considerable time." Whereas Creed was anxious to have *London* back at work, McConnell was less than enthusiastic, even hinting that it was unsafe.

Whatever this reconstruction involved, it gave satisfactory results, for on 9th September McConnell presented a comparative report of the performance of *London* against Jones & Potts long-boiler 4-2-0 175. This must have been favourable, because the Locomotive Committee immediately asked Crampton "for particulars of another engine - modified by his experience with No 200, with the view of another being ordered from him." The next day Crampton wrote agreeing to this and by the end of the year had submitted a set of drawings for his improved engine - the giant 6-2-0 *Liverpool*.

During November 1847 only three trains from Euston were worked by *London*:

Tuesday 2nd: 10.00am express mail, 12 carriages and another added at Tring.
Saturday 27th: 9.00am fast train, 9 carriages.
Monday 29th: 8.30am fast train, 8 carriages.

Apart from these four trains, one in July and three in November, nothing is known of the engine in regular service. It was in the shops for repairs from January to March 1848, back in working order in April, in the shops again for "slight repairs" during May and June and for "general repairs" for almost a year from October 1848.

The "great error" castigated by McConnell must have been the design of the firebox. In the engine as built the grate was 6ft long and 3ft 7in wide but the distance from the back of the firebox to the tubeplate was only 2ft. Below the driving axle, which crossed the footplate below the firehole, the firebox swelled out aft. To place coke on this part of the grate a second firehole was necessary, a big round well at the front of the footplate. It is difficult to see how the firebox could have been improved without drastic rebuilding.

Whatever the case, on 14th December 1848 the Locomotive Committee ordered "that the firebox of No 200 be enlarged and the engine made complete." The work involved must have been considerable, for it was not ready to come out of the Works until sometime in August or September the following year.

In the rebuilding a normally-proportioned firebox was installed, with a grate area reduced to 16 sq ft. This was presumably achieved by removing the rearward bulge of the firebox above the grate, but if the upper firebox was lengthened to match the new grate length, the boiler would have had to be moved forward by two feet or more, probably involving some similar adjustment of the positions of the carrying axles.

McConnell's report of 3rd May 1853 gives the following details of *London* which offer little help towards understanding the nature of the rebuilding:

Heating surface
Tubes (226, 2" dia, 12' 2" long)   1,439.72 sq ft
Firebox   91.80 sq ft
Total   1,531.53 sq ft

At the time of the last available monthly list, 4th December 1849, *London* was working and unlike McConnell's own 227, Stephenson's 233/4 and nineteen others, had not been selected for putting into store. What work *London* was doing is not known but for a time during 1850 it was stored, being brought out in September for working fast trains.

According to McConnell's report of May 1853 *London* was the poorest performer of all the larger passenger engines, but its total mileage (19,834) was 24% higher than that of 'Mac's Mangle'.

Fig. 55   200 rebuilt as an 0-4-2 goods engine, 1855.

Rebuilding as an 0-4-2

London's next appearance in the Locomotive Committee's minutes is on 22nd March 1855 when a £400 outlay was ordered "to improve its efficiency." A drawing dated 1st May 1855 shows the major rebuilding which then took place. It was back at work by 5th June, completely transformed into an 0-4-2 goods engine.

In its new form, 200 had coupled 5ft 6in driving wheels and inside cylinders which were inclined at about 6° upwards towards the front, with the valves underneath worked by valve rods passing under the leading axle. The original oval boiler and a pair of carrying wheels were retained but the inside plate frames, cylinders, driving wheels and much else must have been quite new. In this form it resembled the engines designed by McConnell for the Sydney Railway of New South Wales in 1854 except for a wheelbase longer by 1ft 2in, a different valve layout and a raised firebox. One small feature common to the rebuilt 200 and the Australian engines is the smokebox door, which had a plain locking handle on a single horizontal strap which forked to the hinge; this was unlike McConnell's usual type with two parallel straps and a long L-shaped handle.

Dimensions as 0-4-2

Cylinders (2 inside)	17" x 24"
Boiler	
Diameter, vertical	4' 8"
horizontal	3' 10"
Length of barrel	11' 9½"
Pitch	7' 0"
Length of firebox casing	5' 3"
Grate area	15.17 sq ft
Diameter of wheels	
Coupled	5' 6"
Trailing	3' 9"
Wheelbase	8' 2" + 7' 6" = 15' 8"
Weight	
On leading wheels	12 tons
On middle wheels	11 tons 14 cwt
On trailing wheels	6 tons
Total	29 tons 14 cwt

After this all that is recorded is that it was rebuilt again, during the half-year June - November 1865, and was cut up in July 1874. By then it was listed by Crewe as No 1828 goods engine with 5ft 6in driving wheels, 16 x 24in cylinders, and "altered at Wolverton to Bury's type." This means the Class A engines of 1853-5 whch were superficially similar but had bar frames and 5ft driving wheels.

Summary: Crampton type 4-2-0 built by Tulk & Ley, 1847

No.	Name	Date	Rebuilt	Reno'd	Scrapped
200	London	17/6/1847	5/55 (as 0-4-2)	800(4/62)	
				1201(9/63)	
			b /65	1828(12/71)	7/74

Crampton 6-2-0 Express Passenger Engine, 1848
No 245 *Liverpool*

On 18th June 1847, the day of *London's* first trip on the LNWR, the Board authorised the Southern Division Locomotive Committee (if further trials were satisfactory) to order two more Cramptons. Meanwhile *Great Western* was setting even higher standards, having just taken a train of 100 tons from London to Swindon at almost 60mph; as the leading narrow-gauge company and amid agitation for a broad-gauge line to Birmingham and beyond, the LNWR had to respond. After trials with *London* the S Div Locomotive Committee asked Crampton on 9th September for an engine "of great power ... to be of a power as nearly as possible corresponding to the large one on the Great Western Railway" - and they wanted it quickly. He replied at once.

On 13th January 1848 the S Div Locomotive Committee looked at the "drawings of an improved engine from Mr Crampton which McConnell recommended to the Committee." An order was given (at an unrecorded date) to the firm of Bury, Curtis & Kennedy and, with Bury's steadfast advocacy of four-wheeled engines in mind, it is interesting to see his company chosen to build one with eight wheels - the biggest engine ever. It was completed in June 1848 under BC&K works number 355; the cost was an astronomical £5,002 10s (£5,002.50).

It was built, according to Crampton, "for the purpose of proving that engines of very large power could be constructed for the narrow gauge, combining steadiness with a judicious arrangement of the working parts, however desirous it might be ... to use small engines generally." It was announced as the most powerful locomotive in the world, having a heating surface much greater than that of the GWR engines. It had inside and outside frames, connected by seven transverse plates, all of $1^{1}/_{4}$in iron. There were three sets of carrying wheels - the third pair flangeless - under the low-pitched boiler, with 8ft driving wheels behind the firebox. The carrying axles had outside bearings; the driving axle had inside bearings only. The greater part of the weight was carried on the leading and driving wheels; Crampton claimed that "by relieving the weight from the centre wheels, perfect steadiness when running at high velocities is ensured."

The boiler "designed to receive the largest possible number of tubes" had a cross-section which was not a flat-sided oval like that of *London*, but was of two unequal diameters, the smaller being below, to fit down between the inside frames almost to the carrying axles, thus obtaining a low centre of gravity - lower, in proportion to the track width, than in engines on the broad gauge. There were eighteen cross stays, 4ft 6in long and centred 8in apart, along the boiler at the junction of its two diameters. In the smokebox, a damper in the form of a Venetian blind was placed over the ends of the tubes.

The firebox was not as strange as Crampton's previous 'waisted' type, but had two side-by-side fireholes and a longitudinal midfeather down to six inches above the firebars; it was extended back for a short distance under the driving axle to lengthen the grate, while the outer box was nipped in to clear the driving wheels and swelled out at the front end where it joined the boiler barrel.

Steam was collected in an internal horizontal pipe with a narrow slot along the top and passed, via a regulator on the boiler top, by two external pipes to the outside cylinders, which were mounted above the outer and inner frameplates, alongside the boiler near the middle of the chassis. The regulator control rod passed through the safety valve trumpet to a horizontal lever on the firebox top with a pull-out handle. Outside Stephenson link motion was driven by huge 2ft 9in diameter eccentrics, fixed to the wheel boss and embracing the driving crankpin. These eccentrics were intended to obviate the outside return cranks of earlier Cramptons such as *London*. The pumps were outside and forward of each cylinder, driven by an extension of the piston rod.

The carrying wheels all had underhung springs, the two leading axles having one common spring between them on each side; the driving axle had a

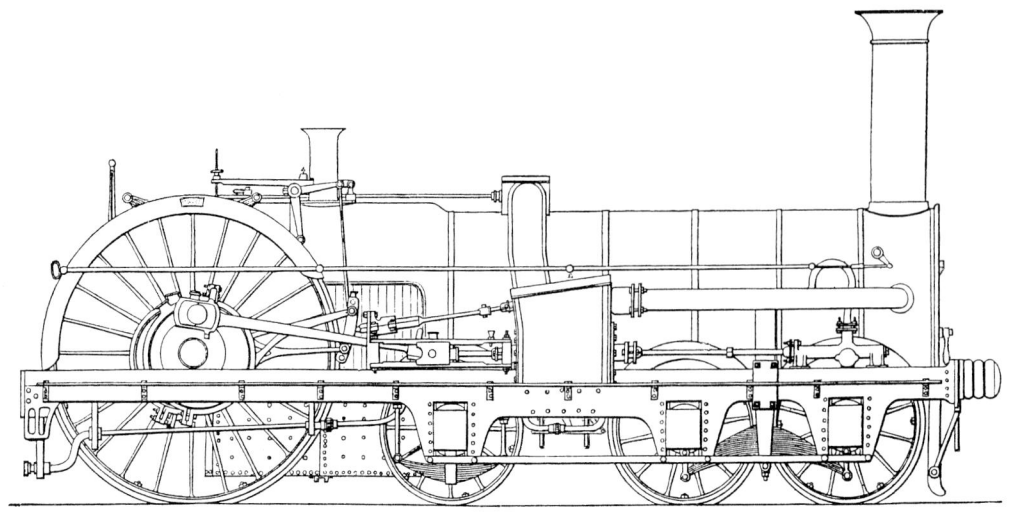

Fig. 56   245, Crampton's 6-2-0 *Liverpool* built by Bury, Curtis & Kennedy, 1848. "The ultimatum for the 4ft 8½ in gauge".

spring high above each journal, reducing the clear width of the footplate, at shoulder height, to about 2ft 10in.

The boiler cleading was sheet-iron and as was usual with BC&K engines the firebox was covered with a sheet of copper. The smokebox had two doors hung on central vertical hinges; the iron buffer beam was directly in front and curved down in the middle to clear the open doors. This precluded a normal drawhook; instead a short length of chain with a central coupling link was fixed by its ends to the beam and hung in a loop between the buffers. *Liverpool* was one of the first engines not to have a wooden bufferplank; the contemporary description puts the term 'buffer-beam' in quotation marks as if something new. The wooden bufferplank shown in some illustrations seems to be an error based on a preliminary drawing.

On each side a narrow footway ran from end to end, supported by brackets from the outer frameplate.

The six-wheeled tender had two auxiliary underfloor tanks between the axles, holding some 220 gallons each.

Dimensions

Cylinders (2 outside)	18" x 24"
Boiler	
Diameter, upper section (210°)	4' 6"
lower section (180°)	4' 3"
Length of barrel	12' 3"
Centre line of upper section above rails	5' 4½"
Heating surface	
Tubes (292, 2 3/16" dia + 8, 1¾" dia, 12' 6" long)	2,136.117 sq ft
Firebox	154.434 sq ft
Total	2,290.551 sq ft
Grate area	21.58 sq ft
Diameter of wheels	
Leading	4' 3"
Intermediate (two axles)	4' 0"
Driving	8' 0"
Tender	3' 9"
Length over buffers	48' 2½"
Wheelbase	
Engine	4' 6" + 6' 7" + 7' 4¾" = 18' 5¾"
Tender	5' 3" + 5' 3" = 10' 6"
Total	38' 1½"
Weight	
On leading two axles	17 tons
On third axle	6 tons
On driving axle	12 tons
Engine, total	35 tons
Tender	21 tons 8 cwt
Total	56 tons 8 cwt
Tender (6 wheel) capacity	water 2,240 gal

Most of the dimensions above are taken from Tredgold, evidently supplied by the makers; McConnell gave the following in 1853:

Heating surface	
Tubes (295, 12' 9" long)	2,090.62 sq ft
Firebox	156.00 sq ft
Total	2,256.47 sq ft

A tube surface figure of 1,874 sq ft is sometimes quoted but this is probably based on the inside tube diameter. The boiler pressure of 120 lb/sq in has been claimed but available records suggest that, officially at least, no LNWR engine had so high a pressure until 1852.

McConnell said that *Liverpool* could be balanced so that there was less than nine tons on any one pair of wheels. He also said the average load taken was 80 tons.

Contemporary illustrations, which differ from each other in detail, include:
(1) A full set of drawings in Tredgold's 10th paper with differences between the pre-production external elevation and the later plan and sections.
(2) A coloured scale drawing by E. T. Lane, dated 20th September 1849, probably based on the Tredgold drawings with additions taken from life, perhaps at Camden.
(3) An outline external drawing in D. K. Clark's *Railway Machinery*, 1855.
(4) A scale drawing in the catalogue of the Great Exhibition of 1851, based on Tredgold's external elevation, but with some changes.

Liverpool was evidently named as a counterpart to the other named engine, *London*, after the northern base of the Company, rather than because it was built in that city. It first appears in the S Div monthly stock return of 10th October 1848 but was not given its number 245 until August 1850, or shortly before. Considering the sensation it was meant to create as "the ultimatum for the narrow gauge" and "the most powerful locomotive in the world" there are surprisingly few references to it in the LNWR archives.

Crampton wrote that "among other feats" very soon after arriving on the line it took a train of forty carriages containing "Franconi's circus troupe and horses" from Rugby to Euston ahead of time; the same train from Liverpool to Rugby "required three engines of the usual size" and arrived late.

With other ordinary heavy trains "the performances were highly satisfactory" but the Permanent Way Report of 25th April 1849 included it in a long list of "engines complained of". The report said that as the speed contests were "now happily over ... there exists no reason why such engines as the [N Div] *Cornwall* and Crampton's engine the *Liverpool* should not be put in store and kept there until, by the adoption of a suitable kind of road, it becomes economical - which at present it is not - to use them." *Liverpool* had a reputation for distorting the track so that following trains were derailed, which is understandable with 56 tons of engine and tender being hurled along at 50mph on track laid down in 1837, much of it still on stone blocks.

By this time *Liverpool* was already in store. It had been reported as in working order every month from its arrival until 30th January 1849. By the end of February it had completely disappeared from the monthly return and was not even listed among the other engines in store. Perhaps this is because it was kept in the roundhouse at Camden and was overlooked by McConnell when preparing his monthly list.

It was certainly LNWR property; BC&K's bill had been paid in two instalments: £4,000 on 9th November 1848 and the balance of £1,002 10s (£1,002.5) on 14th December 1848.

The next mention is found in a minute of 8th August 1850: "That in the event of it being required to meet

Fig. 57   *Liverpool* with added decoration for the Great Exhibition, 1851.

accelerated speed Mr McConnell be allowed to bring out of store Nos 234 and 245 engines for that purpose."

Shortly after this there is a revealing series of letters. On 26th October the Secretary of the Great Exhibition Committee wrote to the LNWR saying he had heard *Liverpool* was to be sent to the Crystal Palace. It is known that the Crewe Committee had "no intention of sending any of the N Div large engines", but when in early February the Board learned that the GWR was sending one of its latest, McConnell was asked to write to Daniel Gooch about its heating surface. Gooch replied that it was about 1,920 sq ft. The Board then asked what was the heating surface of *Liverpool*. Answer: 2,290 sq ft. So to the Crystal Palace *Liverpool* must go! By 13th February the GLC was discussing arrangements for sending it and the N Div *Cornwall* to the Exhibition.

On 11th March 1851 it was ordered that "Crampton's engine (the *Liverpool*) be put in order and sent to the Exhibition." The illustration in the official catalogue shows that some decoration was added to enhance the engine's appearance. A round brass casing with a dished and corniced top covered the plain square box of the regulator; matching this was a brass collar around the base of the chimney. Neither nameplate nor engine number is shown, and there are horizontal lines on the boiler, firebox and smokebox which look like wooden lagging, but are probably only the draughtsman's attempt to suggest curvature.

Each outside cylinder was covered by a rectangular plate which hid the sloping top of the valve chest; in its centre was the badge of the LNWR: Britannia with trident and Union Jack shield, seated beside a lion amid a mass of baroque strapwork and Gothic foliage. This device, the 'cauliflower' as it came to be known, was the variety later used on the sides of carriages; its appearance on *Liverpool* in 1851 is the earliest known example.

The Great Exhibition opened on 1st May and continued until 15th October 1851; *Liverpool* was Exhibit 512 in class V. During this period the stock totals list one engine in store "at the exhibition". The Board was probably glad it was there; at least it was doing no harm and was an imposing advertisement for the LNWR. It was awarded a Council Medal, one of 170 awarded to the most novel or original of over 100,000 exhibits.

After the Exhibition *Liverpool* was returned to stock and evidently did some work, but in its entire career to the end of 1851 it had run a total of only 9,303 miles, the equivalent of a mere 83 trips between London and Birmingham.

It was reported to be "in working order" in a return of 5th June 1855, but its actual work is unknown. The "splendid monster", as D. K. Clark called it, stood out of use in the Camden roundhouse for a long time before its last trip to Wolverton in August 1858. In that month McConnell suggested rebuilding "to reduce her to a suitable engine" and on 9th September he was authorised to proceed "applying the old materials as far as practicable, at a cost not exceeding £1,500, which will make her of the ordinary size and weight of the Company's best engines. The 8ft driving wheels to be offered to the GWR, or any other Company likely to purchase them."

But the wheels were not sold, and stood as an ornament in Wolverton Works yard for many years "an object lesson to young engineers". It is said an attempt was made, but failed, to burst the old boiler by hydraulic pressure. ('Wolvertonian' writing in the *Railway World*, 8th June 1895).

The new engine was completed in April 1859, and came out of the Works bearing the name *Liverpool* and its old number 245. In its new guise it was a standard Wolverton Express Goods 0-6-0 with 5ft 6in wheels and 16in diameter inside cylinders; it can have had little in it of the old Crampton. It was finally scrapped in February 1881.

Livery
E. T. Lane's 1849 drawing is coloured thus:

Frame, smokebox, chimney, wheels, boiler bands, inside of splasher:	black.
Boiler, cylinder, splasher, regulator box:	dark green.
Axleboxes, axle end, safety valve trumpet:	brass.
Firebox, steam pipes:	copper.

Summary: Crampton type 6-2-0 built by Bury, Curtis & Kennedy, 1848

No.	Name	BC&K No.	Date	Rebuilt	Reno'd	Scrapped
245	Liverpool	355	9/1848	9/58-4/59 (as 0-6-0) 2/71	845 (4/62)	2/81

Wolverton 2-2-2 Express Passenger Engine, 1848
No 227 – 'Mac's Mangle'

McConnell took up his duties at Wolverton on 15th February 1847 and within a fortnight the railway papers announced that "the new locomotive superintendent of the L&NW has determined that the narrow gauge shall not be behind, and has an engine building to carry the express train between London and Birmingham in two hours, and we believe he will do it." This was in the *Railway Register* and the *Railway Chronicle* of 27th February.

Three days later McConnell recommended to the Locomotive Committee that engines should be built for passenger traffic with 6ft driving wheels and outside horizontal cylinders of at least 16in x 21in immediately in front of the leading wheels, and with the trailing wheels behind the firebox. Leading, trailing and tender wheels should all be of the same size and pattern and the heating surface should be at least 990 sq ft, 90 sq ft of it in the firebox. On 23rd March 1847 he was asked to submit plans of as large an engine as he considered most suitable for passenger traffic; he quickly produced drawings of an 18in cylinder design and the construction at Wolverton of one engine to this plan was authorised on 8th April 1847. If, as seems likely, the two 2-2-0s 92 and 95 were simply assembled at Wolverton from parts supplied by Bury, Curtis & Kennedy, this was the first engine wholly built there.

It was given the number 227, which suggests a completion date in October 1848, and was added to stock in the second half of December. The cost was £4,744.

It had an outside frame with bearings on all axles, and outside cylinders. The wheelbase was long, with a great distance between the driving and trailing wheels, to allow the firebox to extend outwards to a total width of 5ft 9¼in, filling the space between the outside frameplates. At the front end there was a heavy overhang because the leading wheels were entirely behind the cylinders. The boiler had a big dome on the front ring, immediately behind the chimney, as in Sharp engines.

As usual, McConnell was not slow to extol the virtues of his new design in the right quarters and soon Major-General Pasley was telling the Institution of Civil Engineers about the wide firebox. Although Pasley "was not aware whether that engine had ever made a journey" it would, he thought, be the equal of any of the broad-gauge engines on the GWR. The meeting of the ICE was in April 1849, which may be why this date has usually been given for the completion of 227, but the engine was working on the line before this, with surprising results.

Because the cylinders worked outside the frame they were spaced apart at 7ft 6in between centres, giving the engine an overall width of at least 9ft 3in; it thus fouled some station platforms. Platforms were normally about twenty inches high, but those at Euston were higher, and £300 had to be spent on cutting them back (GLC, 9th March 1849). This, and perhaps other instances elsewhere, earned for 227 its famous nickname 'Mac's Mangle'. The Euston incident led directly to the establishment of a fixed standard of maximum dimensions, when on 10th March the Board ordered the General Manager to "ascertain the size of carriage and engine suitable for the stations and turntables ... and take the necessary steps to guard against the inconvenience complained of consequent upon changes lately made in the sizes of engines and carriages."

The weight of 227 was criticised by the permanent way engineers and contractors: it was the heaviest on the line apart from *Liverpool*. Partly because of this and partly to reduce working costs, it was placed in store in April 1849.

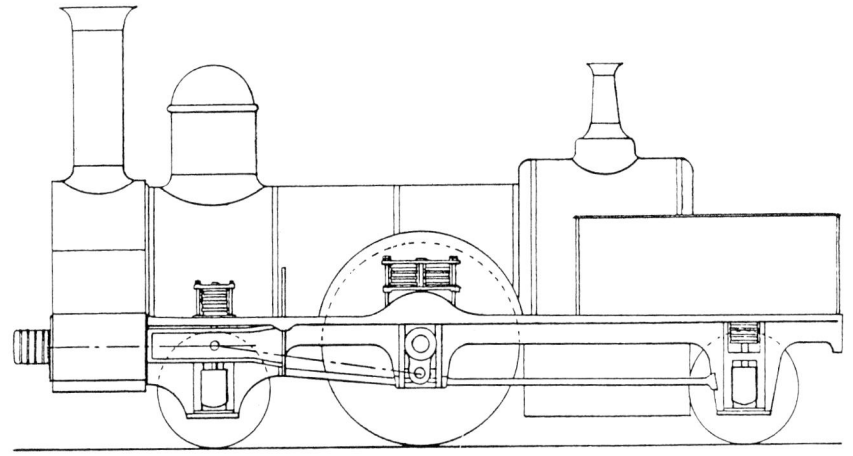

Fig. 58   227 'Mac's Mangle' built at Wolverton, 1848.

Fig. 59
227 after the dome was repositioned in 1850.

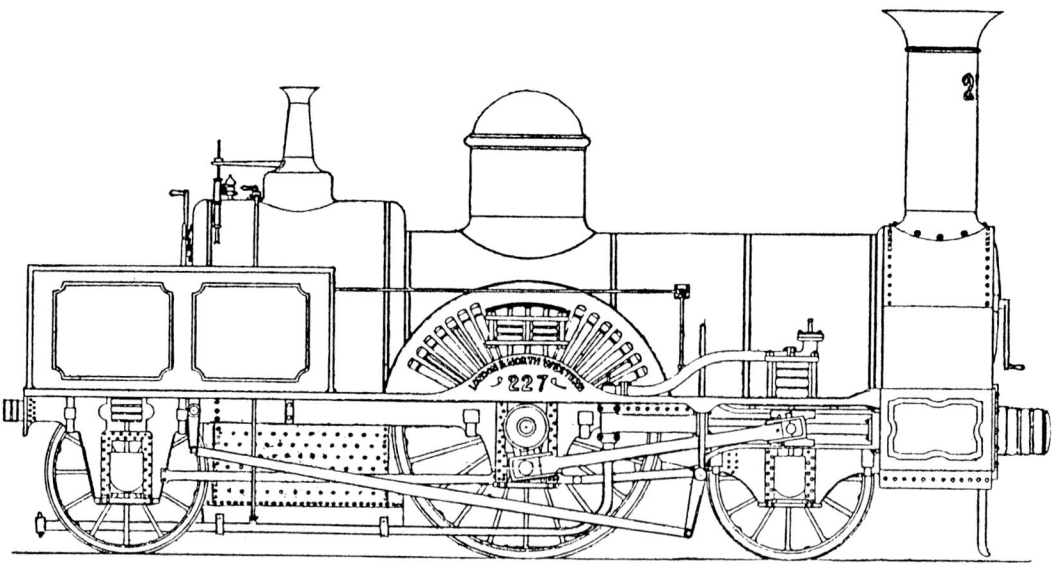

Dimensions

Cylinders (2 outside)	18" x 21"
Boiler	
Diameter	4' 3"
Length of barrel	12' 0"
Pitch	6' 0"
Heating surface	
Tubes (189, 2¼" dia, 12' 7" long)	1,400.97 sq ft
Firebox	130.30 sq ft
Total	1,531.33 sq ft
Diameter of wheels	
Leading	3' 9"
Driving	6' 6"
Trailing	3' 9"
Wheelbase	6' 9¾" + 10' 5" = 17' 2¾"
Weight	
Engine	31 tons 11 cwt
Tender (loaded)	16 tons 16 cwt

Heating surface details are from McConnell's report of May 1853; Ahrons gives a firebox heating surface of 138 sq ft, including a transverse midfeather, and a total of 1539 sq ft. The weights are from a permanent way report of April 1849 but Ahrons says the total weight was 31 tons 19½ cwt, with 13 tons 9½ cwt on the driving axle.

In 1850 the dome was moved to the back ring of the boiler to lessen the weight on the leading wheels. In September of that year 227 was taken out of store, with *London*, for working "the fast trains". A report on its performance was made in February 1851, by Messrs Walker and Johnson, but details are not known. According to McConnell it took a larger average load (89 tons) than any other passenger engine on the S Div, but because it spent so much time in store its total mileage by the end of 1851 was the second lowest of any passenger engine on the line.

As an experiment one S Div engine was fitted with india-rubber springs on all axles in May 1852; the engine concerned may have been 227. Thereafter McConnell was an enthusiastic advocate of their use and in June it was decided to use them in the 2-2-2 Patent class then being ordered. The only known illustrations of 227 show rubber springs.

It was shedded at Camden and regularly worked the 6.30am express from Euston; according to 'Itzaex' it "never used to run any other Down train."

Ramsbottom quickly replaced it in December 1862; the duplicate number was probably 1202. It was scrapped in May 1863.

Summary: McConnell 2-2-2 built at Wolverton Works, 1848

No.	Date	Reno'd 4/62	Renumbered	Scrapped
227	12/1848	827	1202? (12/62)	5/63

Stephenson 4-2-2 Express Passenger Engines, 1848
Nos 233, 234

On 8th June 1848 McConnell reported to the Locomotive Committee that an eight-wheeled engine had arrived on the line from R. Stephenson & Co; this was their works number 729, despatched from Newcastle two days before. This big engine, clearly a response to those of Daniel Gooch and Crampton, was an enlargement of Stephenson's long-boiler 'A' type with a trailing axle added, and weighed about 30 tons with 12½ tons on the 7ft driving wheels. The trailing axle was positioned under the firebox rear, as closely as possible to the driving wheels, and had outside bearings; the wheels on the second carrying axle were flangeless. The dome was immediately behind the chimney and the firebox had a raised top.

In August it was probably parked at Camden, where young E. T. Lane sketched it; in the following month trials of its performance were authorised and these continued through October and November. They must have been satisfactory because another engine, works number 730, was sent from Newcastle on 1st December. Both engines were taken into stock, numbered 233/4, during the month ended 13th December 1848.

Fig. 60   Stephenson 4-2-2 233 and 234, built 1848.

Fig. 61   Stephenson 4-2-2 233, from a woodcut of 1852.

Dimensions

Cylinders (2 outside)	18" x 24"
Boiler	
Diameter	4' 2"
Length of barrel	13' 0"
Pitch	6' 4"
Heating surface	
Tubes (170, 2$\frac{1}{8}$" dia, 13' 6" long)	1,276.96 sq ft
Firebox	94.00 sq ft
Total	1,370.82 sq ft
Grate area	16.125 sq ft
Diameter of wheels	
Leading	4' 0"
Driving	7' 0"
Trailing	3' 6"
Wheelbase	6' 8" + 5' 6" + 5' 4" = 17' 6"
Weight	
On driving wheels	12½ tons
Total	30 tons

The heating surfaces are from McConnell's report of May 1853; Ahrons says the firebox contained a midfeather and contributed 91.5 sq ft to a total of 1,366.5 sq ft. Slightly smaller figures appear on R. Stephenson & Co's drawing (firebox 89.46, total 1,348.67) but this is dated 24th February 1848 and several changes were made before the engines were completed.

The Permanent Way Report of April 1849 complained about damage being caused to the track by heavy engines, but the accompanying list of those over 25 tons did not include these two. Nevertheless, under the GLC's ruling about surplus engines, 233 went into store at the end of 1848, almost immediately after it had been taken into stock, and was joined there by 234 in April 1849. They remained inactive until 1850.

In August 1849 R. Stephenson & Co wrote urging that these two engines should be accepted in place of the last of the Chester & Holyhead order for fourteen 0-6-0 goods engines, of which twelve had already been delivered. These twelve (which carried S Div numbers between 211 and 243) had cost £2,877 each. The price of the passenger engines was £3,200 each, but McConnell was able to get a reduction and payment of £6,000 was authorised on 15th August. Perhaps the makers hoped for orders for more of the same new design, but these were the last passenger engines of the long-boiler type to be taken by the LNWR and no further orders were placed with the firm.

It was not until August 1850 that McConnell was allowed to bring 234 back into traffic "if required" to work the accelerated expresses. There is no mention of 233 which was perhaps already out of store. By the end of 1851 their combined total mileage was almost 37,000.

In 1853/4 the cylinders of both were reduced to 16in diameter.

They went into the duplicate list shortly after Ramsbottom took over; 233 became 1152 and 234 probably became 1191. Both were scrapped in 1864.

Summary: 4-2-2s built by R. Stephenson & Co, 1848

No.	Maker's No. & Date	S Div Date	Renumbered	Withdrawn
233	729, 6/6/48	12/48	833(4/62), 1152(2/63)	Scr /64
234	730, 1/12/48	12/48	834(4/62), 1191?(2/63)	Scr /64

18-inch LONG-BOILER GOODS ENGINES

Sharp Bros 0-6-0 Goods Engine, 'Atlas' type, 1847
No 32

Both Bury and McConnell attended a meeting of the General Locomotive Committee on 4th February 1847. This was McConnell's first such attendance; although he had been appointed Bury's successor, he had not yet started his new job.

One of the items discussed was an offer by Crewe Works to build fifteen goods engines for the S Div during the year. These would have to be of the standard GJR type: Crewe refused to build anything else. A decision on this offer was deferred until McConnell could examine a Crewe 2-4-0 and report on its "peculiar construction". He was also asked to write a report on the sort of goods engines he would recommend for the S Div.

It had been arranged seven weeks before this that the next three 2-4-0s built at Crewe would be sent to the S Div; Trevithick now reported that the first of them was almost ready. At this point McConnell probably suggested an alternative plan because the Committee then decided that "with a view of testing every description of luggage engine" the Crewe engine should go instead to the Manchester & Birmingham Division, and a "large engine" being built by Sharp Bros for the M&B should be sent to the S Div. The M&B Div Locomotive Superintendent John Ramsbottom said it was expected shortly.

This was the second of a pair which had been ordered by the M&B as long ago as November 1844; the first one, No 30, arrived in July 1846 and had achieved great success on that line. On a spectacular test run on 3rd October 1846 it broke all records by hauling a train of 101 wagons (597 tons) for 29 miles from Longsight to Crewe at an average 13.7mph with one stop for water. The neighbouring Manchester, Sheffield & Lincolnshire Railway had two of the same type named *Atlas* and *Hercules* which were also setting new standards on the long inclines over the Pennines.

McConnell was well aware of these engines and would be anxious to try one on the S Div. He was on good terms with their designer, Charles F. Beyer, who was his co-signatory to the circular proposing the creation of the Institution of Mechanical Engineers; in the week prior to his attendance before the GLC, McConnell had been in the chair at the first IMechE general meeting where he and Beyer were elected Vice Presidents.

The new Crewe Goods was duly sent to Longsight in March 1847, losing its N Div name *Marquis* to become M&B Div 31, and in the same month the engine from Sharp Bros arrived on the S Div, bearing the number 32 and with 'M&BR' painted on its tender sides.

A greater contrast with the Crewe Goods would be hard to imagine. It was a large 0-6-0 of the long-boiler type with all wheels in front of the firebox, but it had inside one-piece iron plate frames and 18in diameter cylinders, the biggest yet. The cylinders were inside and inclined upwards at 1 in 10 to the front, with piston rods over the leading axle. The valves were underneath, similarly inclined upwards to the front. Both valves worked in a common steam chest; seen from the front the valve faces were inclined like a flattened inverted **V**. The valve rods worked under the leading axle by drag links which were suspended by two long pendulum levers from brackets on the boiler. The pumps were driven by the crossheads and were fixed inside the frameplates, delivering to the boiler low down on the second ring of

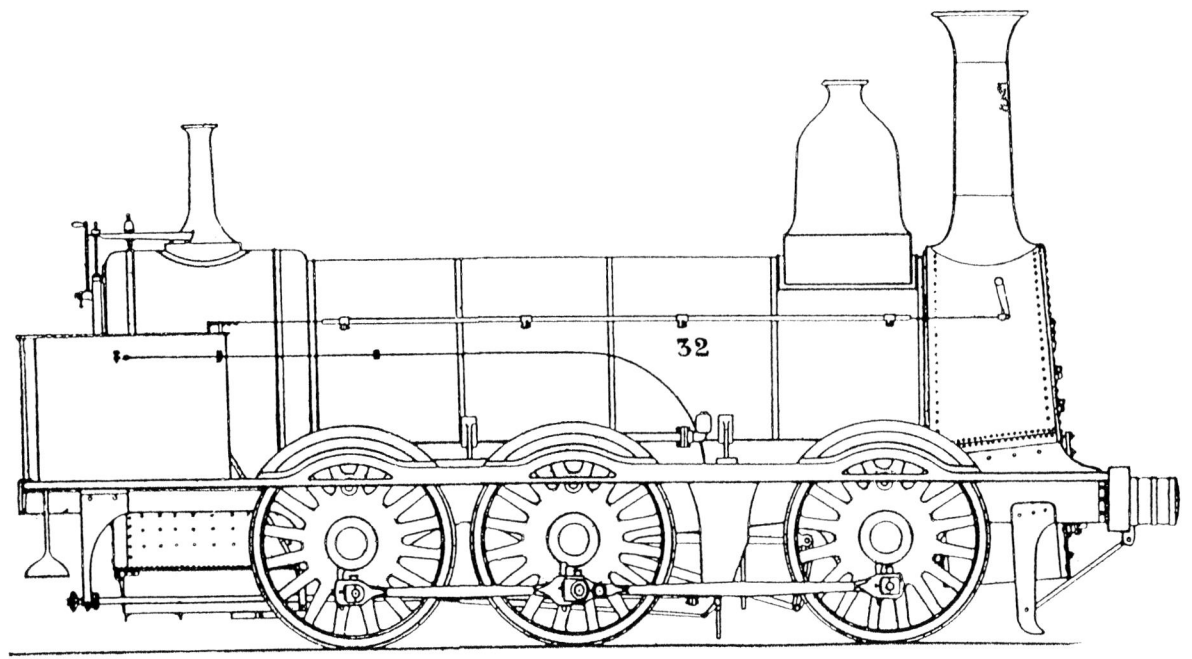

Fig. 62 Sharp Bros 'Atlas' type long-boiler 0-6-0 of 1847, No 32; wheels 4ft 6in dia.

the barrel. The wheels were massive iron castings with balance weights in the bosses opposite the cranks; the spokes were of **T**-section, flat on the outside with a central rib on the back. They had an appearance similar to that of the later **H**-section spokes used at Crewe from 1863. Although the piston stroke was 24in, the coupling rod crankpin circle was 26in diameter; this extra length of coupling rod crank was a feature adopted by McConnell on subsequent coupled engines.

The boiler had four rings, butt-jointed with outside straps, and was fastened to the frame by the motion plate but was supported at the firebox on expansion brackets. A transverse midfeather in the firebox separated the two equal-sized grates. The blastpipe had an adjustable top for sharpening the blast, operated from the footplate by a rod through the left handrail to a crank on the smokebox side. Close behind the chimney was a large dome with a directly-loaded safety valve and a smooth open-topped cover on a square base; on the raised firebox top was a spring balance safety valve in a tall column. The smokebox front sloped at right angles to the incline of the cylinders; this was a characteristic of many Beyer designs and their LNWR derivatives into the 1880s.

Dimensions

Cylinders (2 inside)	18" x 24"
Boiler	
Diameter	3' 6"
Length of barrel	13' 6"
Pitch	6' 0"
Heating surface	
Tubes (146, 1¾" dia, 13' 10" long)	922.30 sq ft
Firebox (3' 8" long, 3' 3¼" wide, 3' 4½" high)	71.00 sq ft
Total	993.30 sq ft
Grate area	10.50 sq ft
Diameter of wheels	4' 6"
Wheelbase	6' 11" + 4' 9" = 11' 8"
Weight	
On leading wheels	8 tons 0.5 cwt
On driving wheels	7 tons 11.5 cwt
On trailing wheels	9 tons 14.0 cwt
Total	25 tons 6.0 cwt

During the month of May 1847 it ran 2,337 miles on the S Div, with a coke consumption of 0.23 lb per ton/mile; in June, 3,004 miles, with a consumption of 0.214 lb per ton/mile. Beyer said that the next most economical S Div engine then at work was burning 0.38 lb.

When the M&B Div obtained an even bigger Sharp goods engine in March 1848, McConnell told Ramsbottom that he intended to return No 32 and asked for the new engine in its place. The new M&B Div engine was the same pattern as engines about to be delivered to the S Div, whereas 32 was the same as the M&B Div's No 30 - and of course McConnell would be exchanging a year-old engine for a bigger new one. The M&B Committee was not impressed and authorised Ramsbottom "to inform McConnell that it is desirable that No 32 remain on the S Div and that the engine last delivered by Sharps be retained on this section."

Even so, it kept its 'M&B 32' identity until October 1848, when it became plain 32 in the S Div list, the old engine with that number (a Bury 2-2-0) having been on the 'condemned for sale' list since the end of 1847.

It was rebuilt in 1860, and entered the duplicate list as 1136 at the end of 1865, becoming 1833 in the reorganisation of the list in December 1871. In September 1872 it was offered to M Lamquet of the Malines & Terneuzen Railway in Belgium for £900, but it remained on the LNWR until it was scrapped in July 1874.

Summary: 'Atlas' type 0-6-0 built by Sharp Bros, 1847

No.	Date	Reno'd 4/62	Rebt	Renumbered	Scrapped
32*	3/1847	632	/60	1136(12/65) 1833(12/71)	7/74

*Listed as M&B 32 until 10/48

Sharp Bros 0-6-0 Goods Engines, 'Sphynx' type, 1848-9
Nos between **210-242** (discontinuous)

After reading McConnell's report on goods engines the S Div Locomotive Committee proposed on 3rd March 1847 to order 40 engines of the most powerful class "similar to Messrs Sharp's now in use on the M&B and Sheffield lines." Twenty of them could be built by Sharp Bros within eighteen months, with delivery starting in 1847. Two days later, with Bury, Curtis & Kennedy offering to build eight goods engines within the year, and learning that the Sharp Bros tender was conditional on an advance payment of £5,000, the GLC reduced their allocation to twelve engines. The advance was paid and the order was placed on 20th March.

These twelve were Charles Beyer's 'Sphynx' type, an enlargement of his 'Atlas' type with 5ft wheels, a longer wheelbase and a bigger five-ring boiler; the firebox was similar in plan but 1ft 3in higher from the firebars to the flat crownplate; again there was a transverse midfeather between the two grates. McConnell's "apparatus for lowering the bars and dropping the fire" was fitted.

Beyer had been making gradual modifications to the size and number of boiler tubes. In the new engines they were fewer but of a larger diameter than before. The original *Atlas* of May 1846 had 175 tubes of 1⅝in diameter; M&B Div 32 of March 1847 had 146 of 1¾in; the published drawings of *Sphynx* show further changes, first 142 tubes and then 133 of 2⅛in diameter. The specification of the S Div engines in the Sharp Bros order book shows a change in the number of the 2⅛in tubes from 141 to 133. Curiously, McConnell's 1853 report says all the 18in cylinder 5ft 0-6-0s had 141 tubes of 2¼in. This, with other evidence, suggests that his boiler details for this group of engines (built by Sharp, Stephenson and Hawthorn) are inexact.

The tenders had six cast-iron wheels and outside sandwich frames; the iron flitch plates had downward projections for the axlebox horns, completely enclosing the springs, and rearward projections to hold the buffers and the rear drawbar spring. With the substitution of a single iron plate for the sandwich assembly, this design was the prototype of McConnell's standard S Div tender.

Sharp's price was £2,400 for each engine and £600 for the tender, but with a deduction of a twelfth of the £5,000 cash advance with interest at 5%, the price actually paid for each engine and tender ranged from

Fig. 63   Sharp Bros 'Sphynx' type long-boiler 0-6-0 of 1848, 210 etc; wheels 5ft dia.

Fig. 64   Sharp Bros 'Sphynx' type 0-6-0 built 1848. Photographed on the South Staffordshire Railway at Bescot in June 1859. Spring buffers, a weatherboard and square sandboxes have been fitted, and the linkage on the smokebox side for adjusting the blast pipe top has been removed.
(Walsall Library)

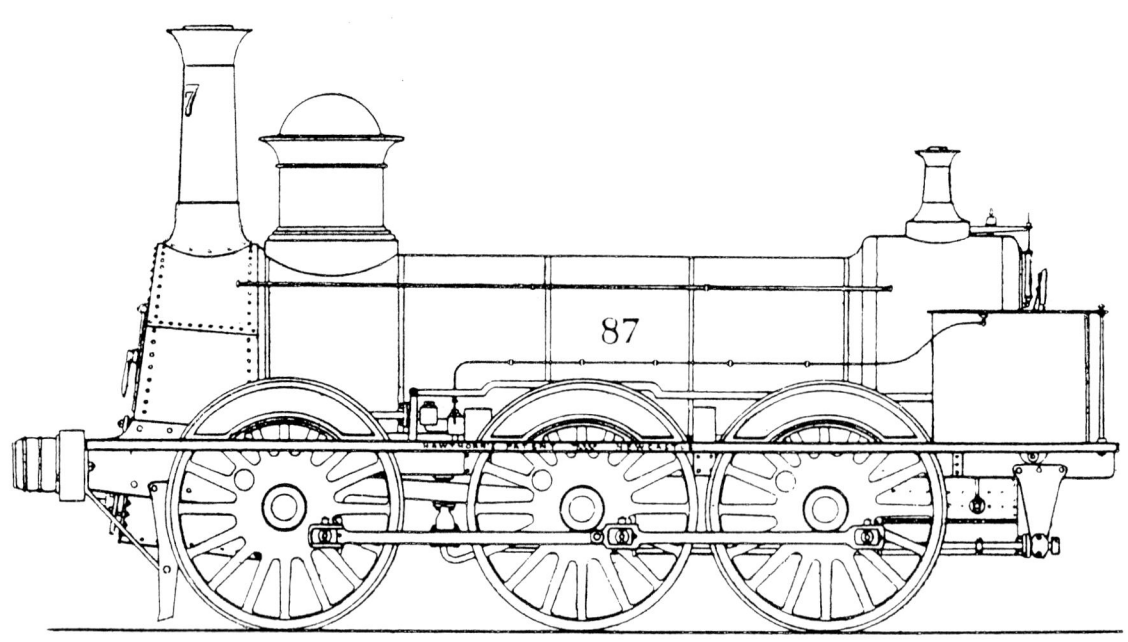

Fig. 65 Hawthorn long-boiler 0-6-0 built for the Huddersfield & Manchester Railway; the three engines of this type became S Div 85, 87 and 246 *Standedge*.

£2,547 to £2,560. Sharp Bros works numbers have been published before but are very doubtful and appear to be guesses from a later date. The engines were delivered from March 1848 to March 1849 and were given S Div numbers interspersed with those of other classes in order of arrival between 210 and 242.

Dimensions

Cylinders (2 inside)		18" x 24"
Boiler		
	Diameter	3' 8"
	Length of barrel	14' 0"
	Pitch	6' 2"
Heating surface		
	Tubes (141, 2¼" dia, 14' 6" long)	1,190.36 sq ft
	Firebox	78.50 sq ft
	Total	1,296.00 sq ft (McC)*
OR:	Tubes (133, 2⅛" dia, 14' 6" long)	1,140.00 sq ft
	Firebox (3' 8" long, 3' 3¼" wide, 4' 7½" high)	81.00 sq ft
	Total	1,220.00 sq ft (Sharp)
Grate area		10.56 sq ft
Diameter of wheels		5' 0"
Wheelbase		6' 11" + 5' 3" = 12' 2"
Weight		
	On leading wheels	8 tons 10 cwt
	On driving wheels	9 tons
	On trailing wheels	8 tons 15 cwt
	Total	26 tons 5 cwt

*McConnell's figure for the total heating surface looks like a misprint for 1,269 sq ft, but is given as above in his report of June 1852, and no fewer than three times (together with these tube and firebox figures) in that of May 1853.

Stephenson 0-6-0 Goods Engines, 1848-9
Nos between **211-243** (discontinuous)
Hawthorn 0-6-0 Goods Engines, 1848-9
Nos 85, 87, between **221-244** (discontinuous), **246** *Standedge*

Orders for twenty goods engines for the Chester & Holyhead Railway were inherited by the S Div in March 1847. Originally these were for Stephenson patent long-boiler 0-6-0s with 15in cylinders and 4ft 6in wheels, similar to the disappointing Longridge and Nasmyth engines which were still being delivered. Fourteen were to be built by R. Stephenson & Co, and six by R. & W. Hawthorn. In August 1847 on McConnell's recommendation the Locomotive Committee requested that the design be altered to that of the Sharp 'Sphynx' type 0-6-0. Hawthorn & Co quoted a new price for the revised design, £2,775 per engine and tender, after a cash advance of £4,550. Stephenson & Co's price was £2,877, and in August 1849 the last two of their order were cancelled and replaced by two big 4-2-2 passenger engines which became S Div 233/4.

Originally the Stephenson engines were allotted maker's numbers 621-34, but when the two 4-2-2 passenger engines (Stephenson 729/30) were substituted, two of the 0-6-0s (632/4) were retained by the firm. These two appear to have been sold to the South Staffordshire Railway in January 1851. The original Hawthorn works numbers for the C&H order were 520-5 but the engines as delivered were 704-9. Twelve Stephenson and six Hawthorn engines were delivered between May 1848 and April 1849, concurrently with the Sharps, and were given S Div numbers in order of arrival between 211 and 244.

Three other Hawthorns of the same type came to the S Div in 1848. They had been ordered by the Huddersfield & Manchester Railway but the LNWR agreed to take this line over while the engines were being built, and when the first of the H&M goods engines was completed it was sent to Crewe. It bore the name *Standedge* after the Pennine ridge pierced by the Huddersfield line's three-mile tunnel. After working for a short time at Crewe, on 13th July 1848 it was ordered to be transferred to the S Div, together with H&M 2-2-2 *Saddleworth*. Meanwhile, the other two engines of the order were ready for delivery and on 31st May the H&M Secretary William Gilmer wrote to the LNWR to propose their exchange for two small engines. Two Bury 13in 0-4-0s 85/7, valued at £800 and £900, were selected in June and sent north in January 1849. The two new 18in 0-6-0s, valued at £2,500 each, came from Hawthorn & Co in July 1848 and took the numbers of the old engines they replaced. Maker's numbers of the three H&M engines were 557/8/9.

Standedge does not seem to have been given an S Div number at first, and is referred to only by its name. Perhaps like *Saddleworth* it carried an H&M number, which would obviously have been a low one probably occupied on the S Div by one of the Bury 2-2-0 engines, and perhaps there was an intention to allow its original number to serve as its S Div number after the old engine was withdrawn - as happened with *Saddleworth* and M&B 31 and 32. This apparent reluctance simply to renumber these engines in the S Div list is puzzling, but in the event *Standedge* was given the number 246 in 1850/1.

The Stephenson and Hawthorn engines were basically the same as the Sharps, all had the sloping smokebox front, a dome close behind the chimney and a raised firebox but the wheelbase was an inch longer and there were dissimilarities in the wheels, splashers and the shape of the boiler mountings. The first three Hawthorns, 85/7 and 246, had cast-iron wheels like the Sharps; the others had wrought-iron wheels. The dome of the Stephenson engines had a lock-up safety valve on top like the Sharps, but the cover was of a different shape; the Hawthorns of the C&H order had that firm's flattish-topped dome cover, while the three from the H&M order had the earlier pattern, round-topped above a prominent concave cornice, like that adopted by McConnell from 1851.

McConnell's drop firegrates were installed by the makers on all except the three H&M engines; these three were given drop grates at Wolverton in 1848.

Dimensions

Cylinders (2 inside)	18" x 24"
Boiler	
Length of barrel	14' 1" (RS & Co)
Heating surface	
Tubes (141, 14' 6" long)	1,190.36 sq ft
Firebox	78.50 sq ft
Total	*1,296.00 sq ft (McC)
OR: Tubes	1,187.30 sq ft
Firebox	97.37 sq ft
Total	1,284.67 sq ft (RS & Co)
Diameter of wheels	5' 0"
Wheelbase	7' 0" + 5' 3" = 12' 3"

See note on heating surfaces in Introduction.

* * * * * *

James Bull says the boilers of engines from the three manufacturers differed, and gives total heating surfaces based on internal tube diameters as:

Sharp 1,023 sq ft, Stephenson 1,140 sq ft, Hawthorn 1,134 sq ft.

These imply variations not recorded by McConnell whose 1853 report shows all three 5ft classes with identical boilers. Despite this he differentiates between them in performance figures:

Maker	Average load	Coke consumption:	
		per mile	per ton/mile
Sharp	178 tons	46.01 lb	0.262 lb
Stephenson	199 tons	53.79 lb	0.272 lb
Hawthorn	191 tons	53.60 lb	0.282 lb

On 13th October 1848 the General Locomotive Committee declared its belief that the LNWR was well stocked with locomotives, and as there were more on order, surplus engines were to be placed in store "to be held as extra stock for new lines." On 14th December six of the 18in goods 226/8/9-32 were put in store, joined almost at once by 235/6/8 when they arrived, and by 211 after a repair. Further new engines were put in store on delivery until by the end of April 1849 there were sixteen lying out of use at Wolverton and at Camden: 211/26/8-32/5/6/8-44.

For the opening of the 'Yorkshire lines' in August 1849 nine were taken out of store at Camden and transferred to Longsight, becoming NE Div 59-67. These nine were 228/9, sent in August, 230/1 in September and 236/8/40/1/2 in October. These dates are from an 1855 report by Ramsbottom; by a typical oversight the nine engines were not taken out of the S Div list until early 1850. On the NE Div, 65/6/7 (formerly S Div 238/40/2) were based at Leeds in 1858/9.

The situation on the S Div in December 1849 was:

	Engines at work	Total
Sharp:	210/2/5/7/9/24	6
Stephenson:	213/4/6/20/3/5	6
Hawthorn:	85/7, 221/2, *Standedge*	5
Total:		17

	Engines in store	Total
Sharp:	232	1
Stephenson:	211/43	2
Hawthorn:	226/35/9/44	4
Total:		7

In January 1850 232/5 were to be taken out of store "if required, for working coal trains when the contracts with the Clay Cross and other companies begin." The others were put to work later in that year.

In the Oxford collision of 3rd January 1853, 220 was the second engine on a 44-wagon coal train; in June 1854 it was fitted with iron tubes and ran 37,510 miles from then until February 1856; later in 1854 it was hired to the Oxford, Worcester & Wolverhampton Railway. Also fitted with iron tubes in 1854 were 224 (April) and 87 (May); their mileages from those dates to February 1856 were 41,642 and 68,776.

LNWR records contain occasional minor references to some of the class: 221 and 223 on main line goods trains in 1853, 222 in an accident while shunting at Camden in 1855, and 235 suffering a burst tube at

Stafford in March 1861.

Three more of this type were built at Wolverton in 1851 as described in the next section. Another four came to the S Div from the South Staffordshire Railway in 1858, two built by Wm Fairbairn & Sons in 1849 (S Div 307/8) and two by Stephenson (S Div 309/10) already mentioned. They will be dealt with later with the other SSR engines.

Rebuilding
Two Sharp engines, 217/9, were given McConnell combustion chamber boilers in the 1850s. In these the boiler contained 199 tubes of 1¾in *inside* diameter, length 11ft 6in. A 3ft long combustion chamber was added to the firebox, whose grate was enlarged to 13.2 sq ft.

Conversion to Saddle Tanks
Several were converted to saddle tanks for shunting. McConnell was authorised to convert six on 9th December 1858, and in 1859 (Sharp) 232 was given a tank of about 850 gallons capacity. In 1859/60 (Sharp) 219 was fitted with an enormous square-topped saddle tank; this was 15ft 5in long by 5ft wide and contained about 1,200 gallons. Differences between them notwithstanding, a Crewe list of the LNWR's heavier engines dated January 1870 gives the weight of these two (renumbered 1177 and 1221) as:

On leading wheels	8 tons	19 cwt
On driving wheels	13 tons	0 cwt
On trailing wheels	14 tons	0 cwt
Total	35 tons	19 cwt

Only these two are known to have been converted by McConnell, but Ramsbottom rebuilt many more to his less ponderous design, whose saddle tank of 530 gallons capacity was on the boiler barrel only and did not cover the smokebox or the firebox.

In December 1858 Ramsbottom reported that he had ten 18in goods engines from the NE Div which would require rebuilding in the next three years; these included the nine transferred from the S Div in 1849. He was authorised to convert them to tanks as they came in for rebuilding and conversions began in November 1859, "the tenders so liberated" to be used by the new DX goods engines being built at Crewe.

On 2nd April 1862, just after the divisions were amalgamated, he was authorised to alter six of the S Div engines to tank engines "to make them available for working the severe gradients on the Merthyr & Abergavenny line". By 1864 this type of engine was also working the 1 in 30 Springs branch at Wigan and the 1 in 40 Coalport branch in Shropshire.

Two Crewe notes dated November 1867 and August 1869 give particulars of 5ft wheel, 18in 0-6-0 tank engines with 12ft 2in and 12ft 3in wheelbase:

Length over buffers	28' 11"
Weight	
On leading wheels	7 tons 18 cwt
On driving wheels	13 tons 4 cwt
On trailing wheels	12 tons 0 cwt
Total	33 tons 2 cwt

The length of the frames on a tank engine of 12ft 2in wheelbase was 25ft 4in, with a front overhang of 4ft 10in and a rear overhang of 8ft 4in.

Rebuilding as Saddle Tanks with 'Long Centres'
In March 1864 Ramsbottom said that 110-ton trains could be worked on the Abergavenny line by 33-ton 0-6-0 tank engines with slightly larger cylinders and a strengthened boiler with a pressure of 130 lb/sq in. (The only difficulty he foresaw was that the brake vans were inadequate to stop runaways; he suggested trying even heavier trains with another big engine behind).

This led immediately to a more radical form of rebuilding of the 18in goods engines as tanks, with a shortened boiler and a lengthened wheelbase. The rear axle was moved from in front of the firebox to a new position behind it. Because the driving and trailing axles were now much further apart these rebuilds became known at Crewe as 'long centres' engines, as opposed to those which retained their original long-boiler characteristics with a 'short centres' wheelbase.

From 1865 several were altered to the 'long centres' form. The boiler barrel had four rings and was 11ft 2¾in long; it contained 134 2⅛in tubes; the dome was on the third ring and Ramsbottom safety valves were on the firebox. As (unlike standard Crewe practice) the firebox retained the raised top of the original, and the barrel rings were all 3ft 8in internal diameter with butt joints, it

Fig. 66
Sharp Bros 0-6-0 rebuilt as a saddle tank in the 1860s retaining its original 'short centres' wheelbase.
Photographed at Crewe in 1875-8.

(LNWR photo)

is clear that the boiler was not entirely new, but a reconstruction of the original five-ring boiler. The grate area was 13.23 sq ft.

The saddle tank held 590 gallons and covered the entire boiler top from the back of the smokebox to the weatherboard. Some were given splashers like those of Ramsbottom's DX class with two cut-outs.

Several of the Stephenson engines (ex-213 'short centres', and 216/20/3/43 'long centres') were noted in the 1870s as having cast-iron wheels; these were probably fitted at the time of conversion to tanks and it seems likely that all the tank engines were so equipped. (Two similarly rebuilt Stephenson engines from the South Staffordshire Railway also had cast wheels at this time: ex-309 'short centres' and 310 'long centres').

Details of the 'long centres' tank engines were:
Sharp:
    Wheelbase   6' 11" + 8' 7" = 15' 6"
    Length over buffers   29' 2½"
    Weight
        On leading wheels   10 tons 13 cwt
        On driving wheels   13 tons
        On trailing wheels   9 tons   6 cwt
        Total   32 tons 19 cwt
Stephenson:
    Wheelbase   7' 0" + 8' 5" = 15' 5"
    Length over buffers   29' 1½"
    Weight
    On leading wheels   7 tons   9 cwt
    On driving wheels   11 tons 10 cwt
    On trailing wheels   10 tons 10 cwt
    Total   29 tons   9 cwt
Hawthorn:
    Wheelbase and length as Stephenson engines
    Weight
        On leading wheels   10 tons   4 cwt
        On driving wheels   13 tons
        On trailing wheels   9 tons   6 cwt
        Total   32 tons 10 cwt

Most of the S Div engines, and all those transferred to the NE Div in 1849 were converted to saddle tanks in one or other of these short or long centres layouts in the 1860s. They proved a very good investment, and after they were superseded by more modern machines on the steep inclines they did a lot of yard shunting; Rosling Bennett recalled seeing several in Camden Goods Yard in the early 1860s and the former S Div 230 and 241 were so employed at Warrington Arpley in 1872.

Disposal

The first to go was a Hawthorn engine, 221, which was replaced in 1859 and all the others from this maker went into the duplicate list in 1863, joining Stephenson 211 which had been replaced in the previous year. Two more Stephensons, 216/20, went into the duplicate list in 1864, the others in 1866/7. All the Sharp engines remained in the capital list until 1866, and it is significant that on the reorganisation of the duplicate list at the end of 1871 whereas all the surviving Stephensons and Hawthorns remained as duplicates, nine of the Sharps were reinstated in the capital list.

When their work on the LNWR was over many were sold for between £1,000 and £1,300 to collieries, ironworks and other railways at home and abroad. In some cases names were put on for the new owners before despatch, as for example *Excelsior* sold to the Pelsall Coal & Iron Co, *Black Tom* to the contractors Scott & Edwards, *Cleveland* to Josiah Hill of Wednesfield, and *Agincourt* and *Black Prince* to the Brownhills Colliery. The Brownhills pair lasted at Grove pit, Wyrley, until 1906 and 1909. *Cleveland* worked at the Chillington Iron Co's Moseley furnaces and is believed to have been transferred to the nearby Willenhall furnaces in 1877, being disposed of in 1882. *Black Tom* worked on the construction of the LNWR Aston-Stechford line, after which it was put up for sale in July 1881. *Excelsior* worked at Pelsall until the ironworks closed; it was offered for sale in November 1892.

Four engines went to Belgium. One of them, ex-S Div 231, a Stephenson engine with short centres, was sold for £1,150 to M Loser of the Hesbaye & Condroz Railway in October 1873; before being despatched it was painted dark green with yellow lines, presumably the H&C livery. It was No 3 on the H&C, but was renumbered 1016 in the État Belge system before being sold to the Societé Turnhout, becoming their No 8 in 1877. Three others, ex-S Div 223, 235 and 243 - two Stephensons and a Hawthorn, all with long centres - were sold for £1,295 each in 1875/6 to "M Bocquean" of Brussels. His name has also been printed as "Mr Badquean" in LNWR lists but he was evidently Ernest Boucquéau, who held the concession of a 6-mile railway from Saint-Ghislain to Erbisoeul, near Mons. This line opened in 1876 with three 0-6-0 tank engines, which are described in a Belgian source as "of unknown origin and probably purchased second-hand". Their recorded dimensions, 18in x 24in inside cylinders, 5ft 1in wheels and 15ft 5in wheelbase, make it virtually certain that they were the three from the LNWR. When the Saint-Ghislain à Erbisoeul line was taken over by the État Belge in 1879, these three were renumbered 1215/6/7, the first two being withdrawn in 1882 and 1217 in 1889.

Another might have gone to Belgium: ex-S Div 217, which had remained a tender engine, was offered to M Lamquet of the Malines & Terneuzen Railway in September 1872, together with the 4ft 6in ex-No 32, for £900 each, but instead of these he bought two ex-Carnarvonshire Railway 2-4-0s. Ex-217 was scrapped as 1834 in March 1874. It was one of the two engines fitted with a McConnell boiler, which both retained to the end. The other, the heavy tank engine ex-219, was sold as capital list 1141 (c/u number unknown) for £1,000 to Kinnersley & Co of Clough Hall Ironworks, Kidsgrove, in May 1873. Both are noted in their last Crewe records as having "McConnell's air chamber".

On 14th February 1873 the former 239 (as 1849, another of the remaining tender engines) was minuted as having been sold to the Northampton & Banbury Junction Railway for £1,000. In November 1875 the N&BJ parted with it to the Severn & Wye Railway where it was named *Ranger*. After being drastically rebuilt as a saddle tank by the Avonside Engine Co it passed into GWR stock and was scrapped in 1897.

Five went to the Alexandra (Newport) Dock Co in 1875-80; four were minuted as sold for £1,295 each on 12th March 1875, but the Newport company found themselves unable to pay for two of them (1802 ex-223

Fig. 67 LNWR S Div 215, Sharp Bros 1848, rebuilt as a saddle tank in 1865 with extended 'long centres' wheelbase. As Alexandra Docks & Railway No 6, *Lady Tredegar* at Newport, c1902.

(W.E. Boyd collection)

Fig. 68 LNWR S Div 220, Stephenson 1848, rebuilt as a saddle tank in 1865 with extended 'long centres' wheel-base. As Alexandra Docks & Railway No 2, *Lord Tredegar* c1890.

(W.E. Boyd collection)

and 1803 ex-243) which went instead to Belgium, as described above, in December. Three others were sold to Newport, one at a time, at gradually reducing prices. Their straight nameplates, fixed to the middle of the saddle tank sides, appear to have been made at Crewe with the names *Sir George Elliot, Lord Tredegar, J. R. McClean, Rhondda* and *Lady Tredegar*.

Their later history has been the subject of a lot of speculation, but it is known that parts of Alexandra Docks Railway No 1 *Sir George Elliot* and No 2 *Lord Tredegar* were used to create a new engine in 1900, which lasted another five years, and that No 6 *Lady Tredegar* survived until November 1906. ADR No 3 *J. R. McClean* was withdrawn in 1900 while No 4 *Rhondda* is believed to have been sold to the dealer C. D. Phillips of Newport in the same year and was probably one of the two ex-ADR engines acquired by the South Hetton Colliery, becoming their Nos 8 and 9. Both were radically rebuilt, No 8 as a side tank and No 9 *Sir George* as a saddle tank, leaving no obvious clues to their original form or identity, and were finally scrapped in 1953.

The last of the saddle tanks on the LNWR was ex-210, which was sold in 1881 (as 1804) to Ackers, Whitley & Co of Leigh, Lancashire, presumably for their Bickershaw Colliery. The last tender engine in traffic, ex-225, was scrapped (as 1812) in the previous year, having been shedded at Longsight latterly.

Summary: 'Sphynx' type 0-6-0s built by Sharp Bros, R. Stephenson, and R. & W. Hawthorn, 1848-9
Engines rebuilt as saddle tanks are noted, where known, by SC (short centres) when the original short wheelbase was retained, or LC (long centres) when the rear axle was relocated behind the firebox.

1. Built by Sharp Bros & Co:

No.	Date	Reno'd 4/62	Rebt tank	Rebt	Renumbered	Withdrawn
210	23/3/1848	810	10/64(SC)		1234(7/66), 1147(12/71), 1804(11/78)	Sold 10/10/81 Ackers, Whitley & Co, Leigh
212	27/5/1848	812	2/66		1235(7/66), 1148(12/71), 1815(11/78)	Scr 19/6/80
215	18/7/1848	815	7/65(LC)		1236(7/66), 1149(12/71), 1821(11/78)	Sold 9/3/80 Alexandra Dock Co, Newport, £1,000 No 6 *Lady Tredegar* Wdn 11/06
217	2/8/1848	817	—	/60	1175(1/66), 1834(12/71)	Scr 14/3/74
219	30/8/1848	819	/59-/60 (SC)		1177(1/66), 1141(12/71)	Sold 27/5/73 Kinnersley & Co, Clough Hall Ironworks, Kidsgrove, £1,000
224	4/10/1848	824	—	/62	1190(1/66), 1832(12/71)	To Machinery & Tools a/c 9/8/75 as Loco Machinery No 4
228	14/10/1848	—	/65(LC)	12/62	NE Div 59(8/49), 459(8/57), 1229(7/66), 1142(12/71)	c/u 1993 Scr 5/7/76
229	19/10/1848	—	/60(SC)		NE Div 60(8/49), 460(8/57), 1230(7/66), 1143(12/71), 1816(8/74)	Sold 20/10/74 Josiah Hill, Wednesfield, £1,110 as *Cleveland*
232	11/1848	832	/59(SC)		1221(1/66)	Scr 2/71
238	1/1849	—	11/60(SC)		NE Div 65(10/49), 465(8/57), 1231(7/66), 1144(12/71), 1825(8/74)	Sold 21/9/74 Scott & Edwards, £1,110 as *Black Tom*
240	2/1849	—	7/61(SC)	/70	NE Div 66(10/49), 466(8/57), 1232(7/66), 1145(12/71), 1833(9/74)	Scr 10/75
242	3/1849	—	3/64(SC)		NE Div 67(10/49), 467(8/57), 1233(7/66), 1146(12/71)	c/u 1963 Scr 20/3/78

2. Built by R. Stephenson & Co:

No.	Date	Reno'd 4/62	Rebt tank	Rebt	Renumbered	Withdrawn
211	18/5/1848	—	—		1166(5/62)	by 9/63
213	10/6/1848	813	6/65(SC)		1151(2/67), 1804(12/71)	Sold 11/72 Vron Colliery Co, £1,000
214	20/7/1848	814	by /65		1150(1/66)	Scr b /71
216	24/7/1848	816	7/65(LC)		1156(8/64), 1805(12/71)	Sold 12/3/75 Alexandra Dock Co, Newport, £1,295 No 1 *Sir George Elliot* Scr /98
220	4/9/1848	820	a /65(LC)		1199(8/64), 1807(12/71)	Sold 12/3/75 Alexandra Dock Co, Newport, £1,295 No 2 *Lord Tredegar* Scr /98
223	15/9/1848	823	b /67(LC)		1133(5/66), 1802(12/71)	Sold 15/12/75 M Boucquéau, Brussels, £1,295
225	10/1848	825	—	/59, 2/69	1224(2/66), 1812(12/71)	Scr 15/11/80
230	13/11/1848	—	2/64(SC)		NE Div 61(9/49), 461(8/57), 1254(1/67), 1808(12/71)	Sold 17/10/73 Pelsall Coal & Iron Co, £1,100 as *Excelsior*
231	22/11/1848	—	2/64(SC)		NE Div 62(9/49), 462(8/57), 1255(1/67), 1809(12/71)	Sold 17/10/73 Hesbaye & Condroz Rly, Belgium, £1,150 État Belge 1016 (11/75)
236	15/12/1848	—	7/64(SC)		NE Div 63(10/49), 463(8/57), 1256(1/67), 1810(12/71)	Sold 18/10/73 W. Harrison, Brownhills Colly, £1,100 as *Black Prince* Scr /09
241	15/2/1849	—	2/64(SC)		NE Div 64(10/49), 464(8/57), 1257(1/67), 1811(12/71)	Sold 29/11/73 W. Harrison, Brownhills Colly, £1,100 as *Agincourt* Scr /06
243	17/3/1849	843	b /67(LC)		1142(5/66), 1803(12/71)	Sold 15/12/75 M Boucquéau, Brussels, £1,295

Stephenson works numbers in order of delivery were 621-9/31/33 and 630.

3. Built by R. & W. Hawthorn & Co:

No.	Date	Reno'd 4/62	Rebt tank	Renumbered	Withdrawn
246*	7/1848	846	—	1216(11/63)	Scr 3/69
85	7/1848	685	b /65	1214(11/63), 1851(12/71)	Scr 23/2/78
87	7/1848	687	a /66(LC)	1215(11/63), 1852(12/71)	Sold 20/5/76 Alexandra Dock Co, Newport, £1,295 No 3 *J. R. McClean* Wdn /00
221	9/1848	—	—	Replaced 7/59	
222	9/1848	822	—	1210(10/63)	? Scr 12/63
226	10/1848	826	—	1211(10/63), 1848(12/71)	Scr 3/75
235	12/1848	835	b /65(LC)	1163(11/63), 1847(12/71)	Sold 2/76 M Boucquéau, Brussels, £1,295
239	2/1849	839	—	1212(11/63), 1849(12/71)	Sold 1/73 Northampton & Banbury Jct Rly, £1,000 Sold 11/75 Severn & Wye Rly & Canal Co, £800 and named *Ranger* Rebt as 0-6-0ST, 1/91 GWR 1358 (10/95) Scr 11/97
244	4/1849	844	5/69(LC)	1213(11/63), 1850(12/71)	Sold 21/2/77 Alexandra Dock Co, Newport £1,135 No 4 *Rhondda* Sold /00 C. D. Phillips, then to South Hetton Colly?

* Named *Standedge* - not numbered 246 until 1850/1.

Hawthorn works numbers were 557/8/9 (S Div 246, 85/7) and 704-9.

Fig. 69   Long-boiler goods engine 228, one of the three built at Wolverton and completed in 1851.

Wolverton 0-6-0 Goods Engines, 1851
Nos 228, 229, 230

Three long-boiler 0-6-0s were begun at Wolverton in 1848, to give work to men taken on as blacklegs during the drivers' strike in August of that year. Work on them was suspended in December because of a trade recession and a surplus of engines on the LNWR. Two years later, with the expectation of a great increase in traffic, McConnell reported that the three engines were "almost half-finished" and that all the materials for completion were on hand. On 12th December 1850 he was authorised to continue them "as may be found convenient" and work was resumed within the next two months.

They cost £2,328 each, and appear to have been completed in December 1851. The numbers given, 228/9/30, were those of engines transferred to the NE Div in 1849.

The design was that of the Sharp 'Sphynx' 0-6-0 apart from the boiler mountings which were of the new McConnell style with the prominently-corniced brass dome and safety valve covers and the matching twin flat bands around the chimney.

On 30th July 1852 228 was working a special cattle train from Rugby to Peterborough when, James Bull tells us "a bridge near Woodford crossing, between Thrapston and Ringstead was in course of renewal, and the driver not being aware of this, ran his engine into the gap; the driver and fireman jumped off and escaped, but the engine plunged headlong into the river Nene." As a result the Works Committee asked that "heavy engines" should not be used in future on the Peterborough or Aylesbury branches. The driver, J. Copley, seems to have been an unlucky individual. On this occasion he forfeited his annual bonus; the year before he was put on half-pay after a brick fell on him in Kilsby tunnel; a year later he was injured in an accident at Blisworth.

All three engines were put on the duplicate list in 1864. In 1870 1168 (ex-229) was scrapped and 1167 (ex-228) became a shunting engine with the Carriage & Wagon Dept. In the same year 1169 (ex-230) was rebuilt as a saddle tank, in its original form with all wheels in front of the firebox. It was scrapped in 1878, being entered in the Crewe ledger as "Sharps 6 wheels coupled goods tank".

Dimensions

Cylinders (2 inside)	18" x 24"
Heating surface, total	1,222.8 sq ft
Diameter of wheels	5' 0"

Summary: 'Sphynx' type 0-6-0s built at Wolverton Works, 1851

No.	Date	Reno. 4/62	Rebt. tank	Renumbered	Scrapped
228	12/1851	828	-	1167(8/64) To C&W Dept 9/70	
229	12/1851	829	-	1168(8/64)	12/70
230	12/1851	830	a /70(SC)	1169(8/64), 1815(12/71)	3/9/78

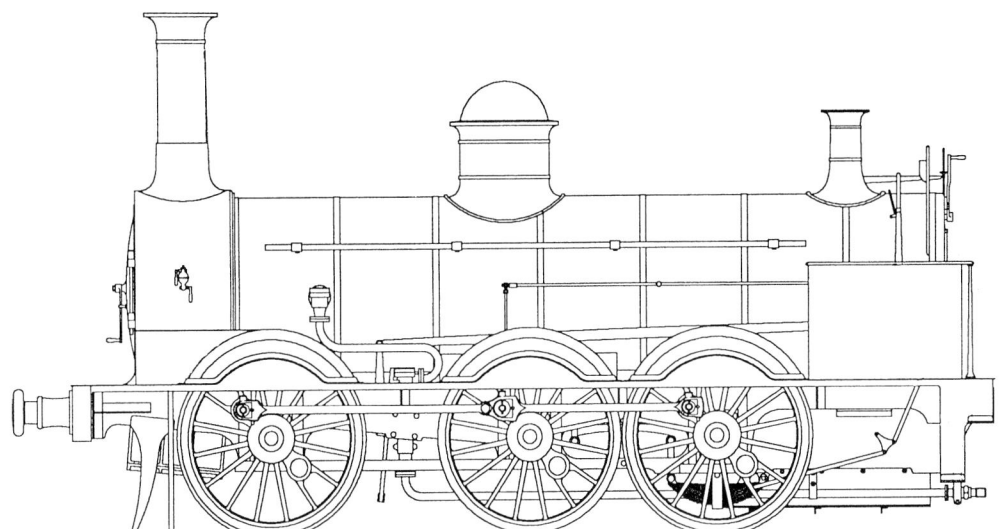

Fig. 70
Fairbairn long-boiler 0-6-0 from a Wolverton drawing of 1856. Probably represents the last four engines of the order, 283-6. *(Richard Powell)*

Fairbairn 0-6-0 Goods Engines, 1851-5
Nos 257-286

At the end of 1850 there were 24 of the splendid 0-6-0 'Sphynx' type on the S Div, built by Sharp Bros, by Stephenson and by Hawthorn, and another three were being built at Wolverton Works. But the period when the S Div was overstocked with locomotives was coming to an end and on 14th March 1851 the General Locomotive Committee decided to order another twenty goods engines, to the 'Sphynx' design as modified by McConnell. Six were to be ordered from private builders and tenders were invited from four firms with whom the LNWR had dealt before and from Wm Fairbairn & Sons, Canal Street Works, Ancoats, Manchester. The other fourteen were to be built at Crewe, at cost price - which was not to exceed the price of those built outside. The six from outside were to be delivered by 1st August, the Crewe engines between October 1851 and March 1852.

On 29th March 1851 offers to build six engines and tenders were considered from the firms and compared with the cost of engines from Crewe:

E. B. Wilson:	£2,290 each
Sharp Bros:	£2,900 each
W. Fairbairn & Sons:	£2,170 each
R. & W. Hawthorn:	£2,475 each
R. Stephenson:	£2,800 each
Crewe Works estimate:	£2,735 each

William Fairbairn was called in and told that the Committee was disposed to accept his tender for six engines and when he offered to reduce the price to £2,100 each for an order for twenty, he was at once given a contract for all the engines. Six were to be built by 1st August, another six by October and the rest by the end of 1851. If any were undelivered by then, the price was to be reduced by £100 each. Crewe was told to cancel preparations for the fourteen engines.

On further reflection the price and the promised dates must have seemed too good to be true and in April 1851 McConnell was sent to Fairbairn's to look around; he reported that all was satisfactory. In May Fairbairn offered to build ten more engines at £2,300 each, but this and another offer in July were declined.

General Manager Mark Huish had written a report with the permanent way engineers, condemning heavy engines. Now he made some "observations" about the forthcoming goods engines. McConnell replied that they would be only 26 tons, as nearly as he could estimate, and the weight would be nearly equally divided among the six wheels. A glance at the table of dimensions will show how unrealistic this estimate proved to be.

These engines were closely based on Beyer's original design as built by Sharp Bros; the main differences were in the wheels. They were of forged iron, rather than cast, and the middle pair were flangeless, like the original Stephenson long-boiler patent engines. This allowed the middle and rear axles to be even closer together (although the overall wheelbase remained the same); the clearance between a new flanged tyre on the rear wheel and the flangeless rim of the middle wheel was less than half an inch. The boiler was slightly fatter, allowing extra tubes and an increased heating surface. As in the Beyer design the coupling-rod cranks were one inch greater in radius than the driving cranks. The most obvious outward differences were the dome, positioned on the middle of the boiler instead of close up behind the chimney, and the footplate valance which was without apertures in the coupling-rod arches.

The first arrived in October 1851, another following in November. Only these two had been delivered when McConnell declared: "In the new merchandise engines we have the most powerful on the narrow gauge; in relation to their weight the most powerful of any now at work." He recommended ordering another ten.

Once more Crewe Works was approached, for ten engines at cost price, but again, on 9th January 1852 and although his price had risen remarkably, the contract went to Fairbairn for ten goods engines at £2,750 each. Delivery was to be by the end of 1852. Then there was a further bill for £840: "Mr Stephenson's account for patent right on 30 engines at £28 each" which was paid on 20th July 1852.

In the ten engines of the second order the heating surface was to be increased by means of more tubes and a bigger firebox, and in 1853 after fifteen of the original

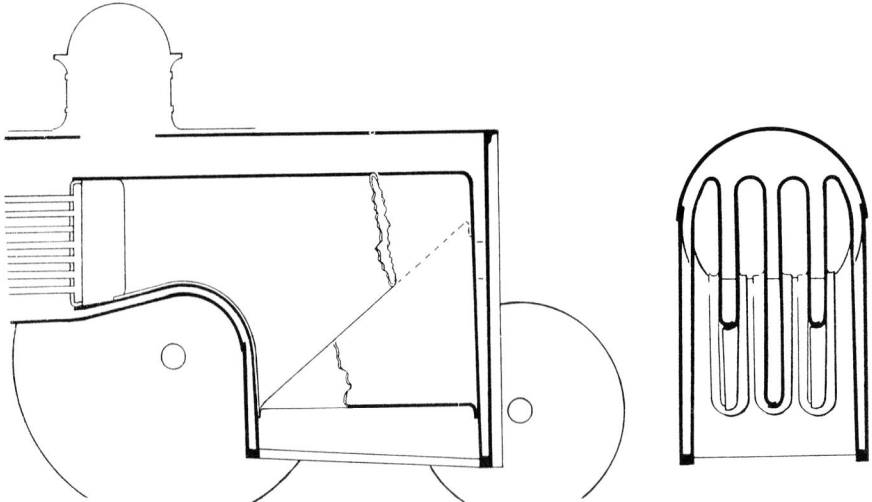

Fig. 71   Firebox with three midfeathers: McConnell's patent of Dec. 1852. Full-depth central midfeather; side midfeathers slope upwards from throatplate to just above each firehole. Boiler recessed over crank-axle to achieve a low centre of gravity.

twenty had been delivered, two of the second batch were rushed out ahead of sequence, apparently so that one of them (277) could take part in the Woods and Marshall trials in the following week. The remaining five of the original order followed in 1853. The building of the second batch coincided with McConnell's firebox experiments and he asked Fairbairn for alterations to the last eight engines whose construction had not yet begun. He now wanted a double firebox with twin combustion chambers, 7ft long, which united so far forward - under the dome - that the tubes were only 7ft 2in long. There were over 300 of these 1¾in tubes. The cylinders were to be enlarged to 19in diameter. This was in July 1852, and the price per engine was now to be £2,860. By the end of the year other changes in the design had put the price up to £2,960.

In February 1853, after McConnell had obtained another patent, further alterations were made to the plans of the last eight engines: the firebox was now to have one grate, but two side-by-side fireholes and *three* longitudinal midfeathers. The central midfeather came down to just above the fire, each of the other two was centred over a firehole, with their bottom edges sweeping diagonally down to the throatplate, rather like thermic syphons. In effect, flames rising from the grate would pass along four parallel passages about seven inches wide by two to three feet high and into a combustion chamber under the dome as before. "With these arrangements" he said "coke or any other fuel may be employed, and anthracite coal which is ordinarily of difficult combustion, may be burned with facility..."

These alterations further delayed the completion of the engines and again put up the cost. Fairbairn's revised contract of 8th February 1853 was for eight goods engines with triple midfeathers at £3,092 10s (£3,092.50) each. But there was a major difficulty: actually making the fireboxes, each with three six-inch partitions seven inches apart and all heavily stayed, was a boilermaker's nightmare and proved to be so very difficult that the coppersmiths refused to try again after struggling with the first four. As Woods and Marshall pointed out in April 1853, not only would these boilers be costly to construct but repairs would be awkward. Reaching the back ends of the tubes would be difficult and "we do not at present see how access is to be obtained to the side plates of the midfeathers and firebox for renewing stays etc, the spaces between being too confined for a man to work in."

By great efforts, in January 1854 the first of the boilers was nearly complete and Fairbairn estimated another seven weeks would suffice for the erection of the engine. The second boiler would take another six weeks; the third and fourth of the 3-midfeather engines could be finished by May.

As for the other four, the copper for the fireboxes had not yet been ordered and Fairbairn was quite unable to forecast when they could be finished. In the light of Woods and Marshall's report of 31st December 1853, which came out in favour of smaller engines, the General Locomotive Committee sent the Manchester directors Matthew Lyon, George R. Chappell and Edward Tootal to visit Fairbairn's works to see the exact state of the engines yet to be delivered. The GLC had been considering cancelling the order but when it was revealed how much work had already been done (and would have to be paid for) Fairbairn was asked what, if any, modification to the design would speed up delivery of the last four engines. He advised dispensing with two of the three midfeathers; if this were done, the second four engines could be finished by August, and would cost £100 less each.

Accordingly the last four engines were built with one midfeather only. The proposal to enlarge the cylinders to 19in was quietly abandoned. McConnell's feelings about these negotiations, conducted well over his head between the directors and Fairbairn, are not difficult to imagine.

In fact, the first of the 3-midfeather engines was not delivered until 4th April 1854 and it was another seven months before the last one was finished. The remaining four did not appear until the following year, almost four years from ordering. The delay could only be blamed on

McConnell's changes in boiler and firebox design, as Fairbairn complained in January 1854: "We may observe that ever since 1852 we have had in our place the whole of the following parts for *all* the engines viz.: tubes, wheels, frames, axles, tyres, slide bars, springs, motion etc."

When the last instalment of the bill for the engines was paid, the LNWR made a deduction because of the long delay. Fairbairn objected to this and the LNWR was obliged to concede payment in full - "as it appeared some of the delay might have been caused by this Company altering the specification of the engines".

The first 22 engines (257-78) had raised outer fireboxes like the prototype Sharp 0-6-0, but in the eight engines with longitudinal midfeathers (279-86) the boilers had flush tops. All had the new distinguishing feature of the S Div, McConnell's brass dome with its prominent cornice, and a matching safety valve trumpet. None had the extra lock-up safety valve as built, but this was fitted later, and probably all had it by the time they were rebuilt. Some (at least) had a brass segmental numberplate on the coupling-rod arch of the valance over the middle wheel. The earlier series had sloping smokebox fronts like the Sharp engines but drawings from 1853 show vertical fronts. In the later series sandboxes were built onto the front splashers, extending forward to the smokebox front; the earlier engines were so fitted later. A peculiar feature was the extremely short footplate which measured only 1ft 4in from the firebox to the rear edge.

The leading and driving axles had laminated springs behind the splashers, but the firebox was so close behind the axleboxes that an alternative method was adopted for the trailing axle. At first volute springs were probably used, but a Wolverton drawing of 1856 shows a laminated spring under the rear axle, with an equalising lever between it and the overhung middle axle spring.

They were the last engines of the long-boiler type built for the S Div, but others were acquired in 1858 from the South Staffordshire Railway.

Dimensions

Cylinders (2 inside)					18" x 24"
Boiler					
Diameter (internal)	middle ring				4' 3"
	first and third rings				4' 2$\frac{1}{8}$"
Length of barrel					13' 10"
Pitch					6' 6"
Length of firebox casing					5' 1$\frac{1}{2}$"
Heating surface	*Nos 257-76*	*277/8*		*279-86*	
Tubes, number:	200	251	or 237	305	
dia:	2$\frac{1}{8}$"	2$\frac{1}{8}$"	2$\frac{1}{8}$"	1$\frac{3}{4}$"	
length:	14' 4"	14' 4"	14' 8"	7' 2"	
sq ft:	1,595	2,001	1,939	978	

Firebox
    Midfeathers: 1 transverse in some of Nos 257-78
               3 longitudinal in Nos 279-82
               1 longitudinal in Nos 283-6
Quoted heating surfaces vary wildly and are difficult to reconcile with details given for tubes.

Firebox heating surface	
without midfeather	101 sq ft
with transverse midfeather	121 or 143 sq ft
with 3 longitudinal midfeathers	339 sq ft
Total heating surface	
first series	1,700 sq ft
No 278	2,082 sq ft
with 3 midfeathers	1,252 or 1,317 sq ft
Grate area	16 sq ft, 15 sq ft with divided grate.
Boiler pressure	100 lb/sq in (1851), 110 lb/sq in (1852), 120 lb/sq in (1856)
Diameter of wheels	5' 0"
Wheelbase	7' 0" + 5' 2" = 12' 2"
Length over bufferbeam	first series 24' 9", second series 25' 1"
Weight (259, 1st Jan 1853):	
On leading wheels	8 tons 4.4 cwt
On driving wheels	9 tons 1.9 cwt
On trailing wheels	12 tons 11.0 cwt
Total	29 tons 17.3 cwt
Weight (277, 18th March 1853):	
Engine	33 tons
Tender	17 tons
Tender (6 wheel) capacity	coke 2$\frac{1}{2}$ tons water 2,000 gal

Rebuilding

They were all rebuilt by Ramsbottom, after which the grate area was 14.2 sq ft and the weight, according to two official sources, was:

	January 1870	April 1877
On leading wheels	8 tons 7 cwt	8 tons 14 cwt
On driving wheels	10 tons 10 cwt	10 tons 10 cwt
On trailing wheels	13 tons 2 cwt	11 tons 6 cwt
Total	31 tons 19 cwt	30 tons 10 cwt

Some were given rectangular-section coupling rods jointed behind the middle crank in place of the original front-jointed round-section rods. By the end of their careers, the Webb type of wheel-operated reverse had been fitted to engines of this class, and the equalising levers had been removed. None were converted to saddle tanks.

Work

As the most powerful goods class they worked the heaviest trains all over the S Div. In 1854/5 at least three of them, 260/7 and 276, were hired to the Oxford, Worcester & Wolverhampton Railway.

One of their shortest jobs was working wagons - up to 100 at a time - between Curzon Street yard and the Midland Railway exchange sidings in Birmingham. In their last years they worked chiefly in the South Staffordshire area; photographs of three of them (1824, 1850 and 1905) were taken in the vicinity of Bushbury shed in 1877. An official photograph of the last survivor, 1965 (ex-273) was taken outside the Paint Shop at Crewe in 1881.

Accidents

Driver Hosker was on 268 with the 12.45am Down goods train at Rugby on 9th February 1854 when he rammed a Midland train passing from the Up to the Down line on an unsignalled crossing. On 3rd June in the same year a tube burst on 269 while on a train near Roade. Fireman Wallace jumped clear and was killed under a passing express; Driver Micklethwaite was sacked. On the afternoon of 29th October 1856, 277 was on an Up coal train which included two dead engines being taken from the South Staffordshire Railway to Wolverton for repair. Between Roade and Hanslope, in a fog so dense that "he could not see the length of his engine" the driver realised he had broken away from his train. He stopped, and according to one account, drove slowly back to look for it. The train - 27 loaded wagons, ten empties and a brake van - was rolling down the 1 in 330 gradient led by its two dead goods engines, Stothert 0-6-0 55 and SSR 22 *Bilston*, both of them heavy modern machines. In the crash all three engines overturned, "driven together in one inextricable mass"; 277's fireman Ben Pike was killed. The Up line was soon filled for five miles back with a continuous line of halted trains, with more held on the Down line to the south. The wreckage stopped all Up and Down traffic for 36 hours, the longest stoppage ever on the S Div.

278 was involved in an accident at Wolverton on 16th December 1859; its total mileage then was 115,842.

On 11th June 1861 282 was running tender first on a train of empty coal wagons from Leamington to Victoria Colliery, Coventry. About 7.00am the bridge over Leek Wootton crossroads gave way just after 282's tender had passed over. James Bull says: "the engine and tender went down, doubled together, the driver and fireman being pinned against the firebox and there burned to death." Driver George Rowley lived at Brockhall, near Weedon; his fireman John Wade came from Preston.

On 5th May 1862 while 878 was shunting a Camden-Rugby goods train at Harrow Station about 1.30am its boiler exploded; the right side ripped open, tubes were torn out and bent backwards, hitting both enginemen, severely injuring Driver James Beckwith of Camden and killing Fireman Henry Cowdry. The engine had been retubed at Wolverton in October 1860 and had run 66,272 miles since then.

862 was on a Stoke-Birmingham goods train on 13th January 1875 in fog and on greasy rails south of Four Ashes when it smashed into the rear of an Up Liverpool goods.

Fig. 72
Fairbairn long-boiler 0-6-0 1824 (ex-270) built 1853. After rebuilding, but retaining original round-section coupling rods; rubber springs on tender. Photograph taken at Bushbury, 1877. (R.H. Bleasdale)

Fig. 73
Fairbairn long-boiler 0-6-0 1965 (ex-273) built 1853. The last survivor of the class, at Crewe before scrapping in November 1881. *(LNWR photo)*

Fig. 74
Fairbairn long-boiler 0-6-0 1850 (ex-275) built 1853. At Bushbury, 1877.
(R.H. Bleasdale)

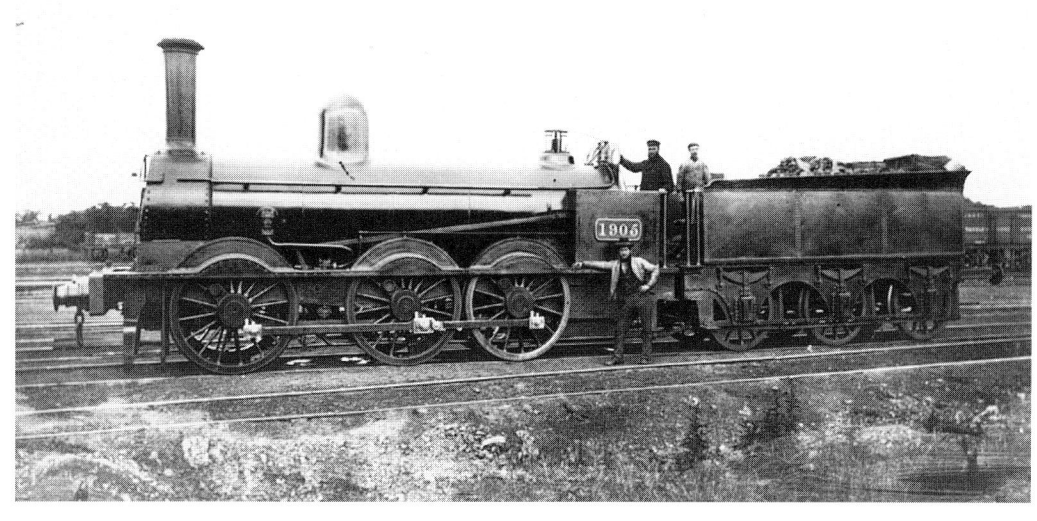

Fig. 75
Fairbairn long-boiler 0-6-0 1905 (ex-280) built 1854. At Bushbury, 1877.

(R.H. Bleasdale)

Disposal

Strangely - by comparison with other goods engine classes - none of them were sold. The first to be scrapped went in 1874, and three more in 1875/6. In 1877 all but one of the 25 remaining went into the duplicate list and the last three were scrapped in 1881.

Annual totals:

	capital	duplicate
30/11/1871:	29	1
30/11/1872:	30	-
30/11/1873:	30	-
30/11/1874:	29	-
30/11/1875:	27	-
30/11/1876:	26	-
30/11/1877:	1	22
30/11/1878:	-	17
30/11/1879:	-	13
30/11/1880:	-	4
30/11/1881:	-	-

Summary: 0-6-0s built by Wm Fairbairn & Sons, 1851-5

No.	Date	Reno'd 4/62	Rebt	Reno'd	Withdrawn
257	10/1851	857	11/64	1847(4/77)	Scr 17/12/79
258	11/1851	858	2/71	1882(4/77)	To Loco Mach'y, 11/77
259	1/1852	859	10/69	1225(2/66), 1138(12/71), 1929(5/78)	Scr 9/10/80
260	1/1852	860	a /67	1884(5/77)	Scr 5/1/78
261	5/1852	861	5/68	1902(5/77)	Scr 20/2/80
262	8/1852	862	b /65	1960(5/77)	Scr 26/7/80
263	8/1852	863	12/67, /70	1927(5/77)	Scr 17/3/80
264	4/10/1852	864		1944(5/77)	Scr 28/2/80
265	11/1852	865	12/63	1962(5/77)	Scr 10/12/78
266	12/1852	866	11/69	1964(5/77)	Scr 5/10/78
267	1/1853	867	b /63	1843(6/77)	Scr 30/8/81
268	1/1853	868	12/63	1878(6/77)	Scr 15/8/77
269	2/1853	869	a /65	1805(6/77)	Scr 26/7/80
270	2/1853	870	4/68	1824(6/77)	Scr 30/6/80
271	3/1853	871		1828(6/77)	Scr 12/5/78
277	7/3/1853	877	b /63	c/u 1980	Scr 6/75
278	28/3/1853	878	b /63	1943(6/77)	Scr 10/12/78
272	4/1853	872	b /67	1835(6/77)	Scr 9/10/80
273	5/1853	873	b /67	1965(6/77)	Scr 21/11/81
274	5/1853	874	12/67	1896(6/77)	Scr 14/8/79
275	7/1853	875	b /64	1850(6/77)	Scr 27/6/78
276	7/1853	876	a /65	1887(6/77)	Scr 18/4/78
279	4/4/1854	879	b /65	1916(6/77)	Scr 21/11/81
280	30/5/1854	880	a /65	1905(6/77)	Scr 18/4/78
281	17/7/1854	881	a /65	1980(7/77)	Scr 18/12/80
282	11/11/1854	882	b /64	1981(7/77)	Scr 7/11/79
283	9/1855	883	a /64	c/u 1986	Scr 12/4/77
284	10/1855	884	a /65	c/u 1999	Scr 6/76
285	12/1855	885	b /64	c/u 1828	Scr 7/74
286	12/1855	886	a /65	c/u 1984	Scr 10/75

The BLOOMERS

Sharp Bros 2-2-2 Express Passenger Engines, 1851-3
Nos 247-256, 287-296

Early in 1851 the LNWR Board suddenly realised they would shortly face competition on both flanks, from the GNR for the Yorkshire traffic and from the GWR reaching up towards Birmingham. The Great Exhibition seemed likely to produce heavy extra traffic. Express engines of proven reliability were wanted quickly.

A report on the working of McConnell's 227 by Messrs Walker and Johnson was submitted to the S Div Locomotive Committee on 11th February 1851; nine days later an order was placed with Sharp Bros & Co, Atlas Works, Manchester, for ten engines. There was no question of building more 'Mac's Mangles'; the new design was virtually that of the six Bury, Curtis & Kennedy 'Low-dome' singles of 1848 except for larger driving wheels (7ft) and proportionately increased cranks, which meant raising the boiler by several inches. The boiler requested was identical, except that the firebox was slightly bigger.

	Bury single	*New engine - as ordered*	*as delivered.*
Cylinders	16" x 20"	16" x 24"	16" x 22"
Boiler			
Diameter	4' 1"	4' 1"	4' 1"
Length	12' 8"	12' 8"	11' 9"
Pitch	6' 6"		7' 1"
Heating surface			
Tubes	1,363.55 sq ft	1,363.55 sq ft	1,306.30 sq ft
number	178	178	195
dia	2¼"	2¼"	2⅛"
length	13' 0"	13' 0"	12' 0½"
Firebox	86.70 sq ft	122.62 sq ft	142.30 sq ft
Total	1,450.25 sq ft	1,486.17 sq ft	1,448.60 sq ft
Grate area	16.00 sq ft	17.00 sq ft	18.00 sq ft
Diameter of wheels			
Leading	4' 6"	4' 6"	4' 6"
Driving	6' 0"	7' 0"	7' 0"
Trailing	3' 7"	4' 0"	4' 0"
Wheelbase	8' 2" + 7' 10"		8' 4" + 8' 6"

Sharp Bros quoted a price of £1,900 per engine and £400 per tender, and they promised delivery of the first one on 1st May - only ten weeks away - and the other nine by the end of June.

At this time Sharp Bros were paying off a retiring partner and were short of ready cash; they wrote on 27th February asking for an advance of £4,000 on the strength of pushing on with the ten engines, and got it. It was to be repaid at £400 per engine plus 5% interest.

When by 10th June no engines had appeared, the LNWR Secretary was instructed to complain urgently about the non-delivery; the Committee was evidently unaware that the delay was at least partly caused by its own Locomotive Superintendent. While the engines were being built McConnell asked for a bigger firebox, then for a transverse midfeather, then for the addition of the grate-dropping apparatus. The tubes were to be increased in number and decreased in size, first to 200 at 2in diameter, then to 195 at 2⅛in.

These alterations took time and cost money, and the first engine was not delivered to the LNWR at Manchester until 30th August, with the others following at intervals to the end of the year. They were placed on the line without any of the leaks to the press which preceded McConnell's 'Mangle' or his dismal 'Patents'. For a class which has since been his main claim to fame, their beginnings were very quiet.

From the speed at which the order was placed, the fact that the design was closely based on the Bury 'Low-domes', that Beyer was in charge of the manufacture at Sharp Bros, and that the engines were simple and straightforward and with a high centre of gravity, it can be concluded that McConnell had very little to do with their design. At a meeting of the Locomotive Subcommittee at Wolverton on 28th October 1851 he was asked what was the boiler pressure of the six new engines by then in stock. He had to go and find out and a fortnight later was able to report that it was 100 lb/sq in, an increase of 15 lb/sq in on that of the previous engines.

The ten engines were given running numbers 247-56 and on 6th January 1852, shortly after the last of them had been delivered, McConnell gave his opinion: "I believe we have now in the latest passenger engines by Sharp the best description yet constructed as regards speed, power and economy." The Board ordered payment of the outstanding account "less £13 9s 8d for repairs of defects" (£13.48) and decided to order ten more.

Before asking for tenders for these from other firms, McConnell was authorised to write to Sharp Bros on 25th January. On 3rd February their offer to build ten more engines at £2,450 each was accepted. It is hardly surprising that the price had been increased, for various improvements had suggested themselves during the day-to-day running of the first ten. Thicker cylinder faces were specified, also larger pump valves and stronger trailing axle springs. On the Bury engines the trailing springs were coiled, whereas the longer wheelbase of the Sharps allowed just enough room behind the firebox to squeeze in very short leaf springs only 1ft 9in in length. These were to be strengthened by adding extra plates. The main change was in the firebox, where McConnell now wanted a longitudinal midfeather down to about a foot above the grate, necessitating two fireholes side by side.

Sharp Bros promised to deliver three in July and the rest by the end of September, a schedule more realistic than before, perhaps because they foresaw a repetition of their previous experience with McConnell.

Fig. 76 Sharp Bros Bloomer 249 built 1851. In virtually original condition, at Camden shed facing north with a coke-filled tender, 1856-61. Right-hand drive, leather buffers, flat smokebox door; without sanding gear or weatherboard, but equalising levers have been fitted to engine and tender.   (J.E. Kite collection)

Sure enough, on 20th March, McConnell asked for changes in the midfeathers, which may account in part for delayed completion dates. The first engine was handed over to the LNWR on 13th October, the last not until the end of February 1853. Another reason for the delay may be that all was not well at Sharp Bros; new partners had come into the firm, which was renamed Sharp, Stewart & Co from mid-1852. Charles F. Beyer, who had done so much for the firm and for the development of the locomotive, left them at this time.

On learning that the engines would be delayed the Locomotive Committee wrote to Sharp expressing disappointment and promising to remember the firm's lack of punctuality when placing further orders. In reply, Sharp wrote that the first two engines would be ready in August, and asked for an advance of £4,000. No money was sent and no engines arrived. On 21st September Sharp wrote again: the two engines would definitely be ready in the next fortnight. Just over three weeks later the first arrived, followed in two days by the second.

They had been a rush job. The ashpans had been badly fixed and "the engines were not properly painted". These matters must be put right at Sharp's expense, they were told, or the £4,000 advance would not be forthcoming.

The third engine was found to have a defective steam pipe. The others were examined and Sharp, Stewart & Co were cautioned about the engines under construction. To no avail: the fifth also had a defective steam pipe. "Defects in recent Sharp engines" was already an item on the Committee's agenda when in January 1853 a leading wheel tyre burst off one of the engines at Harrow, causing an accident. Out of eighteen engines delivered to 11th February it was found that there had been four such failures. The firm disclaimed responsibility, McConnell was ordered to take the engines off the road for all leading wheel tyres to be tested, legal proceedings were instituted, and payment was withheld pending the outcome. Claims and denials ground on until October, when the LNWR abandoned the action, and the outstanding balance, including £10 per engine for midfeather alterations was paid in January 1854.

The second ten engines were given running numbers 287-96.

The nickname 'Bloomer'.
Although the six similar Bury singles were already working the LNWR expresses, the new engines were outwardly very different, and from the first took on a quite distinct identity.

When the first engine arrived at Camden in early September 1851, the 'Bloomer' furore was at its height. In the previous month a few daring young women had appeared on the London streets clad in the costume advocated by the American feminist, Mrs Amelia Bloomer. Instead of tightly-laced corsets, yards of flannel petticoats and crinolines which were then considered normal and decent female attire, these modernists wore loose knee-length frocks and lightweight pants down to the ankles. This was sensational; the press went wild; the ladies were followed by gaping crowds, guffaws and catcalls. After their mentor, they and their dresses were called *Bloomers*. Suddenly the word was heard everywhere. Concurrently three London theatres put on Bloomer farces. A brewery clad all its barmaids in Bloomer costume. Mrs Bloomer, Bloomerism and Bloomers preoccupied the British autumn of 1851. Anything novel and striking was likely to be labelled *Bloomer* and because the new engine looked different it was given the inevitable nickname. Few nicknames have caught on so quickly or so completely and within a very short time it was used in official correspondence; the engines have never been known as anything else.

Efforts have since been made to rationalise the meaning by referring to "clearing away the decent skirting of the underframe" but this makes no sense in an LNWR context; at the time of the engines' debut most of the others on the line had *naked* wheels. The reason for the nickname is simply that the engines looked unusual and arrived at the height of the Bloomer excitement.

Design features.

The cylinder and steam chest arrangement of the Bury design was copied in the Bloomer. This layout has often been claimed as the reason for the success of the latter; notably it was later used by F. W. Webb in his Precursors and Precedents - the famous 'Jumbos'. Most of the other constructional details were likewise taken directly from the Bury engine.

The principal difference was that the Bloomer was mounted on plate frames. This is easily understandable, as the man in charge at Sharp Bros was Beyer, the German who more than anyone gave the British locomotive its characteristic clean lines and who had introduced the one-piece plate frame. Bury, Curtis & Kennedy's works had just closed down so it was unlikely that bar frames would have been used, whoever built the engines. Beyer also held modern ideas about the centre of gravity of a locomotive, so he was unworried by the 7ft wheels and inside cranks which necessitated a high-pitched boiler. McConnell by contrast was still striving for a low centre of gravity years after this time.

Bury's double-beat regulator in the smokebox with its long collecting-pipe was replaced by a similar regulator in a large dome on the boiler barrel. The blast pipe top was lower. This was because Beyer's friend and later business partner Richard Peacock had discovered by experiment in 1850 that the best position was just above the level of the top tubes and not, as in previous practice, up to the base of the chimney.

On the Bury engine the reversing lever was on the right-hand side of the footplate and the reversing rod passed over the driving axle between the inside of the wheel and the frame to an arm which projected upwards from the weighshaft. Because the plate frame was at the outer end of the axle bearing (unlike the bar frame, whose top member was centred over the bearing) there was insufficient room to copy this exactly. Instead the reversing lever was made longer and extended down beyond its fulcrum to a position below the frame, whence the reversing rod passed behind the wheel *under* the axle to an arm projecting downwards from the weighshaft. This reversing rod sloping down to within 15in above the rail was a prominent feature of all S Div express engines thereafter. Between the frames the Stephenson link-motion was arranged as in the Bury engine except that there were two counterweights balancing the box links: in the Bury engine one centrally-mounted weight was sufficient for the shorter eccentric rods and links. The box links were carried from the weighshaft underneath, and the valve rods were likewise supported from below by suspension links. In the bar-framed Bury engine the suspension links were mounted on a cross shaft which, like the weighshaft, was carried in bearings let into the lower member of the frame on each side. In the Bloomer the suspension links were pivoted in brackets at the bottom of the motion plate, and the weighshaft was carried in downward lugs from the frame. The positions of these two supporters of the valve gear, hanging in space below the plate frame, marked the site of the absent bottom bar frame member.

The site of the bar frame of the prototype had its memorial also in the position of the pumps, which in the Bury were bolted directly along the inside of the wide top frame-bar, fitting snugly between it and the outside of the cylinder slide bar. They were copied exactly in the Bloomer, so were given long brackets which placed them inboard some six inches from the frame-plate.

There was one real difference in the cylinder layout. In the Bloomer the cylinders and valves were parallel to the rails, whereas the Bury piston rod and valve spindle diverged from each other by about 4°, the cylinders being very slightly down at the front, while the valves inclined upwards. McConnell reverted to the Bury arrangement when he came to design the Patents in 1852 and the Small Bloomers in 1853. The Small Bloomer layout closely copied that of the Bury, but in the Patent the valves were horizontal and the cylinders hung down at an angle of 6° in order to achieve a low boiler.

The Bloomer footplate was very simple, as on all engines of this period. The reversing lever was on the right; this had been the engine driver's traditional side and with a clear view ahead over a low boiler it hardly mattered which side he occupied. With the arrival of the Bloomers whose firebox top was 5ft 8in above the floor it became apparent that a position on the left had obvious advantages and subsequent classes, from the Patents on, had left-hand drive.

The space on the left was taken up with the handle of McConnell's drop-grate device which was evidently an elaboration of the Bury design. The grate consisted of two fire-frames, one behind the other, which were free to drop open in the centre like a double door when the locking mechanism was released. The general arrangement drawing of the first ten shows the fire-frames pivoted on trunnions at the bottom of the firebox sides. The horizontal handle of the vertical operating shaft was a foot long and out of sight behind the side fender. The difficulties of getting the ash and clinker-encrusted grates to budge must have caused some rethinking; the second ten (in a partial reversion to the Bury type) had their grates loosely hooked at their outer ends, and the operating handle - lengthened to two feet for extra purchase - appeared over the fender side. The Patents had the same device with a different handle, but it seems to have been quietly forgotten and no trace of it can be found in later engines.

In the first ten Bloomers the firehole had to be high above the footplate to get the fuel onto the front grate over the transverse midfeather. In the second series, with the longitudinal midfeather, the twin fireholes were lower by a couple of inches, centred at 2ft 6in above the footplate.

High up, between the two vertical brass tubes housing

the Salter safety valve springs, was the upright regulator handle in its quadrant, with the word SHUT on the left and OPEN on the right. The Bury singles were like this and from photographs the 'closed on the left' position remained standard on the S Div, despite the changeover to left-hand drive. The Bloomer regulator valve was the double-beat type, worked by an eccentric. This arrangement is usually ascribed to Ramsbottom, but Sharp Bros had been using it since 1846.

On the left side of the firebox a pull-rod operated the cylinder and steam chest drain cocks, passing through the boiler handrail to a **T**-shaped bell-crank on the smokebox side. This crank became quite a McConnell trademark.

A 'warming-cock' was provided on the left side of the firebox top to let steam from the boiler into the tender tank. This was on the Bury singles, and the original Bloomer order had specified "heating apparatus from boiler to tender, with sufficient strength of plate in the tanks". Sharp's standard engines also had this appliance, and the pattern supplied on the Bloomers was their design.

The smokebox door on the first general arrangement drawing is also the Sharp pattern - hinged at the top, below a horizontal handrail - and probably the first ten were like this, with six or eight separate catches distributed round the perimeter - but the second ten had a side-hinged door, with the long **L**-shaped locking handle which McConnell normally used. This door was a reversion to the type used on the Bury singles, with a central handle operating four radial bolts. The McConnell door was circular; the Bury had a round top and bottom with straight sides. Both were hinged on the right. All these doors were quite flat, without the familiar dishing adopted on the S Div in 1853.

A contemporary onlooker would have been impressed by an apparently top-heavy engine, and a lot of polished brasswork. The boiler looked high, but the firebox rose above it, swelling out above the footplate side fender, with prominent rounded brass edging at front and back, and crowned by a large brass safety valve cover with generous, well-proportioned curves. On the running board over the driving wheel stood a broad double-edged brass splasher of the Sharp/Beyer pattern - seven feet long and three feet high.

The most striking feature of all was the large brass dome cover with its cove-cornice and two flat mouldings at the top and bottom of the central cylindrical portion. This was like the dome on Hawthorn's three Huddersfield & Manchester goods engines delivered in 1848 but with a smooth base; from 1851 it quickly became a Wolverton standard and was fitted to all new and many older engines as the most obvious characteristic feature of the S Div until 1862.

In many ways the Bloomers were ahead of their time. In the year of their introduction the LNWR was showing off two engines at the Crystal Palace: the underslung-boiler *Cornwall* and the 6-2-0 Crampton *Liverpool*. On the S Div there were no fewer than 45 engines with cylinders as small as 13in diameter and five with only 12in. There were 92 four-wheeled engines. In the matter of cylinder size the N Div was even worse, with 71 engines of 13in or smaller. Only three N Div engines weighed over 20 tons; by contrast a Bloomer weighed 29 tons.

In many ways however they were typical products of 1851. There was no protection for the enginemen, not even a weatherboard; the front buffers were two leather pouffes stuffed with horsehair; there was no sanding gear and the only brakes were on the tender.

Dimensions

Cylinders (2 inside)	16" x 22"
Boiler	
Diameter (inside)	
Middle ring	4' 1¾"
Front and back rings	4' 1"
Length of barrel	11' 9"
Pitch	7' 1"
Length of firebox casing	5' 9½"
Heating surface	
Tubes (195, 2⅛" dia, 12' 0½" long)	1,306.3 sq ft
Firebox	
Nos 247-256, transverse midfeather	142.3 sq ft
Nos 287-296, longitudinal midfeather	163.57 sq ft
Total	
Nos 247-256	1,448.6 sq ft
Nos 287-296	1,469.87 sq ft
Grate area	
Nos 247-256	18.0 sq ft
Nos 287-296	18.9 sq ft
Boiler pressure	100 lb/sq in (1851), 110 lb/sq in (1852), 120 lb/sq in (1856)
Diameter of wheels	
Leading	4' 6"
Driving	7' 0"
Trailing	4' 0"
Tender	3' 9"
Wheelbase	
Engine	8' 4" + 8' 6" = 16' 10"
Tender	5' 6" + 5' 6" = 11' 0"
Tender (6 wheel, with well) capacity	coke 2½ tons or coal 2 tons water 2,000 gal
Weight	
On leading wheels	9 tons 18 cwt
On driving wheels	12 tons 7 cwt
On trailing wheels	6 tons 15 cwt
Total, engine	29 tons 00 cwt

In March 1853 the weight of 291 was given as 30 tons, tender 16 tons.

Detail alterations

An extra lock-up safety valve was fitted behind the dome and centred over the driving axle from about 1855-6. Probably most of the class were so equipped by 1862. The cover looked like a small model of the McConnell dome barrel, straight sided with mouldings, but later a curved type which matched the Salter safety valve cover was sometimes used.

The Bloomers "rode like a swing" as David Joy put it, but this probably referred to the period after equalising levers had been fitted. In the tests conducted in 1853 the Patent and the Crewe engines were said to have had "great and equal steadiness at all speeds" but the Bloomer had "a rougher motion, especially at higher speeds".

In the mid 1850s compensating or equalising levers were fitted to some - perhaps all - engines. A cantilever connected the back end of the leading axle spring through a central pivot on the frame to the front end of the driving axle spring, thus enabling correct weight distribution despite variations in spring characteristics and rails. Thus equipped they should have ridden very well with minimal disturbance to the track, and have been very sure-footed as the adhesive weight would not vary on uneven rails. A drawing and photograph of 249 show that the Bloomers had the compensating lever fitted in behind the frame above the pump and arched at the front end to clear the motion plate. Tenders were similarly equipped between the middle and rear axle springs by curved levers outside and inside the frame. These levers were all removed in Ramsbottom's day; improved track had probably made them superfluous.

From about 1855 very small weatherboards were fitted and were probably regarded as normal by the end of the decade.

Samuel S. Bateson's patent feed-water heater was fitted to 248 in May 1861. Water was forced by the pumps through a tube inside the firebox, looped round the sides and throatplate, just below the bottom row of tubes, before entering the boiler. A 27.9% fuel saving was claimed and at least two other engines were fitted but nothing is known of it after 1862.

As built short footsteps were fitted whose bottom step was 1ft 9in above rail level, but from 1854 a longer pattern came in which was 1ft 2½in from the rail, matching the tender steps. Some engines kept their short footstep to the end.

Sandboxes were fitted from about 1854. At first the delivery pipe was vertical, but by 1861 was bent closer to the driving wheel tyre.

Bloomer 247 was fitted with iron tubes in August 1854 and ran with them until at least February 1856, having covered 39,497 miles in that period.

A few Krupp weldless steel tyres were purchased by the LNWR from March 1857; they were very expensive at £55 a pair, plus £7.90 customs duty, but came with a 400,000 miles guarantee. They were fitted on 293 and 294 according to a report of their comparative performance of July 1859.

One of the second batch of Bloomers was fitted with McConnell's patent steam brake in March 1857 for what were said to be successful tests. From a speed of 45mph, a train of sixteen loaded carriages was brought to a stand in 560 yards by the steam brake plus the brakes on the tender and in two vans "without reversing the engine or throwing it out of gear." From 27mph the train stopped in 330 yards.

The brake was in the form of a 4ft long wrought-iron sledge or skid fitted on each side between the driving and trailing wheels and bearing on the latter and the rail when steam was turned on. Capt Huish told the Institution of Civil Engineers that it was the best brake he had seen, adding, in his equivocal way: "It was very powerful; it certainly did injury to the rails but it was only intended to be used in exceptional cases." Another trial was held on 19th January 1858 with a Bloomer pulling over 127 tons including the tender. The train ran up and down on the Oxford branch, applying the various brakes, singly and in combination, at speeds from 13 to 43mph. The steam brake acting alone stopped the train from 39mph in 1,320 yards on the level, from 37.5mph in 1,194 yards approaching Claydon from the west on an uphill gradient of 1/209 and from 25mph in 623 yards near Marsh Gibbon on an uphill 1/1430.

At the end of 1858 when five other engines had been fitted the LNWR was threatened with a lawsuit if the use of this brake was continued, because McConnell's patent 591 of 1857 appeared to be an infringement of Fitzpatrick's patent 519 of 1852. No more is heard of it after 1859.

Bloomer 247 was fitted with a form of screw reversing gear on the right side of the firebox in October 1857, apparently preceding Ramsbottom's first application. It is not known how long it remained on 247, or if any others were fitted.

Perhaps from as early as 1857 some engines were given front cover plates to their open splashers, partly hiding and giving some protection from the spokes. The three prominent cut-outs were a contrast to the radial apertures on the splashers of Crewe engines. The earliest known drawings are dated 1861, but photographs show that earlier engines had been so fitted at some time, perhaps as late as the Ramsbottom period.

Other changes were made in the normal course of repairs: dished smokebox doors, spring buffers and more elegant and slightly shorter chimneys. The feed-water delivery shown on the Sharp drawings led directly to the underside of the middle boiler ring, a simple variation of the Bury arrangement, but McConnell favoured a clack box low down on the front ring. This can be seen in the earlier photograph of 249, but the same engine after reboiling in 1861 seems to have some other layout - perhaps a reversion to the original or Bateson's feed-water heater which had backhead delivery. From 1861 Giffard injectors were added to the right side of some engines, leaving the pump on the left; later some engines had injectors on both sides.

In March 1861 Bloomers working the Scotch and Irish Mails were equipped with whistles which could be operated from the guard's van by a cord which passed along the tender frame to a bell-crank on the engine footplate. The rest of the class were fitted by 1862. This whistle was bigger and deeper-toned than the driver's whistle; in McConnell's time the two were mounted side by side in front of the weatherboard, with the guard's whistle on the right. After rebuilding with Ramsbottom boilers the Crewe position was used, in front of and just below the safety valve casing and angled radially on the right side of the firebox.

Accidents

The earliest recorded incident was on 7th July 1852, when 253 broke away from its train, the 9.15am Down express, in Primrose Hill tunnel. The engine ran on to Sudbury before stopping but then returned on the Down line to look for the missing train. Driver Jonathan Hill and his fireman lost their annual gratuities as punishment.

Fig. 77 Bloomer 249 as rebuilt following the boiler explosion of July 1861. Changes include left hand drive, extra lock-up safety valve, sanding gear, ornamental splasher infill, deeper footstep, spring buffers, dished smokebox door, weatherboard and a neater and slightly shorter chimney. At Wolverton, with the station refreshment room and kitchen behind, December 1861. *(LNWR Society)*

On 14th January 1861, when on the Up Limited Mail from Scotland (departing Bletchley at 4.40am) 248 was parted from its train by the derailment of a carriage at Pinner. The train consisted of two composite carriages, five post office vehicles and two brake vans. One of the brake vans came from the Caledonian, a post office van and tender from the Midland.

One unlucky engine was in two serious accidents. 249 was on the eight-vehicle Up Scotch Limited Mail on 16th November 1860 when at about 2.00am it ran into a special cattle train from Holyhead which was being shunted at the south end of Atherstone. The engine burst through the guard's van, then through a van full of drovers and into a cattle wagon before falling on its left side on the embankment. It suffered bent frames and axles, broken frame stays and a lot of superficial damage. Fireman James Cherry and nine of the drovers were killed; Driver E. Barber escaped, but despite his nine years as a driver and his "long meritorious service and high character" attested by McConnell, he was downgraded because he was believed to have run past a red signal. Foreman Moorcroft of Tamworth was sacked for not informing him of the cattle train ahead. The forthright remarks of the investigating officer led to the fitting of guard-operated whistles on engines.

The same engine was on the Down Irish Mail on Thursday, 4th July 1861. About 10.40pm it was four miles north of Rugby and just coming up to Easenhall bridge when the boiler exploded. The boiler was blown to pieces, some of which were driven into the bridge, bringing down five tons of brickwork; the crank axle was torn in two, the right-hand driving wheel and a big chunk of the frame shot across the Up line at the bridge abutment. Bits of locomotive were found a hundred yards away. Driver William Atterbury was thrown off to the left, hitting a telegraph post which broke his collar bone, but he survived. Fireman Henry Robinson, trapped on the engine, was so badly crushed that he only lived long enough to be carried to the New Inn at Brinklow.

The boiler was found to have become so pitted above a lap-joint that in places it was only a sixteenth of an inch thick. The boiler pressure was 120 lb/sq in. The engine had run 336,368 miles in its $9\frac{3}{4}$ years, and had been once retubed, in October 1857.

Following the accident the engine was completely rebuilt at Wolverton. Others of the class were rebuilt there, retaining their outward McConnell appearance, after Ramsbottom took over.

* * * * * *

The Bloomers were very successful express engines, the best on the S Div, where they ran most of the fast trains for a quarter of a century. They were so good that another twenty of the same class were built ten years after the first batch. The later engines were virtually the same as the earlier ones, which says much for the quality of the original design in this period of rapid development and improvement.

In order not to depart too far from chronological sequence, several other classes acquired up to 1861 must first be described, before dealing with the later Bloomers. Details of the earlier Bloomers after that date, and a summary of the whole class, will be found on pp240-49.

The PATENTS

2-2-2 Express Passenger Engines, 1852-4
E. B. Wilson & Co   Nos 297, 298
Wm Fairbairn & Sons   Nos 300-309

In June 1852 the S Div had ten Bloomers at work and another ten on order, as well as the six prototype Bury 6ft singles. Apart from teething troubles the Bloomers had given a performance "satisfactory in all respects" in the Locomotive Committee's words. Future demands could have been met simply by building more of them as required, which is demonstrated by the fact that in 1861/2 another twenty were built, basically the same as the original engines of ten years before. But McConnell seems to have been unable to leave well alone. Having been given an excellent design by Bury and Beyer, he set about trying to improve it.

During 1851/2 he experimented with boilers, not at this stage with a view to burning coal, but to improve the steaming capacity. Stephenson had claimed in 1841 for his patent long-boiler type that the longer tubes increased thermal efficiency by reducing the amount of heat lost up the chimney; the draught was of course more sluggish. McConnell took a different approach; he proposed a much bigger firebox and very short tubes, so that although the heating surface was less, more of it was exposed directly to the fire and "the generation of steam with upwards of 60% less heating surface could be as plentiful as before." In May 1852 he declared that by this "complete change in the arrangement" he had achieved a 13% economy in fuel, and anticipated further savings in the reduced wear and tear of the tubes and firebox.

The S Div Locomotive Committee was impressed by McConnell's arguments and on 8th June 1852 reported: "We have come to the conclusion that to run express trains at the weight and at the speed which is required a class of engine must be employed of greater power and speed than the 16in cylinder engines last made [the Bloomers] and have accordingly obtained tenders, on a specification and drawing prepared by Mr McConnell." The engines proposed were to have 18in cylinders and 7ft 6in driving wheels; heating surface of the firebox would be a hefty 260 sq ft, of the tubes only 970 sq ft; the engine would weigh under 30 tons, and - most importantly - would have a centre of gravity six inches below that of the previous express engines. They would be capable of taking fifteen carriages at about 56mph; in other words, from London to Birmingham in two hours. The Committee recommended ordering ten engines.

The General Locomotive Committee considered this report at its monthly meeting on 11th June, and looked at the bids from four manufacturers:

Sharp Bros:	£3,050 each
E. B. Wilson & Co:	£2,580 each
R. Stephenson & Co:	£3,100 each
Wm Fairbairn & Sons:	£2,940 each

The GLC agreed with the S Div suggestion that small engines be sold in part exchange for the large ones as they were delivered.

Hardman Earle (N Div) then moved that the new passenger engines about to be ordered should be limited to the weight of those ordered from Sharp on 6th February - the second batch of Bloomers. On a vote, the GLC was split: four for, four against. As chairman, Moorsom used his casting vote in favour of McConnell's patent design. It was therefore resolved that Fairbairn's tender be accepted on condition that two engines would be delivered by 25th September on penalty of £1,000 and that Fairbairn take away "at least six of the least serviceable locomotives *as they stand* on satisfactory terms."

Fairbairn eventually agreed to take ten old engines, five of them 12in cylinder 2-2-2 tanks, at £450 each in part payment for the new express engines. "Were it not for the great interest we take in the success of this new engine we should scarcely have felt justified in making this offer" Fairbairn wrote. The contract was agreed on 22nd June. At the time it was hoped to dispose of the other old engines by the same semi-barter system, but this was the only contract of its kind.

On 28th June E. B. Wilson & Co of the Railway Foundry, Leeds, wrote offering to make two engines in the time specified and repeating their price of £2,580 each. This was accepted by the GLC on 9th July.

The new design was an enlarged version of the Bloomer mounted on an outside frame, but there were many new features. The most curious was the indentation of the underside of the boiler over the cranks to secure a low centre of gravity. This was covered by McConnell's patent 13729 of February 1852, and was simply a repetition of an 1846 patent of W. Stubbs & J. I. Grylls of Llanelly, who had since become bankrupt. The cylinder and valve layout of the Bloomers was retained but the cylinders were enlarged by two inches in bore and stroke and were inclined downwards at about 6° toward the front end; the total wheelbase was the same, but the driving wheel with its bigger diameter was centred two inches farther back. Thanks to the recess, the boiler centre line was three inches lower than on the Bloomers; a normal boiler would have been pitched at 7ft 5in or more above the rails.

The simple inside frame was discarded in favour of an outside frame with bearings on all three axles. Two inside sub-frame members between firebox and smokebox lay alongside and parallel with the piston rods and held additional smaller bearings on the driving axle. The sub-frame thus absorbed the reaction forces developed between cylinder block and crank axle. Support for the cylinders, smokebox, boiler and firebox was by three forged brackets bolted to the outside frame on each side; the weighshaft supporting the Stephenson link motion was carried by downward lugs from the inside sub-frame.

The firebox was huge, with a grate area 30% bigger than that of the first Bloomers. There were two fireholes, a longitudinal midfeather down to 1ft 2in above the grate and a long combustion chamber which shortened the tubes to 7ft; there were more than 300 of these. The boiler pressure was 120 lb/sq in, not 150 as usually claimed. Although crosshead pumps are shown on drawings prepared before the first engines were

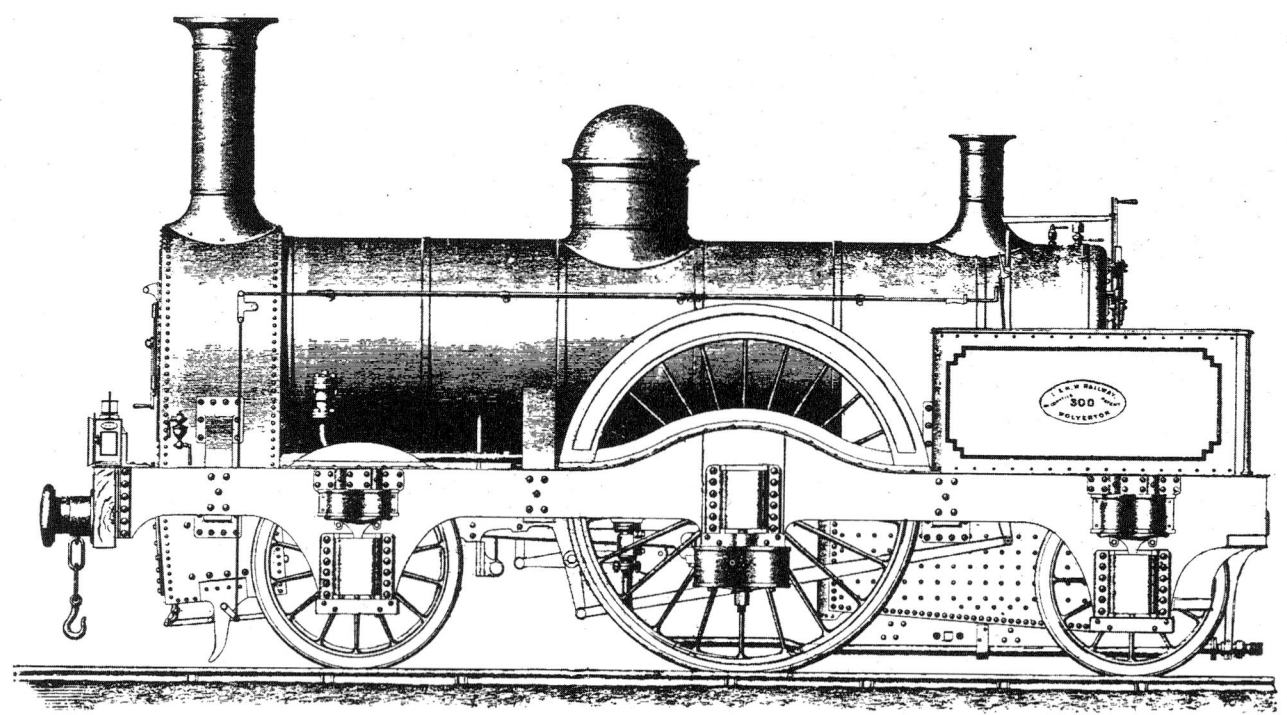

Fig. 78   McConnell's Patent express engines built by E.B. Wilson & Co and Wm Fairbairn & Sons, 1852-4; 297/8 and 300-9.

Fig. 79   Patent class 300 in Fairbairn's works, 1852.

completed, as built each was equipped with a donkey engine and feed pumps on the footplate. Various other innovations - McConnell's patent wrought-iron pistons, his patent "surcharger" or smokebox steam-dryer, his patent tubular carrying axles, hollow stays with valves to admit air to the front of the firebox and Coleman's rubber springs and buffers - justified D. K. Clark's description: "a bundle of novelties".

The engines were widely publicised in the press, and a great future was predicted. "*There need be no more top-heavy engines made* and those that are can be readily altered" the *Railway Journal* exulted and even the *Illustrated London News* printed an engraving of the first one standing in Fairbairn's workshop and a description of this "important step in progress". The claim that the engines would be able to run express trains from London to Birmingham in two hours was made over and over again, even an article in the *Practical Mechanic's Journal* about Coleman's india-rubber springs included: "as made for the large express locomotives which Mr McConnell intends to run in two hours..." The *Artizan* went further: the tenders would carry 3,000 gallons of water and two tons of coke so that the run to Birmingham would be non-stop. When the first two engines appeared, the *Illustrated Magazine of Art* enthused about the "excellence and novelty of the design as well as the beauty and finish of the workmanship" of these "new magnificent express engines".

The design of the Patents has worried commentators on McConnell. From the time of Stretton it has often been claimed for McConnell that he was an advocate of a high centre of gravity in locomotives; he did not claim this himself and in fact was concerned to achieve a low centre of gravity until well after this period. Ahrons wrote in 1925: "The arrangement of outside framing and cylinder attachment was so completely at variance with McConnell's prior and subsequent practice in which simple inside plate frames were always the feature, that one can only conceive that he was forced to this design by some definite instruction in regard to the height of the boiler." Likewise P. C. Dewhurst, who described the design as "decidedly freaky" and wrote in 1950: "It appears inexplicable why McConnell, whose machinery and running-gear designing was usually so straightforward, came to produce this potentially troublesome example."

These difficulties vanish when it is realised that the straightforward designs were not his. The Bloomer was simply the Bury single enlarged under Beyer's direction, with only minimal involvement by McConnell in firebox alterations. When McConnell was given his head, and time to prepare his own designs, he tended towards complication and strove for a low centre of gravity, as in 'Mac's Mangle' and the Patent class.

The Fairbairn engines were allotted numbers from 300 upwards by jumping ahead from 296 which was the last engine then on order; large oval numberplates were fitted by the maker, with the words McCONNELL'S PATENT in addition to the usual information. The two Wilson engines were then given 297/8 in the gap (299 was a vacant number until 1859). The first two, one Wilson and one Fairbairn, arrived at Wolverton on the same day, 8th November 1852. Fairbairn's deliveries were slow, partly because of a long engineers' strike in 1851/2 and another in 1853, so that the last of their ten engines did not arrive until the end of 1854.

Dimensions

Cylinders (2 inside)	18" x 24"
Boiler	
Diameter (external)	4' 3¼"
Length of barrel	11' 9"
Pitch	6' 10"
Heating surface	
Tubes (303, 1¾" dia, 7' 0" long)	971.74 sq ft
Firebox	260.00 sq ft
Total	1,231.74 sq ft
Grate area	23.5 sq ft
Boiler pressure	120 lb/sq in
Diameter of wheels	
Leading	4' 6"
Driving	7' 6"
Trailing	4' 0"
Wheelbase	8' 6" + 8' 4" = 16' 10"
Weight (298, January 1853)	
On leading wheels	11 tons 12.7 cwt
On driving wheels	12 tons 3.9 cwt
On trailing wheels	7 tons 7.8 cwt
Total	31 tons 4.4 cwt

The weight of 300 was given in March 1853 as engine: 31 tons, tender: 17 tons.

The first Wilson engine was tried out on 11th December 1852 and is said to have run to Euston at 60mph. It was claimed that sufficient steam could be raised to move the engine within 45 minutes of lighting the fire. From 4th to 8th March 1853, as part of the Woods and Marshall trials, 300 hauled trains of 17 and 34 carriages between Camden and Birmingham; it ran to time with the smaller load at the prescribed speed of 38mph but lost 8 minutes with the longer train, averaging 36.39mph with a maximum of 54mph.

D. K. Clark was unimpressed; in the same month he spoke about the new engines before the Institution of Civil Engineers and said the loss of heat by the chimney "has been observed to be prodigious".

In January 1854 some engines were stuck in snowdrifts and coal was taken from nearby wagons to keep the fires going. This seems to have shown that the large firebox could burn ordinary coal effectively and in March McConnell said two of Fairbairn's engines were using coal instead of coke without nuisance or inconvenience; in May he reported using coal alone in five engines. Edward Woods and William P. Marshall were again summoned to investigate and in June and July they tested Patent class 303 on six consecutive days from Rugby to Camden and back from Euston to Rugby; trains worked were the 12.55pm Up express and the 5.45pm Down stopping train. Then for three days 303 took the heavy 6.30am Down and the 11.46am Up. Fuel used was alternately Pease's West coke and Hawkesbury Main coal from Coventry ("hard, clean and free from clinker"); on one day the coal used was "cobbles". The engine had no difficulty maintaining its pressure and speed, and because of the much greater "care and labour on the part of the fireman" produced little smoke. The fire was kept thin, 4in to 6in thick, and each grate was fed with a small quantity of coal alternately once every two or three

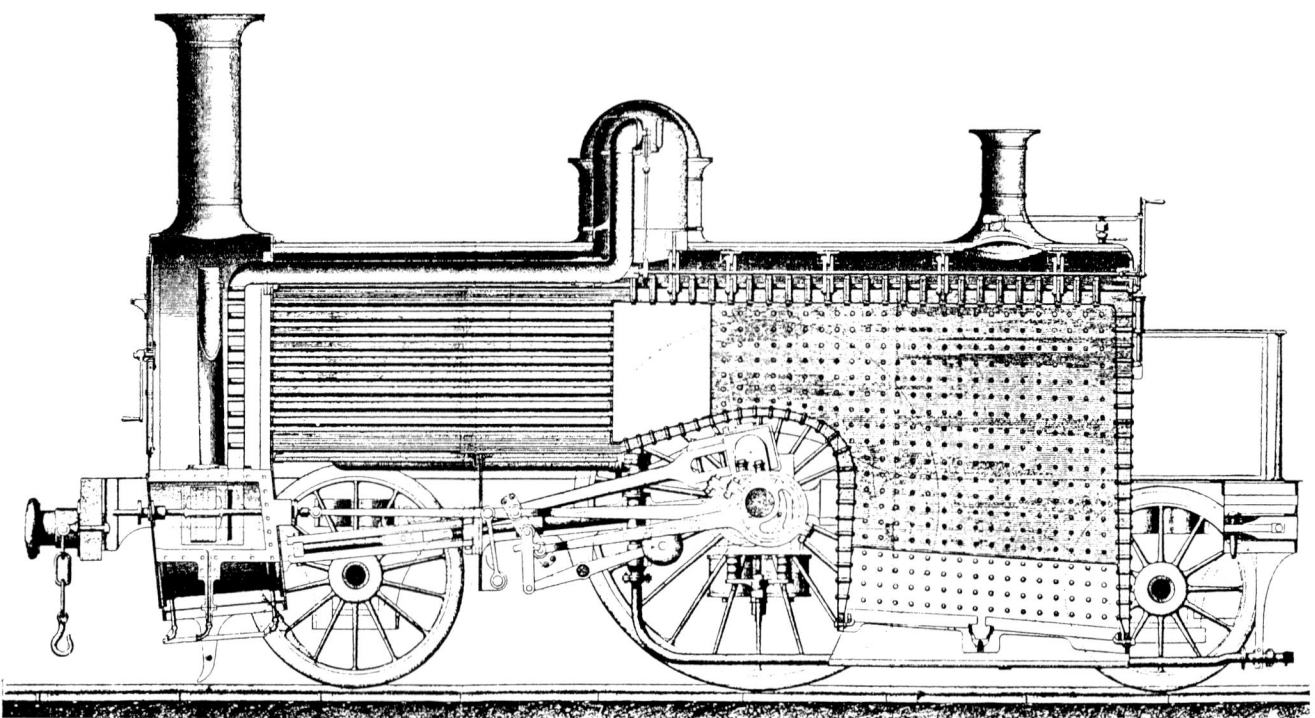

Fig. 80   Patent class, longitudinal section. Boiler recessed to clear cranks, large firebox with central midfeather and combustion chamber, steam drier in smokebox, hollow leading and trailing axles, rubber springs.

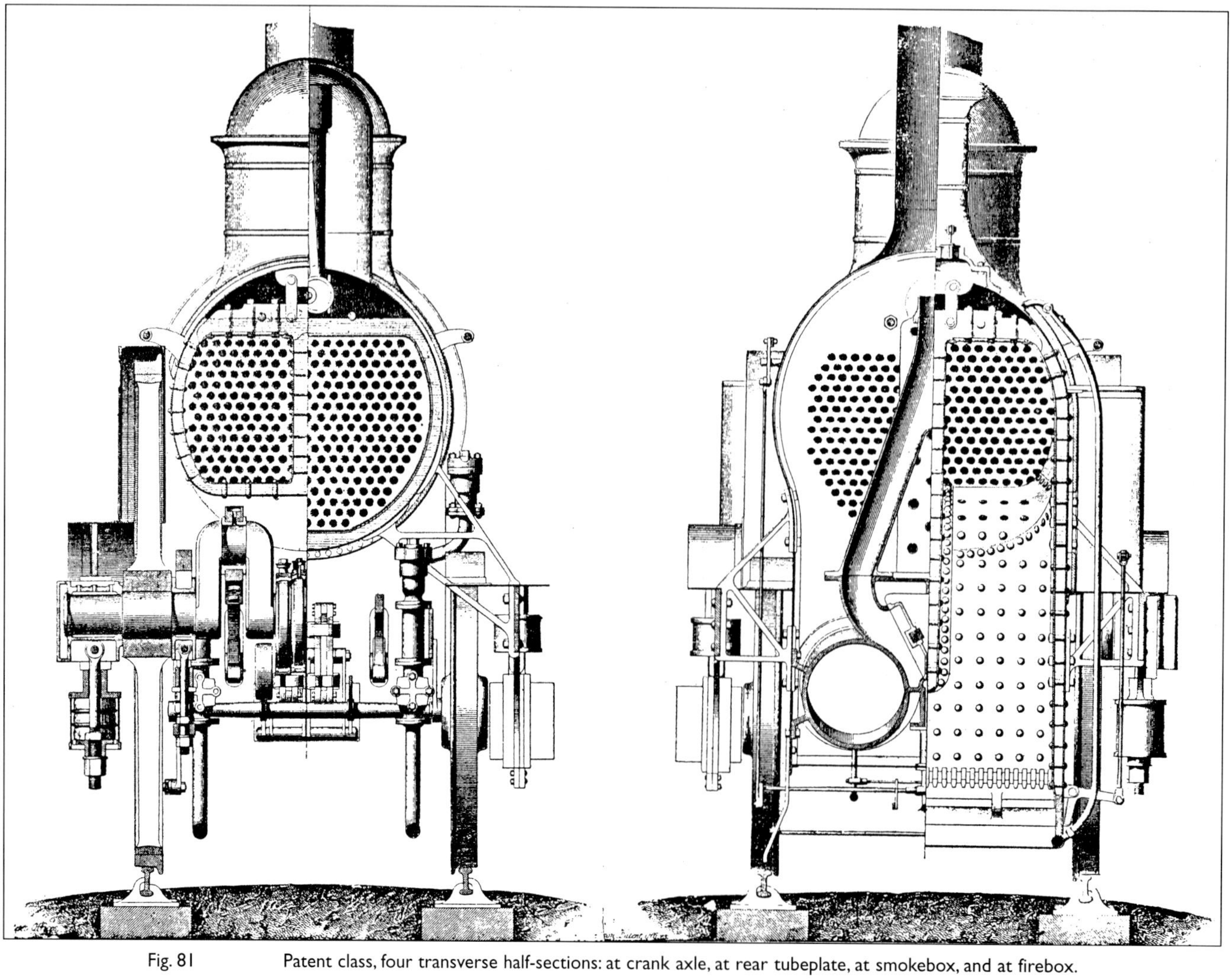

Fig. 81   Patent class, four transverse half-sections: at crank axle, at rear tubeplate, at smokebox, and at firebox.

miles instead of once every ten or twelve miles with coke. Woods and Marshall reported on 14th July that the combustion chamber "combined with the double firebox renders McConnell's engine a more perfect smoke consumer than the common engine."

All the same, only 5.83 lb of water were evaporated per 1 lb of coal, and the temperature of the waste gases in the smokebox sometimes reached 1,100°F.

On 22nd December 1857 two American observers took a footplate trip from Euston to Bletchley on Patent class 43 (formerly 304), fresh out of the works. They described the two fireholes, which had been modified and no longer had normal doors; instead each led directly into a sheet iron box protruding 3ft into the firebox. The bottom of the box was hinged at the back and could be raised by a chain, opening directly over the fire. This "horizontal trap or scuttle door" and the far end of the box were pierced by numerous air holes. The original air passages into the combustion chamber via hollow stays had been blocked up (this had also been observed as early as February 1853 on a coke-burning engine; they may have been blocked by the footplatemen). There were no firebricks in the firebox. After the fires had got going, all subsequent firing was into each firehole alternately, so that unburnt gas from one grate was ignited in the combustion chamber by flames from the other grate.

The coal in the tender was described as "clean externally, compact lumps, little slack but very bituminous" which burned with a deep flame. Whenever the engine stopped the blower was turned on. A lot of smoke was given out when the engine was standing unless care was taken.

The observers, Alexander Lyman Holley and Zerah Colburn (later editor of *The Engineer* and founder of *Engineering*) concluded that the combustion was very good, but the engine did not steam as well as expected. They criticised the short tubes "by which, no doubt, much fuel is wasted" and this was confirmed by the great heat of the smokebox.

Not much more is heard about the Patent class after this.

They did not live up to their promise. As early as May 1853 the *Artizan* reported a rumour that "they do not fulfil their proposed end." After, as G. A. Sekon wrote "being introduced with a vast amount of publicity, they became a nine days' wonder, then sank into quiescent mediocrity, and after a brief career, were seen no more."

In the 1856 renumbering 297/8 and 300-9 became 37-48, taking the numbers of old Bury 2-2-0 engines withdrawn or themselves renumbered lower in the list. In May 1860 they were still regarded as a "standard class" of passenger engines on the S Div. A photograph of 47 taken in 1861/2 shows that by then only the leading axle retained the rubber springs; the driving and trailing wheels had been fitted with leaf springs above the footplating.

No 42 was rebuilt at Wolverton in 1860 with a Krupp cast-steel crank axle and 16in x 20in cylinders. Despite their very short working life Ramsbottom swiftly consigned the other eleven engines to the duplicate list in 1862/3, beyond which their precise fate is unknown. All were probably scrapped in 1863/4.

It has been claimed that one of them was the engine 1165 sent to the Cromford & High Peak line (of all places) in August 1864; this seems very unlikely, as does another story that two of them were sold in that year. These must be mistaken attributions of numbers in the rapidly changing duplicate list at that period.

The rebuilt engine, 642, was itself put into the duplicate list in 1864 as 1170. It was working from Camden in 1869 when it was reported on 26th July as one of the engines to be fitted with the guard's whistle communication system. In 1873 it was transferred to Crewe steelworks, where it was set up as a stationary engine to drive the merchant mill which rolled bar iron in the spring-making shop. Its fuel bunker was part of an old S Div tender with a flared top. Latterly the boiler was fitted with Webb safety valves and dome and there was a locking wheel on its Wolverton smokebox door. It was there until 1926, when it was replaced by a Coal Engine boiler.

Fig. 82 Patent class 47, formerly 308. From an ambrotype taken at an unidentified location in 1861/2. The original rubber springs have been retained on the leading axle but replaced by steel springs on the driving and trailing axles. Other changes include the addition of a blower for coal burning, weatherboard and large guard's whistle.
(D.E. Jones collection)

Euston – Bletchley, 22nd December 1857
from notes by Zerah Colburn and A. L. Holley

Train: 17 carriages, about 102 tons
Engine: Patent class 43, with front-end assistance from Euston to Camden

Time	*Boiler pressure* lb/sq inch		*Exhaust*
3.30pm	105	Depart from Euston.	A little discolouration.
3.32	85		” ” ”
3.38	105		A little more discolouration, not amounting to offensive smoke.
3.40	110		
3.42	115	Blowing off.	Slowly diminishing discolouration.
3.43		Fired right door.	Some smoke after one minute, for one minute only.
3.45	115	Blowing off. Fired left door.	No increase of smoke.
3.48	115	Fired right door.	No more smoke than before.
3.50	105		
3.53		Raked left fire.	Slight increase of smoke after door was closed.
3.54	110	Cut-off 2/3 stroke.	
3.56	95		Discolouration same as before.
3.57		Raked right fire.	No more smoke than before.
3.59	90		
4.03	85		
4.04		Fired left door.	Same general result.
4.05	80		
4.07	85	Slips very considerably in Watford tunnel.	
4.09		Raked left fire and fired.	Few sparks.
4.11	80	Raked right fire.	Steam and smoke the same.
4.15	75		
4.16			Smoke scarcely perceptible, but at no previous time unless for a few moments was there smoke enough to constitute an objection.
4.16	75	Fired right door.	No more smoke than before, steam pressure did not fall.
4.17	85		
4.19	80		
4.23	80	Fired left door, steam fell to 77.	
4.24	75		
4.26	73		
4.30	70		
<u>4.31</u>	68	Arrived at Tring. Shut off, blower on. Fired both boxes, jet on slightly, raked fire underneath.	More smoke.
4.36	95	Started, slipped considerably.	
4.37	80		
4.40	85	Fired right door.	
4.42	90		
4.44	85		
4.45	80		
<u>4.50</u>		Arrived at Leighton. Shut off, blower on. Fired both sides, turned steam into tender.	Smoke about same.
4.55	120	Started.	
4.58	100		
5.02	95	Smokebox quite hot.	
5.04	90		
5.06	90	Fired left door.	
<u>5.07</u>		Arrived at Bletchley. Shut off.	

Summary: Patent class 2-2-2s built by E. B. Wilson and Wm Fairbairn & Sons, 1852-4

No.	Maker	Date	Reno'd 4/56	Reno'd 4/62	Rebt	Reno'd	Withdrawn
297	Wilson	8/11/1852	37	-		1187(5/62)	by 2/64
298	Wilson	12/1852	38	-		1189(5/62)	by 11/67
300	Fairbairn	8/11/1852	39	639		1164(8/63)	by 2/65
301	Fairbairn	2/1853	40	640		1165(8/63)	by 8/64
302	Fairbairn	6/1853	41	641		1166(9/63)	by 5/64
303	Fairbairn	17/9/1853	42	642	/60	1170(8/64), 1923(12/71)	To Loco Machinery, Crewe, 10/73
304	Fairbairn	22/12/1853	43	643		1167(9/63)	by 8/64
305	Fairbairn	4/3/1854	44	644		1168(9/63)	by 8/64
306	Fairbairn	3/5/1854	45	645		1169(9/63)	by 8/64
307	Fairbairn	5/6/1854	46	646		1170(9/63)	by 5/64
308	Fairbairn	18/8/1854	47	647		1171(9/63)	by 3/64
309	Fairbairn	30/12/1854	48	648		1199(9/63)	by 8/64

Other McConnell Patent 2-2-2 Designs

1. "Express Locomotive on the LNWR"

Although further applications of his patent boiler had been blocked by the General Locomotive Committee in May 1853 and it had been decided that the next passenger engines were to be a smaller version of the Bloomer type, McConnell persisted. He produced drawings of a quite different and smaller patent-boiler 2-2-2, which were published in William Johnston's *Imperial Cyclopædia of Machinery* in 1855. The accompanying text describes the engine as having been built to run from London to Birmingham in two hours and the drawings consist of longitudinal and cross-sections and end elevations of the locomotive to a scale of ³⁄₄in to 1ft, with larger-scale details. A corniced dome is prominent among other typical S Div features, and each page is headed: "Express Locomotive on the London and North Western Railway, J. E. McConnell, Engineer, Wolverton". With such credentials it is not surprising that these drawings have been taken at face value by writers about LNWR engines.

In fact no such engines were built for the LNWR. The drawings might represent some design which was aborted after the GLC decision, but there is nothing in any of the reports or other records to suggest that engines with these dimensions were ever proposed. The engine depicted is an inside-framed 2-2-2 with 7ft driving wheels and 15in x 21in inside cylinders. Gooch stationary-link motion operates the valves, each in a separate valve chest placed at an angle above and outside each cylinder, quite unlike the arrangement in the Bloomers and Patents. A low centre of gravity is achieved by the cylinders hanging down at the front end, and by a huge recess in the underside of the boiler to clear the cranks, thus allowing the boiler pitch to come down to 6ft 2in. The firebox and combustion chamber layout is similar to that on the Patent class, but the midfeather extends further down to create two entirely separate grates, and the boiler has 410 tubes (or 404 in the text) each of 1¼in outside diameter and 6ft long. As in the Patents there are rubber springs and hollow leading and trailing axles. A curious decorative feature is the arching of the footplating over the driving wheel centre.

2. C F du Nord 164 *Eugénie*

McConnell was a director in the firm of Wm Fairbairn & Sons which may have some bearing on their building a patent 2-2-2, rather like that in the *Imperial Cyclopædia of Machinery*, for the Paris Exhibition of 1855. This engine also had inside frames; the driving wheels were 7ft 1in, the cylinders were 15in x 22in and there were no fewer than 414 tubes of 1¼in outside diameter in the recessed boiler. The typical S Div tender was on four wheels with rubber springs. Engine and tender were finished in an elaborately lined livery like that of the Bloomers and Patents with a McConnell brass dome and the name *Eugénie* (after the French Empress) in large letters on the splasher. Before going to France it ran trials with "express and mixed trains on the Southern Division" according to a puff in the *Illustrated London News* "and has amply realised all expectations..." The fuel used was coke. These trials are nowhere mentioned in surviving LNWR records. *Eugénie* was bought by the Chemin de Fer du Nord and numbered 164, but the complications of the firebox led to frequent and expensive repairs and it was withdrawn in 1866.

The earliest-known photograph of a McConnell engine is in the National Railway Museum collection and is of *Eugénie* (Fig 145). This photograph was the basis of a wood-engraving in the *Illustrated London News* of 30th June 1855 and shows the engine on steam trials before final painting.

At least two other photographs of *Eugénie* have been published. A small reproduction of the earlier, taken somewhere in France and showing the elaborate S Div livery and NORD No 164 on the tender, appeared in *La Machine Locomotive en France* by Jacques Payen (Lyon, 1988); the later photograph - together with an outline drawing - was printed in *The Locomotive* of May 1930.

Class A

Wolverton 0-4-2 Goods Engines, 1853-5
Nos 28, 124. 148, 164, 192-195, 231, 236

New lines totalling some 87 miles were opened in 1850 and more were expected soon; connections were anticipated shortly with the GWR at Oxford and Leamington, and with the North London line to the docks. An unpredictable amount of extra traffic would be generated by the Great Exhibition and the S Div Locomotive Department could expect to be hard pressed in 1851. Whereas in March 1850 there had been 31 engines in store, at the end of that year there there were only five, and McConnell was told to get all his engines into a state of readiness "and if possible to have on 1st May 1851 every engine on the list in working order."

On 12th December 1850 he reported "a large amount of material, consisting of parts of engines" in the stores at Wolverton. "By an additional expenditure of about £4,859 for further materials eight luggage engines of the class of 117 and two of the class of No 33 may be constructed." He was authorised to proceed with these at Wolverton, as they would probably be required "at no distant period".

The building of the first of the Wolverton/Bury engines began in March 1851, and two more were in hand by August. Eight of them were intended to be numbered 192 to 199 to fill the gap still empty up to 200 awarded to *London*, but in the event four took lower numbers left vacant by engines removed from stock, three of them having been destroyed in accidents. Two others took the numbers of Stephenson long-boiler 0-6-0s transferred to the NE Div in 1849. It might be inferred from this that these two engines, 231/6, were those built to the type of No 33, but available records treat all ten as being identical. The cost was £2,877 per engine.

The first one was delivered between 7th January and 18th April 1853 and all were on the line by 5th June 1855. The dates of delivery are not precisely known and some of those given in the summary are estimated. S.S. Scott compiled a list in the 1870s, either from observation of the actual engines or from a source in Crewe, which gives the years of building. These confirm the years given here except for 236 which he dates as 1852. Perhaps this date was on the engine, but it did not enter traffic until January 1853 at the earliest. James Bull gives building dates which are either partly wrong (the previous 164 was not scrapped until 1855) or imply some renumbering of which nothing is known:

    First lot: 28, 124/48/64, 236   built 1852/3.
    Second lot: 192-5, 231   built 1853/4.

Crewe recorded the building dates of 194/5 as October and December 1854, but their date for 148 (September 1855) must be an error.

The engines were mounted on bar-frames, which may have been acquired from Bury, Curtis & Kennedy. In April 1851 Kennedy had written offering to sell the patterns for the engines built for the LNWR and McConnell was authorised to attend the sale at Clarence Foundry to purchase what he required. Perhaps he was also able to secure ten sets of bar-frame parts at a knock-down price.

The inside cylinders hung low down at the front, with the piston rods working beneath the leading axle as in the original Bury goods engines but, unlike them, the new class was built with outside footplating and closed splashers. The firebox had a raised top and McConnell's cornished brass dome was mounted on the middle of the boiler barrel. They were known as Class A in the series given to engines built at Wolverton.

Dimensions

Cylinders (2 inside)	16" x 24"
Boiler	
Diameter	4' 1"
Length of barrel	11' 8"
Length of firebox casing	4' 6"
Heating surface	
Tubes (178, $2\frac{1}{8}$" dia, 11' $11\frac{1}{2}$" long)	1,181 sq ft
Firebox	89 sq ft
Total	1,270 sq ft
Grate area	14.75 sq ft
Diameter of wheels	
Coupled	5' 0"
Trailing	3' 4"
Wheelbase (1853)	8' 0" + 6' 9" = 14' 9"

(given in Crewe records of 1867 and 1877 as
8' 0" + 6' $7\frac{3}{4}$" = 14' $7\frac{3}{4}$")

Very little is known of these engines in service, although they lasted into the late 1870s.

In a fuel emergency caused by snowstorms, 193 was sent to the York, Newcastle & Berwick Railway in January or early February 1854 to work trains of coke from Durham for the S Div.

The rather unclear photograph of 236 (Fig 83) was taken at an unidentified location, possibly Vauxhall shed, Birmingham.

All were placed on the duplicate list in 1864, but in 1867 they were considered worth fitting with new flush-top boilers. The drawing of the proposed arrangement was dated 13th August and shows a barrel made of four rings, rather than Ramsbottom's normal three; the dome is on the second ring. The barrel was 11ft 8in long and 4ft 2in diameter. Confirmation of these details was found in Ramsbottom's letter book which contained a list of boiler plates ordered for the first rebuilds on 20th December 1867.

Nine engines were reboilered and were reinstated in the capital list at the end of 1871 but 1860 (ex-28) was never rebuilt and was scrapped in 1873.

1167 (ex-124) was shedded at Bangor in the early 1870s, and an unidentified member of the class was photographed on a ballast train at Northampton c1878, with a Webb chimney, open Ramsbottom safety valves and a Crewe-pattern weatherboard.

Unusually, 1171 (ex-195) was sold directly from the capital list to William Moss of Stafford for £150, in

Fig. 83   Class A 236, built at Wolverton 1853; photographed 1856-62. The tender has equalising levers between the middle and rear springs.
(W.E. Boyd collection)

Fig. 84   Class A 231, built at Wolverton 1853.

Fig. 85 Unidentified Class A 0-4-2 built at Wolverton 1853-5. After rebuilding at Crewe with Ramsbottom boiler and weatherboard and later given a Webb chimney. At Northampton Castle station, late 1870s. *(L. Hanson collection)*

exchange for his old engine, a Bury 0-4-2 (formerly 206, see p143) which had been badly damaged in a collision on the LNWR between Northampton and Billing Road on 18th October 1877. This exchange was made in order to avoid the expense to the LNWR of repairing Moss's old engine. It seems likely that 1171 was sold to Moss under cut-up number 2000.

Annual totals:

	capital	duplicate
to 30/11/1863:	10	-
30/11/1864	-	10
to 30/11/1871:	-	10
30/11/1872:	9	1
30/11/1873:	9	-
to 30/11/1876:	9	-
30/11/1877:	8	-
30/11/1878:	1	2
30/11/1879:	-	1
30/11/1880:	-	-

Summary: Class A 0-4-2s built at Wolverton Works, 1853-5

No.	Built	Reno'd 4/62	Rebt.	Renumbered		Withdrawn
236	a /1853	836	b /68	1162(3/64), 1169(12/71), 1834(11/78)		Scr 7/11/79
192	6/1853	792	/69	1218(2/64), 1173(12/71)	c/u 1878	Scr 24/8/78
231	7/1853	831	a /69	1220(2/64), 1175(12/71)	c/u 1868	Scr 13/7/78
193	12/1853	793	a /69	1219(2/64), 1174(12/71)	c/u 1841	Scr 17/12/78
194	10/1854	794	4/71	1153(3/64), 1165(12/71), 1832(11/78)		Scr 24/3/80
195	12/1854	795	b /68	1161(3/64), 1171(12/71)	c/u 2000?	Sold 12/77 Wm Moss, £150 plus his old engine.
28	5/1855	628	—	1191(2/64), 1860(12/71)		Scr 4/3/73
164	5/1855	764	b /68	1217(2/64), 1172(12/71)	c/u 1903	Scr 8/5/78
124	a /1855	724	b /68	1159(2/64), 1167(12/71)	c/u 1985	Scr 6/7/77
148	a /1855	748	a /69	1187(2/64), 1170(12/71)	c/u 1886	Scr 4/10/78

The SMALL BLOOMERS

1. Hawthorn and Vulcan Foundry 2-2-2 Passenger Engines, 1854 Nos 310-320

The S Div Locomotive Committee proposed to order ten passenger engines with McConnell's patent boiler and 7ft driving wheels and on 25th January 1853 tenders were accepted from the Vulcan Foundry for four at £2,850 each and from R. & W. Hawthorn for six at £3,200. These orders were suspended by the General Locomotive Committee and after Woods and Marshall's report the design was changed to a reduced version of the Bloomer, very like the Bury, Curtis & Kennedy 'Low-dome' prototype; in fact McConnell referred to the design on 3rd May 1853 as "Bury's Improved".

The new engine was slightly shorter than the Bury 'Low-dome', with a wheelbase reduced by six inches, but the layout of the cylinders was exactly the same, with V-shaped steam chest above and between, the cylinder centre line inclined slightly down to the front and the valve rods inclined upwards. The frame plates were $7/8$in thick, $1/8$ in less than on the Bloomer and the driving wheels were 6ft 6in diameter, half way between the Bury at 6ft and the Bloomer at 7ft; the length of stroke, 21in, likewise fell between the two. The smaller driving wheels allowed the boiler to be centred 4in lower than on the Bloomer and the firebox was flush with the boiler top. Dished smokebox doors and spring buffers were fitted from new and the carrying springs were Coleman's india-rubber pads, located under the driving axleboxes and over the carrying and tender axles. They had the same copper-capped chimneys, corniced brass domes and brass splashers as the Bloomers.

The taller chimney on a lower boiler emphasised the reduced bulk of the engine and it is not surprising that the class became known officially as the Small Bloomers.

In May fresh negotiations began with Vulcan and Hawthorn for these smaller and more straightforward engines and, after some weeks of haggling, lower prices and new contracts were agreed on 10th June 1853. Vulcan Foundry were to supply two engines in January 1854 and two in February for £2,700 each. R. & W. Hawthorn reduced their price to £2,743, which meant that seven engines could be had for the previous cost of six, and their order was accordingly increased to seven: one to be delivered in January 1854, three in February and three in March.

Vulcan's four were working numbers 128-31 (engines) and 132-5 (tenders); in the firm's new 'locomotives-only' works list they were given 'rotation numbers' 358-61. Hawthorn's seven were works numbers 842-7 and 865.

As usual, deliveries were late and the first engines did not arrive until April 1854, but all eleven were on the line by the end of July.

They were given S Div numbers 310-20, but in April 1856 were all renumbered to fill gaps left by the simultaneous renumbering, or withdrawal, of Bury 2-2-0 passenger engines, 13/4/5/7/23-7/9/30.

Dimensions

Cylinders (2 inside)	16" x 21"
Boiler	
Diameter	4' 0$7/8$"
Length of barrel	10' 3"
Pitch	6' 9"
Length of firebox casing	5' 5"
Heating surface	
Tubes (205, 2" dia, 10' 6" long)	1,128 sq ft
Firebox	102 sq ft
Total	1,230 sq ft
Grate area	17.4 sq ft
Boiler pressure	120 lb/sq in
Diameter of wheels	
Leading	4' 0"
Driving	6' 6"
Trailing	4' 0"
Length	
Engine, over bufferbeam	22' 1$1/2$"
Tender, excluding buffers	18' 5"
Wheelbase	
Engine	7' 9" + 7' 9" = 15' 6"
Tender	5' 6" + 5' 6" = 11' 0"
Weight	
On leading wheels	8 tons 13 cwt
On driving wheels	10 tons 0 cwt
On trailing wheels	5 tons 0 cwt
Total	23 tons 13 cwt
Tender (6 wheel) capacity	coke 105 cu ft
	water 1,500 gal

2. Wolverton 2-2-2 Passenger Engines, 1857-61 Classes C, E and K
Nos 2, 3, 7, 21, 66, 103, 117, 140, 165, 168, 180, 189, 238, 240, 317, 377-381

As a result of the explosion of long-boiler goods engine 140 in December 1856, McConnell was given authority to lay down ten engines (in addition to the sixteen he was already building at Wolverton) to replace the long-boilers, which he said "might be expected to fail almost simultaneously." These ten were Small Bloomers, and were known as Class C; they were turned out from about March 1857 to the end of 1858 at a cost which McConnell estimated in November 1859 to have been £1,750 each.

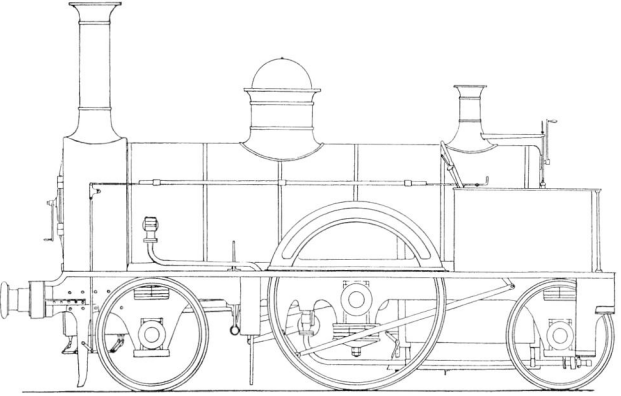

Fig. 86   Small Bloomer as built by Vulcan Foundry, 1854.

Fig. 87
Small Bloomer Class C 103, the first of the type built at Wolverton Works, May 1857. Rubber springs on tender and on the engine's carrying axles, steel springs on driving axle, coal fired. Photograph taken 1857-62.

Fig. 88
Small Bloomer Class K 381, the last of the type built at Wolverton, November 1861. Steel springs throughout; painted in the short-lived dark red livery. At Wolverton, December 1861.
(Stephenson Locomotive Society)

Fig. 89
Small Bloomer Class E 603 (ex-3) built at Wolverton, October 1859. Painted in N Div livery, green with black lines, but before other Ramsbottom alterations: there is no front handrail and S Div lamp irons and equalising levers are still fitted. In 1862 or soon after.
(W.E. Boyd collection)

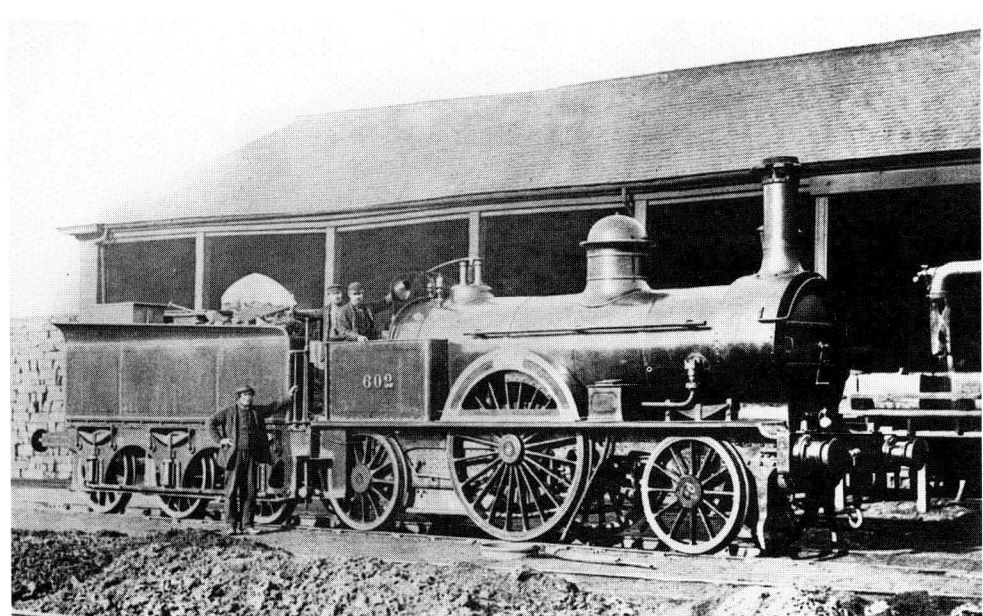

Fig 90
Small Bloomer Class C 602 (ex-2) built at Wolverton, July 1858. At Rugby coaling shed c1868. Ramsbottom changes include new safety valves, chimney cap, displacement lubricator, leading springs and front handrail. Equalising levers removed from tender. The brasswork and the old S Div numberplate on the splasher have been stripped of their paint and polished.
(C.R. Clinker collection)

They were similar to the Vulcan and Hawthorn engines except that only the springs on the leading and trailing axles were rubber whereas the crank axle had underhung laminated plate springs. A lock-up safety valve was fitted behind the dome, and the sand container, which in the earlier engines had been tucked in below, was now a prominent square box on the running plate. The weight of the engine was 25 tons 9 cwt.

Ten more were built at Wolverton in 1859-61; five in 1859/60 were known as Class E and another five ordered on 10th January 1861 as "engines of the 2nd class weighing about 24 tons" were known as Class K. The inner firebox was slightly shorter in Class K engines, giving a grate area of 17 sq ft, but other significant differences (if any) between the three groups are not known. The letters seem to have been used at Wolverton like those used for orders at Crewe Works.

Externally Class E were like Class C in that they had plain splashers with one large segmental opening; a brass numberplate was fixed at the top of each splasher like a wide keystone, about 17in long by 4in deep. The engine number, in elaborate numerals, was in the middle, with "London & North Western Railway" along the top edge and "Manufactured at the Engine Works, Wolverton" along the bottom. To the left and right of the number scrolled ribbons were engraved, containing the month and year of building. Class K had shorter chimneys, about 4ft 6in tall instead of the 4ft 10in of the earlier batches, giving the engines a bulkier appearance, and had the more elaborate three-aperture splashers and small oval numberplates on the footplate side sheets.

Eight Class C engines were given numbers made available by withdrawals, but two were numbered 238 and 240, left blank at the 1856 renumbering scheme and last used on engines transferred to the NE Div in 1849. The first four of Class E were also given replacement numbers. At the end of 1859 the S Div number list was at last completely filled from 1 to 316, so the capital and replacement system of numbering as long practised at Crewe could begin. The last of Class E was given a new number 317, following the South Staffordshire engines at the end of the list. The five Class K engines of 1861 were also given new numbers, 377-81.

Soon after Ramsbottom took over in 1862 Crewe's standard fittings began to appear: chimneys, safety valves, lubricators, bigger weatherboards. A handrail was added around the top of the smokebox front and remaining rubber springs on engines were replaced by steel plate springs, those on the leading axle being mounted above the footplate. In 1865 a programme of rebuilding was begun. The new boiler was the same size as the original, 10ft 3in long and 4ft 0½in diameter; the weight of the rebuilt engines was:

On leading wheels	9 tons	8 cwt
On driving wheels	11 tons	10 cwt
On trailing wheels	6 tons	6 cwt
Total	27 tons	4 cwt

Three, 623/5 and 615, were rebuilt at Wolverton during 1865/6; 613 and 624 were scrapped at the end of 1866 but the other 26 were rebuilt at Crewe between 1868 and 1876. 977 and 603 were rebuilt for a second time in 1877 and 1878. Rebuilds from 1873 were fitted with cabs, and from 1874 the last five were given steel boilers.

On 18th April 1872 names were allotted to the 29 engines then remaining; all the names had been used before on the N Div, mostly on Old Crewe type goods engines.

Work

These 31 Small Bloomers worked the secondary fast trains on the main line, and were much used on branch lines, where some were coupled to 1,000 gallon four-wheeled tenders. A Small Bloomer identified only as "one of the regular passenger engines" was derailed at Watford on 22nd March 1858. The following week, on the night of 2nd April 1858, 240 was working a mail train through Blisworth when it was badly damaged by colliding with a goods train.

The first LNWR engine to run all the way from Euston to Manchester was 980 on 5th January 1863 with Thomas

Fig 91
Small Bloomer 630 (ex-320 and 30) built by Hawthorn in July 1854. After rebuilding at Crewe with new boiler and standard fittings. Photographed c1870 just north of Leamington (Milverton) station; the bridge has since been removed.
(A.G. Dunbar collection)

Wheatley, Ramsbottom's Outdoor Assistant at Wolverton, on the footplate.

A partial return of July 1869 has two of the class at Northampton and six at Rugby, including two of the Crewe rebuilds.

Something of their shed allocation and work was recorded by observers in 1870-85:

602	Camden.
603	Rugby; Nuneaton; Bletchley.
607	Bletchley.
614	Rugby; Bletchley, on Euston-Bletchley slow trains c1877.
615	Rugby; Nuneaton, on Ashby and Leicester branches c1878.
617	Rugby.
621	Stafford, on Trent Valley slow trains c1879; Bletchley.
623	Rugby.
625	Rugby.
626	Rugby.
629	Rugby, on Rugby-Birmingham slow trains.
630	Rugby; on Leamington branch c1870.
703	Rugby.
717	Rugby; Nuneaton, on Leicester and Ashby branches; Bletchley.
740	Rugby, on Rugby-Birmingham slow trains; Northampton /79.
765	Rugby, on Rugby-Birmingham slow trains; Monument Lane /81; Burton /82.
768	Rugby, on Rugby-Birmingham slow trains.
780	Rugby; then on Euston-Bletchley slow trains.
789	Rugby; then on Euston-Bletchley slow trains; Northampton /79.
838	On Euston-Bletchley slow trains; Derby /78, on Derby-Lichfield-Birmingham trains.
840	Stafford.
917	Rugby; Bletchley.
977	Rugby.
978	Rugby; Northampton; Nuneaton /82, on Leicester and Ashby branches.
979	Rugby.
980	Rugby.
981	Rugby; Derby /81, on Derby-Lichfield-Birmingham trains.

Some worked on the Peterborough, Oxford-Bletchley and Bletchley-Cambridge lines; "several" were shedded at Milverton c1876.

Disposal

After the first two were scrapped in 1866, eleven years went by before scrapping began again in December 1877 and continued gradually until 1887. Those surviving in 1884 were put on the 18xx duplicate list and lost their nameplates. The last to go, S Div 380 built at Wolverton in 1861, was renumbered in the 30xx series of duplicates for a short period before being scrapped in March 1887.

Annual totals:

	capital	duplicate
to 30/11/1866:	31	-
to 30/11/1877:	29	-
30/11/1878:	25	-
30/11/1879:	22	-
30/11/1880:	20	-
30/11/1881:	16	-
30/11/1882:	13	-
30/11/1883:	8	-
30/11/1884:	1	5
30/11/1885:	-	3
30/11/1886:	-	2
30/11/1887:	-	-

Summary: Small Bloomer 2-2-2s, 1854-61

1. Built by The Vulcan Foundry Co and R. & W. Hawthorn, 1854

No.	Maker	Date	Reno'd 4/56	Reno'd 4/62	Name 4/72	Rebt*	Reno'd	Scr.
310	Vulcan	1/6/1854	13	613	—	—	1127(12/66)	12/66
311	Vulcan	12/6/1854	14	614	*Wyre*	10/68		2/79
312	Vulcan	14/7/1854	15	615	*Lune*	/66(W)		2/83
313	Vulcan	31/7/1854	17	617	*Partridge*	5/71		6/83
314	Hawthorn	2/4/1854	23	623	*Medea*	/65(W)		12/77
315	Hawthorn	18/4/1854	24	624	—	—	1196(12/66)	12/66
316	Hawthorn	6/5/1854	25	625	*Mastodon*	/65(W)		7/78
317	Hawthorn	7/6/1854	26	626	*Earl*	1/70		5/79
318	Hawthorn	18/6/1854	27	627	*Bulldog*	8/69		8/81
319	Hawthorn	20/6/1854	29	629	*Swan*	1/74(c)		1/83
320	Hawthorn	23/7/1854	30	630	*Ribble*	10/68		2/82

Vulcan working numbers were 128-31 (engines) and 132-5 (tenders).
Vulcan rotation numbers were 358-61.
Hawthorn works numbers were 842-7/65.

2. Classes C, E and K built at Wolverton Works, 1857-61

No.	Date	Reno'd 4/62	Name 4/72	Rebt*	Reno'd	Scr
103	5/1857	703	*Osprey*	after /69		9/81
21	7/1857	621	*Bela*	11/70		2/82
7	8/1857	607	*Inglewood*	8/68		2/83
140	8/1857	740	*St David*	9/73(c)	1947(11/84)	11/86
238	10/1857	838	*Petrel*	5/70		3/79
240	b /1857	840	*Lonsdale*	5/69		3/78
168	2/1858	768	*Glyn*	11/70	1963(3/84)	3/84
2	7/1858	602	*Caliban*	8/69		8/81
165	10/1858	765	*Herald*	4/76(S,c)	1952(11/84)	3/85
180	12/1858	780	*Bucephalus*	1/72		8/83
117	5/1859	717	*Swift*	8/70		9/82
189	7/1859	789	*Cadmus*	10/68		12/80
66	8/1859	666	*Pheasant*	8/68		12/77
3	10/1859	603	*Langdale*	4/68, 2/78(S,c)	1941(11/84)	12/84
317	1/1860	917	*Napier*	12/68		6/80
377	9/1861	977	*Sultan*	8/69, 11/77(S,c)	1954(11/84)	2/87
378	10/1861	978	*Mammoth*	6/74(S,c)	1957(11/84)	2/85
379	10/1861	979	*Wasp*	5/69		6/80
380	11/1861	980	*Vandal*	12/73 (c)	1816(12/84), 3038(11/86)	3/87
381	11/1861	981	*Councillor*	3/76(S,c)	1925(12/83)	1/84

*Rebuilds: W - at Wolverton; S - with steel boiler; c - with cab.

STOTHERT GOODS

0-6-0 Mineral Engines, 1855
Nos 321-331

Ten goods engines were ordered from Stothert, Slaughter & Co of the Avonside Ironworks, Bristol, on 25th January 1853; they were to have McConnell's patent firebox and would cost £3,200 each. The firm refused to submit to the usual penalties for late delivery and some form of written guarantee was arranged. Then the General Locomotive Committee suspended the order on 11th February to await Woods and Marshall's investigation and possible changes to the design, at which a worried Edward Slaughter wrote asking for details of the proposed alterations because his firm had already purchased a large quantity of material for the ten engines. On learning that McConnell's patent firebox was no longer required he lowered his price by £100 per engine. The LNWR then offered £32,000 for eleven engines (£2,909 each), with a cash advance of £6,000; this was accepted on 28th May 1853. The engines were to be 0-6-0s for mineral traffic with 18in cylinders and 5ft wheels. It may be that some attempt was then made to make further changes to the design because McConnell's printed list of 1853, showing locomotives in stock and on order, describes the eleven Stothert engines as having 16in cylinders.

None of them had arrived by October 1854 and the LNWR called in the solicitors. Slaughter wrote in November that "five-sixths of the eleven engines" were complete and delivery would be "before long". This last vague promise did little to mollify the Locomotive Committee and in January 1855 the firm was served with notice of legal action.

On 27th February 1855 three engines were reported delivered. It was then discovered that they had not been built to the specification and a bill for the expense of the alterations was sent to the makers who were told that their "work in many instances was not first class, for which an allowance would be claimed." These deductions, with 5% interest on the £6,000 advance, reduced the amount finally paid for each engine to about £2,700. Eight had been delivered by 5th June, and the last three came shortly after. They were numbered 321-31 on arrival, in a gap kept for them between the Hawthorn Small Bloomers and the Kitson Goods, engines which were ordered at the same time and had all been delivered in the previous year.

They have been wrongly described as long-boiler engines, and the drawing of 321 in that form in the 1898 *Locomotive Magazine* was evidently based on a very rough sketch or a faulty memory. Full dimensional details have not survived, but it seems clear that the design was basically like the Kitson 0-6-0 goods engine but with bigger cylinders and smaller wheels. James Bull quotes the same heating surface of 1209 sq ft for this class and for the Kitsons (figures probably based on inside tube diameters) which suggests that the boilers of the two classes were similar.

Dimensions

Cylinders (2 inside)	18" x 24"
Boiler	
Length of barrel	10' 9"
Heating surface	
Tubes	1,266 sq ft
Firebox	101 sq ft
Total	1,367 sq ft
Grate area	16.9 sq ft
Diameter of wheels	5' 0"
Wheelbase	7' 6" + 7' 6" = 15' 0"

In the renumbering of April 1856 they became Nos 54-64. Although they were ordered as mineral engines, later references describe them simply as Stothert (or Slaughter) goods engines.

Reputedly they were not very successful, being underboilered for the large cylinders. Soon after delivery they were sent to the South Staffordshire line and stationed at Walsall and Wichnor "where the loads were big and the distances short" (*Locomotive Magazine* 1911, p113).

No 55 was working on the SSR in 1856 and was being taken, along with SSR *Bilston*, to Wolverton for repair when both were involved in the collision south of Roade on 29th October.

No 63 was scrapped in 1865 but the other ten went into the duplicate list in 1866 and were reinstated as capital stock at the end of 1871. Nos 57 (1240) and 62 (1136) were rebuilt as saddle tanks in 1868 and 1873, the latter receiving a cab. In 1872 Nos 55 (1129) and 59 (1133) were rebuilt, remaining as tender engines; both were reboilered and 1129 was given new cylinders.

One of the saddle tanks, ex-57 by then carrying its sixth number, 1801, was sold to the Wigan coalowners Dewhurst, Hoyle & Smethurst for £1,100 in June 1875. Possibly it went to their Anderton Hall Colliery near Horwich, where the engine *Hannah* was later said to be a large cabless inside-cylinder 0-6-0 saddle tank, apparently from a main line. *Hannah* survived at the nearby Ellerbeck Colliery until about 1916.

All the others were scrapped at Crewe; the last two, by then numbered 1838 and 1842, lasted until March 1882.

Annual totals:

	capital	duplicate
to 30/11/1864:	11	-
30/11/1865:	10	-
30/11/1866:	-	10
to 30/11/1871:	-	10
30/11/1872:	10	-
30/11/1873:	8	-
30/11/1874:	8	-
30/11/1875:	-	7
30/11/1876:	-	6
30/11/1877:	-	5
30/11/1878:	-	4
30/11/1879:	-	3
30/11/1880:	-	3
30/11/1881:	-	2
30/11/1882:	-	-

Summary: 0-6-0s built by Stothert, Slaughter & Co, 1855

No.	Date	Reno'd 4/56	Reno'd 4/62	Rebt	Reno'd	Withdrawn
321	2/1855	54	654	a /63	1237(7/66), 1128(12/71) 1825(4/75)	Scr 30/7/79
322	2/1855	55	655	3/72	1238(7/66), 1129(12/71), 1807(4/75)	Scr 23/9/81
323	2/1855	56	656		1239(8/66), 1130(12/71) c/u?	Scr 2/73
324	3/1855	57	657	a /68(ST)	1240(8/66), 1131(12/71), 1801(3/75)	Sold 24/6/75, Dewhurst, Hoyle & Smethurst, Wigan, £1,100
325	3/1855	58	658		1241(8/66), 1132(12/71) c/u?	Scr 6/73
326	3/1855	59	659	3/72	1242(8/66), 1133(12/71), 1838(4/75)	Scr 13/3/82
327	5/1855	60	660	a /63	1243(8/66), 1134(12/71), 1828(3/75)	Scr 15/3/77
328	5/1855	61	661		1244(8/66), 1135(12/71), 1829(4/75)	Scr 29/9/76
329	6/1855	62	662	1/73(ST,c)	1245(8/66), 1136(12/71), 1842(5/75)	Scr 13/3/82
330	7/1855	63	663		c/u?	Scr 10/65
331	8/1855	64	664	a /63	1246(8/66), 1137(12/71), 1860(4/75)	Scr 14/8/78

EXPRESS GOODS ENGINES

Kitson, Thompson & Hewitson 0-6-0 Goods Engines, 1854   Nos 332-342

McConnell reported in December 1852 that the speeds then required for through express goods trains were too high for 5ft wheels and he recommended goods engines "of the Fairbairn type" but with a wheel diameter of 5ft 6in. Not long after this, on 25th January 1853, ten goods engines with McConnell patent fireboxes were ordered from Kitson, Thompson & Hewitson of the Airedale Foundry, Leeds. After the Woods and Marshall report changes were made in the design: the engines were to be smaller and without patent fireboxes and on learning this Kitson offered eleven engines for their previous total price for ten. This offer was accepted and a revised order was placed on 24th May for eleven goods engines with 5ft 6in wheels and 16in cylinders for £2,909 each. They arrived at regular intervals from March to September 1854 and a payment of £2,900 was made for each.

Hitherto most six-wheel coupled goods engines on the S Div had been of the long-boiler type with all axles in front of the firebox; the only exceptions were the solitary Jones & Potts outside-framed 174 and the four Bury, Curtis & Kennedy engines 168-71. The new engines from Kitson were like the BC&K design with the rear axle behind the firebox, the same cylinder dimensions, total heating surface and equally-divided wheelbase. If reliable drawings of the two classes ever come to light it will be interesting to see if a similar relationship exists between the Bury and McConnell goods engines as that which can be recognised between the Bury singles and the Bloomers.

The Kitson engines were modern in appearance; the boiler was of large diameter with a flush-top firebox, spring buffers and dished smokebox door; the cylinders were inclined 5° upwards to the front with the piston rods working over the leading axle; the steam chest had inclined **V**-shaped valve faces above and between the cylinders. On each side the sandbox was in front of the middle wheel and beneath the running plate whose valance had very large segmental apertures in the coupling-rod arches; there was a very short single footstep at the footplate end. The corniced brass dome was on the middle of the boiler; the two flat mouldings at the top and bottom of the dome barrel were repeated on the safety valve casing and on the chimney.

The engines were Kitson works numbers 372-82, the tenders were 383-93. They were given S Div numbers 332-42 after the block allotted to the Stothert mineral engines. In the half-year ending 31st May 1854, five had been delivered; three of these were charged to revenue account as replacements, and two to capital account as additions to stock, but the engine numbers 332-6 do not reflect this. The Crewe system of giving old numbers to replacement engines was not yet in force on the S Div.

Dimensions

Cylinders (2 inside)	16" x 24"
Boiler	
Diameter (outside)	4' 4"
Length of barrel	10' 0"
Pitch	6' 9½"
Length of firebox casing	5' 3"
Heating surface	
Tubes (234, 1⅞" dia, 10' 5" long)	1,200 sq ft
Firebox	109 sq ft
Total	1,309 sq ft
Grate area	16.3 sq ft
Diameter of wheels	5' 6"
Length over bufferbeam	22' 9"
Wheelbase	7' 6" + 7' 6" = 15' 0"
Weight	
On leading wheels	10 tons
On driving wheels	10 tons
On trailing wheels	7 tons
Total	27 tons

The weight of 332 was recorded when new as 26 tons 12 cwt.

McConnell's original design had been reduced in size and his patent firebox had been discarded to conform to the General Locomotive Committee's wishes, so it is not surprising that he was lukewarm in his appreciation of the new engines. On 5th December 1854 he reported that "they have not sufficient adhesion to work their trains, or sufficient heating surface to keep up their steam." In the same month Kitson & Co offered to build more, but this was not taken up.

It seems likely that they later had their wheelbase lengthened to make them standard with the similar Wolverton-built engines of 1856.

In April 1856 the whole class was renumbered, becoming 68-71, 73 and 76-81, numbers which had belonged to old Bury goods engines withdrawn or themselves renumbered.

LNWR Wolverton (86 built 1856-63)
Kitson & Hewitson (5 built 1862)
Wm Fairbairn & Sons (5 built 1862)

In mid-1854, with 0-4-2 engines of Class A being successfully turned out, there was some rearrangement at Wolverton to allow engine building there on a regular basis. At the end of that year McConnell reported that he had commenced building ten "express goods engines", similar to those by Kitson, as replacements of old engines.

This came to a sudden stop in March 1855 when, because of falling traffic receipts, the Board ordered a period of "retrenchment". Locomotive building at Crewe was to be slowed down, and suspended altogether at Wolverton. Because of this, the first of the Express Goods engines could not be finished until the summer of 1856, but all ten were on the line by the end of the year.

Fig. 92 Express Goods Engine built by Kitson, Thompson & Hewitson, 1854.

Fig. 93 Express Goods Engine built by Kitson & Hewitson, 1862.

In February 1857 McConnell was questioned by the LNWR Executive Committee about the goods engines he was building. They were, he said "of the proportions recommended by Woods and Marshall."

Wolverton turned out engines of this class in every year from 1856 until 1863 and no fewer than 86 were built there. With the original eleven from Kitson and ten more built outside in 1862, the total was 107. Despite this large number, they are very mysterious engines; they lasted well into the 1880s but few photographs and only scanty dimensional details have survived.

The later engines differed from the original Kitsons in having a slightly longer wheelbase; the rear axle was placed four inches rearwards so that its centre was ten inches away from the firebox back. The cylinders of some were two inches shorter in stroke. There was a lock-up safety valve on the boiler top midway between the dome and the spring balance valve, which was positioned nine inches farther back on the firebox; the apertures in the valance over the wheels were smaller, and there was a footstep of normal depth. A square sandbox was mounted on the running plate behind the leading wheel splasher, instead of underneath the running plate as on the Kitsons.

Under the N Div accountancy system which was now in force most of the engines were built as replacements with running numbers scattered between 5 and 245; additions to stock were built at Wolverton as 196-9 and 241/2, filling gaps in the list, and with new numbers 318/9 and 355-71.

The first batch was described as Class B, and by 1859 further engines of the same type were being described as Class D. McConnell said in November of that year that an engine of Class D cost £1,795 to build. It may be inferred from the known allocation of other class letters that later batches of this type would have been styled Classes F, I and J, but so far there is no evidence of this.

One curious member of the class was the former 6-2-0 Crampton *Liverpool* which was 'rebuilt' at Wolverton from September 1858 to April 1859, emerging as a normal express goods 0-6-0 with its old number 245 and its old nameplates. How long it kept its name is not known.

Early in 1861, with 52 in stock and Wolverton fully occupied, tenders for ten more were sought from outside firms. On 23rd January Kitson & Hewitson (as

Fig. 94 New Express Goods 0-6-0 371, about to be backed into the Wolverton painting shop, December 1861. The water tank is at the south end of the station platform; the cottages in the left background are in Young Street with the church spire beyond. The engine at the right is Small Bloomer 381.

(Stephenson Locomotive Society)

the firm was now known) of Leeds were given an order for five at £2,950 each for delivery in July-September 1861; these were maker's numbers 909-13, the tenders being 914-8.

On the same day an order was placed with Wm Fairbairn & Sons of Manchester who promised five engines at £2,740 each by February 1862. The Kitson and Fairbairn engines were given S Div numbers 409-18 and by the time they arrived in January-March 1862 another 35 had been built at Wolverton, where production was almost catching up with that of Crewe. These completed the class built by the separate S Div, but in December 1862 ten more were authorised to use up parts already in store. They were the last engines built at Wolverton Works. Their numbers were 1056-60 and 1071-5 in the all-LNWR list. As built they are said to have had plain Ramsbottom domes and his pattern of safety valves.

Dimensions

Cylinders (2 inside)	16" x 24" (some were 16" x 22" originally)
Boiler	
Diameter	4' 0" inside, 4' 4" over cleading.
Length of barrel	10' 0"
Pitch	6' 9⅞"
Length of firebox casing	5' 3"
Heating surface	
Tubes (10.4' long)	1,107.28 sq ft
Firebox	101.75 sq ft
Total	1,209.03 sq ft
Grate area	16.5 sq ft
Diameter of wheels	5' 6"
Length over bufferbeam	23' 1"
Wheelbase	7' 6" + 7' 10" = 15' 4"
Weight	27 tons 14 cwt

Engines built in 1861 had 229 tubes with a heating surface of 1,163 sq ft; the firebox added 103 sq ft to give a total of 1,266 sq ft.

Between 1862 and 1867 all were given 17in x 24in cylinders. Most were rebuilt by Ramsbottom and Webb in 1866-76, the last five with steel boilers. From the end of 1872 cabs were fitted, those recorded are indicated in the summary, but probably the others got them by 1880. As rebuilt, with the Crewe sloping-fronted smokebox and matching sandboxes built onto the leading splashers, they looked like a large-wheeled version of the DX class, except for having a reversing lever instead of Ramsbottom's wheel, the reversing rod under the rear and middle axles and a prominent Wolverton-pattern footstep.

Weights given in a Crewe diagram of April 1877 were:

On leading wheels	11 tons 4 cwt
On driving wheels	10 tons 10 cwt
On trailing wheels	8 tons 0 cwt
Total	29 tons 14 cwt

One of the very few photographs of this large class was taken in the late 1870s at Bletchley, showing 678 coupled to a tender with rubber springs.

In January 1873 one of the class, 961, was altered to a 2-4-0 by removing the front coupling rods for trials with fast trains. This was apparently successful; Webb's Precursor and Precedent classes appeared shortly afterwards, and were obviously based on the Wolverton design. 961 reverted to its 0-6-0 status in December 1873, and Webb's 5ft 6in 2-4-0 *Precursor* was completed at Crewe in April 1874.

Work

For such a large number of engines there are surprisingly few records of their activities and none at all

Fig. 95
Accident near north end of Watford tunnel, 21st May 1866. Unidentified Wolverton Express Goods lying on its side; tender with rubber springs. Crewe Goods 2-4-0 89 *Bela* in front.
(David Patrick collection)

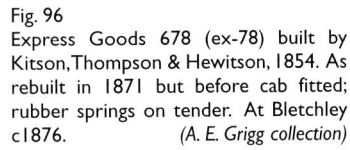

Fig. 96
Express Goods 678 (ex-78) built by Kitson, Thompson & Hewitson, 1854. As rebuilt in 1871 but before cab fitted; rubber springs on tender. At Bletchley c1876. *(A. E. Grigg collection)*

Fig. 97 One of the last batch of engines built at Wolverton Works, Express Goods 1073 completed in August 1863. As rebuilt in 1874 with standard Webb fittings and cab; photographed at Crewe in that year.
(LNWR photo)

from the early period, though the name 'Express Goods' indicates their class of work. One of the very rare references to any of them in the LNWR archives is a note from the Chairman, Lord Chandos, to McConnell complaining that he had just seen "the driver and stoker of engine 150 with the Up coal train on the 3rd line" passing Boxmoor about 12.30pm on 27th June 1860: they were both *smoking*.

In 1862 No 93 was stationed at Oxford and was in a collision at Wolvercot Jct on 17th January.

Other sightings recorded by enthusiasts were:

In 1863: 1010 was at Rugby.
In 1865: 714 was at Vauxhall.
Early 1870s: 677, 963/5-8, 1009-16, 1056-9 and 1073/4 were at Camden shed;
955 was at Bletchley;
704/70 were at Northampton;
969 and 1017 were at Derby.
In 1877: 672, 798, 965/9 and 1011 were at Longsight.
In 1880: 747 was on hire to the Northampton & Banbury Jct Railway.
About 1880: 605, 678 and 691 were at Bletchley.

Because of their large wheels the engines of this class were also used on passenger trains and seem to have specialised in excursion working.

On 21st May 1866 one of them brought an excursion train from Northampton, to which carriages from Oxford and Banbury were added at Bletchley, and was being piloted by Crewe Goods No 89 *Bela*, when it was involved in the Watford Tunnel accident. The damaged engines were photographed but it is not possible to identify the Wolverton Express Goods beyond saying that it had the longer wheelbase, appears to be in original condition (apart from the Ramsbottom chimney and lubricator) and its tender had rubber springs. Damage in the accident may have made it a candidate for rebuilding; if so it was perhaps one of those rebuilt in 1866: 649, 779/82.

In 1883, 751 was at Northampton, working excursion trains; 1012 was on this duty at Birmingham in the same year and, unusually for a goods engine at that period, was in lined-out passenger engine livery.

Disposal

The entire class was scrapped at Crewe, the first to go being ex-159 in 1868, when it was less than twelve years old. The other 106 engines remained in stock until 1875, from which date they were slowly withdrawn; the survivors went into the duplicate list in 1884/5. The last two were scrapped at the end of 1887, ex-182 (built in 1857) and ex-370 (built in 1862).

Annual totals:

	capital	duplicate
to 30/11/1867:	107	-
to 30/11/1874:	106	-
30/11/1875:	105	-
30/11/1876:	97	-
30/11/1877:	93	-
30/11/1878:	83	-
30/11/1879:	72	-
30/11/1880:	70	-
30/11/1881:	54	-
30/11/1882:	38	-
30/11/1883:	21	-
30/11/1884:	14	-
30/11/1885:	-	10
30/11/1886:	-	4
30/11/1887:	-	1
30/11/1888:	-	-

Summary: 0-6-0 Express Goods Engines, 1854-63

1. Built by Kitson, Thompson & Hewitson, 1854

No.	Date**	Reno'd 4/56	Reno'd 4/62	Rebt*	Scrapped
332	25/3/1854	68	668	4/69	1/79
333	11/4/1854	69	669	8/69	1/79
334	3/5/1854	70	670	12/69	7/79
335	13/5/1854	71	671	4/69	2/83
336	30/5/1854	73	673	10/72	12/82
337	27/6/1854	76	676	3/70	12/77
338	17/7/1854	77	677	2/72	6/80
339	28/7/1854	78	678	6/71, 10/80(c)	6/83
340	15/8/1854	79	679	12/69	9/82
341	4/9/1854	80	680	7/66	3/79
342	24/9/1854	81	681	5/66	8/77

Kitson works numbers were 372-82 (engines) and 383-93 (tenders).

2. Built at Wolverton, 1856-62

No.	Date	Reno'd 4/62	Rebt*	Renumbered	Scrapped
11	5/1856	611	12/70		9/82
150	5/1856	750	2/67		3/81
19	7/1856	619	2/72		12/80
20	8/1856	620	9/68	c/u 1982	12/76
149	8/1856	749	12/69		9/78
159	8/1856	759	—	c/u 1158	6/68
90	9/1856	690	7/72		2/83
49	11/1856	649	8/66	c/u 1981	12/76
147	12/1856	747	4/66		1/83
167	12/1856	767	—		6/76
151	6/1857	751	10/73(c)	c/u 1937	8/84
179	6/1857	779	/66		3/79
166	7/1857	766	1/73		9/81
182	7/1857	782	7/66	1963(2/85)	11/87
196	8/1857	796	1/70	1964(2/85)	6/85
197	10/1857	797	8/75(S,c)		12/82
198	11/1857	798	1/69		3/82
199	11/1857	799	11/74(c)		7/78

No.	Date	Reno'd 4/62	Rebt*	Renumbered	Scrapped
241	12/1857	841	6/69		1/79
242	1/1858	842	—		9/77
82	12/1858	682	7/70		9/82
172	12/1858	772	—	c/u 1994	4/76
245 *Liverpool*	4/1859	845	2/71		2/81
91	8/1859	691	10/69		3/83
120	10/1859	720	10/70		2/81
183	10/1859	783	2/72		6/81
50	11/1859	650	—	c/u 1989	3/76
175	11/1859	775	—		2/76
83	b/1859	683	8/70		9/80
318	1/1860	918	—		8/76
319	1/1860	919	3/70		10/78
5	9/1860	605	12/69		9/82
51	9/1860	651	10/68		8/78
104	9/1860	704	3/71		3/81
101	10/1860	701	11/71		9/82
169	10/1860	769	5/71		5/83
170	10/1860	770	1/71		9/82
171	10/1860	771	7/72	1962(2/85)	7/86
100	11/1860	700	1/72		2/81
105	11/1860	705	9/70		3/82
107	11/1860	707	11/70		7/82
74	1/1861	674	11/71		7/82
93	1/1861	693	7/72		10/82
108	1/1861	708	11/71	c/u 1971	3/84
109	1/1861	709	1/72		11/79
114	3/1861	714	2/69		3/81
115	3/1861	715	5/71		6/78
173	3/1861	773	2/71		8/79
118	4/1861	718	3/71		5/79
92	6/1861	692	9/70		6/83
94	6/1861	694	11/70		6/83
98	6/1861	698	8/70		6/83
113	6/1861	713	12/69		7/79
52	7/1861	652	2/76(S,c)	1960(2/85)	3/86
86	7/1861	686	8/72		4/83
99	7/1861	699	7/73(c)	1965(2/85)	11/86
97	8/1861	697	7/69		10/78
355	8/1861	955	2/70		2/82
356	8/1861	956	7/72		4/81
357	8/1861	957	3/70		9/81
358	9/1861	958	8/72	1967(2/85)	5/86
359	9/1861	959	10/73(c)		8/83
360	9/1861	960	—	c/u 1997	6/76
361	10/1861	961	12/72(c) as 2-4-0 1/73-12/73		3/81
362	10/1861	962	—		8/76
363	10/1861	963	1/73(c)		7/81
72	11/1861	672	—		2/78
89	11/1861	689	—		12/77
364	11/1861	964	—	c/u 1965	4/75
365	11/1861	965	11/73(c)		3/82
366	11/1861	966	11/71	1971(2/85)	7/85
367	11/1861	967	4/69		12/77
368	12/1861	968	3/69		2/79
369	12/1861	969	5/70		3/82
371	1/1862	971	b/72		9/81
370	2/1862	970	6/73(c)	1972(3/85)	12/87

3. Built by Kitson & Hewitson, 1862

No.	Date**	Reno'd 4/62	Rebt*	Renumbered	Scrapped
409	18/1/1862	1009	6/71		1/83
410	25/1/1862	1010	5/70		2/81
411	1/2/1862	1011	7/73(c)		3/82
412	8/2/1862	1012	5/76(S,c)	1975(3/85)	9/86
413	15/2/1862	1013	12/74(c)	c/u 1807	1/84

Kitson works numbers in order of delivery were 909-13 (engines) and 914-8 (tenders).

4. Built by Wm Fairbairn & Sons, 1862

No.	Date	Reno'd 4/62	Rebt*	Renumbered	Scrapped
414	2/1862	1014	6/74(c)		2/83
415	3/1862	1015	7/72		2/83
416	3/1862	1016	2/73(c)	1976(3/85)	7/87
417	3/1862	1017	11/74(c)	c/u 1959	3/84
418	3/1862	1018	8/70		4/76

5. Built at Wolverton, 1863

No.	Date	Rebt*	Renumbered	Scrapped
1056	4/1863	10/72	1806(4/84)	4/84
1057	4/1863	1/74	1905(7/84)	7/84
1058	5/1863	9/75(S,c)	1908(12/84)	9/87
1059	5/1863	5/73(c)		4/83
1060	5/1863	11/71		9/81
1071	7/1863	11/72		4/82
1072	8/1863	5/73(c)	1917(12/84)	9/86
1073	8/1863	6/74(c)	1805(4/84)	4/84
1074	9/1863	—	1919(3/85)	11/85
1075	9/1863	8/75(S,c)	1983(1/85)	4/85

* Rebuilding: S - with steel boiler; c - with cab.
** Dates of the 1854 Kitson engines are of receipt at Wolverton.
Those of the 1862 Kitson engines are of works trial before delivery.

ENGINES FROM THE SOUTH STAFFORDSHIRE RAILWAY, 1858

Not long after Wolverton had settled down to producing its two standard types of engine, further variety was added to the S Div stock by the acquisition of 29 engines from the South Staffordshire Railway.

The SSR was a small independent line of 24 miles which ran from the Oxford, Worcester & Wolverhampton Railway at Dudley across the Black Country in a north-easterly direction to join the Midland Railway at Wichnor Jct, some five miles short of Burton-on-Trent. This undulating route passed through Wednesbury, Walsall and Lichfield, giving access to many mines and ironworks, and had an important interchange with the Birmingham canal system. It crossed and connected with the LNWR's Stour Valley, Grand Junction and Trent Valley lines.

The first section of only $1^{3}/_{4}$ miles, from the Grand Junction line at Bescot to Walsall, opened in November 1847 with a service of trains between Birmingham and Walsall worked by the LNWR Northern Division. Before this short stub was extended for seventeen miles to join the Midland at Wichnor, the SSR ordered its first locomotives from Wm Fairbairn & Sons in June 1848, four 2-2-2s and two 0-6-0s. They were all big engines and after the first of the singles arrived the SSR Board seems to have become alarmed at the prospect of the even heavier goods engines, which were the Sphynx long-boiler type, and would weigh about 26 tons. In May 1849 Fairbairn & Sons were asked to delay further deliveries, while attempts were made to offload "as many of the heavy engines as may not be required" to the LNWR "or any other willing party". At the same time an offer by Sharp Bros of three of their standard 2-2-2s was accepted. Unfortunately the attempt to dispose of the Fairbairns coincided with a surplus of engines on the LNWR; the makers were naturally unwilling to hold on to their new products, and so by the end of August 1849 there were nine engines in SSR stock.

The seven passenger engines were more than enough for Locomotive Superintendent George Wells to operate a weekday service of four trains each way between Birmingham Curzon Street and Burton-on-Trent; this was a distance of 33 miles, only about half of which - the middle section between Bescot and Wichnor - was over SSR metals. With the opening of the southern five miles of the line to Dudley in March 1850, goods traffic began. With only two goods engines available, the company was immediately in trouble.

The SSR workshop facilities were quite inadequate and George Wells, a former Wolverton employee, asked McConnell as early as September 1849 for help with small repairs. Seventy miles away, Wolverton was hardly convenient for the SSR and although Fairbairn single No 2 *Walsall* was repaired there in 1850, most of the engines in need of attention were sent the forty-odd miles north to Crewe Works. The chief clerk of the SSR was George P. Neele, who said that they "were far from welcome at Crewe, the engines were none of theirs; the type of engine not only dissimilar to any others under the superintendence of Mr Trevithick, but themselves varying in style; the attention bestowed on these unwelcome visitors was at best but meagre, and it not unfrequently happened that almost immediately after the return of our engines, some further failure took place and complaints of inattention were rife."

From 1st August 1850 the working of the line was leased for 21 years to John Robinson McClean, the SSR's Engineer: "a man of restless enterprise" later to open up the Cannock Chase coalfield and to become involved in a dozen other ventures, including the Anglo-American Telegraph Co; he became President of the Institution of Civil Engineers and was elected MP for East Staffordshire. McClean took over the SSR engines at a valuation made by Matthew Kirtley of the Midland Railway. But the problem of inadequate workshops remained and McClean often found himself short of engine power; on these occasions he would hire engines from Wolverton or Crewe, at £5 per day, plus one shilling (5p) per mile after 100 miles.

Working by the LNWR Northern Division

After a few months of struggle even the able and active McClean was driven to ask the LNWR to take over the working. The tripartite negotiations, conducted between the SSR, McClean as lessee, and the LNWR, occupied some further months until on 18th November 1851 it was decided that the LNWR N Div would work the line, and for that purpose an inventory and valuation of the stock was made by John Viret Gooch of the Eastern Counties Railway. The working agreement was approved on 10th February 1852; all SSR engines were to be transferred "forthwith" to the N Div and Crewe was to be responsible for all repair work.

By this time McClean had increased the number of his engines to fifteen but they were in a terrible state. On 23rd March Trevithick reported that the first three had been handed over to him but that repairs would cost £1,000 (some engines had parts missing) and he could not yet undertake the working of the line. To help out, four engines were sent from Wolverton in April 1852.

Another request was issued for the engines to be handed over "forthwith" and Trevithick officially took charge of the SSR engines on 5th July 1852; on 30th November the N Div stock included "twelve SS engines which do not work over the L&NW line". These were Nos 1, 3-7 and 10-15. The others, Nos 2, 8 and 9 were probably still undergoing repair and were taken over during the next half-year period.

Nos 10-15, four goods engines and two shunting tanks, had been ordered by the lessee, McClean, and paid for by the SSR after vetting and agreement by referees Richard Peacock and J. V. Gooch. As soon as he took over, Trevithick lost no time in asking the SSR for more; an official return of March 1853 gave a total of seventeen SSR engines, and by the end of May nineteen were in his hands. A report of all N Div engines in stock in March 1855 listed Nos 1-19 with their names and building dates, except for Nos 10 and 11 whose dates were "not known". The engines retained their SSR identities and were not renumbered into the N Div list; despite the various parties involved in the working arrangement, they remained SSR property.

According to Neele, Trevithick's man on the spot was "Mr Parker (junior)" of Vauxhall, but Vauxhall shed was too small even for LNWR purposes and although additional engine accommodation was requested there in July 1852, nothing was done. Despite Crewe's official responsibility for repairs sometimes Wolverton became involved, as shown by the correspondence between McConnell and Trevithick about repairs to No 3 *Wednesbury* in November 1852 and to No 8 *Birmingham* which was sent first to Wolverton then transferred to Crewe in January 1853.

Neither the stock of locomotives nor the supply of train crews was ever adequate; long continuous hours of work led to accidents, culminating just before Christmas 1854 when two goods trains, held up by signals outside Walsall, were rammed by a heavy double-headed coke train. The inquiry revealed gross misuse of both engines and men. It was, as Neele put it, unlikely that the LNWR would have sent its best drivers to the SSR, "but the very frequent instances we experienced of careless mishaps forced the conclusion that the men relegated to our service were not up to the normal standard of capability..." They were a wild bunch and Mr Parker (junior) was unable to control "the rough staff of the engine shed". In June 1855 a spate of robberies on the SSR led to the arrest of four suspected enginemen. Neele says that goods trains were regularly halted at night in Cannock Chase, where the train staff "rifled the most promising truck and hid the spoils in a regular smuggler's cave". Later that month eight drivers, four firemen and a cleaner were sacked for complicity.

To tame the unruly LNWR enginemen and bring some order to this chaotic little railway Frank Holt arrived from Crewe. He was a cousin of John Ramsbottom, had been apprenticed at Sharp, Roberts & Co in Ramsbottom's time and became a foreman there before following him to the LNWR. "His admiration for Mr Ramsbottom was remarkable" says Neele "and his prediction that that gentleman would ultimately become the sole Locomotive Engineer of the L&NW, superseding both Mr Trevithick and Mr McConnell came perfectly true." Holt was a tall, gaunt Yorkshireman "somewhat peculiar in manner" and with a mordant humour. He was also a strict disciplinarian and "worked a remarkable change" on the SSR locomotive department in his short period there, but in the absence of local workshop facilities, mere discipline was not enough.

Twice negotiations were begun for the Midland Railway to take over, but at the end of 1855 the SSR was still in Crewe's care and engines were still breaking down from overwork. Trevithick complained in November that he was working the full contract mileage, and that the SSR wanted extra trains. He said the SSR would have to provide more engines. Hearing this, McConnell offered an old Bury engine for £500.

The railway was in dire straits. Amid complaints of chronic lack of power and heavy repairs, three trains were withdrawn in December. Six more engines were loaned from Crewe in January 1856 but made little difference; in March it was reported that as many as 600 loaded wagons were stranded and there was no means of moving them. But Trevithick had his hands full and had other worries; he was now also working the Shropshire Union line and simply had no more engines to lend as substitutes for the SSR engines sent away for repair.

Working by the LNWR Southern Division

In this crisis the LNWR Manager Mark Huish asked if Wolverton could help. The S Div Committee instructed McConnell to send "two of his engines to Mr Holt to assist him out of his present difficulty" and recommended to the Executive Committee "with a view of preventing the constant complaints of insufficient power" that McConnell should take over the entire SSR working. Trevithick was glad to be rid of it, and the transfer was arranged. This involved yet another valuation of the stock, this time by Trevithick and McConnell, with Ramsbottom as "umpire". McConnell made two or three visits of inspection - not enough, as things turned out, but he was keen to expand his area.

"There was undoubtedly" says Neele "some keen difference in *esprit de corps* between the Wolverton men and the Crewe men, and there was some hesitancy as to how far the latter working on the South Stafford would quietly accept the transfer." Then, on Monday 21st April 1856 "a long series of engines with steam up, sixteen in number, arrived at Walsall" - McConnell was never one to do things by halves - "and as each of those engaged in the daily work came to the station, the Crewe men were instructed to drop their fire and cross over to the respective engine from Wolverton appointed to continue the day's work. The order was given to each man in Mr Holt's firm style, so that whatever rumours might have existed as to mutiny, the change was effected with complete success and from that time the grasshopper style of engines, with their distinctive nameplates, *Sylph*, *Stork*, *Saracen* etc, disappeared, the heavier McConnell type took their place and certainly worked more efficiently over the gradients of the South Stafford than those they had superseded." Frank Holt resigned a week later.

Neele's description records two of the Trevithick engines hired to the SSR, both built at Crewe in 1852: N Div No 1 *Saracen* was a 6ft single, 136 *Stork* was a goods 2-4-0. The other engine, *Sylph*, was SSR No 14, a Sharp 2-4-0 tank which remained on the line despite the welcome arrival of the S Div engines. It is an indication of the proportion of SSR locomotives normally away for repair that Neele was under the impression that the line was worked entirely by LNWR engines.

There were now 21 engines in SSR stock and these were transferred to McConnell on 21st April. The N Div stock total was reduced by this number in the next half-yearly return, specifically "by discontinuance of South Staffs working" but by a typical oversight the engines were not then added to the S Div total. Two more engines arrived in July 1856.

McConnell was surprised by the enormous amount of shunting which had to be done every day and soon found himself in Trevithick's position, short of engines. The traffic demanded more but having rid himself of the day-to-day problems of working the line, McClean was now as unwilling as the SSR to add to the locomotive stock. It was only after a lot of argument that in June 1857 the reluctant company agreed to order six 0-6-0s from Wm Fairbairn & Sons for £2,950 each.

SSR Engines Acquired

These discussions probably led to the agreement of 21st January 1858 between the three parties to transfer McClean's lease to the LNWR. Although Parliament refused to sanction this transfer, the LNWR agreed to purchase the existing stock of 23 locomotives outright for £49,486 13s 7d (£49,486.68) and also to take over the outstanding order for the six Fairbairn goods engines. All 29 SSR engines were paid for by the LNWR in the half year ending 31st May 1858. Most of them remained on their own line, although *Wednesbury* was recorded on a St Albans - Euston train in June 1858 and *Dudley* was on the Peterborough branch from 1859. In effect the SSR became a branch of the LNWR, worked as part of the S Div, although McClean's lease was not legally transferred until February 1861 and it was not until 1867 that the SSR was officially absorbed into the LNWR.

In February 1858 two SSR branches, three and seven miles long, were opened into the Cannock Chase coalfield. As well as giving access to collieries, the longer of these also had a passenger service and was extended in the following year by the Cannock Mineral Railway, which ran another seven miles to join the Trent Valley line at Rugeley. The LNWR leased the CM from its opening, and ran passenger trains between Walsall and Stafford via Cannock with S Div engines working on the TV line for three miles as far as Colwich. Other developments in 1858 were the erection of a new engine shed at Walsall and an enlargement of that at Vauxhall which was used by the SSR engines.

The engines purchased by the LNWR were all named and carried numbers 1-23; the six on order were delivered after the purchase with names chosen by the SSR and were almost certainly numbered 24-9. On 9th September 1858 it was "ordered that the whole of the engines delivered over by the SSR be entered in the Stock Register of the Southern Division." This may only have been a reminder to McConnell to put his paperwork in order, and it seems most probable that the engines were entered in the list under their SSR names with the numbers 1-29.

That they remained on the SSR is shown by a curious Stores Committee minute of 7th April 1859 saying that McClean now had six more engines than necessary. This seems to indicate that the new Fairbairns were doing very well, or perhaps that Wolverton was taking better care of the engines now that they were LNWR property. The minute goes on to suggest that four of the surplus engines be sold to reduce the amount charged to McClean for interest. McConnell urged further consideration, and a month later it was resolved that the interest paid by McClean on the cost of the six engines beyond the LNWR's average rate of interest be set aside, to reduce the cost charged to capital account to the amount they would have cost if built at Wolverton. Mark Huish, forced to resign from his position as General Manager in November 1858, acted as referee between McClean and the LNWR in these negotiations.

A chronic shortage of engines had suddenly become a surplus, and by September 1859 the line was being worked by eighteen engines in steam, eight passenger engines averaging 70 miles per day, and ten goods averaging only 48 miles. McConnell claimed that these eighteen under-used engines would be sufficient to work the N Div Stour Valley line as well as the SSR.

Renumbering

The minute-books tell us nothing explicit about the renumbering of the SSR engines into the S Div list and the slender evidence they offer might be open to other interpretations, but it seems quite clear that the engines were not renumbered when purchased. A clue is contained in a Locomotive Committee minute about seven old S Div engines for sale on 5th August 1858. These are listed as Nos 7(A), 53, 86, 160, 165, 180 and 182(A); the suffix (A) indicates engines which had then been replaced. Two (53 and 160) of those unreplaced bore numbers later carried by SSR engines, which implies that the renumbering took place after that date.

On 22nd January 1859 McConnell, in forecasting the number of engines he would have to build in the next three years said "the SSR stock must now be considered as coming in for renewal." This might suggest the engines were by then renumbered into the S Div list, as perhaps a strict adherence to the Crewe accountants' system would require, but there are some later hints that a separate SSR list had been kept.

On 26th May 1859 he reported the hiring of No 84 engine at £5 per day to Brassey to ballast the Cannock Mineral line. This must surely be the Bury 0-4-0 (ex-79), not the SSR Sharp 2-2-2 which became 84 on renumbering. If the SSR engines had been renumbered by then, the Bury should have been 84(A), but of course this could be a clerical omission.

On 22nd June 1859 the SSR engine *Cannock* (no number quoted) was reported as having fallen into Elwell's Pool at Bescot. At the same meeting it was resolved "that stock of engines be taken and that a complete list be prepared of engines in working stock and in store, that all blank numbers be filled up from engines in working stock including South Staffordshire engines so that the stock numbers shall range from 1 to 316 inclusive." The new list was laid before the Stores Committee on 7th July, but was not entered in the minute-book and has not survived.

The implication seems to be that the SSR engines had been kept in a separate list and had retained their old numbers from the time of their purchase in February 1858 and that they were renumbered into the LNWR list in July 1859.

By this time one of the SSR engines had been scrapped. The others were given the numbers of eight withdrawn S Div engines: 53, 84, 111/2/6, 160/81, 221, and new numbers 297-316.

There is no record of when the names were taken off. The last mention of an engine name in the minute-books is *Cannock* on 7th July 1859; reports of an accident to *Dudley* in May 1864 refer to it only by its number 897. It is likely that *Derby* would have lost its name no later than the 1862 amalgamation, as there was a Crewe engine with the same name.

On 20th March 1861, after McClean's lease had been legally transferred to the LNWR, McConnell was told to discontinue keeping separate accounts for the SSR locomotives, and it was at that time that other SSR stock, wagons, sheets and carriages, were ordered to be renumbered in the LNWR lists.

South Staffordshire Railway Locomotives 1849-58

SSR No.	Name	Type			Maker	Date	Reno'd LNWR S Div 7/1859
1	Dudley	2-2-2	5' 9"	16x20"	Fairbairn	2/1849	297
2	Walsall	"	"	"	"	3/1849	298
3	Wednesbury	"	"	"	"	4/1849	299
4	Lichfield	"	"	"	"	5/1849	300
5	Burton	2-2-2	5' 6"	15x20"	Sharp	5/1849	53
6	Stafford	"	"	"	"	5/1849	84
7	Bescot	"	"	"	"	6/1849	116
8	Birmingham	0-6-0	5' 0"	18x24"	Fairbairn	7/1849	307
9	Wolverhampton	"	"	"	"	7/1849	308
10	Belvidere	0-4-2	5' 0"	16x22"	Garforth	/1850	*
11	Angerstein	"	"	"	"	/1850	221
12	Pelsall	0-6-0	5' 0"	18x24"	Stephenson	1/1851	309
13	Alrewas	"	"	"	"	1/1851	310
14	Sylph	2-4-0T	5' 0"	16x20"	Sharp	7/1851	111
15	Safety	"	"	"	"	7/1851	112
16	Viper	0-6-0	5' 0"	16x24"	Wilson	12/1852	301
17	Stag	"	"	"	"	1/1853	302
18	Esk	2-4-0	5' 9"	16x20"	Wilson	5/1853	160
19	Justin	"	"	"	"	5/1853	181
20	Priam	0-6-0	5' 0"	17x24"	Vulcan	4/1855	305
21	Ajax	"	"	"	"	4/1855	306
22	Bilston	0-4-2	5' 0"	16x24"	Beyer	7/1856	304
23	Derby	"	"	"	"	7/1856	303
24	Cannock	0-6-0	5' 0"	18x24"	Fairbairn	3/1858	311
25	Bloxwich	"	"	"	"	3/1858	312
26	McConnell	"	"	"	"	4/1858	313
27	Vauxhall	"	"	"	"	5/1858	314
28	Aston	"	"	"	"	5/1858	315
29	Tipton	"	"	"	"	6/1858	316

* No 10 was scrapped before being allotted a number by the LNWR.

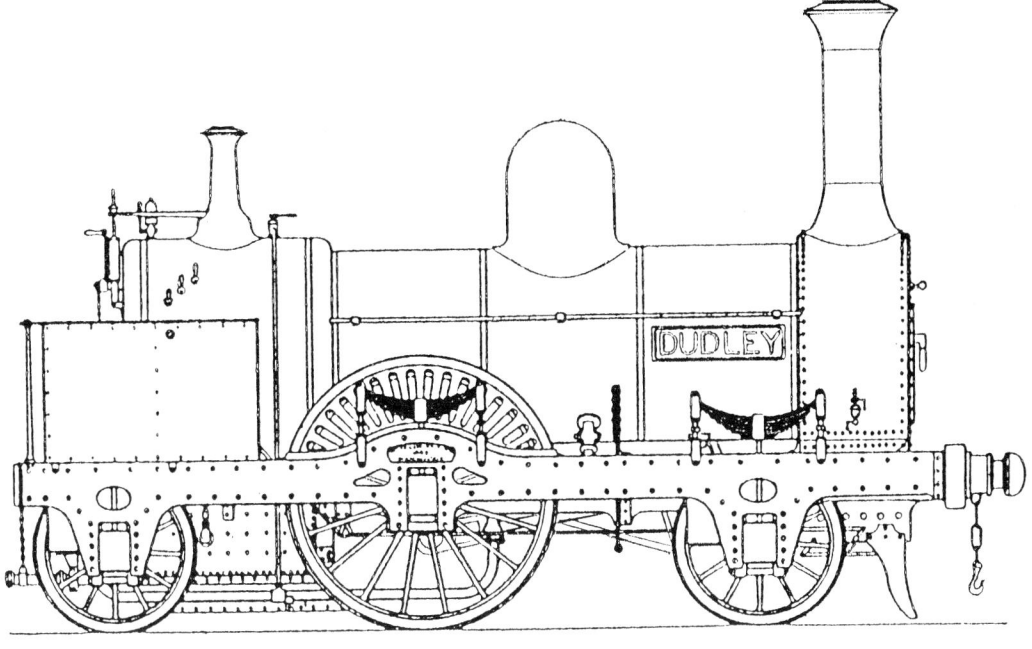

Fig. 98
South Staffordshire Railway No 1 *Dudley* built by Fairbairn in 1849; LNWR S Div No 297.

Fairbairn 2-2-2 Passenger Engines (SSR Nos 1-4)
Nos 297-300

These four engines were ordered from William Fairbairn & Sons by the SSR on 29th June 1848 at a cost of £2,070 each, with tenders. They appear to have been to the same design as the better-documented *Vulcan* built by this maker for the Shrewsbury & Birmingham Railway in 1849, an enlarged version of the Sharp standard single. They had inside cylinders and outside sandwich frames plus inside iron plate frames between the bufferplank and the front of the firebox. The crank axle had four bearings and all carrying springs were above the running plate. The firebox had a raised top and there was a plain polished dome on the middle of the three-ring boiler.

Their names were those of the principal towns served by the SSR.

Dimensions

Cylinders (2 inside)	16" x 20"
Boiler	
Diameter	3' 11"
Length of barrel	10' 0"
Pitch	6' 0½"
Heating surface	
Tubes	1,104 sq ft
Firebox	89 sq ft
Total	1,193 sq ft
Grate area	13.75 sq ft
Diameter of wheels	
Leading	3' 6"
Driving	5' 9"
Trailing	3' 6"
Wheelbase	7' 2" + 6' 10" = 14' 0"

The weight of the similar Shrewsbury & Birmingham *Vulcan* was 22 tons 8¼ cwt.

Curiously, McConnell used drawings of this class instead of a Wolverton engine to illustrate one of his steam-drying patents in February 1859. In this patent, steam was led from the regulator to the cylinders via a pipe which jacketed the entire length of one of the top fire tubes. There appears to be no record of this device actually being applied to a Fairbairn single, or to any other engine.

The cylinders of No 1 *Dudley* and No 2 *Walsall* were altered to 16in x 21in at Wolverton about 1860.

No 2 *Walsall* was involved in a collision at Vauxhall in December 1850, following which it was repaired at Wolverton.

No 3 *Wednesbury* broke its leading axle at Sudbury while on the 8.20pm St Albans - Euston train on 29th June 1858.

From 1859 No 1 *Dudley* worked on the Peterborough branch. It was on the 11.55am passenger train from Peterborough on 30th May 1864 and had just drawn into the station at Overton when the boiler exploded. The entire rear boiler ring was thrown 50 yards and the crank axle was broken, but both enginemen survived.

The engine was rebuilt at Wolverton in 1864 with a Ramsbottom boiler:

Length of barrel	10' 0"
Tubes	190, 2" dia, 10' 2" long
Grate area	13.4 sq ft

Nos 2 and 3 were similarly rebuilt in 1869 and 1867 after being placed in the duplicate list. All were scrapped at Crewe in 1874-81.

The duplicate numbers of January 1867 have been confused in previous accounts; those given in the summary are all taken from a Crewe list of 1872.

Summary: SSR 2-2-2s built by Wm Fairbairn & Sons, 1849

SSR No	Name	Built	LNWR 7/59	4/62	Rebt	Reno'd	Scrapped
1	*Dudley*	2/1849	297	897	12/64	1122(1/67), 1921(12/71)	12/3/81
2	*Walsall*	3/1849	298	898	a /69	1124(1/67), 1919(12/71)	30/4/78
3	*Wednesbury*	4/1849	299	899	12/67	1248(1/67), 1920(12/71)	23/9/81
4	*Lichfield*	5/1849	300	900	/60	1249(1/67), 1922(12/71)	4/74

Sharp Bros 2-2-2 Passenger Engines (SSR Nos 5, 6, 7)
Nos 53, 84, 116

"Three light engines" were offered by Sharp Bros from stock and were accepted by the SSR on McClean's recommendation on 3rd May 1849. Delivery was promised for 17th May (Sharp order No 227) and the first was delivered on 19th but the third engine was not taken into stock until June. They were standard Sharp singles; each engine cost £1,500 plus £390 for the tender.

The Sharp works numbers are problematical because at this period there were lots of cancelled and postponed orders, with engines diverted from one order to another. Although the Sharp order book contains the pencilled numbers 589 and 654 against two of the engines, these look like much later guesswork. E. Craven, whose thorough and wide-ranging research uncovered so much of early locomotive history, considered that the SSR order was more likely to have consisted of Sharp Nos 581/4/5.

Dimensions

Cylinders (2 inside)	15" x 20"
Boiler	
Diameter	3' 6"
Length of barrel	10' 0"
Tubes	147, 1¾" dia
Firebox	3' x 3' 6" x 3' 11" high
Grate area	10.5 sq ft
Diameter of wheels	
Leading	3' 6"
Driving	5' 6"
Trailing	3' 6"
Wheelbase	5' 8" + 7' 0" = 12' 8"
Tender (6 wheel) capacity	1,000 gal

In 1859 No 84 was rebuilt at Wolverton and in 1869/71 all three were converted to saddle tanks. During the 1870s 684/1913 worked on the South Leicestershire branch.

They went into the duplicate list in 1875 and were scrapped at Crewe in 1877/9.

Summary: SSR 2-2-2s built by Sharp Bros, 1849

SSR No.	Name	Date	LNWR 7/59	4/62	Rebt	Reno'd	Scrapped
5	*Burton*	19/5/1849	53	653	5/69(ST)	1887(1/75)	26/3/77
6	*Stafford*	5/1849	84	684	/59, 5/71(ST)	1913(1/75)	20/1/79
7	*Bescot*	6/1849	116	716	9/69(ST)	1924(1/75)	4/4/79

Fairbairn 0-6-0 Goods Engines (SSR Nos 8, 9)
Nos 307, 308

These were two long-boiler engines of Sharp's Sphynx type ordered from Wm Fairbairn & Sons on 29th June 1848 at a price of £2,240 each, including tender. Before they were delivered the Board became anxious about the weight of the engines, perhaps having heard about the LNWR report on this subject of April 1849, and perhaps worrying about the SSR's wooden viaducts. On 3rd May 1849 Fairbairn & Sons were asked to delay their delivery while efforts were made to dispose of them to the LNWR or some other railway. No buyer could be found and the engines arrived on the SSR in July 1849.

Dimensions

Cylinders (2 inside)	18" x 24"
Diameter of wheels	5' 0"

Other dimensions were probably as the Sharp Bros S Div engines, 210 etc.

No 8 *Birmingham* was involved in a collision at Wednesbury on 19th September 1853 and a year later was listed among engines being overworked.

Both went into the duplicate list in 1866; the allocation of duplicate numbers given in the summary contradicts earlier accounts and is from official sources.

In 1868 both were rebuilt as saddle tanks, and in December 1871 reverted to the capital list.

No 9 was sold in 1875 under cut-up number 1982 to Richard Evans & Co of Haydock Colliery, Lancashire, probably becoming their No 4 *Newton*. If this identification is correct its rebuilding in 1868 was with 'long centres' having the rear axle behind the firebox.

In 1877 No 8 went back into the duplicate list with its sixth number, 1935, and was scrapped at Crewe in 1880.

Summary: SSR 0-6-0s built by Wm Fairbairn & Sons, 1849

SSR No.	Name	Date	LNWR 7/59	4/62	Rebt tank	Reno'd	Withdrawn
8	*Birmingham*	7/1849	307	907	a /68	1165(5/66), 1156(12/71), 1935(3/77)	Scr 30/4/80
9	*Wolverhampton*	7/1849	308	908	a /68(LC?)	1173(5/66), 1157(12/71),	as c/u 1982 Sold 17/8/75 Richd Evans & Co, £1,295

Garforth 0-4-2 Goods Engines (SSR Nos 10, 11)
No 221

These two inside-framed engines were added to SSR stock in 1850, and were paid for in the second half of that year. They were built by W. J. & J. Garforth & Co of the Dukinfield Foundry, near Ashton-under-Lyne, probably to Sharp's design and similar to Garforth's engines for the Manchester, Sheffield & Lincolnshire Railway - Nos 37 and 39-43 of 1848 and 1849.

The names of these engines *Angerstein* and *Belvidere* perhaps had some personal significance for the lessee of the SSR, J. R. McClean. He lived in Kent, where a local industrialist John Angerstein built a branch line from the SER to Angerstein's Wharf on the Thames in 1852; Belvedere is six miles away. The name of the engine is spelled *Belvidere* in all old references.

Dimensions

Cylinders (2 inside)	16" x 22"
Diameter of wheels	
Coupled	5' 0"
Trailing	3' 6"

No 10 *Belvidere* was among the engines described as "overworked" in 1854, being used for almost 21 hours at a stretch; it was withdrawn and probably scrapped in 1859, and was the only SSR engine not to receive an LNWR number.

In 1863 ex-No 11 *Angerstein* went into the duplicate list and, although not known to have been rebuilt, lasted until 1876 when it was scrapped at Crewe.

Summary: SSR 0-4-2s built by W. J. & J. Garforth & Co, 1850

SSR No.	Name	Date	LNWR 7/59	4/62	Reno'd	Scrapped
10	*Belvidere*	/1850	—			/59
11	*Angerstein*	/1850	221	821	1179 (5/63), 1865 (12/71)	10/2/76

Stephenson 0-6-0 Goods Engines (SSR Nos 12, 13)
Nos 309, 310

These two long-boiler engines are untraced in Stephenson & Co's list but were probably their 632 and 634, part of an order for the Chester & Holyhead Railway. The original order was for six goods engines (with tenders) at £2,100 each, to be delivered in January 1848, plus another eight at £2,380 from January to July of the same year. These fourteen were allotted works numbers 621 to 634. When this order was diverted to the S Div, only twelve goods engines were sent; at Stephenson & Co's request two 4-2-2 passenger engines (S Div 233 and 234) were substituted for two of the goods engines, which appear to be those sold to the SSR in January 1851. The SSR paid £3,944 18s (£3,944.90) to R. Stephenson & Co on 22nd February and the firm's records show deliveries to "Lancaster" of 634 on 10th January and 632 on 20th January, 1851. Perhaps this was meant to be "Lancaster & Carlisle Railway" because Lancaster itself seems an unlikely delivery point for engines from Newcastle to the SSR; maybe McClean or the SSR had an arrangement with the L&C and the LNWR to convey the engines south to Walsall.

The names of the engines are of places on the SSR.

Dimensions

Cylinders (2 inside)	18" x 24"
Diameter of wheels	5' 0"

Other dimensions were presumably as the Stephenson S Div engines, 211 etc.

Both engines were fitted with saddle tanks in the 1860s, 909 retaining its original long-boiler wheel arrangement with all wheels below the boiler barrel ('short centres'), 910 being rebuilt with the rear axle behind the firebox ('long centres'). Both had cast-iron Sharp-type wheels in the 1870s, probably fitted during their rebuilding as tanks.

No 12, by then renumbered 1806, was sold on 10th February 1874 to the Wrexham, Mold & Connah's Quay Railway for £1,100, where it became No 7. It was renumbered 3 in 1878 and was rebuilt as an 0-6-2ST in 1882. Substantial parts of it were used in the building of a 'new' 2-6-0T in 1901 which became Great Central Railway 400B in January 1905 and was scrapped in June 1907.

No 13, as 1801, was sold on 13th April 1875 to Barber, Walker & Co of Eastwood, Nottingham, for £1,065 "including injector".

Summary: SSR 0-6-0s built by R. Stephenson & Co, 1851

SSR No.	Name	Date	LNWR 7/59	4/62	Rebt tank	Reno'd	Withdrawn
12	*Pelsall*	1/1851	309	909	1/65 (SC)	1188 (2/67), 1806 (12/71)	Sold 10/2/74 WM&CQR, £1,100
13	*Alrewas*	1/1851	310	910	a /68 (LC)	1143 (5/66), 1801 (12/71)	Sold 13/4/75 Barber, Walker & Co, £1,065

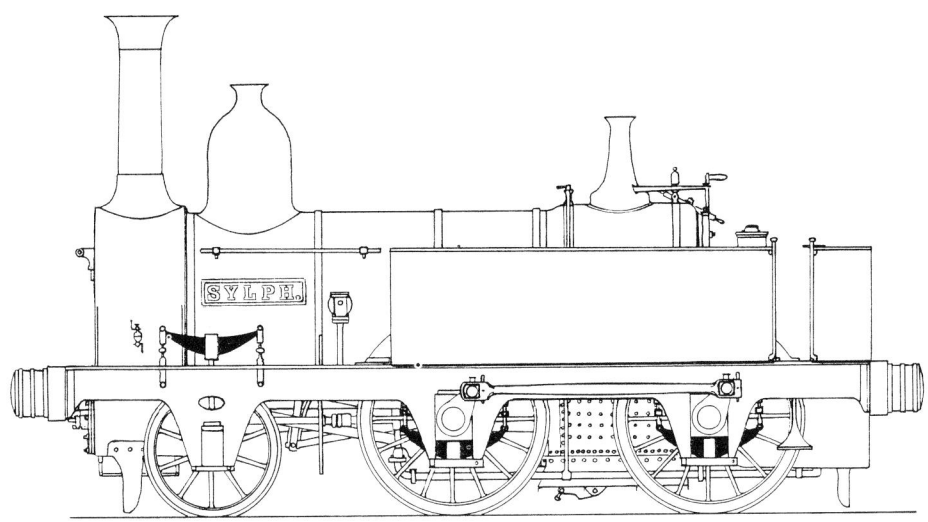

Fig. 99
South Staffordshire Railway No 14 *Sylph* 2-4-0T built by Sharp Bros in 1851; LNWR S Div No 111.

Sharp Bros 2-4-0 Tank Engines (SSR Nos 14, 15)
Nos 111, 112

These two were ordered from Sharp Bros on 7th December 1850 (Sharp order No 245, progressive numbers 675/6) at a cost of £1,720 each. They had inside cylinders and outside sandwich frames, with inside iron plate frames between the front bufferplank and the firebox. The leading axle springs were above the running plate but those on the driving wheel axles were underhung. There were short side tanks with a well tank under the footplate and bunker. The dome with a safety valve on top was placed just behind the chimney in Sharp Bros' usual style. Both were delivered in July 1851.

Dimensions

Cylinders (2 inside)	16" x 20"
Boiler	
Diameter	3' 10"
Length of barrel	9' 9"
Pitch	5' 10"
Heating surface	
Tubes (162, 2" dia, 10' 3" long)	864 sq ft
Firebox (3' 6" long x 3' 7" wide)	66 sq ft
Total	930 sq ft
Diameter of wheels	
Leading	3' 6"
Coupled	5' 0"
Wheelbase	6' 6" + 7' 0" = 13' 6"
Capacity	Coke 10 cwt
	Water 600 gal

They were given 16" x 22" cylinders by 1867.

It seems likely that they were mainly used for shunting, of which an inordinate amount was necessary on the SSR and No 14 *Sylph* was among the "overworked" engines listed in 1854; they were classed as goods engines by the LNWR.

Both went into the duplicate list in 1863; the numbers in the summary are from the Crewe 1872 list and other official records and modify some previously published versions.

No 14 was sold (as 1831) to the Northampton & Banbury Junction Railway in March 1873 for £700 and was probably scrapped in 1875.

No 15 was sold (as 1830) to the contractors Scott & Edwards in August 1873 for £900 and may have become their *Lady Cornewall*, hired to the Golden Valley Railway about 1887. This engine later worked on the Nottingham Suburban Railway and was advertised for sale in 1890 as "*Lady Cornwall*, 16in, by LNWR".

Summary: SSR 2-4-0T built by Sharp Bros, 1851

SSR No.	Name	Date	LNWR 7/59	4/62	Rebt	Reno'd	Withdrawn
14	*Sylph*	8/7/1851	111	711	-	1208(10/63), 1831(12/71)	Sold 3/73 N&BJ Rly, £700
15	*Safety*	14/7/1851	112	712	a /65	1209(10/63), 1830(12/71)	Sold 9/8/73 Scott & Edwards, £900

Sharp progressive numbers were 675/6.

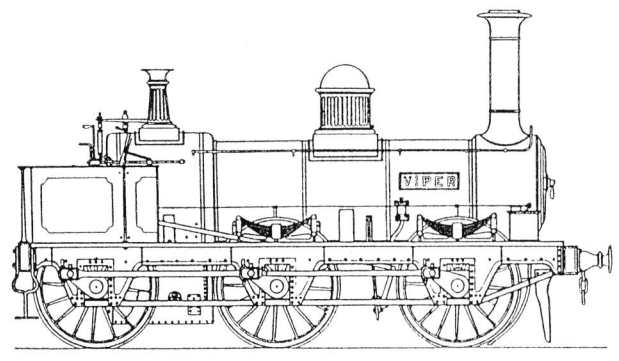

Fig. 100 South Staffordshire Railway No 16 *Viper* built by E.B. Wilson in 1852; LNWR S Div 301.

E. B. Wilson 0-6-0 Goods Engines (SSR Nos 16, 17) Nos 301, 302

These (and Nos 18 and 19) were obtained from E. B. Wilson & Co of the Railway Foundry, Leeds, in response to Trevithick's request for additional power. They were to Wilson's standard design of 0-6-0 with outside sandwich frames.

Dimensions

Cylinders (2 inside)	16" x 24"
Diameter of wheels	5' 0"

No other details are known to survive, but similar contemporary engines on the GNR had a wheelbase 7ft 9in + 7ft 9in = 15ft 6in, and weighed 29 tons 10 cwt.

The eventual disposal of these two engines is mysterious. They were replaced early in 1864 and would have gone into the duplicate list at that time, but their duplicate numbers are not known. Two possible numbers are 1166 and 1170, which would explain why the Wilson 0-6-0s are never heard of again, and why there is no mention of their scrapping in the Crewe records. 1166 was sold on 1st July 1864 to the Grand Trunk Railway of Canada for £700, and 1170 went for £600 on 2nd August 1864 to Eckersley & Bayliss, contractors for the Rowsley and Buxton extension line of the Midland Railway, which opened in October 1866.

Summary: SSR 0-6-0s built by E. B. Wilson & Co, 1852-3

SSR No.	Name	Date	LNWR 7/59	4/62	Replaced	Reno'd	Withdrawn
16	*Viper*	12/1852	301	901	1/64	1166?	/63-64?
17	*Stag*	1/1853	302	902	2/64	1170?	/63-64?

Fig. 101 South Staffordshire Railway No 19 *Justin* built by E.B. Wilson in 1853; LNWR S Div 181.

E. B. Wilson 2-4-0 Passenger Engines (SSR Nos 18, 19) Nos 160, 181

These two outside-framed engines followed Nos 16 and 17 from E. B. Wilson & Co, arriving on the line in May 1853.

Dimensions

Cylinders (2 inside)	16" x 20"
Diameter of wheels	
Leading	3' 9"
Coupled	5' 9"
Wheelbase	8' 0" + 7' 6" = 15' 6"

The above wheel and cylinder sizes are from the Crewe records; as built the engines may have had 6ft 6in driving wheels and 16 x 22in cylinders as described by James Bull.

The names *Justin* and *Esk* seem to have a Scottish association. Some accounts spell *Esk* as 'Eske' but this derives from an 1855 list of Trevithick's, whose clerk habitually added a curl to the letter k at the end of names - as in *Turke*, *Cossacke* etc.

781 (ex-*Justin*) was shedded at Bushbury in 1863 and acted as the pilot engine at Wolverhampton. In the same year it went into the duplicate list as 1207 and was scrapped in 1874.

760 (ex-*Esk*) went into the duplicate list as 1205 in 1863 but was reboilered in 1867. It was scrapped in 1876.

Summary: SSR 2-4-0s built by E. B. Wilson & Co, 1853

SSR No.	Name	Date	LNWR 7/59	4/62	Rebt	Reno'd	Scrapped
18	*Esk*	5/1853	160	760	b /67	1205(10/63), 1935(12/71)	4/76
19	*Justin*	5/1853	181	781	-	1207(10/63), 1936(12/71)	10/74

Fig. 102
South Staffordshire Railway No 21 *Ajax* built by Vulcan Foundry in 1855; LNWR S Div 306.

Vulcan Foundry 0-6-0 Goods Engines (SSR Nos 20, 21) Nos 305, 306

Thomas Brassey, as lessee of the Shrewsbury & Hereford Railway, ordered six engines from Vulcan Foundry (maker's working Nos 590-5, tenders 596-601, rotation Nos 377-82) but did not take the last two, which were instead delivered direct to the SSR in April 1855. They had 5ft coupled wheels and double frames of half-inch iron; the inner and outer plates were curved upwards to form the sides of the splashers. As built they each had a donkey engine to drive the feed pump.

By 1863 both had been given 5ft 6in wheels at Wolverton and they were described as "Express Goods"; several Crewe records mention 5ft 0in wheels but it is not known whether this is a repeated error or if smaller wheels were fitted later. 906 (ex-21 *Ajax*) was rebuilt with a Ramsbottom boiler in 1864.

Both went into the duplicate list in February 1866; 1226 (ex-20 *Priam*) was withdrawn in 1867, but 1227 (ex-21) was sold in May 1872 to the Northampton & Banbury Junction Rly for £700. It was probably scrapped soon after the LNWR took over the working of the line in 1875.

Dimensions

Cylinders (2 inside)	17" x 24"
Boiler	
Diameter	4' 0"
Length of barrel	11' 1"
Heating surface	
Tubes (183, 2⅛" dia, 11' 5" long)	1,134.6 sq ft
Firebox (4' 1" long x 3' 5" wide x 5' 2¼" high, with longitudinal midfeather)	85.0 sq ft
Total	1,219.6 sq ft
Grate area	13.75 sq ft
Diameter of wheels	5' 0"
Wheelbase	7' 7½" + 7' 8½" = 15' 4"
Weight	
On leading wheels	10 tons 0 cwt
On middle wheels	10 tons 0 cwt
On rear wheels	8 tons 10 cwt
Total	28 tons 10 cwt
Tender (6 wheel) capacity	Coke 100 cu ft
	Water 1,400 gal

Summary: SSR 0-6-0s built by the Vulcan Foundry Co, 1855

SSR No.	Name	Date	LNWR 7/59	4/62	Rebt	Reno'd	Withdrawn
20	*Priam*	4/1855	305	905	-	1226(2/66)	-/67
21	*Ajax*	4/1855	306	906	5/64	1227(2/66), 1827(12/71)	Sold 5/72, N&BJ Rly, £700

Vulcan rotation numbers were 381/2.

Fig. 103　South Staffordshire Railway Nos 22/3 *Bilston* and *Derby* built by Beyer, Peacock & Co, 1856; LNWR S Div 304 and 303.

Beyer, Peacock 0-4-2 Goods Engines (SSR Nos 22, 23) Nos 303, 304

These two were offered by Beyer, Peacock & Co on 3rd November 1855 for delivery in February 1856; this was accepted (BP order No 84) but they did not arrive on the SSR until July. They were part of an original order for four engines, but the other two were sold to the Oppeln-Tarnowitzer Eisenbahn in Prussia. The cost was £2,750 each and the SSR pair bore maker's numbers 29 and 30. (Incidentally Beyer's number 28 was a smaller saddle tank version of the same type, for the SSR lessee's Cannock Chase Colliery. Named *McClean*, it survived until 1955 when it was believed to be the oldest locomotive then working in Britain). They were inside-framed engines of typical Beyer design with a domeless boiler, a conical brass safety valve trumpet on the raised firebox, and a smokebox with a sloping front. The inside cylinders were inclined upwards at 1 in 12 towards the front, with piston and valve rods working over the leading axle.

Dimensions

Cylinders (2 inside)	16" x 24"
Boiler	
Diameter (inside)	
Middle ring	4' 0$\frac{7}{8}$"
Front and back rings	4' 0"
Length of barrel	11' 0"
Pitch	6' 5"
Length of firebox casing	4' 7"
Heating surface	
Tubes (192, 2" dia, 11' 3½" long)	1130 sq ft
Firebox	82 sq ft
Total	1212 sq ft
Grate area	14 sq ft
Diameter of wheels	
Coupled	5' 0"
Trailing	3' 6"
Tender	3' 6"
Wheelbase	
Engine	7' 9" + 7' 1" = 14' 10"
Tender	5' 6" + 5' 6" = 11' 0"
Weight	
On leading wheels	9 tons 10 cwt
On driving wheels	9 tons 5 cwt
On trailing wheels	4 tons 15 cwt
Total	23 tons 10 cwt

With these two the SSR reverted to giving its engines local placenames: *Bilston* and *Derby*.

No 22 *Bilston* was one of the dead engines being taken to Wolverton for repair when it was involved in the disastrous collision south of Roade on 29th October 1856.

They entered the duplicate list at the end of 1867 as 1268 (ex-23) and 1269 (ex-22) although one of them had already been given a new Ramsbottom boiler - like that put on 906 - and the other (1269) was similarly reboilered in 1869.

In 1871 they were taken back into the capital list, becoming 1176 (ex-23) and 1177 (ex-22). 1176 was shedded at Bangor in the early 1870s; both were scrapped at Crewe under cut-up numbers in 1877.

Summary: SSR 0-4-2s built by Beyer, Peacock & Co, 1856

SSR No.	Name	Date	LNWR 7/59	4/62	Rebt	Reno'd	Scrapped
22	*Bilston*	7/1856	304	904	4/69	1269(12/67), 1177(12/71) c/u 1984	26/3/77
23	*Derby*	7/1856	303	903	a /67	1268(12/67), 1176(12/71) c/u 1986	14/7/77

Beyer works numbers were 29 and 30.

Fairbairn 0-6-0 Goods Engines (SSR 24-29) Nos 311-316

When the LNWR agreed in January 1858 to purchase the SSR's locomotive stock, an outstanding order for six engines was also taken over. These had been ordered from William Fairbairn & Sons on 5th June 1857 at £2,950 each. They were delivered from March 1858, so were never actually SSR property, but appear to have been given numbers in the SSR list. The engines' names were again local placenames with one exception, *McConnell* - presumably selected when ordered (as O. S. Nock put it) "by an appreciative management".

They were long-boiler engines like the S Div Fairbairn Goods, with flush-top fireboxes but there were differences in detail. The middle wheels had flanged tyres, which must have involved some increase in the middle-to-rear wheelbase; the splashers were slightly bigger and the coupling-rod arches in the valance had segmental apertures; the large brass dome cover was plain as on the Fairbairn passenger engines. The extra lock-up safety valve behind the dome was not fitted on the engines as built.

Dimensions

Cylinders (2 inside)	18" x 24"
Diameter of wheels	5' 0"

One of these engines suffered a spectacular mishap while working on the SSR Walsall - Dudley section. At Bescot the line went over a timber viaduct across a reservoir which served Edward Elwell's Wednesbury Forge. The viaduct was already known to be in poor condition when in June 1859 part of it collapsed under *Cannock*, which was thrown into Elwell's Pool. The photograph of the half-submerged engine confirms its flush top firebox and the absence of the lock-up safety valve and possibly shows the nameplate on the side of the boiler just below the dome. The tender is the McConnell type with an equalising lever between the middle and rear axle springs. Recovery and repair of the engine cost £110 17s 7½d (£110.88); the bill was sent to the SSR.

Like the S Div Fairbairns, none of them became tank engines but all were rebuilt with Ramsbottom boilers in the 1860s. One of R. H. Bleasdale's photographs shows 914 (ex-*Vauxhall*) in this form at Bushbury in 1877.

All were scrapped in 1878-81 after a short period in the 18xx duplicate list.

Summary: SSR 0-6-0s built by Wm Fairbairn & Sons, 1858

SSR No.	Name	Date	LNWR 7/59	4/62	Rebt	Reno'd	Scrapped
24	*Cannock*	3/1858	311	911	b /65	1982(7/77)	30/7/79
25	*Bloxwich*	3/1858	312	912	b /65	1808(4/78)	1/12/79
26	*McConnell*	4/1858	313	913	/66	1809(4/78)	12/3/81
27	*Vauxhall*	5/1858	314	914	b /67	1829(4/78)	14/1/81
28	*Aston*	5/1858	315	915	12/63	1871(5/78)	17/10/78
29	*Tipton*	6/1858	316	916	b /68	1879(5/78)	26/8/78

Fig. 104 Accident at Elwell's Pool, Bescot, June 1859. Looking south-east with the chimney of Elwell's Wednesbury Forge in the background. The half-submerged engine is the South Staffordshire Railway Fairbairn long-boiler 0-6-0 *Cannock* (LNWR S Div 311) built in 1858. On the viaduct is one of the seven Sharp 'Sphynx' type of 1848, S Div 210 etc.
(Walsall Library)

Fig. 105 Fairbairn long-boiler 0-6-0 of 1858, 914 (ex-South Staffordshire Railway *Vauxhall*) after rebuilding. At Bushbury, 1877.
(R.H. Bleasdale)

ENGINES FROM THE NORTHERN DIVISION, 1860

The Southern Division expanded northwards to Stafford on 16th January 1860, and it was arranged that 34 of the 73 N Div engines which had worked between there and Rugby would be handed over to McConnell. The engines actually transferred were 32 of the 'Old Crewe' type: three 7ft singles, twenty 6ft singles and nine 2-4-0 Crewe Goods; the other two were new 0-6-0 goods engines built by Beyer, Peacock & Co.

These 34 engines were given S Div numbers 320-53, following engines built at Wolverton which entered stock in January 1860.

1. Beyer, Peacock 0-6-0 Goods Engines
Nos 321, 322

Ramsbottom visited Beyer, Peacock & Co's Gorton Foundry, Manchester, on 28th December 1859 and found that they had four goods engines available for sale at £2,550 each. He at once wrote to the Chairman, Lord Chandos, telling him they were "very similar in size and type to those we are now making." He was told to buy them, and this was ratified on 2nd January.

They were from a batch of six built in 1859 (BP order No 362, works Nos 120-5) for the Danube & Black Sea Railway in (present-day) Romania. The first two had been sent there, but as the line did not open until October 1860 four remained in Manchester. After they were sold to the LNWR, another four were built in 1860 for the Danube line. They were of typical Beyer 0-6-0 design and, as Ramsbottom said, very like the DX class but slightly smaller, and with the firm's standard boiler mountings: a large brass dome with spring balance safety valves on the middle of the boiler and a raised manhole cover on the firebox top carrying only a whistle. Inside cylinders were inclined upwards at 1 in 10, and the smokebox had the usual sloping front. The engines were handed over to the LNWR at Ardwick, Manchester: BP Nos 122/3 on 12th January and 124/5 on 17th. It is not known how the LNWR numbers were distributed among them; the two to be transferred were immediately sent south; the other two became N Div 133 *Ostrich* and 199 *Castor*.

Dimensions

Cylinders (2 inside)	16" x 22"
Boiler	
Diameter (outside)	
Middle ring	4' 1"
Front and back rings	3' 11¾"
(plates thickened to ⅝" at lap joints)	
Length of barrel	10' 3"
Pitch	6' 6"
Length of firebox casing	4' 7"
Heating surface	
Tubes (168, 2" dia, 10' 6½" long)	927.2 sq ft
Firebox	81.9 sq ft
Total	1009.1 sq ft
Grate area	14 sq ft
Diameter of wheels	5' 0"
Wheelbase	6' 9" + 7' 11" = 14' 8"
Weight	
On leading wheels	9 tons 11½ cwt
On driving wheels	8 tons 1½ cwt
On trailing wheels	7 tons 10 cwt
Total	25 tons 3 cwt

Both S Div engines went into the duplicate list in 1867 as 1252/3, but were restored to capital stock as 1180/1 in December 1871. They were rebuilt with Crewe boilers in 1869 and 1874; the drawing dated 7th August 1868 is of a three-ring telescopic barrel 10ft 1in long, increasing in external diameter from a 3ft 11¾in front ring to a 4ft 1in back ring, and with a firebox casing 4ft 9in long.

Latterly they seem to have done odd jobs; 1181 was working as a ballast engine on the Peterborough line in August 1875 when it was derailed at Oundle ballast pit.

Fig. 106
Beyer, Peacock 0-6-0 built for the Danube & Black Sea Railway but acquired instead by the LNWR; S Div 321 and 322.

Fig. 107   Beyer, Peacock 0-6-0 formerly S Div 321, on Tyneside in the 1890s.

(R.H. Inness photo, Frank Jones collection)

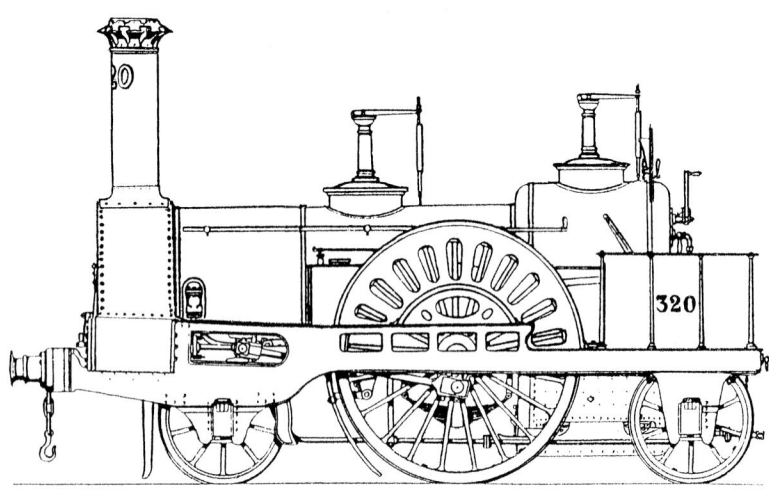

Fig. 108   Crewe 2-2-2 with 7ft driving wheels, transferred to S Div in 1860: 320, 323 and 324.

This engine was scrapped in 1879. In that year 1180 went back into the duplicate list as 1882 and was used as a shunter in Crewe Works yard. It was sold on 10th July 1884 to the Rhondda & Swansea Bay Railway for £823, being sent from Crewe to Swansea on 3rd February 1885 with "R&SBR" painted on its tender side. It became R&SBR No 2, but was sold in February 1891 to William Westlake, a haulage contractor at Swansea Docks, for £550. He quickly resold it to the Neath Low Level Haulage Co and shortly afterwards it appears to have been sold again (perhaps via the Mersey Engineering Works of Swansea who advertised a similar engine for sale in November 1894) to a colliery on Tyneside. A photograph taken in the 1890s by R. H. Inness shows the engine as No 11, with buffers repositioned for chaldron wagons and fitted with heavy wooden brake blocks on the middle and rear wheels. Various Crewe modifications are evident but it is still coupled to its original Beyer, Peacock tender. It seems likely that it was No 11 of the Backworth Coal Co, and that it might have lasted until about 1909; another possibility is that it belonged to the Cramlington Coal Co, in which case it would have gone by 1901.

2. Crewe 7ft 2-2-2 Passenger Engines
   Nos 320, 323, 324

The three 7ft singles had been built at Crewe in 1853/4 and were simply the 'Old Crewe' large firebox (LFB) type with bigger driving wheels. The higher axle allowed almost horizontal cylinders which involved a slightly different shape of outside frame. At the time they were transferred all three had the original domeless Trevithick boiler with two Dewrance spring balance safety valves, one on the boiler top and the other on the raised firebox.

Fig. 109
Crewe 2-2-2 with 6ft driving wheels and small firebox; transferred to S Div in 1860: 329-344. 325-328 were similar but had a longer firebox and boiler mountings like the 7ft Crewe engines.

Dimensions

Cylinders (2 outside)	15¼" x 20"
Boiler	
Diameter	3' 6"
Length of barrel	9' 8¾"
Pitch	6' 1"
Length of firebox casing	4' 5"
Heating surface	
Tubes (158, 1¾" dia, 9' 11⅞" long)	721.0 sq ft
Firebox	65.8 sq ft
Total	786.8 sq ft
Grate area	13.1 sq ft
Boiler pressure	100 lb/sq in
Diameter of wheels	
Leading	3' 7½"
Driving	7' 0"
Trailing	3' 7½"
Wheelbase	6' 10" + 6' 6" = 13' 4"
Weight	21 tons 10 cwt

3. Crewe 6ft 2-2-2 Passenger Engines
Nos 325-344

The twenty 6ft engines had been built between 1845 and 1857, three at Edge Hill (334/6/7) the remainder at Crewe. The newest four were the large firebox (LFB) type; of the other small firebox (SFB) type, two had 'direct action' valve gear while fourteen had 'indirect action' and intermediate rocking shafts. Typically, the LFB engines had domeless boilers like the 7ft class, while the SFB type had a dome on the firebox. The oldest of the engines, *Mersey*, was built in Grand Junction days and had been loaned to the London & Birmingham back in 1846.

They were renumbered into the S Div list as 325-44 in order of size and age, the LFB engines coming first, then the SFB direct action, with the SFB indirect action engines last. The last group (for whatever reason) was arranged only roughly in order of seniority.

Dimensions

LFB Engines 325-8:

Cylinders (2 outside)	15¼" x 20"
Boiler	
Diameter	3' 6"
Length of barrel	9' 8¾"
Pitch	5' 7"
Length of firebox casing	4' 5"
Heating surface	
Tubes (158, 1¾"dia, 9' 11⅞")	721.0 sq ft
Firebox	65.8 sq ft
Total	786.8 sq ft
Grate area	13.1 sq ft
Boiler pressure	100 lb/sq in
Diameter of wheels	
Leading	3' 6"
Driving	6' 0"
Trailing	3' 6"
Wheelbase	6' 10" + 6' 6" = 13' 4"
Weight	21 tons 3 cwt

SFB Engines 329-44

As above, except:

Cylinders (2 outside)	15" x 20"
Boiler	
Length of barrel	9' 9"
Length of firebox casing	3' 7½"
Heating surface	
Tubes (158, 1¾" dia, 9' 11⅝" long)	720 sq ft
Firebox	55 sq ft
Total	775 sq ft
Grate area	10.5 sq ft
Boiler pressure	75/85 lb/sq in
Wheelbase	
Nos 329-42/4	6' 0" + 7' 0" = 13' 0"
No 343	5' 6" + 7' 6" = 13' 0"
Weight	18 tons 0 cwt

Fig. 110
Crewe Goods 2-4-0 with small firebox; transferred to S Div in 1860: 351-353. 345-350 were similar but had a longer firebox.

4. Crewe 2-4-0 Goods Engines
Nos 345-353

These nine Crewe Goods engines were all built at Crewe from 1852 to 1857, six LFB and three SFB but all had 'direct action' link motion. They were renumbered S Div 345-53 in age order, newest first.

Dimensions

LFB Engines 345-50

Cylinders (2 outside)	15¼" x 20"
Boiler	
Diameter	3' 6"
Length of barrel	9' 4"
Pitch	5' 7"
Length of firebox casing	4' 5"
Heating surface	
Tubes (158, 1¾" dia, 9' 10½" long)	715 sq ft
Firebox	81 sq ft
Total	796 sq ft
Grate area	13.1 sq ft
Boiler pressure	100 lb/sq in
Diameter of wheels	
Leading	3' 6"
Coupled	5' 0"
Wheelbase	5' 10" + 7' 8" = 13' 6"
Weight	
On leading wheels	6 tons 15 cwt
On driving wheels	9 tons 1 cwt
On trailing wheels	5 tons 14 cwt
Total	21 tons 10 cwt

SFB Engines 351-3

As LFB, except:	
Cylinders (2 outside)	15" x 20"
Boiler	
Length of barrel	9' 4½"
Pitch	5' 3"
Length of firebox casing	3' 7½"
Heating surface	
Tubes (158, 1¾" dia, 9' 7½" long)	697 sq ft
Firebox	59 sq ft
Total	756 sq ft
Grate area	10.5 sq ft
Boiler pressure	80/85 lb/sq in
Wheelbase	5' 4" + 7' 4" = 12' 8"
Weight	
On leading wheels	5 tons 16 cwt
On driving wheels	9 tons 0 cwt
On trailing wheels	4 tons 16 cwt
Total	19 tons 12 cwt

According to the drawings which accompanied James Bull's article in the 1898 *Locomotive Magazine* the S Div numbers were painted on the footplate side fenders and brass numerals were fixed to the chimney fronts. The nameplates were removed, and when Ramsbottom told the Locomotive & Stores Committee on 2nd February that "the nameplates of engines transferred to the S Div might be made available for the new engines about to be built, if not required by Mr McConnell", they were sent back to Crewe.

The names were all used again at Crewe during 1860. Twenty of them went to new engines: eight Problems, ten DX Goods and the two N Div Beyer goods; the other twelve went to engines taken over from the Birkenhead Railway in November. Whether these nameplates were actually re-used seems doubtful in the case of the Problems, with their 4ft radius splashers. Some names went from engine to engine with bewildering rapidity in the early 1860s and eventually six came back to the engines they started with.

Four of the SFB singles were rebuilt at Wolverton in 1860/2, two of them (334/5) with Crewe-type large fireboxes and non-Crewe domes while retaining their original frames. Crewe Goods 353 was also rebuilt there in October 1862.

One of the Crewe engines was on the 9.30pm passenger train from Birmingham to Wolverhampton on 21st April 1861 near Soho when its leading axle broke, derailing the train. No-one was hurt but the S Div Committee called the attention of the Stores Committee to "Mr McConnell's report upon the condition of the axles of the engines received from Crewe, which he considered it was necessary to replace." On 16th May the report was passed to Ramsbottom.

This was McConnell's last thrust. Ten days later the Chairman, Admiral Moorsom - his supporter from his first days on the LNWR - collapsed and died, and was succeeded by Richard Moon. Thereafter McConnell could only react defensively while Moon and his Special Committee began to look closely into S Div Locomotive Department expenditure. Their report came out early in 1862 and was followed quickly by McConnell's resignation and the amalgamation of the two locomotive departments under Ramsbottom.

The N Div engines, after their 27 months in southern hands, went back under Crewe control and were renumbered into the all-LNWR list as 920-953. Possibly 330 went directly into the duplicate list as 1195 in May 1862; it was replaced in October.

Most of them, all of the goods engines and most of the SFB passenger engines, ran nameless for the rest of their lives; those that were given nameplates had to wait a few years. The three 7ft engines were renamed in 1864, *Etna* and *Chandos* receiving their old names back after they had, in the interim, adorned the splashers of ex-Birkenhead and DX engines. The other 7ft engine, *Owl*, was given a new name, *Marathon*, its old name having been given to a Problem. *Latona*, one of the 6ft LFB engines, also got its name back in 1864, but the others were renamed later, *Prince Eugene* not until 1872. Webb seems to have started a scheme to name all the passenger engines and perhaps *Sefton* and *Glendower* got their old nameplates back about this time, when old *Majestic* became *Ant*. *Glendower* appears to have been the only one of the SFB engines to be renamed.

The more recent of the passenger engines were rebuilt with 16in cylinders and Ramsbottom boilers in the 1860s. The three oldest goods engines were converted to side tanks in 1868-72; one of them was fitted with a steam crane at the same time and was later sent to the Carriage Department at Wolverton. Five other goods engines were altered to saddle tanks in 1873/4; one of these, 946, was painted in passenger livery when photographed in 1877 and was probably used as the station pilot at New Street.

Evidently the transferred Crewe engines continued working on the S Div; some of them were still in the south in the 1870s when the 6ft LFB 925-8 were all shedded at Bletchley for a time.

In 1878 928 *Prince Eugene* was at Camden, working on the Euston-St Albans trains and 927 *Latona* was at Birmingham, working to Derby. Both later went to Rugby. 926 *Ant* went to Warrington, then Longsight; *Sefton* was also at Longsight in the 1880s.

Of the 7ft engines, 920 *Etna* was at Stafford latterly, while 923 *Chandos* went to Edge Hill.

All were eventually scrapped at Crewe in 1872-95, apart from the two oldest goods engines, the former *Quicksilver* and *Croxteth* (S Div 352/3) which were sold in 1892 for £600 each. 353 went to J. H. Hurman of Cardiff; 352 went to the Abram Colliery at Bickershaw, Lancashire, where it is believed to have survived until about 1925.

Fig. 111
Crewe 6ft 2-2-2 *Sefton* which was S Div 325 in 1860-2. At Prestbury c1886, as rebuilt with a Webb boiler and renumbered in the duplicate list as 1848.
(*LNWR Society*)

Fig. 112
Crewe Goods 2-4-0 which was S Div 353 in 1860-2. As converted to a side tank in 1872; photographed at Walsall shed c1882.
(*R.H. Bleasdale*)

Fig. 113
Crewe Goods 2-4-0 which was S Div 346 in 1860-2. As converted to a saddle tank in 1874; photographed at Monument Lane shed, Birmingham, in 1877.
(*R.H. Bleasdale*)

Summary: Engines acquired from the Northern Division, January 1860

1. Beyer, Peacock & Co 0-6-0 goods engines

No.	Date	Reno'd 4/62	Rebt*	Reno'd	Withdrawn
321	1/1860	921		1252(1/67), 1180(12/71)	
			11/74(c)	1882(2/79)	Sold 10/7/84, Rhondda & Swansea Bay Rly, £823, sent 3/2/85
322	1/1860	922		1253(1/67), 1181(12/71)	
			a /69		c/u 1828 Scr 14/1/79

2. Crewe 7ft 2-2-2 passenger engines

S Div No.	ex-N Div	Built	Motion No.	Name to 1/60	Reno'd 4/62	Rebt	Renamed	Reno'd	Scrapped
320	343	8/54	289	Etna	920	8/67	Etna (/64)	1853(11/76)	5/1/78
323	325	1/54	284	Chandos	923	9/64	Chandos (9/64)	1835(5/76)	31/4/77
324	134	11/53	282	Owl	924	7/68	Marathon (/64)	1880(11/76)	20/8/77

3. Crewe 6ft 2-2-2 passenger engines

S Div No.	ex-N Div	Built	Motion No.	Name to 1/60	Reno'd 4/62	Rebt*	Renamed	Reno'd	Scrapped
325	285	11/57	391	Sefton	925	3/75	Sefton (/73?)	1848(1/84), 3068(2/87)	11/88
326	368	6/55	337	Majestic	926	7/75	Ant (/73)	1858(1/84), 3075(5/87)	11/89
327	364	4/55	332	Latona	927	8/70	Latona (/64)	1863(1/84)	8/85
328	316	8/53	256	Prince Eugene	928	1/68	Prince Eugene (/72)	1870(1/84)	7/86
329	280	4/52	202	Glendower	929	11/63	Glendower (/73?)	1831(3/73)	10/12/78
330	278	4/52	200	Locke	930?	1/64		1195(/62), 1890(12/71)	14/8/78
331	61	11/50		Phosphorus	931	6/68		1849(3/73)	4/9/78
332	236	4/49		Hawkstone	932	12/63		1959(3/73)	1/78
333	224	9/48		Violet	933	1/64		1910(3/73)	4/10/78
334	211	5/48**		Onyx	934	6/62(W,LFB)		1107(1/66), 1893(12/71)	20/2/79
335	192	1/48		Hero	935	/62(W,LFB)		1135(1/66), 1894(12/71)	14/8/78
336	231	12/48**		Firefly	936	11/59		1906(3/73)	1/74
337	60	11/49**		Tantalus	937	5/59		1958(12/72)	20/1/73
338	220	8/48		Waterloo	938	1/59, 8/70		1949(9/72)	15/12/77
339	33	10/46		Erebus	939	1/58		1900(3/73)	8/73
340	111	7/47		Russell	940	2/58		1860(4/73)	10/74
341	221	9/48		Trafalgar	941	/58		1841(8/73)	18/4/78
342	44	9/46		Harlequin	942	10/59			8/73
343	77	11/45		Mersey	943	5/60(W)		c/u 1910	Scr 22/6/72
344	97	12/46		Atalanta	944	8/60(W)			17/10/72

** built at Edge Hill

4. Crewe 2-4-0 goods engines

S Div 1/60	ex-N Div	Built	Motion No.	Name to 1/60	Reno'd 4/62	Rebt*	Reno'd	Withdrawn	
345	199	3/57	375	Castor	945	5/69	1834(1/81), 3058(12/86)		Scr 7/87
346	215	8/56	366	Spitfire	946	5/74(ST)		c/u 1814	Scr 4/84
347	356	2/55	324	Memnon	947	2/73(ST)	1913(10/84)		Scr 8/85
348	345	9/54	301	Turk	948	6/73(ST)		c/u 1917	Scr 7/84
349	133	5/54	280	Ostrich	949	11/74(ST)	1916(10/84), 3035(6/89)		Scr 7/91
350	312	5/53	248	Tubal	950	12/73(ST,S)	1925(10/84)		Scr 4/85
351	296	11/52	228	Bellerophon	951	8/68(T & steam crane) To Carriage Dept, Crewe, as CD4, 8/77 To Wolverton, as CD2, 3/86.			Scr 3/95
352	293	11/52	225	Quicksilver	952	3/70(T)	1841(5/83), 3062(2/87)	Sold 4/92 Abram Colly Co, Bickershaw, Wigan, £600 ?Scr /25	
353	283	4/52	206	Croxteth	953	10/62(W), 12/72(T)	1982(5/83), 3030(2/91)	Sold 6/92 J. H. Hurman, Cardiff, £600	

*Rebuilding:
W - rebuilt at Wolverton; T - side tank; ST - saddle tank; S - steel boiler; c - cab.

Class G

Wolverton 0-4-2 Tank Engines, 1860
Nos 102, 110, 125, 174, 354

The year 1858 saw a renewed interest in tank engines on the S Div. In April the 6½-mile branch from the main line at Watford to St Albans was finished and ready for Board of Trade inspection before opening. A turntable had been put down at the far end of the line but the inspecting officer, Lt Col Yolland, insisted on another at Watford; he was told that until this could be installed, the LNWR intended working the line *with tank engines only*. That was on 24th April; the branch was opened on 5th May, using tender engines working through from Euston, and on 13th May the directors asked McConnell about tank engines. By this time all the old Bury 2-2-2T rebuilds had been disposed of and he had only two tank engines in stock, Sharp's *Sylph* and *Safety* from the South Staffordshire Railway. He proposed altering six others to tank engines but was told to convert two only. Meanwhile a 40ft turntable was ordered for Watford.

The Northern Division likewise possessed only a very few tank engines, but a programme of altering the oldest and smallest of the 2-4-0 Crewe Goods had begun. Ten conversions had been authorised when Ramsbottom reported in January 1859 that they were such a success for shunting and working short trains that 40 more were ordered "to be converted to tank engines as they come in for new boilers".

At the next meeting of the Locomotive Committee on 22nd January, McConnell was authorised to "prepare to lay down ... six passenger tank engines but gradually throwing over the expenditure so that they may be completed only during the two half-years of 1860." In October it was ordered that the five tank engines which had been begun should be completed in the first half of 1860, but so much work was being done at Wolverton that they were still under construction in March and were not completed until the second half of the year. In the end only those five were built, charged to the replacement account and thus taking old numbers. However it was ruled on 23rd January 1861 that one of them would be charged to capital, and it was presumably then renumbered 354; the others were 102/10/25/74.

They were inside-framed, inside-cylinder 0-4-2s with a well tank under the footplate and bunker as in the Bury 2-2-2T rebuilds; the boiler was built for a pressure of 150 lb/sq in, which was the standard for new Wolverton engines from 1860. It had McConnell's patent arrangement of twin grates separated by a longitudinal midfeather and a long combustion chamber. A corniced brass dome was on the boiler barrel, with a lock-up safety valve towards the front of the long raised firebox top. The valve gear was Gooch stationary link motion.

The cost of each engine was £2,146 5s (£2,146.25)

Dimensions

Cylinders (2 inside)	15" x 24"
Boiler	
Length of barrel	7' 6"
Length of firebox + combustion chamber	8' 0"
Grate area	11.4 sq ft
Boiler pressure	150 lb/sq in
Diameter of wheels	
Coupled	5' 6"
Trailing	4' 0"
Wheelbase	7' 6" + 9' 6" = 17' 0"

Fig. 114
The only known photograph showing a Class G 0-4-2T. At Hinckley station c1865 on a westbound train; the engine number is illegible. As fitted with Crewe chimney cap, displacement lubricators and front handrail.
(Gordon Webster collection)

These were the first LNWR tank engines to be used on local trains in the London area. They were also used on branch lines and one of them was photographed on the Nuneaton-Leicester line at Hinckley with a six-carriage passenger train in the mid-1860s, by which time it had been given Ramsbottom modifications. Crewe classed them as goods engines. They were all put into the duplicate list in 1867/8, and were scrapped in 1874-6. Two accountants' lists of 1874 and 1875 describe these Class G engines as having 16in x 24in cylinders, but this may be only a repeated clerical error as no record of such enlargement has survived, and the contemporary duplicate list clearly shows 15in x 24in for all five.

All of them retained McConnell's "air chamber boiler" until the end.

Annual totals:

	capital	duplicate
to 30/11/1867:	5	-
30/11/1868:	-	5
to 30/11/1873:	-	5
30/11/1874:	-	3
30/11/1875:	-	2
30/11/1876:	-	-

Summary: 0-4-2T Class G built at Wolverton, 1860

No.	Date	Reno'd 4/62	Renumbered		Scrapped
125	7/1860	725	1265(6/68),	1853(12/71)	7/76
102	8/1860	702	1270(12/67),	1855(12/71)	8/75
110	8/1860	710	1271(12/67),	1856(12/71)	8/74
174	9/1860	774	1266(6/68),	1854(12/71)	6/3/76
354	b /1860	954	1272(6/68),	1857(12/71)	1/74

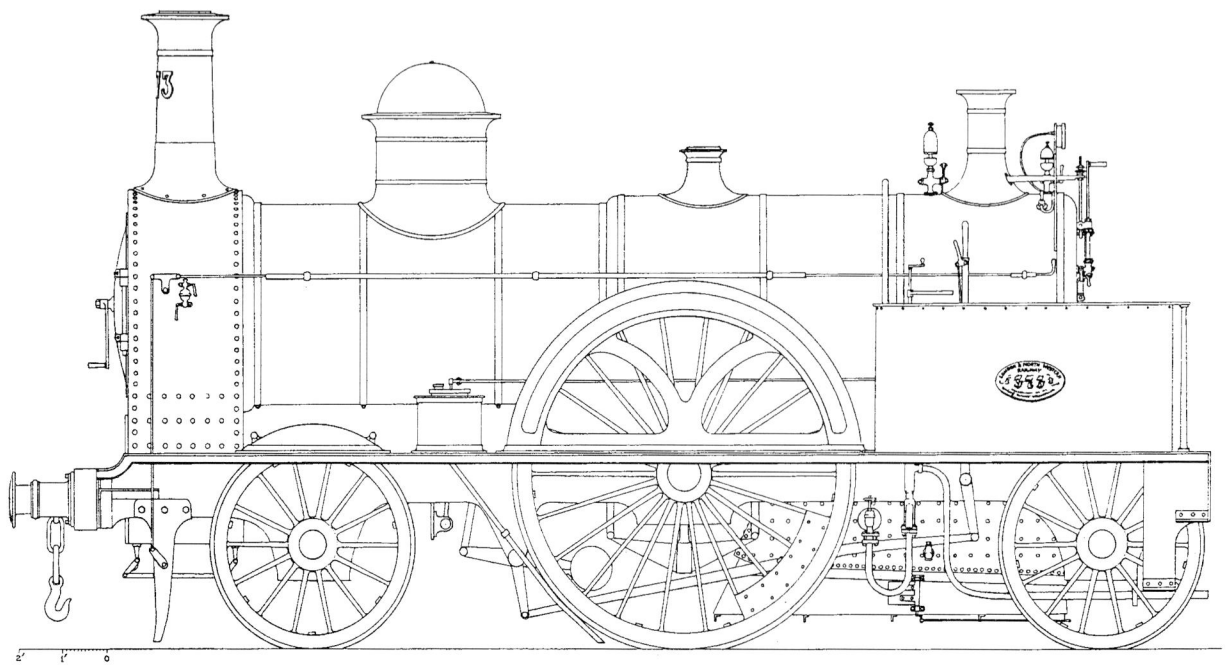

Fig. 115   Class H Special Large Bloomer built at Wolverton, 1861.

Class H

Wolverton 2-2-2 Passenger Engines - Special Large Bloomers, 1861
Nos 372, 373, 375

On 2nd March 1860 the Locomotive Committee approved McConnell's recommendation to build five 7ft Bloomers at Wolverton. Two months later he gave his opinion that the weight of the engines working on the S Div need not be exceeded, but rumours of Sturrock's big new singles for the Great Northern had reached the LNWR and on 10th May, two days before the first of the GNR engines (229 class) was delivered, the Committee seems to have been panicked into a decision to go for a bigger engine. While approving the weights and specifications of "the present standard classes" - the N Div Problem at $26\frac{3}{4}$ tons, the 7ft Bloomer at $29\frac{1}{2}$ tons and the Patent at $31\frac{1}{4}$ tons - the Committee resolved that "in view of the probable requirements of the traffic the proposal of Mr McConnell to build the five passenger engines (already ordered) with 18in cylinders, 24in stroke be approved, of the weight of 33 tons, as an experiment."

Drawings for the revised design were completed on 13th June 1860; as normal Bloomers they would have had 16in cylinders but the GNR engines had 17in: the new Class H Special Bloomers would have 18in. Then, having got his way with the Committee over increasing the size of these five engines, two weeks later McConnell went on to propose that the order should be increased to ten. The Committee did not agree and he was reminded that "the engines were intended as an experiment".

The five were put in hand in the New Erecting Shop at Wolverton, and were to be numbered 372-6, after the last of the Express Goods then on order. In May 1861 the first was completed and was given the number 375.

The original Bloomer design was enlarged to accommodate cylinders two inches bigger in bore and stroke, with driving wheels increased to 7ft 6in. The frameplates were thicker, increased from 1in to $1\frac{1}{8}$in and the wheelbase was lengthened by fourteen inches to 18 feet, the same as the new GNR engine and the longest for a six-wheeler at that time. The pistons were made of wrought iron, to a McConnell patent, and the valve gear was Stephenson, not Gooch as has sometimes been stated. The boiler was mounted very high to clear the cranks, without any of the recessing of the Patent class, but it was the firebox which provoked the most comment at the time. It was enormous, with two grates completely separated by a longitudinal midfeather; twin fireholes, side by side, were to be fed with coal alternately, like Fairbairn's Lancashire boiler. Hot gases from both grates mixed in a combustion chamber, which left only a comparatively short distance of 9ft 4in between the tubeplates.

Describing this firebox, in June 1862 *The Engineer* commented: "The plan hardly needs criticism now, for its evils are so well understood that there can be very little danger of its being further reproduced. Any resident in the neighbourhood [of Camden Shed] has the opportunity every hour of the day of witnessing its smoke emitting capabilities, and the boilermakers at the Wolverton shops know well the weeping habits of the midfeathers, ever lachrymose with percolations which caulking cannot check nor patches dam the flow..."

The working pressure was 150 lb per square inch which McConnell, like Sturrock, only began using in 1860 - repeated claims of much earlier adoption notwithstanding.

Authority to fit Giffard injectors to new engines was given to McConnell and Ramsbottom on 20th February 1861; these were obtained from Sharp, Stewart & Co, the British patent-holder, at prices from £32 to £40 each. Each engine of the H class had two injectors of the largest (10mm) size. These were fitted on the firebox sides, with delivery just above grate level.

Another great improvement of the period was the weldless steel tyre produced by Krupp of Essen. Each of the H class had these tyres on all wheels, engine and tender. With an eye to publicity in the British market, Krupp made a sporting offer: less than half-price on delivery, with the balance to be paid *after* the tyres had outlived the average Farnley tyre, in instalments every 10,000 miles until paid in full, or until the tyres wore out. This was accepted for the five engines, the full price of the tyres being £4 5s (£4.25) per cwt. Krupp also offered six steel crank axles at £180 each "in the forged state, roughly turned" with a ten-year guarantee. This also was accepted.

Following McConnell's usual practice, the leading and driving axle springs were connected by equalising levers; the tender was similarly equipped between the middle and the rear axles. The tender itself was an enlarged version of the usual Wolverton standard.

Outwardly a Special Large Bloomer must have been striking to 1861 eyes. The high, fat boiler was adorned with a lot of polished brasswork - the corniced dome, two safety valve covers and two ring-mouldings around the barrel. One of these was next to the smokebox, the other was midway along the boiler where the barrel increased in diameter around the combustion chamber. This rear portion was elliptical in cross-section, slightly higher than wide, whose outline continued smoothly over the firebox to the footplate end, where there was a third prominent brass moulding. There was more polished brass in the double flat bands outlining the immense splasher. The chimney was short (for those days) with a copper cap, and the paintwork was probably a rich dark red.

The engines were big and showy, but not everyone was favourably impressed: G. P. Neele contrasted them with Ramsbottom's "more elegant" Problem class.

Dimensions

Cylinders (2 inside)	18" x 24"
Steam ports	14" x 1⅞"
Exhaust ports	14" x 3¾"
Boiler	
Diameter of barrel, front section	4' 0"
rear section, elliptical, vertical	4' 4"
horizontal	4' 3"
Length of barrel, front section	8' 7"
rear section	3' 2"
Firebox, mean length	6' 6"
mean width	3' 8"
height from firebars to crown	6' 2½"
Combustion chamber, length	2' 4½"
width	3' 8"
Firebox casing, length	7' 2"
mean width	4' 2¼"
Pitch	7' 5½"
Heating surface	
Tubes (214, 1⅞" dia, 9' 4" long)	980.35 sq ft
Firebox	242.50 sq ft
Total	1,222.85 sq ft
Grate area	26.00 sq ft
Boiler pressure	150 lb/sq in
Diameter of wheels	
Leading	4' 6"
Driving	7' 6"
Trailing	4' 6"
Tender	3' 9"
Wheelbase	
Engine	8' 6" + 9' 6" = 18' 0"
Tender	6' 7½" + 6' 7½" = 13' 3"
Length over buffers	
Engine	27' 4"
Tender	21' 9½"
Total	49' 1½"
Tender (6 wheel) capacity	coal 2 tons; water 2,500 gal
Weight (in working order)	
On leading wheels	11 tons 18 cwt
On driving wheels	14 tons 6 cwt
On trailing wheels	8 tons 10 cwt
Total, engine	34 tons 14 cwt
Tender, loaded	25 tons 2 cwt
Total, engine and tender	59 tons 16 cwt

The weight of the engine in working order was thus 1 ton 14 cwt heavier than had been stipulated by the Locomotive Committee. On 11th June, only a few days after 375 had started work, a bridge near Kenilworth collapsed under one of the heavy Fairbairn Goods engines and at the next meeting it was "ordered that Mr McConnell's attention be specially called" to a previous minute requiring him to report the weights of new engines each half-year.

Another engine (372) appeared in August, and in November a third (373) which got off to a bad start by killing a Wolverton fitter after its second trial trip to Bletchley and back on 14th December 1861. The engine, with five people on the footplate, had just drawn up on the turntable at the entrance to the Works; the fitter, James Davey, was reaching between the spokes to feel the connecting rod big end when the fireman opened the regulator.

A week later Moon's motion of censure on McConnell was placed before the Board; in January it was put to the vote, and McConnell was given the bad news, but he remained in post. Then on 19th February 1862 orders were issued that owing to damage to the track, the three H class engines were to be withdrawn from the line and, if possible, sold. Work was stopped on the remaining two. The next day, McConnell wrote out his resignation.

In all, 375 had worked for nine months and had run 23,906 miles; 372 for six months and had run 10,560 miles; 373 had hardly worked at all. Average coal consumption per mile had been 41.68 lb, per ton/mile 0.71 lb. The three engines went into store at Wolverton.

In the previous year the organisers of the forthcoming International Exhibition asked if the LNWR wished to participate, as at the Crystal Palace ten years before. Admiral Moorsom was then alive, McConnell was in high esteem and some promise was probably given at that time that one of the new Special Large Bloomers would be exhibited; by the end of 1861 it was common knowledge in Wolverton that 373 was intended for the Exhibition. But with Moon in the chair and McConnell suddenly out of favour, the scheme seems to have been countermanded and 373 was not included in the official catalogue of exhibits. Then, after McConnell's departure and with the H class lying idly in store, it was decided to show 373 after all and it was taken through the streets to South Kensington behind William Bray's big traction engine. By the time the Exhibition opened on 1st May it was displayed on its own short length of track, facing down an aisle which was flanked by a long line of the other exhibited locomotives, including Ramsbottom's *Lady of the Lake* about 60 feet away. The McConnell engine, as a late entry, had to share the same catalogue number 1269 as *Lady of the Lake*, whose tender was exhibited under the separate number 1270.

Although the other S Div engines had been renumbered into the all-LNWR list, at the Exhibition it kept its old number 373 and presumably its old livery, but the only known reference to this is somewhat confused. Wilfred L. Steel in his 1914 *History of the L&NWR* (p183) said that *Lady of the Lake* was at the Crystal Palace in 1851, painted blue. In a list of corrections to Steel's book, S. S. Scott said that *Lady of the Lake* was actually shown at the 1862 Exhibition, painted green, and that the blue engine there was 373. This unsatisfactory statement seems to be the only comment on the livery of 373 while on display.

When the Exhibition closed on 1st November, 373 went back to join the other two in store at Wolverton.

In the following year Ramsbottom was asked what he thought should be done with them and in August 1863 he suggested that the three completed engines might be given ordinary boilers to reduce the weight to about 31½ tons - "under all the circumstances he does not see what can be done better." The cost of the new boilers would be "very trifling" because of the large quantity of valuable copper in the McConnell fireboxes. He could not recommend completing the other two. In September the reboilering was deferred while an attempt was made to find a buyer. Not surprisingly no buyer was found.

In 1864 Krupp of Essen enquired about the steel tyres which had been supplied for the H class four years

Fig. 116 Newly built Class H Special Large Bloomer 373 – the International Exhibition engine. At Wolverton, December 1861. *(Stephenson Locomotive Society)*

before. A minute of 17th November records that "as the engines practically never ran" it was impossible to settle Krupp's bill on a mileage basis; the amount outstanding (£1,250) was paid off in a lump sum.

Then in March 1865 the LNWR Auditor, Henry Crosfield, brought up the question of the "Engines 'H' at Wolverton". He suggested putting the three finished engines in the duplicate list, valued at £200 each "and when they are sold, if they realise a profit over and above the £600, putting the excess to the credit of the Capital Account in reduction of the original extraordinary charge. As respects the amount spent upon the two in progress, the material might be taken for what it is worth and the balance charged out to Locomotive Power Account." Accordingly duplicate numbers 1152/5/66 were allotted in July and the capital list numbers were given to three DX 0-6-0 goods engines built at Crewe on Replacement Account in October.

1866 came and still there were no buyers, so Ramsbottom began to rebuild them with smaller boilers and 16in x 24in cylinders. The new boiler barrel was telescopic, with four rings of ⅜in plate increasing from 3ft 11¾in external diameter at the smokebox to 4ft 2in at the firebox end; the dome was on the third ring. There were 178 tubes of 1⅞in diameter and the firebox was of normal size and shape, with one firehole. This design of boiler was also used when the 7ft Bloomers came to be rebuilt, but on the H class it was pitched three inches higher and the regulator handle hung downwards.

After Webb had taken over the engines were put back into the capital list at the end of 1871, and in the following year were given names. Two of these, *Delamere* and *Maberley*, had been used before on Crewe Goods engines but the other was a new name, that of one of the more recently appointed directors, the Earl of Caithness.

They went back into the duplicate list in October 1879 and were scrapped in 1880/2. They never received cabs.

Work

When they finally started work after their long period in storage, they were sent to Camden Shed, and were still there in 1878, "doing an undue share of piloting work" according to Ahrons; Driver Button recalled 1199 (late 373) as a regular passenger pilot in the 1870s. They also hauled secondary expresses and were often used on the Sunday 5pm Down train, sometimes piloted by a 7ft Bloomer. Ahrons gives a log of 1199 on a twelve-carriage Up Scotch express in 1877, running non-stop from Nuneaton to Willesden at an average speed of 49.17mph.

About the time the first one was scrapped, early in 1880 the others were transferred to Rugby for their last two years.

The *Trent* Special

There is only one description of the work of an H class engine in original condition. The famous *Trent* special was worked by 372 from Stafford to London in January 1862, and much has been made of its non-stop 133-mile run at an alleged average speed of 57.2mph, including a "tremendous spurt" of very nearly 80mph between Tring and Boxmoor. These claims appeared in the *Locomotive Magazine* in 1905 but a somewhat different story was given by *The Times* on the day after the event.

This was during the anxious period, early in the American Civil War, when it seemed likely that Britain would be embroiled in the conflict. On 8th November 1861 a US warship had stopped the British steamer *Trent* at sea and forcibly removed two passengers, Confederate envoys travelling to London. The British Government was outraged by this "act of piracy on the high seas" and immediately demanded an apology from the USA and the return of the prisoners. There were some tense weeks as troops embarked for Canada and Britain waited for Abraham Lincoln's response. His reaction to the ultimatum might mean war.

A transatlantic cable had been laid in 1858 but had failed; the swiftest available communication was by steamship. Elaborate arrangements had to be set up to transmit the American reply to London. After crossing the Atlantic the message would be taken by special train across Ireland from Cork to Dublin, then by steamer across the Irish Sea to Holyhead, where the LNWR kept engines in readiness to convey the news to London.

On 1st January 1862 a special train ran from Holyhead to Euston in 5 hours 43 minutes and although it brought no decisive news, the overall speed of 46mph was thought to be a record and created its own excitement. This was eclipsed on 7th January when a special train arrived at Euston five hours after leaving Holyhead, having attained speeds of up to 70mph according to *The Times*. On that day the Problem class *Watt* arrived at Stafford with the special, consisting of a saloon and two vans, having come from Holyhead non-stop at an average 54mph, picking up water from the trough at Mochdre en route. From Stafford the train was taken by H class 372 over the S Div to Euston. Almost all accounts of the run agree that arrival at Euston was at 1.13pm, but the other timings differ wildly. These and other features of the vivid *Locomotive Magazine* article make its claims for this epic 57.2mph run very suspect.

This account, which has been quoted and requoted ever since, seems to have been written up on the basis of a mistake in the timings at Holyhead. According to the *Locomotive Magazine* the train left Holyhead station at 8.28am and arrived at Stafford at 10.52am; the engine change took 1½ minutes, so that only 2 hours 19½ minutes were spent travelling over the S Div to Euston. By contrast, *The Times* stated that departure from Holyhead was at 8.13am and arrival at Stafford was at 10.38am. A correspondent 'W. J.' in the *English Mechanic* of 13th January 1871 gave the same arrival time and added that departure from Stafford was at 10.41am, that there was a two minute delay at Rugby, a slack through Kilburn and a signal stop at Primrose Hill tunnel. His time for the arrival at Euston was 1.16pm.

The Times mentioned the speed of 54mph from Holyhead to Stafford and commented that "so high a speed was judiciously not attempted over the more crowded portion of the line from Stafford to London." A 10.41am departure from Stafford would give an average speed to Euston of about 52mph rather than the doubtful 57.2mph.

* * * * * *

Of all big express engines, those of Class H have been the most obscure and the most surrounded by fantasy.

After a statement appeared in the engineering press in 1890 that drawings no longer existed, Clement Stretton published an absurd sketch of 373 which he claimed was from an official source. Unfortunately this has been reprinted in several books.

The only known photograph of the class - 373 in works grey - came to light subsequently and was used as the basis for the small drawing in the *Locomotive Magazine* in 1898 and for an F. Moore oil painting of about the same period which is now in the Science Museum. This painting shows 373 (with a small tender, from a photograph of Small Bloomer 381) in a quite mythical scarlet livery, whose vividness alone has ensured its frequent reproduction.

Many years after they were scrapped the engines were awarded the facetious nickname 'Extra-large Bloomers'.

Summary: 2-2-2 Class H built at Wolverton, 1861

No.	Built	Reno'd /62	Rebt	Reno'd	Name	Scrapped
375	5/1861	975(4/62)	b /66	1166(7/65), 1200(12/71), 1871(10/79)	Maberley (/72)	3/82
372	8/1861	972(4/62)	a /67	1152(7/65), 1198(12/71), 1940(10/79)	Delamere (/72)	1/80
373	11/1861	973(11/62)	a /66	1155(7/65) 1199(12/71) 1885(10/79)	Caithness (5/72)	3/82

The BLOOMERS - later series

Wolverton, Sharp and Kitson 2-2-2 Passenger Engines, 1861-2   Nos 389-408

By the end of 1860 several new lines were in prospect: Bedford to Cambridge; the South Leicestershire; branches to Sutton Coldfield and Rickmansworth. McConnell estimated these would require 24 additional engines and increasing traffic would need a further 40 engines. On 10th January 1861 he was authorised "to lay down 10 passenger engines of the Bloomer type ... and the Secretary was instructed to invite tenders by advertisement for ... 10 passenger engines of the Bloomer type." The emphasis is striking; fancy boilers and patent 'improvements' were not wanted.

Ten were accordingly built at Wolverton in 1861/2. A tender from Kitson & Hewitson, Leeds, to build five for £2,920 each, two to be delivered in July and the rest by September, was accepted on 23rd January. Sharp, Stewart & Co's tender was accepted on the same day; their contract dated 29th January promised two in September, two in October and one in November for £3,092 each, with a £10 penalty per engine per week for late delivery. Despite the penalty clause the Sharp engines and also the Kitson engines were delivered some weeks late, but all were in LNWR hands by the middle of November, taking numbers 399-408, after those allocated to the ten Wolverton-built Bloomers. Sharp, Stewart's works numbers were 1289-93; Kitson's were 899-903 for the engines and 904-8 for the tenders.

Completion dates of the Wolverton engines are not known precisely; the month and year which later appeared on their nameplates (March-May 1862) were apparently 'dates to traffic' which suggests that at least two of the engines never carried S Div numbers. The last three from Sharp Stewart and the last two (or three) from Kitson may have been stored for four months after their arrival as their nameplate dates were March/April 1862.

These engines were basically the same as those of ten years before; the main differences were in the boiler and the suspension; other minor changes were the improvements of the period.

The boilers of the 1851 Bloomers were of $3/8$in plate with single-riveted lap joints. The 1861 boiler plates were one sixteenth inch thicker with double-riveted joints; the firebox outer wrapper was similarly increased to $1/2$in thick. The working pressure was raised to 150 lb/sq in, and a lock-up safety valve was on the barrel, behind the dome. There were nine fewer tubes, slightly increasing the circulation space. The firebox was at last free of midfeathers so there was only one firehole, some 7in lower than on the earlier single-firehole engines. The troublesome trailing axle springs were replaced by one large transverse spring over the axle. Compensating levers between leading and driving axle springs were mounted on the same downwards frame-lug which carried the weighshaft, which was lower than before - so low that the reversing rod at its forward end came down to $6 1/2$in above rail level. Leading and driving axle springs were longer by 3in at 2ft 9in, and the driving axle springs were underhung.

In the earlier Bloomers the bracket for the front hanger of the driving wheel spring was at each end of a large forging which stretched between the frameplates and incorporated a curved saddle to support the boiler. In the 1861 engines the presence of compensating levers removed the need for these hanger brackets, so a different boiler support was employed. This consisted of a gusset plate on each side, held by angle irons, stretching up to the boiler saddle from the arch of the frame above the driving axle.

Similarly, for the leading axle, the spring hangers had been mounted on the ends of cross stays. These were eliminated in the 1861 engines. The earlier Bloomers could be recognised by the kinks in the horns where the cross stays were fastened.

Weatherboards, dished smokebox doors, spring buffers, cut-out splashers and muzzle-loader chimneys gave the engines a more up-to-date look: mid-Victorian compared with the Spartan lines of Bury's originals and the clean,

Fig. 117   A 7ft Bloomer from a Wolverton drawing of 1861.

uncluttered earlier Bloomers.

The earlier series had been troubled with leading wheel tyre failures; Beattie's tyres, which had a safeguarding lip on the outside, were specified for the leading wheels of the 1861 engines.

Pumps were being superseded by Giffard's injector at this period, but the Sharp order book reveals the uncertainty that was still felt: two pumps or two injectors, or one of each, were to be supplied; the size of the injector, 9mm or 10mm, was left to the maker's discretion. The general arrangement drawing shows a pump on the left, delivering through a clack on the front boiler ring, and an injector on the right, delivering to the firebox side, just above the grate. They were turned out with this layout - pump on the left, injector on the right - but later photographs show delivery from both through long pipes to the front or middle ring of the boiler.

Their appearance when new can be gauged from the photograph (Fig 77) of the rebuilt 249 of the 1851 series. This had been wrecked by a boiler explosion in July 1861 and the photograph shows the completely reconstructed engine about to enter the paint shop at Wolverton in December 1861.

Dimensions

Cylinders (2 inside)	16" x 22"
Boiler	
Diameter (inside)	
Middle ring	4' 2"
Front and back rings	4' 1⅛"
Length of barrel	11' 9"
Pitch	7' 1"
Length of firebox casing	5' 9½"
Heating surface	
Tubes (186, 2⅛" dia, 12' long)	1,248.24 sq ft
Firebox	118.00 sq ft
Total	1,366.24 sq ft
Grate area	18.75 sq ft
Boiler pressure	150 lb/sq in
Diameter of wheels	
Leading	4' 6"
Driving	7' 0"
Trailing	4' 0"
Tender	3' 9"
Wheelbase	
Engine	8' 4" + 8' 6" = 16' 10"
Tender	5' 6" + 5' 6" = 11' 0"
Weight	
On leading wheels	11 tons 2 cwt
On driving wheels	14 tons 6 cwt
On trailing wheels	6 tons 1 cwt
Total	31 tons 9 cwt
Tender (6 wheel) capacity	coke 2¾ tons or coal 2 tons water 2,000 gal

Alterations and Rebuilding

Changes which took place to Bloomers of both series in the Ramsbottom period include the removal of the compensating levers between the leading and driving axle springs, and the usual Crewe additions - spherical displacement lubricators, a short handrail above the smokebox door, the 'castellated' chimney cap, the blower pipe moved from the right to the left side of the boiler. From 1868 engines were rebuilt with Crewe boilers having standard domes and Ramsbottom safety valves, and with taller side sheets whose top rails were at a safer height than the previous 2ft 10in above the footplate.

The new boilers were to the same design as those put on the H class when rebuilt, with four telescoped rings:

Diameter (inside):	
Front ring:	3ft 11in
2nd ring:	3ft 11¾in
3rd ring:	4ft 0½in
4th ring:	4ft 1¼in
Length of barrel	12ft 1½in
Pitch	7ft 1in

The dome was on the third ring, centred 7ft 6in from the front of the barrel; there were 178 tubes of 1⅞in diameter.

Under Webb rebuilding continued until all but three had Crewe boilers. In his first trial programme using Crewe-made boiler plates 999 was turned out with a steel boiler. The next two rebuilds (888 and 995) in 1874 are said to have been given "old (DX) boilers" presumably with an extra ring added, but the six subsequent reboilerings used steel plates. Crewe steel tyres were fitted from November 1871.

Backhead injectors began to replace the old firebox-side Giffard injectors in 1872, eliminating the long exterior pipes so prominent on the Bloomers. Sandboxes were cleared away from the footplating and tucked underneath, hidden behind plain flat plates. Very soon after Webb took over, all engines were given his neat chimney which at once gave them a more modern look, as did the cabs added to all the engines rebuilt from September 1872 and to the others surviving in 1878/9.

In 1872 all the Bloomers were given names, each plate inscribed with the usual reference to Crewe Works and a date which in some cases was as much as five months after the building date. The engines of 1851-3 were given a selection of names all of which had been used previously on Crewe engines; these were applied in March. In June the later engines were named, again with old N Div names apart from two new ones, *Japan* and *Burmah*. Both nations were in the news in 1872; in April - surprisingly for such a recently feudal state - an industrial exhibition opened at Kyoto, followed by the first Japanese railway, and later in the year Japanese and Burmese delegations arrived to meet Queen Victoria.

None of the Bloomers are known to have received Webb's closed safety valves, but they might have done so in the 1880s. Front screw couplings also belong to this period and can be seen in the official photograph of 895 *Torch* taken at Crewe c1880. Also visible is the chain brake-cord pulley on the side sheet; this prompts the thought that some of the last Bloomers could have been fitted with the vacuum brake towards the end of their lives.

In Southern Division days the 7ft engines were known simply as Bloomers, but from 1862 Crewe referred to them as Large Bloomers.

Fig. 118 Bloomer 890 (ex-290) built by Sharp Bros, 1852. At Bletchley, 1863-70. McConnell additions include lock-up safety valve and weatherboard. Ramsbottom changes include N Div livery, castellated cap on shortened chimney, new buffers, displacement lubricator on valve chest, front handrail. The engine still has right-hand drive and there are equalising levers on the long-wheelbase tender. *(W.E. Boyd collection)*

Fig. 119 Bloomer 992 (ex-392) built at Wolverton in 1862. Equalising levers between the leading and driving axle springs have been removed; screw reverse fitted and blower now on left side; c1870.
(E. Pouteau photo, W.E. Boyd collection)

Fig. 120　　1007 (ex-407) built by Kitson in 1861; named *President* in 1872. Photographed just before scrapping at Crewe in December 1877 – the last surviving unrebuilt Bloomer. With Webb chimney and livery of black with red, white and pale blue lining, numberplate painted red and yellow. Injector on right side, pump on left.　　*(LNWR photo)*

Fig. 121　　Bloomer 1008 (ex-408) *Rowland Hill* built by Kitson in 1861. In the early form of black livery with pale blue lines on the boiler bands; Crewe-pattern weatherboard; injector on right side, pump on left. At Camden shed early in 1876, with the Roundhouse – by this time Gilbey's gin store – prominent in the background. The driver is Sammy Lovesey, who came to Camden some ten years before this with a South Staffordshire Railway engine.
(Stephenson Locomotive Society)

Fig. 122
Bloomer 887 (ex-287) *Knowsley* built by Sharp Bros in 1852. As rebuilt with a Crewe boiler; injector on right side, pump on left. Outside Monument Lane shed, Birmingham, 1877.
(R.H. Bleasdale)

The weight of the rebuilt engines was given in Crewe records as:

	January 1870	April 1877
On leading wheels	10 tons 7 cwt	11 tons 6 cwt
On driving wheels	12 tons 10 cwt	12 tons
On trailing wheels	6 tons 14 cwt	7 tons 10 cwt
Total	29 tons 11 cwt	30 tons 16 cwt

Work

The Bloomers continued in their role as the best of the S Div express engines and from first to last their service covered 37 years.

They seldom worked north of Crewe, but 997 *Baronet* was noted working through to Manchester via Stoke on an occasion when the relieving engine failed, and W. B. Thompson once saw one at Carlisle. Until the Precedents arrived in 1875, the Bloomers handled almost all the main line expresses, although a few Problems made their way into S Div schedules after 1862. In 1876 Bloomers took twelve trains daily out of Euston, but the Precedents were gradually taking over. There was a brief resurgence in 1878, when several Precedents were taken out of service for repairs and had to be replaced by Bloomers - at Crewe by 991/2/4/8/1001 and at Rugby by 847/87/94. In August an *English Mechanic* correspondent wrote: "I saw 998 on the 10am Down a few days back with fifteen on, running in fine style." But once the Precedents returned there was a steady decline in Bloomer express work and by 1881 they took only four regular daily trains from Euston, reduced to three at the end of 1882.

It was said that a Bloomer could take nine carriages up Camden bank without assistance, but a scene recorded in 1878 is probably more typical of this period. Bloomer 1005 *Achilles* was piloting 864 *Pilot* (Precedent) on a fourteen-carriage train. After it started and the tail of the train reached the platform end, Wolverton 0-4-2 Class N tank 1906 ran after it and pushed as far as Chalk Farm. All trains over eight carriages were apparently started like this.

Up to 1884 a Bloomer worked the fastest LNWR express, the 2.10pm seven-carriage Birmingham to London on which Charles Rous-Marten recorded a maximum speed of 72mph with 989 *Archimedes*. The same top speed was logged in 1876 with 889 *Camilla* on the eight-carriage 2.45pm Euston to Liverpool and Manchester. The Scotch Expresses could consist of fourteen to eighteen carriages (172 to 220 tons) and one or two Bloomers were timed on these trains in the 1870s showing good work.

The working of the four Bloomers at Bushbury in May and June 1878 was published at the time:

Engines 996 *Raglan*, 999 *Medusa*, 1000 *Umpire* and 1002 *Theseus* (one spare).

	Monday	Tuesday	Wednesday	Thursday	Friday	Saturday
1.	11.45am	—	7.05am	7.05am	11.45am	—
2.	7.05am	8.55am	11.45am	—	7.05am	8.55am
3.	8.55am	11.45am	—	8.55am	8.55am	11.45am
4.	—	7.05am	8.55am	11.45am	—	7.05am

Wolverhampton dep:	7.05am	Wolverhampton dep:	8.55am	11.45am
Rugby arr:	8.22	Rugby arr:	10.20	—
dep:	9.40	dep:	10.45	—
Wolverhampton arr:	11.15	Euston arr:	12.50pm	2.50pm
dep:	1.30pm	dep:	3.00	6.00
Rugby arr:	2.55	Rugby arr:	5.10	—
dep:	4.55	dep:	5.53	—
Wolverhampton arr:	7.05	Wolverhampton arr:	7.20	10.00

Fig. 123　　Bloomer 998 *Una*, built at Wolverton in 1862. As rebuilt with a Crewe boiler; injector on both sides, long-wheelbase tender. Outside Bushbury shed, 1877.　　*(R.H. Bleasdale)*

Fig. 124　　Bloomer 995 *Briareus*, built at Wolverton in 1862. At Crewe, probably just after rebuilding in 1874 with new boiler, cab and standard fittings.　　*(LNWR photo)*

By 1883 they were generally piloting and W. B. Thompson noted that one or two of them were kept at Rugby exclusively for pushing out southbound trains.

Their last journeys were between Rugby and Bletchley, and Rugby and Birmingham.

Some record of shed allocations has survived from their later years. A partial return of 1869 gives these incomplete totals:

Camden	3
Bletchley	4
Rugby	10 (including 6 rebuilt)
Monument Lane	5

The other eighteen were probably at Camden, Rugby, Wolverton and perhaps Bushbury. Northampton had none. At Camden in the 1860s the Euston pilot engine was 889; this job was done by 896 *Dædalus* and 1007 *President* for some years before scrapping in 1877.

The following shed allocations are based on the records of observers from about 1872:

847	Rugby.
848	Rugby.
849	Rugby; Monument Lane /79.
850	Camden; Rugby /78.
851	Rugby; Monument Lane /79.
852	Rugby.
853	Rugby.
854	Rugby.
855	Rugby.
856	Rugby.
887	Monument Lane; Rugby /78; Camden /81.
888	Monument Lane; Rugby /78.
889	Camden; Crewe /83.
890	Bletchley.
891	Rugby; Camden /81.
892	Rugby.
893	Rugby; Monument Lane (later?)
894	Monument Lane; Rugby /78.
895	Monument Lane; Rugby /78.
896	Camden.
989	Rugby.
990	Camden; Crewe /79; Northampton /80; Rugby /82.
991	Camden; Crewe /78; Monument Lane?
992	Rugby; Crewe /78; Northampton /80; Rugby /83.
993	Bletchley? Rugby /80.
994	Bletchley? Crewe /78; Camden /81.
995	Monument Lane; Northampton /78.
996	Camden; Bushbury /78.
997	Camden.
998	Camden? Bushbury /77; Crewe /78; Camden /81.
999	Camden? Bushbury /78; Crewe /80; Rugby /81.
1000	Northampton? Bushbury /77.
1001	Camden; Crewe /78; Bushbury /83?
1002	Camden; Bushbury /78.
1003	Camden; Rugby /83.
1004	Camden; Rugby /83.
1005	Camden; Rugby /83.
1006	Camden.
1007	Camden.
1008	Camden; Crewe /81.

Harrow Accident

There was a major accident at Harrow on Saturday 26th November 1870. The 5.00pm express from Euston to Liverpool and Manchester, nineteen carriages long and double headed, ran past red signals in fog and crashed into the rear of a goods train. The leading engine was Bloomer 850, the train engine was Problem 833 *Clyde*. There were 44 injured and seven killed, including 850's Driver William Shelvey, who was blamed for reckless driving in such poor visibility. The 39-year old Shelvey was a well-known character who always took his pet dog Snatch with him on the footplate and was nicknamed 'Duke' because he had a nose like Wellington's. Snatch survived the crash but Shelvey was buried in Wolverton churchyard. Presumably 850 was shedded at Wolverton at that period.

Disposal

The first of the class to be scrapped went in June 1876, after a life of 24½ years, and another eight had gone by the end of 1877. Eleven were left at the end of November 1884 ten of which were then placed on the duplicate list with numbers above 1800; the eleventh was scrapped immediately. In 1885 the nameplates were taken off.

By this time duplicate list engines fully occupied numbers 1801-2000 and numbers from 2001 into the 2500s were already in use by new engines built from 1871 onwards; as old engines were still being added to the duplicate list a new series of numbers above 3000 was started. After a few months there was some rearrangement of the list and in November 1886 two of the four surviving Bloomers were renumbered again. The engines were listed at the end of that month as 1882/98, 3050/71.

The first of these, the former S Div 392, renumbered 992 and named *Stork*, put into the duplicate list as 1882 and finally renumbered 3023 in 1887, was the last Bloomer. It was also the last of the Wolverton-built engines and the last of all the Southern Division engines on the line.

Its scrapping in November 1888 symbolised the end of the troubled first half of LNWR locomotive history.

Annual totals:

	capital	duplicate
to 30/11/1875:	40	-
30/11/1876:	38	-
30/11/1877:	34	-
30/11/1878:	31	-
30/11/1879:	28	-
30/11/1880:	27	-
30/11/1881:	24	-
30/11/1882:	18	-
30/11/1883:	14	-
30/11/1884:	11	-
30/11/1885:	-	6
30/11/1886:	-	4
30/11/1887:	-	1
30/11/1888:	-	-

Fig. 125 Bloomer 895 (ex-295) *Torch*, built by Sharp Bros in 1853. At Crewe c1880, with front screw-coupling, chain-brake pulley on footplate fender and long-wheelbase tender. (*LNWR photo*)

Fig. 126 Bloomer 895 (ex-295) *Torch*. At Monument Lane shed in 1877, with standard short-wheelbase tender. (*R.H. Bleasdale*)

Fig. 127   Bloomer 1002 (ex-402) *Theseus*, built by Sharp, Stewart in 1861. Long-wheelbase tender; ash pipes for emptying smokebox char fitted behind guard irons. At Camden shed, early 1876.   *(Stephenson Locomotive Society)*

Fig. 128   Bloomer 894 (ex-294) *Trentham*, built by Sharp Bros in 1853. With new 20-spoke steel driving wheels fitted by Webb and later re-used in his 7ft compounds. At Monument Lane shed, 1877.   *(R.H. Bleasdale)*

Summary: Bloomer 2-2-2s

No.	Maker	Date	Reno'd 4/62	Name	Rebt * /72	Reno'd	Scrapped
247	Sharp 677	30/8/1851	847	Odin	a /68		12/78
248	Sharp 678	9/9/1851	848	Hecate	b /67(W)		10/83
249	Sharp 679	18/9/1851	849	Æolus	12/61(W), 2/72		12/79
250	Sharp 680	29/9/1851	850	Columbine	8/71		11/81
251	Sharp 681	6/10/1851	851	Apollo	b /68		3/81
252	Sharp 682	20/10/1851	852	Basilisk	a /67(W)		9/79
253	Sharp 683	8/11/1851	853	Vulture	b /68		1/77
254	Sharp 684	22/11/1851	854	Dalemain	a /69		12/77
255	Sharp 685	16/12/1851	855	Sandon	a /69		12/77
256	Sharp 686	31/12/1851	856	Ingestre	b /68		6/76
287	Sharp 700	13/10/1852	887	Knowsley	11/71		5/82
288	Sharp 701	15/10/1852	888	Hydra	6/74(c)		4/82
289	Sharp 702	2/11/1852	889	Camilla	3/72	c/u 1941	2/84
290	Sharp 703	19/11/1852	890	Helvellyn	a /63(W)		3/77
291	Sharp 704	26/11/1852	891	Duke	b /67(W)	c/u 1828	4/83
292	Sharp 705	24/12/1852	892	Polyphemus	b /68	c/u 1989?	9/77
293	Sharp 710	24/12/1852	893	Harpy	b /67(W), 4/76(S,c)	1817(12/84)	3/85
294	Sharp 712	8/2/1853	894	Trentham	9/72(c)		4/83
295	Sharp 713	14/2/1853	895	Torch	a /63(W), 10/73(c)	1828(12/84), 3050(11/86)	3/87
296	Sharp 715	28/2/1853	896	Dædalus	—	c/u 1988?	7/77
389	Wolverton	3/1862	989	Archimedes	(rebt)	1853(12/84), 3071(11/86)	9/87
390	Wolverton	3/1862	990	Alaric	7/73(c)	1881(12/84)	6/86
391	Wolverton	3/1862	991	Japan	11/71		1/82
392	Wolverton	3/1862	992	Stork	9/76(S,c)	1882(12/84), 3023(5/87)	11/88
393	Wolverton	4/1862	993	Burmah	3/76(S,c)		2/81
394	Wolverton	4/1862	994	Ariel	7/72	c/u 1965	9/84
395	Wolverton	4/1862	995	Briareus	10/74(c)		9/79
(396)	Wolverton	5/1862	996	Raglan	11/71		6/82
397	Wolverton	4/1862	997	Baronet	11/72(c)		1/82
(398)	Wolverton	5/1862	998	Una	12/70	1897(12/84)	6/85
399	Sharp 1289	21/10/1861	999	Medusa	11/73(S,c)	1898(12/84)	9/87
400	Sharp 1290	28/10/1861	1000	Umpire	4/75(S,c)	1902(12/84)	3/85
401	Sharp 1291	2/11/1861	1001	Leviathan	5/73(c)	c/u 1959	12/84
402	Sharp 1292	7/11/1861	1002	Theseus	8/73(c)		6/82
403	Sharp 1293	13/11/1861	1003	Tamerlane	6/71	1905(12/84)	5/86
404	Kitson 899	14/9/1861	1004	Lucifer	4/73(c)		7/83
405	Kitson 900	19/9/1861	1005	Achilles	9/75(S,c)		10/84
406	Kitson 901	5/10/1861	1006	Proserpine	—		10/76
407	Kitson 902	16/10/1861	1007	President		—	12/77
408	Kitson 903	25/10/1861	1008	Rowland Hill	4/76(S,c)	1907(12/84)	2/85

*Rebuilding: W - rebuilt at Wolverton; S - with steel boiler; c - cab.

Sharp dates are those of delivery to the LNWR at Manchester.
Kitson dates are those of works trial before delivery.
Wolverton dates are those on the 1872 nameplates.
Other nameplate dates were:

847-56:	10/51	889:	12/52	999, 1000/4/5:	10/61
887:	10/52	893:	1/53	1001/2/7/8:	3/62
888/90/1/2:	11/52	894/5/6:	2/53	1003:	4/62

Life after Death

The Bloomers were popular with railway watchers, but in those days news spread slowly and in any case there was a reluctance to believe they were extinct. Thus in 1890 both the *English Mechanic* and the *Railway Herald* assured readers that some Bloomers were still working. Even *The Engineer* said: "Bloomers ... are even now in use, though their comparatively light weight precludes them from express work." This appeared in 1897.

A recurring story that driving wheel centres from scrapped Bloomers were re-used in Webb's Teutonics and Greater Britains was mentioned in a paragraph in the *Locomotive Magazine* of July 1903; in 1924 J. G. B. Sams published his recollections of Crewe Works in the *Railway Magazine* and said he heard the story from workmates in 1897-1902. The original wheels were forged, with 22 spokes, but the compounds had cast-steel wheels with 20 spokes, so the story seemed unbelievable. In fact, Webb provided new cast wheels for some of the surviving Bloomers and it was these which were re-used in the compounds.

The influence of the Bloomer design was far-reaching. Webb used the cylinder and **V**-shaped valve layout in his Jumbos and even Ramsbottom borrowed it for his 2-4-0 Ironclads on the South Eastern Railway. LNWR tank engines derived from the 2-4-0 design appeared in 1876 and were built in quantity at Crewe until 1898. The last of these - apart from the preserved *Hardwicke*, the last engine with this cylinder layout by Webb via McConnell from Edward Bury - ran on British Railways until 1955, just as the steam locomotive was coming to the end of its long career.

New Bloomers

1. Working Replica 670

Thirty years later plans were laid in Birmingham to celebrate the forthcoming 150th anniversary of the L&BR, and Birmingham (Tyseley) Railway Museum looked around for a suitable subject to build as a working replica. After considering an H class, the 7ft Bloomer was selected. One of these, as well as being most suitable for the immediate purpose, would fill an obvious gap among preserved and museum locomotives in Britain with one of the best of the mid-Victorian period.

The engineer of the scheme was Robert Meanley, and his first task was the reconstitution of dozens of lost detail drawings from sparse and scattered information.

The first item completed was the tender, using an original Wolverton tender frame and wheels from an old oil tank wagon at Northwich. During cleaning it was discovered that this frame came from the tender of Small Bloomer 603. By March 1987 a new tender tank, complete with well, had been made by Mercia Fabrications of Dudley. The tender was completed and painted in S Div green, lined in the style used at Wolverton until 1861. The engine number selected is from the address of the Birmingham Railway Museum, 670 Warwick Road, Tyseley.

The boiler was made by Babcock Energy and was completed in January 1988. It is believed to be the first all-steel, all-welded standard gauge locomotive boiler in Britain, and although thus structurally different, it follows the dimensions of the prototype as far as possible. Other components - frames, cylinders, motion, wheels and axles - were made by several industrial firms in Birmingham and the West Midlands, and a McConnell corniced brass dome cover was made at Wolverton Works, probably the first since 1862.

Despite a lot of dedicated work, it was found impossible to have the engine ready for the L&B 150th anniversary. The frames were erected at the end of 1989 and the boiler was mounted in 1990. At the time of writing, although not much more work is required, construction is at a standstill because of financial problems.

2. Non-Working Replica 1009 *Wolverton*

Meanwhile, using much of the information gathered in the research for the working engine, an accurate full-size non-working replica was commissioned by Milton Keynes Development Corporation and was built by apprentices at the Milton Keynes Training Centre. It was unveiled as a static monument in front of Milton Keynes Central Station on 3rd October 1991. It had always been intended to finish the working engine in c1860 condition, with the S Div green livery and polished brasswork; by contrast the static engine was painted in the better-known LNWR black, lined in the style of 1873-6, with a Webb chimney, number and nameplates. As if to follow the last Bloomer of 1862 it was numbered 1009, and by a happy inspiration was named *Wolverton* - to commemorate the railway works and town which now fall within the boundary of Milton Keynes.

Class M

Wolverton 0-4-2 Tank Engines, 1862
Nos 734, 974, 976, 982-988

At the end of October 1861 McConnell reported a stock of 363 engines (146 passenger, 217 goods); 20 more were on order from outside builders and 38 were under construction at Wolverton. He considered that these would be required for the 502 miles of the enlarged Southern Division "without providing for additional mileage or new lines", but 43 miles of new branches would be ready for opening in the next twelve months and General Manager William Cawkwell was afraid that the 1862 Exhibition might generate so much extra traffic that the locomotive departments, especially Wolverton, would be "hard pressed to provide adequate power". The average daily train mileage for each locomotive on the S Div was already high, at 52.41, and that on the N Div was 44.07. In view of this McConnell was authorised to complete the 38 engines being built and build another fifteen, ten of which were to be tank engines for branch lines.

The ten Class M engines were 0-4-2 well tanks, similar to Class G with inside cylinders and Gooch valve gear, but unlike Class G the boilers were domeless and were without McConnell's patent divided firebox and combustion chamber. Other McConnell trademarks had also disappeared. In place of the usual corniced dome there was a manhole on the middle of the boiler with a lock-up safety valve, whose shallow cover was similar in outline to those on Beattie's engines on the London & South Western. The spring balance safety valve on the flush firebox top had a small conical cover like some of Beyer, Peacock's. The chimney was the standard S Div type. Although the piston stroke was 20in, the coupling rod crankpin circle was 26in diameter. The coupled wheels were braked, with the brakeblocks in front of each wheel. Giffard injectors were fitted on each side with prominent steam pipes arching over the firebox in front of the safety valve. As built there was no rear weatherboard; one was fitted later on the bunker front.

Because of the normal firebox, without the complications of midfeather or combustion chamber, they were cheaper than Class G, each costing just £1,784 15s 6d (£1,784.77).

As they were not completed until after the amalgamation of the divisions, none of them carried S Div numbers and they were all put straight into the combined list above 600. One was a replacement, 734, but the nine others all had new numbers, 974/6 and 982-8. The first two of these were numbers which would have gone to McConnell's large Class H engines, but work on them had stopped, and under the new regime would never be resumed.

Fig. 129 Class M 0-4-2T 734, built at Wolverton, 1862. As built: S Div chimney and lamp irons, no rear weatherboard; N Div livery, green with black lines. At Sutton Coldfield, 1863. *(W.E. Boyd collection)*

Fig. 130 Class M 0-4-2T 1857 (ex-983) built at Wolverton, 1862. In green livery with painted number; Crewe alterations include front handrail, blower on left side, displacement lubricator, Webb chimney, rear weatherboard, new buffers and lamp irons. The engine is standing on gauntletted track alongside the GJ line platform at Bushbury in 1877; LNWR and GWR trains ran on separate sets of rails though the station to the junction with the Stafford-Wolverhampton line.
(R.H. Bleasdale)

Dimensions

Cylinders (2 inside)	15" x 20"
Boiler	
Length of barrel	10' 6"
Length of firebox casing	4' 10"
Grate area	13.4 sq ft
Diameter of wheels	
Coupled	5' 6"
Trailing	4' 0"
Wheelbase	7' 6" + 9' 6" = 17' 0"
Length over buffers	29' 7½"
Weight	
On leading wheels	11 tons 0 cwt
On driving wheels	11 tons 0 cwt
On trailing wheels	7 tons 14 cwt
Total	29 tons 14 cwt

Crewe classified them as goods engines. 734 was photographed on a seven-carriage passenger train at Sutton Coldfield in 1863. This engine was rebuilt at Wolverton in 1867 with a Crewe boiler, a plain dome and Ramsbottom safety valves. In 1874 it was renumbered with the other survivors of the class in the duplicate list and as 1811 it worked as a station pilot at Euston, painted black and lined-out like a passenger engine. By the summer of 1877, it was at Bushbury shed, as was the former 983, still in green livery with a painted duplicate number 1857, and in original condition apart from the addition of a rear weatherboard, a Webb chimney and other minor modifications. Several were shedded at Walsall, 986/7/8 being there in the early 1860s.

Two were scrapped in 1873, the boiler of one of them, 974, being transferred to 987. They were all scrapped within the next five years.

Annual totals:

	capital	duplicate
to 30/11/1872:	10	-
30/11/1873:	9	-
30/11/1874:	-	6
30/11/1875:	-	4
30/11/1876:	-	4
30/11/1877:	-	1
30/11/1878:	-	-

Summary: 0-4-2T Class M built at Wolverton, 1862

No.	Date	Rebt	Renumbered	Scrapped
974	4/1862	—		5/73
734	5/1862	/67	1811(1/74)	4/9/78
976	5/1862	—	1816(1/74)	6/74
982	5/1862	—		12/73
983	5/1862	—	1857(1/74)	10/10/77
984	6/1862	—	1866(1/74)	6/74
985	6/1862	—	1880(1/74)	7/75
986	6/1862	—	1808(1/74)	7/6/77
987	6/1862	—	1809(1/74) (Given boiler from 974 5/73)	2/8/77
988	6/1862	—	1905(1/74)	9/75

Fig. 131 Class M 0-4-2T 1811 (ex-734) built at Wolverton, 1862. As rebuilt with a Crewe boiler; in black livery, lined like a passenger engine for station pilot duties at Euston. At Bushbury, 1877.
(R.H. Bleasdale)

Class N

Wolverton 0-4-2 Mixed Traffic Engines, 1862
Nos 601/6/16/88/95/6, 741/78/84/7/90, 811, 1019/20/1

These fifteen engines were the last new engines ordered from Wolverton, apart from ten Express Goods 0-6-0s built in 1863 to use up spare parts. The Class N 0-4-2 was simply a tender engine version of the Class M tank, and dimensions were virtually the same except that the distance between the driving and trailing axles was reduced by two feet. The tender was the S Div four-wheeled type, with the brakes behind the wheels in the usual Wolverton manner. Apart from the chimney, which was the Crewe standard 'castellated' pattern, the boiler mountings and most of the other details were the same as in Class M. With their low-set domeless boilers and short tenders they looked uncharacteristically small for Wolverton tender engines; perhaps this was a gesture from McConnell of compliant conformity in the suddenly chilly climate of Richard Moon's chairmanship. A drawing dated December 1861 refers to "15-inch Mixed Traffic Engines" and it seems unlikely that Ramsbottom seriously modified the design, although other drawings were dated 29th April 1862, a month after McConnell's departure, and the first engine was not completed until July.

All fifteen were delivered in the second half of 1862, three with new numbers 1019/20/1 and the others with replacement numbers. The cost was £2,276 10s (£2,276.5) each.

Dimensions

Cylinders (2 inside)	15" x 20"
Boiler	
Length of barrel	10' 9"
Length of firebox casing	4' 6"
Heating surface	
Tubes	839 sq ft
Firebox	78 sq ft
Total	917 sq ft
Grate area	14 sq ft
Diameter of wheels	
Coupled	5' 6"
Trailing	3' 9"
Wheelbase	
Engine	7' 6" + 7' 6" = 15' 0"
Tender	8' 0"
Tender (4 wheel) capacity	water 1,000 gal

When new, 741 is believed to have worked between Wichnor Jct and Birmingham; 601 was at Monument Lane shed in the 1860s.

Two (811 and 606) were rebuilt in 1867/9, remaining as tender engines, but commencing in August 1868 four were converted to saddle tanks at an average cost of £684 each. These were 601 and 695, whose rebuilding was completed in 1869, and 688 and 1021 in 1871. In these rebuilds, the wheelbase remained the same as originally, 15ft equally divided, but the frame was extended rearwards to 3ft 8½in from the trailing axle to carry a short bunker; the length over the buffers was 26ft 9½in. Ramsbottom safety valves and dome were fitted, with weatherboards before and behind the footplate.

Four unrebuilt engines were scrapped in 1873; the others went into the duplicate list in the following year and the remainder of the unrebuilt engines were scrapped in 1874-6.

The four tank rebuilds lasted longer and were used as station pilots; 1906 (ex-601) and 1822 (ex-1021) were at Euston in the late 1870s, banking trains up to Camden. One of the four is said to have worked from Whaley Bridge on the Buxton line. Three were scrapped in 1886, but 1822 was renumbered 3044 in the duplicate list reorganisation and was the last but one of all the Wolverton engines to be withdrawn. It was scrapped in September 1888.

Annual totals:

	capital	duplicate
to 30/11/1872:	15	-
30/11/1873:	11	-
30/11/1874:	-	9
30/11/1875:	-	9
30/11/1876:	-	7
30/11/1877:	-	5
30/11/1878:	-	5
30/11/1879:	-	4
to 30/11/1885:	-	4
30/11/1886:	-	1
30/11/1887:	-	1
30/11/1888:	-	-

Summary: 0-4-2 Class N built at Wolverton, 1862

No.	Date	Rebt	Renumbered	Scrapped
606	7/1862	/69	1923(2/74)	11/7/79
741	8/1862	—	1960(2/74)	14/12/76
778	8/1862	—	1961(3/74)	6/74
790	8/1862	—		7/73
811	8/1862	/67	1963(3/74)	15/8/77
1019	8/1862	—	1806(3/74)	7/76
1020	8/1862	—		7/73
601	9/1862	6/69(ST)	1906(2/74)	6/8/86
616	9/1862	—	1810(2/74)	23/12/75
784	9/1862	—	1962(3/74)	4/74
688	10/1862	4/71(ST)	1938(2/74)	12/11/86
695	10/1862	6/69(ST)	1942(2/74)	21/9/86
696	11/1862	—		7/73
787	11/1862	—		7/73
1021	11/1862	4/71(ST)	1822(3/74), 3044(11/86)	9/88

Fig. 132
Class N 0-4-2 601 built at Wolverton, 1862. Outside Monument Lane shed, 1863-9. The shed is under the bridge to the right; the Stour Valley line is behind the engine.
(Anthony Parkes collection)

Fig. 133   Class N 0-4-2 778 built at Wolverton, 1862. *(LNWR Society)*

Fig. 134.   Class N 0-4-2 778. *(A.G. Ellis collection)*

LOCOMOTIVE CLASSIFICATION

Class Numbers
In 1852 and 1853 two reports identify locomotive classes by number, from 1 to 51. Classes omitted are the Nasmyth singles, which were transferred away in 1849, and new engines which arrived from 1851, the Bloomers, the Patents and the Fairbairn 0-6-0s. It is not known how long this class number system existed or if it was ever extended to cover the later classes.

Class	Maker	Type	Cylinders	DW	Boiler	Nos. & Names
1	Hick etc	2-2-2T	12" x 18"	5' 6"	1a	5/27/191/8/9
2	Bury	2-2-0	13" x 18"	5' 0"	3c	58
3	Bury etc	2-2-0	13" x 18"	5' 6"	2a	1/3/4/10/5/20/1/5/49
4	Bury	2-2-0	13" x 18"	5' 6"	3c	37/8/9/41/2/4/6/7/53/4/5/7
5	Bury	2-2-0	13" x 18"	5' 6"	6d	237
6	Bury etc	2-2-0	13" x 18"	5' 9"	4b	2/7/11/7/9/29
7	Bury	2-2-0	13" x 18"	5' 9"	4h	48
8	Haigh	2-2-0	13" x 18"	6' 0"	4b	24
9	Bury etc	0-4-0	13" x 18"	5' 0"	3c	61/2/3/6/8/77/83/4/8/90
10	Hick etc	2-2-0	14" x 8"	5' 9"	6d	13/4/23/6/8/30/43/50/1/2
11	Wolverton	2-2-0	14" x 18"	5' 9"	9g	92/5
12	BC&K	2-2-0	14" x 18"	5' 9"	5f	59/60/91
13	BC&K	2-2-0	14" x 18"	5' 9"	8f	93/4/6-9
14	Bury	2-2-0	14" x 18"	6' 0"	7e	40
15	Bury etc	0-4-0	14" x 18"	5' 0"	9g	64/9/70/6/8/9/80/1
16	BC&K	0-4-0	15" x 20"	5' 0"		111-6
17	BC&K	0-4-2	15" x 20"	5' 0"		117/8
18	Sharp	2-2-2	15" x 20"	5' 0"		4 (*Saddleworth*)
19	Sharp	2-2-2	15" x 20"	5' 6"		31/5/6/145/6/205/7
20	BC&K	2-2-2	15" x 20"	6' 0"		100-10
21	Wilson	2-2-2	15" x 20"	5' 6"		201
22	Wilson	2-2-2	15" x 20"	6' 0"		208/9
23	Tayleur	4-2-0	15" x 22"	6' 0"		159-67
24	Tayleur	4-2-0	15" x 22"	6' 0"		176-81
25	Jones	4-2-0	15" x 22"	6' 0"		182-5
26	Jones	4-2-0	15" x 22"	6' 5"		175
27	Haigh	4-2-0	15" x 22"	6' 5"		202/3/4
28	Jones	4-2-0	15" x 22"	6' 6"		186-90
29	BC&K	0-4-0	15" x 20"	4' 0"		172/3
30	Tayleur	0-6-0	15" x 24"	4' 6"		119/24
31	Tayleur	0-6-0	15" x 24"	4' 6"		120-3
32	Nasmyth	0-6-0	15" x 24"	4' 6"		137-44
33	BC&K	0-4-0	15" x 24"	4' 9"		72/4/86/9
34	Longridge	0-6-0	15" x 24"	5' 0"		125-36
35	Jones	4-2-0	15" x 24"	6' 6"		147-52
36	Stephenson	4-2-2	15" x 24"	6' 6"		153/7
37	Stephenson	4-2-0	15" x 24"	7' 0"		154/5/6/8
38	BC&K	0-4-2	16" x 24"	5' 0"		6/16/22/33/4/206
39	Sharp	2-2-2	16" x 20"	5' 6"		8
40	Sharp	2-2-2	15" x 20"	6' 0"		9
41	BC&K	2-2-2	16" x 20"	6' 0"		12/8/65/7/75/218
42	Jones	0-6-0	16" x 22"	5' 0"		174
43	BC&K	0-6-0	16" x 24"	5' 0"		168-71
44	Tulk & Ley	4-2-0	18" x 20"	8' 0"		200 (*London*)
45	Wolverton	2-2-2	18" x 21"	6' 6"		227
46	Stephenson	4-2-2	18" x 24"	7' 0"		233/4
47	BC&K	6-2-0	18" x 24"	8' 0"		245 (*Liverpool*)
48	Sharp	0-6-0	18" x 24"	4' 6"		32
49	Stephenson	0-6-0	18" x 24"	5' 0"		211/3/4/6/20/3/5/43
50	Sharp	0-6-0	18" x 24"	5' 0"		210/2/5/7/9/24/32
51	Hawthorn	0-6-0	18" x 24"	5' 0"		85/7/221/2/6/35/9/44 and 246 (*Standedge*)

Class Letters

Engines built at Wolverton were given class letters, in alphabetical and chronological order from Class A to Class N. Not all have been positively identified, and they seem to refer to works orders rather than discrete classes.

Class	Date	Type		Total
A	1853/4	0-4-2	Wol/Bury goods	10
B	1856-	0-6-0	Express Goods	*
C	1857/8	2-2-2	Small Bloomer	10
D	c1859	0-6-0	Express Goods	*
E	1859	2-2-2	Small Bloomer	5
F			*	
G	1860	0-4-2T	Patent tank	5
H	1861	2-2-2	Special large Bloomer	3 (+ 2 cancelled)
I			*	
J			*	
K	1861	2-2-2	Small Bloomer	5
L	1862	2-2-2	Bloomer	10
M	1862	0-4-2T	Branch line tank	10
N	1862	0-4-2	Mixed Traffic	15

*Classes B and D were Wolverton Express Goods but there seems to be no mention anywhere of classes (or orders) F, I or J. As no fewer than 75 of the Express Goods (plus the rebuilt *Liverpool*) were built at Wolverton in 1856-61 it seems likely that these letters covered the later batches of this class.

Confusingly, the 1862 Class L Bloomers were also known as Class B, which may be because the original Class B had been relettered by then for some unknown reason.

Wolverton Works Numbers

There is no official evidence that works numbers were ever used at Wolverton. At least four distinct versions of a 'works list' have been in circulation for many years; not only do they differ, but all contain errors sufficient to show that they were concocted from inaccurate data long after Wolverton had ceased to build locomotives.

ENGINES BUILT AT WOLVERTON, 1845-63

Date	Type	Cyls	DW	Running No.	Remarks
11/1845	2-2-0	14" x 18"	5' 9"	92	Bury type
1/1846				95	
10/1848	2-2-2	18" x 21"	6' 6"	227	McConnell
12/1851	0-6-0	18" x 24"	5' 0"	228	Sharp type long-boiler
12/1851				229	
12/1851				230	
a /1853	0-4-2	16" x 24"	5' 0"	236	Bury/Wolverton type Class A
6/1853				192	
7/1853				231	
12/1853				193	
10/1854				194	
12/1854				195	
5/1855				28	
5/1855				164	
a /1855				124	
a /1855				148	
5/1855	0-4-2	17" x 24"	5' 6"	200	(nominal rebuild of 4-2-0 *London*)
5/1856	0-6-0	16" x 24"	5' 6"	11	Express Goods Class B
5/1856				150	
7/1856				19	
8/1856				20	
8/1856				149	
8/1856				159	
9/1856				90	
11/1856				49	
12/1856				147	
12/1856				167	
5/1857	2-2-2	16" x 21"	6' 6"	103	Small Bloomer Class C
7/1857				21	
8/1857				7	
8/1857				140	
10/1857				238	
b /1857				240	
6/1857	0-6-0	16" x 24"	5' 6"	151	Express Goods
6/1857				179	
7/1857				166	
7/1857				182	
8/1857				196	
10/1857				197	
11/1857				198	
11/1857				199	
12/1857				241	
2/1858	2-2-2	16" x 21"	6' 6"	168	Small Bloomer Class C
7/1858				2	
10/1858				165	
12/1858				180	
1/1858	0-6-0	16" x 24"	5' 6"	242	Express Goods
12/1858				82	
12/1858				172	

Date	Type	Cyls	DW	Running No.	Remarks
4/1859	0-6-0	16" x 24"	5' 6"	245	(nominal rebuild of 6-2-0 *Liverpool*)
5/1859	2-2-2	16" x 21"	6' 6"	117	Small Bloomer Class E
7/1859				189	
8/1859				66	
10/1859				3	
8/1859	0-6-0	16" x 24"	5' 6"	91	Express Goods Class D
10/1859				120	
10/1859				183	
11/1859				50	
11/1859				175	
b /1859				83	
1/1860	2-2-2	16" x 21"	6' 6"	317	Small Bloomer Class E
1/1860	0-6-0	16" x 24"	5' 6"	318	Express Goods
1/1860				319	
9/1860				5	
9/1860				51	
9/1860				104	
10/1860				101	
10/1860				169	
10/1860				170	
10/1860				171	
11/1860				100	
11/1860				105	
11/1860				107	
7/1860	0-4-2T	15" x 24"	5' 6"	125	Patent Tank Class G
8/1860				102	
8/1860				110	
9/1860				174	
b /1860				354	
5/1861	2-2-2	18" x 24"	7' 6"	375	Special Large Bloomer Class H
8/1861				372	
11/1861				373	
				(374)	not completed, scrapped 1863
				(376)	not completed, scrapped 1863
9/1861	2-2-2	16" x 21"	6' 6"	377	Small Bloomer Class K
10/1861				378	
10/1861				379	
11/1861				380	
11/1861				381	
1/1861	0-6-0	16" x 24"	5' 6"	74	Express Goods
1/1861				93	
1/1861				108	
1/1861				109	
3/1861				114	
3/1861				115	
3/1861				173	
4/1861				118	
6/1861				92	
6/1861				94	
6/1861				98	
6/1861				113	
7/1861				52	
7/1861				86	

Date	Type	Cyls	DW	Running No.	Remarks
7/1861	0-6-0	16" x 24"	5' 6"	99	Express Goods
8/1861				97	
8/1861				355	
8/1861				356	
8/1861				357	
9/1861				358	
9/1861				359	
9/1861				360	
10/1861				361	
10/1861				362	
10/1861				363	
11/1861				72	
11/1861				89	
11/1861				364	
11/1861				365	
11/1861				366	
11/1861				367	
11/1861				368	
12/1861				369	
12/1861				371	
1/1862				371	
2/1862				370	
3/1862	2-2-2	16" x 22"	7' 0"	389	Bloomer Class L (or B)
3/1862				390	
3/1862				391	
3/1862				392	
4/1862				393	
4/1862				394	
4/1862				395	
4/1862				397	
5/1862				996	
5/1862				998	
4/1862	0-4-2T	15" x 20"	5' 6"	974	Tank Class M
5/1862				734	
5/1862				976	
5/1862				982	
5/1862				983	
6/1862				984	
6/1862				985	
6/1862				986	
6/1862				987	
6/1862				988	
7/1862	0-4-2	15" x 20"	5' 6"	606	Mixed Traffic Class N
8/1862				741	
8/1862				778	
8/1862				790	
8/1862				811	
8/1862				1019	
8/1862				1020	
9/1862				601	
9/1862				616	
9/1862				784	
10/1862				688	
10/1862				695	
11/1862				696	
11/1862				787	
11/1862				1021	

Date	Type	Cyls	DW	Running No.	Remarks
4/1863	0-6-0	16" x 24"	5' 6"	1056	Express Goods
4/1863				1057	
5/1863				1058	
5/1863				1059	
5/1863				1060	
7/1863				1071	
8/1863				1072	
8/1863				1073	
9/1863				1074	
9/1863				1075	

Total: 166 (including two 'rebuilds' of Crampton express passenger engines as coupled goods engines).

Notes

1. In dates:
   'a' is the first half-year (six months to 31st May),
   'b' is the second half-year (six months to 30th November).

2. Some dates are 'to traffic', some are from numberplate building dates and others are estimates from the alleged age of the engine when scrapped at Crewe. Reconciliation of these sources is complicated by the building of ten engines in 1857/8 "in advance" without the Board's authorisation. Six of these were built in the half-year ending November 1857, the other four by the end of May 1858. They seem likely to have been ten of the eleven engines 196-9, 238, 240/1/2 and 317/8/9, but certainty is impossible. Four of them appear to have been taken into stock in 1858; two more were taken into stock in June 1859, charged to the revenue account. The other four entered stock in January 1860, charged to capital.

3. Renumbering into the all-LNWR list by the addition of 600 took place in mid-April 1862 but the precise date is not known; some S Div engines completed in April 1862 might have carried numbers in the 600 series from new, like those completed in and after May 1862.

LOCOMOTIVE NUMBERING
and the Duplicate Lists

Engine Numbering on the S Div

In L&B days series of numbers had been allotted to engines ordered from a particular builder and had been numbered within each series in order of receipt. Thus batches of engines from Bury & Co were numbered 1-9, from Hick 10-15, from Hawthorn 16-21 and so on. This system continued on the S Div apart from a period in 1847-9 when most engines were numbered in order of receipt irrespective of class or maker. At this time some new engines were given the numbers of old engines which had been disposed of, but this was not done in a systematic way and several blanks remained in a list which grew longer and longer. Two curious gaps were left before 200, Crampton's *London*, and 300, the first of McConnell's Patents, presumably to give these engines 'prestige' numbers and in both cases the series of numbers then ran on, leaving the preceding blanks apparently overlooked.

By mid-1855, there were 283 S Div engines in a list whose highest-numbered engine was 342. There were 41 blanks, and eighteen engines on the sales list, withdrawn from working stock but still bearing numbers.

The list was fairly tight above 90, with spaces allowed for new engines on order (283-6 and 329/30/1), gaps where engines transferred to the NE Div had not yet been replaced (238 and 240/1/2) and the 'overlooked' 299. The nine numbers preceding 200 are more complicated. Numbers 191-6 were originally taken by Nasmyth singles but these were transferred to the Huddersfield & Manchester line in May 1849. During 1850-2 some small 12in Bury passenger engines, rebuilt as tanks, were renumbered into this 191-9 space; Nos 191, 198 and 199 are so recorded in June 1852, and although they were shortly to be taken away by Fairbairn & Sons as part-payment for new engines, they were still in LNWR hands when Wolverton-built engines of Class A were allocated Nos 192-5. Four other Class A engines were intended for (or may have briefly carried) Nos 196-9, but were instead given the numbers of withdrawn engines 28, 124, 148 and 164.

The list below 91 was very ragged, with 24 blanks and all eighteen of the "condemned for sale" engines. Within the next few months four more blanks appeared by the withdrawal of Nos 13, 20, 50 and 54 from the working stock. Meanwhile new construction filled 283-6 and 329/30/1 and the first of the Wolverton-built Express Goods engines were nearing completion.

In the main, S Div engines of one class occupied blocks of consecutive numbers. This was quite unlike the N Div system, where engines of a class were scattered throughout the list and no number was left vacant for long; an old engine disposed of was 'replaced' by a new engine, paid for from revenue, which took the running number of the old engine. New engines which increased the total stock were paid for out of capital (which had to be justified at a General Meeting where the approval of the shareholders was required) and these were the only engines to be given new numbers. By this system the highest engine number in use was that of the total number of engines in stock. After a few years of these 'revenue replacements' an engine's number gave no clue to its classification; engines with consecutive numbers could belong to any type. This would have been awkward at times for the men who actually worked among the engines (the engine names would be a memory aid) but it was a simple system for accountancy purposes. To accountants accustomed to Crewe's tight and tidy system the Wolverton list must have seemed a mess.

McConnell's carefree way with figures and stock totals is very evident in the surviving records. The presentation of clear, accurate and unambiguous data does not seem to have been one of his priorities. But at the end of 1854 departmental accounts were being looked into very carefully, following the conviction for embezzlement (and transportation to Australia for fourteen years) of the head of the Audit Department, Thomas Goalen. Errors were discovered in the Wagon Department accounts whereupon the Superintendent, Henry H. Henson, was sacked. Other faults were exposed and dismissals of senior executives followed. In January 1855 there was a fire in McConnell's office which destroyed "old accounts etc". Not surprisingly, the suspicious and vigilant auditors immediately requested a verification of the locomotive and ballast engine stock. Their investigation probably led to a decision to extend the orderly Crewe replacement system to the S Div.

The 1856 Renumbering

Before the Crewe system could begin, the S Div locomotive list had to be put in order and in 1856 a wholesale scheme of renumbering was undertaken. James Bull's eye-witness description is the only evidence of what then took place; strangely there is no mention of it in the surviving LNWR records. The day selected for the renumbering was All Fools' Day, which McConnell may have thought very appropriate.

In the scheme drawn up, the 'for sale' engines were cleared out from the list, and most of the remaining old Burys with numbers below 91 were regrouped. All engines from 297 upwards were renumbered into the gaps. After all this, there were still ten blank numbers (20/49, 196-9, 238/40/1/2) apparently scheduled for new Express Goods engines being built at Wolverton.

Bull says: "For some time previous ... the new numbers were painted on the buffer-planks as opportunity occurred... On the morning of April 1st the brass figures on the chimney were blacked over, and as soon after as convenient were taken off and the new numbers put on." He (or the *Locomotive Magazine* editor) goes on to say that this was the only time known when S Div engines had bufferplank numbers and that they were then painted over. This must be wrong because all photographs showing the front of an engine show a number between the buffers, and Sharp's order from McConnell for five engines in 1861 contains this note: "Name plates to pattern - Nos 399, 400, 401, 402, 403. Nos to be painted upon the buffer plank of engines."

So it would appear that from 1856 until 1862 numbers were carried in both places, on the chimney-front and on the bufferplank. Fig 33 demonstrates the somewhat overpowering effect.

Renumbering, 1st April 1856

Old No. 31/3/1856	Type	New No. 1/4/1856	Old No. 31/3/1856	Type	New No. 1/4/1856
14	Hick 2-2-0	1	309	Patent 2-2-2	48
23	Haigh 2-2-0	2	60	BC&K 2-2-0	50
26	Rothwell 2-2-0	3	70	Bury 0-4-0	53
30	"	5	321	Stothert 0-6-0	54
40	Bury 2-2-0	7	322	"	55
43	"	10	323	"	56
47	"	11	324	"	57
310	Small Bloomer 2-2-2	13	325	"	58
311	"	14	326	"	59
312	"	15	327	"	60
313	"	17	328	"	61
48	Bury 2-2-0	19	329	"	62
59	BC&K 2-2-0	21	330	"	63
314	Small Bloomer 2-2-2	23	331	"	64
315	"	24	76	Bury 0-4-0	66
316	"	25	332	Kitson 0-6-0	68
317	"	26	333	"	69
318	"	27	334	"	70
319	"	29	335	"	71
320	"	30	336	"	73
297	Patent 2-2-2	37	337	"	76
298	"	38	338	"	77
300	"	39	339	"	78
301	"	40	340	"	79
302	"	41	341	"	80
303	"	42	342	"	81
304	"	43	78	Bury 0-4-0	83
305	"	44	79	Maudslay 0-4-0	84
306	"	45	80	"	88
307	"	46	81	"	90
308	"	47	69	Bury 0-4-0	191

The S Div Duplicate List

The introduction of the Crewe system to the S Div, following the April 1856 renumbering scheme, initiated what was to become known as the Duplicate List. Each half-year a number of new engines were authorised as replacements for old engines, which were then 'condemned for sale'.

At first the condemned engines retained their old numbers. Thus, old 42 was sold in August 1856, apparently with that number, although it had been replaced by a new 42 in April. Not long after this, engines which had been replaced were given the suffix 'A'. Hence in August 1858 two old engines are referred to as 7(A) and 182(A), while 53, 86, 160, 165 and 180 in the same list of engines on offer to the Portsmouth Railway are without the suffix, not yet having been replaced.

Although many were scrapped without finding a buyer there was a slow turnover among the 'for sale' engines, and it was possibly to avoid the confusion of having two engines in the sales list with the same number - one having been put there at the renumbering joined all-too-soon by *its* replacement - that a 'letter' series was begun. An auction sale held on 20th August 1858 featured four engines from Wolverton listed simply as E, G, H and Q. From the miserably low prices realised they were evidently old, small engines, probably from the pre-1856 'condemned' list. Confirmation of the existing practice was given on 11th November 1858, when the Locomotive Committee discussed the "mode of replacing engines and the numbers affixed to them." It was ordered that "the originals of duplicates Nos 7, 166 and 182 be lettered A, B and C and that in future when a number is replaced by a new engine and the old one still kept running, the latter should lose its number and have an alphabetical letter in lieu thereof." A month later it was agreed to keep the original number as well as the letter; Ramsbottom proposed this, and thereafter *his* duplicate engines merely had the letter 'A' added to the number. In the south the 'duplicate-duplicate' problem remained, so for a short time sales list engines on the S Div carried letters from A to Z as well as their old number. The only ones known, apart from 7A, 166B and 182C, are 117D (mentioned in July 1859) and 2S and

58Z (in October 1859).

With a steadily growing list of duplicates and only 26 letters in the alphabet, a new scheme of simply adding 1000 to the old number was authorised on 22nd June 1859. The existing lettered engines were not altered, but future duplicates went into the 1000 series. Of these, 1083 (sold Nov 1859), 1066 (sold Dec 1859), and 1172 (sold April 1860) are known from the minutes. This 1000 series no doubt continued until the amalgamation of the two divisions in 1862, when the S Div duplicates were renumbered into Ramsbottom's duplicate list.

The 1862 Renumbering
John Ramsbottom took over at Wolverton on 29th March 1862 and during the following month the S Div engines in working stock were renumbered into the N Div list. In 1857 he had conducted a similar exercise with the NE Div engines by adding 400 to each number "so as to preserve the present numbers so far as tens and units were concerned" as he carefully explained to the Executive Committee. In April 1862 the highest-numbered N Div engine was 596 and Crewe was turning out more every month, so on this occasion it was appropriate to add 600 to the number of each of the engines taken over, and the S Div engines thus became 601-1018. The precise date is not known but the new numbers were in use by 25th April. During the year new construction at Wolverton filled gaps in this series and added three more numbers by November, 1019-21. In May, June and July new engines from Crewe took the numbers 597-600 and continued from 1022 onwards.

By the end of 1862 the total locomotive stock in the LNWR capital list was 1031, of which exactly 400 had come from the S Div. Other S Div engines had been immediately condemned for replacement and had joined those from the old 1000 series in the new all-LNWR duplicate list.

The Duplicate List from 1862
In April 1862 a block of numbers from 1101 upwards was set aside for duplicate stock. The 33 engines in the N Div 'A' list - 7A, 28A etc - were renumbered 1101 to 1133. Another nine engines were replaced by new engines built at Crewe in May, so by the end of that month the N Div contribution to the new list comprised 1101 to 1142. Numbers from 1143 upwards were allocated to the S Div duplicates.

The precise number of S Div duplicates from the old 1000 series is unknown, but the total of both divisions at 31st December 1861 was 70, which suggests that the S Div list contained about 37. On Ramsbottom's taking over, several other S Div engines were removed from capital stock and immediately added to the duplicates, well in advance of the building of new engines as replacements. Some were scrapped, but even so the new list consisted of 84 engines by 30th June 1862; a further purge of S Div stock brought the total to 101 by the end of November. During 1863-4 another 81 S Div engines were replaced, but scrapping and sales kept the total of duplicate engines down to around 121 throughout this period. While doubt surrounds the identity of the first duplicates from the S Div at least we know which engines were placed on the duplicate list after 1862 - and approximately when - because each new engine carried the number of the engine it replaced, and an old engine had to be given an 11xx series number before its old number could be taken by the new replacement engine. Some of the duplicate numbers are not known and there has been a lot of guesswork, with many spurious numbers getting into print.

Some of these bad guesses can be identified and corrected from a list found at Crewe in the 1960s, which gives the earlier numbers of each engine which had survived until 1872. Others, which had a shorter stay in the 11xx list before sale or scrapping, are sometimes known from archive sources and sometimes can be deduced. Many versions of these numbers have been circulated in the past, and it is often difficult to sort out those for which there was - at one time - some actual evidence.

The full and complicated story of the duplicate list will be dealt with in another volume in this series, but the following should suffice to give an explanation of the later renumberings of the S Div engines.

When an engine in the duplicate list was sold or scrapped, its 11xx number was used again for another engine entering the duplicate list, and with some numbers this happened over and over again. The system worked on a six-monthly basis; at the beginning of each half-year vacant numbers in the list were awarded to engines which were about to become duplicates. Sometimes the number of an engine sold or scrapped was immediately transferred to another engine, but sometimes the number lay vacant until the end of the current half-year; then the next engine to hold the same number was entered in the list at the start of the following six months period. The accountants who allotted the duplicate numbers controlled the system so that in their books the list was tightly filled at the start of each half-year.

From 1863 a fixed proportion of engines was replaced each year, irrespective of whether the old engines were fully worn out or not, so that by February 1870 the block of numbers from 1101 to 1300 was completely filled with duplicates. By this time capital stock already occupied numbers from 1301 into the 1700s so Ramsbottom "in the absence of instructions to the contrary" took the block from 1801 to 2000 for further additions to the duplicate stock.

At 30th November 1871 the total number of duplicates was 234, over 12% of the entire stock, and most of them were still hard at work. It was realised that far too many had been written off prematurely so 100 of the best were restored to capital stock, including several ex-S Div engines, notably the Bury, Curtis & Kennedy singles which had been in the duplicate list for nine years. These 100 engines were renumbered as capital list 1101-1200 in December 1871 - the rest of the former duplicate block up to 1300 being filled by new engines built at Crewe in 1872/3. Each of the remaining duplicate engines (including those already carrying numbers in the 18xx series) was renumbered into a new 1801-2000 block.

By 1886 the duplicate stock had again grown to 200, and a new block of numbers from 3001 upwards was allocated. There was some reshuffling of the duplicate numbers in 1886/7 in order to have all the duplicate DX goods engines together in the 1801 series, with the miscellaneous duplicate engines in the 3001 series. A handful of old S Div engines acquired numbers in the latter group for their last year or so.

'Cut-up Numbers'
Under the Crewe system from 1862 every engine scrapped or sold by the LNWR had, for accountancy reasons, to be from the duplicate list. Those scrapped without having been renumbered into the list were awarded a notional 'cut-up' number which was simply a vacant number in the current half-year's duplicate list; it was not applied to the engine before scrapping, unless scribbled on with chalk. Occasionally, engines were sold to outside purchasers directly from capital stock and these also were given 'cut-up' numbers to keep the books straight.

Summary - Duplicate List

Date		Numbering of old engines when replaced
	1856	Engine kept its old number
	1857	Suffix A added to number, 7A etc
	1858	Engines identified by letter only, A, B, C etc
Dec	1858	Engine kept old number with letter added, 7A, 166B, 182C, 117D etc
Jun	1859	Number & letter series retained but later duplicates to have 1000 added to the old number, 1083, 1172 etc
May	1862	All-LNWR renumbering. Duplicate list allocated 1101-1300
Feb	1870	Duplicate list filled 1101-1300; new allocation 1801-2000
Dec	1871	Duplicate list 1801-2000 only, 1101-1300 taken by capital list engines
Mar	1886	Duplicate list 1801-2000, 3001-

London & Birmingham Railway & LNWR Southern Division
Locomotives from 1837 to the renumbering of April 1856

ORIGINAL ENGINES

No.	Maker	Type	Date
1	Bury	2-2-0	7/37
2	”	”	7/37
3	”	”	8/38
4	”	”	8/38
5	”	”	7/38
6	”	”	8/38
7	”	”	9/38
8	”	”	9/38
9	”	”	10/38
10	Hick	”	7/37
11	”	”	1/38
12	”	”	2/38
13	”	”	4/38
14	”	”	6/38
15	”	”	7/38
16	Hawthorn	”	7/37
17	”	”	10/37
18	”	”	11/37
19	”	”	12/37
20	”	”	2/38
21	”	”	3/38
22	Haigh	”	8/37
23	”	”	9/37
24	”	”	10/37
25	Rothwell	”	12/37
26	”	”	3/38
27	”	”	3/38
28	”	”	8/38
29	”	”	4/38
30	”	”	8/38
31	Mather	”	10/37
32	”	”	12/37
33	”	”	3/38
34	”	”	3/38
35	”	”	4/38
36	”	”	7/38
37	Bury	”	10/39
38	”	”	10/39
39	”	”	11/39
40	”	”	1/40
41	”	”	1/40
42	”	”	2/40
43	”	”	2/40
44	”	”	3/40
45	”	”	3/40
46	”	”	4/40
47	”	”	10/40
48	”	”	10/40
49	Hick	”	1/40
50	”	”	1/40
51	”	”	2/40
52	”	”	3/40
Ayl 1	”	”	1/40
Ayl 2	”	”	1/40
53	Bury	”	2/41
54	”	”	3/41

REPLACEMENTS, 1847-1855

Maker	Type	No'd
Hick (ex-Aylesbury 2)	2-2-0	9/48
Sharp *Saddleworth*	2-2-2	/50-/52
Hick (ex-12)	2-2-2T	/50
BC&K	0-4-2	11/47
Sharp	2-2-2	10/47
Sharp	2-2-2	11/48
BC&K	2-2-2	8/48
BC&K	0-4-2	1/48
BC&K	2-2-2	8/48
BC&K	0-4-2	10/47
Haigh (ex-22)?	2-2-2T	/50
Wol Class A	0-4-2	5/55
Sharp (ex-M&B 31)	2-2-2	10/48
Sharp (ex-M&B 32)	0-6-0	10/48
BC&K	0-4-2	10/47
BC&K	0-4-2	11/47
Sharp	2-2-2	12/47
Sharp	2-2-2	12/47

ORIGINAL ENGINES				**REPLACEMENTS, 1847-1855**		
No.	Maker	Type	Date	Maker	Type	No'd
55	Bury	2-2-0	3/41			
56	"	"	3/41			
57	"	"	5/41			
58	"	"	6/41			
59	BC&K	2-2-0	2/45			
60	"	"	2/45			
61	Bury	0-4-0	11/38	Bury (ex-*Kennedy*)	0-4-0	/52-/53?
62	"	"	11/38			
63	"	"	11/38			
64	"	"	1/39			
65	"	"	1/39	BC&K	2-2-2	5/48
66	"	"	2/39			
67	"	"	2/39	BC&K	2-2-2	6/48
68	"	"	3/39			
69	"	"	4/39			
70	"	"	4/39			
71	"	"	5/39	(unidentified)	2-2-0	/50-/52
72	"	"	5/39	BC&K	0-4-0	9/47
73	"	"	6/39			
74	"	"	7/39	BC&K	0-4-0	9/47
75	"	"	7/39	BC&K	2-2-2	6/48
76	"	"	8/39			
77	"	"	9/39			
78	"	"	11/39			
79	Maudslay	"	9/38			
80	"	"	10/38			
81	"	"	11/38			
82	"	"	12/38	Bury (ex-*Bury*)	0-4-0	/52-/53?
83	"	"	2/39			
84	"	"	2/39			
85	"	"	7/39	Hawthorn	0-6-0	7/48
86	"	"	8/39	BC&K	0-4-0	6/47
87	"	"	9/39	Hawthorn	0-6-0	7/48
88	"	"	10/39			
89	"	"	11/39	BC&K	0-4-0	10/47
90	"	"	11/39			
91	BC&K	2-2-0	5/45			
92	Wol	"	11/45			
93	BC&K	"	12/45			
94	"	"	1/46			
95	Wol	"	1/46			
96	BC&K	"	3/46			
97	"	"	4/46			
98	"	"	7/46			
99	"	"	7/46			
100	BC&K	2-2-2	8/46			
101	"	"	9/46			
102	"	"	9/46			
103	"	"	9/46			
104	"	"	9/46			
105	"	"	10/46			
106	"	"	10/46			
107	"	"	10/46			
108	"	"	11/46			
109	"	"	11/46			
110	"	"	12/46			
111	BC&K	0-4-0	9/45			
112	"	"	10/45			
113	"	"	10/45			
114	"	"	11/45			

ORIGINAL ENGINES				**REPLACEMENTS, 1847-1855**			
No.	Maker	Type	Date	Maker		Type	No'd
115	BC&K	0-4-0	12/45				
116	"	"	12/45				
117	BC&K	0-4-2	2/46				
118	"	"	2/46				
119	Tayleur	0-6-0	10/46				
120	"	"	12/45				
121	"	"	2/46				
122	"	"	2/46				
123	"	"	2/46				
124	"	"	3/46	Wol		Class A	0-4-2	a /55
125	Longridge	0-6-0	5/46				
126	"	"	5/46				
127	"	"	6/46				
128	"	"	7/46				
129	"	"	10/46				
130	"	"	9/46				
131	"	"	/47				
132	"	"	/47				
133	"	"	10/47				
134	"	"	12/47				
135	"	"	12/47				
136	"	"	3/48				
137	Nasmyth	0-6-0	4/47				
138	"	"	4/47				
139	"	"	4/47				
140	"	"	5/47				
141	"	"	6/47				
142	"	"	7/47				
143	"	"	7/47				
144	"	"	11/47				
145	Sharp	2-2-2	10/46				
146	"	"	12/46				
147	J&P	4-2-0	5/46				
148	"	"	7/46	Wol		Class A	0-4-2	a /55
149	"	"	7/46				
150	"	"	8/46				
151	"	"	9/46				
152	"	"	12/46				
153	RS	4-2-0	2/47				
154	"	"	1/47				
155	"	"	2/47				
156	"	"	2/47				
157	"	"	3/47				
158	"	"	3/47				
159	Tayleur	4-2-0	12/46				
160	"	"	12/46				
161	"	"	12/46				
162	"	"	1/47				
163	"	"	1/47				
164	"	"	2/47	Wol		Class A	0-4-2	5/55
165	"	"	2/47				
166	"	"	2/47				
167	"	"	3/47				
168	BC&K	0-6-0	12/46				
169	"	"	12/46				
170	"	"	12/46				
171	"	"	12/46				
172	BC&K	0-4-0	12/46				
173	"	"	12/46				
174	J&P	0-6-0	3/47				
175	"	4-2-0	4/47				

ORIGINAL ENGINES				**REPLACEMENTS, 1847-1855**			
No.	Maker	Type	Date	Maker		Type	No'd
176	Tayleur	4-2-0	3/47				
177	"	"	3/47				
178	"	"	3/47				
179	"	"	4/47				
180	"	"	4/47				
181	"	"	5/47				
182	J&P	4-2-0	5/47				
183	"	"	6/47				
184	"	"	6/47				
185	"	"	8/47				
186	"	"	5/48				
187	"	"	6/48				
188	"	"	8/48				
189	"	"	9/48				
190	"	"	10/48				
191	Nasmyth	2-2-2	11/47	Mather (ex-31)?		2-2-2T	/50
192	"	"	12/47	Wol	Class A	0-4-2	6/53
193	"	"	12/47	Wol	Class A	0-4-2	12/53
194	"	"	1/48	Wol	Class A	0-4-2	10/54
195	"	"	1/48	Wol	Class A	0-4-2	12/54
196	"	"	3/48				
198	Mather (ex-32)?	2-2-2T	/50				
199	" (ex-35)?	"	/50				
200	T&L *London*	4-2-0	6/47	Wol (rebuild)		0-4-2	5/55
201	Wilson	2-2-2	11/47				
202	"	"	11/47	Haigh		4-2-0	1/49
203	"	"	11/47	Haigh		4-2-0	7/49
204	"	"	11/47	Haigh		4-2-0	9/49
205	Sharp	"	12/47				
206	BC&K	0-4-2	12/47				
207	Sharp	2-2-2	12/47				
208	Wilson	2-2-2	3/48				
209	"	"	3/48				
210	Sharp	0-6-0	3/48				
211	RS	"	5/48				
212	Sharp	"	5/48				
213	RS	"	6/48				
214	"	"	7/48				
215	Sharp	"	7/48				
216	RS	"	7/48				
217	Sharp	"	8/48				
218	BC&K	2-2-2	8/48				
219	Sharp	0-6-0	8/48				
220	RS	"	9/48				
221	Hawthorn	"	9/48				
222	"	"	9/48				
223	RS	"	9/48				
224	Sharp	0-6-0	10/48				
225	RS	"	10/48				
226	Hawthorn	"	10/48				
227	Wol	2-2-2	10/48				
228	Sharp	0-6-0	10/48	Wol		0-6-0	12/51
229	"	"	10/48	Wol		0-6-0	12/51
230	RS	"	11/48	Wol		0-6-0	12/51
231	"	"	11/48	Wol	Class A	0-4-2	7/53
232	Sharp	"	11/48				
233	RS	4-2-2	12/48				
234	"	"	12/48				
235	Hawthorn	0-6-0	12/48				
236	RS	"	12/48	Wol	Class A	0-4-2	a /53

ORIGINAL ENGINES

No.	Maker	Type	Date
237	Bury (ex-2)	2-2-0	1/49
238	Sharp	0-6-0	1/49
239	Hawthorn	"	2/49
240	Sharp	"	2/49
241	RS	"	2/49
242	Sharp	"	3/49
243	RS	"	3/49
244	Hawthorn	"	4/49
245	BC&K	6-2-0	*Liverpool* built 9/48, numbered in /50
246	Hawthorn	0-6-0	*Standedge* built 7/48, numbered in /50-/51
247	Sharp	2-2-2	8/51
248	"	"	9/51
249	"	"	9/51
250	"	"	9/51
251	"	"	10/51
252	"	"	10/51
253	"	"	11/51
254	"	"	11/51
255	"	"	12/51
256	"	"	12/51
257	Fairbairn	0-6-0	10/51
258	"	"	11/51
259	"	"	1/52
260	"	"	1/52
261	"	"	5/52
262	"	"	8/52
263	"	"	8/52
264	"	"	10/52
265	"	"	11/52
266	"	"	12/52
267	"	"	1/53
268	"	"	1/53
269	"	"	2/53
270	"	"	2/53
271	"	"	3/53
272	"	"	4/53
273	"	"	5/53
274	"	"	5/53
275	"	"	7/53
276	"	"	7/53
277	"	"	3/53
278	"	"	3/53
279	"	"	4/54
280	"	"	5/54
281	"	"	7/54
282	"	"	11/54
283	"	"	9/55
284	"	"	10/55
285	"	"	12/55
286	"	"	12/55
287	Sharp	2-2-2	10/52
288	"	"	10/52
289	"	"	11/52
290	"	"	11/52
291	"	"	11/52
292	"	"	12/52
293	"	"	12/52
294	"	"	2/53
295	"	"	2/53
296	"	"	2/53

ORIGINAL ENGINES

No.	Maker	Type	Date
297	Wilson	2-2-2	11/52
298	"	"	12/52
300	Fairbairn	2-2-2	11/52
301	"	"	2/53
302	"	"	6/53
303	"	"	9/53
304	"	"	12/53
305	"	"	3/54
306	"	"	5/54
307	"	"	6/54
308	"	"	8/54
309	"	"	12/54
310	VF	2-2-2	6/54
311	"	"	6/54
312	"	"	7/54
313	"	"	7/54
314	Hawthorn	2-2-2	4/54
315	"	"	4/54
316	"	"	5/54
317	"	"	6/54
318	"	"	6/54
319	"	"	6/54
320	"	"	7/54
321	Stothert	0-6-0	2/55
322	"	"	2/55
323	"	"	2/55
324	"	"	3/55
325	"	"	3/55
326	"	"	3/55
327	"	"	5/55
328	"	"	5/55
329	"	"	6/55
330	"	"	7/55
331	"	"	8/55
332	Kitson	0-6-0	3/54
333	"	"	4/54
334	"	"	5/54
335	"	"	5/54
336	"	"	5/54
337	"	"	6/54
338	"	"	7/54
339	"	"	7/54
340	"	"	8/54
341	"	"	9/54
342	"	"	9/54

LNWR Southern Division
Locomotives from 1856 to 1862

ENGINES at 1st April 1856

No.	Former No.	Maker	Type
1	14	Hick	2-2-0
2	23	Haigh	2-2-0
3	26	Rothwell	2-2-0
4		Sharp	2-2-2
5	30	Rothwell	2-2-0
6		BC&K	0-4-2
7	40	Bury	2-2-0
8		Sharp	2-2-2
9		Sharp	2-2-2
10	43	Bury	2-2-0
11	47	Bury	2-2-0
12		BC&K	2-2-2
13	310	VF	2-2-2
14	311	VF	2-2-2
15	312	VF	2-2-2
16		BC&K	0-4-2
17	313	VF	2-2-2
18		BC&K	2-2-2
19	48	Bury	2-2-0
21	59	BC&K	2-2-0
22		BC&K	0-4-2
23	314	Hawthorn	2-2-2
24	315	Hawthorn	2-2-2
25	316	Hawthorn	2-2-2
26	317	Hawthorn	2-2-2
27	318	Hawthorn	2-2-2
28		Wol	0-4-2 A
29	319	Hawthorn	2-2-2
30	320	Hawthorn	2-2-2
31		Sharp	2-2-2
32		Sharp	0-6-0
33		BC&K	0-4-2
34		BC&K	0-4-2
35		Sharp	2-2-2
36		Sharp	2-2-2
37	297	Wilson	2-2-2
38	298	Wilson	2-2-2
39	300	Fairbairn	2-2-2
40	301	Fairbairn	2-2-2
41	302	Fairbairn	2-2-2
42	303	Fairbairn	2-2-2
43	304	Fairbairn	2-2-2
44	305	Fairbairn	2-2-2
45	306	Fairbairn	2-2-2
46	307	Fairbairn	2-2-2
47	308	Fairbairn	2-2-2
48	309	Fairbairn	2-2-2
50	60	BC&K	2-2-0
51		Hick	2-2-0
52		Hick	2-2-0
53	70	Bury	0-4-0
54	321	Stothert	0-6-0
55	322	Stothert	0-6-0
56	323	Stothert	0-6-0

REPLACEMENTS and ADDITIONS

No.	Maker	Type	Date
601	Wol	0-4-2 N	9/62
	Wol	2-2-2 C	7/58
	Wol	2-2-2 E	10/59
	Wol	0-6-0	9/60
606	Wol	0-4-2 N	7/62
	Wol	2-2-2 C	8/57
	Wol	0-6-0 B	5/56
616	Wol	0-4-2 N	9/62
	Wol	0-6-0 B	7/56
20	Wol	0-6-0 B	8/56
	Wol	2-2-2 C	7/57
49	Wol	0-6-0 B	11/56
	Wol	0-6-0 D	11/59
	Wol	0-6-0	9/60
	Wol	0-6-0	7/61
	Sharp	2-2-2 SSR	7/59

ENGINES at 1st April 1856 | | | | ## REPLACEMENTS and ADDITIONS | | | |
No.	Former No.	Maker	Type	No.	Maker	Type	Date
57	324	Stothert	0-6-0				
58	325	Stothert	0-6-0				
59	326	Stothert	0-6-0				
60	327	Stothert	0-6-0				
61	328	Stothert	0-6-0				
62	329	Stothert	0-6-0				
63	330	Stothert	0-6-0				
64	331	Stothert	0-6-0				
65		BC&K	2-2-2				
66	76	Bury	0-4-0		Wol	2-2-2 E	8/59
67		BC&K	2-2-2				
68	332	Kitson	0-6-0				
69	333	Kitson	0-6-0				
70	334	Kitson	0-6-0				
71	335	Kitson	0-6-0				
72		BC&K	0-4-0		Wol	0-6-0	11/61
73	336	Kitson	0-6-0				
74		BC&K	0-4-0		Wol	0-6-0	1/61
75		BC&K	2-2-2				
76	337	Kitson	0-6-0				
77	338	Kitson	0-6-0				
78	339	Kitson	0-6-0				
79	340	Kitson	0-6-0				
80	341	Kitson	0-6-0				
81	342	Kitson	0-6-0				
82		Bury	0-4-0		Wol	0-6-0	12/58
83	78	Bury	0-4-0		Wol	0-6-0	b /59
84	79	Maudslay	0-4-0		Sharp	2-2-2 SSR	7/59
85		Hawthorn	0-6-0				
86		BC&K	0-4-0		Wol	0-6-0	7/61
87		Hawthorn	0-6-0				
88	80	Maudslay	0-4-0	688	Wol	0-4-2 N	10/62
89		BC&K	0-4-0		Wol	0-6-0	11/61
90	81	Maudslay	0-4-0		Wol	0-6-0 B	9/56
91		BC&K	2-2-0		Wol	0-6-0 D	8/59
92		Wol	2-2-0		Wol	0-6-0	6/61
93		BC&K	2-2-0		Wol	0-6-0	1/61
94		BC&K	2-2-0		Wol	0-6-0	6/61
95		Wol	2-2-0	695	Wol	0-4-2 N	10/62
96		BC&K	2-2-0	696	Wol	0-4-2 N	11/62
97		BC&K	2-2-0		Wol	0-6-0	8/61
98		BC&K	2-2-0		Wol	0-6-0	6/61
99		BC&K	2-2-0		Wol	0-6-0	7/61
100		BC&K	2-2-2		Wol	0-6-0	11/60
101		BC&K	2-2-2		Wol	0-6-0	10/60
102		BC&K	2-2-2		Wol	0-4-2T G	8/60
103		BC&K	2-2-2		Wol	2-2-2 C	5/57
104		BC&K	2-2-2		Wol	0-6-0	9/60
105		BC&K	2-2-2		Wol	0-6-0	11/60
106		BC&K	2-2-2				
107		BC&K	2-2-2		Wol	0-6-0	11/60
108		BC&K	2-2-2		Wol	0-6-0	1/61
109		BC&K	2-2-2		Wol	0-6-0	1/61
110		BC&K	2-2-2		Wol	0-4-2T G	8/60
111		BC&K	0-4-0		Sharp	2-4-0T SSR	7/59
112		BC&K	0-4-0		Sharp	2-4-0T SSR	7/59
113		BC&K	0-4-0		Wol	0-6-0	6/61
114		BC&K	0-4-0		Wol	0-6-0	3/61
115		BC&K	0-4-0		Wol	0-6-0	3/61
116		BC&K	0-4-0		Sharp	2-2-2 SSR	7/59
117		BC&K	0-4-2		Wol	2-2-2 E	5/59

ENGINES at 1st April 1856 — REPLACEMENTS and ADDITIONS

No.	Former No.	Maker	Type	No.	Maker	Type	Date
118		BC&K	0-4-2		Wol	0-6-0	4/61
119		Tayleur	0-6-0				
120		Tayleur	0-6-0		Wol	0-6-0 D	10/59
121		Tayleur	0-6-0				
122		Tayleur	0-6-0				
123		Tayleur	0-6-0				
124		Wol	0-4-2 A				
125		Longridge	0-6-0		Wol	0-4-2T G	7/60
126		Longridge	0-6-0				
127		Longridge	0-6-0				
128		Longridge	0-6-0				
129		Longridge	0-6-0				
130		Longridge	0-6-0				
131		Longridge	0-6-0				
132		Longridge	0-6-0				
133		Longridge	0-6-0				
134		Longridge	0-6-0	734	Wol	0-4-2T M	5/62
135		Longridge	0-6-0				
136		Longridge	0-6-0				
137		Nasmyth	0-6-0				
138		Nasmyth	0-6-0				
139		Nasmyth	0-6-0				
140		Nasmyth	0-6-0		Wol	2-2-2 C	8/57
141		Nasmyth	0-6-0	741	Wol	0-4-2 N	8/62
142		Nasmyth	0-6-0				
143		Nasmyth	0-6-0				
144		Nasmyth	0-6-0				
145		Sharp	2-2-2				
146		Sharp	2-2-2				
147		J&P	4-2-0		Wol	0-6-0 B	12/56
148		Wol	0-4-2 A				
149		J&P	4-2-0		Wol	0-6-0 B	8/56
150		J&P	4-2-0		Wol	0-6-0 B	5/56
151		J&P	4-2-0		Wol	0-6-0	6/57
152		J&P	4-2-0				
153		RS	4-2-2				
154		RS	4-2-0				
155		RS	4-2-0				
156		RS	4-2-0				
157		RS	4-2-2				
158		RS	4-2-0				
159		Tayleur	4-2-0		Wol	0-6-0 B	8/56
160		Tayleur	4-2-0		Wilson	2-4-0 SSR	7/59
161		Tayleur	4-2-0				
162		Tayleur	4-2-0				
163		Tayleur	4-2-0				
164		Wol	0-4-2 A				
165		Tayleur	4-2-0		Wol	2-2-2 C	10/58
166		Tayleur	4-2-0		Wol	0-6-0	7/57
167		Tayleur	4-2-0		Wol	0-6-0 B	12/56
168		BC&K	0-6-0		Wol	2-2-2 C	2/58
169		BC&K	0-6-0		Wol	0-6-0	10/60
170		BC&K	0-6-0		Wol	0-6-0	10/60
171		BC&K	0-6-0		Wol	0-6-0	10/60
172		BC&K	0-4-0		Wol	0-6-0	12/58
173		BC&K	0-4-0		Wol	0-6-0	3/61
174		J&P	0-6-0		Wol	0-4-2T G	9/60
175		J&P	4-2-0		Wol	0-6-0 D	11/59
176		Tayleur	4-2-0				
177		Tayleur	4-2-0				
178		Tayleur	4-2-0	778	Wol	0-4-2 N	8/62

ENGINES at 1st April 1856

No.	Former No.	Maker	Type
179		Tayleur	4-2-0
180		Tayleur	4-2-0
181		Tayleur	4-2-0
182		J&P	4-2-0
183		J&P	4-2-0
184		J&P	4-2-0
185		J&P	4-2-0
186		J&P	4-2-0
187		J&P	4-2-0
188		J&P	4-2-0
189		J&P	4-2-0
190		J&P	4-2-0
191	69	Bury	0-4-0
192		Wol	0-4-2 A
193		Wol	0-4-2 A
194		Wol	0-4-2 A
195		Wol	0-4-2 A
200		Wol (rebuild)	0-4-2
201		Wilson	2-2-2
202		Haigh	4-2-0
203		Haigh	4-2-0
204		Haigh	4-2-0
205		Sharp	2-2-2
206		BC&K	0-4-2
207		Sharp	2-2-2
208		Wilson	2-2-2
209		Wilson	2-2-2
210		Sharp	0-6-0
211		RS	0-6-0
212		Sharp	0-6-0
213		RS	0-6-0
214		RS	0-6-0
215		Sharp	0-6-0
216		RS	0-6-0
217		Sharp	0-6-0
218		BC&K	2-2-2
219		Sharp	0-6-0
220		RS	0-6-0
221		Hawthorn	0-6-0
222		Hawthorn	0-6-0
223		RS	0-6-0
224		Sharp	0-6-0
225		RS	0-6-0
226		Hawthorn	0-6-0
227		Wol	2-2-2
228		Wol	0-6-0
229		Wol	0-6-0
230		Wol	0-6-0
231		Wol	0-4-2 A
232		Sharp	0-6-0
233		RS	4-2-2
234		RS	4-2-2
235		Hawthorn	0-6-0
236		Wol	0-4-2 A
237		Bury	2-2-0
239		Hawthorn	0-6-0

REPLACEMENTS and ADDITIONS

No.	Maker	Type	Date
	Wol	0-6-0	6/57
	Wol	2-2-2 C	12/58
	Wilson	2-4-0 SSR	7/59
	Wol	0-6-0	7/57
	Wol	0-6-0 D	10/59
784	Wol	0-4-2 N	9/62
787	Wol	0-4-2 N	11/62
	Wol	2-2-2 E	7/59
790	Wol	0-4-2 N	8/62
196	Wol	0-6-0	8/57
197	Wol	0-6-0	10/57
198	Wol	0-6-0	11/57
199	Wol	0-6-0	11/57
811	Wol	0-4-2 N	8/62
	Garforth	0-4-2 SSR	7/59
238	Wol	2-2-2 C	10/57

ENGINES at 1st April 1856

No.	Former No.	Maker	Type
243		RS	0-6-0
244		Hawthorn	0-6-0
245		BC&K	6-2-0
246		Hawthorn	0-6-0
247		Sharp	2-2-2
248		Sharp	2-2-2
249		Sharp	2-2-2
250		Sharp	2-2-2
251		Sharp	2-2-2
252		Sharp	2-2-2
253		Sharp	2-2-2
254		Sharp	2-2-2
255		Sharp	2-2-2
256		Sharp	2-2-2
257		Fairbairn	0-6-0
258		Fairbairn	0-6-0
259		Fairbairn	0-6-0
260		Fairbairn	0-6-0
261		Fairbairn	0-6-0
262		Fairbairn	0-6-0
263		Fairbairn	0-6-0
264		Fairbairn	0-6-0
265		Fairbairn	0-6-0
266		Fairbairn	0-6-0
267		Fairbairn	0-6-0
268		Fairbairn	0-6-0
269		Fairbairn	0-6-0
270		Fairbairn	0-6-0
271		Fairbairn	0-6-0
272		Fairbairn	0-6-0
273		Fairbairn	0-6-0
274		Fairbairn	0-6-0
275		Fairbairn	0-6-0
276		Fairbairn	0-6-0
277		Fairbairn	0-6-0
278		Fairbairn	0-6-0
279		Fairbairn	0-6-0
280		Fairbairn	0-6-0
281		Fairbairn	0-6-0
282		Fairbairn	0-6-0
283		Fairbairn	0-6-0
284		Fairbairn	0-6-0
285		Fairbairn	0-6-0
286		Fairbairn	0-6-0
287		Sharp	2-2-2
288		Sharp	2-2-2
289		Sharp	2-2-2
290		Sharp	2-2-2
291		Sharp	2-2-2
292		Sharp	2-2-2
293		Sharp	2-2-2
294		Sharp	2-2-2
295		Sharp	2-2-2
296		Sharp	2-2-2

REPLACEMENTS and ADDITIONS

No.	Maker	Type	Date
240	Wol	2-2-2 C	b /57
241	Wol	0-6-0	12/57
242	Wol	0-6-0	1/58
	Wol (rebuild)	0-6-0	4/59

ADDITIONS from 1859

No.	Maker	Type	Date
297	Fairbairn	2-2-2 SSR	7/59
298	Fairbairn	2-2-2 SSR	7/59
299	Fairbairn	2-2-2 SSR	7/59
300	Fairbairn	2-2-2 SSR	7/59

ADDITIONS from 1859

No.	Maker	Type	Date	No.	Maker	Type	Date
301	Wilson	0-6-0 SSR	7/59	362	Wol	0-6-0	10/61
302	Wilson	0-6-0 SSR	7/59	363	Wol	0-6-0	10/61
303	Beyer	0-4-2 SSR	7/59	364	Wol	0-6-0	11/61
304	Beyer	0-4-2 SSR	7/59	365	Wol	0-6-0	11/61
305	VF	0-6-0 SSR	7/59	366	Wol	0-6-0	11/61
306	VF	0-6-0 SSR	7/59	367	Wol	0-6-0	11/61
307	Fairbairn	0-6-0 SSR	7/59	368	Wol	0-6-0	12/61
308	Fairbairn	0-6-0 SSR	7/59	369	Wol	0-6-0	12/61
309	RS	0-6-0 SSR	7/59	370	Wol	0-6-0	2/62
310	RS	0-6-0 SSR	7/59	371	Wol	0-6-0	1/62
311	Fairbairn	0-6-0 SSR	7/59	372	Wol	2-2-2 H	8/61
312	Fairbairn	0-6-0 SSR	7/59	373	Wol	2-2-2 H	11/61
313	Fairbairn	0-6-0 SSR	7/59	974	Wol	0-4-2T M	4/62
314	Fairbairn	0-6-0 SSR	7/59	375	Wol	2-2-2 H	5/61
315	Fairbairn	0-6-0 SSR	7/59	976	Wol	0-4-2T M	5/62
316	Fairbairn	0-6-0 SSR	7/59	377	Wol	2-2-2 K	9/61
317	Wol	2-2-2 E	1/60	378	Wol	2-2-2 K	10/61
318	Wol	0-6-0	1/60	379	Wol	2-2-2 K	10/61
319	Wol	0-6-0	1/60	380	Wol	2-2-2 K	11/61
320	Crewe	2-2-2 N Div	1/60	381	Wol	2-2-2 K	11/61
321	Beyer	0-6-0	1/60	982	Wol	0-4-2T M	5/62
322	Beyer	0-6-0	1/60	983	Wol	0-4-2T M	5/62
323	Crewe	2-2-2 N Div	1/60	984	Wol	0-4-2T M	6/62
324	Crewe	2-2-2 N Div	1/60	985	Wol	0-4-2T M	6/62
325	Crewe	2-2-2 N Div	1/60	986	Wol	0-4-2T M	6/62
326	Crewe	2-2-2 N Div	1/60	987	Wol	0-4-2T M	6/62
327	Crewe	2-2-2 N Div	1/60	988	Wol	0-4-2T M	6/62
328	Crewe	2-2-2 N Div	1/60	389	Wol	2-2-2	3/62
329	Crewe	2-2-2 N Div	1/60	390	Wol	2-2-2	3/62
330	Crewe	2-2-2 N Div	1/60	391	Wol	2-2-2	3/62
331	Crewe	2-2-2 N Div	1/60	392	Wol	2-2-2	3/62
332	Crewe	2-2-2 N Div	1/60	393 (993?)	Wol	2-2-2	4/62
333	Crewe	2-2-2 N Div	1/60	394 (994?)	Wol	2-2-2	4/62
334	Edge Hill	2-2-2 N Div	1/60	395 (995?)	Wol	2-2-2	4/62
335	Crewe	2-2-2 N Div	1/60	996	Wol	2-2-2	5/62
336	Edge Hill	2-2-2 N Div	1/60	397 (997?)	Wol	2-2-2	4/62
337	Edge Hill	2-2-2 N Div	1/60	998	Wol	2-2-2	5/62
338	Crewe	2-2-2 N Div	1/60	399	Sharp	2-2-2	10/61
339	Crewe	2-2-2 N Div	1/60	400	Sharp	2-2-2	10/61
340	Crewe	2-2-2 N Div	1/60	401	Sharp	2-2-2	11/61
341	Crewe	2-2-2 N Div	1/60	402	Sharp	2-2-2	11/61
342	Crewe	2-2-2 N Div	1/60	403	Sharp	2-2-2	11/61
343	Crewe	2-2-2 N Div	1/60	404	Kitson	2-2-2	9/61
344	Crewe	2-2-2 N Div	1/60	405	Kitson	2-2-2	9/61
345	Crewe	2-4-0 N Div	1/60	406	Kitson	2-2-2	10/61
346	Crewe	2-4-0 N Div	1/60	407	Kitson	2-2-2	10/61
347	Crewe	2-4-0 N Div	1/60	408	Kitson	2-2-2	10/61
348	Crewe	2-4-0 N Div	1/60	409	Kitson	0-6-0	1/62
349	Crewe	2-4-0 N Div	1/60	410	Kitson	0-6-0	1/62
350	Crewe	2-4-0 N Div	1/60	411	Kitson	0-6-0	2/62
351	Crewe	2-4-0 N Div	1/60	412	Kitson	0-6-0	2/62
352	Crewe	2-4-0 N Div	1/60	413	Kitson	0-6-0	2/62
353	Crewe	2-4-0 N Div	1/60	414	Fairbairn	0-6-0	2/62
354	Wol	0-4-2T G	b /60	415	Fairbairn	0-6-0	3/62
355	Wol	0-6-0	8/61	416	Fairbairn	0-6-0	3/62
356	Wol	0-6-0	8/61	417	Fairbairn	0-6-0	3/62
357	Wol	0-6-0	8/61	418	Fairbairn	0-6-0	3/62
358	Wol	0-6-0	9/61	1019	Wol	0-4-2 N	8/62
359	Wol	0-6-0	9/61	1020	Wol	0-4-2 N	8/62
360	Wol	0-6-0	9/61	1021	Wol	0-4-2 N	11/62
361	Wol	0-6-0	10/61				

WOLVERTON TENDERS

The earlier S Div tenders were simply the types supplied by the various firms of locomotive makers, but in 1851 McConnell adopted a standard type of tender which was used thereafter with all engines built at Wolverton or ordered from outside firms. According to Ahrons, writing in 1925, this was the first example of the "present-day standard British tender" with springs above the axleboxes but below the tank so that "not only are the springs visible and accessible, but the tank can be widened to the edge of the platforms."

There were four sizes of tender but all were to the same basic design. All had outside one-piece frames of ¾in iron plate which had an arch on its lower edge between each wheel, with stays between the horns and a segmental opening for the springs over each axlebox. This was similar in outline to the sandwich plates on some Hawthorn tenders. The back end was like that on Sharp tenders in that there was no bufferplank; instead, the outside frameplate was prolonged to form the outer side of the buffer socket. At the front end the plate carried the footsteps, offset to match those of the locomotive.

Just inside the wheels another long plate, ½in thick and 10 to 12in deep, was secured to the outside frame at a distance of 9½in by gusset plates; each double frame was connected to that on the opposite side by a sturdy box-structure enclosing the drawbar and buffer spring at the front, and at the back by a single ¾in plate. Behind this lay a transverse plate spring with the rear drawhook buckled at its centre and a buffer shaft on each end. Above and below this spring, two horizontal plates 6in apart connected the rear extensions of the outside frameplates, forming the top and bottom of the buffer sockets. The top of this assembly also provided a flat footplate, useful when shunting and coupling.

A simple horseshoe tank whose wings enclosed the fuel space was mounted on the frame and was supported by transverse angle irons. The fuel space was quite open at the front end, flat bottomed and 3ft 6in wide. The outer tank sides were built up from three plates with single-riveted lap joints, but some earlier tenders had double-riveted butt joints. In these, built by Fairbairn's and Vulcan Foundry, the rivets were hardly noticeable, being countersunk into a 3in-wide iron strip. This strip, around the edges of the sides and back, and on the two vertical butt joints, formed three conspicuous panels on the tank side.

A concave coping was fixed along the top outer edge of the tank, tapering at the sides and rising from 4in at the front to a prominent 12in at the back. The whole tank was easily detachable from the frame and four lifting-shackles were fixed to the top, two on the rear corners and two on the side wings. On each side two pillars and a handrail fixed to the front of the tank protected the footplate; on the right side a hollow third pillar held the vertical shaft of the brake screw handle. Turning this handle to apply the brakes lifted a crank on a cross shaft mounted between the outside frameplates just above the bottom footsteps. Cranks on the cross shaft worked four long horizontal pull rods, just inside and outside the wheels, to the lower ends of the brake hangers which held the wooden brake blocks behind each wheel.

Hollow axles were used on most tenders; the wheels were all 3ft 9in diameter with twelve spokes.

This tender in its basic 6-wheel form contained 1,500 gallons, but on those for the Bloomers an auxiliary well tank was added beneath the tender floor, between the inner frameplates and above the axles, which increased the capacity to 2,000 gallons. The well was fixed directly beneath the floor of the upper tank; a large hole in the floor below the filling manhole connected the two. The long drawbar passed from the front to the back couplings in a tube which ran through the well from end to end.

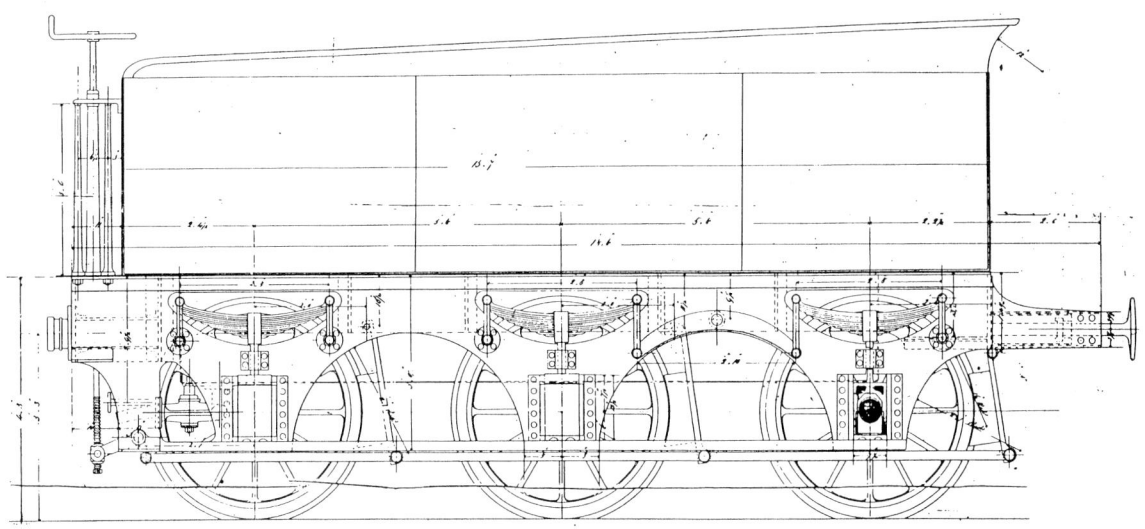

Fig. 135   Standard McConnell tender (11ft wheelbase), Wolverton drawing of 1861.

McConnell tender frames in use with water tanks on the Cromford & High Peak section.

Fig. 136   Six-wheel tender as Tank No 16. At Middleton Top, March 1967.   *(H. Jack)*

Fig. 137   Four-wheel tender as Tank No 11. At Middleton Top, March 1967.   *(H. Jack)*

McConnell tenders – rear buffer arrangement.

Fig. 138　Four-wheel tender (Tank No 5) at left. At Longcliffe, September 1962.　*(H. Jack)*

Fig. 139　The same, viewed from above.　*(H. Jack)*

Fig. 140　Rear of six-wheel tender (Tank No 16). At Longcliffe, June 1963.　*(H. Jack)*

The idea of adding a well probably came from the tender of the Crampton *Liverpool* which also had extra underfloor water storage, but its two well tanks hanging between the axles were separate from the main tank and connected by pipes, a long drawbar passing between the main tank and the well tanks to diagonal cross-bracing attached to the rear bufferplank.

Rubber springs
A tender with rubber springs was introduced for the Small Bloomers and the Stothert mineral engines in 1854. This was basically the same as the 1851 tender except for the different shape of the apertures in the frameplate above the wheels. A brass canister above each axlebox, shaped in plan like a figure 8, contained two vertical rubber cylinders bound with iron rings, each fitting inside one of the 6in diameter halves of the canister. The canister was held in a 9in high x 12in wide rectangular opening in the frameplate, with a smaller triangular aperture on each side. Rubber springs were also used on the back and front buffers.

Four-wheeled tenders
Also in 1854 a four-wheeled version of the rubber-sprung tender was produced; this was very similar but had a shorter and lower 1,000 gallon tank with two-plate sides. These tenders were built for "15in express engines" which probably means the Sharp singles; a photograph shows a four-wheeled tender with rubber springs coupled to 31 of this class. A tender of the same type was built by Fairbairn for McConnell's patent *Eugénie* in 1855.

The same design of four-wheeled tender but with steel springs was built for the N class in 1862, and this type of tender is believed to have been coupled to Small Bloomers for branch line work.

Long-wheelbase tenders
In 1860 Wolverton began building a bigger six-wheeled tender with a total wheelbase increased by 3ft and a tank capacity, including a longer and wider well, of 2,500 gallons. These were built for some Express Goods; a variation on this big tender, reduced in length by nine inches, was built for the three H class engines.

Later these long tenders were sometimes attached to Bloomers.

Compensating levers
On tenders with steel springs compensating levers were added, from about 1854, between the springs of the middle and rear axles. The levers were crescent-shaped, curved to match the arch of the outside frame, to which they were pivoted in their centre, with each end attached to a spring hanger.

Look-out boxes
The tenders of 23 S Div passenger engines were fitted with lookout boxes from January 1859. These had been used on the GWR since 1847, but characteristically the LNWR went in for a cheaper version - £7 each to the GWR's £10. They only lasted a year or two and were taken off on the introduction of communication cords and guards' whistles from 1861.

Changes after 1862
From 1863 many tenders were rebuilt; the wells were taken out and some tanks were widened by 6in overall to give a capacity of 1,700 gallons. Water pick-up scoops were fitted to 174 tenders.

In the mid-1860s standard Crewe lamp sockets were bolted to the rear footplate, one above each buffer, replacing the two on the back of the tank; the driver's handlamp socket was also removed. Compensating levers were taken off about this time.

During the Webb period some tenders had the brakes rehung in the standard Crewe position, in front of the wheels.

A few S Div tenders ended up behind Crewe engines. Two six-wheelers were sold in 1883 to the Eastern & Midlands Railway with ex-Lancaster & Carlisle 2-4-0 goods engines; one of them (it was probably from Fairbairn 0-6-0 914 of the South Staffordshire Railway) became M&GN Fresh Water Tank 42A, and lasted at Stratford Works into the 1950s.

The tender frames had a surprising longevity, and many uses were found for them after their engines were scrapped and the tanks were no longer worth renewing. Singly, they conveyed boilers about Crewe Works and were used as crane match-trucks; in teams of four they were used to transport 68-ton naval guns. Cylindrical tanks were fitted to them for oil storage; box tanks were fitted for taking drinking water into the Derbyshire hills; one set ended its days supporting an old Webb boiler for the Middleton Incline winding engine, another formed the foundations of a lineside hut at the north end of Kilsby Tunnel.

They were used as bogies for boiler trolleys: D83, to carry 50 tons, had a 6-wheel (short wheelbase) tender frame at each end. Other boiler trolleys used only part of a tender frame as a four-wheeled bogie: D76, to carry 20 tons and D77, to carry 25 tons, had rear sections of 6-wheel (short wheelbase) tender frames at each end; D78, to carry 30 tons, had similarly amputated long-wheelbase frames. These carried extraordinary loads, as for example Lancashire boilers, miles of cable, and lifeboats.

Thirteen Wolverton tender frames were fitted with box tanks and sent to the Cromford & High Peak line as water carriers; eleven of them were four-wheeled, some of which probably came from Class N 0-4-2s. The two six-wheelers ran with their centre axle removed; one of these and six of the four-wheelers were still in daily use in the mid-1960s, the last being broken up in 1968. Some tender frames fitted with oil storage tanks lasted longer and fortunately two of them were rescued from Northwich MPD in September 1986. One of these, with the original brake gear from a third example at Machynlleth, will be used with the working Bloomer replica being constructed at Tyseley.

Dimensions

1. 4-wheel tender:
Diameter of wheels	3' 9"
Wheelbase	8' 0"
Length (excluding buffers)	15' 3"
Tank	
Length	12' 3"
Width	6' 6"
Height	3' 0"
Fuel space	
Length	7' 3"
Width	3' 6"
Water capacity	1,000 gal
Weight empty (in 1874)	7 tons 15 cwt
loaded	12 tons 16 cwt

2. 6-wheel tender, short wheelbase:
Diameter of wheels	3' 9"
Wheelbase	5' 6" + 5' 6" = 11' 0"
Length (excluding buffers)	18' 4"
Tank	
Length	15' 6"
Width	6' 6"
Height	3' 6"
Fuel space	
Length	8' 6"
Width	3' 6"
Water capacity	1,500 gal
Well	
Length	12' 6"
Width	3' 6"
Depth	1' 10"
Water capacity	500 gal
Total capacity with well	2,000 gal
Weight loaded	16 tons

3. 6-wheel tender, long wheelbase:
Diameter of wheels	3' 9"
Wheelbase	7' 0" + 7' 0" = 14' 0"
Length (excluding buffers)	21' 5¾"
Tank	
Length	18' 6"
Width	7' 0"
Height	3' 6"
Fuel space	
Length	9' 6"
Width	3' 6"
Well	
Length	15' 0"
Width	4' 3"
Depth	1' 9"
Total water capacity	2,500 gal

4. H class tender:
As 3 above, except:
Wheelbase	6' 7½" + 6' 7½" = 13' 3"
Length (excluding buffers)	20' 9"
Tank	
Length	17' 9"
Fuel space	
Length	8' 9"
Fuel capacity	2 tons
Total water capacity with well	2,500 gal
Weight, empty	13 tons 10 cwt
loaded	
On front wheels	7 tons 12 cwt
On middle wheels	8 tons 12 cwt
On rear wheels	8 tons 18 cwt
Total	25 tons 2 cwt

5. 6-wheel short wheelbase tender, as rebuilt at Crewe:
As 2 above, except:
Tank	
Length	15' 6½"
Width	7' 0"
Height	3' 6"
Fuel space	
Length	8' 6¼"
Width	3' 6"
Water capacity	1,700 gal
Pick-up gear fitted	

LIVERIES and NUMBERPLATES

Edward Bury

The livery adopted by the L&B was green with broad black bands and this was continued under the LNWR.

In the earliest engines the boiler, bufferplank, wheels, footplate side-sheets and tender were painted green; boiler bands were black and there were broad black lines, perhaps 2in wide, forming three rectangular panels on the tender side. The smokebox, chimney, frame-bars and tender axle-guards were black. The domed firebox top of the Bury engines was covered with a sheet of polished copper; safety valves, splashers and the smokebox door surround were polished brass. The engines built at Bury's Clarence Foundry (and perhaps those from other builders) had a brass disc engraved with the maker's name in the centre of the driving wheel nave. Nos 59, 60, 91/3/4 and 96-118 had copper-capped chimneys.

In the centre of the boiler side was a flat oval brass plate about 22in wide and 12in high with engraved lettering: **LONDON &** around the top edge and **BIRMINGHAM** around the lower edge with the engine number in the centre. The number was also displayed in cut-out brass numerals high on the chimney front. Fixed centrally on the side of the tender frame was a cast-iron plate, consisting of an 8in diameter disc containing the engine number, flanked by the shields of London and Birmingham. The shields were probably painted in their heraldic colours; the number seems to have been painted in a light colour on a darker background.

After 1846 the oval brass numberplate on the boiler side was continued for a short time with the lower legend changed to **NORTH WESTERN**. One of Lane's 1849 sketches shows a plate like this on Sharp Bros No 9, and there is an oval plate on Bury, Curtis & Kennedy 102 in the 1850 Roade accident report diagram. By then these numberplates had been abandoned for new engines.

James Edward McConnell

Under McConnell the engine number was displayed in a variety of ways. By 1848 painted numerals were the normal style, and in most cases these were on the boiler side, either on the middle ring or toward the front end. An exception to this seems to have been the Vulcan Foundry long-boiler singles, one of which (176) is shown in Leitch's drawing with the number on the side of the dome.

McConnell's own first engine, 227, had its number on the connecting-rod splasher, with the words **LONDON & NORTH WESTERN** in an arc above it. Later McConnell classes had brass plates of various types: elliptical on the footplate side-sheet, shaped like a keystone on the driving-wheel splasher, or segmental on the middle coupling rod splasher. From drawings and photographs all were flat, with the engine number and surrounding legends engraved in various layouts. In some cases the month and year of building were on a scroll to left and right of the engine number, which was in figures about 2in high. The numerals were in fancy styles, outlined and shaded; the most elaborate were on H class 373, where the engraver evidently decided to show off by inventing his own freakish typeface.

The one standard and unchanging feature was the number on the chimney-front. The cut-out brass numerals continued from the first engines in 1837 to the end of the separate Southern Division in 1862. These were $7\frac{1}{2}$in high in a chunky, square-serif style.

On the back of the tender tank the engine number was painted in numerals of the same size and style as the chimney number. Perhaps this practice began with Bury, but evidence is lacking.

Green continued as the basic colour; it is described as "Brunswick green" or "light Brunswick green" in the stores orders of the 1850s, and "bright green" by Frank S. Hennell whose memory of locomotive matters went back to that period. On the evidence of paint scrapings from old tender frames the S Div shade was the same as that used on the LNWR after 1862 and like that of preserved Great Northern Railway locomotives. The plain black lining of the Bury period was probably continued on most of the engines; the black banded panels on the tender and side-sheet had incurved corners by the late 1840s. This is the only lining visible - on the tender - in the photograph of Jones & Potts 4-2-0 189 taken in 1858/9 (Fig 45).

On certain engines McConnell introduced variety in the layout and colouring of the lining bands in some lighter shades, with the corners of the panels arranged as three right-angled steps. These panels appear in several drawings of the Patents and on the earliest Bloomer photograph (Fig 76). A different arrangement is seen on the photograph of Small Bloomer 103 (Fig 87); here the lines alternate from light to dark to simulate the appearance of panels, seen as though lit from the upper left. The inner space, with incurved $2\frac{1}{2}$in radius corners, represents a raised panel; outside this is a 'recessed' area surrounded by a 'raised' frame. This painted imitation of relief was perhaps inspired by the real panels on the tanks of tenders made by Fairbairn and Vulcan Foundry; to Victorian eyes a plain tender side may have required some decoration to break up the flat expanse.

The lining colours of the tender and side sheets of the Bloomers are said to have been red and yellow, with a panel "in the same style" on the green bufferplank. Latterly some engines had a white line forming a rectangle with similarly incurved or stepped corners inside the other lines. Boiler bands were black.

From 1856 the engine number was painted on the bufferplank in the same size and style as the chimney numerals (Fig 33), probably in yellow with black shading whose width was 1in to the right and $1\frac{1}{2}$in below. This was begun for the renumbering scheme; the new number was painted on the bufferplank before the night of 31st March and on the following morning the brass chimney numerals were blacked over, to be taken off and replaced with new figures later. Apparently all engines, whether to be renumbered or not, were given bufferplank numbers, and the practice continued until 1862; they appear in all known photographs and were

Fig. 141 Bury, Curtis & Kennedy regulator quadrant of 1847. (GS&W Rly No 36)
(A.G. Ellis collection)

stipulated for engines ordered from Sharp, Stewart & Co in 1861. The engine number also appeared in small figures on the tender frame, near the front end, and on the wheel naves, with suffixes L for leading and T for trailing wheel.

The bufferplank was still green at this period, with a plain one-inch black border; buffer sockets were black.

From the end of 1860 some engines were painted a very dark red, believed to be Foulger's metallic oxide paint. The colour of the lining used is not known; only one photograph seems to show this red livery, that of Small Bloomer 381 taken in December 1861 (Fig 88). Here the lining is even more elaborate than the earlier McConnell schemes. The lines forming the panels are again alternately light and dark, and apparently intended to suggest a raised panel on a flat surround, with a recessed central area. In this case the light and dark lines are arranged as if the panel were lit from the upper right. The central 'recess' has 2½in radius incurved corners and contains a plain white line, 2½in from the edge, forming a rectangle with similarly incurved corners. The 2in boiler bands are dark (black?) with a light line on each edge and another light (white?) line 1¾in away on the boiler cleading on each side. The remainder of the lining (on the footplate edge, bufferplank end, sandbox, splasher, in bands around the barrel of the lock-up safety valve, on the wheel centres and rims, around the footstep and the edges of the tender frame) consists of two parallel light lines, about ¾in apart, perhaps containing or being contained by a darker band.

There is no foundation at all for the widespread belief that engines were painted vermilion. This description first appeared in the *Locomotive Magazine* of 1898 but seems to have been a mistake on the part of the editor, probably when copying a note about McConnell's livery from the *English Mechanic* of 1879. In its issue of 14th March that paper included a letter from one 'Helios' saying that "Mr Maconnell, when on the L&NW, used to paint his engines a rich red, which looked very handsome". Immediately above the word "Maconnell", but in a quite different context, "red (vermilion?)" is printed. It looks likely that some hasty transcription introduced this word into the *Locomotive Magazine* article, and into LNWR lore. Not long afterwards the magazine's proprietors, the Locomotive Publishing Co, produced an 'F. Moore' painting of H class 373 in bright red with black and white lining, which was acquired by the Science Museum in 1949. Since then this painting has been reproduced very many times and its bright, attractive and unusual colour has been copied by other artists, so that pictures of S Div engines in vermilion and scarlet have appeared in books and magazines, above the seats in railway carriages, on postcards, birthday cards, calendars, china plates, matchboxes, gift-wrap paper and even on foreign postage stamps (Fujeira, United Arab Emirates, 75c, 1969).

In addition to coloured pictures, written descriptions of this mythical vermilion livery have been printed over and over again in recent years, despite a complete lack of evidence. The actual shade of "rich red" used was described as "brick red" by Ahrons (a term he also used for the Midland Railway livery) and by the LNWR Chief Mechanical Engineer Bowen Cooke as "a kind of plum colour". While Ahrons (born 1866) was not old enough to remember the colour, Cooke (born 1859) just might have done so; in any case both would certainly have known many who had seen it. Paint scrapings from two old tender frames indicate a colour rather darker than LMS red.

Chimney caps of BC&K 'Low-dome' singles, Bloomers of all three types and Patents were copper; some of the Patents had "a thick or double-rimmed copper top to the funnel, of Mr McConnell's invention" - whatever that means. This is according to Mr C. H. Harben who wrote to *The Railway World* in August 1895 and recalled seeing the Woods and Marshall trials engines arriving, from his policeman's box at the east end of Primrose Hill Tunnel. Some engines had a brass or copper collar around the base of the chimney. The lock-up safety valve cover was usually painted, but sometimes was made of brass and polished like the dome and Salter safety valve trumpet.

Fig. 142 Plate on wheel centre of BC&K engine of 1846. (Furness Rly No 3). (H. Jack)

Some splashers had a polished brass rim; the back (and where fitted, front) corner mouldings of fireboxes were also polished.

John Ramsbottom

Most engines would still have been green at Ramsbottom's takeover in 1862 when the livery changed to what had remained the N Div style: green with plain black lines. The ½in lines formed panels with 3½in radius incurved corners on the sides and back of the tender and on the footplate side-sheets. The sandboxes also had a similar black-lined panel and there was a black line on each edge of the boiler bands. Most of the brasswork was painted over. The numberplates and chimney numerals were removed; instead the engine number was painted in the Crewe style, 6¼in yellow figures with ¾in black shading to the right and below, on the footplate side sheets and on the bufferplank. The front of the bufferplank was painted red; its top and ends were green, as were the buffer sockets.

A small innovation from 1st January 1863 was an oval label 5in wide by 3¾in high indicating by a numerical code the shed to which the engine belonged. It was fastened to the rear face of the weatherboard near the top and bore the shed number in figures about 2in high. At first these had light (yellow?) numerals on a dark (green?) ground but from the early 1870s the labels were enamelled white with black numerals. When an engine was fitted with a cab the label was transferred to the back edge of the cab roof.

Francis William Webb

From 1873 engines were painted in Webb's well-known all-over black with cast-iron numberplates which had raised yellow-painted numerals on a red background surrounded by a raised yellow border. The plain red front bufferplank was decorated only with black edging and a black line forming a round-cornered rectangle between the black buffer sockets. The sockets were sometimes given a red line around the end to warn of an unusual type of spring within. The rear bufferplank of tank engines was also red, but those of tenders were black.

Passenger engines, and some goods engines used as station pilots or for excursion traffic, were additionally lined out with red, white and pale blue lines, which beneath coats of varnish were seen as scarlet, cream and blue-grey. This lining was applied on the tender sides and on the footplate side-sheets in a single panel with round corners of 4in radius to the outer edge. The outer line was a ⅝in band of pale blue, with a ⅛in line of white on its inner edge; 1½in inside this was a ¼in red line, so that the whole series was 2½in wide. The boiler bands had a central red line, flanked at a short distance on each side by the white and blue lines; adaptations of this pattern, with the blue always on the outside edge, were applied to the footplate valance, splashers, footsteps and the tender frame.

In 1876 the lining was simplified: boiler bands were black, edged in red only, and usually lining was omitted below the footplate on engine and tender.

Nameplates added to S Div passenger engines in 1872 were the standard LNWR pattern and bore the misleading legend: L&NWR Co - CREWE WORKS above the month and year of building.

LAMPS & LAMP IRONS

Oil-burning headlamps were carried on L&B engines from the beginning. Early regulations mention "the front buffer light" without any indication as to where on the bufferplank the lamp was to be located, but it seems likely that the single front lamp was always on the right end of the plank, looking forwards. The lamp was in the form of a box about 1ft high topped by a chimney and a side-to-side carrying handle, with a lens about 9in diameter. The front lamp iron was a stout L-shaped casting, the 7in upright leg of which was shaped on its rear face to receive a vertical tongue on the back of the lamp. Another lamp iron was riveted to the back of the tender tank above the left buffer (looking forward); this was a rectangular plate with a central vertical slot to hold the headlamp when running tender-first.

All L&B and S Div engines carried a small handlamp, used for signalling the driver's intention to pointsmen at night. When out of use this handlamp sat in a socket which projected on a stem from the left side of the tender or bunker, within reach of the footplate. A fourth lamp holder projected from the back of the tender tank; this was the same pattern as the handlamp socket, was fixed centrally near the top of the tank, and was used for the red tail-lamp when running light or when banking at the rear of a train.

The headlamp code was simple: a white light on passenger trains, a green light on goods trains.

Small sockets were fixed to the sides of some engine chimneys by the end of 1861; they were for disc and diamond headcodes in the London area and can be seen on the photographs of Express Goods 371, M class 734 and N class 601 (Figs 94, 129, 132).

Within a few years after 1862, the large S Div lamp was superseded by the standard Crewe type; the front and back lamp irons were removed and were replaced by four cast-iron sockets, one over each buffer. The driver's handlamp socket and the tail-lamp socket were taken off at the same time.

Probably the last surviving S Div lamp irons were those on the Engineer's Department engine *Dwarf*, which was acquired in 1863. Presumably because it would have to run from Stafford over both S Div and N Div lines, it was fitted with both types of lamp iron at the chimney foot and also with the S Div sockets on the bunker side and rear. These are visible on a photograph taken outside Crewe Paint Shop about 1880.

A new headlamp code was introduced on 1st January 1873 which involved an extra lamp at the chimney foot. On S Div engines which had received Crewe-pattern smokeboxes a new design of lamp socket was fixed at the top of the smokebox front; it incorporated a holder for the short chain which supported the horizontally-hinged door when open. On engines which retained their original smokeboxes the lamp socket used was the old S Div stem type which was slightly smaller than the Crewe pattern. This was fixed to the top of the smokebox front or on the smokebox door. On the tender or bunker back, a lamp socket was attached centrally to the top edge of the coping.

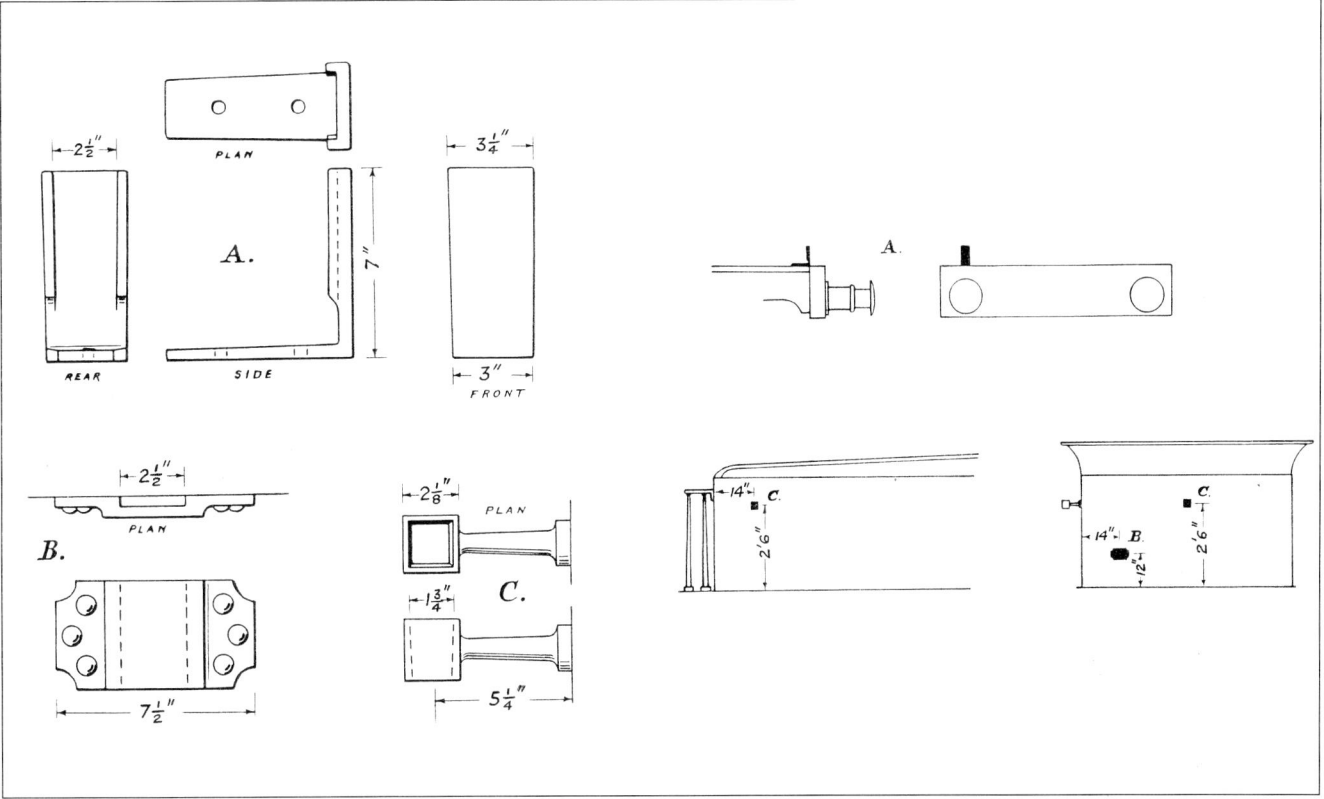

Fig. 143   Southern Division lamp irons based on a Wolverton drawing of June 1861.

OTHER ALTERATIONS FROM 1862

Shallow Ashpans
Following the installation of water troughs at Mochdre on the Chester & Holyhead line in 1860, and in 1861 at Parkside between Liverpool and Manchester, on 20th March 1862 Ramsbottom suggested laying troughs "at some suitable point between Rugby and London". But after taking over at Wolverton at the end of that month he discovered that 83 of the S Div engines "run too near the ground to admit the use of the Trough". These were the Patents, Bloomers and Small Bloomers, whose ashpans, supported by three transverse angle irons, were only a few inches above rail level.

These engines were quickly fitted with the Crewe pattern of firebar supports and new shallow ashpans of $3/8$in iron without supporting angle irons. The clearance above rail level "when the engine is worn down" was to be not less than five inches. Other classes similarly dealt with were the Stephenson 4-2-2s, the Bury 2-2-2s of 1848, the Fairbairn South Staffordshire singles and at least two of the Sharp 2-2-2s, 631 and 746. The work must have been done very swiftly, because troughs were ordered for Castlethorpe, just north of Wolverton, in July 1862 and were installed soon afterwards.

Front Handrail
Wolverton-built engines had no handrail on the front of the smokebox, but the Bloomers built by Sharp and Kitson in 1861 had a 4ft length of curved $1\frac{1}{2}$in pipe on two pillars, above the smokebox door. From May 1863 Ramsbottom fitted all S Div engines without front handrails with a curved $1\frac{1}{4}$in rod above the door, held by a single central pillar at the top and with the ends bent back and riveted to the smokebox sides.

Blower Pipe
On coal-burning S Div engines the pipe from the blower-cock on the firebox top to the smokebox passed through the hollow handrail, or just above it, on the right side of the boiler. After 1862 the blower pipe was moved to the left side which was the standard Crewe position. Because the left handrail contained the cylinder-cock linkage, the pipe ran along the boiler behind the handrail, supported by the handrail pillars.

Chimney
Even when they kept their original chimneys most S Div engines were quickly given the standard Crewe chimney cap, an elaborate construction of ten identical castings which surrounded the top of the chimney barrel. These ten separate projections had a profile which was convex on top and concave below, and when riveted in place the outer edge of the complete assembly had ten large oval cut-outs around its outer edge. Because of a fancied resemblance to battlements and machicolations it has been called the 'castellated' chimney.

After F. W. Webb took over as Locomotive Superintendent in 1871 his simpler design of chimney soon became universal. The cap was a smaller and much neater one-piece casting.

Safety Valves
Some engines retained their old spring-balance and lock-up safety valves throughout their lives - as late as 1877 - or until rebuilt with Crewe boilers. Others had the S Div valves replaced by open Ramsbottom valves on their old boilers. A few of the survivors had Webb's enclosed type in the 1880s.

Weatherboard
The shape of weatherboards on S Div engines varied, but a common type (used on Bloomers, Small Bloomers, M and N classes and some Express Goods) had straight vertical sides and a top which had a raised central curve behind the pressure gauge, with two small vertical oval windows (Fig 129). Many of these weatherboards were replaced by the bigger Crewe design with a smooth, curved outline and round windows with rain shields - also known as 'sun visors'. S Div tank engines had no rear weatherboards as built, but the wide type used on Old Crewe tanks was fitted later.

Smokebox
On rebuilding with Crewe boilers some engines were given Crewe smokeboxes with horizontally-hinged doors; many others retained the Wolverton smokebox with its round side-hinged door until the end. The S Div cylinder-cock linkage with its prominent **T**-shaped bell crank on the left side of the smokebox was taken away on reboilering and replaced by rods passing down behind the frameplate.

Lubricators
Ramsbottom displacement lubricators, prominent 6in diameter brass spheres, were fitted to the front of the valve chest or on the smokebox sides from 1862, and were replaced by Webb's less obtrusive type in the 1870s.

Cabs
From 1872 some S Div engines were fitted with standard Crewe cabs with a roof 3ft 8in long; these included most of the Bloomers, at least eight of the Small Bloomers and at least eleven of the Express Goods.

Buffers
The front buffers of S Div engines had large cast-iron sockets, each secured directly to the bufferplank by four bolts, one at each corner of the rectangular base. These buffers were gradually replaced by Crewe's standard type whose sockets were much shorter, with a circular flange mounted on a circular wooden pad and fastened by six bolts.

Reversing
Many S Div engines had their reversing levers removed and replaced by Crewe reversing wheels of the Ramsbottom or Webb types.

APPENDIX 1

LOCOMOTIVE PERFORMANCE, 1851

A Locomotive Committee report of June 1852 contains details of mileage, average loads, coke consumption and cost of repairs of the various classes. The mileage figures are probably to the end of 1851.

Passenger Engines			*Average per engine:* Total miles	Load tons	*Coke consumed (lbs)* per mile	per ton	*Repair costs (pence)* per mile	per ton
Bury type, 12in cylinders								
5/27 etc		2-2-2T	—	41	31.18	0.779	2.663	0.0665
Bury type, 13in cylinders								
58		2-2-0	217,927	37	29.47	0.807	1.416	0.0388
1/3/4/10 etc		2-2-0	156,486	44	30.58	0.738	1.655	0.0400
37/8/9 etc		2-2-0	201,947	44	32.04	0.740	1.995	0.0461
237		2-2-0	203,504	47	32.60	0.706	2.142	0.0464
2/7/11 etc		2-2-0	161,769	40	28.25	0.733	1.658	0.0430
48		2-2-0	37,941	33	25.62	0.792	6.138	0.1897
24		2-2-0	114,127	41	28.83	0.714	1.795	0.0445
Bury type, 14in cylinders								
13/4/23 etc		2-2-0	125,603	42	29.85	0.743	2.704	0.0673
92/5		2-2-0	82,888	43	35.46	0.867	2.051	0.0502
59/60/91		2-2-0	169,173	44	31.51	0.725	1.892	0.0436
93/4/6-9		2-2-0	115,957	47	30.06	0.644	1.379	0.0296
40		2-2-0	197,199	45	29.65	0.671	2.123	0.0480
15in cylinders								
4	SB	2-2-2	74,190	35	28.14	0.818	1.248	0.0363
31 etc	SB	2-2-2	118,607	57	28.67	0.514	1.159	0.0208
100-10	BC&K	2-2-2	102,763	64	35.63	0.574	1.966	0.0317
201	EBW	2-2-2	38,202	45	32.85	0.784	1.773	0.0423
208/9	EBW	2-2-2	86,879	62	32.25	0.536	1.459	0.0243
159-67	VF	4-2-0	90,569	64	30.70	0.498	2.136	0.0347
176-81	VF	4-2-0	93,564	62	31.55	0.528	2.059	0.0345
182-5	J&P	4-2-0	79,725	62	31.59	0.522	1.865	0.0308
175	J&P	4-2-0	75,926	65	33.94	0.547	2.222	0.0358
202/3/4	HF	4-2-0	21,003	54	31.43	0.612	1.585	0.0309
186-90	J&P	4-2-0	69,854	62	31.69	0.519	1.607	0.0263
147-52	J&P	4-2-0	87,521	60	33.19	0.575	2.468	0.0428
153/7	RS	4-2-2	90,915	64	33.83	0.546	2.348	0.0379
154/5/6/8	RS	4-2-0	101,337	64	31.96	0.510	1.830	0.0292
9	SB	2-2-2	26,558	68	34.38	0.524	1.588	0.0236
16in cylinders								
8	SB	2-2-2	73,420	64	32.45	0.525	1.583	0.0256
12 etc	BC&K	2-2-2	82,837	66	33.94	0.511	1.653	0.0256
18in cylinders								
200	T&L	4-2-0	19,834	64	42.54	0.672	5.886	0.0930
227	Wol	2-2-2	15,996	89	41.36	0.473	2.997	0.0343
233/4	RS	4-2-2	18,478	80	36.44	0.457	4.064	0.0510
245	BC&K	6-2-0	9,303	80	41.56	0.529	1.101	0.0140

Goods Engines

			Average per engine: Total miles	Load tons	Coke consumed (lbs) per mile	per ton	Repair costs (pence) per mile	per ton
Bury type, 13in cylinders								
61/2/3 etc		0-4-0	—	83	38.56	0.477	2.611	0.0323
Bury type, 14in cylinders								
64/9/70 etc		0-4-0	72,449	81	31.92	0.400	2.408	0.0302
15in cylinders								
111-6	BC&K	0-4-0	101,828	113	44.12	0.402	2.064	0.0188
117/8	BC&K	0-4-2	82,717	125	51.54	0.423	2.351	0.0193
172/3	BC&K	0-4-0	91,480	59	32.27	0.552	2.165	0.0370
119/24	VF	0-6-0	80,066	132	41.79	0.327	2.551	0.0200
120-3	VF	0-6-0	86,470	130	43.84	0.341	2.730	0.0213
137-44	NG	0-6-0	51,010	117	36.63	0.327	2.469	0.0221
72 etc	BC&K	0-4-0	66,102	111	43.92	0.409	1.794	0.0167
125-36	RBL	0-6-0	67,959	132	44.72	0.346	2.684	0.0208
16in cylinders								
6 etc	BC&K	0-4-2	70,362	152	45.77	0.305	1.100	0.0133
174	J&P	0-6-0	32,470	146	42.02	0.296	4.296	0.0303
168-71	BC&K	0-6-0	75,101	160	49.51	0.316	2.709	0.0173
18in cylinders								
32	SB	0-6-0	63,754	178	50.49	0.287	2.049	0.0119
211 etc	RS	0-6-0	52,894	199	53.79	0.272	1.764	0.0089
210 etc	SB	0-6-0	59,713	178	46.01	0.262	1.439	0.0082
221 etc	RWH	0-6-0	35,892	191	53.60	0.282	2.533	0.0133

Abbreviations:

BC&K	Bury, Curtis & Kennedy
EBW	E. B. Wilson
HF	Haigh Foundry
J&P	Jones & Potts
NG	Nasmyth, Gaskell
RBL	R. B. Longridge
RS	Robert Stephenson
RWH	R. & W. Hawthorn
SB	Sharp Bros
T&L	Tulk & Ley
VF	Vulcan Foundry (Tayleur)
Wol	Wolverton LNWR

FUEL - FROM COKE TO COAL

APPENDIX 2

On the London & Birmingham Railway, coke was the normal fuel for locomotives from the beginning. Coal was cheaper but produced an unacceptable amount of smoke and more sparks than good quality coke. Good coke was made at Camden from Newcastle coal brought in by canal, but almost a quarter of that used in 1839 was an inferior grade made at Birmingham from Staffordshire coal. 'Smokeless' anthracite coal was tried in locomotives without much success and Bury investigated Samuel Hall's patent coal-burning system in 1836 and again in June 1842, when it was arranged to adapt goods engine 78, but this was probably abandoned after Josiah Kearsley's adverse report on the system in August. No results are known of any trial on the L&B.

The Birmingham coke ovens did not last long, but 50 were erected by the L&B at Peterborough in 1846. The eighteen Camden ovens were closed down in 1851, and by the following year Peterborough was producing about 9% of S Div requirements. All the rest came ready-made from County Durham, from the immense coking establishments at Marley Hill, Pease's West and Brancepeth collieries; this was said to be the best coke in the world. By 1854 the LNWR was having to pay £114,000 a year to other railway companies for the carriage of locomotive coke.

The constant comparison and criticism of S Div locomotive expenses stimulated experimentation at Wolverton, where some attempts were made to burn coal efficiently as early as 1850. At that time coke was 39% more expensive on the S Div than in the north, where for Trevithick and Ramsbottom there was no economic advantage in changing to coal, but in the south a saving of 6s 9d (34p) per ton of fuel was anticipated if the change could be made.

In March 1854 McConnell reported that he was using coal in two of Fairbairn's engines; the other two divisions were asked to try it in their fireboxes. In April coal formed as much as 9% by weight of the fuel used in the S Div Locomotive Dept. Comparative figures were N Div: 1.5%, NE Div: 1.2%, but both abandoned coal after a few months. By May McConnell was using coal alone in five engines "without nuisance or inconvenience" whereupon on 9th June the General Locomotive Committee brought in as investigators Edward Woods and William P. Marshall, who had recently reported on McConnell's heavy engines. In the Woods and Marshall fuel experiments, Patent class 303 was tried on expresses and heavy trains, using coke alternately with coal of various kinds. It was found that too much coal had to be used, but smoke consumption was pronounced satisfactory. Coal was also tried in a Bloomer, but the driver and fireman were unused to it and 293's smokebox quickly filled up with burning coal dust, resulting in some "very objectionable brown smoke". After this report in July 1854 the use of coal was discontinued everywhere on the LNWR except in S Div engines 125, 132, 175 and 179 which had been fitted with McConnell's large firebox.

From then until early 1858 hardly any coal was burned on the other divisions, but its use continued on the S Div. In December 1856 coal was 6.5% of S Div fuel, but less than 1% on the rest of the LNWR. During 1857 coal's share increased on the S Div from 9% in February to almost 32% in June. Despite restrictions on its use from July, it accounted for over 21% of fuel in the rest of the year. Meanwhile no coal at all was used on the N Div or the NE Div.

In April 1857 McConnell tried South Wales anthracite at Oxford, apparently with success. Direct rail communication opened to the anthracite mines of the Aberdare and Rhondda valleys at the end of the year and within eight months the weight of coal consumed on the S Div equalled that of coke. Coal burning was resumed on the N Div in January 1858 and by September amounted to 27% of all fuel used there; the figure for the entire LNWR was then 38%.

There were temporary setbacks to this steady and rapid progress, as in July 1857 when after complaints by passengers the use of coal was banned south of Watford on passenger trains, and when the Corporation of Birmingham gave notice that it would levy a fine of £2 per day on every LNWR engine "not consuming its own smoke" after 23rd April 1859.

In June 1859 Ramsbottom was ordered to discontinue the use of coal in passenger engines "except those adapted for its consumption" between Rugby and Liverpool, Preston and Manchester and in those on fast trains on the Stour Valley "until luggage compartments are made in the second-class carriages which will remove luggage from roofs and at the same time the objection to coal burning." This ban on coal did not apply between Crewe and Holyhead, where luggage vans were provided. Luggage, covered by sheets and held down by straps, was still being carried on the roofs of some trains well into the 1860s.

By July 1859 all the railways between Preston and Edinburgh - the Lancaster & Carlisle, the Caledonian and the North British - had gone over to burning coal in their engines, and the LNWR soon followed suit.

In August 1859 and again in June 1861 the residents of Ampthill Square, just outside Euston, complained about smoke from engines, and in October of the latter year it was officially asserted that no coal at all was used at Camden shed. Nevertheless, a year later the use of coke was almost extinct; the fuel consumption of the entire LNWR in 1862 amounted to 370,762 tons of coal, with only 32,801 tons of coke, just over 8%.

Engines which burned coal were fitted with a steam ejector, or blower, which maintained the draught while the engine was at rest, and could be used to liven up a coal fire in a way that was not possible with coke. In McConnell's day the blower pipe was taken along the right side of the boiler to the smokebox. On Ramsbottom's engines this pipe was on the left side and after 1862 this became standard on S Div engines.

As soon as he took over the S Div engines, Ramsbottom began fitting their fireboxes with firebrick arches. Crewe drawings of the arrangement for the

Express Goods, Bloomers and Small Bloomers are dated 2nd June 1862, and show a long arch, rising from the throatplate and almost meeting a very long deflecting plate coming down from the firehole. A month later another drawing shows a different arrangement for the Class M "mixed traffic tank engines": a very short arch, sloping downwards from a throatplate which had been modified with Ramsbottom's square air-holes and dampers. This short arch was also fitted to the Fairbairn 0-6-0s, Class A, Class N and the Sharp 2-2-2s. Some Bloomers, Stothert 0-6-0s and Express Goods were given long downward-sloping arches and throatplate air-holes.

These simple brick arches quite superseded all the complications of big double fireboxes, midfeathers and combustion chambers, and led very quickly to the use of coal exclusively throughout the LNWR.

Fig. 144   The only surviving McConnell engine; built by R. Stephenson & Co for the Sydney Railway in 1854 and now preserved in the Powerhouse Museum, Sydney.

LNWR ENGINES ON THE NORTH LONDON RAILWAY

The original title was the East & West India Docks & Birmingham Junction Railway and as such it opened a ten-mile line in 1850-52, running east from Chalk Farm and giving the LNWR access to the docks at Poplar. The simpler title 'North London Railway' was adopted on 8th July 1853.

The LNWR put up most of the capital for this nominally independent railway and, having agreed to work it, provided some of the first locomotives. Before opening, it was reported on 5th March 1850 that 172 (Bury 4ft 0-4-0) had been hired to the E&WID&BJR for the use of a contractor at £50 per month.

It was estimated that the line would need eight locomotives; four 12in engines from the 'for sale' list ("now lying unemployed") were altered to 2-2-2 tanks at Wolverton in the summer of 1850, and four drivers and four firemen were transferred from the LNWR in September. The London & Blackwall Railway also supplied eight footplatemen, and presumably four engines.

The first section, from Islington eastwards around the northern outskirts of London to Bow, where it joined the London & Blackwall Railway to reach the latter's Fenchurch Street terminus, was opened in September 1850. On 15th February 1851 the connection west from Islington to the LNWR at Chalk Farm was completed. The last portion opened from Bow to the docks on 1st January 1852.

From the opening of the connection, the Camden roundhouse which had been built for main line goods engines was the shed used for all the LNWR engines on the Docks Line.

After only a few days working, the engines were found to be inadequate. In April 1851 the E&WID&BJR complained about "irregularity" in the working of the line and McConnell was told to look into this and provide additional engines. He blamed the lack of watering facilities - the only water crane was at Stepney on the Blackwall line - but otherwise he seemed satisfied with the way the line was being worked. He must have made some changes: originally 12in engines had been sent but by August he was saying that 14in engines were too small for the work and that 15in engines had to be used; the following month he reported that the Docks Line working was improved.

0-4-0 15in engines 112, 113 and 114 "known as the Little Burys" were recalled as having worked the line in its early days. ('Itzaex', writing in the *English Mechanic* 8.12.1876).

The improvement did not last. In January 1852, just after the opening to Poplar, there were more complaints. The line was described as difficult to work; 66 (Bury 13in goods) was found incapable of working the goods traffic at the docks; on 3rd January an engine with only eleven wagons stalled on the 1 in 87 incline at Highbury and had to be pushed forward by a following passenger train. McConnell thought he would soon be forced to use bigger engines, and in February he was told to carry out the change as soon as possible.

Other unrecorded engines must have worked the Docks line at this period, for in June 1853 an *additional* 18in engine was sent to work the Highbury incline. Light 4-wheeled engines were still being used for goods trains over the sharp curves and weak bridges at Poplar. A derailment at Minories on the Blackwall line on 28th July 1853 led the Board of Trade inspector to remark that the LNWR engines were "scarcely in a condition fit for conducting passenger trains".

By this time the NLR had ordered ten engines of its own. To accommodate them Harry Chubb (NLR Manager) asked in January 1854 for space in the Camden roundhouse. McConnell said he could spare 12 pits there (out of 23) which were offered on a short-notice let for £500 a year. In March the NLR explained that workshops and an engine shed were being erected at Bow, which were expected to be finished by June; they really only wanted free temporary "standing room" for their engines until then. This was allowed.

Despite a growing stock of engines, and the appointment in 1854 of William Adams as Locomotive Superintendent, there were still acute shortages of power. At least one S Div engine was on the NLR in December 1854 and two more were loaned in February 1855 "for three weeks." In a list dated 12 April 1855 four LNWR engines were recorded as working for the NLR but a month later they were asked to return six LNWR engines. The reply came on 8th June: the four passenger engines would be returned forthwith but they would like to keep the two goods "for a time". On 28th June the NLR asked to retain three passenger engines for another three months, which was agreed.

On 14th July the boiler of one of the NLR's own engines exploded; this was a 2-4-0 tank No 10, recently built by Stothert, Slaughter & Co. Immediately McConnell examined all the LNWR engines on the NLR - five passengers and three goods - which were then taken back. The bill for various repairs to the engines was sent to the NLR, whose Board returned it, objecting to paying for repairs after having paid for the hire of the engines. McConnell reported to the LNWR Secretary C. E. Stewart on 27th July 1855:

"North London Railway have no reason to complain as the Engines were returned to this Dept, as Mr Rowland (Chief Foreman, Wolverton) says, almost complete wrecks, one or two having been smashed by an accident on the NL line and actually sent back to us in that condition." All had been "in 1st rate condition" when sent from Wolverton. He listed the following:

Nos.	Repairs done
25	26th January and 7th April 1855
50	4th and 25th May 1855 (sent back minus all wheels)
52	2nd March and 4th to 30th May 1855 (india-rubber springs)
54	21st Dec 1854 (130 feet of deal)
112	18th to 26th May 1855
113	April and May 1855 (72 feet of elm)
115	March, April and May 1855 (india-rubber springs, 15 feet of deal)
145	28th May 1855 (hand railing and framing broken, new connecting rods, all wheels torn from under tender)

Total repair cost: £655 2s 4d (£655.12)

25 and 54 were 13in 2-2-2 tanks;
50/2 were 14in 2-2-0s;
112/3/5 were 15in 0-4-0s;
145 was Sharp 15in 2-2-2.

Perhaps connected with the settlement of this account, No 25 was sold to the NLR in October 1855 for £500. It worked on the NLR and latterly on the N&SWJR Hammersmith branch, was given a new boiler in 1864 and was withdrawn c1877.

In September 1855 it was agreed that the LNWR would work cattle trains twice a week over the NLR from Camden to "the Market Station" (Caledonian Road) using S Div engines. After this there seems to have been no further involvement by the S Div Locomotive Department in NLR affairs.

In 1859 the N Div stepped in, with results just as unhappy. In May of that year the Locomotive Committee discussed engines for the new Hampstead Junction line. This line was to run from Camden Road on the NLR to the N&SWJR south of Willesden Jct, avoiding Chalk Farm by a route to the north through Hampstead and bridging over the main line at Willesden; it was built by the LNWR but was intended to be worked by the NLR. Ramsbottom suggested that "the ordinary Crewe Goods engines will suit" and was instructed to send one for trial at £3 per day. He sent N Div 100 *Earl*, a 2-4-0 built in February 1847 and recently converted to a tank engine, but it was returned quickly because the NLR people found that many of the working parts were very old and would shortly require repairs. On 7th July 1859 Ramsbottom was told to alter six of "the most recent" Crewe Goods into tanks "under the NLR Engineer's inspection and to his satisfaction" for the Hampstead Junction line. The price was to be £1,600 each, chargeable to the capital of the HJ Co. Ramsbottom replaced these with six new DX Goods for LNWR use, built at Crewe from October 1859 to April 1860.

The Crewe Goods involved were *Samson, Menai, Bee, Ellesmere, Hercules* and *Sutherland*, all of the 'Small Firebox' type with 'indirect action' and none of which could be described as "the most recent", having been built in 1847-51.

Samson began on the NLR on 22nd November 1859 as No 32 but on 16th May 1860 it was derailed at Bow Jct on the London & Blackwall Railway and after uncomplimentary remarks by the Board of Trade inspector, Harry Chubb wrote to ask the LNWR to take back the six engines "the Blackwall Co having given notice they will not allow them to run over any part of their line." Ramsbottom reported that the NLR road was in poor condition, and that since leaving Crewe india-rubber auxiliary springs had been removed from the rear axle and replaced by cork and that the flanges had been turned off the middle wheels. It was decided to compel the NLR to return the engines in the state in which they were sent from Crewe. In October, with the prospect of delay if Bow did the repairs, it was arranged that the engines be sent back to Crewe immediately with the NLR paying the costs. Four were returned before the end of the financial year, 30th November, the other two in December; they were taken into stock in these half-years, so four of them were renumbered in November and two in December 1860.

N Div No.	Name	Built	Rebt tank	NLR No.	Date	to N Div 11/ or 12/60 No.	Name
240	Bee	4/50	10/59	31	(11/59)	37	Hawk
120	Samson	11/47	10/59	32	(22/11/59)	364	Buffalo
261	Hercules	10/50	12/59	33	(1/60)	529	—
266	Sutherland	2/51	11/59	34	(11/59)	233	Unicorn
245	Ellesmere	8/49	11/59	35	(2/60)	141	Pheasant
206	Menai	6/48	2/60	36	(2/60)	45	Sybil

There is some doubt about the names given to NLR 32 and 33 on their return to the N Div and they may have been named *Charon* and *Martin* for a short time until the DX engines No 65 and 129 with these names were built in October and September 1861. Perhaps some unrecorded renumbering took place. The name *Buffalo* was already carried by a new DX when the engines came back, so it seems likely that this name and perhaps others were given some time later. An old ledger found at Crewe contains a list of the NLR numbers (in order 31, 33, 35, 36, 32, 34) with original names and the later numbers and names (apart from 529, which has no name) under the heading: "Tank Engines returned from North London line Sepr/61... Nos and Names given them March/65." The September 1861 date is presumably the date the particulars were entered in the book; the precise significance of "March/65" is not known. 529 is said to have been named *Langdale* but another source suggests it became *Commodore*. All were scrapped in 1880-6.

INTERIOR OF THE GREAT ENGINE-HOUSE, CAMDEN.

APPENDIX 4

LNWR ENGINES ON THE
OXFORD, WORCESTER & WOLVERHAMPTON RAILWAY

Promoted with the backing of the Grand Junction when it and the London & Birmingham had fallen out, the OW&W was intended as an alternative route from the Black Country to the South. By the time construction began, the GJR and the L&B had settled down together as the LNWR. The new line had become a potentially dangerous competitor which would syphon traffic away to the GWR. But before the line was completed the OW&W and the GWR were on unfriendly terms.

In September 1853 it was agreed between the OW&W and the LNWR that all London traffic would be routed away from the GWR and onto the main line to Euston. To facilitate this the LNWR built a 1½-mile loop from their Bletchley-Oxford line to the OW&W at Yarnton, and a service of through coaches between Wolverhampton and Euston via Worcester began in April 1854. LNWR engines worked the trains over the loop and on 3½ miles of the OW&W's track between Yarnton Jct and Handborough. To bypass Bletchley and obviate having to reverse there, a short west-to-south spur from the Oxford branch to the main line was opened in October 1854.

Other connections from the OW&W to the LNWR were opened, at Tipton on the Stour Valley line in December 1853 and at Bushbury on the old GJR line north of Wolverhampton in July 1854.

The OW&W locomotives were operated by a contractor, C. C. Williams, with the famous David Joy as his Superintendent. Too few engines and inadequate workshops soon caused trouble. In 1854 there were 31 engines of which 20 were either under or wanting repair and in September of that year the OW&W manager W. T. Adcock asked if the LNWR could help. McConnell said he would do all he could and sent three goods engines from Wolverton, but in October the OW&W asked for more.

By December 1854 four S Div goods engines had been loaned: Fairbairn 0-6-0s 260/7/76 and Stephenson 0-6-0 220; in January 260 was damaged at Worcester. Early in March 1855 Adcock asked if the LNWR could work the passenger trains between Handborough and Worcester for the next two months. It was agreed that provided no shunting was required and there was a guaranteed minimum daily run of 166 miles, trains of seven carriages including a van would be conveyed by the LNWR for 11d (4½p) per mile plus ½d for each additional vehicle. Working on these terms came into effect at the beginning of April and on the 12th there were six S Div engines on the OW&W, all at Worcester shed.

The N Div had likewise been asked to work the OW&W north of Worcester but Trevithick said he could not do it without disrupting the South Staffordshire traffic - in other words he had no spare power. In May the OW&W asked for faster trains on the Worcester-Handborough section.

Two of the goods engines were returned in May 1855 in a poor condition and in September Archibald Sturrock (GNR Locomotive Superintendent, acting as arbitrator) awarded the sum of £82 17s 7d (£82.88) against the OW&W for the deterioration of three of them.

Sturrock and McConnell made a valuation of the entire OW&W stock in 1855 prior to the ending of the contract with Williams. David Joy's *Diary* tells how they overestimated the value of his engines by 14%.

By this time the OW&W locomotive position had improved slightly, but Adcock requested occasional help from the S Div and engines were sent when required until 1858.

From the line's opening the OW&W engines had the use of the LNWR shed at Oxford and a goods engine was being regularly watered there in July 1853. In October 1857 one OW&W engine was stabled at Oxford at a cost of £1 16s (£1.80) per week for firelighting and cleaning. Normally OW&W passenger trains ran into the GWR station at Oxford but from October to December 1857 they passed over the Yarnton loop and into the LNWR station.

Not long after this the OW&W began patching up its differences with the Great Western and in 1860 amalgamated with the Worcester & Hereford and the Newport, Abergavenny & Hereford lines to form the West Midland Railway. From July 1861 the West Midland and the GWR began working in close co-operation; narrow gauge rails were quickly laid on the GWR to allow through running between the WMR and London. When these were complete in September, the old OW&W train service over the LNWR to Euston came to an end.

The Newport, Abergavenny & Hereford Railway had figured earlier in an LNWR scheme to enter South Wales. In 1852 the LNWR undertook to work the NA&H from its opening and in October 1853 McConnell said he could have six 14in cylinder engines ready by 1st December. In the event, none of these were needed and the line was worked by Thomas Brassey, as subcontractor, with his own engines from the opening on 2nd January 1854.

ENGINES ON TRIAL

APPENDIX 5

From the time of McConnell's arrival, several makers sent engines for trial on the line. Tulk & Ley's Crampton *Namur* arrived in February 1847 and worked until April as already described.

Stephenson & Co asked to try out their patent three-cylinder engine on the LNWR and this was agreed on 8th April 1847. The engine was the second of two built under Stephenson and Howe's patent 11086 of 1846, a long-boiler 4-2-0 with 6ft 6in driving wheels. It had two small outside cylinders, $10\frac{1}{2}$in diameter by 22in stroke, whose cranks were in the same position so that both pistons moved in the same direction simultaneously. One large inside cylinder, $16\frac{3}{8}$in diameter by 18in stroke, had its central crank at right angles to the other two. The purpose of this arrangement was to eliminate the swaying or nosing motion characteristic of outside-cylinder engines.

It arrived at Wolverton on 24th April and was tried with a train on Monday 26th. Two days later it took a five carriage special from Wolverton to Coventry in 42 minutes, or $58\frac{1}{2}$mph; at its top speed of 64mph its motion was perfectly steady, according to McConnell and Winter ("Superintendent of Mr Stephenson's patent engines") who were on the footplate.

During the month of May it ran 331 miles and continued working on the LNWR for a year but was not taken into stock. On 17th April 1848 it was reported to have broken its crank axle. No doubt it was then taken back to Newcastle for repair; it was later sold to the York, Newcastle & Berwick Railway.

Bury, Curtis & Kennedy's request to try a new engine was sanctioned on 7th September 1848. It was reported as on trial during October - December, and described as a four-wheeled engine with 15in cylinders. BC&K's offer to sell it was declined by the S Div Locomotive Committee on 9th November; Kennedy asked for its return and on 2nd January 1849 it was ordered to be sent back free of charge "in view of the use the LNW had of it". It was probably an 0-4-0 but its ultimate fate is not known.

On 12th October 1848 the S Div Locomotive Committee allowed "Adams & Co" (presumably William Bridges Adams) to try out an engine on the West London Railway, permission having already been given by the GWR. This was probably the *Fairfield* railcar for the broad gauge Bristol & Exeter Railway.

Jones & Potts arranged on 7th November 1849 to try out an engine of theirs "on a new plan". This was *Newton* which after trial McConnell reported was no improvement on LNWR engines; Jones & Potts' offer to sell it (including the tender) for £2,000 was declined in April 1850. It was probably an inside-framed 2-2-2 with 6ft 6in driving wheels, inside $15\frac{1}{2}$in x 20in cylinders and outside steam chests and valve gear. Included in the clearance sale in March 1852, when the firm was wound up, it was eventually sold by Arthur Potts to the Shrewsbury & Chester Railway for £2,000 in November 1852. As S&C No 32 it became known as 'The Flying Flogger', lasting on the GWR until 1873.

Timothy Hackworth's last engine *Sanspareil* was also given a trial. Built at his Soho Engine Works, Shildon, and completed in October 1849 it was a 2-2-2 with 15in x 22in inside cylinders, 6ft 6in driving wheels and had many innovations including a partly-welded boiler and Hackworth's patent slide valves. It had been tried out on the York, Newcastle & Berwick where Hackworth claimed a saving of 25% in fuel consumption. It was then sent to the LNWR but McConnell reported adversely on 5th December 1849 and a month later he said that *Sanspareil* showed no advantage in coke consumption. Advertised for sale in December 1849, the engine was not sold until May 1851, after Hackworth's death. It went to the York, Newcastle & Berwick Railway, became NER 135 and lasted until 1881.

"NAMUR," THE FIRST ENGINE BUILT ON CRAMPTON'S PRINCIPLE

CAUTION

It hardly needs saying that the vast and largely untapped LNWR archives in the Public Record Office are an invaluable source of railway history, but for researchers into early locomotives a note of warning is necessary: the official records contain some very misleading material.

There are monthly stock lists of S Div locomotives in the handwritten minute-books from September 1847 to December 1849 but this 'primary source' contains many demonstrable errors, some of which are isolated mistakes in copying. Others are more serious, such as the continued listing of engines known (from other sources) to have been transferred elsewhere, or the omission of engines now known to have been in stock. The monthly totals of passenger and goods engines which were also entered in the minutes were derived from these lists, and are therefore frequently inaccurate. These stock totals continue to appear in the minutes after 1849 but, without detailed lists to check them by, are probably just as unreliable.

In January 1850 a new method of presenting the regular locomotive stock return came into use, but only one example of this type of list has survived in the LNWR archives. Indexed as BTC R 352/13, this is a four-page foolscap proforma booklet with a printed list of engine numbers, grouped in classes with cylinder diameters and makers' names. Three blank columns are headed "Wanting Repair", "Under General Repair" and "Slight Repair" and were intended for manuscript additions, to present the current state of each engine to the S Div Locomotive Committee each month. Evidently this surviving copy is one of a batch printed soon after 10th June 1853 because engines ordered on that day are included, but so (unaccountably) are two engines scrapped after the Oxford collision of 3rd January 1853. Engines withdrawn 'for sale' are not included in the printed details.

The form is filled in and dated "5th June 1855" in ink, and *at first sight* appears to be a very useful piece of evidence for the period, but unfortunately it cannot be taken at face value. Three engines known to have been destroyed long before this date, Jones & Potts 4-2-0 148, Tayleur 0-6-0 124 and 4-2-0 164 are shown "in working order". The explanation of this can only be that these numbers are those of the Wolverton 0-4-2 Class A engines which replaced them. Among the 13in Bury passenger engines No 28 "in working order" has been added in manuscript. But Bury No 28 was a *14in* engine which disappeared from working stock in 1853, so again the likely explanation is that the listed 28 is the Class A replacement. Among the 18in passenger engines is "200 Crampton - in working order" - which ought to have been listed among the goods engines by this date.

It becomes clear that the list had been used as a number list without any regard for the makers' names or types as printed. It may not have been an official stock return at all, but merely the use of a handy form for totalling engines for some purpose where class details were immaterial. Nevertheless, the form is carefully completed, with subtotals of passenger and goods engines in working order and under repair. Because engines have been placed in the wrong classes the totals of passenger and goods engines so diligently added up at the end of the return - passengers 145, goods 138 - are wrong. The true totals at that date were probably passengers 141, goods 142.

This document is useful as a list of numbers carried by engines in working stock on 5th June 1855 and as a list of engines on sale at that time, but is quite misleading for the allocation of numbers among classes. The *printed* details give an approximation of the engines in stock and on order around the second half of 1853; it seems impossible to be more precise, or to understand why two scrapped engines were included.

During the remainder of the separate existence of the S Div occasional stock totals are given in the minutes but, apart from their basic unreliability mentioned above, they are not easy to interpret because only incomplete details of new engine construction have survived, and very little about the disposal of old engines. The situation is complicated by ten engines which were built at Wolverton in 1857-8 without Board authorisation, and which were kept in store for a time before being added to stock, the last four not until January 1860.

The last two lists of S Div engines among the archives show totals of types of engines in stock in 1861 by maker and cylinder diameter, and at the end of 1862 by maker and driving wheel diameter. The earlier of these lists, like most paperwork from the McConnell era, contains many errors, anomalies and mysteries.

It is hoped that this note will be enough to alert researchers to some not-so-obvious pitfalls, which have already wasted so much time.

Bibliography

Ahrons, Ernest Leopold:
    The British Steam Railway Locomotive 1825-1925 (1927).
    Locomotive & Train Working in the Latter Part of the Nineteenth Century (1915).

Bennett, Alfred Rosling:
    The Chronicles of Boulton's Siding (1927).

Bury, Edward:
    On the Locomotive Engines of the London & Birmingham Railway (1840: Transactions of the Institution of Civil Engineers, vol 3).

[Bury, Mrs Priscilla Susan]:
    Recollections of Edward Bury, by His Widow (1859).

Clark, Daniel Kinnear:
    Railway Machinery (1855).
    Railway Locomotives (1860).
    The Exhibited Machinery of 1862 (1862).

Clark, Daniel Kinnear, and Colburn, Zerah:
    Recent Practice in the Locomotive Engine (1860).

Colburn, Zerah, and Holley, Alexander Lyman:
    The Permanent Way, and Coal-burning Locomotive Boilers... (1858).

Dempsey, George Drysdale:
    A Rudimentary Treatise on the Locomotive Engine... (1856).

Edinburgh Review:
    Inland Transport (Oct 1832).
    Answer of the Directors of the Liverpool & Manchester Railway (April 1833).

Harris, W. L.:
    The First 182 Engines Built at Crewe. (LNWR Society 'Premier News', Dec 1992).

Lecount, Lieut Peter:
    A Practical Treatise on Railways (1839).

Locomotive Magazine:
    The Southern Division Engines of the L&NWR. (Series from April 1897 to April 1898, based on notes of James Bull, with preliminary articles from January 1897).

McConnel, David C.:
    Facts & Traditions collected for a Family Record (1861).

Marshall, C. F. Dendy:
    Centenary History of the Liverpool & Manchester Railway (1930).
    A History of Railway Locomotives to the end of 1831 (1953).

Marshall, William Prime:
    Description of the Patent Locomotive Engine made by Robert Stephenson & Co (1838).
    Evolution of the Locomotive Engine (1898).

Neele, George P.:
    Railway Reminiscences (1904).

Reed, Malcolm C.:
    The London & North Western Railway, a History (1996).

Roscoe, Thomas:
    The London & Birmingham Railway (1839)

Sekon, G. A.:
    The Evolution of the Steam Locomotive 1803-1898 (1898).
    Locomotion in Victorian London (1938).

Smith, G. Royde:
    Old Euston (1938).

Steel, Wilfred L.:
    The History of the London & North Western Railway (1914).

Stevenson, David:
    Fifty Years on the London & North Western Railway (1891).

Stuart, Donald H. and Reed, Brian:
    The Crewe Type (1971).

Thomas, R. H. G.:
    The Liverpool & Manchester Railway (1980).
    London's First Railway - the London & Greenwich (1972).

Tredgold, Thomas:
    Locomotive & Stationary Engines (1850).

'Veritas Vincit':
    Railway Locomotive Management (1847).

Warren, J. G. H.:
    A Century of Locomotive Building by Robert Stephenson & Co (1923).

West, Theodore:
    The Evolution of the Locomotive Engine (1900).

Whishaw, Francis:
    The Railways of Great Britain and Ireland (1842).

Acknowledgement of Photographs

Photography began soon after the London & Birmingham Railway opened, but if any early attempts were made to record the first engines they have not survived. The earliest known LNWR photographs were taken in the 1850s and although some of them are of poor quality, either because of the difficulty of the complicated wet-plate process or because of the effects of time, each provides some useful knowledge. The names of most of the early photographers have been forgotten, so it is not possible to give them proper credit, but all who are interested in locomotive history are in debt to them for having recorded so much, at a time when photography was expensive, cumbersome, messy and uncertain. The work of Robert H. Bleasdale is outstanding, for he photographed locomotives systematically all over Britain. Two of the locations he visited with his camera were Monument Lane shed and Bushbury, where he captured several old engines in the 1870s. The official LNWR photographer at Crewe Works took some S Div engines after rebuilding, and others just before scrapping, recording some famous types in their final state.

The prints used in this book have been provided by the following people and institutions, to whom grateful acknowledgement is made:

Title page:	Coventry Library
Fig. 5	Science & Art Institute, Wolverton
Figs. 14, 24, 66, 73, 77, 97, 105, 111, 112, 113, 122, 124, 131, 133	LNWR Society
Figs. 20, 72, 74, 75, 88, 94, 116, 121, 123, 126, 127, 128, 130	Stephenson Locomotive Society
Fig. 31	Ian Jack
Fig. 33	J. C. Davies
Fig. 41	Mike Williams
Figs. 42, 91, 120	Alan G. Dunbar
Fig. 45	W. H. Whitworth
Figs. 64, 104	Walsall Library
Figs. 67, 68, 83, 89, 118, 119, 129	W. E. Boyd
Fig. 76	J. E. Kite
Fig. 82	D. E. Jones
Fig. 85	L. Hanson
Figs. 87, 125	British Railways, LM Region
Fig. 90	C. R. Clinker
Fig. 95	David Patrick
Fig. 96	A. E. Grigg
Fig. 105	Neil Fraser
Fig. 107	Frank Jones
Fig. 114	Gordon Webster
Fig. 132	Anthony Parkes
Figs. 134, 141	Bruce Ellis
Fig. 145	National Railway Museum

Fig. 145 McConnell's *Eugénie* built by Wm. Fairbairn & Sons in 1855 for the Paris Universal Exhibition, with patent boiler recessed over the cranks to achieve a low centre of gravity; became Chemin de Fer du Nord 164. Photographed early in 1855 during trials and before final painting. *(National Railway Museum)*

SOME OTHER RCTS BOOKS

LMS LOCOMOTIVE NAMES
The Named Locomotives of the LMS and its Constituent Companies

The LNWR had a vigorous naming policy and the Midland Railway an equally determined anti-naming stance. The 1923 grouping set the stage for an absorbing battle within the management teams over naming policy with Derby's early policy success followed by Crewe's ultimate victory. Author John Goodman's absorbing read presents the full story of the LMS and its constituent companies' naming policies and the history of each named engine owned by the LMS, a total of 812. The LNWR contributed 668 of these and a complete presentation of its complex re-naming system is an invaluable inclusion. *Casebound. 211 pages, 124 photographs, 25 drawings.*

HIGHLAND RAILWAY LOCOMOTIVES
Book One – Early Days to the Lochs

David Jones was in at the start of the Highland, assisting its first two locomotive superintendents, Barclay and Stroudley, equip the company with an inadequate fleet that struggled with increasing loads. In 1870 he took command and his excellent Duke 4-4-0 conversions introduced his trade mark louvred chimney. After enlarging the design into the capable Clyde Bogies, Straths and Lochs came his famous long-lived Big Goods, the first 4-6-0s in Britain. The two local authors, J.R.H. Cormack and J.L. Stevenson, include much new research in this book on the important 41-year period in locomotive history, 1855-96. Board covers, 160 pages, 116 photographs give a complete history of each locomotive's design, modifications, livery, allocation and use, also a description of routes and other features.

Book Two – The Drummond, Smith and Cumming Classes

The early twentieth century was a most eventful period for the Highland. Drummond introduced inside cylinder designs with the Bens and the Barneys. George Smith followed with the contentious River class, designed for the enormously increased wartime loads but refused by the civil engineer. They were sold to the Caledonian, proved themselves successful, and after grouping many were used by the LMS over Highland metals!

James Cormack and James Stevenson detail the three engineers' designs from 1895 to the Clans, the battle to serve the demands of wartime, individual engine design modifications, shed allocations and operating history, projected designs and the preservation initiatives – both successful and otherwise – in a most readable style.
Casebound, 190 pages, 149 illustrations.

THE BIRKENHEAD RAILWAY
(LMS & GW Joint)

Today's successful electric railway between Chester and Birkenhead is in sharp contrast to the earlier story of the line. At first passengers were the major earner, but opening of other lines at Chester and the development of Ellesmere Port brought major freight operations. The main line was quadrupled, and the dock system eventually grew to 48 miles. Author Bruce Maund brings to life the detailed and fascinating tale of the complete system, the machinations of expanding railway companies to get control and, in the end, an object lesson in how two great rivals found a satisfactory *modus operandi* to run it with reasonable harmony for almost 90 years. Compulsory reading for all those involved in today's fragmented railways!
Page size 277 x 212mm, laminated cover, 136 pages, 140 illustrations.

RAISING STEAM ON THE LMS
The Evolution of LMS Locomotive Boilers

This absorbing read opens at Grouping with an LMS locomotive fleet of poor steaming designs unsuited to the heavy and growing traffic levels. The Board's historic decision to hire Stanier from the rival Great Western and his revolutionary work to equip the LMS with a more suitable fleet revolved around more effective raising and use of steam. The complete story is presented here, from early LMS practice based on pre-Grouping designs, through Stanier's importation of GWR practices, early results and comprehensive details of his design improvements culminating in the largest British pacifics, the Coronation class. The necessary technical content is presented by author Arthur Cook concisely in useful tables and an Appendix, allowing the text to be presented in an infectious, readable style. Readers can almost imagine themselves in the mutual improvement classes at the running shed!

Casebound, page size 180 x 235mm, 233 pages, 138 photographs and drawings, including one in colour

LMS DIESELS
Locomotives and Railcars

Today's British motive power fleet is a tribute to the pioneering work of the LMS. Cl 56, 58, 60 and HST power cars use AC generators based on the 10800 *Hawk* development and Cl 77 electrics used LMS designed bogies. Cl 40, 50 and DP2 used LMS designed engines and Peak Cl 44-46 used cab design from the famous 10000 and 10001. Our first generation dmmus owe much to the 1938 80000-2 LMS railcars. And, of course, our Cl 08 and 11 bear testimony to the quality of their LMS design 60 years ago. Author Edgar Richards takes readers through the fascinating history of LMS diesel development. From the first steam conversion in 1932 to the rugged 0-6-0 shunters built in large numbers for war service at home and abroad, the revolutionary main line 10000, 10001 10100 and 10800, and the Michelin, Coventry and LMS railcars, in total 208 locomotives, 15 railcars and 5 trolleys were operated by the LMS. Full details of their design, construction, modification, liveries, allocation and use are included. The book includes much new material and is highly recommended. *Casebound, 219 pages, 125 illustrations.*

GREAT NORTHERN LOCOMOTIVE HISTORY

This major four volume work covers the complete story of the Great Northern Railway, Doncaster Works and its locomotives, from earliest days to The Grouping. Each class is covered from all six designers – Cubitt, Bury, Sturrock, Stirling, Ivatt and Gresley. 1,553 Doncaster built engines are covered, plus those bought in. Their robust design was demonstrated by almost half of the GN stock passed to the LNER at Grouping surviving into British Railway ownership 25 years later.

The set totals 804 pages with 738 illustrations. Buy the complete set or individual volumes.

BRITISH RAILWAYS STANDARD STEAM LOCOMOTIVES
Volume 1 Background to Standarisation and the Pacific Classes
Volume 3 The Tank Engine Classes

Immediately British Railways was formed in January 1948, Robert Riddles was instructed to design a series of standard locomotives to modernise secondary route power. Railway enthusiasts from Penzance to Wick became familiar with their high running plates. The Society presents for the first time the complete story of British locomotive standardisation from the days of the Robinson ROD 2-8-0s to the twelve BR Standard designs totalling 999 locomotives. Paul Chancellor and Peter Gilbert present the Standards design history and for each of the 66 locomotives in the popular Britannia, Duke and Clan classes (Vol 1) and the 230 engines of the three tank classes (Vol 3) its complete construction, modification, diagram, allocation and use. With their construction at all six main workshops, local livery variations and national use, there is something for everyone to savour in these books. *Page size 212 x 272mm, Casebound, Vol 1 184 pages, 151 illustrations including 17 in colour, Vol 3 168 pages, 189 photographs incl. 16 colour.*

RCTS Publication List

*UK Post Free
Overseas add 25%

Title of Book	ISBN No	*Price
Locomotives of the LMS		
Locomotives of the LNWR Southern Division		
L & BR, LNWR and Wolverton Loco Works	0901115894	£27.95
Raising Steam on the LMS	0901115851	£24.95
LMS Diesels	0901115762	£19.95
LMS Locomotive Names	0901115797	£18.95
Highland Railway Locomotives 1855-1895	0901115649	£12.95
Highland Railway Locomotives 1895-1923	090111572X	£16.95

SPECIAL OFFER set of Highland Railway Locomotives		£23.50

Title of Book	ISBN No	*Price
The Birkenhead Railway	0901115878	£14.95
BR Standard Steam Locomotives:		
Vol 1 Background and the Pacifics	0901115819	£19.95
Vol 3 The Tank Engine Classes	0901115770	£19.95

SPECIAL OFFER BUY THIS BOOK WITH ANOTHER FOR JUST £5.00		
Western Change-Summer Saturdays in the West	0901115789	£15.95

Title of Book	ISBN No	*Price
The Railways of Keynsham	0901115827	£16.95
The Great Northern Railway in the East Midlands		
The Erewash Valley lines, Pinxton Branch, Awsworth-Ilkeston, Heanor & Stanton Branches	0901115886	£15.95
Nottingham Vic, GC, Leen Valley Network	090111586X	£14.95
Colwick Yards, London Rd-Gedling-Basford	0901115843	£13.95
The High Level Bridge and Newcastle Central Station	1873513283	£9.95
Gt. Northern Locomotive History		
1: 1847-1866	0901115614	£12.95
2: 1867-1895	0901115746	£19.95
3A: 1896-1911	090111569X	£19.95
3B: 1911-1923	0901115703	£16.95

Special Offer Set of Gt Northern Loco History		£40.95

Title of Book	ISBN No	*Price
A Travellers Guide to Robin Hood line	0901115835	£2.95
Locomotives of the LNER:		
Part 1 Preliminary Survey	0901115118	£12.95
Part 2A Tender Engines A1-A10	0901115258	£14.95
Part 2B Tender Engines Classes B1-B19	0901115738	£13.95
Part 9A Tank Engine Classes L1-L19	0901115401	£10.95
Part 10A Departmental Stock, Engine Sheds, Boiler and Tendering Numbering	0901115657	£10.95

Available from:–
Hon Assistant Publications Officer
Hazelhurst
Tiverton Road
Bampton
Devon EX16 9LJ

When ordering please quote reference LNWS1